Crossing Cultures

Readings for Composition

Sixth Edition

Annie Knepler
University of Illinois, Chicago

Ellie Knepler

Myrna Knepler
Northeastern Illinois University

Longman

New York San Francisco Boston
London Toronto Sydney Tokyo Singapore Madrid
Mexico City Munich Paris Cape Town Hong Kong Montreal

Senior Vice President/Publisher: Joseph Opiela
Executive Marketing Manager: Ann Stypuloski
Production Manager: Denise Phillip
Project Coordination, Text Design, and Electronic Page Makeup: WestWords, Inc.
Cover Design Manager: John Callahan
Cover Designer: Maria Ilardi
Cover Photo: © Frans Lemmens/ Getty Images / The Image Bank
Senior Manufacturing Buyer: Dennis J. Para
Printer and Binder: Courier Corporation
Cover Printer: Coral Graphics

For permission to use copyrighted material, grateful acknowledgment is made to the copyright holders on pp. 458–460 which are hereby made part of this copyright page.

Library of Congress Cataloging-in-Publication Data

Crossing cultures : readings for composition / [compiled by] Myrna Knepler, Annie Knepler, Ellie Knepler.— 6th ed.
     p. cm.
  Includes index.
  ISBN 0-205-33167-X
   1. College readers. 2. Pluralism (Social sciences)—Problems, exercises, etc. 3. Report writing—Problems, exercises, etc. 4. Culture—Problems, exercises, etc. 5. English language—Rhetoric. 6. Readers—Social sciences. I. Knepler, Myrna. II. Knepler, Annie. III. Knepler, Ellie.

PE1417 .C75 2002
808'.0427—dc21

2002066111

Copyright © 2003 by Pearson Education, Inc.

Please visit our website at http://www.ablongman.com

ISBN 0-205-33167-X

1 2 3 4 5 6 7 8 9 10—CRW—05 04 03 02

Contents

PART II   Education   79

PART VIII   Communicating   403

Rhetorical Contents

Narration (Observation and reporting)

Definition

Classification and Division

Comparison and Contrast

Cause and Effect

Argument and Persuasion

Irony, Humor, and Satire

Poetry

Preface

The year 2003 marks the twentieth anniversary of the publication of *Crossing Cultures*. In revising the sixth edition, we were struck by the enduring quality of the anthology. While the general structure of the book remains the same, the themes have expanded and shifted to adapt to changes in the ways we think about multiculturalism. For this edition, we have chosen fourteen new pieces that we think reflect new ways of thinking about culture and add to this ongoing conversation. Also, when we reread the pieces that have been in *Crossing Cultures* for many years, we found new relevance and meaning as we read them in a different context. As the newly added chapter on critical reading points out, reading is always a process of exploration and discovery.

Not only does each of us interpret what we read differently, but a piece may take on new meaning as situations and events in the world change. As we were preparing the manuscript for this book, the events of September 11, 2001, and the conflicts that succeeded it were vivid in our minds. We considered including a piece that specifically addressed the events, but decided that the issue was too raw and the outcome too uncertain. There is no question, though, that many of the essays included in *Crossing Cultures* can help us talk about these events. We have a new context in which to read them. We hope the essays in this anthology can help students raise issues of culture in complex ways that encourage meaningful discussion.

NEW FEATURES

Besides the new pieces, the most important new feature to the sixth edition of *Crossing Cultures* is a section on critical reading, which appears at the beginning of the book. We felt it was important not only to emphasize the essential connection between reading and writing, but also to guide students through strategies and techniques that will help them become more active and critical readers. Although critical reading is something that needs to be practiced and not simply explained, this chapter provides composition instructors with a starting point for guiding students toward becoming better readers and writers.

NEW SELECTIONS

The results of the 2000 census revealed some significant changes in the ethnic and racial landscape of the United States. According to census data, one in five U.S. residents is either foreign born or first generation, the highest level in U.S. history. Furthermore, the questions asked in the census itself seem to reflect our changing attitudes towards race and ethnicity, acknowledging that many of us identify with more than one group. For the first time the census allowed each person to check off more than one box for race or ethnicity.

The census was only one of the many things we were thinking of when we selected new pieces for this edition. Robin D.G. Kelley and Roxane Farmanfarmaian speak to the complexity of multiracial and multiethnic identity. Bharati Mukherjee explores some of the diverse paths immigrants may take as they come to a new country. Other pieces, like those by Ian Buruma and Alexis Bloom, explore the influence that technology and global communication have on language and culture.

Other pieces look at new ways of defining the family. Dan Savage explores the implications of gender roles through looking at his own experience as a gay parent. Stephanie Coontz debunks the myth of the "traditional" family, arguing that the "ideal" family that we hold as an example never really existed.

Other new pieces round out themes that we felt needed strengthening or help broaden the notion of how culture can be discussed. Through the use of vignettes, Sherman Alexie documents one Native American child's education in racism and stereotyping. Michael Pollan visits Celebration, Florida, a town built and managed by the Disney Corporation, and critiques their attempts to manufacture community. Susan Douglas and Meredith Michaels take aim at the media, analyzing the rhetoric surrounding gushing portrayals of celebrity mothers. In all, the new edition includes fifteen new selections, all written within the past five years.

USING CROSS-CULTURAL THEMES

The success of this book and our experiences teaching have convinced us that cross-cultural subjects work well in a composition course. They provide strong and meaningful topics for discussion and writing both by broadening students' perspectives and by allowing them to draw on stories and themes from their own lives. Multicultural selections challenge accepted beliefs by asking students to consider the lives, ideas, aspirations, and prejudices of people who may be very different from them. At the same time reading, and having one's classmates read, selections from one's own culture is likely to heighten students' self-assurance and prompt them to reflect on the meaning of their own experience. This reflection and reaction to reading and class discussion can often be the starting point for writing that "belongs" to the student, yet extends beyond his or her own (perhaps limited) experience of the world.

The readings in *Crossing Cultures* have been collected from a variety of sources and are meant to reflect a broad range of perspectives, ideas, and rhetorical styles. Each selection has also been chosen because it is a "good read" whose subject and style will engage college students and provide thought-provoking material for class discussion as well as compelling ideas for writing.

USING *CROSSING CULTURES* AS A COMPOSITION TEXT

Clearly, students produce stronger writing when they are motivated to write—engaged by content that is thematically interesting and challenging. However, more is needed to turn that interest into good writing. *Crossing Cultures* provides many tools to help students develop stronger reading and composition skills. Each selection in the book is followed by a set of questions that can be used for class discussions or as writing prompts. "Some of the Issues" aids students in careful reading by providing questions that help them clarify and analyze the meaning of the essay. The questions in "The Way We Are Told" ask students to examine the author's rhetorical strategies and point out the significance and effect of stylistic choices we make when we compose. Each exercise section concludes with "Some Subjects for Writing," prompts that can be used for essays and/or journal entries. Asterisks indicate questions or writing topics that refer to more than one selection, giving students the chance to compare and contrast two different views of the same subject. In response to reviewers' feedback, we have retailored some of the questions to prompt responses from students that are more analytical than narrative.

The arrangement of the book allows the instructor both flexibility and structure. *Crossing Cultures* contains selections of varying length, difficulty, and style. Selections are arranged thematically; each section begins with an accessible essay, moving on to more challenging and difficult readings. There is also a supplementary Rhetorical Contents that organizes the readings based on the writers' stylistic patterns.

ACKNOWLEDGMENTS

We wish to thank the editorial and production staff at Longman. Joe Opiela devoted his considerable enthusiasm and expertise to initiating the project and to seeing it through from beginning to end. Julie Hallett provided thoughtful and thorough answers to sometimes thorny questions, always with cheerful encouragement. Jared Sterzer and Denise Phillip skillfully coordinated the many details involved in the production of this book.

Several readers and reviewers gave us expert advice and suggestions for improving the text. We thank the reviewers: Anne Bliss, University of Colorado at

Boulder; David Elias, Eastern Kentucky University; Vicki Holmsten, San Juan College; Joyce Marie Miller, Collin County Community College; James Murphy, Southern Illinois University Edwardsville; Patricia Nebrida, DeVry Institute of Technology; Johnnie Scott, California State University Northridge; and Chesley Spring, DeVry Institute of Technology.

Several colleagues, students and friends generously offered ideas, expertise, encouragement, and support at various stages throughout the book. Some shared their syllabi so we could get a better idea of the variety of ways teachers use the book in the classroom. Hal Adams, Joe Alter, Martha Bayne, Ralph Cintron, Jennifer Cohen, Dan Collins, Jamie Owen Daniel, Ann Feldman, Chris Glomski, Sharon Haar, Jim Hall, Claude Mark Hurlbert, Camille Isabell, David Jolliffe, Carmen Manning, Paula Mathieu, Ifeyemi O Oyelami, Derek Owens, David Schaafsma, Kendra Sisserson, Janet Smith, and Sue Weinstein all contributed in a variety of ways. Deborah Epstein, Kate Ingold, Lenora Warren and Pat Guy at the Neighborhood Writing Alliance, and all the writers in the *Journal of Ordinary Thought* groups, were a constant source of inspiration. A big thanks to Carla Cenker, Miriam Golden, Ellen Grimes, Eileen Hess, Amy Ludwig, Rashmi Ramaswamy, Christine Tarkowski, Helen Tsatsos, and Dinah Wayne for consistently keeping our spirits up and our minds active.

We have dedicated this book to Henry Knepler, who was one of the founding editors of *Crossing Cultures* and died one year after the last edition was published. Not only are his words and ideas still literally present in the book, but the stories and thoughts he passed on to us became an integral part of our conversations as we revised it.

Annie Knepler
Ellie Knepler
Myrna Knepler

READING AND THINKING CRITICALLY

You might be asking yourself why a textbook for a writing class would begin with a chapter on reading. The answer is simple: reading and writing are connected in a fundamental way.

In your writing courses, you will be asked to respond to what you read and to use your reading as a source for ideas and information. Keep in mind that, in general, good writers are good readers. They read often and from a wide variety of sources. As they read, or after they finish a selection, they note down interesting passages or write a response to the reading in a journal. Good writers pay attention to the author's style and note the techniques the author uses to make his or her points. They think about where they agree and disagree with the author and why. And, they read to find new topics and ideas for their own writing.

For most of you, reading has become an essential part of your everyday life both in and out of school. However, we read differently depending on our purpose. We read a traffic sign to know which way to go, or an instruction manual to learn how to program our new DVD player. A newspaper is something we might read both to gather information and to begin to reflect on the events of the world around us. In this case, we process what we are reading with a more critical eye.

Sometimes we think of ourselves as reading simply for pleasure, such as when we read a novel, a short story or poem, but even then we are often making connections and analyzing, even if we don't realize that's what we're doing. A character's experience in a novel might help us think through a similar experience we've had, or to consider why someone we know acted in a particular way. By making those connections, we are reading critically, asking questions about what we've read and comparing the concepts in a reading to other ideas we've encountered.

As a student, it is important that you approach your academic readings as an *active* critical reader. Being an active critical reader generally means that you are taking more formal and deliberate steps to analyze what you read. Simply put, you should read the essays in this book differently than you would read your computer manual or than you might casually read a novel by your favorite writer. You will be encouraged to write down and think through your responses to the essays, stories, and poems in *Crossing Cultures*. Your primary goal in reading critically and actively should be to incorporate new ideas and perspectives into your own understanding of the world around you by engaging in a conversation with what you're reading. This in no way means that you should not find pleasure in the readings in this book, only that you are engaging with them on a different and deeper level.

WHAT DOES IT MEAN TO READ CRITICALLY?

In order to effectively incorporate ideas from what you read into what you write, you need to develop the strategies and skills to read critically. Critical readers ask questions as they read. They note down ideas and comparisons they find striking. They work to question and to figure out the author's perspective, keeping in mind what they know about the author's background and values. They consider the author's style of writing, and the writing techniques the author uses in order to develop his or her thesis.

Ultimately, critical readers attempt to form a clear and accurate understanding of what the author is trying to say in order to come up with their own purposeful analysis of what they've read.

You might think of your writing, therefore, as a way to interact or converse with what you read. Even if what you write does not directly respond to something you've read, the essays you write should somehow reflect the way the reading has influenced your approach to a specific topic. Writing is generally a process of moving back and forth between your reading and your computer or pen and paper, particularly if you are incorporating specific ideas or quotations from your reading.

In order to fully absorb a reading and integrate it into your own writing, you generally need to read it more than once (perhaps several times). You will notice different aspects of the reading each time you look at it. New passages will stand out to you and ideas that didn't seem clear will come into focus. Even if the words on a page don't change, your reading of them does as your ideas evolve. Good writers often reread the material they're working with even after they've finished a draft of their paper.

LOOKING AHEAD

Many of us are taught to approach our reading as if it were a mystery novel. We come to think that looking ahead will spoil the reading somehow, and that we should only read something beginning to end. But good critical readers skim a piece before reading it carefully in order to develop a sense of what the piece is about and to get a glimpse of the author's perspective.

Before you sit down to read and take notes on your reading, take some time to read the headnote (the introductory information that precedes the selection), which will give you some background on both the author and the piece itself. Look through the piece, and read passages that stand out to you. Also take note of keywords that you see are repeated throughout the reading. Then, ask yourself what you already know about the topic and what assumptions you might already hold about that topic. Consider the title and ask yourself what it might tell you about the reading. For example, think about the title of the first piece in the book, Elizabeth Wong's, "The Struggle to Be an All-American Girl." What do you think she means by the phrase "All-American"? Can you think of a reason this might be a struggle?

Once you have skimmed through the piece and have done some initial thinking about it, sit down in a comfortable setting with a pen or pencil and a notebook, and prepare to read closely and carefully.

IDENTIFYING THE THESIS

A thesis is the main point that the author wants to convey to the reader. Sometimes an author will state his or her thesis directly; in other cases, the thesis will be implied. You will see examples of both throughout this reader. You can think of the thesis as representing the author's purpose in writing the piece. Whether or not the author tells you straight out what he or she wants to convey, or implies his or her purpose through examples and illustrations, all good writers have something they want to say.

In many cases, the author will state a thesis within the first few paragraphs. A writer may set up the thesis in such a way that the reader is drawn in to the piece and becomes curious about the author's topic or perspective. Sometimes authors will start with an anecdote, a question, or a brief scenario that relates to some aspect of their thesis. In other cases, the author will present an idea in order to argue against it. Below are the first five paragraphs from Stephanie Coontz's "Where Are the Good Old Days," an essay that traces the history of the American family. It appears in Chapter 3 of this book. As you read the paragraphs below, try to identify the author's thesis. Also consider how Coontz sets up her main point and guides the reader toward her thesis:

> The American family is under siege. To listen to the rhetoric of recent months, we have fallen down on the job. We're selfish; too preoccupied with our own gratification to raise our children properly. We are ungrateful; we want a hand-out, not a hand.
>
> If only we'd buckle down, stay on the straight and narrow, keep our feet on the ground, our shoulder to the wheel, our eye on the ball, our nose to the grindstone. Then everything would be all right, just as it was in the family-friendly '50s, when

we could settle down in front of the television after an honest day's work and see our lives reflected in shows like *Ozzie and Harriet* and *Father Knows Best.*

But American families have been under siege more often than not during the past 300 years. Moreover, they have always been diverse, both in structure and ethnicity. No family type has been able to protect its members from the roller-coaster rides of economic setbacks or social change. Changes that improve the lives and fortunes of one family type or individual often resulted in losses for another.

A man employed in the auto industry, for example, would have been better off financially in the 1950s than now, but his retired parents would be better off today. If he had a strong taste for power, he might prefer Colonial times, when a man was the undisputed monarch of the household and any disobedience by wife, child, or servant was punishable by whipping. But woe betide that man if he wasn't born to property. In those days, men without estates could be told what to wear, where to live, and whom to associate with.

His wife, on the other hand, might have been happier in the 1850s, when she might have afforded two or three servants. We can be pretty sure, though, that the black or Irish servants of that day would not have found the times so agreeable. And today's children, even those scarred by divorce, might well want to stay put rather than live in the late 19th century, when nearly half of them died before they reached their late teens.

In this case, Coontz states her thesis directly in the third paragraph. She questions the idea that the family is currently "in crisis" by arguing that there has never been such a thing as a "normal" or "ideal" family and that families have always struggled, though with different issues at different times in history. Coontz sets up her thesis by playing on what she feels might be our assumptions. She mimics what she sees as commonly held perspectives on the contemporary family. Coontz goes on to provide evidence of this and we can assume that she will further develop this argument in her essay. A thesis often appears toward the beginning of an essay, but it doesn't have to.

Sometimes an author will imply the thesis rather than state it directly. In many of the narrative essays you will read in this text, the authors develop a point through recounting specific incidents or events. Instead of *telling* you what they want to say, they *show* you through illustration and examples. Although an author may not tell you his purpose directly, he has an idea that he wants to get across. You might ask yourself why an author describes something in a specific way. What kinds of details does the author give? Does she present the subject in a positive or negative light? What language does she use? Authors' reasons for choosing whether to state their thesis directly or indirectly may depend on a number of factors: the audience they're writing for; the topic of their piece; the genre they prefer; as well as their own personal style of writing.

IDENTIFYING CLAIMS AND EVIDENCE

How the author develops the thesis determines how the piece is organized. In order to understand the organization and structure of the reading, you will need to identify the claims the author makes throughout the piece in order to support the thesis and consider the kinds of evidence the author uses to back up those claims. Evidence can appear in various forms: authors might use statistics or numbers to back up their points; they might relate an anecdote or story that serves as an example of their claim; or they might quote from another source or authority on the topic. In her essay "Less Is More: A Call for Shorter Work Hours," Barbara Brandt argues that Americans spend too much time at work compared to many industrialized countries where the standards of living are just as high, but where workers have more time to devote to community, family, and other pursuits.

In the following paragraph, which appears in the middle of her essay, try to identify both Brandt's claim and the evidence she uses to back up her claim:

> In our era, almost every other industrialized nation (except Japan) has fewer annual working hours and longer vacations than the United States. This includes all of Western Europe, where many nations enjoy thriving economies and standards of living equal to or higher than ours. Jeremy Brecher and Tim Costello, writing in *Z Magazine* (Oct. 1990), note that "European unions during the 1980s made a powerful and largely successful push to cut working hours. In 1987 German metalworkers struck and won a 37.5-hour week; many are now winning a 35-hour week. In 1990, hundreds of thousands of British workers have won a 37-hour week."

Brandt states her claim in the first sentence by telling us that we should look to other industrialized nations whose work hours are shorter. To back up her claim, she quotes from another source, one that provides statistical information confirming the fact that workers in other industrialized nations have successfully fought for a shorter work week.

IDENTIFYING PATTERNS AND TECHNIQUES

Depending on their purpose in writing a piece, authors apply various techniques in order to argue a point or convey a certain mood or feeling. Some authors rely a great deal on detailed description that allows the reader to "see" and "feel" the experiences they recount, while others might compare and contrast two people or events. Another technique is to demonstrate cause and effect by showing how one event affected another. Strong writing generally follows certain *patterns*, where an author uses certain identifiable techniques in order to support a thesis and develop an idea or argument. In other words, the piece follows a certain logic and there is a clear and thought-out reason for why the author has chosen to write that way.

One example of a technique that you may already be familiar with is "compare and contrast." We often use comparison and contrast to formulate arguments and make decisions in our daily lives. For example, you might try to persuade your parents that you should be allowed a certain privilege (staying out later, using the car) because your friends have that right, or you might compare one teacher to another in order to decide what class to take. Authors compare and contrast to demonstrate how both the differences *and* the similarities between two examples reveal something about the point they want to make. For instance, a writer might compare two cities with similar populations in order to show the impact of a specific regulation that one city has enacted but the other has not. If the author were to compare a large city with a small town or rural area, the comparison would not have the same effect.

In "The Mommy Wars" Susan Douglas and Meredith Michaels compare newspaper and magazine descriptions of what they refer to as "celebrity moms" with depictions of welfare mothers, to make a point about how these images help reinforce negative stereotypes of mothers who receive public aid. In the following paragraph, notice how they make a claim then back it up with a series of comparisons:

> As the push "to end welfare as we know it" gained momentum and reached its climax in the welfare reform of 1996, the canonized celebrity mom and the demonized welfare mother became ever more potent symbols, working in powerful opposition to each other. We rarely saw these mothers in the same publication, or even considered them in the same breath. Celebrity moms graced the covers of magazines designed for self-realization and escape; welfare mothers were the objects of endless stories in newspapers and newsmagazines and on the nightly news that focused on public policy and its relation to the tenuous state of morality in America.

Whether or not you agree with their conclusion, the authors' comparison works because the examples are both similar and different. If they were to compare profiles of childless fashion models with welfare mothers, their argument would not hold up. The effectiveness of their argument relies on their ability to point out how these two images of motherhood play against each other to formulate public opinion.

Writers also control the tone and the language of their writing in order to demonstrate their point. Descriptive writing is a technique that allows the reader to show you what they want to say by giving you a visual image that sets a certain mood. The way an author describes an object or an incident can tell you a lot about how they feel about it. In "The Jacket," Gary Soto wants to convey the narrator's disappointment when, instead of giving him a tough leather jacket like "bikers wear," his mother presents him with a jacket several sizes too large and "the color of day-old guacamole." In the following passage, the author describes the first time he tries on the jacket:

> I put the jacket on. I zipped it up and down several times and rolled the cuffs up so they didn't cover my hands. I put my hands in the pockets and flapped the jacket like a bird's wings. I stood in front of the mirror, full face, then profile, and then looked over my shoulder as if someone had called me. I sat on the bed, stood against the bed, and combed my hair to see what I would look like doing something natural. I looked ugly. I threw it on my brother's bed and looked at it for a long time before I slipped it on and went out to the backyard, smiling a "thank you" to my mom as I passed her in the kitchen. With my hands in my pockets I kicked a ball against the fence, and then climbed it to sit looking into the alley. I hurled orange peels at the mouth of an open garbage can, and when the peels were gone I watched the white puffs of my breath thin to nothing.

How does the narrator feel about the jacket? Furthermore, how does the jacket make him feel about himself? If we picture the narrator with his hands in his pockets, looking down at the ground (how else would he see the ball that he kicks?) we can imagine a boy who feels far from "tough" in his new jacket.

Though you will be able to identify certain patterns, every writer is unique and uses different techniques in different ways. Furthermore, you are unlikely to find a piece that relies solely on one technique. Ultimately, although one might be able to characterize a piece of writing as primarily "descriptive" or "persuasive," most strong writing contains a number of identifiable patterns and techniques. It is important to look for and be able to identify these patterns and techniques since they are essential to understanding not only *what* the author's purpose is, but *how* the author chooses to convey his or her point. Most important, they provide examples and models for techniques you might apply in your own writing.

MAKING YOUR MARK

As a critical reader, it is important that you keep track of the observations and questions that come up as you read and reread. Though you may not be used to writing in your textbooks, making notes in pencil on the text itself is often the best way to keep track of your responses and keep your ideas flowing. Of course you cannot write in a library book or a book that you've borrowed from a friend or an instructor, but you can write in your own books.

Here is an example of how one reader marked the opening paragraphs by Stephanie Coontz that you saw earlier:

?

The American family is under siege. To listen to the (rhetoric) of recent months, we have fallen down on the job. We're selfish; too preoccupied with our own gratification to raise our children properly. We are ungrateful; we want a handout, not a hand.

when was this written?

does she believe this?

If only we'd buckle down, stay on the straight and narrow, keep our feet on the ground, our shoulder to the wheel, our eye on the ball, our nose to the grindstone. Then everything would be all right, just as it was in the family-friendly '50s, when we could settle down in front of the television after an honest day's work and see our lives reflected in shows like *Ozzie and Harriet* and *Father Knows Best.*[1]

clichés

I think these are TV shows about families, but look them up. Maybe compare to Simpsons?

thesis?

But American families have been under siege more often than not during the past 300 years. Moreover, they have always been diverse, both in structure and ethnicity. No family type has been able to protect its members from the roller-coaster rides of economic setbacks or social change. Changes that improve the lives and fortunes of one family type or individual often resulted in losses for another.

what types is she talking about?

comparison and contrast

A man employed in the auto industry, for example, would have been better off financially in the 1950s than now, but his retired parents would be better off today. If he had a strong taste for power, he might prefer Colonial times, when a man was the undisputed monarch of the household and any disobedience by wife, child, or servant was punishable by whipping. But woe betide that man if he wasn't born to property. In those days, men without estates could be told what to wear, where to live, and whom to associate with.

when was this?

__?

how does the author know this? will she prove it?

what political perspective is she coming from?

His wife, on the other hand, might have been happier in the 1850s, when she might have afforded two or three servants. We can be pretty sure, though, that the black or Irish servants of that day would not have found the times so agreeable. And today's children, even those scarred by divorce, might well want to stay put rather than live in the late 19th century, when nearly half of them died before they reached their late teens.

Notice that the reader circled words or phrases she didn't know and wrote a question mark in the margin. She also made notes to herself to look into references she wasn't sure about so that she could ask the instructor about them in class. The reader identified the thesis and noticed that the author used comparison and contrast to begin to back up each point. She also questioned whether or not the evidence so far was substantial, which will help her look for further evidence as she moves along. Finally, she started to think about the theme of families and the media, making way for a possible writing topic.

Though you will ultimately develop your own style and strategies for making marks in your readings, here are some key guidelines for what to look for:

- underline passages that stand out to you or in which the author makes key claims.
- make notes in the margin when you have a specific reaction to a point or when a point relates to something else you've read.
- identify unfamiliar words you need to look up and passages you do not fully understand.

READING NEW OR DIFFICULT MATERIAL

We all struggle when we read new and difficult material. Even college professors have a tough time understanding readings on a new subject or in a different field. But a reading may not only be difficult because it contains difficult vocabulary or complicated sentence structures. A reading may be difficult to *you* because the subject itself is completely unfamiliar.

However, even if you don't fully understand what an author is trying to say, you can often pick out the writer's key claims. Once you identify these claims, a good strategy is to try and paraphrase these passages by putting them into your own words. After you gain a better understanding of certain key claims, you can try to fit these ideas into the larger point the author is trying to make.

USING THE QUESTIONS

The questions at the end of each selection will help you both comprehend and analyze the reading. The "Some of the Issues" questions help you identify key issues in the reading and consider how the ideas in the reading relate to each other. Often, these questions ask you to paraphrase or summarize a section of the reading in order to better understand the author's meaning. These questions may also ask you to analyze some of the author's ideas and think about why the author came to a certain conclusion or made a specific point. In other cases, the questions call for you to compare some aspect of the reading with a personal experience, or to other readings.

The questions in the section called "The Way We Are Told" address issues of style and technique. These questions ask you to consider the author's specific writing choices. Essentially they call for you to think about why the author stated or organized something the way he or she did.

The section called "Some Subjects for Writing" offers ideas and topics for more extended writing. Your instructor may assign or ask you to choose one of these topics for a more formal essay, but you should also consider writing more informally in response to some of these prompts. If you keep a reading journal for your class, you should use some of the writing prompts to help develop your journal responses to each reading and to help you move from reading to writing.

PART **I**

GROWING UP

A s we grow up, our awareness of the world around us gradually expands. The learning process begins at birth and never stops. We get to know our physical surroundings—a crib, perhaps, then a room, a house. We become aware of a parent and learn that if we cry, that parent will do something for us. We also learn that others want things from us; much of the time these demands are designed to stop us from doing what we want at that moment. Communication, we find, works in both directions.

What we learn depends of course on our environment, although we do not know that in our early lives. Then, we believe that our way of talking—our language—is the only one, and that the way things happen is the only way they can be done. For many Americans, these earliest experiences are confined to one culture. Sooner or later we learn, however, that we coexist with people whose experience or upbringing differs from ours. The discovery of that fact may come as a shock, particularly when we find at the same time that our culture is in some way not welcomed or accepted, that there is a barrier between ours and "theirs," a barrier that we cannot readily cross.

Each author in Part One confronts that barrier while growing up. Elizabeth Wong wants to be an "all-American girl" and fights her mother's attempt to have her keep her Chinese background. Gary Soto's despised jacket, ugly, torn, and several sizes too large, becomes inflated in importance in the author's mind into a symbol of what keeps him from fitting in. Maya Angelou, an African-American student in a segregated elementary school in Arkansas in the 1940s, recoils from the condescending attitude of the white speaker at her graduation from the eighth grade.

In Harry Mark Petrakis's story "Barba Nikos," the narrator illustrates the conflict that often arises between first- and second-generation immigrants when the ways of the Old Country—and their parents' accented English—become a source of embarrassment. Maxine Hong Kingston, brought up in a Chinese environment, turns silent when she enters public school. In "Scents," Maria Laurino uses a humiliating incident from her high school gym class as a jumping off point for examining how smells relate to culture, ethnicity, and class. Grace Paley's short story tells of school administrators who, with great unconcern, impose a Christmas pageant on children whose culture is not Christian.

The next two essays look at teenage life. Lindsy Van Gelder, by looking at her own life and at important sociological studies, analyzes the changes girls go through when they reach age eleven, and lose their boldness and spontaneity in an effort to conform to society's notion of how women should behave. Vendela Vida investigates the world of the quinceañera, a coming of age ritual for many Latina girls, and explores its role and function in contemporary teenage culture. Finally, Countee Cullen speaks simply but tellingly of his first confrontation, at age eight, with prejudice.

The Struggle to Be an All-American Girl

Elizabeth Wong

Elizabeth Wong's mother insisted that she learn Chinese and be aware of her cultural background. In her essay, which first appeared in the Los Angeles Times, *Wong vividly portrays her childhood resistance to her mother's wishes and the anger and embarrassment she felt. Chinese school interfered with her being, as she puts it, "an all-American girl." Here, writing as a young adult, she recognizes in herself a sense of loss.*

Elizabeth Wong is a playwright and television writer who grew up in Los Angeles's Chinatown and worked as a news reporter for ten years before quitting in 1988 to write plays. Her first play premiered off Broadway in 1991. She received a B.A. from the University of Southern California in 1980 and an M.F.A. from New York University in 1991. She has written for television, and her plays have been produced throughout the country.

1   It's still there, the Chinese school on Yale Street where my brother and I used to go. Despite the new coat of paint and the high wire fence, the school I knew 10 years ago remains remarkably, stoically the same.

2   Every day at 5 P.M., instead of playing with our fourth- and fifth-grade friends or sneaking out to the empty lot to hunt ghosts and animal bones, my brother and I had to go to Chinese school. No amount of kicking, screaming, or pleading could dissuade my mother, who was solidly determined to have us learn the language of our heritage.

3   Forcibly, she walked us the seven long, hilly blocks from our home to school, depositing our defiant tearful faces before the stern principal. My only memory of him is that he swayed on his heels like a palm tree, and he always clasped his impatient twitching hands behind his back. I recognized him as a repressed maniacal child killer, and knew that if we ever saw his hands we'd be in big trouble.

4   We all sat in little chairs in an empty auditorium. The room smelled like Chinese medicine, an imported faraway mustiness. Like ancient mothballs or dirty closets. I hated that smell. I favored crisp new scents. Like the soft French perfume that my American teacher wore in public school.

5   There was a stage far to the right, flanked by an American flag and the flag of the Nationalist Republic of China, which was also red, white and blue but not as pretty.

6   Although the emphasis at the school was mainly language—speaking, reading, writing—the lessons always began with an exercise in politeness. With the entrance of the teacher, the best student would tap a bell and everyone would get up, kowtow, and chant, "Sing san ho," the phonetic for "How are you, teacher?"

7   Being ten years old, I had better things to learn than ideographs copied painstakingly in lines that ran right to left from the tip of a *moc but*, a real ink pen that had to be held in an awkward way if blotches were to be avoided. After all, I could do the multiplication tables, name the satellites of Mars, and write reports on *Little Women* and *Black Beauty*. Nancy Drew, my favorite book heroine, never spoke Chinese.

8   The language was a source of embarrassment. More times than not, I had tried to disassociate myself from the nagging loud voice that followed me wherever I wandered in the nearby American supermarket outside Chinatown. The voice belonged to my grandmother, a fragile woman in her seventies who could outshout the best of the street vendors. Her humor was raunchy, her Chinese rhythmless, patternless. It was quick, it was loud, it was unbeautiful. It was not like the quiet, lilting romance of French or the gentle refinement of the American South. Chinese sounded pedestrian. Public.

9   In Chinatown, the comings and goings of hundreds of Chinese on their daily tasks sounded chaotic and frenzied. I did not want to be thought of as mad, as talking gibberish. When I spoke English, people nodded at me, smiled sweetly, said encouraging words. Even the people in my culture would cluck and say that I'd do well in life. "My, doesn't she move her lips fast," they would say, meaning that I'd be able to keep up with the world outside Chinatown.

10   My brother was even more fanatical than I about speaking English. He was especially hard on my mother, criticizing her, often cruelly, for her pidgin speech—smatterings of Chinese scattered like chop suey in her conversation. "It's not 'What it is,' Mom," he'd say in exasperation. "It's 'What *is* it, what *is* it, what *is* it!'" Sometimes Mom might leave out an occasional "the" or "a," or perhaps a verb of being. He would stop her in mid-sentence: "Say it again, Mom. Say it right." When he tripped over his own tongue, he'd blame it on her: "See, Mom, it's all your fault. You set a bad example."

11   What infuriated my mother most was when my brother cornered her on her consonants, especially "r." My father had played a cruel joke on Mom by assigning her an American name that her tongue wouldn't allow her to say. No matter how hard she tried, "Ruth" always ended up "Luth" or "Roof."

12   After two years of writing with a *moc but* and reciting words with multiples of meanings, I finally was granted a cultural divorce. I was permitted to stop Chinese school.

13   I thought of myself as multicultural. I preferred tacos to egg rolls; I enjoyed Cinco de Mayo[1] more than Chinese New Year.

---

[1]Fifth of May. Mexican national holiday marking Mexico's victory over France at Puebla in 1862.

14   At last, I was one of you; I wasn't one of them.
15   Sadly, I still am.

EXERCISES

Some of the Issues

1. Cite some of the characteristics of the Chinese school as Wong describes it; how does it differ from her American school?
2. Why was the Chinese language "a source of embarrassment" to Wong? What are her feelings about speaking English?
3. Consider the last sentence: "Sadly, I still am." Why "sadly"?
*4. Read Maxine Hong Kingston's "Girlhood among Ghosts." Compare Kingston's attitude toward Chinese school with Wong's.
*5. Read Maria Laurino's "Scents" and Harry Mark Petrakis's "Barba Nikos." What similarities do you notice between their experiences and Wong's? What differences?

The Way We Are Told

6. Consider the title. To what extent does Wong succeed in becoming the "all-American girl" she wanted to be? Explain why the title could be considered ironic.
7. What details does Wong give about her experience in Chinese school to make her feelings explicit? What senses does she appeal to?
8. How does the description of the principal in paragraph 3 reflect the fact that Wong sees him through the eyes of a child?
9. In paragraph 14, whom do "you" and "them" refer to?
10. Wong does not state a thesis directly. Nevertheless, a thesis statement that sums up the essay could be constructed. What might the thesis be? What do you think the author would gain or lose by stating it directly?

Some Subjects for Writing

11. Describe an experience you disliked. Try, like Wong, to build your case by the way you describe the details.
12. What does one gain or lose by assimilating into the mainstream culture? How might it affect one's family ties and self-awareness? Base your conclusions on both observation of others and personal knowledge.

---

*Asterisks used in this context denote questions and essay topics that draw on more than one selection.

*13. Read Maria Laurino's "Scents." Compare Wong's and Laurino's attitudes toward their respective cultures. How does each woman's experience explain her attitude?

The Jacket

Gary Soto

Gary Soto is a poet and prose writer influenced by his working-class Mexican-American roots. His writing style captures the particulars of everyday life while at the same time offers a glimpse of larger, more universal themes.

This selection takes a specific object, a jacket, and uses it to describe a feeling and mood at a particular time in the author's life. Most of us have shared the experience of having a piece of clothing take on a significance beyond its practical purpose.

Soto, born in 1952, has published numerous works of fiction and poetry for young adults and children, as well as several volumes of poetry for adults. He has chronicled his childhood in three volumes of memoirs: Living Up the Street *(1985),* Lesser Evils *(1988), and* Small Faces *(1986), from which this essay is taken. His most recent book, a comic novel, is* Poetry Lover, *published in 2001. He teaches creative writing at the University of California, Riverside.*

1   My clothes have failed me. I remember the green coat that I wore in fifth and sixth grade when you either danced like a champ or pressed yourself against a greasy wall, bitter as a penny toward the happy couples.

2   When I needed a new jacket and my mother asked what kind I wanted, I described something like bikers wear: black leather and silver studs, with enough belts to hold down a small town. We were in the kitchen, steam on the windows from her cooking. She listened so long while stirring dinner that I thought she understood for sure the kind I wanted. The next day when I got home from school, I discovered draped on my bedpost a jacket the color of day-old guacamole. I threw my books on the bed and approached the jacket slowly, as if it were a stranger whose hand I had to shake. I touched the vinyl sleeve, the collar, and peeked at the mustard-colored lining.

3   From the kitchen mother yelled that my jacket was in the closet. I closed the door to her voice and pulled at the rack of clothes in the closet, hoping the jacket on the bedpost wasn't for me but my mean brother. No luck. I gave up. From my bed, I stared at the jacket. I wanted to cry because it was so ugly and so big that I knew I'd have to wear it a long time. I was a small kid, thin as a young tree, and it would be years before I'd have a new one. I stared at the jacket, like an enemy, thinking bad things before I took off my old jacket, whose sleeves climbed halfway to my elbow.

4   I put the big jacket on. I zipped it up and down several times and rolled the cuffs up so they didn't cover my hands. I put my hands in the pockets and flapped the jacket like a bird's wings. I stood in front of the mirror, full face, then profile,

and then looked over my shoulder as if someone had called me. I sat on the bed, stood against the bed, and combed my hair to see what I would look like doing something natural. I looked ugly. I threw it on my brother's bed and looked at it for a long time before I slipped it on and went out to the backyard, smiling a "thank you" to my mom as I passed her in the kitchen. With my hands in my pockets I kicked a ball against the fence, and then climbed it to sit looking into the alley. I hurled orange peels at the mouth of an open garbage can, and when the peels were gone I watched the white puffs of my breath thin to nothing.

5   I jumped down, hands in my pockets, and in the backyard, on my knees, I teased my dog, Brownie, by swooping my arms while making bird calls. He jumped at me and missed. He jumped again and again, until a tooth sunk deep, ripping an L-shaped tear on my left sleeve. I pushed Brownie away to study the tear as I would a cut on my arm. There was no blood, only a few loose pieces of fuzz. Damn dog, I thought, and pushed him away hard when he tried to bite again. I got up from my knees and went to my bedroom to sit with my jacket on my lap, with the lights out.

6   That was the first afternoon with my new jacket. The next day I wore it to sixth grade and got a D on a math quiz. During the morning recess Frankie T., the playground terrorist, pushed me to the ground and told me to stay there until recess was over. My best friend, Steve Negrete, ate an apple while looking at me, and the girls turned away to whisper on the monkey bars. The teachers were no help: they looked my way and talked about how foolish I looked in my new jacket. I saw their heads bob with laughter, their hands half covering their mouths.

7   Even though it was cold, I took off the jacket during lunch and played kick-ball in a thin shirt, my arms feeling like braille from goose bumps. But when I returned to class I slipped the jacket on and shivered until I was warm. I sat on my hands, heating them up, while my teeth chattered like a cup of crooked dice. Finally warm, I slid out of the jacket but put it back on a few minutes later when the fire bell rang. We paraded out into the yard where we, the sixth graders, walked past all the other grades to stand against the back fence. Everybody saw me. Although they didn't say out loud, "Man, that's ugly," I heard the buzz-buzz of gossip and even laughter that I knew was meant for me.

8   And so I went, in my guacamole-colored jacket. So embarrassed, so hurt, I couldn't even do my homework. I received C's on quizzes and forgot the state capitals and the rivers of South America, our friendly neighbor. Even the girls who had been friendly blew away like loose flowers to follow the boys in neat jackets.

9   I wore that thing for three years until the sleeves grew short and my forearms stuck out like the necks of turtles. All during that time no love came to me—no little dark girl in a Sunday dress she wore on Monday. At lunchtime I stayed with the ugly boys who leaned against the chainlink fence and looked around with propellers of grass spinning in our mouths. We saw girls walk by alone, saw couples, hand in hand, their heads like bookends pressing air together. We saw them and spun our propellers so fast our faces were blurs.

10   I blame that jacket for those bad years. I blame my mother for her bad taste and her cheap ways. It was a sad time for the heart. With a friend I spent my

sixth-grade year in a tree in the alley, waiting for something good to happen to me in that jacket, which had become the ugly brother who tagged along wherever I went. And it was about that time that I began to grow. My chest puffed up with muscle and, strangely, a few more ribs. Even my hands, those fleshy hammers, showed bravely through the cuffs, the fingers already hardening for the coming fights. But that L-shaped rip on the left sleeve got bigger; bits of stuffing coughed out from its wound after a hard day of play. I finally Scotch-taped it closed, but in rain or cold weather the tape peeled off like a scab and more stuffing fell out until that sleeve shriveled into a palsied arm. That winter the elbows began to crack and whole chunks of green began to fall off. I showed the cracks to my mother, who always seemed to be at the stove with steamed-up glasses, and she said that there were children in Mexico who would love that jacket. I told her that this was America and yelled that Debbie, my sister, didn't have a jacket like mine. I ran outside, ready to cry, and climbed the tree by the alley to think bad thoughts and watch my breath puff white and disappear.

11   But whole pieces still casually flew off my jacket when I played hard, read quietly, or took vicious spelling tests at school. When it became so spotted that my brother began to call me "camouflage," I flung it over the fence into the alley. Later, however, I swiped the jacket off the ground and went inside to drape it across my lap and mope.

12   I was called to dinner: steam silvered my mother's glasses as she said grace; my brother and sister with their heads bowed made ugly faces at their glasses of powdered milk. I gagged too, but eagerly ate big rips of buttered tortilla that held scooped-up beans. Finished, I went outside with my jacket across my arm. It was a cold sky. The faces of clouds were piled up, hurting. I climbed the fence, jumping down with a grunt. I started up the alley and soon slipped into my jacket, that green ugly brother who breathed over my shoulder that day and ever since.

EXERCISES

Some of the Issues

1. How does the narrator describe the jacket he wants? How does he describe the jacket his mother buys for him? What do these descriptions say about the narrator's self-image as an adolescent?
2. Why does the narrator call the jacket a "stranger whose hand I had to shake" in paragraph 2?
3. Why do you think the narrator's mother buys him such a large jacket?
4. How does the incident in paragraph 5 foreshadow events later in the story?
5. What problems or misfortunes does the narrator attribute to the jacket? To what extent do you think his perceptions differ from reality?
6. Although there is little or no direct discussion of class and ethnicity in the story, there is a sense that both are important. How is this apparent?
7. Throughout the essay, Soto refers to the jacket in many different ways: "a stranger" (paragraph 2), "an enemy" (paragraph 3). Make a list of the

various words and phrases he uses to describe the jacket. How do his perceptions of the jacket change? What does the jacket come to symbolize by the last line of the story?

*8. Read Malcolm X's "Hair." Compare Malcolm's attitude toward his hair with Soto's view of the jacket. How do their approaches differ? How are they similar?

The Way We Are Told

9. Throughout the essay, Soto uses short, simple sentences in combination with longer, more complex ones. How or why are these short sentences effective?

10. Soto uses many similes and metaphors in the story. Find as many of them as you can and discuss which ones you feel are most effective. How do they work as a stylistic tool?

*11. Read Piri Thomas's "Alien Turf." Whereas Soto uses vivid images throughout the story, allowing the reader to visualize certain scenes or moments, Thomas uses dialogue that lets the reader "hear" the action. Discuss the difference between these two methods of description. Why might one author choose to emphasize one over the other?

Some Subjects for Writing

12. Soto uses the jacket to provide focus and continuity in his story. Write an essay or story in which, like Soto, you focus on one object and its significance in your life. What did this object mean to you? What metaphors and similes would you use to describe this object?

13. Some people feel that clothes make the person. How true is the statement, "You are what you wear"? What kinds of judgments do we make about individuals based on the way they dress? Write an essay in which you analyze the importance placed on clothing in our society. Depending on the focus of your essay, you may want to take into consideration some of the following issues: school uniforms; gang-related clothing and insignias; fashion magazines and the fashion industry; or the relationship between clothing and musical/artistic taste.

14. Keeping in mind Soto's use of visual imagery, create a comic book based on the story of the jacket. Which scenes would you illustrate? In what places would you use captions or bubbles for dialogue?

Graduation

Maya Angelou

Maya Angelou was born Marguerite Johnson in St. Louis in 1928, and was raised by her grandmother in Stamps, Arkansas. She grew up in a rigidly segregated society. The Civil War had ended slavery but had not eliminated segregation. In fact, several decisions of the Supreme Court reaffirmed its legality. In the case of Plessy v. Ferguson *(1896) in particular, the Court gave its approval to segregation, declaring it to be constitutional as long as the affected facilities, such as public schools, were "separate but equal." Schools were separate after that in large parts of the country, but not equal, as Angelou's memory of the early 1940s demonstrates. In 1954 the Supreme Court reversed itself in* Brown v. Board of Education, *declaring that segregation was "inherently unequal" and, therefore, unconstitutional.*

Angelou—writer, actor, and civil rights activist—is the author of numerous books of poetry, which have been collected in The Complete Collected Poems *(1994).* I Know Why the Caged Bird Sings *(1970), from which this selection is taken, is the first in a series of autobiographical prose works that includes* Gather Together in My Name *(1975),* Singin' and Swingin' and Merry Like Christmas *(1976),* The Heart of a Woman *(1981) and* A Song Flung Up to Heaven *(2002).*

1 The children in Stamps trembled visibly with anticipation. Some adults were excited too, but to be certain the whole young population had come down with graduation epidemic. Large classes were graduating from both the grammar school and the high school. Even those who were years removed from their own day of glorious release were anxious to help with preparations as a kind of dry run. The junior students who were moving into the vacating classes' chairs were tradition-bound to show their talents for leadership and management. They strutted through the school and around the campus exerting pressure on the lower grades. Their authority was so new that occasionally if they pressed a little too hard it had to be overlooked. After all, next term was coming, and it never hurt a sixth grader to have a play sister in the eighth grade, or a tenth-year student to be able to call a twelfth grader Bubba. So all was endured in a spirit of shared understanding. But the graduating classes themselves were the nobility. Like travelers with exotic destinations on their minds, the graduates were remarkably forgetful. They came to school without their books, or tablets or even pencils. Volunteers fell over themselves to secure replacements for the missing equipment. When accepted, the willing workers might or might not be thanked, and it was of no importance to the pregraduation rites. Even teachers were respectful of the now quiet and aging seniors, and tended to speak to them, if not as

equals, as beings only slightly lower than themselves. After tests were returned and grades given, the student body, which acted like an extended family, knew who did well, who excelled, and what piteous ones had failed.

2   Unlike the white high school, Lafayette County Training School distinguished itself by having neither lawn, nor hedges, nor tennis court, nor climbing ivy. Its two buildings (main classrooms, the grade school and home economics) were set on a dirt hill with no fence to limit either its boundaries or those of bordering farms. There was a large expanse to the left of the school which was used alternately as a baseball diamond or a basketball court. Rusty hoops on the swaying poles represented the permanent recreational equipment, although bats and balls could be borrowed from the P.E. teacher if the borrower was qualified and if the diamond wasn't occupied.

3   Over this rocky area relieved by a few shady tall persimmon trees the graduating class walked. The girls often held hands and no longer bothered to speak to the lower students. There was a sadness about them, as if this old world was not their home and they were bound for higher ground. The boys, on the other hand, had become more friendly, more outgoing. A decided change from the closed attitude they projected while studying for finals. Now they seemed not ready to give up the old school, the familiar paths and classrooms. Only a small percentage would be continuing on to college—one of the South's A & M (agricultural and mechanical) schools, which trained Negro youths to be carpenters, farmers, handymen, masons, maids, cooks and baby nurses. Their future rode heavily on their shoulders, and blinded them to the collective joy that had pervaded the lives of the boys and girls in the grammar school graduating class.

4   Parents who could afford it had ordered new shoes and ready-made clothes for themselves from Sears and Roebuck or Montgomery Ward. They also engaged the best seamstresses to make the floating graduating dresses and to cut down secondhand pants which would be pressed to a military slickness for the important event.

5   Oh, it was important, all right. Whitefolks would attend the ceremony, and two or three would speak of God and home, and the Southern way of life, and Mrs. Parsons, the principal's wife, would play the graduation march while the lower-grade graduates paraded down the aisles and took their seats below the platform. The high school seniors would wait in empty classrooms to make their dramatic entrance.

6   In the Store I was the person of the moment. The birthday girl. The center. Bailey had graduated the year before, although to do so he had to forfeit all pleasures to make up for his time lost in Baton Rouge.

7   My class was wearing butter-yellow piqué dresses, and Momma launched out on mine. She smocked the yoke into tiny crisscrossing puckers, then shirred the rest of the bodice. Her dark fingers ducked in and out of the lemony cloth as she embroidered raised daisies around the hem. Before she considered herself finished she had added a crocheted cuff on the puff sleeves, and a pointy crocheted collar.

8   I was going to be lovely. A walking model of all the various styles of fine hand sewing and it didn't worry me that I was only twelve years old and merely graduating from the eighth grade. Besides, many teachers in Arkansas Negro schools had only that diploma and were licensed to impart wisdom.

9   The days had become longer and more noticeable. The faded beige of former times had been replaced with strong and sure colors. I began to see my classmates' clothes, their skin tones, and the dust that waved off pussy willows. Clouds that lazed across the sky were objects of great concern to me. Their shiftier shapes might have held a message that in my new happiness and with a little bit of time I'd soon decipher. During that period I looked at the arch of heaven so religiously my neck kept a steady ache. I had taken to smiling more often, and my jaws hurt from the unaccustomed activity. Between the two physical sore spots, I suppose I could have been uncomfortable, but that was not the case. As a member of the winning team (the graduating class of 1940) I had outdistanced unpleasant sensations by miles. I was headed for the freedom of open fields.

10   Youth and social approval allied themselves with me and we trammeled memories of slights and insults. The wind of our swift passage remodeled my features. Lost tears were pounded to mud and then to dust. Years of withdrawal were brushed aside and left behind, as hanging ropes of parasitic moss.

11   My work alone had awarded me a top place and I was going to be one of the first called in the graduating ceremonies. On the classroom blackboard, as well as on the bulletin board in the auditorium, there were blue stars and white stars and red stars. No absences, no tardinesses, and my academic work was among the best of the year. I could say the preamble to the Constitution even faster than Bailey. We timed ourselves often: "WethepeopleoftheUnitedStatesinorder toformamoreperfectunion . . ." I had memorized the Presidents of the United States from Washington to Roosevelt in chronological as well as alphabetical order.

12   My hair pleased me too. Gradually the black mass had lengthened and thickened, so that it kept at last to its braided pattern, and I didn't have to yank my scalp off when I tried to comb it.

13   Louise and I had rehearsed the exercises until we tired out ourselves. Henry Reed was class valedictorian. He was a small, very black boy with hooded eyes, a long, broad nose and an oddly shaped head. I had admired him for years because each term he and I vied for the best grades in our class. Most often he bested me, but instead of being disappointed I was pleased that we shared top places between us. Like many Southern Black children, he lived with his grandmother, who was as strict as Momma and as kind as she knew how to be. He was courteous, respectful and soft-spoken to elders, but on the playground he chose to play the roughest games. I admired him. Anyone, I reckoned, sufficiently afraid or sufficiently dull could be polite. But to be able to operate at a top level with both adults and children was admirable.

14   His valedictory speech was entitled "To Be or Not to Be." The rigid tenth-grade teacher had helped him write it. He'd been working on the dramatic stresses for months.

15   The weeks until graduation were filled with heady activities. A group of small children were to be presented in a play about buttercups and daisies and bunny rabbits. They could be heard throughout the building practicing their hops and their little songs that sounded like silver bells. The older girls (non-graduates, of course) were assigned the task of making refreshments for the night's festivities. A tangy scent of ginger, cinnamon, nutmeg and chocolate wafted around the home economics building as the budding cooks made samples for themselves and their teachers.

16   In every corner of the workshop, axes and saws split fresh timber as the woodshop boys made sets and stage scenery. Only the graduates were left out of the general bustle. We were free to sit in the library at the back of the building or look in quite detachedly, naturally, on the measures being taken for our event.

17   Even the minister preached on graduation the Sunday before. His subject was, "Let your light so shine that men will see your good works and praise your Father, Who is in Heaven." Although the sermon was purported to be addressed to us, he used the occasion to speak to backsliders, gamblers and general ne'er-do-wells. But since he had called our names at the beginning of the service we were mollified.

18   Among Negroes the tradition was to give presents to children going only from one grade to another. How much more important this was when the person was graduating at the top of the class. Uncle Willie and Momma had sent away for a Mickey Mouse watch like Bailey's. Louise gave me four embroidered handkerchiefs. (I gave her three crocheted doilies.) Mrs. Sneed, the minister's wife, made me an underskirt to wear for graduation, and nearly every customer gave me a nickel or maybe even a dime with the instruction "Keep on moving to higher ground," or some such encouragement.

19   Amazingly the great day finally dawned and I was out of bed before I knew it. I threw open the back door to see it more clearly, but Momma said, "Sister, come away from that door and put your robe on."

20   I hoped the memory of that morning would never leave me. Sunlight was itself still young, and the day had none of the insistence maturity would bring it in a few hours. In my robe and barefoot in the backyard, under cover of going to see about my new beans, I gave myself up to the gentle warmth and thanked God that no matter what evil I had done in my life He had allowed me to live to see this day. Somewhere in my fatalism I had expected to die, accidentally, and never have the chance to walk up the stairs in the auditorium and gracefully receive my hard-earned diploma. Out of God's merciful bosom I had won reprieve.

21   Bailey came out in his robe and gave me a box wrapped in Christmas paper. He said he had saved his money for months to pay for it. It felt like a box of chocolates, but I knew Bailey wouldn't save money to buy candy when we had all we could want under our noses.

22   He was as proud of the gift as I. It was a soft-leather-bound copy of a collection of poems by Edgar Allan Poe, or, as Bailey and I called him, "Eap." I turned

to "Annabel Lee" and we walked up and down the garden rows, the cool dirt between our toes, reciting the beautifully sad lines.

23   Momma made a Sunday breakfast although it was only Friday. After we finished the blessing, I opened my eyes to find the watch on my plate. It was a
dream of a day. Everything went smoothly and to my credit. I didn't have to be
reminded or scolded for anything. Near evening I was too jittery to attend to
chores, so Bailey volunteered to do all before his bath.

24   Days before, we had made a sign for the Store, and as we turned out the
lights Momma hung the cardboard over the doorknob. It read clearly: CLOSED,
GRADUATION.

25   My dress fitted perfectly and everyone said that I looked like a sunbeam in
it. On the hill, going toward the school, Bailey walked behind with Uncle
Willie, who muttered, "Go on, Ju." We wanted him to walk ahead with us because it embarrassed him to have to walk so slowly. Bailey said he'd let the
ladies walk together, and the men would bring up the rear. We all laughed,
nicely.

26   Little children dashed by out of the dark like fireflies. Their crepe-paper
dresses and butterfly wings were not made for running and we heard more than
one rip, dryly, and the regretful "uh uh" that followed.

27   The school blazed without gaiety. The windows seemed cold and unfriendly from the lower hill. A sense of ill-fated timing crept over me, and if
Momma hadn't reached for my hand I would have drifted back to Bailey and
Uncle Willie, and possibly beyond. She made a few slow jokes about my feet
getting cold, and tugged me along to the now-strange building.

28   Around the front steps, assurance came back. There were my fellow
"greats," the graduating class. Hair brushed back, legs oiled, new dresses and
pressed pleats, fresh pocket handkerchiefs and little handbags, all homesewn.
Oh, we were up to snuff, all right. I joined my comrades and didn't even see my
family go in to find seats in the crowded auditorium.

29   The school band struck up a march and all classes filed in as had been rehearsed. We stood in front of our seats, as assigned, and on a signal from the
choir director, we sat. No sooner had this been accomplished than the band
started to play the national anthem. We rose again and sang the song, after
which we recited the pledge of allegiance. We remained standing for a brief
minute before the choir director and the principal signaled to us, rather desperately I thought, to take our seats. The command was so unusual that our carefully rehearsed and smooth-running machine was thrown off. For a full minute
we fumbled for our chairs and bumped into each other awkwardly. Habits
change or solidify under pressure, so in our state of nervous tension we had
been ready to follow our usual assembly pattern: the American national anthem,
then the pledge of allegiance, then the song every Black person I knew called
the Negro National Anthem. All done in the same key, with the same passion
and most often standing on the same foot.

30   Finding my seat at last, I was overcome with a presentiment of worse things to come. Something unrehearsed, unplanned, was going to happen, and we were going to be made to look bad. I distinctly remember being explicit in the choice of pronoun. It was "we," the graduating class, the unit, that concerned me then.

31   The principal welcomed "parents and friends" and asked the Baptist minister to lead us in prayer. His invocation was brief and punchy, and for a second I thought we were getting back on the high road to right action. When the principal came back to the dais, however, his voice had changed. Sounds always affected me profoundly and the principal's voice was one of my favorites. During assembly it melted and lowed weakly into the audience. It had not been in my plan to listen to him, but my curiosity was piqued and I straightened up to give him my attention.

32   He was talking about Booker T. Washington,[1] our "late great leader," who said we can be as close as the fingers on the hand, etc . . . Then he said a few vague things about friendship and the friendship of kindly people to those less fortunate than themselves. With that his voice nearly faded, thin, away. Like a river diminishing to a stream and then to a trickle. But he cleared his throat and said, "Our speaker tonight, who is also our friend, came from Texarkana to deliver the commencement address, but due to the irregularity of the train schedule, he's going to, as they say, 'speak and run.'" He said that we understood and wanted the man to know that we were most grateful for the time he was able to give us and then something about how we were willing always to adjust to another's program, and without more ado—"I give you Mr. Edward Donleavy."

33   Not one but two white men came through the door offstage. The shorter one walked to the speaker's platform, and the tall one moved over to the center seat and sat down. But that was our principal's seat, and already occupied. The dislodged gentleman bounced around for a long breath or two before the Baptist minister gave him his chair, then with more dignity than the situation deserved, the minister walked off the stage.

34   Donleavy looked at the audience once (on reflection, I'm sure that he wanted only to reassure himself that we were really there), adjusted his glasses and began to read from a sheaf of papers.

35   He was glad "to be here and to see the work going on just as it was in the other schools."

36   At the first "Amen" from the audience I willed the offender to immediate death by choking on the word. But Amens and Yes, sir's began to fall around the room like rain through a ragged umbrella.

[1]African-American leader (1856–1915) and founder of Tuskegee Institute who advocated economic self-reliance.

37   He told us of the wonderful changes we children in Stamps had in store. The Central School (naturally the white school was Central) had already been granted improvements that would be in use in the fall. A well-known artist was coming from Little Rock to teach art to them. They were going to have the newest microscopes and chemistry equipment for their laboratory. Mr. Donleavy didn't leave us long in the dark over who made these improvements available to Central High. Nor were we to be ignored in the general betterment scheme he had in mind.

38   He said that he had pointed out to people at a very high level that one of the first-line football tacklers at Arkansas Agricultural and Mechanical College had graduated from good old Lafayette County Training School. Here fewer Amens were heard. Those few that did break through lay dully in the air with the heaviness of habit.

39   He went on to praise us. He went on to say how he had bragged that "one of the best basketball players at Fisk sank his first ball right here at Lafayette County Training School."

40   The white kids were going to have a chance to become Galileos and Madame Curies and Edisons and Gauguins, and our boys (the girls weren't even in on it) would try to be Jesse Owenses[2] and Joe Louises.[3]

41   Owens and the Brown Bomber were great heroes in our world, but what school official in the white-goddom of Little Rock had the right to decide that those two men must be our only heroes? Who decided that for Henry Reed to become a scientist he had to work like George Washington Carver, as a bootblack, to buy a lousy microscope? Bailey was obviously always going to be too small to be an athlete, so which concrete angel glued to what county seat had decided that if my brother wanted to become a lawyer he had to first pay penance for his skin by picking cotton and hoeing corn and studying correspondence books at night for twenty years?

42   The man's dead words fell like bricks around the auditorium and too many settled in my belly. Constrained by hard-learned manners I couldn't look behind me, but to my left and right the proud graduating class of 1940 had dropped their heads. Every girl in my row had found something new to do with her handkerchief. Some folded the tiny squares into love knots, some into triangles, but most were wadding them, then pressing them flat on their yellow laps.

43   On the dais, the ancient tragedy was being replayed. Professor Parsons sat, a sculptor's reject, rigid. His large, heavy body seemed devoid of will or willingness, and his eyes said he was no longer with us. The other teachers examined the flag (which was draped stage right) or their notes, or the windows which opened on our now-famous playing diamond.

[2](1913–1980) African-American winner of four Olympic gold medals in track and field.
[3]African-American boxer (1914–1981) and heavyweight champion of the world from 1937 through 1949. Also known as the Brown Bomber.

44   Graduation, the hush-hush magic time of frills and gifts and congratulations and diplomas, was finished for me before my name was called. The accomplishment was nothing. The meticulous maps, drawn in three colors of ink, learning and spelling decasyllabic words, memorizing the whole of *The Rape of Lucrece*[4]—it was for nothing. Donleavy had exposed us.

45   We were maids and farmers, handymen and washerwomen, and anything higher that we aspired to was farcical and presumptuous.

46   Then I wished that Gabriel Prosser and Nat Turner had killed all white-folks in their beds and that Abraham Lincoln had been assassinated before the signing of the Emancipation Proclamation, and that Harriet Tubman had been killed by that blow on her head and Christopher Columbus had drowned in the *Santa María*.

47   It was awful to be Negro and have no control over my life. It was brutal to be young and already trained to sit quietly and listen to charges brought against my color with no chance of defense. We should all be dead. I thought I should like to see us all dead, one on top of the other. A pyramid of flesh with the whitefolks on the bottom, as the broad base, then the Indians with their silly tomahawks and teepees and wigwams and treaties, the Negroes with their mops and recipes and cotton sacks and spirituals sticking out of their mouths. The Dutch children should all stumble in their wooden shoes and break their necks. The French should choke to death on the Louisiana Purchase (1803) while silk-worms ate all the Chinese with their stupid pigtails. As a species, we were an abomination. All of us.

48   Donleavy was running for election, and assured our parents that if he won we could count on having the only colored paved playing field in that part of Arkansas. Also—he never looked up to acknowledge the grunts of acceptance—also, we were bound to get some new equipment for the home economics building and the workshop.

49   He finished, and since there was no need to give any more than the most perfunctory thank-you's, he nodded to the men on the stage, and the tall white man who was never introduced joined him at the door. They left with the attitude that now they were off to something really important. (The graduation ceremonies at Lafayette County Training School had been a mere preliminary.)

50   The ugliness they left was palpable. An uninvited guest who wouldn't leave. The choir was summoned and sang a modern arrangement of "Onward, Christian Soldiers," with new words pertaining to graduates seeking their place in the world. But it didn't work. Elouise, the daughter of the Baptist minister, recited "Invictus," and I could have cried at the impertinence of "I am the master of my fate, I am the captain of my soul."

51   My name had lost its ring of familiarity and I had to be nudged to go and receive my diploma. All my preparations had fled. I neither marched up to the

[4]Shakespeare's poem (1594) based on a Roman legend.

stage like a conquering Amazon, nor did I look in the audience for Bailey's nod of approval. Marguerite Johnson, I heard the name again, my honors were read, there were noises in the audience of appreciation, and I took my place on the stage as rehearsed.

52 I thought about colors I hated: ecru, puce, lavender, beige and black.

53 There was shuffling and rustling around me, then Henry Reed was giving his valedictory address, "To Be or Not to Be." Hadn't he heard the whitefolks? We couldn't *be*, so the question was a waste of time. Henry's voice came out clear and strong. I feared to look at him. Hadn't he got the message? There was no "nobler in the mind" for Negroes because the world didn't think we had minds, and they let us know it. "Outrageous fortune"? Now, that was a joke. When the ceremony was over I had to tell Henry Reed some things. That is, if I still cared. Not "rub," Henry, "erase." "Ah, there's the erase." Us.

54 Henry had been a good student in elocution. His voice rose on tides of promise and fell on waves of warnings. The English teacher had helped him to create a sermon winging through Hamlet's soliloquy. To be a man, a doer, a builder, a leader, or to be a tool, an unfunny joke, a crusher of funky toadstools. I marveled that Henry could go through with the speech as if we had a choice.

55 I had been listening and silently rebutting each sentence with my eyes closed; then there was a hush, which in an audience warns that something unplanned is happening. I looked up and saw Henry Reed, the conservative, the proper, the A student, turn his back to the audience and turn to us (the proud graduating class of 1940) and sing, nearly speaking,

> "Lift ev'ry voice and sing
> Till earth and heaven ring
> Ring with the harmonies of Liberty . . ."

56 It was the poem written by James Weldon Johnson. It was the music composed by J. Rosamond Johnson. It was the Negro national anthem. Out of habit we were singing it.

57 Our mothers and fathers stood in the dark hall and joined the hymn of encouragement. A kindergarten teacher led the small children onto the stage and the buttercups and daisies and bunny rabbits marked time and tried to follow:

> "Stony the road we trod
> Bitter the chastening rod
> Felt in the days when hope, unborn, had died.
> Yet with a steady beat
> Have not our weary feet
> Come to the place for which our fathers sighed?"

58 Every child I knew had learned that song with his ABC's and along with "Jesus Loves Me This I Know." But I personally had never heard it before.

Never heard the words, despite the thousands of times I had sung them. Never thought they had anything to do with me.

59   On the other hand, the words of Patrick Henry had made such an impression on me that I had been able to stretch myself tall and trembling and say, "I know not what course others may take, but as for me, give me liberty or give me death."

60   And now I heard, really for the first time:

> "We have come over a way that with tears
> has been watered,
> We have come, treading our path through
> the blood of the slaughtered."

61   While echoes of the song shivered in the air, Henry Reed bowed his head, said "Thank you," and returned to his place in the line. The tears that slipped down many faces were not wiped away in shame.

62   We were on top again. As always, again. We survived. The depths had been icy and dark, but now a bright sun spoke to our souls. I was no longer simply a member of the proud graduating glass of 1940; I was a proud member of the wonderful, beautiful Negro race.

EXERCISES

Some of the Issues

1. How does Angelou establish the importance of the graduation? How does she build it stage by stage?
2. Why does Angelou distinguish between the high school graduates (paragraph 3) and the eighth-graders like herself? How do their attitudes differ? Why is she happier?
3. How does Angelou describe her rising expectations for "the great day" in paragraphs 15 through 28?
4. At what point in the narrative do we first get the idea that things may be going wrong with the "dream of a day"? What are later indications that something is wrong?
5. In paragraph 29 the children are confronted with a change in the usual order of things. Why does Angelou make this seem important? Why does the principal "rather desperately" signal for the children to sit down?
6. How do the first words Mr. Donleavy says indicate what his attitude is?
7. In paragraphs 50 through 60 Angelou describes her shifting thoughts and emotions. Explain them in your own words and relate them to the conclusion reached in paragraph 62.

*8. Read Jamaica Kincaid's "On Seeing England for the First Time." How does Angelou's anger after hearing Mr. Donleavy's speech resemble Kincaid's anger at the end of her article? What is the source of anger in each case?

The Way We Are Told

9. Paragraph 1 talks about the graduates and their schoolmates. Paragraphs 2 and 3 describe the school. Why does Angelou write in that order? What distinguishes paragraph 1 from 2 and 3 in addition to the content?
10. Explain the irony Angelou sees in Henry Reed's "To Be or Not to Be" speech.

Some Subjects for Writing

11. Have you ever experienced an event—a dance, a party, a trip—that you looked forward to and that turned out to be a disaster? Or have you ever dreaded an event, such as an interview or a blind date, that turned out better than you had expected? Tell it, trying to make the reader feel the anticipation and the change through the specific, descriptive details you cite, rather than by direct statements. (You will find that the indirect way—making the reader feel or see the event—is more effective than simply saying, "I was bored" or "I found out it was a great evening after all.")
12. In his speech, Mr. Donleavy offers only sports figures like Jesse Owens and Joe Louis as cultural heroes for African-American students. Reflect on famous persons whom you have admired as role models. Write an essay in which you examine the importance of role models and cultural heroes in determining how we see ourselves.
13. Describe a ceremony you have witnessed or participated in. Do it in two separate essays. In the first, describe the event simply in a neutral way. In the second, tell it from the point of view of a witness or participant.
*14. Read Grace Paley's "The Loudest Voice." Compare Mr. Donleavy's insensitivity to that shown by Shirley's teachers in the story. Cite specific instances to explain similarities and differences.

Barba Nikos

Harry Mark Petrakis

Harry Mark Petrakis was born in St. Louis in 1923 but has spent most of his life in and around Chicago. A novelist and short story writer, his books in-clude Pericles on 31st Street *(1965),* A Dream of Kings *(1966), and* Stelmark: A Family Recollection *(1970), from which the following selec-tion is an excerpt.*

In more recent years he has written a memoir, Tales of the Heart: Dreams and Memories of a Lifetime *(1999). Petrakis, himself of Greek descent, often sets the scene of his writing among Greek Americans and immigrants.*

The story Petrakis tells describes the strains that can come between first- and second-generation immigrants, when the ways of the Old Country—and their parents' accented English—become a source of embarrassment. Young people, trying to conform with their peers, may find this situation particularly trying.

Located in the eastern Mediterranean, Greece has some ten million in-habitants. It gained its independence in the nineteenth century after centuries of rule by the Turkish empire. It is a relatively poor country, many of whose people have sought their fortunes elsewhere, often in the United States, which has a large population of Greek descent.

Ancient Greece, the Greece Barba Nikos talks about so proudly, has of-ten been called "the cradle of Western civilization." Among its many small city states, Athens stands out as the first representative democracy. Of the earliest philosophers, poets, historians, and scientists whose works have been preserved, most are Athenians. Achilles, whom Barba Nikos mentions, is a mythical warrior who plays a central role in Homer's Iliad, *the epic poem about the war between the Greek city states and Troy. Alexander the Great, King of Macedonia, conquered the Middle East as far as India some 2,300 years ago. Marathon was not a race but a city in Greece where, in 490 B.C., the Athenians won a major battle against the invading Persians. According to legend, a Greek soldier ran from Marathon to Athens to carry the news of victory—before collapsing dead from the strain. He ran the same distance as the thousands who now run in marathons all over the world, ex-cept he ran it in full armor.*

1   There was one storekeeper I remember above all others in my youth. It was shortly before I became ill, spending a good portion of my time with a motley group of varied ethnic ancestry. We contended with one another to de-ride the customs of the old country. On our Saturday forays into neighborhoods beyond our own, to prove we were really Americans, we ate hot dogs and drank

Cokes. If a boy didn't have ten cents for this repast he went hungry, for he dared not bring a sandwich from home made of the spiced meats our families ate.

2   One of our untamed games was to seek out the owner of a pushcart or a store, unmistakably an immigrant, and bedevil him with a chorus of insults and jeers. To prove allegiance to the gang it was necessary to reserve our fiercest malevolence for a storekeeper or peddler belonging to our own ethnic background.

3   For that reason I led a raid on the small, shabby grocery of old Barba Nikos, a short, sinewy Greek who walked with a slight limp and sported a flaring, handlebar mustache.

4   We stood outside his store and dared him to come out. When he emerged to do battle, we plucked a few plums and peaches from the baskets on the sidewalk and retreated across the street to eat them while he watched. He waved a fist and hurled epithets at us in ornamental Greek.

5   Aware that my mettle was being tested, I raised my arm and threw my half-eaten plum at the old man. My aim was accurate and the plum struck him on the cheek. He shuddered and put his hand to the stain. He stared at me across the street, and although I could not see his eyes, I felt them sear my flesh. He turned and walked silently back into the store. The boys slapped my shoulders in admiration, but it was a hollow victory that rested like a stone in the pit of my stomach.

6   At twilight when we disbanded, I passed the grocery alone on my way home. There was a small light burning in the store and the shadow of the old man's body outlined against the glass. Goaded by remorse, I walked to the door and entered.

7   The old man moved from behind the narrow wooden counter and stared at me. I wanted to turn and flee, but by then it was too late. As he motioned for me to come closer, I braced myself for a curse or a blow.

8   "You were the one," he said, finally, in a harsh voice.

9   I nodded mutely.

10   "Why did you come back?"

11   I stood there unable to answer.

12   "What's your name?"

13   "Haralambos," I said, speaking to him in Greek.

14   He looked at me in shock. "You are Greek!" he cried. "A Greek boy attacking a Greek grocer!" He stood appalled at the immensity of my crime. "All right," he said coldly. "You are here because you wish to make amends." His great mustache bristled in concentration. "Four plums, two peaches," he said. "That makes a total of 78 cents. Call it 75. Do you have 75 cents, boy?"

15   I shook my head.

16   "Then you will work it off," he said. "Fifteen cents an hour into 75 cents makes"—he paused—"five hours of work. Can you come here Saturday morning?"

17   "Yes," I said.

18   "Yes, Barba Nikos," he said sternly. "Show respect."

19   "Yes, Barba Nikos," I said.

20   "Saturday morning at eight o'clock," he said. "Now go home and say thanks in your prayers that I did not loosen your impudent head with a solid smack on the ear." I needed no further urging and fled.

21   Saturday morning, still apprehensive, I returned to the store. I began by sweeping, raising clouds of dust in dark and hidden corners. I washed the windows, whipping the squeegee swiftly up and down the glass in a fever of fear that some member of the gang would see me. When I finished I hurried back inside.

22   For the balance of the morning I stacked cans, washed the counter, and dusted bottles of yellow wine. A few customers entered, and Barba Nikos served them. A little after twelve o'clock he locked the door so he could eat lunch. He cut himself a few slices of sausage, tore a large chunk from a loaf of crisp-crusted bread, and filled a small cup with a dozen black shiny olives floating in brine. He offered me the cup. I could not help myself and grimaced.

23   "You are a stupid boy," the old man said. "You are not really Greek, are you?"

24   "Yes, I am."

25   "You might be," he admitted grudgingly. "But you do not act Greek. Wrinkling your nose at these fine olives. Look around this store for a minute. What do you see?"

26   "Fruits and vegetables," I said. "Cheese and olives and things like that."

27   He stared at me with a massive scorn. "That's what I mean," he said. "You are a bonehead. You don't understand that a whole nation and a people are in this store."

28   I looked uneasily toward the storeroom in the rear, almost expecting someone to emerge.

29   "What about olives?" he cut the air with a sweep of his arm. "There are olives of many shapes and colors. Pointed black ones from Kalamata, oval ones from Amphissa, pickled green olives and sharp tangy yellow ones. Achilles carried black olives to Troy and after a day of savage battle leading his Myrmidons, he'd rest and eat cheese and ripe black olives such as these right here. You have heard of Achilles, boy, haven't you?"

30   "Yes," I said.

31   "Yes, Barba Nikos."

32   "Yes, Barba Nikos," I said.

33   He motioned at the row of jars filled with varied spices. "There is origanon there and basilikon and daphne and sesame and miantanos, all the marvelous flavorings that we have used in our food for thousands of years. The men of Marathon carried small packets of these spices into battle, and the scents reminded them of their homes, their families, and their children."

34   He rose and tugged his napkin free from around his throat. "Cheese, you said. Cheese! Come closer, boy, and I educate your abysmal ignorance." He motioned toward a wooden container on the counter. "That glistening white de-

light is feta, made from goat's milk, packed in wooden buckets to retain the flavor. Alexander the Great demanded it on his table with his casks of wine when he planned his campaigns."

35   He walked limping from the counter to the window where the piles of tomatoes, celery, and green peppers clustered. "I suppose all you see here are some random vegetables?" He did not wait for me to answer. "You are dumb again. These are some of the ingredients that go to make up a Greek salad. Do you know what a Greek salad really is? A meal in itself, an experience, an emotional involvement. It is created deftly and with grace. First, you place large lettuce leaves in a big, deep bowl." He spread his fingers and moved them slowly, carefully, as if he were arranging the leaves. "The remainder of the lettuce is shredded and piled in a small mound," he said. "Then comes celery, cucumbers, tomatoes sliced lengthwise, green peppers, origanon, green olives, feta, avocado and anchovies. At the end you dress it with lemon, vinegar, and pure olive oil, glinting golden in the light."

36   He finished with a heartfelt sigh and for a moment closed his eyes. Then he opened one eye to mark me with a baleful intensity. "The story goes that Zeus himself created the recipe and assembled and mixed the ingredients on Mount Olympus[1] one night when he had invited some of the other gods to dinner."

37   He turned his back on me and walked slowly again across the store, dragging one foot slightly behind him. I looked uneasily at the clock, which showed that it was a few minutes past one. He turned quickly and startled me. "And everything else in here," he said loudly. "White beans, lentils, garlic, crisp bread, kokoretsi, meat balls, mussels and clams." He paused and drew a deep, long breath. "And the wine," he went on, "wine from Samos, Santorini, and Crete, retsina and mavrodaphne, a taste almost as old as water . . . and then the fragrant melons, the pastries, yellow diples and golden loukoumades, the honey custard galatobouriko. Everything a part of our history, as much a part as the exquisite sculpture in marble, the bearded warriors, Pan[2] and the oracles at Delphi,[3] and the nymphs dancing in the shadowed groves under Homer's glittering moon." He paused, out of breath again, and coughed harshly. "Do you understand now, boy?"

38   He watched my face for some response and then grunted. We stood silent for a moment until he cocked his head and stared at the clock. "It is time for you to leave," he motioned brusquely toward the door. "We are square now. Keep it that way."

39   I decided the old man was crazy and reached behind the counter for my jacket and cap and started for the door. He called me back. From a box he drew out several soft, yellow figs that he placed in a piece of paper. "A bonus because

---

[1]Highest point in Greece. Believed to be the home of the gods in early Greek mythology.
[2]Greek god of woods, fields, and fertility. Pan was part human and part goat.
[3]The ancient Greeks believed Delphi to be the site of the oracle who spoke the words of the god Apollo.

you worked well," he said. "Take them. When you taste them, maybe you will understand what I have been talking about."

40   I took the figs and he unlocked the door and I hurried from the store. I looked back once and saw him standing in the doorway, watching me, the swirling tendrils of food curling like mist about his head.

41   I ate the figs late that night. I forgot about them until I was in bed, and then I rose and took the package from my jacket. I nibbled at one, then ate them all. They broke apart between my teeth with a tangy nectar, a thick sweetness running like honey across my tongue and into the pockets of my cheeks. In the morning when I woke, I could still taste and inhale their fragrance.

42   I never again entered Barba Nikos's store. My spell of illness, which began some months later, lasted two years. When I returned to the streets I had forgotten the old man and the grocery. Shortly afterwards my family moved from the neighborhood.

43   Some twelve years later, after the war, I drove through the old neighborhood and passed the grocery. I stopped the car and for a moment stood before the store. The windows were stained with dust and grime, the interior bare and desolate, a store in a decrepit group of stores marked for razing so new structures could be built.

44   I have been in many Greek groceries since then and have often bought the feta and Kalamata olives. I have eaten countless Greek salads and have indeed found them a meal for the gods. On the holidays in our house, my wife and sons and I sit down to a dinner of steaming, buttered pilaf like my mother used to make and lemon-egg avgolemono and roast lamb richly seasoned with cloves of garlic. I drink the red and yellow wines, and for dessert I have come to relish the delicate pastries coated with honey and powdered sugar. Old Barba Nikos would have been pleased.

45   But I have never been able to recapture the halcyon flavor of those figs he gave me on that day so long ago, although I have bought figs many times. I have found them pleasant to my tongue, but there is something missing. And to this day I am not sure whether it was the figs or the vision and passion of the old grocer that coated the fruit so sweetly I can still recall their savor and fragrance after almost thirty years.

EXERCISES

Some of the Issues

1. Why do the gang members attack immigrants of their own ethnic group?
2. What is the first sign that the narrator will change his mind about his deed?
3. What is the boy's first reaction to the olives? How does it set the scene for later reactions?

4. What does Barba Nikos mean when he says, "a whole nation and a people are in this store"?
5. In what way do the last two paragraphs sum up the theme of the essay?

The Way We Are Told

6. In the first four paragraphs the author uses a number of rather unusual words and phrases for simple events: *motley, repast, untamed, bedevil, malevolence, to do battle.* What effect is achieved by this choice?
7. Contrast the tone of the narrative frame at the beginning and end of the selection with the telling of the story through dialog in the middle. What is the effect?
8. Examine the various references to Barba Nikos throughout the selection. What impression do we have of him in the beginning? How does it change?
9. List the various references linking food and drink to mythology. What is their purpose?

Some Subjects for Writing

10. Write an essay about a traditional family celebration that was important to you as a child. Describe in detail the rituals, ceremonies, and foods associated with it. Was symbolism involved? What meaning did the ceremony have for you in early life? Has that meaning changed as you have grown older?
11. Interview several second-generation children of immigrants about their relationship to their family and their feelings about their identity. Using Petrakis as a starting point, write an essay in which you analyze and compare the similarities and differences between their experiences and beliefs.

Girlhood among Ghosts

Maxine Hong Kingston

Maxine Hong Kingston's parents came to America from China in the 1930s. She was born in Stockton, California, in 1940 and graduated from the University of California at Berkeley.

The following selection comes from The Woman Warrior: Memories of a Girlhood among Ghosts *(1976), for which Kingston received the National Book Critics Circle Award. The ghosts she refers to are of several kinds: the spirits and demons that Chinese peasants believed in, the ghosts of the dead, and, more significantly, the whole of non-Chinese America, peopled with strange creatures who seem very powerful but not quite human, and whose behavior is often inexplicable.*

Kingston continued her autobiography with China Men *(1981). Since then she has also written* Hawaii One Summer *(1981) and a novel,* Tripmaster Monkey *(1988).*

1   Long ago in China, knot-makers tied string into buttons and frogs, and rope into bell pulls. There was one knot so complicated that it blinded the knot-maker. Finally an emperor outlawed this cruel knot, and the nobles could not order it anymore. If I had lived in China, I would have been an outlaw knot-maker.

2   Maybe that's why my mother cut my tongue. She pushed my tongue up and sliced the frenum. Or maybe she snipped it with a pair of nail scissors, I don't remember her doing it, only her telling me about it, but all during childhood I felt sorry for the baby whose mother waited with scissors or knife in hand for it to cry—and then, when its mouth was wide open like a baby bird's, cut. The Chinese say "a ready tongue is an evil."

3   I used to curl up my tongue in front of the mirror and tauten my frenum into a white line, itself as thin as a razor blade. I saw no scars in my mouth. I thought perhaps I had had two frena, and she had cut one. I made other children open their mouths so I could compare theirs to mine. I saw perfect pink membranes stretching into precise edges that looked easy enough to cut. Sometimes I felt very proud that my mother committed such a powerful act upon me. At other times I was terrified—the first thing my mother did when she saw me was to cut my tongue.

4   "Why did you do that to me, Mother?"

5   "I told you."

6   "Tell me again."

7   "I cut it so that you would not be tongue-tied. Your tongue would be able to move in any language. You'll be able to speak languages that are completely dif-

ferent from one another. You'll be able to pronounce anything. Your frenum looked too tight to do those things, so I cut it."

8   "But isn't 'a ready tongue an evil'?"

9   "Things are different in this ghost country."

10   "Did it hurt me? Did I cry and bleed?"

11   "I don't remember. Probably."

12   She didn't cut the other children's. When I asked cousins and other Chinese children whether their mothers had cut their tongues loose, they said, "What?"

13   "Why didn't you cut my brothers' and sisters' tongues?"

14   "They didn't need it."

15   "Why not? Were theirs longer than mine?"

16   "Why don't you quit blabbering and get to work?"

17   If my mother was not lying she should have cut more, scraped away the rest of the frenum skin, because I have a terrible time talking. Or she should not have cut at all, tampering with my speech. When I went to kindergarten and had to speak English for the first time, I became silent. A dumbness—a shame— still cracks my voice in two, even when I want to say "hello" casually, or ask an easy question in front of the check-out counter, or ask directions of a bus driver. I stand frozen, or I hold up the line with the complete, grammatical sentence that comes squeaking out at impossible length. "What did you say?" says the cab driver, or "Speak up," so I have to perform again, only weaker the second time. A telephone call makes my throat bleed and takes up that day's courage. It spoils my day with self-disgust when I hear my broken voice come skittering out into the open. It makes people wince to hear it. I'm getting better, though. Recently I asked the postman for special-issue stamps; I've waited since childhood for postmen to give me some of their own accord. I am making progress, a little every day.

18   My silence was thickest—total—during the three years that I covered my school paintings with black paint. I painted layers of black over houses and flowers and suns, and when I drew on the blackboard, I put a layer of chalk on top. I was making a stage curtain, and it was the moment before the curtain parted or rose. The teachers called my parents to school, and I saw they had been saving my pictures, curling and cracking, all alike and black. The teachers pointed to the pictures and looked serious, talked seriously too, but my parents did not understand English. ("The parents and teachers of criminals were executed," said my father.) My parents took the pictures home. I spread them out (so black and full of possibilities) and pretended the curtains were swinging open, flying up, one after another, sunlight underneath, mighty operas.

19   During the first silent year I spoke to no one at school, did not ask before going to the lavatory, and flunked kindergarten. My sister also said nothing for three years, silent in the playground and silent at lunch. There were other quiet Chinese girls not of our family, but most of them got over it sooner than we did. I enjoyed the silence. At first it did not occur to me I was supposed to

talk or to pass kindergarten. I talked at home and to one or two of the Chinese kids in class. I made motions and even made some jokes. I drank out of a toy saucer when the water spilled out of the cup, and everybody laughed, pointing at me, so I did it some more. I didn't know that Americans don't drink out of saucers.

20   I liked the Negro students (Black Ghosts) best because they laughed the loudest and talked to me as if I were a daring talker too. One of the Negro girls had her mother coil braids over her ears Shanghai-style like mine; we were Shanghai twins except that she was covered with black like my paintings. Two Negro kids enrolled in Chinese school, and the teachers gave them Chinese names. Some Negro kids walked me to school and home, protecting me from the Japanese kids, who hit me and chased me and stuck gum in my ears. The Japanese kids were noisy and tough. They appeared one day in kindergarten, released from concentration camp, which was a tic-tac-toe mark, like barbed wire, on the map.

21   It was when I found out I had to talk that school became a misery, that the silence became a misery. I did not speak and felt bad each time that I did not speak. I read aloud in first grade, though, and heard the barest whisper with little squeaks come out of my throat. "Louder," said the teacher, who scared the voice away again. The other Chinese girls did not talk either, so I knew the silence had to do with being a Chinese girl.

22   Reading out loud was easier than speaking because we did not have to make up what to say, but I stopped often, and the teacher would think I'd gone quiet again. I could not understand "I." The Chinese "I" has seven strokes, intricacies. How could the American "I," assuredly wearing a hat like the Chinese, have only three strokes, the middle so straight? Was it out of politeness that this writer left off strokes the way a Chinese has to write her own name small and crooked? No, it was not politeness; "I" is a capital and "you" is lowercase. I stared at the middle line and waited so long for its black center to resolve into tight strokes and dots that I forgot to pronounce it. The other troublesome word was "here," no strong consonant to hang on to, and so flat, when "here" is two mountainous ideographs. The teacher, who had already told me every day how to read "I" and "here" put me in the low corner under the stairs again, where the noisy boys usually sat.

23   When my second grade class did a play, the whole class went to the auditorium except the Chinese girls. The teacher, lovely and Hawaiian, should have understood about us, but instead left us behind in the classroom. Our voices were too soft or nonexistent, and our parents never signed the permission slips anyway. They never signed anything unnecessary. We opened the door a crack and peeked out, but closed it again quickly. One of us (not me) won every spelling bee, though.

24   I remember telling the Hawaiian teacher, "We Chinese can't sing 'land where our fathers died.'" She argued with me about politics, while I meant be-

cause of curses. But how can I have that memory when I couldn't talk? My mother says that we, like the ghosts, have no memories.

After American school, we picked up our cigar boxes, in which we had arranged books, brushes, and an inkbox neatly, and went to Chinese school, from 5:00 to 7:30 P.M. There we chanted together, voices rising and falling, loud and soft, some boys shouting, everybody reading together, reciting together and not alone with one voice. When we had a memorization test, the teacher let each of us come to his desk and say the lesson to him privately, while the rest of the class practiced copying or tracing. Most of the teachers were men. The boys who were so well behaved in the American school played tricks on them and talked back to them. The girls were not mute. They screamed and yelled during recess, when there were no rules; they had fistfights. Nobody was afraid of children hurting themselves or of children hurting school property. The glass doors to the red and green balconies with the gold joy symbols were left wide open so that we could run out and climb the fire escapes. We played capture-the-flag in the auditorium, where Sun Yat-sen[1] and Chiang Kai-shek's[2] pictures hung at the back of the stage, the Chinese flag on their left and the American flag on their right. We climbed the teak ceremonial chairs and made flying leaps off the stage. One flag headquarters was behind the glass door and the other on stage right. Our feet drummed on the hollow stage. During recess the teachers locked themselves up in their office with the shelves of books, copybooks, inks from China. They drank tea and warmed their hands at a stove. There was no play supervision. At recess we had the school to ourselves, and also we could roam as far as we could go—downtown, Chinatown stores, home—as long as we returned before the bell rang.

At exactly 7:30 the teacher again picked up the brass bell that sat on his desk and swung it over our heads, while we charged down the stairs, our cheering magnified in the stairwell. Nobody had to line up.

Not all of the children who were silent at American school found voice at Chinese school. One new teacher said each of us had to get up and recite in front of the class, who was to listen. My sister and I had memorized the lesson perfectly. We said it to each other at home, one chanting, one listening. The teacher called on my sister to recite first. It was the first time a teacher had called on the second-born to go first. My sister was scared. She glanced at me and looked away; I looked down at my desk. I hoped that she could do it because if she could, then I would have to. She opened her mouth and a voice came out that wasn't a whisper, but it wasn't a proper voice either. I hoped that she would not cry, fear breaking up her voice like twigs underfoot.

[1](1866–1925) Chinese statesman and revolutionary leader.
[2](1887–1975) Chinese politician and general.

She sounded as if she were trying to sing though weeping and strangling. She did not pause or stop to end the embarrassment. She kept going until she said the last word, and then she sat down. When it was my turn, the same voice came out, a crippled animal running on broken legs. You could hear splinters in my voice, bones rubbing jagged against one another. I was loud, though. I was glad I didn't whisper. There was one little girl who whispered.

EXERCISES

Some of the Issues

1. After reading the selection explain why Kingston says in the first paragraph, "In China, I would have been an outlaw knot-maker." Why does she call herself an outlaw? And, considering the legend she tells, why would she have been a knot-maker?
2. "Maybe that's why my mother cut my tongue." That startling sentence introduces a remembered conversation with her mother. Is it possible that the tongue-cutting never took place? What evidence do you find either way?
3. Kingston is silent in some situations but not in others. When is she silent and when not?
4. How did the American and the Chinese schools differ in the way they were run? In the way they affected the children?

The Way We Are Told

5. Kingston uses several symbols: the knot, the tongue, the Chinese word for *I.* Explain their meaning and use.
6. What is the effect of the first sentence of paragraph 2? Were you startled by it?
7. Kingston departs from strict chronological order in telling her story. What is the effect?

Some Subjects for Writing

8. Kingston describes times when she was embarrassed or "tongue-tied." Describe a time when you were afraid to speak. Include descriptions of your feelings before, during, and after the incident.
9. Kingston suggests that, in Chinese-American culture, girls are brought up very differently from boys. In your own experience of the culture in which you were raised does gender make an important difference in upbringing? Give examples in your answer.

*10. In Maxine Hong Kingston's story and in Grace Paley's "The Loudest Voice," the question of voice plays a major role. In an essay, compare and contrast the two central characters' experience of losing and finding a voice.

Scents

Maria Laurino

*In this essay, Maria Laurino begins by describing a scene in her high school
gym class, a site of almost universal adolescent humiliation and embarrassment, and ends in an upscale perfumery in Paris. In between she takes the
reader on a journey that describes the scents that are the emotional markers
of her growing up. From her early adolescent efforts to distance herself from
her Italian heritage to her efforts as an adult to reconnect to what she has
lost, the sensuality of her culture plays an ever-present role.*

Laurino, a New York journalist who wrote for the Village Voice *for
many years, grew up in Short Hills, the suburban New Jersey town she describes here, and attended college at Georgetown University in Washington,
DC. This essay is the opening chapter of her memoir* Were You Always an
Italian? Ancestors, and Other Icons of Italian America *(2000), a national bestseller. The title of the book comes from a question posed to her by
former New York governor Mario Cuomo, as she was interviewing him on his
own Italian roots. At the time, she says, her honest answer was no. The book
is an attempt to explore her memories and impressions of growing up Italian-
American, and perhaps an attempt to answer that question for herself.*

1   I can still remember the day when my ethnicity no longer felt like the tag line
of my narrative, reluctantly affixed to my American self, but instead signified
an inescapable me. I was a teenager standing in line before gym class, and we
began to strut in sync, bare legs and barely covered bodies, to the gymnasium.
Our uniforms were the baby blue of surgeons' gowns and prison uniforms. I felt
both sick (or I feigned physical illness) and trapped (excuses about stomachaches
rarely worked) during those fifty forced minutes of exercise.

2   Gym class, humiliating gym class, had provoked earlier difficult episodes.
Once, in junior high—that particular place and time in which sameness is the
prize, and a seed of adolescent difference could sprout into a field of skunk
cabbage—a blond girl who had already developed curves that had captured the
attention of a league of boys mentioned with a bored nonchalance how she
needed to shave her legs. The blond girl's legs were as smooth and silky as a
newly varnished oak floor, and I couldn't imagine why she'd put a razor to her
skin. The hair on my legs, however, looked like a bed of wilted grass dipped in
black ink.

3   "I need to shave too," I naïvely replied. To share the truth—that my mother
thought I was too young to have a woman's legs—would have been mortifying,
but I also lacked the instinct to distract her with a line like "You know, Cybill

Shepherd couldn't hold a candle to your thighs," and quickly change the topic. The look of horror on that girl's face when she peered down at my calves is as clear to me today as it was back then in 1973. I'm sure she had never encountered the hirsute beauty of the Italian-American body.

4   The girl, too young to be tactful, revealed her thoughts in wide-eyed disbelief. At about the same time, I received a more discreet reaction to my appearance from a motherly neighbor who casually mentioned that I should bleach my dark arm hair blond. For much of my childhood I stood out in homogenized suburbia (hard as I tried to mask the Italian side of my hyphen); I grew up in a neighborhood where, in every other home, Mazola poured from clear plastic bottles, while we lifted heavy golden-colored tins of olive oil. To a child who wished to imitate others with the precision of a forger's brush, that was a clumsy, humiliating distinction. While such incidents embarrassed me, none was as difficult as this conversation before gym class:

5   "You were shopping at Saks the other day?" the popular girl next to me asked.

6   "Uh-huh," I meekly replied. (She had never spoken to me before; in retrospect the visit to Saks probably provided a necessary credential.)

7   "Yeah, I told my mother, 'That's the smelly Italian girl who stands in front of me in gym class'."

8   I was stunned. I didn't move quickly enough in class even to perspire. But instead of challenging her, I just stood there. Silently. As she continued to chatter, I yearned to shed my smell, my self, that very instant. Standing in the powerless world of childhood, a world in which the words and actions of peers cast the parts that we play for years, I intuitively understood that I was bound to the sweat of my ancestors, peasants from southern Italy. Even the name of the region, the Mezzogiorno, or "midday," invokes an oppressive afternoon heat that parches the skin and then showers it with drops of sweat.

9   Yet despite my deep self-consciousness, the part of me that recognized the significance of a school social hierarchy was flattered: this pretty, popular girl was talking to me. Sloe-eyed with chocolate brown hair, she was Jewish; I could never be like the Waspy girls, but I could see myself as a darker, rawer version of her. We were both slightly above average height, but she was thin, shaved her legs, plucked her eyebrows, and dyed unwanted lip hairs blond with a jar of Jolene. I, on the other hand, was chubby, and had the leg hairs of a grizzly, a light mustache, and a bristly black feather of an eyebrow that rested proudly at the bottom of my forehead.

10   Comprising our basic similarities, I saw the potential for my own reform. So I decided that if she continued to befriend me, I would ignore the nasty comment. In the following weeks, I tried to ingratiate myself into her world and she began to accept me. But always she'd tell classmates about the incident that sparked our first conversation. "I saw her shopping at Saks," she would say with a high-pitched giggle, "and I told my mother, 'That's the smelly Italian girl who stands in front of me in gym class'."

11   She never talked about the smelly girl, or that smelly girl who is Italian, but rather that "smelly Italian girl"—in other words, I was smelly *because* I was Italian. She also acted surprised to have seen me at Saks; with a popular girl's unfailing instinct for the social ladder, perhaps she found it amusing that an Italian girl, who should have been on the bottom rung, would shop in the town's fanciest store.

12   Soon sympathetic friends pulled me aside to say that I never smelled and she must have confused me with someone else. I burned with embarrassment, but politely nodded as they defended me. Looking back on those days, I must have believed them, since I did not begin to shower three times a day to escape my odors. Instead, I continued the same bath regimen (although I can't say precisely if it was every day or every other) and sprayed myself with a fragrance called Love's Fresh Lemon, marketed for teens with a popular Donovan song about wearing your love like heaven. Did I smell like hell and rotten lemons? Probably not. Rather than believing that I smelled, I accepted the definition of being smelly. That is, if someone thought I had a body odor, there must be something unpleasant about me that needed to be changed.

13   Gym class wasn't the only time I heard the words "Italian" and "smelly" placed together, like a pungent clove of garlic sweating in a pan of warm olive oil. A few months later, I was sitting in the cafeteria with my new gym pal and a friend of hers, sharing gossip and news between bites of our sandwiches. The other girl mentioned that her father was planning a trip to Italy, and my friend and I swayed in delight at the idea of traveling to Europe.

14   "Are you going with him?" we asked in an enthusiastic chorus.

15   "Are you kidding?" she replied with a girlish laugh. "And be around all those smelly Italians?"

16   Suellen Hoy, the author of a book on cleanliness, tells this anecdote: In 1957, when she was a teenager and had recently begun to shave, she was lounging at a pool with several other bare-legged friends. There they saw an older woman in a beautiful bathing suit reveal her hairy legs and armpits. Hoy was "shocked and repulsed" to see this woman's unsightly hair in public, and her girlfriends decided that the woman must be "foreign" because European women didn't shave. The incident, Hoy explains, first taught her about America's obsession with being clean. Not much has changed—she also cites a "Dear Abby" column from 1985 in which a reader advises that if "'Rapunzel Legs' [is] too lazy to shave, she should move to Europe." Another woman wrote in that Europeans who don't shave also "think sweat and other natural body odors are sexy. Pee-ooey!"

17   It may be a peculiarly American habit to associate leg hair with dirt. Ultimately, however, looking dark and unkempt because of unwanted body hair is very different from being called smelly. I wonder if I earned that label because I seemed more foreign than the rest of the girls in my class. Not that we were recent Italian immigrants; I am third-generation, the youngest of my grandparents' youngest-born. Yet around the same time as the gym incident, a teacher

who called out my name for attendance on the first day of class asked if I spoke English.

18   The label "smelly Italian" was acceptable to many teenagers in my high school for another reason: body odor suggests that you are ill-bred, a member of the lower class. For centuries, the sweet scents of the upper class and the earthy smells of the lower class differentiated both groups in body and spirit. More than the clothes one wears or the language one speaks, the stink that fills the air of an unwashed person, the dirt and sweat that turn underarms and loins into a triangular estuary of odor, a repository of the unwanted emissions of our bodies, separates the classes. The "basement odor of the masses," as Flaubert once wrote, serves as one of the clearest demarcations between rich and poor.

19   The issue of smell and class plagued George Orwell for many years. In *The Road to Wigan Pier*, his treatise for a socialist state, Orwell wrote with characteristic bluntness that there are "four frightful words which people nowadays are chary of uttering," that is, "the lower classes smell." Orwell reasoned that class equality could never be achieved if the bourgeoisie continued to consider the lower classes "inherently dirty," making olfactory distinctions between *us* and *them*. Such a judgment can be impenetrable, he claimed, because a physical feeling of dislike is far more difficult to transcend than an intellectual one.

20   Orwell may have paid particular attention to odors because as a child he had his own fears that he smelled bad. Describing his experiences as a scholarship student in an elite public school, Orwell wrote in his essay "Such, Such Were the Joys . . .": "A child's belief in its own shortcomings is not much influenced by facts. I believed, for example, that I 'smelt' but this was based simply on general probability. It was notorious that disagreeable people smelt, and therefore presumably I did so too."

21   Orwell thought that he was "disagreeable" because his family was poorer than those of the other boys at his school, who came from the highest quarters of English society. The writer, with his flawless understanding of England's class system, famously described his family's economic status as "lower-upper-middle class." But because class distinction is relative and children want more than anything to be like their peers, Orwell must have imagined that a lower-class boy smelled—and that he took on this trait.

22   I may have accepted my classmates' assumptions because my family's economic position could be described as deep in the basement of upper-middle-class life, or, more accurately, we lived a middle-middle class life—in the strict American sense of annual income. (Orwell came from an established English family whose fortunes had dwindled.) The notion that I was called smelly because I was Italian seemed as logical a matter of cause and effect as that I was chubby because I ate brownies at lunch. Growing up in Short Hills, New Jersey, a suburb that produced debutantes just as Detroit manufactured steel, I learned as a child that the shrill whistle sounding every hour at the station signaled more than an approaching train: the town's dividing line was drawn at the railroad, and we were on the wrong side of the tracks. While many of my friends lived in

sprawling ranch houses with stone patios and outdoor pools, our little split-level house in a new development had a modest lawn that blended into the same-sized property of our neighbors, who were mostly small businessmen, middle managers, and teachers. As my neighborhood pal would remind me, we lived in "the ghetto of Short Hills."

23   Perhaps any child who is poor among the rich learns to kowtow to the needs of the wealthy, and in doing so carries a deep sense of shame over her own inadequacies. The child intuits the sense of privilege that the rich share, and knows she'll be rewarded by indulging them, commenting on how lovely their house is, oohing and aahing at the wall of mirrors in the bathroom, enthusiastically accepting the gracious invitation to swim in their pool. Her role is to be a constant reminder, like a grandfather clock that chimes reassuringly, of just how much they have.

24   But people pride themselves on degrees of wealth, so I never forgot that the real "ghetto" was in a section of Millburn, the neighboring town where my father had grown up, that housed an enclave of Italian-Americans. Because Short Hills was part of Millburn Township, the poor kids and young gents went to school together (the public school was so good that there was not the usual channeling of the elite to private schools). In both junior high and high school, there were mainly middle-, upper-middle-, and upper-class teens. Latinos and African-Americans were still excluded back then, so the only people of color in my high school were the children of the housekeeper at the local Catholic church. That left the largest dark ethnic group: the lower-middle-class Italians from Millburn, and the only kids labeled with an ethnic slur.

25   In high school, the Italian-American boys were known as the "Ginzo Gang"; they were greasers with beat-up cars that first chugged, then soared, thanks to their work at the local gas station (Palumbo's), owned by the father of one of them. Olive-skinned and muscular, they were sexy in their crudeness; and their faint gasoline scent and oiled-down hair defined the image of Italian-Americans in our school. The young women who hung out with them had little separate identity other than as the girlfriends of the Ginzos.

26   The Ginzos were my rearview mirror, a reflection of the near past that I wished to move beyond. They were an acknowledgment of my heritage, a recognition that the small sum of money my mother had inherited from her parents, used as the down payment on our house in a neighborhood a mile away, allowed me to escape from their world. But who was I fooling? My grandfather, who started a small construction company, earned his money by digging the earth; sweat and dirt were part of me, an oath of fealty to my family's peasant past. Yet I preferred to bury the memories of his labor, which provided us with some material comforts but not enough to rid me of the label of the "smelly Italian girl."

27   In the interval between the accusation of being smelly and an unspoken admission of my guilt, a denial of my ethic self emerged. Unprepared to confront my fears, I responded like a criminal who'd do anything to get the charges

dropped. If the cause of being called smelly were my Italian roots, then I would pretend not to be Italian.

28   At first I rejected the smells of my southern European heritage. Gone were the tastes and aromas of my youth: the sweet scent of tomato sauce simmering on the stove, soothing as a cup of tea on a rainy night; the paper-thin slices of prosciutto, salty and smooth on the tongue; and my own madeleine,[1] oil-laden frying peppers, light green in color with long, curvaceous bodies that effortlessly glide down the throat and conjure up memories of summer day trips to Asbury Park, where we ate ham, Swiss, and fried pepper sandwiches prepared by my mother. Instead, I began to savor the old flavors of eastern Europe, new to my tongue: pickled herring and cured fish, sour and smoky, and the brisket I was served when I ate holiday meals with my new friend from gym class.

29   Decades later, when I told my Jewish husband that in high school I tried to assimilate by imitating his culture, he laughed. But in the uninformed world of the adolescent, narrow assumptions get made about the scheme of things. At the time, I didn't understand that the Jewish girls who zealously booked plastic surgery appointments with Howard Diamond, the Manhattan doctor famous for creating identical pug noses in Short Hills and Great Neck,[2] Long Island, were undergoing a similar identity struggle.

30   Stripped of familiar smells, next I wanted to eliminate the extra baggage of vowels, those instant markers of ethnicity.

31   "Mom, why did you name me Maria?" went my familiar dinner-table question.

32   "Hun, why did we choose Maria?" she'd say, deferring to my father. He had wanted to name me Denise, after a Belgian child who greeted his troop during World War II and remained etched in his memory.

33   "Mama's name was Maria," my mom would add, interrupting her own question and recognizing that she was the keeper of tradition, the holder of the deciding vote. "Your father's mother was Maria, and I loved the actress Maria Montez."

34   Her last explanation was the consolation prize, the frayed ticket to the American scene that she had won and wished to hand to me. Naming me after a beautiful, vapid actress (Spanish, no less) would have revealed an unseen side of my mother, one that had rebelled against the expectation of having to show respect. A momentary fantasy, a chimera. I'm certain that I was named after my mother's mother.

35   But I would adopt the Montez interpretation. That both my grandmothers were named Maria bore little relevance at the time; a grade B movie actress, however, at least sounded glamorous.

---

[1]In Marcel Proust's novel *Remembrance of Things Past*, the narrator eats a madeleine (a French cookie), which triggers a flood of memories.
[2]Wealthy towns near New York City.

36   "Why didn't you change your last name to Laurin?" I continued in my teenage whine. During these end-of-the-day efforts to sanitize myself, washing off an *o* seemed a clean, decisive stroke.

37   Only years later did I begin the precarious work of trying to replace the layers of ethnicity I had stripped away in order to dissociate myself from the smelly Italians. The alien surroundings of college fostered a nostalgia for familiar tastes and allowed me to appreciate the foods I had grown up with, although not everyone shared my enthusiasm. Once my freshman roommate approached me, her face a picture of compassion and concern, as I entered our tiny dorm room. How was my weak stomach? she asked. Momentarily befuddled, I soon realized that she had confused the pungent aroma of the provolone I had recently eaten with that of vomit, and believed that I had thrown up in our room.

38   By my early twenties, I learned more about the girl at the cafeteria table who talked about the smelly Italians. According to the local grapevine, her parents were getting divorced because her father had been making seasonal trips to Italy to visit his secret mistress and their two children. Now I realize that she probably was never invited on her father's frequent sojourns, and the thoughtless remark was the defense of an insecure child, rejected by a man too busy sniffing the earthy scents of Italians to spend much time with her.

39   Today I have a new fear about smell; I fear that I lack a defining odor. I feel removed from my own sense of smell and the images it could conjure. I feel a languorous appreciation for everyday scents, like my pots of dried lavender, whose wildflower fragrance has faded to a docile sachet, as its deep purple buds grew pale with streaks of beige, a graceful bow to domesticity and old age. I refuse to linger by the coffeepot and sniff my carefully chosen beans, or inhale their smoky end, first ground, then muddied and scorched by a hot rain; instead, I quickly dump the grounds and wash the pot in soapy water, just as I will rush to lather the summer heat off my body. No smell, no mess. Life is measured, careful, far removed from the chaos of dirt and its primitive pleasures, and the smelly label of my youth.

40   Clean, but without texture; scrubbed of the salty drops that tell our singular stories. I fear that after years of trying to rid myself of the perceived stench of my ethnic group and its musty basement-class status, I sanitized my own voice, washed it away.

41   Certain incidents in life—like being told during gym class that you smell—become emotional markers, and around these events a series of reactions are set in motion: giving up pizza for pickled herring can take years to undo. I have recently come to notice how much time I spend scenting my body, covering it with colognes, milks, and creams, giving it a pleasant but artificial character, or voice, you could say. At first I was unaware that I had become perfume-obsessed, as people can often be unaware of their obsessions. But now I think I can link its beginnings to a time and a place.

42   Initially, I didn't realize the connection between a fragrance fixation and a freelance writing career, but neither did I fully understand that a spray of

cologne can provide a narrative for your body in case your own story lacks luster. My aromatic addiction began when I decided not to return (after a brief stint in government) to the newspaper I had worked at for nearly a decade, which was as familiar as family. I was nervous about the decision to freelance, because it not only took away an important piece of identity but would force me to choose my subjects, instead of writing about what others expected of me. And perhaps even worse, telling people that you are a full-time freelancer sounds more like a euphemism for unemployment than an adult career choice. So I acted a bit like the child who leaves home for the first time: one part wants to go while the other kicks and drags his way down the stairs, clutching the newel post. The final decision to step out the door and not return to my old work home coincided with a surprise birthday gift from my husband, a five-day trip to Paris. A perfect distraction, except that I found myself spending a good part of the time thinking about a particular French cologne.

43   I would like to chalk it up to coincidence rather than to Freud that I had occasionally been wearing a French cologne with a light lemon scent and Roman emperor's name Eau d'Hadrien, which seemed like an elegant version of the Love's Fresh Lemon of my youth. But maybe the alchemy of a new affection for Europe and my old need to hide Italian smells with lemons conjured an odd sensory experience—reluctance, relief!—when I first sniffed this cologne.

44   I went to a small Left Bank perfumery filled with fluted glass bottles capped in gold and bought my scent, one of my tasks in Paris, because it was cheaper there than back home. The saleswoman handed me the bag and then made an irresistible gesture: she sprayed my body, from my neck to my thighs, with cologne. Her hands flowed gently yet confidently around me, and the idea of being covered in fragrance, not frugally dabbed behind the ears, was so enticing that I went back to the store every day for a purchase and another spray. I had discovered a scented balm to soothe a shaky ego.

45   "Is this a gift for someone?" she asked upon my return.

46   "No it's for me," I happily responded, waiting for the soft mist to drape me like a gossamer veil.

47   After that trip, I became even more attached to the fragrance, or perhaps the idea of this fragrance. In department stores, I allowed myself one indulgent purchase: hand cream, body lotion, perfumed body cream (my favorite—it's as if I'm covered in lemons and cream), soaps, other colognes to mix with my fragrance to create a new, layered smell—the possibilities seemed endless. I no longer just sprayed behind the ears but covered myself completely in the scent, letting the perfume conquer the blandness of a scrubbed self, an elixir to enliven a diffident voice.

48   I used to think that my guilt-free desire for an expensive French cologne meant that I was at least coming to terms with the embarrassing bourgeois side of myself, which capitalized on the chic of a European heritage rather than my real-life peasant roots. But now I realize that, like the young girl who wanted to deny her heritage, again I was ducking for cover. I never quite unlearned the lesson from gym class long ago, when the voices of my family and my past were

silenced as I altered the scents surrounding me. It's easier to shower away a smell, to censor yourself with a scent, than to accept your body's signature, the rawness of odor and sweat.

49   The smelly Italian girl no longer exists, if she ever did. In addition to my fragrance, my body is practically hairless, waxed from lip to toe by a Gallic woman who says "Voilà" after finishing each leg and who reminisces about her country, sharing with me that she knows the colorist who knows the colorist who mixes the blond hair dye for Catherine Deneuve (her six strands of separation from true glamour). During the months between waxings, I let my leg hair grow long and I run my fingers through it, still mystified by the abundance of those dark strands that I wish to find beautiful, but that I ultimately decide to remove once again.

50   I have tried to escape the class boundaries of my youth, but sometimes, in that lonely space between me and the bathwater, I wonder what has become of my own smell, and what it would be like to uncover a voice that could tell the stories of my past.

EXERCISES

Some of the Issues

1. After you have finished reading the essay, look again at the first sentence. What does Laurino mean when she states: "Ethnicity no longer felt like the tag line of my narrative, reluctantly affixed to my American self, but instead signified an inescapable me"?
2. What does Laurino see as some of the physical and sensory markers of her Italian identity? Does she describe these markers in a positive or negative light?
3. What does unmanaged hair symbolize in American culture, according to Laurino? What do people associate it with and how are these associations symbolic of social and economic status?
4. Ultimately, how does Laurino describe herself in terms of class (paragraph 22)? What do you feel Laurino is trying to say about class, particularly as it relates to American culture?
5. Why does Laurino refer to the Ginzos as her "rearview mirror" (paragraph 26)? What is trying she trying to move beyond?
6. Why does Laurino's husband laugh when she tells him that she tried to assimilate by imitating Jewish culture (paragraph 29)?
7. What is Laurino's "new fear about smell" (paragraph 39)?
8. What voices does Laurino want to uncover (paragraph 50)? How were they silenced? In your answer, use examples from throughout the essay.

The Way We Are Told

9. To what does Laurino compare the blue of the gym uniforms (paragraph 1)? What does the comparison imply?

10. Are there sections of Laurino's narrative that you find humorous? Which sections are they and why are they funny? How might humor help her set the tone in her essay?

11. At what points does Laurino use dialogue in her narrative? Is this effective?

12. As with many narratives, Laurino does not state her thesis directly. She does, however, want to convey specific messages about class, ethnic heritage, and identity. Summarize two or three of the claims you feels she is making.

13. Reflect on the title. Does the word "scents" usually carry negative or positive connotations? Why doesn't Laurino use the word "smells" as a title?

*14. From what perspective is Laurino writing: that of a teenager, an adult, or both? Where do you see indications of either of these perspectives? Compare her point of view to that of Gary Soto in "The Jacket."

Some Subjects for Writing

15. Of all the senses, smell has been thought to be the one that evokes our most vivid memories. Write a narrative about an incident, person, or place brought back to you by a certain smell. It might be the aroma of a specific food, a fragrance a person you knew wore, or a smell from a natural setting. Try to apply some of the same techniques Laurino uses such as dialogue, metaphor and simile, and detailed description to make your narrative vivid.

*16. How and why do certain attributes become markers of economic class? Using specific examples from "Scents" as well as from other essays in the book (for example, Gary Soto's "The Jacket") write an essay in which you examine the relationship between class and specific material markers (clothing, looks, or odors) in your own current environment or in the environment in which you grew up.

*17. How does food help reinforce and develop a sense of cultural, ethnic and class identity? Using Laurino's essay, Harry Mark Petrakis's "Barba Nikos," and your own experience as examples, write an essay in which you explore some aspect of the relationship between food and identity.

The Loudest Voice

Grace Paley

Grace Paley grew up in the Bronx, New York, where she was born in 1922. Her first published collection of short stories, The Little Disturbances of Man, *which appeared in 1959, contained this story. Since then she has published* Enormous Changes at the Last Minute *(1974),* Later the Same Day *(1985),* Leaning Forward *(1985),* Long Walks and Intimate Talks *(1991), and* Just As I Thought *(1998). A complete volume of her fiction,* The Collected Stories, *was published in 1994.* Begin Again, *her collected poems, was published in 2000.*

Most of Paley's stories are set in New York and treat the lives of a great range of people of different backgrounds, Jews, African-Americans, Italians, Puerto Ricans, and Irish. She is noted particularly for her ability to capture the flavor of American speech, and for using dialogue as a way to establish character.

In her short story "The Loudest Voice," Grace Paley tells how an unthinking school administration dealt with the children under its authority. There are almost no Christian children in Shirley Abramowitz's grade school, but the teachers find it natural to foist a Christmas pageant on them. The results are hilarious as well as thought provoking.

1   There is a certain place where dumb-waiters boom, doors slam, dishes crash; every window is a mother's mouth bidding the street shut up, go skate somewhere else, come home. My voice is the loudest.

2   There, my own mother is still as full of breathing as me and the grocer stands up to speak to her. "Mrs. Abramowitz," he says, "people should not be afraid of their children."

3   "Ah, Mr. Bialik," my mother replies, "if you say to her or her father 'Ssh,' they say, 'In the grave it will be quiet.'"

4   "From Coney Island[1] to the cemetery," says my papa. "It's the same subway; it's the same fare."

5   I am right next to the pickle barrel. My pinky is making tiny whirlpools in the brine. I stop a moment to announce: "Campbell's Tomato Soup. Campbell's Vegetable Beef Soup. Campbell's S-c-otch Broth . . ."

6   "Be quiet," the grocer says, "the labels are coming off."

7   "Please, Shirley, be a little quiet," my mother begs me.

---

[1]Brooklyn amusement park on the Atlantic Ocean.

8   In that place the whole street groans: Be quiet! Be quiet! but steals from the happy chorus of my inside self not a tittle or a jot.

9   There, too, but just around the corner, is a red brick building that has been old for many years. Every morning the children stand before it in double lines which must be straight. They are not insulted. They are waiting anyway.

10   I am usually among them. I am, in fact, the first, since I begin with "A."

11   One cold morning the monitor tapped me on the shoulder. "Go to Room 409, Shirley Abramowitz," he said. I did as I was told. I went in a hurry up a down staircase to Room 409, which contained sixth-graders. I had to wait at the desk without wiggling until Mr. Hilton, their teacher, had time to speak.

12   After five minutes he said, "Shirley?"

13   "What?" I whispered.

14   He said, "My! My! Shirley Abramowitz! They told me you had a particularly loud, clear voice and read with lots of expression. Could that be true?"

15   "Oh yes," I whispered.

16   "In that case, don't be silly; I might very well be your teacher someday. Speak up, speak up."

17   "Yes," I shouted.

18   "More like it," he said. "Now, Shirley, can you put a ribbon in your hair or a bobby pin? It's too messy."

19   "Yes!" I bawled.

20   "Now, now, calm down." He turned to the class. "Children, not a sound. Open at page 39. Read till 52. When you finish, start again." He looked me over once more. "Now, Shirley, you know, I suppose, that Christmas is coming. We are preparing a beautiful play. Most of the parts have been given out. But I still need a child with a strong voice, lots of stamina. Do you know what stamina is? You do? Smart kid. You know, I heard you read 'The Lord is my shepherd' in Assembly yesterday. I was very impressed. Wonderful delivery. Mrs. Jordan, your teacher, speaks highly of you. Now listen to me, Shirley Abramowitz, if you want to take the part and be in the play, repeat after me, 'I swear to work harder than I ever did before.'"

21   I looked to heaven and said at once, "Oh, I swear." I kissed my pinky and looked at God.

22   "That is an actor's life, my dear," he explained. "Like a soldier's, never tardy or disobedient to his general, the director. Everything," he said, "absolutely everything will depend on you."

23   That afternoon, all over the building, children scraped and scrubbed the turkeys and the sheaves of corn off the schoolroom windows. Goodbye Thanksgiving. The next morning a monitor brought red paper and green paper from the office. We made new shapes and hung them on the walls and glued them to the doors.

24   The teachers became happier and happier. Their heads were ringing like the bells of childhood. My best friend Evie was prone to evil, but she did not get a single demerit for whispering. We learned "Holy Night" without an error.

"How wonderful!" said Miss Glacé, the student teacher. "To think that some of you don't even speak the language!" We learned "Deck the Halls" and "Hark! The Herald Angels.". . . They weren't ashamed and we weren't embarrassed.

25   Oh, but when my mother heard about it all, she said to my father: "Misha, you don't know what's going on there. Cramer is the head of the Tickets Committee."

26   "Who?" asked my father. "Cramer! Oh yes, an active woman."

27   "Active? Active has to have a reason. Listen," she said sadly, "I'm surprised to see my neighbors making tra-la-la for Christmas."

28   My father couldn't think of what to say to that. Then he decided: "You're in America! Clara, you wanted to come here. In Palestine the Arabs would be eating you alive. Europe you had pogroms.[2] Argentina is full of Indians. Here you got Christmas. . . . Some joke, ha?"

29   "Very funny, Misha. What is becoming of you? If we came to a new country a long time ago to run away from tyrants, and instead we fall into a creeping pogrom, that our children learn a lot of lies, so what's the joke? Ach, Misha, your idealism is going away."

30   "So is your sense of humor."

31   "That I never had, but idealism you had a lot of."

32   "I'm the same Misha Abramovitch, I didn't change an iota. Ask anyone."

33   "Only ask me," says my mama, may she rest in peace. "I got the answer."

34   Meanwhile the neighbors had to think of what to say too.

35   Marty's father said: "You know, he has a very important part, my boy."

36   "Mine also," said Mr. Sauerfeld.

37   "Not my boy!" said Mrs. Klieg. "I said to him no. The answer is no. When I say no! I mean no!"

38   The rabbi's wife said, "It's disgusting!" But no one listened to her. Under the narrow sky of God's great wisdom she wore a strawberry-blond wig.

39   Every day was noisy and full of experience. I was Right-hand Man. Mr. Hilton said: "How could I get along without you, Shirley?"

40   He said: "Your mother and father ought to get down on their knees every night and thank God for giving them a child like you."

41   He also said: "You're absolutely a pleasure to work with, my dear, dear child."

42   Sometimes he said: "For God's sakes, what did I do with the script? Shirley! Shirley! Find it."

43   Then I answered quietly: "Here it is, Mr. Hilton."

44   Once in a while, when he was very tired, he would cry out: "Shirley, I'm just tired of screaming at those kids. Will you tell Ira Pushkov not to come in till Lester points to that star the second time?"

---

[2]Organized massacres of Jews in turn-of-the-century Russia and in Nazi Germany.

45   Then I roared: "Ira Pushkov, what's the matter with you? Dope! Mr. Hilton told you five times already, don't come in till Lester points to that star the second time."

46   "Ach, Clara," my father asked, "what does she do there till six o'clock she can't even put the plates on the table?"

47   "Christmas," said my mother coldly.

48   "Ho! Ho!" my father said. "Christmas. What's the harm? After all, history teaches everyone. We learn from reading this is a holiday from pagan times also, candles, lights, even Chanukah. So we learn it's not altogether Christian. So if they think it's a private holiday, they're only ignorant, not patriotic. What belongs to history, belongs to all men. You want to go back to the Middle Ages? Is it better to shave your head with a secondhand razor? Does it hurt Shirley to learn to speak up? It does not. So maybe someday she won't live between the kitchen and the shop. She's not a fool."

49   I thank you, Papa, for your kindness. It is true about me to this day. I am foolish but I am not a fool.

50   That night my father kissed me and said with great interest in my career, "Shirley, tomorrow's your big day. Congrats."

51   "Save it," my mother said. Then she shut all the windows in order to prevent tonsillitis.

52   In the morning it snowed. On the street corner a tree had been decorated for us by a kind city administration. In order to miss its chilly shadow our neighbors walked three blocks east to buy a loaf of bread. The butcher pulled down black window shades to keep the colored lights from shining on his chickens. Oh, not me. On the way to school, with both my hands I tossed it a kiss of tolerance. Poor thing, it was a stranger in Egypt.

53   I walked straight into the auditorium past the staring children. "Go ahead, Shirley!" said the monitors. Four boys, big for their age, had already started work as propmen and stagehands.

54   Mr. Hilton was very nervous. He was not even happy. Whatever he started to say ended in a sideward look of sadness. He sat slumped in the middle of the first row and asked me to help Miss Glacé. I did this, although she thought my voice too resonant and said, "Show-off!"

55   Parents began to arrive long before we were ready. They wanted to make a good impression. From among the yards of drapes I peeked out at the audience. I saw my embarrassed mother.

56   Ira, Lester, and Meyer were pasted to their beards by Miss Glacé. She almost forgot to thread the star on its wire, but I reminded her. I coughed a few times to clear my throat. Miss Glacé looked around and saw that everyone was in costume and on line waiting to play his part. She whispered, "All right . . ." Then:

57   Jackie Sauerfeld, the prettiest boy in first grade, parted the curtains with his skinny elbow and in a high voice sang out:

> *"Parents dear*
> *We are here*
> *To make a Christmas play in time.*
> *It we give*
> *In narrative*
> *And illustrate with pantomime."*

58   He disappeared.

59   My voice burst immediately from the wings to the great shock of Ira, Lester, and Meyer, who were waiting for it but were surprised all the same.

60   "I remember, I remember, the house where I was born . . ."

61   Miss Glacé yanked the curtain open and there it was, the house—an old hayloft, where Celia Kornbluh lay in the straw with Cindy Lou, her favorite doll. Ira, Lester, and Meyer moved slowly from the wings toward her, sometimes pointing to a moving star and sometimes ahead to Cindy Lou.

62   It was a long story and it was a sad story. I carefully pronounced all the words about my lonesome childhood, while little Eddie Braunstein wandered upstage and down with his shepherd's stick, looking for sheep. I brought up lonesomeness again, and not being understood at all except by some women everybody hated. Eddie was too small for that and Marty Groff took his place, wearing his father's prayer shawl. I announced twelve friends, and half the boys in the fourth grade gathered round Marty, who stood on an orange crate while my voice harangued. Sorrowful and loud, I declaimed about love and God and Man, but because of the terrible deceit of Abie Stock we came suddenly to a famous moment. Marty, whose remembering tongue I was, waited at the foot of the cross. He stared desperately at the audience. I groaned, "My God, my God, why hast thou forsaken me?" The soldiers who were sheiks grabbed poor Marty to pin him up to die, but he wrenched free, turned again to the audience, and spread his arms aloft to show despair and the end. I murmured at the top of my voice, "The rest is silence, but as everyone in this room, in this city—in this world—now knows, I shall have life eternal."

63   That night Mrs. Kornbluh visited our kitchen for a glass of tea.

64   "How's the virgin!" asked my father with a look of concern.

65   "For a man with a daughter, you got a fresh mouth, Abramovitch."

66   "Here," said my father kindly, "have some lemon, it'll sweeten your disposition."

67   They debated a little in Yiddish, then fell in a puddle of Russian and Polish. What I understood next was my father, who said, "Still and all, it was certainly a beautiful affair, you have to admit, introducing us to the beliefs of a different culture."

68   "Well, yes," said Mrs. Kornbluh. "The only thing . . . you know Charlie Turner—that cute boy in Celia's class—a couple others? They got very small parts or no part at all. In very bad taste, it seemed to me. After all, it's their religion."

69   "Ach," explained my mother, "what could Mr. Hilton do? They got very small voices; after all, why should they holler? The English language they know from the beginning by heart. They're blond like angels. You think it's so important they should get in the play? Christmas . . . the whole piece of goods . . . they own it."

70   I listened and listened until I couldn't listen any more. Too sleepy, I climbed out of bed and kneeled. I made a little church of my hands and said, "Hear, O Israel . . ." Then I called out in Yiddish, "Please, good night, good night. Ssh." My father said, "Ssh yourself," and slammed the kitchen door.

71   I was happy. I fell asleep at once. I had prayed for everybody: my talking family, cousins far away, passersby, and all the lonesome Christians. I expected to be heard. My voice was certainly the loudest.

EXERCISES

Some of the Issues

1. In paragraphs 1 through 8 Paley tells about "a certain place." How does she describe it? Do we know what it looked like? What it sounded like? How do we know that it is a place in Shirley's memory?
2. In paragraph 9 we move to another place, just around the corner. How are we told about that place?
3. Shirley has the loudest voice in the school, but at some points she whispers or talks softly. When and why?
4. Mr. Hilton has a number of ways of getting Shirley and the other children to do what he wants them to do. What techniques does he use? How sincere do you think he is? How much do he and the other teachers seem to understand or care about the children in the school?
5. Shirley's mother and father disagree with one another at several points in the story. Find the points where they disagree. What position does the father take consistently? The mother?
6. In paragraph 24 Miss Glacé, the student teacher, makes a comment. Does she believe it is a compliment? Is it really? Does her remark, and others made by teachers in the school, give any indication of their attitudes toward the children and their families?
7. Read the last sentences of paragraph 24; who is referred to as "we"? As "they"?
8. Paragraphs 34 through 38 tell how the neighbors react to the upcoming school play. What is their reaction? Why does no one pay attention to the rabbi's wife?
9. Read paragraph 52. Explain the people's reaction to "the tree." Why is it a stranger in Egypt?
10. Paragraphs 57 through 62 tell about the actual performance of the Christmas play. What is the story being told in the play? What parts are each of

the children playing? How well do the children seem to understand the story and their parts?

11. Examine the last paragraph. Whom does Shirley pray for and why? In what way can Shirley be said to have triumphed?

The Way We Are Told

12. Grace Paley is known for her good ear for dialog. She is said to create dialog that sounds natural and conveys a sense of her characters' personalities. A large part of this story is told through dialog. Examine it, and show how it conveys the sense of each character who speaks and how it carries the story along.

13. Did you find the story funny? If so, why? Does the humorous tone help or hinder its serious purpose?

Some Subjects for Writing

14. We know Shirley, and indeed all of the characters in the story, through their voices. Unlike many authors, Paley gives few visual descriptions. We are not told the color of Shirley's hair, or how tall she is, or even exactly how old she is. We may, however, be able to form images in our minds about what she and others are like, from our knowledge of what they say and how they say it. Imagine that "The Loudest Voice" is to be filmed. You are the casting director. Tell how you would visualize Paley's characters: Shirley, her parents, and the various teachers.

15. In this story Paley describes people and places by means of sound, not appearance. Write a paragraph giving a vivid description of a place you know well, using primarily sounds to describe it, and avoiding visual details as much as possible.

16. Have you ever, as a child or as an adult, participated in a cultural or religious ceremony that was unfamiliar to you, in which you perhaps felt out of place? Describe it in an essay.

*17. Like Paley, Maya Angelou in "Graduation" describes a school ceremony in which officials are insensitive to the lives of the children and their parents. How do the two situations differ? In what way are they the same? Explain in an essay.

The Importance of Being Eleven: Carol Gilligan Takes on Adolescence

Lindsy Van Gelder

In this 1990 Ms. *article, Lindsy Van Gelder reviews the results of a study on adolescent girls undertaken by a group of educational psychologists at Harvard University (known as the Harvard Project) and published in* Making Connections: The Relational Worlds of Adolescent Girls at Emma Willard School *(1989). Their findings indicate that as girls approach adolescence, they undergo a crisis in response to what they perceive as the demands placed on girls and women in mainstream American culture. As a consequence, girls learn to "think in ways that differ from what they really think," and turn from outspoken to self-doubting.*

Van Gelder notes in this essay that as recently as a decade ago, there was not enough research on adolescent girls to "fill even a chapter in a psychology textbook." Recently there has been a small explosion of books published about the issues facing adolescent girls. Several of these books, including another book written by members of the Harvard Project, Meeting at the Crossroads: Women's Psychology and Girls' Development *(1992), have become national bestsellers.*

Van Gelder is chief writer for Allure *magazine and coauthor with Pamela Robin Brandt of* Are You Two . . . Together?: A Gay and Lesbian Travel Guide to Europe *(1991) and* The Girls Next Door: Into the Heart of Lesbian America *(1996). She was born in 1944 and has two daughters.*

1   The summer before sixth grade, I grew six inches. So, probably, did my breasts. In June, my nickname was "Ace," and my favorite possession was a pair of boys' black hightoppers with a decal of the Lone Ranger on the ankle; by September, I had given up sports (this being the pre-aerobics 1950s), changed my name to "Lyn," learned to sleep in iron maiden hair rollers, and begun getting crushes on boys instead of on their haberdashery. The adults in my life were visibly relieved at my "decision," and I remember being happy

that I apparently seemed to be the one in control. On the inside it felt more like putting a gun to my own head just before the enemy army burst through the ramparts. Around the same time as my fall from tomboy grace, but seemingly unrelated to it, I also stopped doing something else I loved: writing poetry. There was no reason to leave it behind; the poetry was the one part of my smart-ass fifth-grade self that teachers and parents wholeheartedly approved of. Nonetheless, it simply disappeared.

2   According to the ongoing research of Harvard University's Project on the Psychology of Women and the Development of Girls, I was hardly the only girl in our culture who, in one way or another, choked off her own voice at adolescence. The project—whose best known member is Carol Gilligan, author of *In a Different Voice*—has uncovered strong evidence that girls at puberty get the message that the culture doesn't value their experience; it literally doesn't want to listen to what they have to say. They "adjust" by stifling themselves. Indeed, in self-defense most of them stop even consciously knowing the things that the choked-off voice would want to say.

3   At 10 or 11, girls have clear-eyed views of the world and their own right to be heard, says Gilligan. "At this age, they're often called 'bossy'—a word that virtually disappears later on. They're not afraid of conflict. They care deeply about relationships, but they understand that there's often jealousy and anger in relationships as well as joy and comfort." Above all, they aren't worried about being "nice."

4   Consider the girl who is asked to complete the sentence "What gets me into trouble is" and adds: "Chewing gum and not tucking my shirt in (but it's usually worth it)." Or the girl who's mad at her friend for ignoring her when a third friend is around and who plans to "get even" by doing the same thing—at which point her friend will empathize with how *she* felt, and they can be friends again. Or the girl who gets annoyed when she thinks her family isn't paying enough attention to what she has to say at the dinner table—and whips out a whistle and blows it. In the stunned silence that follows, she cheerfully notes in a normal voice: "That's much nicer."

5   But by seventh grade, the girls have started to use the phrase "I don't know" as a sort of conversational mantra ("I thought it was, like—I don't know—a little unfair") or later, even to preface their opinions with remarks like "This may sound mediocre, but . . ." Instead of living comfortably inside their own skin, they measure themselves against an idealized, perfect girl. And they start to frame dilemmas in relationships not in terms of conflicts between two people but in terms of how "nice" and "good" and self-sacrificing they can be. One legacy of all this shoehorning into an impossible ideal is that girls' relationships (precisely the thing they really *were* "good" at) may become inauthentic—since one's "real" self needs constantly to be tamed, denigrated, glossed over, or buried. It's an endless loop—or it will be if we don't find our way back to what we all knew, effortlessly, in fifth grade.

6   As recently as a decade ago, according to Gilligan, there wasn't enough adolescent girl-specific research to fill even a chapter in a psychology textbook. "The study of adolescence had been the study of males," Gilligan notes. "You'd have titles like 'The Psychological World of the Teenager: A Study of 175 Boys.' These studies were passing government review boards and peer review boards, and they were being published in journals, and they weren't studying girls. I think it's one of the most interesting pieces of intellectual history of this century that nobody saw this, neither women nor men."

7   Then in 1980 Robert Parker moved from a New England boys' prep school to become headmaster of Emma Willard, a girls' private high school near Albany, New York. Parker did notice that the trajectory into adulthood for his new female students seemed to be very different from that of boys. He invited Gilligan (whose *In a Different Voice* had focused on variations in the way men and women approach moral choices) to study his students. The book based on that research (*Making Connections: The Relational Worlds of Adolescent Girls at Emma Willard School*, edited by Gilligan, Nona P. Lyons, and Trudy J. Hanmer) has just been published by Harvard University Press.

8   "What could you possibly learn," one of the Emma Willard girls asked the researchers early on, "by studying *us*?" The girl may have been asking the question out of a typical conviction that girls don't really count, but the researchers themselves didn't have an agenda. The most basic question at the time was simply: "What will we hear about adolescence if we start listening to girls?" As the project grew, the group listened to girls beyond the Emma Willard sample: black, Irish, and Hispanic girls at after-school clubs in three inner-city Boston neighborhoods, as well as girls in public, private, coed, and all-girls school settings.

9   In hindsight, the breakthrough probably came when project member Lyn Mikel Brown began studying girls at a private school in the Midwest. Because it was an elementary as well as a secondary school, Brown had the opportunity to mount a five-year longitudinal comparative study of girls in four different age groups: second, fifth, seventh, and tenth grades. Brown saw changes among the age groups, and over time, saw individual girls change. As Gilligan notes, "It was as if we had been filling in a mosaic piece by piece. With Lyn's pieces, a real picture emerged: and the picture was of an 11-year-old."

10   That the 11-year-old's sea change might be a pivotal life event was also radical news. "As psychologists we're used to thinking of early childhood as the most crucial time," Gilligan explains. The project's research certainly suggests, however, that psychologists should look at adolescence when they look at girls. Gilligan also finds cultural clues pointing in the same direction: "Look at all the coming-of-age stories written by men, from *David Copperfield* to *Tom Jones* to *Portrait of the Artist.* They almost always begin in infancy or childhood. Then look at what women write. Jane Eyre was ten at the beginning of the novel. Claudia in Toni Morrison's *The Bluest Eye* is nine. Or look at Margaret Atwood's

Cat's Eye or Jamaica Kincaid's *Annie John* or Carson McCullers's *Member of the Wedding*. It's much more likely that *our* stories start at nine or ten." The new work is likely to invite controversy precisely because the team members at this stage analyze only girls' responses. Ironically, Gilligan's *In a Different Voice*, which did compare men and women, was attacked for providing ammunition to those who would use differences between men and women as a basis for discrimination.

11   I deliberately began this article with my own personal experience because, ultimately, research on girls doubles back to our own ten-year-old selves. I learned to write, and you learned to read, and the Harvard researchers learned to collect and interpret data precisely in the language of the culture that didn't hear what we had to say. The Journalism Voice I learned was one that insisted on pretending that the writer was "objective" and not part of the story. The Researcher Voice assumes no personal connection between interviewer and subject (in this case a girl who may in fact be looking for clues about life from a former girl—or vice versa).

12   Traditional research also assumes that interviews proceed in a linear way and can be codified according to long-standing traditions of social science. Project members felt in their guts that this approach wasn't fine-tuned to the way girls really talk about themselves—but what was the alternative? For several years, literally, the group wrestled with this basic dilemma of language. Ultimately, they came up with a method of interpreting interviews that proceeds from a metaphor not of language at all, but of music. Each interview is gone over four times, like a song played in four different keys, with researchers listening for different elements: the "plot" of whatever story is being told, the teller's sense of self, her concern for justice, and her sensitivity to caring. Researchers also listen for what *isn't* said.

13   "We now see what's said as polyphonic, and we listen for the counterpoint and the orchestration of voices," Gilligan explains. The metaphor seemed even more apt when project member Annie Rogers researched the etymology of the word "counterpoint" and found that it came from *contre-point*—or quilt-making.

14   Another image that project members are using a lot these days is that of "resistance." Not all girls stop knowing what they knew in fifth grade; some girls simply take that knowledge "underground" without losing it. "It's a brilliant but risky strategy," says Gilligan, "because when you're thirteen years old, it really *is* hard to confront the authority of the culture. So you keep your mouth shut, and you take a deep dive. Friendships become treacherous, because who do you trust? Will they turn out to be double agents?"

15   Current project work includes research into the role of friendships in adolescence and workshops on how to build resistance in girls. (Writing helps, since it keeps girls in touch with their own voice, as do activities that emphasize group efforts rather than competition.) The group is also studying girls whom society has labeled "at risk." Much preliminary research indicates that it may be precisely those "trouble-making" girls who are among the strongest resisters—and who may even drop out of school as a way to protect their sense of self.

16   Adds Gilligan: "It's often the ones who seem to be doing *well* who may, from our perspective, be the ones who are in trouble."

EXERCISES

Some of the Issues

1. What analogy does Van Gelder use to describe her internal response to the "decision" she made in the sixth grade (paragraph 1)? What does this image say about her feelings?
2. What can you infer about Van Gelder's parents' attitude toward her behavior at that time?
3. According to the research findings, why do girls change their personalities at adolescence (paragraph 2)?
4. How would you characterize the behavior of the girls cited in paragraph 4?
5. What are the noticeable features of the speech of seventh-grade girls quoted in paragraph 5? How do you interpret these patterns of speech?
6. Why do you suppose research on adolescence before 1980 focused only on male behavior?
7. Describe the procedure used to interpret the girls' responses to the interviewers. How does it differ from traditional research methods in the social sciences?
8. What strong claims about at-risk girls does the preliminary research purport?
9. Explain the significance of Gilligan's comment in the last lines of the article.

The Way We Are Told

10. What strategies does Van Gelder use in the first paragraph to capture the reader's attention?
11. What further motivation does she give (paragraph 11) for beginning in this way?
12. In paragraph 10, what other kinds of evidence does Gilligan examine to support the claim that age eleven is a critical psychological period for girls?
13. In paragraph 11, Van Gelder characterizes the "language" of our culture, i.e., the "Journalism Voice" and the "Researcher Voice." How is her "voice" different?

Some Subjects for Writing

14. Journal writing, poetry writing, and free writing are ways to stay in touch with our own voices. For one week, write for at least 10 minutes a day to see what you can discover about yourself. You might wish to begin by reflecting on some of the questions asked in the Harvard University Project:

a. How would you describe yourself to yourself?

b. A woman should always . . .

c. A man should always . . .

d. What gets me into trouble is . . .

15. Examine several current magazines aimed at teenagers or young men or women. Looking at both the text and the photos, what images are presented of young men and young women? Write an essay in which you examine how these images might shape our views of gender roles.

16. In your opinion, is the development of boys radically different from that of girls? Use your own family history or that of friends and relatives to support your idea.

Bikinis and Tiaras: Quinceañeras

Vendela Vida

In Girls on the Verge, *the collection of essays from which this selection is taken, Vendela Vida, a young writer who currently makes her home in New York, travels around the country documenting firsthand the initiation rites and rituals of contemporary American girls. In this essay she travels to Miami to interview girls and their families about their quinceañera, an event that marks a Latina girl's fifteenth birthday and also her symbolic transition into womanhood. Vida describes how some of these celebrations have become so elaborate and expensive that many families cannot afford the actual celebration, and instead opt simply for a photographic record of an event that never happened.*

Vida has been published in, among others, The Chicago Sun-Times, Jane, *and* Vogue. *She attended Middlebury College in Vermont and received her Masters of Fine Arts in writing from Columbia University.*

1 With a Giotto[1] blue ceiling sprinkled with gold stars, gargoyles (the only ones I've seen both indoors and with wholly intact ears), and two fountain-sized cages in which colorful birds chirp along to Vivaldi's "Four Seasons" and pick at artfully prepared plates of lettuce and fresh fruit, the lobby of the Biltmore Hotel in Miami, Florida, has clearly been designed to scream "luxury." Three times a day—ten, noon, and two o'clock—use of the space is rented out for $175 to brides and *quinceañeras* who want to have a room—or rather, an opulent backdrop—of their own.

2 It's one of my first days in Miami and I've come to the Biltmore to observe the noon photo session because that's when fifteen-year-old Monica is scheduled to pose for her *quinceañera (Keen-se-an-yeh-ra)* photographs. The *quinceañera*, or *quince (keen-say)* as it's commonly referred to in America, is the coming-of-age ritual for Latin American girls that transforms them from *niñas* to *señoritas* when they're fifteen years old—*quince años*. In fact, many girls simply refer to the ritual as "having their fifteens." The reason I'm down in Miami, a hotbed of *quince* activity, is to learn more about the current state of the ritual in America.

3 Although the *quince* is often considered akin to the debutante ball, there are some substantial differences between the two fêtes: Unlike the debutante ball, in

[1]14th century Italian painter, many of whose frescoes feature an intense blue background.

which upper-middle- to upper-class girls are presented to society, *quinceañeras* can be of any class (tales of cars being sold and second mortgages taken out on homes to cover the cost of a *quince* are not uncommon), and while the debutante ball is usually held in honor of a group of girls, the *quince* party is typically thrown for one girl, who, as symbolized by her tiara, is queen for the day.

4   In addition to the requisite tiara, for her photo session today Monica is sporting a cotton-candy pink dress. The dress has six layers of organza ruffles that drape out around her like a multi-tiered cake. A heavyset woman who's wearing blue jeans and red high heels, Monica's mother issues stage directions to both Monica, her sister, and the photographer. "Have her stand over there," she commands. "Would you mind moving over there?" the sister says to hotel guests sitting in couches that could conceivably edge their way into a photograph's border. "*Gracias. Muchas gracias.*"

5   The *quinceañera* holds a rose in her gloved right hand and leans against a piano she doesn't know how to play. Next, she stands beside a gargoyle, her non-rose-holding hand resting on its head as though it's a child, or a dog. Some photos are meant to showcase the back of her dress, with its elaborate stitching and beading, and for these, Monica glances back at the camera over the puff of her leg-of-mutton sleeve.

6   All this is merely preparation for an even more impressive backdrop. For about half an hour Monica's mother has been eyeing the window that a large party of hotel guests has been congregated in front of, lounging and drinking. When they finally disperse, Monica's mother wobbles over to the window and stands there territorially, the way someone might save a parking space. Monica takes her position in front of a curtain held back with a wide sash and looks wistfully out a window she's never looked out before. The window affords her, and more important, the camera, a view of the hotel's manicured grounds—complete with fountains—and beyond, the upscale neighborhood of Coral Gables.

7   Like mannequin dressers in a department store, Monica's mother and sister tend to her. Her mother pushes back her shoulders to fix her posture and secures one of Monica's curling-ironed ringlets behind the tiara. Backing away, so as not to miss the spectacle for a moment, she smiles exaggeratedly at her daughter, the way mothers smile at babies whose pictures are being taken, hoping that this will encourage them to smile back.

8   The photographer glances at the mother and she nods and then holds her hands together, as though in prayer. "Smile," the photographer says to Monica. "You're not always going to be fifteen."

9   From the way Monica is dressed and the way her mother and sister are acting, I'm sure that she is headed off for the biggest party of her fifteen-year life. So when the photo session is over, I ask Monica where the *quince* festivities will be held.

10   Wearing perfume that smells like hibiscus, she smiles an equally sweet smile and says, "I decided not to have a party. Instead, my mom and I agreed that for my fifteens I would have my pictures."

11   This is it, she is telling me, and this, I think, is bizarre.

12   After a few more days in Miami I learn that increasingly, many Cuban girls who turn fifteen forego the ritual of the *quince* altogether and instead, like Monica, opt for what is known as "having your pictures." This isn't because the *quince* parties are any less popular than they used to be, but rather the opposite, because *quince* parties have become so important and elaborate and costly and competitive, many lower- to middle-class families in Miami today opt to devote all their time and effort to the end result: the photos.

13   No one knows the precise origins of the *quince*—some say it dates back to the Aztecs and Mayans. Michele Salcedo, author of *Quinceañera!: The Essential Guide to Planning the Perfect Sweet Fifteen Celebration*, writes that the Duchess of Alba, in eighteenth-century Spain, is credited with starting the custom.

> The duchess would invite girls on the cusp of womanhood to the palace and dress them up as adults for the first time. Similarly, although a century later, the Empress Carlota of Mexico invited the daughters of the members of her court to be presented as young ladies eligible for marriage. In both cases, there would be a party, with a feast and the dancing of intricate figures, as was the custom of the time, a custom that is carried over to the *quinceañera* celebration today.

14   Whatever its origins, in most Latin American cultures when a girl celebrates her *quince* she has a church ceremony, followed by a reception at which she has a court of fourteen couples, one representing each year of her life. Once the *quinceañera* has made her entrance in her simple white gown and her father has crowned her head with a tiara, removed her flat shoes, and fitted her feet with high heels, and she has waltzed with him, then boys her age, and finally with her escort, her *chambelán de honor*, it is finally understood that she is now an adult. What being an adult in *quince* terms means is that as of the day of the ritual, the young woman is allowed to start wearing makeup, high heels, and more revealing clothing; shaving her legs; going to parties; and dating men.

15   But much of this simplicity and tradition is a thing of the past.

16   "*Quinces* are all different now," says Angela Lopez, a fifty-year old Miami woman who went through her *quince* in Havana, Cuba, before her family moved to America. "It used to be the *experience* of the day of your *quince* that was important," she says. "My parents kept me at home all the time before I turned fifteen. My *quince* was a ritual that said I was allowed to start going out and be seen. I was allowed to start painting my lips and wear makeup in public."

17   "*Quince* parties today have turned into carnival theme shows with women in Marie Antoinette dresses pulling elaborate stunts," concurs Dulce Goldberg, a teacher at Miami High who went through her own *quince* in Cuba and is now regularly invited to her students' *quinces* in Miami. "I've been to *quinces* where the girls even make their entrance in a hot air balloon." She shakes her head. "Hot air balloons!"

18   These days the presentations compete to be more inventive and expensive than the *quince* the guests attended only the week before. This is especially the case in Miami, where most of the young *quinceañera's* families are from Cuba.

Salecedo, author of *Quinceañera!*, told me that in her research of *quince* parties across the country she found that Cubans in Miami often went to much greater, more elaborate and costly lengths for *quinces* than other Latinas celebrating their *quinces* in, say, San Antonio or Chicago.

19   "A lot of Cuban mothers who wanted to have *quinces* when they were young never got the chance to [because of the political situation]," Salcedo told me. "When they left Cuba, they left with nothing. When they came to America, however, a lot of them became successful, and their daughter's *quince* has become an important way of showing their friends and family that they've made it. While Mexican Americans in Texas might celebrate a *quince* with a rented dress and a five-dollar-per-person barbecue plate, Cubans in Miami buy the dress and even middle-class families can spend $100,000 a pop on the parties."

20   In Miami today, it's not uncommon for the *quinceañera* to make a formidable entrance to her party that entails, yes, a hot air balloon, a Cinderella-like horse-drawn carriage, a spinning carousel on which she sits side-saddle on a horse, or a large seashell that whirls around electronically and from which the *quinceañera* emerges like Botticelli's Venus.[2] In fact, in some of the photos I've seen, the *quinceañera* is almost as scantily dressed as the Renaissance beauty: Posing in a bikini, her legs shaved, her lips red, she smiles seductively, as if to advertise her new status as a *señorita*/Lolita.

21   Of course, the extravagance of *quinces* exists all around the country, and so do its critics—many of whom are church officials and educators. Although, unlike the bat mitzvah, the *quince* doesn't have a particular religious significance, many families choose to have a private mass for their daughters on the day of the party so they can thank God for bringing them into the world. But many in the Catholic community feel that this is not enough, that the dress often becomes more important than God, and that the ritual—not to mention the photographs of bikini-clad poses—can emphasize a girl's sexuality. Addressing these concerns, in the past ten years many archdioceses, such as the archdioceses of Phoenix, Arizona, Los Angeles, California, and San Antonio, Texas, have begun issuing guidelines. The guidelines vary, but they can include advising that girls take five classes of Bible study, Hispanic history, *quince* history, and modern morals, and that the girls go on a church-sponsored retreat with their parents before the event.

22   After Father Antonio Sotelo, a vicar for Hispanic affairs and a pastor at Immaculate Heart in Phoenix, Arizona, circulated his guidelines around the diocese, several churches, including Immaculate Heart, started sponsoring *quince* classes and retreats. When I call Father Sotelo to ask what he thinks of *quinceañeras* who opt not to include a mass in their *quince* celebration, he bluntly

[2]Painting by 15th century Italian painter Sandro Botticelli, in which the figure of Venus seems to float on a clamshell.

tells me, "That's not a *quince*, that's just a party. The mass shows their special relationship to the Lord, to the community, to their parents."

23   "Do you think people should have to have masses as part of their *quinces*?" I ask.

24   "Well, it's a free country," he says. Despite his words, there's disapproval in his voice. Then his tone changes as he adds, "But all the girls who come here to Immaculate Heart are really committed to the *quince* mass. We have them write letters saying why they want to be a *quinceañera* and some of the letters are so personal you can hardly read them. In the letters they thank the Lord for their families and, if they've been fighting with their families they talk about how they want to start getting along, they talk about mistakes they've made, how they want to renew their baptismal vows, about how they miss their grandparents who have died.

25   "The girls are all so *sincere* in what they say," Father Sotelo continues. As his enthusiasm and praise for these young women increases, so does the speed with which he speaks. "People say the wild years are twelve, thirteen, fourteen years old. I think the wild years are eighteen and up. Some of the young brides who come to me to get married are spoiled brats. At least with the *quinceañeras* they mean what they say. I'd rather do ten *quinces* than one wedding. I could do *quinces* all day long."

26   One person in the Catholic Church who makes it her crusade, as she calls it, to educate and assist parents with their preparation of the *quince* is Sister Angela Erevia. Sister Angela, who has written a book about *quinces* entitled *Quince Años: Celebrating a Tradition*, travels around the country leading workshops that encourage parents of all religions and nationalities to plan at least one coming-of-age celebration for their daughters *and* their sons. In fact, she calls the *quinceañera*, the *quince años*, because she suggests young men go through a ritual at age fifteen as well.

27   When I ask Sister Angela what she thinks about the amount of money families put into their children's *quinces*, she says, "There's not a right way or a wrong way to celebrate. I don't tell people how much to spend on their weddings, so I don't tell them how much to spend on their child's *quince años*. But," she adds, "it doesn't have to cost a lot. In Dallas I helped the diocese organize a *quince años* for seventy-five teenagers and it only cost twenty dollars per family."

28   "Five hundred years ago in pre-Christian times in Mexico, kids went through ordeals to test their maturity and if they were successful they were considered mature members of their community," Sister Angela says to me during a phone conversation. Her voice was patient yet firm and I can't help but envision her as a Hispanic Julie Andrews in a modern adaptation of *The Sound of Music*. "Today we don't have to put our kids through ordeals. There is already so much pressure in the environment, with alcohol, divorce, suicide, premarital sex, teenage pregnancy, and there's nothing that affirms teenagers' presence."

29   In her workshops Sister Angela encourages parents to use the *quince años* to help their children understand who they are and where they come from. "It's an opportunity to develop their identity," she says.

30   Esther Nodarse who, with her husband, Aurelio, runs a successful party planning service in Miami called Pretty Party, says that she's seen a change in the *quince* in the twenty-five years since she started her company. It used to be that girls born in the U.S. thought the *quince* was "a tacky, Cuban tradition, and they wanted to be more American than Cuban and celebrate their sweet sixteen." But today, she says, many of the girls encourage their parents to have *quinces*, and therefore in Miami it's becoming more popular than ever before. She estimates that nowadays about 90 percent of Cuban girls have some sort of celebration.

31   I spent some time at Miami High, talking to girls about the *quince* to find out what it meant to them. Miami High is an inner-city high school with a primarily Latino student body. It's not famous for much except that *Porky's* was filmed there. No one really knows for sure if the peephole still exists in the boys' locker room; many of the students haven't seen *Porky's*, they just know that an American movie was filmed at their school.

32   "I'm having my fifteens next month," says one sophomore in a pink halter top and denim miniskirt that exposes cheerleading-toned thighs. All the other girls in the room—those who have yet to have their fifteens, and especially those who have had their fifteens—ooh and ahh as though this weren't something they all went through.

33   But while these young women believe that getting their driver's license, or graduating high school, or even turning sixteen will all be significant transition points in their future lives, they don't pretend that turning fifteen is in and of itself transformative, because it doesn't give them any new sought-after independence.

34   So if it's not a big day in that it grants them license to wear makeup, or shave their legs, or date boys—most Miami High students have been doing all of the above for years—then why do they make such a big deal about their fifteens? One reason is that they have inherited their mothers' love for *quinces*. (This is where the oohing and ahhing comes from.) Their mothers are the ones with the memories and the stories of their *quinces* or the regret at not having one, and they are the ones with the dreams of their daughters' celebrations, and their daughters are born into these dreams. As one young woman with manicured red nails tells me, "I wasn't even born yet and my mother was already saying 'I can't wait for her to have her fifteens.'"

35   Just as they don't pretend that it means anything more to them than that they're fifteen, these young women don't pretend they go through their *quince* for the sake of tradition. As one young Cuban girl wearing a tight T-shirt with a Betty Boop decal says, "Your parents want it to be as important to you as it is to them, but it's not. Like, we want it because of the party, and they want it because of tradition so their friends will be 'Oh, wow.' To us, it's just a party."

36   "Yeah," says another, "Having my fifteens wasn't a turning point. It was just a way to celebrate."

37   A well-groomed young woman who has charm bracelets from both her *quince* and her sweet sixteen, explains why she wanted to have a party, even

though her parents offered her a car or a cruise instead, simply to avoid the hassle: "I like to party, and I like being the center of attraction."

38 The prospect of being the center of attraction is one of the most appealing aspects of the *quince* for these girls. For a day, they get to have their photographs taken by professionals who specialize in child models. For a day they get to pose in bikinis as though for a fashion spread in *Seventeen* magazine. For a day, they get to wear ball gowns and tiaras and hold roses and when the camera snaps they look like they have just been crowned Miss America.

39 Even those who are at first reluctant usually enjoy their night in the spotlight. "I didn't want to have a *quince*, because I'm a liberal kind of girl," says Juanita, a sixteen-year-old of Columbian descent who lives in New Jersey. "I always thought that the *quince* was a way for people to say, 'Look at how pretty my daughter is. Look how much money I have. Don't you want to marry my daughter?' When I was fourteen, my mother asked me if I wanted to have one, and I told her 'Look, we're living comfortable, why waste the money?' and I thought she would leave it at that."

40 But Juanita's mother, Yolanda, who had four hundred people to her own *quince* in Columbia, did not leave it at that. For her daughter's sixteenth birthday, she threw her a combination surprise birthday party and *quince* because she wanted to keep up the tradition and also, she said, "It was more to have the pictures to send back home."

41 I went to the party, held at a banquet hall in Union City, New Jersey, complete with disco ball, a DJ who spun salsa, and figurines of Venus de Milo. There I saw an unsuspecting but happily surprised Juanita greeted with a chorus of "Surprise!" and colorful ribbons thrown in her direction before she was ushered off to the ladies' room to be changed by her mother into clothing fit for a *quinceañera*—a white gown, long white gloves, and slippers. (Yolanda took Juanita's measurements for the dress a few weeks earlier, under the guise of saying, "Juanita, you look like you've lost weight. Let me take your measurements so we can have a record.") When Juanita reentered the banquet hall, Yolanda stalled the start of the ceremony so she could load her camera with film (an oversight in all the excitement) and instructed the guests to make sure to give her their negatives so she could send the pictures to *her* mother, and then the ritual commenced.

42 Because Juanita's father left when she was three months old, his duties were fulfilled by a cousin who changed her slippers into size 8 white high heels (her mother tried them on Juanita, a heavy sleeper, in the middle of the night to make sure they fit) and crowned her curly-haired head with a tiara. All the while, Juanita held a rose in her gloved hand and sat upright in a wicker chair decorated with pink bows that had been placed in the middle of the banquet hall. "The chair is her temporary throne," her mother explained to me. "Tonight she is queen, but tomorrow she will be a regular person again."

43 After her shoes had been changed her mother made a toast: "I am toasting the birthday girl because I have been a mother and a father. Juanita, we are here

to toast your future because you are starting a new future that's going to be harder." Then she danced the *quinceañera* waltz with her daughter—traditionally reserved for the father—and there were tears in her eyes and tears in Juanita's eyes and tears in *my* eyes. At the end of the waltz, Juanita spun her mother around because even at that moment, she knew the ritual was more about her mother than her.

44   I spoke with Juanita the day after the party, and she said she now understood why the *quince* tradition was alive. While it made her want to celebrate her own daughter's sweet sixteen, however, she maintained that she won't incorporate elements of the *quince* into her daughter's party. "I think the *quince* is sort of a lost tradition among the second generation," she explained.

45   "For my fifteens I had my pictures," says a young Cuban woman named Rosa. When I ask her why she thinks young women are increasingly having their pictures taken in lieu of a party she says, "So we can have a memory. We could have a party but we can't, like, keep that to show our children. But if we have the pictures we can show our children, our grandchildren, and they can see, like, our favorite age."

46   Rosa is a nice girl but she hardly strikes me as having an easy time as a teenager. She complains that she's never been asked out by a boy and she suffers some standard teenage afflictions like being overweight, having a poor complexion, and wearing heavy glasses.

47   "Is fifteen *really* your favorite age?" I ask.

48   She gives me a winsome smile and answers, "You're only young once."

49   I am sitting in the courtyard of Miami High during a recess with Rosa and Melissa, a petite seventeen-year-old beauty with aqua eyes who also opted to just "have her pictures" for her fifteens. Unlike Rosa, Melissa has had an easy time making friends at Miami High, an easy time being a teenager. While Melissa's role model is Gloria Estefan, Rosa loves the Colorado Rockies, and she's wearing a jacket with their name across the back. The black jacket is much too hot for the Miami sun, but Rosa will do anything to show her loyalty to the team. Melissa's wearing a spaghetti-strapped sundress. What's striking is that both these girls—one thin, one fat, one popular, one with few friends—are prematurely nostalgic about the fifteenth year of their life that *quince* photographs capture.

50   "The day of your pictures is just the best," gushes Melissa. "It's the biggest rush and everything. Everyone's pampering you and everybody's helping you get dressed and the photographer's super nice and he's saying 'Look here' and 'Do this' and you feel like a model."

51   "Yeah," chimes in Rosa, "you feel like a model. For the one day you look beautiful—you're like, yeah, I know it, it's cool. You want to see some pictures?"

52   Before I respond Rosa pulls out a photo album from her backpack. The photo album says *"Mis Quince Años"* on the front and a gold-encircled peephole features her favorite picture. It's a little like looking through the peephole in

Porky's because there is something prurient about the way Rosa has been made up. She's wearing a low-cut white dress and smiling seductively, leaning against a column that looks like it could be part of a costly mansion but isn't (it's just a solitary column in Coral Gables that doesn't support anything; it is, however, a popular spot for many photo shoots of *quinceañeras*).

53   The first page of the album is designed for filling in the details of the party; it has spaces in which the names of all the fourteen couples who make up the *quinceañera's* court of honor are to be written. Since Rosa didn't have a party, this page is blank, as it is in the photo albums of all the other young Latinas who increasingly decide just to "have their pictures." In the back of her album are pictures of other girls' photo sessions. Students at Miami High exchange *quince* photos the way schoolgirls trade stickers. The other photos show the *quinceañeras* posing in front of fake backgrounds, blown-up photographs of waterfalls, white sand beaches, castles. Some even have magazine-like headings embossed on top: "Get attention"; "Looking good"; "Super body."

54   One of the photos in Rosa's album is of her sister with the president of a club she was trying to get into. "They took pictures and everything, but they didn't end up letting my sister in," Rosa says accusingly, as though they did something deceitful. "My father bought the pictures anyway."

55   There's something sad about this but not unexpected. This is, after all, a place and an environment where pictures mean more than the truth, where a day in a young woman's life is special because photographs are taken of her in various poses.

56   Of course, photographs from a young woman's fifteens aren't just collected in her album and wallet and those of her friends, they're sent to all the family's friends and relatives. Rosa sent some of the photographs to her grandmother and her parents' friends in Cuba. She says that she saw some of the photographs from girls' fifteens that were taken "over there" (Cuba) and that "the color was faded and the dress wasn't so pretty and the hotel where the pictures were taken was a cheap motel, a roach motel."

57   For Rosa and others who see the difference between *quince* pictures taken in Miami and their parents' homelands, that is really the issue—the difference in the quality of the photographs and the difference in their dresses. To these girls' parents, however, the difference is that between two worlds, and two social classes. Their parents send the photographs to all their friends in the countries they have left behind as though they were Hallmark cards. This is America— America!—these photographs say, and we have made it.

EXERCISES

Some of the Issues

1. How does Vida describe Monica and Monica's mother and sister in the opening section of the essay? What is your impression of them?

2. What did the author find "bizarre" about Monica's photo session (paragraph 11)? Did you also find it bizarre?
3. Why is "having your pictures" in lieu of an actual party becoming more common?
4. How are quinceañeras for Cuban Americans different now than they were in the past in Cuba?
5. In groups of three or four, describe and discuss other coming of age rituals that you have participated in or attended. Make a list of how are they similar to or different from the quinceañera.
6. Why are Cuban quinceañeras more elaborate than those of other Latino girls, according to Michele Salcedo (paragraph 19)?
7. Why is Father Antonio Sotelo critical of the elaborate quinceañeras and why is Sister Angela Erevia supportive of them? What is your response to their ideas and their reasoning?
8. Why is turning fifteen not a life-changing transformation for the girls Vida talks to at Miami High? Why do they still feel excited about it?
9. Whose words does Rosa echo in paragraph 48 when she says, "You're only young once"?
10. What do you feel is Vida's attitude towards the girls she interviews? Give specific examples to back up your point.
11. What is the significance of the quinceañera photographs for many Cuban families?

The Way We Are Told

12. How does Vida describe the lobby of the Biltmore Hotel? What impression do you have of it?
13. Why do you think Vida chooses to write in the first person at times? How does this affect what she says and how she says it?
14. How does Vida give the reader a sense of the personalities of the people she interviews? Give specific examples.

Some Subjects for Writing

15. Write up a personal observation of a rite of passage or an event that marks a particular occasion. It might be a wedding, a funeral, a confirmation, a bar or bat mitzvah, or a quinceañera. Detail your impressions of the event. Through your description and tone, try to give the reader a feel for what it was like to be there.
16. Think of a rite of passage that is of particular interest to you. Using personal interviews with family members and acquaintances, as well as your own experience, investigate whether or not the rite has changed over time, or as the people who practice it move to a different place. Write an essay in which you analyze the possible significance of those changes.

*17. Several of the selections in this chapter explore the ways in which immigrant parents or elders influence (or attempt to influence) second-generation children and teach them about their culture. Elizabeth Wong's parents send her to Chinese school; in "Barba Nikos" the grocer educates the Greek boy about Greek history, food, and mythology; and in "Bikinis and Tiaras" Vida shows how important it is for the Cuban girls' mothers that they celebrate their quinceañeras. Read each of these responses. How are the children both similar and different in their responses to the wishes of their parents and elders?

Incident

Countee Cullen

Countee Cullen (1903 – 46) gained recognition for his poetry while still in high school and published his first volume of poetry at the age of twenty-two. He attended New York University and Harvard and continued to publish poetry and fiction. "Incident" first appeared in Color *(1925).*

Once riding in old Baltimore
   Heart-filled head-filled with glee,
I saw a Baltimorean
   Keep looking straight at me.

5   Now I was eight and very small,
   And he was no whit bigger,
And so I smiled, but he poked out
   His tongue, and called me, "Nigger."

10   I saw the whole of Baltimore
   From May until December;
Of all the things that happened there
   That's all that I remember.

EXERCISES

Some of the Issues

1. What are the author's feelings toward the Baltimorean at the beginning of the poem? Why are these feelings significant?
2. How old is the Baltimorean? How is age significant in the poem?
3. Why is the incident the only thing the author remembers?
4. Read the poem aloud several times. Does his insistent meter and rhyme remind you of poems that children may recite? How does the music of the poem contrast with its subject?

Some Subjects for Writing

5. Write about an incident in which someone called you a name. Describe the incident and your reaction.
6. There is a saying: "Sticks and stones will break my bones, but names will never hurt me." Is this statement true? Write an essay in which you examine whether or not words and names can be harmful.

II

EDUCATION

For most of us, school is one of our most formative experiences growing up. Our thoughts, opinions, and attitudes are shaped not only by what we learn in school, but also by our social interactions with our classmates and teachers. We carry with us fond memories of those teachers who fed our curiosity, inspiring us to learn more, and less fond memories of those who stifled it. There were probably some times when school felt like a broadening experience, and others when it felt simply like a test of both our intellectual and social skills. Sometimes it was simply a test of our patience.

One reason school is such a key reference point for most people is that it's an experience we all share. Education is one of the most equalizing forces in American society since, at least until a certain age, every child has access to schooling. But, as many of the writings in this chapter demonstrate, educational experiences can also prove to be a clear demonstration of our society's inequalities.

The writings in this chapter look at education from the perspective of both students and teachers. Sun Park explores the often confining expectations placed on Asian students, who are assumed to be "geniuses" by their parents and teachers whether they really are or not. In "One Man's Kids" Daniel Meier writes about his choice to become a first grade teacher and describes his day in the classroom. Having chosen a profession that has historically been regarded as "female," Meier questions the degree to which we are confined by our definition of "traditional" male work.

Sherman Alexie, in his story "Indian Education," presents a series of vignettes that demonstrate that much of what we learn in school, for better or worse, happens outside of the classroom. Mike Rose, with the help of a dedicated teacher, overcomes the limiting boundaries of working-class life and under-education. In "Living in Two Worlds," Marcus Mabry, as a college junior, writes about the gap between his earlier and his present life. Returning home to his lower-class neighborhood in New Jersey from prestigious Stanford University in California, he finds himself with two identities that are hard to reconcile.

In the poem that closes this chapter, Martin Espada looks back on his days as a worker in a factory that makes legal pads. Now a law student, he realizes that he knows something about paper, and labor, that other law students may not know.

Don't Expect Me to Be Perfect

Sun Park

This essay first appeared in a 1990 special edition of Newsweek *for teenagers. Sun Park writes about some of the problems she and others face in trying to meet parental expectations.*

1   I am a 16-year-old Korean-American. My family has been in the United States for six years now. I'll be a junior next fall.

2   When I first came to the States, it took two years before I could speak English fluently. By the time I started middle school, I realized that most of my fellow students had never met many kids like me before. They had this idea, probably from TV and movies, that all Asians are nerds and all Asians are smart. It's true that some are. I know many smart people. But what about those Asians who aren't so smart? Having a reputation for brains is nice, I guess, but it can also be a pain. For instance, sometimes when my classmates do not know something, they come to me for the answer. Often I can help them. But when I can't, they get these weird expressions on their faces. If I were a genius, I would not mind being treated like one. But since I am not, I do.

3   The problem isn't just limited to the classroom. My mother and father expect an awful lot from me, too. Like so many Korean parents, and many ambitious American parents, they're very competitive and can't help comparing me with other kids. Mine always say to me, "So and so is smart, works so hard and is so good to his or her parents. Why can't you be more like him or her?" Because I am the oldest kid in my family, they expect me to set a good example for my younger sisters and relatives. They'd rather I concentrate on schoolwork than dating. They want me to be No. 1.

4   Most of the time I want to do well, too. I'm glad I take all honors classes. But now that I am at those levels, I have to be on my toes to keep doing well. The better I do, the more pressure I seem to place on myself. Because my parents want me to be perfect—or close to perfect—I find myself turning into a perfectionist. When I do a project and make one little error, I can't stand it. Sometimes I stay up as late as 2 A.M. doing homework.

5   I don't think I would be like this if my parents weren't motivating me. But I don't think they know what pressure can do to a teenager. It's not that they put me down or anything. They have plenty of faith in me. But to tell the truth, sometimes I really like to be lazy, and it would be nice just to take it easy and not worry so much about my grades all the time. Maybe my parents know this.

Maybe that's why they encourage me to be better. Well, it still drives me crazy when they compare me with others. I wonder if those smart kids have parents like mine.

6   Sure, I'm proud of who I am, and I love my parents very much. But then there are times I just feel like taking a break and going far away from parents and teachers. Of course that's impossible, but it's always nice to dream about it.

EXERCISES

Some of the Issues

1. What image of Asians do most of Park's classmates have? How does this image affect her relationships with other students?
2. How does she react to her parents' wishes that she achieve high marks?
3. What are some of the manifestations of her "perfectionism"? Do you think there is anything wrong with this behavior?
4. What is the author's attitude toward her parents? How do you know?

The Way We Are Told

5. Sun Park opens her essay with a short description of herself. Why might this be an effective way to begin?
6. How would you describe the tone of this essay? How does the author's audience affect her tone? Find specific phrases and words from the text to illustrate your answer.
7. What do you think is the author's purpose in writing this essay? What lines best express it?

Some Subjects for Writing

8. Do you know any perfectionists? Describe their behavior and characteristics. What is your own attitude toward perfectionism?
9. Sun Park wonders if other "smart kids have parents like mine." Have you ever felt this way? From your own school experiences, have you noticed any connection between academic achievement and parental involvement?
10. What were the attitudes in your household toward personal achievement? Were they stated explicitly or were they implicit? What was the attitude toward failure and how was failure defined?
11. Park dreams of "going far away from parents and teachers" as a solution to her problem. Have you ever had these feelings? Can you think of better options?

*12. Read Sherman Alexie's "Indian Education" in which the author recounts the negative impressions many teachers have of Native American students. Park believes that Asians are also subject to teachers' preconceived notions, though in ways that many would view as positive. After reading both pieces, write an essay in which you explore how both positive and negative stereotypes impact students' education. Use specific examples from both the essays as well as from your own experiences.

One Man's Kids

Daniel Meier

"One Man's Kids" originally appeared in The New York Times *"About Men" series in 1987, when Daniel Meier was teaching at a public elementary school in Boston. Meier begins this essay by describing part of his typical day as a first-grade teacher. He goes on to describe how, as a man who works with small children, his career choice sets him apart from other men he knows. Meier shows us that teaching can be a continual process or education for both teacher and student.*

Meier received a bachelor's degree in English from Wesleyan University and a master's degree in education from Harvard University. After this essay was written, Meier went on to earn a Ph.D. in education from the University of California, Berkeley. He is currently Assistant Professor of Education at San Francisco State University. He is the author of two books, Learning in Small Moments: Life in an Urban Classroom *(1997) and* Scribble Scrabble: Learning to Read and Write *(2000).*

1   I teach first graders. I live in a world of skinned knees, double-knotted shoelaces, riddles that I've heard a dozen times, stale birthday cakes, hurt feelings, wandering stories and one lost shoe ("and if you don't find it my mother'll kill me"). My work is dominated by 6-year-olds.

2   It's 10:45, the middle of snack, and I'm helping Emily open her milk carton. She has already tried the other end without success, and now there's so much paint and ink on the carton from her fingers that I'm not sure she should drink it at all. But I open it. Then I turn to help Scott clean up some milk he has just spilled onto Rebecca's whale crossword puzzle.

3   While I wipe my milk- and paint-covered hands, Jenny wants to know if I've seen that funny book about penguins that I read in class. As I hunt for it in a messy pile of books, Jason wants to know if there is a new seating arrangement for lunch tables. I find the book, turn to answer Jason, then face Maya, who is fast approaching with a new knock-knock joke. After what seems like the 10th "Who's there?" I laugh and Maya is pleased.

4   Then Andrew wants to know how to spell "flukes" for his crossword. As I get to "u," I give a hand signal for Sarah to take away the snack. But just as Sarah is almost out the door, two children complain that "we haven't even had ours yet." I stop the snack mid-flight, complying with their request for graham crackers. I then return to Andrew, noticing that he has put "flu" for 9 Down, rather than 9 Across. It's now 10:50.

5   My work is not traditional male work. It's not a singular pursuit. There is not a large pile of paper to get through or one deal to transact. I don't have one

area of expertise or knowledge. I don't have the singular power over language of a lawyer, the physical force of a construction worker, the command over fellow workers of a surgeon, the wheeling and dealing transactions of a businessman. My energy is not spent in pursuing, climbing, achieving, conquering or cornering some goal or object.

6   My energy is spent in encouraging, supporting, consoling and praising my children. In teaching, the inner rewards come from without. On any given day, quite apart from teaching reading and spelling, I bandage a cut, dry a tear, erase a frown, tape a torn doll and locate a long-lost boot. The day is really won through matters of the heart. As my students groan, laugh, shudder, cry, exult and wonder, I do too. I have to be soft around the edges.

7   A few years ago, when I was interviewing for an elementary-school teaching position, every principal told me with confidence that, as a male, I had an advantage over female applicants because of the lack of male teachers. But in the next breath, they asked with a hint of suspicion why I chose to work with young children. I told them that I wanted to observe and contribute to the intellectual growth of a maturing mind. What I really felt like saying, but didn't, was that I loved helping a child learn to write his name for the first time, finding someone a new friend, or sharing in the hilarity of reading about Winnie the Pooh getting so stuck in a hole that only his head and rear show.

8   I gave that answer to those principals, who were mostly male, because I thought they wanted a "male" response. This meant talking about intellectual matters. If I had taken a different course and talked about my interest in helping children in their emotional development, it would have been seen as closer to a "female" answer. I even altered my language, not once mentioning the word "love" to describe what I do indeed love about teaching. My answer worked; every principal nodded approvingly.

9   Some of the principals also asked what I saw myself doing later in my career. They wanted to know if I eventually wanted to go into educational administration. Becoming a dean of students or a principal has never been one of my goals, but they seemed to expect me, as a male, to want to climb higher on the career stepladder. So I mentioned that, at some point, I would be interested in working with teachers as a curriculum coordinator. Again, they nodded approvingly.

10   If those principals had been female instead of male, I wonder whether their questions, and my answers, would have been different. My guess is that they would have been.

11   At other times, when I'm at a party or a dinner and tell someone that I teach young children, I've found that men and women respond differently. Most men ask about the subjects I teach and the courses I took in my training. Then, unless they bring up an issue such as merit pay, the conversation stops. Most women, on the other hand, begin the conversation on a more immediate and personal level. They say things like "those kids must love having a male teacher" or "that age is just wonderful, you must love it." Then, more often than not,

they'll talk about their own kids or ask me specific questions about what I do. We're then off and talking shop.

12   Possibly, men would have more to say to me, and I to them, if my job had more of the trappings and benefits of more traditional male jobs. But my job has no bonuses or promotions. No complimentary box seats at the ball park. No cab fare home. No drinking buddies after work. No briefcase. No suit. (Ties get stuck in paint jars.) No power lunches. (I eat peanut butter and jelly, chips, milk and cookies with the kids.) No taking clients out for cocktails. The only place I take my kids is to the playground.

13   Although I could have pursued a career in law or business, as several of my friends did, I chose teaching instead. My job has benefits all its own. I'm able to bake cookies without getting them stuck together as they cool, buy cheap sewing materials, take out splinters, and search just the right trash cans for useful odds and ends. I'm sometimes called "Daddy" and even "Mommy" by my students, and if there's ever a lull in the conversation at a dinner party, I can always ask those assembled if they've heard the latest riddle about why the turkey crossed the road. (He thought he was a chicken.)

EXERCISES

Some of the Issues

1. Meier begins his essay by listing many specific things he does in his work as a first-grade teacher. What are they? In what way do they contribute to the children's lives?
2. How does Meier define "traditional male work" and how does he contrast it with his own work? Do you agree with his definition?
3. Meier tells us that he was not completely frank when he interviewed for his job. What reasons does he state for giving a "male" response to the principal's questions?
4. Meier claims that when he mentions his job to acquaintances, men and women respond differently. How does he characterize the different responses?
5. Do you think Meier's students are lucky to have a teacher like him? Why or why not?
6. Advertising and the media often reinforce, or call into question, gender stereotypes. Find two print advertisements, one focusing on male and one on female stereotypes. Working in groups of three to five, compare and discuss your advertisements with other students.

The Way We Are Told

7. Many writers believe that one can present an idea more effectively through description than through direct statements. Meier begins and ends his es-

say by describing specific activities, showing rather than telling about his daily routine. What does he gain by starting with specific details?

8. Much of Meier's analysis depends on his use of comparison and contrast. What does he compare and how does this technique strengthen his argument?

Some Subjects for Writing

9. In paragraph 6, Meier shows us what he feels a teacher should do beyond "teaching reading and spelling." Write an essay in which you develop your own philosophy of a teacher's role beyond reading, writing, and arithmetic. In other words, what can teachers teach us beyond academics?

10. As Meier implies, the majority of primary school teachers are female, while the majority of principals are male. Work in small groups or brainstorm with the entire class to determine other jobs that are typically held by either men or women. Choose one of these jobs to write about, either justifying the present situation or arguing for change.

*11. Meier demonstrates how gender can impact our career choices. Clearly there are ways in which culture, education, and gender influence our career decisions, although those influences may be subtle at times. Consider the career choice of a family member or friend and write an essay in which you analyze the choice in relation to the person's gender, cultural background, or educational experience.

Indian Education

Sherman Alexie

Sherman Alexie was born in Washington in 1966 and grew up on the Wellpinit Indian reservation, about 50 miles from Spokane. Alexie's mother is a Spokane Indian; his father is from the Coeur D'Alene tribe. Alexie was born hydroencephalic (with water on the brain) and underwent surgery as a small child. He was not expected to survive, and when he did, his doctors predicted he would be mentally retarded. Despite this prediction he learned to read at age three and soon became an avid reader, reading novels on his own by age five.

Like the narrator of his story, Alexie attended an Indian school for the primary grades but made a conscious decision as a teenager to attend high school off the reservation, where he thought he would get a better education. He graduated from Washington State University and has written prolifically since then, publishing more than a dozen books including poetry, novels, and short stories. He is also the author of a movie script, for Smoke Signals, *which was released in 1998 and won several awards. Alexie also reads his work on the poetry slam circuit, and won the World Heavyweight Poetry competition in 1998. This selection is taken from his collection of short stories,* The Lone Ranger and Tonto Fistfight in Heaven *(1993).*

The history of Indian schools in America is a long, varied and complicated one. Over the course of its history from 1778 through 1871, the United States Government entered into over 370 treaties with the various Indian nations it displaced. These treaties included agreements that the United States government would provide various services to the Native American communities, including education.

The Indian schools were originally conceived as a way to assimilate young children and make them accept the white man's belief and value systems. Communities had little control over school curriculum and treatment of students was often harsh. Native languages and dress were forbidden, and there was little or no acknowledgment or understanding of Native traditions.

In more recent years, beginning in the early 20th century, there have been movements to make Indian schools more sensitive to Native American cultures and to use teaching methods and curricula adapted to the unique characteristics and needs of Native communities. Indian schools in America, however, still remain often underfunded and ignored.

FIRST GRADE

1   My hair was too short and my U.S. Government glasses were horn-rimmed, ugly, and all that first winter in school, the other Indian boys chased me from one corner of the playground to the other. They pushed me down, buried me in the snow until I couldn't breathe, thought I'd never breathe again.

2   They stole my glasses and threw them over my head, around my out-stretched hands, just beyond my reach, until someone tripped me and sent me falling again, facedown in the snow.

3   I was always falling down; my Indian name was Junior Falls Down. Sometimes it was Bloody Nose or Steal-His-Lunch. Once, it was Cries-Like-a-White-Boy, even though none of us had seen a white boy cry.

4   Then it was a Friday morning recess and Frenchy SiJohn threw snowballs at me while the rest of the Indian boys tortured some other *top-yogh-yaught* kid, another weakling. But Frenchy was confident enough to torment me all by himself, and most days I would have let him.

5   But the little warrior in me roared to life that day and knocked Frenchy to the ground, held his head against the snow, and punched him so hard that my knuckles and the snow made symmetrical bruises on his face. He almost looked like he was wearing war paint.

6   But he wasn't the warrior. I was. And I chanted *It's a good day to die, it's a good day to die*, all the way down to the principal's office.

SECOND GRADE

7   Betty Towle, missionary teacher, redheaded and so ugly that no one ever had a puppy crush on her, made me stay in for recess fourteen days straight.

8   "Tell me you're sorry," she said.

9   "Sorry for what?" I asked.

10   "Everything," she said and made me stand straight for fifteen minutes, eagle-armed with books in each hand. One was a math book; the other was English. But all I learned was that gravity can be painful.

11   For Halloween I drew a picture of her riding a broom with a scrawny cat on her back. She said that her God would never forgive me for that.

12   Once, she gave the class a spelling test but set me aside and gave me a test designed for junior high students. When I spelled all the words right, she crumpled up the paper and made me eat it.

13   "You'll learn respect," she said.

14   She sent a letter home with me that told my parents to either cut my braids or keep me home from class. My parents came in the next day and dragged their braids across Betty Towle's desk.

15   "Indians, indians, indians." She said it without capitalization. She called me "indian, indian, indian."

16   And I said, *Yes, I am. I am Indian. Indian, I am.*

THIRD GRADE

17   My traditional Native American art career began and ended with my very first portrait: *Stick Indian Taking a Piss in My Backyard.*

18   As I circulated the original print around the classroom, Mrs. Schluter intercepted and confiscated my art.

19   *Censorship*, I might cry now. *Freedom of expression*, I would write in editorials to the tribal newspaper.

20   In third grade, though, I stood alone in the corner, faced the wall, and waited for the punishment to end.

21   I'm still waiting.

FOURTH GRADE

22   "You should be a doctor when you grow up," Mr. Schluter told me, even though his wife, the third grade teacher, thought I was crazy beyond my years. My eyes always looked like I had just hit-and-run someone.

23   "Guilty," she said. "You always look guilty."

24   "Why should I be a doctor?" I asked Mr. Schluter.

25   "So you can come back and help the tribe. So you can heal people."

26   That was the year my father drank a gallon of vodka a day and the same year that my mother started two hundred different quilts but never finished any. They sat in separate, dark places in our HUD house and wept savagely.

27   I ran home after school, heard their Indian tears, and looked in the mirror. *Doctor Victor*, I called myself, invented an education, talked to my reflection. *Doctor Victor to the emergency room.*

FIFTH GRADE

28   I picked up a basketball for the first time and made my first shot. No. I missed my first shot, missed the basket completely, and the ball landed in the dirt and sawdust, sat there just like I had sat there only minutes before.

29   But it felt good, that ball in my hands, all those possibilities and angles. It was mathematics, geometry. It was beautiful.

30   At the same moment, my cousin Steven Ford sniffed rubber cement from a paper bag and leaned back on the merry-go-around. His ears rang, his mouth was dry, and everyone seemed so far away.

31   But it felt good, that buzz in his head, all the colors and noises. It was chemistry, biology. It was beautiful.

32   Oh, do you remember those sweet, almost innocent choices that the Indian boys were forced to make?

SIXTH GRADE

33   Randy, the new Indian kid from the white town of Springdale, got into a fight an hour after he first walked into the reservation school.

34   Stevie Flett called him out, called him a squawman, called him a pussy, and called him a punk.

35   Randy and Stevie, and the rest of the Indian boys, walked out into the playground.

36   "Throw the first punch," Stevie said as they squared off.

37   "No," Randy said.

38   "Throw the first punch," Stevie said again.

39   "No," Randy said again.

40   "Throw the first punch!" Stevie said for the third time, and Randy reared back and pitched a knuckle fastball that broke Stevie's nose.

41   We all stood there in silence, in awe.

42   That was Randy, my soon-to-be first and best friend, who taught me the most valuable lesson about living in the white world: *Always throw the first punch.*

SEVENTH GRADE

43   I leaned through the basement window of the HUD house and kissed the white girl who would later be raped by her foster-parent father, who was also white. They both lived on the reservation, though, and when the headlines and stories filled the papers later, not one word was made of their color.

44   *Just Indians being Indians,* someone must have said somewhere and they were wrong.

45   But on the day I leaned through the basement window of a HUD house and kissed the white girl, I felt the good-byes I was saying to my entire tribe. I held my lips tight against her lips, a dry, clumsy, and ultimately stupid kiss.

46   But I was saying good-bye to my tribe, to all the Indian girls and women I might have loved, to all the Indian men who might have called me cousin, even brother.

47   I kissed that white girl and when I opened my eyes, she was gone from the reservation, and when I opened my eyes, I was gone from the reservation, living in a farm town where a beautiful white girl asked my name.

48   "Junior Polatkin," I said, and she laughed.

49   After that, no one spoke to me for another five hundred years.

EIGHTH GRADE

50   At the farm town junior high, in the boys' bathroom, I could hear voices from the girls' bathroom, nervous whispers of anorexia and bulimia. I could

hear the white girls' forced vomiting, a sound so familiar and natural to me after years of listening to my father's hangovers.

51   "Give me your lunch if you're just going to throw it up," I said to one of those girls once.

52   I sat back and watched them grow skinny from self-pity.

53   Back on the reservation, my mother stood in line to get us commodities. We carried them home, happy to have food, and opened the canned beef that even the dogs wouldn't eat.

54   But we ate it day after day and grew skinny from self-pity.

55   There is more than one way to starve.

NINTH GRADE

56   At the farm town high school dance, after a basketball game in an overheated gym where I had scored twenty-seven points and pulled down thirteen rebounds, I passed out during a slow song.

57   As my white friends revived me and prepared to take me to the emergency room where doctors would later diagnose my diabetes, the Chicano teacher ran up to us.

58   "Hey," he said. "What's that boy been drinking? I know all about these Indian kids. They start drinking real young."

59   Sharing dark skin doesn't necessarily make two men brothers.

TENTH GRADE

60   I passed the written test easily and nearly flunked the driving, but still received my Washington State driver's license on the same day that Wally Jim killed himself by driving his car into a pine tree.

61   No traces of alcohol in his blood, good job, wife and two kids.

62   "Why'd he do it?" asked a white Washington State trooper.

63   All the Indians shrugged their shoulders, and looked down at the ground.

64   "Don't know," we all said, but when we look in the mirror, see the history of our tribe in our eyes, taste failure in the tap water, and shake with old tears, we understand completely.

65   Believe me, everything looks like a noose if you stare at it long enough.

ELEVENTH GRADE

66   Last night I missed two free throws which would have won the game against the best team in the state. The farm town high school I play for is nicknamed the "Indians," and I'm probably the only actual Indian ever to play for a team with such a mascot.

67   This morning I picked up the sport page and read the headline: INDIANS LOSE AGAIN.

68   Go ahead and tell me none of this is supposed to hurt me very much.

TWELFTH GRADE

69   I walk down the aisle, valedictorian of this farm town high school, and my cap doesn't fit because I've grown my hair longer than it's ever been. Later, I stand as the school board chairman recites my awards, accomplishments, and scholarships.

70   I try to remain stoic for the photographers as I look toward the future.

71   Back home on the reservation, my former classmates graduate: a few can't read, one or two are just given attendance diplomas, most look forward to the parties. The bright students are shaken, frightened, because they don't know what comes next.

72   They smile for the photographer as they look back toward tradition.

73   The tribal newspaper runs my photograph and the photograph of my former classmates side by side.

POSTSCRIPT: CLASS REUNION

74   Victor said, "Why should we organize a reservation high school reunion? My graduating class has a reunion every weekend at the Powwow Tavern."

EXERCISES

Some of the Issues

1. What is the significance of the narrator's glasses in the first-grade scenario?
2. What can you assume from the narrator's first-grade school? Who were his fellow classmates?
3. What does the narrator mean when he tells us that his teacher said "indian" without capitalization (paragraph 15)? What is the significance of the narrator's response?
4. What does the narrator mean by the line "I'm still waiting" in paragraph 21?
5. What effect does kissing the white girl have on the narrator in seventh grade? Why does he say after that "no one spoke to me for another five hundred years"?
6. The narrator switches to a new school for junior high. What is different about the new school?
7. How do you interpret the line "There is more than one way to starve" (paragraph 55)?
8. What stereotypes do the teachers in the story have of Native Americans?

9. Why does the narrator tell us of the teacher who assumed he was drunk in the eighth grade was Chicano? How did you respond to the narrator's assertion in paragraph 59?
10. What do you think the postscript means?

The Way We Are Told

11. Find examples of where Alexie uses humor. How would you characterize his sense of humor?
12. Why do you think Alexie chooses to write his story as a series of vignettes? How else might he have written it?
13. Consider the title. Is it meant to be ironic? Why or why not?
14. How does the author juxtapose optimistic scenes of possibility with bleaker ones? Give specific examples from the text. Why do you think he does this?
15. How would you characterize Alexie's tone? Is it appropriate to the story? Why or why not?

Some Subjects for Writing

16. Using Alexie's story as a model, retell the story of your own education from first through twelfth grade. Focus on specific incidents that taught you a lesson you could not have learned from a textbook.
17. With the help of your instructor, research the history of Native American schools in the United States. Write a paper in which you examine some aspect of the schools. You may choose to focus on such topics as changes in the school over time, the level of student retention in high schools, and the reasons why students stay or drop out, or innovative approaches to education in Native American schools.

I Just Wanna Be Average

Mike Rose

Mike Rose was born in Chicago in 1938 and, when he was seven, moved with his parents to the south side of Los Angeles. His parents, who had immigrated from Italy and arrived at Ellis Island in the 1910s and 1920s, never escaped poverty; however, they managed to save enough money to send Rose to a parochial school. He was an average student but, after junior high, was misplaced in the vocational education track in high school, where he "drifted to the level of a really mediocre and unprepared student." His experience in "Voc. Ed." illustrates how students placed in the lower tracks live down to the expectations of their classrooms. Fortunately, Rose's biology teacher noticed his ability, looked at his academic record, and discovered that his grades had been switched with those of another student named Rose. Subsequently, he was reassigned to the college track. In his senior year, he encountered a nontraditional teacher who opened up the world of poetry, ideas, and language, and who helped Rose to get a scholarship to Loyola University in Los Angeles.

Rose became a teacher and worked with others on the margins of society: inner-city kids, Vietnam veterans, and underprepared adults. He is now the associate director of the writing program at UCLA, where he continues to teach underprepared students to enter and succeed in the academic world.

In the following excerpt from his book Lives on the Boundary *(1989), he relates how poverty contributes to deep, lasting feelings of self-doubt, and how one caring person can make a fundamental difference in the lives of others. Rose is also the author of* Possible Lives: The Promise of Public Education in America *(1995).*

1 The house was on a piece of land that rose about four feet up from heavily trafficked Vermont Avenue. The yard sloped down to the street, and three steps and a short walkway led up the middle of the grass to our front door. There was a similar house immediately to the south of us. Next to it was Carmen's Barber Shop. Carmen was a short, quiet Italian who, rumor had it, had committed his first wife to the crazy house to get her money. In the afternoons, Carmen could be found in the lot behind his shop playing solitary catch, flinging a tennis ball high into the air and running under it. One day the police arrested Carmen on charges of child molesting. He was released but became furtive and suspicious. I never saw him in the lot again. Next to Carmen's was a junk store where, one summer, I made a little money polishing brass and rewiring old lamps. Then came a dilapidated real estate office, a Mexican restaurant, an empty lot,

and an appliance store owned by the father of Keith Grateful, the streetwise, chubby boy who would become my best friend.

2   Right to the north of us was a record shop, a barber shop presided over by old Mr. Graff, Walt's Malts, a shoe repair shop with a big Cat's Paw decal in the window, a third barber shop, and a brake shop. It's as I write this that I realize for the first time that three gray men could have had a go at your hair before you left our street.

3   Behind our house was an unpaved alley that passed, just to the north, a power plant the length of a city block. Massive coils atop the building hissed and cracked through the day, but the doors never opened. I used to think it was abandoned—feeding itself on its own wild arcs—until one sweltering afternoon a man was electrocuted on the roof. The air was thick and still as two firemen— the only men present—brought down a charred and limp body without saying a word.

4   The north and south traffic on Vermont was separated by tracks for the old yellow trolley cars, long since defunct. Across the street was a huge garage, a tiny hot dog stand run by a myopic and reclusive man named Freddie, and my dreamland, the Vermont Bowl. Distant and distorted behind thick lenses, Freddie's eyes never met yours; he would look down when he took your order and give you your change with a mumble. Freddie slept on a cot in the back of his grill and died there one night, leaving tens of thousands of dollars stuffed in the mattress.

5   My father would buy me a chili dog at Freddie's, and then we would walk over to the bowling alley where Dad would sit at the lunch counter and drink coffee while I had a great time with pinball machines, electric shooting galleries, and an ill-kept dispenser of cheese corn. There was a small, dark bar abutting the lanes, and it called to me. I would devise reasons to walk through it: "'Scuse me, is the bathroom in here?" or "Anyone see my dad?" though I can never remember my father having a drink. It was dark and people were drinking and I figured all sorts of mysterious things were being whispered. Next to the Vermont Bowl was a large vacant lot overgrown with foxtails and dotted with car parts, bottles, and rotting cardboard. One day Keith heard that the police had found a human head in the brush. After that we explored the lot periodically, coming home with stickers all the way up to our waists. But we didn't find a thing. Not even a kneecap.

6   When I wasn't with Keith or in school, I would spend most of my day with my father or with the men who were renting the one-room apartments behind our house. Dad and I whiled away the hours in the bowling alley, watching TV, or planting a vegetable garden that never seemed to take. When he was still mobile, he would walk the four blocks down to St. Regina's Grammar School to take me home to my favorite lunch of boiled wieners and chocolate milk. There I'd sit, dunking my hot dog in a jar of mayonnaise and drinking my milk while Sheriff John tuned up the calliope music on his "Lunch Brigade." Though he

never complained to me, I could sense that my father's health was failing, and I began devising child's ways to make him better. We had a box of rolled cotton in the bathroom, and I would go in and peel off a long strip and tape it around my jaw. Then I'd rummage through the closet, find a sweater of my father's, put on one of his hats—and sneak around to the back door. I'd knock loudly and wait. It would take him a while to get there. Finally, he'd open the door, look down, and quietly say, "Yes, Michael?" I was disappointed. Every time. Somehow I thought I could fool him. And, I guess, if he had been fooled, I would have succeeded in redefining things: I would have been the old one, he much younger, more agile, with strength in his legs.

7   The men who lived in the back were either retired or didn't work that much, so one of them was usually around. They proved to be, over the years, an unusual set of companions for a young boy. Ed Gionotti was the youngest of the lot, a handsome man whose wife had run off and who spoke softly and never smiled. Bud Hall and Lee McGuire were two out-of-work plumbers who lived in adjacent units and who weekly drank themselves silly, proclaiming in front of God and everyone their undying friendship or their unequivocal hatred. Old Cheech was a lame Italian who used to hobble along grabbing his testicles and rolling his eyes while he talked about the women he claimed to have on a string. There was Lester, the toothless cabbie, who several times made overtures to me and who, when he moved, left behind a drawer full of syringes and burnt spoons. Mr. Smith was a rambunctious retiree who lost his nose to an untended skin cancer. And there was Mr. Berryman, a sweet and gentle man who eventually left for a retirement hotel only to be burned alive in an electrical fire.

8   Except for Keith, there were no children on my block and only one or two on the immediate side streets. Most of the people I saw day to day were over fifty. People in their twenties and thirties working in the shoe shop or tile garages didn't say a lot; their work and much of what they were working for drained their spirits. There were gang members who sauntered up from Hoover Avenue, three blocks to the east, and occasionally I would get shoved around, but they had little interest in me either as member or victim. I was a skinny, bespectacled kid and had neither the coloring nor the style of dress or carriage that marked me as a rival. On the whole, the days were quiet, lazy, lonely. The heat shimmering over the asphalt had no snap to it; time drifted by. I would lie on the couch at night and listen to the music from the record store or from Walt's Malts. It was new and quick paced, exciting, a little dangerous (the church had condemned Buddy Knox's "Party Doll"), and I heard in it a deep rhythmic need to be made whole with love, or marked as special, or released in some rebellious way. Even the songs about lost love—and there were plenty of them—lifted me right out of my socks with their melodious longing. In the midst of the heat and slow time the music brought the promise of its origins, a promise of deliverance, a promise that, if only for a moment, life could be stirring and dreamy.

9   But the anger and frustration of South Vermont could prove too strong for music's illusion; then it was violence that provided deliverance of a different order. One night I watched as a guy sprinted from Walt's to toss something on our lawn. The police were right behind, and a cop tackled him, smashing his face into the sidewalk. I ducked out to find the packet: a dozen glassine bags of heroin. Another night, one August midnight, an argument outside the record store ended with a man being shot to death. And the occasional gang forays brought with them some fated kid who would fumble his moves and catch a knife.

10   It's popular these days to claim you grew up on the streets. Men tell violent tales and romanticize the lessons violence brings. But, though it was occasionally violent, it wasn't the violence in South L.A. that marked me, for sometimes you can shake that ugliness off. What finally affected me was subtler, but more pervasive: I cannot recall a young person who was crazy in love or lost in work or one old person who was passionate about a cause or an idea. I'm not talking about an absence of energy—the street toughs and, for that fact, old Cheech had energy. And I'm not talking about an absence of decency, for my father was a thoughtful man. The people I grew up with were retired from jobs that rub away the heart or were working hard at jobs to keep their lives from caving in or were anchorless and in between jobs and spouses or were diving headlong into a barren tomorrow: junkies, alcoholics, and mean kids walking along Vermont looking to throw a punch. I developed a picture of human existence that tendered it short and brutish or sad and aimless or long and quiet with rewards like afternoon naps, the evening newspaper, walks around the block, occasional letters from children in other states. When, years later, I was introduced to humanistic psychologists like Abraham Maslow and Carl Rogers, with their visions of self-actualization, or even Freud with his sober dictum about love and work, it all sounded like a glorious fairy tale, a magical account of a world full of possibility, full of hope and empowerment. Sindbad and Cinderella couldn't have been more fanciful.

11   Some people who manage to write their way out of the working class describe the classroom as an oasis of possibility. It became their intellectual playground, their competitive arena. Given the richness of my memories of this time, it's funny how scant are my recollections of school. I remember the red brick building of St. Regina's itself, and the topography of the playground: the swings and basketball courts and peeling benches. There are images of a few students: Erwin Petschaur, a muscular German boy with a strong accent; Dave Sanchez, who was good in math; and Sheila Wilkes, everyone's curly-haired heartthrob. And there are two nuns: Sister Monica, the third-grade teacher with beautiful hands for whom I carried a candle and who, to my dismay, had wedded herself to Christ; and Sister Beatrice, a woman truly crazed, who would sweep into class, eyes wide, to tell us about the Apocalypse.

12   All the hours in class tend to blend into one long, vague stretch of time. What I remember best, strangely enough, are the two things I couldn't under-

stand and over the years grew to hate: grammar lessons and mathematics. I would sit there watching a teacher draw her long horizontal line and her short, oblique lines and break up sentences and put adjectives here and adverbs there and just not get it, couldn't see the reason for it, turned off to it. I would hide by slumping down in my seat and page through my reader, carried along by the flow of sentences in a story. She would test us, and I would dread that, for I always got Cs and Ds. Mathematics was a bit different. For whatever reasons, I didn't learn early math very well, so when it came time for more complicated operations, I couldn't keep up and started day-dreaming to avoid my inadequacy. This was a strategy I would rely on as I grew older. I fell further and further behind. A memory: The teacher is faceless and seems very far away. The voice is faint and is discussing an equation written on the board. It is raining, and I am watching the streams of water form patterns on the windows.

13   I realize now how consistently I defended myself against the lessons I couldn't understand and the people and events of South L.A. that were too strange to view head-on. I got very good at watching a blackboard with minimum awareness. And I drifted more and more into a variety of protective fantasies. I was lucky in that although my parents didn't read or write very much and had no more than a few books around the house, they never debunked my pursuits. And when they could, they bought me what I needed to spin my web.

14   One early Christmas they got me a small chemistry set. My father brought home an old card table from the secondhand store, and on that table I spread out my test tubes, my beaker, my Erlenmeyer flask, and my gas-generating apparatus. The set came equipped with chemicals, minerals, and various treated papers—all in little square bottles. You could send away to someplace in Maryland for more, and I did, saving pennies and nickels to get the substances that were too exotic for my set, the Junior Chemcraft: Congo red paper, azurite, glycerine, chrome alum, cochineal—this from female insects!—tartaric acid, chameleon paper, logwood. I would sit before my laboratory and play for hours. My father rested on the purple couch in front of me watching wrestling or *Gunsmoke* while I measured powders or heated crystals or blew into solutions that my breath would turn red or pink. I was taken by the blends of names and by the colors that swirled through the beaker. My equations were visual and phonetic. I would hold a flask up to the hall light, imagining the veils of a million atoms dancing. Sulfur and alcohol hung in the air. I wanted to shake down the house.

15   One day my mother came home from Coffee Dan's with an awful story. The teenage brother of one of her waitress friends was in the hospital. He had been fooling around with explosives in his garage "where his mother couldn't see him," and something happened, and "he blew away part of his throat. For God's sake, be careful," my mother said. "Remember poor Ada's brother." Wow! I thought. How neat! Why couldn't my experiments be that dangerous? I really lost heart when I realized that you could probably eat the chemicals spread across my table.

16   I knew what I had to do. I saved my money for a week and then walked with firm resolve past Walt's Malts, past the brake shop, across Ninetieth Street, and into Palazolla's market. I bought a little bottle of Alka-Seltzer and ran home. I chipped up the wafers and mixed them into a jar of white crystals. When my mother came home, dog tired, and sat down on the edge of the couch to tell me and Dad about her day, I gravely poured my concoction into a beaker of water, cried something about the unexpected, and ran out from behind my table. The beaker foamed ominously. My father swore in Italian. The second time I tried it, I got something milder—in English. And by my third near-miss with death, my parents were calling my behavior cute. Cute! Who wanted cute? I wanted to toy with the disaster that befell Ada Pendleton's brother. I wanted all those wonderful colors to collide in ways that could blow your voice box right off.

17   But I was limited by the real. The best I could do was create a toxic antacid. I loved my chemistry set—its glassware and its intriguing labels—but it wouldn't allow me to do the things I wanted to do. St. Regina's had an all-purpose room, one wall of which was lined with old books—and one of those shelves held a row of plastic-covered space novels. The sheen of their covers was gone, and their futuristic portraits were dotted with erasures and grease spots like a meteor shower of the everyday. I remember the rockets best. Long cylinders outfitted at the base with three slick fins, tapering at the other end to a perfect conical point, ready to pierce out of the stratosphere and into my imagination: X-fifteens and Mach 1, the dark side of the moon, the Red Planet, Jupiter's Great Red Spot, Saturn's rings—and beyond the solar system to swirling wisps of galaxies, to stardust.

18   Students will float to the mark you set. I and the others in the vocational classes were bobbing in pretty shallow water. Vocational education has aimed at increasing the economic opportunities of students who do not do well in our schools. Some serious programs succeed in doing that, and through exceptional teachers—like Mr. Gross in *Horace's Compromise*—students learn to develop hypotheses and troubleshoot, reason through a problem, and communicate effectively—the true job skills. The vocational track, however, is most often a place for those who are just not making it, a dumping ground for the disaffected. There were a few teachers who worked hard at education; young Brother Slattery, for example, combined a stern voice with weekly quizzes to try to pass along to us a skeletal outline of world history. But mostly the teachers had no idea of how to engage the imaginations of us kids who were scuttling along at the bottom of the pond.

19   And the teachers would have needed some inventiveness, for none of us was groomed for the classroom. It wasn't just that I didn't know things—didn't know how to simplify algebraic fractions, couldn't identify different kinds of clauses, bungled Spanish translations—but that I had developed various faulty and inadequate ways of doing algebra and making sense of Spanish. Worse yet, the years of defensive tuning out in elementary school had given me a way to escape quickly while seeming at least half alert. During my time in Voc. Ed., I devel-

oped further into a mediocre student and a somnambulant problem solver, and that affected the subjects I did have the wherewithal to handle: I detested Shakespeare; I got bored with history. My attention flitted here and there. I fooled around in class and read my books indifferently—the intellectual equivalent of playing with your food. I did what I had to do to get by, and I did it with half a mind.

20   But I did learn things about people and eventually came into my own socially. I liked the guys in Voc. Ed. Growing up where I did, I understood and admired physical prowess, and there was an abundance of muscle here. There was Dave Snyder, a sprinter and halfback of true quality. Dave's ability and quick wit gave him a natural appeal, and he was welcome in any clique, though he always kept a little independent. He enjoyed acting the fool and could care less about studies, but he possessed a certain maturity and never caused the faculty much trouble. It was a testament to his independence that he included me among his friends—I eventually went out for track, but I was no jock. Owing to the Latin alphabet and a dearth of *R*s and *S*s, Snyder sat behind Rose, and we started exchanging one-liners and became friends.

21   There was Ted Richard, a much-touted Little League pitcher. He was chunky and had a baby face and came to Our Lady of Mercy as a seasoned street fighter. Ted was quick to laugh and he had a loud, jolly laugh, but when he got angry he'd smile a little smile, the kind that simply raises the corner of the mouth a quarter of an inch. For those who knew, it was an eerie signal. Those who didn't found themselves in big trouble, for Ted was very quick. He loved to carry on what we would come to call philosophical discussions: What is courage? Does God exist? He also loved words, enjoyed picking up big ones like *salubrious* and *equivocal* and using them in our conversation—laughing at himself as the word hit a chuckhole rolling off his tongue. Ted didn't do all that well in school—baseball and parties and testing the courage he'd speculated about took up his time. His textbooks were *Argosy* and *Field and Stream,* whatever newspapers he'd find on the bus stop—from the *Daily Worker* to pornography—conversations with uncles or hobos or businessmen he'd meet in a coffee shop, *The Old Man and the Sea.* With hindsight, I can see that Ted was developing into one of those rough-hewn intellectuals whose sources are a mix of the learned and the apocryphal, whose discussions are both assured and sad.

22   And then there was Ken Harvey. Ken was good-looking in a puffy way and had a full and oily ducktail and was a car enthusiast...a hodad. One day in religion class, he said the sentence that turned out to be one of the most memorable of the hundreds of thousands I heard in those Voc. Ed. years. We were talking about the parable of the talents, about achievement, working hard, doing the best you can do, blah-blah-blah, when the teacher called on the restive Ken Harvey for an opinion. Ken thought about it, but just for a second, and said (with studied, minimal affect), "I just wanna be average." That woke me up. Average?! Who wants to be average? Then the athletes chimed in with the clichés that make you want to laryngectomize them, and the exchange became a platitudinous melee. At the time, I thought Ken's assertion was stupid, and I wrote

him off. But his sentence has stayed with me all these years, and I think I am finally coming to understand it.

23   Ken Harvey was gasping for air. School can be a tremendously disorienting place. No matter how bad the school, you're going to encounter notions that don't fit with the assumptions and beliefs that you grew up with—maybe you'll hear these dissonant notions from teachers, maybe from the other students, and maybe you'll read them. You'll also be thrown in with all kinds of kids from all kinds of backgrounds, and that can be unsettling—this is especially true in places of rich ethnic and linguistic mix, like the L.A. basin. You'll see a handful of students far excel you in courses that sound exotic and that are only in the curriculum of the elite: French, physics, trigonometry. And all this is happening while you're trying to shape an identity, your body is changing, and your emotions are running wild. If you're a working-class kid in the vocational track, the options you'll have to deal with this will be constrained in certain ways: You're defined by your school as "slow"; you're placed in a curriculum that isn't designed to liberate you but to occupy you, or, if you're lucky, train you, though the training is for work the society does not esteem; other students are picking up the cues from your school and your curriculum and interacting with you in particular ways. If you're a kid like Ted Richard, you turn your back on all this and let your mind roam where it may. But youngsters like Ted are rare. What Ken and so many others do is protect themselves from such suffocating madness by taking on with a vengeance the identity implied in the vocational track. Reject the confusion and frustration by openly defining yourself as the Common Joe. Champion the average. Rely on your own good sense. Fuck this bullshit. Bullshit, of course, is everything you—and the others—fear is beyond you: books, essays, tests, academic scrambling, complexity, scientific reasoning, philosophical inquiry.

24   The tragedy is that you have to twist the knife in your own gray matter to make this defense work. You'll have to shut down, have to reject intellectual stimuli or diffuse them with sarcasm, have to cultivate stupidity, have to convert boredom from a malady into a way of confronting the world. Keep your vocabulary simple, act stoned when you're not or act more stoned than you are, flaunt ignorance, materialize your dreams. It is a powerful and effective defense—it neutralizes the insult and the frustration of being a vocational kid and, when perfected, it drives teachers up the wall, a delightful secondary effect. But like all strong magic, it exacts a price.

25   Jack MacFarland couldn't have come into my life at a better time. My father was dead, and I had logged up too many years of scholastic indifference. Mr. MacFarland had a master's degree from Columbia and decided, at twenty-six, to find a little school and teach his heart out. He never took any credentialing courses, couldn't bear to, he said, so he had to find employment in a private system. He ended up at Our Lady of Mercy teaching five sections of senior English. He was a beatnik who was born too late. His teeth were stained, he tucked his sorry tie in between the third and fourth buttons of his shirt, and his pants were chroni-

cally wrinkled. At first, we couldn't believe this guy, thought he slept in his car. But within no time, he had us so startled with work that we didn't much worry about where he slept or if he slept at all. We wrote three or four essays a month. We read a book every two to three weeks, starting with the *Iliad* and ending up with Hemingway. He gave us a quiz on the reading every other day. He brought a prep school curriculum to Mercy High.

26   MacFarland's lectures were crafted, and as he delivered them he would pace the room jiggling a piece of chalk in his cupped hand, using it to scribble on the board the names of all the writers and philosophers and plays and novels he was weaving into his discussion. He asked questions often, raised everything from Zeno's[1] paradox to the repeated last line of Frost's "Stopping by Woods on a Snowy Evening." He slowly and carefully built up our knowledge of Western intellectual history—with facts, with connections, with speculations. We learned about Greek philosophy, about Dante, the Elizabethan world view, the Age of Reason, existentialism. He analyzed poems with us, had us reading sections from John Ciardi's *How Does a Poem Mean?*, making a potentially difficult book accessible with his own explanations. We gave oral reports on poems Ciardi didn't cover. We imitated the styles of Conrad, Hemingway, and *Time* magazine. We wrote and talked, wrote and talked. The man immersed us in language.

27   Even MacFarland's barbs were literary. If Jim Fitzsimmons, hung over and irritable, tried to smart-ass him, he'd rejoin with a flourish that would spark the indomitable Skip Madison—who'd lost his front teeth in a hapless tackle—to flick his tongue through the gap and opine, "good chop," drawing out the single "o" in stinging indictment. Jack MacFarland, this tobacco-stained intellectual, brandished linguistic weapons of a kind I hadn't encountered before. Here was this *egghead*, for God's sake, keeping some pretty difficult people in line. And from what I heard, Mike Dweetz and Steve Fusco and all the notorious Voc. Ed. crowd settled down as well when MacFarland took the podium. Though a lot of guys groused in the schoolyard, it just seemed that giving trouble to this partic-ular teacher was a silly thing to do. Tomfoolery, not to mention assault, had no place in the world he was trying to create for us, and instinctively everyone knew that. If nothing else, we all recognized MacFarland's considerable intelli-gence and respected the hours he put into his work. It came to this: The trou-blemaker would look foolish rather than daring. Even Jim Fitzsimmons was reading *On the Road*[2] and turning his incipient alcoholism to literary ends.

28   There were some lives that were already beyond Jack MacFarland's minis-trations, but mine was not. I started reading again as I hadn't since elementary school. I would go into our gloomy little bedroom or sit at the dinner table while, on the television, Danny McShane was paralyzing Mr. Moto with the

---

[1]Zeno, a Greek philosopher, developed paradoxes to demonstrate that our common-sense no-tions of time and space are deceptive.
[2]Semiautobiographical novel by American Beat writer Jack Kerouac (1922–1969) about his travels through the United States and Mexico.

atomic drop, and work slowly back through *Heart of Darkness*, trying to catch the words in Conrad's sentences. I certainly was not MacFarland's best student; most of the other guys in College Prep, even my fellow slackers, had better backgrounds than I did. But I worked very hard, for MacFarland had hooked me. He tapped my old interest in reading and creating stories. He gave me a way to feel special by using my mind. And he provided a role model that wasn't shaped on physical prowess alone, and something inside me that I wasn't quite aware of responded to that. Jack MacFarland established a literacy club, to borrow a phrase of Frank Smith's, and invited me—invited all of us—to join.

29   There's been a good deal of research and speculation suggesting that the acknowledgment of school performance with extrinsic rewards—smiling faces, stars, numbers, grades—diminishes the intrinsic satisfaction children experience by engaging in reading or writing or problem solving. While it's certainly true that we've created an educational system that encourages our best and brightest to become cynical grade collectors and, in general, have developed an obsession with evaluation and assessment, I must tell you that venal though it may have been, I loved getting good grades from MacFarland. I now know how subjective grades can be, but then they came tucked in the back of essays like bits of scientific data, some sort of spectroscopic readout that said, objectively and publicly, that I had made something of value. I suppose I'd been mediocre for too long and enjoyed a public redefinition. And I suppose the workings of my mind, such as they were, had been private for too long. My linguistic play moved into the world; like the intergalactic stories I told years before on Frank's berry-splattered truck bed, these papers with their circled, red B-pluses and A-minuses linked my mind to something outside it. I carried them around like a club emblem.

30   One day in the December of my senior year, Mr. MacFarland asked me where I was going to go to college. I hadn't thought much about it. Many of the students I teach today spent their last year in high school with a physics text in one hand and the Stanford catalog in the other, but I wasn't even aware of what "entrance requirements" were. My folks would say that they wanted me to go to college and be a doctor, but I don't know how seriously I ever took that; it seemed a sweet thing to say, a bit of supportive family chatter, like telling a gangly daughter she's graceful. The reality of higher education wasn't in my scheme of things: No one in the family had gone to college; only two of my uncles had completed high school. I figured I'd get a night job and go to the local junior college because I knew that Snyder and Company were going there to play ball. But I hadn't even prepared for that. When I finally said, "I don't know," MacFarland looked down at me—I was seated in his office—and said, "Listen, you can write."

31   My grades stank. I had As in biology and a handful of Bs in a few English and social science classes. All the rest were Cs—or worse. MacFarland said I would do well in his class and laid down the law about doing well in the others. Still, the record for my first three years wouldn't have been acceptable to any four-year school. To nobody's surprise, I was turned down flat by USC and

UCLA. But Jack MacFarland was on the case. He had received his bachelor's degree from Loyola University, so he made calls to old professors and talked to somebody in admissions and wrote me a strong letter. Loyola finally accepted me as a probationary student. I would be on trial for the first year, and if I did okay, I would be granted regular status. MacFarland also intervened to get me a loan, for I could never have afforded a private college without it. Four more years of religion classes and four more years of boys at one school, girls at another. But at least I was going to college. Amazing.

32   In my last semester of high school, I elected a special English course fashioned by Mr. MacFarland, and it was through this elective that there arose at Mercy a fledgling literati. Art Mitz, the editor of the school newspaper and a very smart guy, was the kingpin. He was joined by me and by Mark Dever, a quiet boy who wrote beautifully and who would die before he was forty. MacFarland occasionally invited us to his apartment, and those visits became the high point of our apprenticeship: We'd clamp on our training wheels and drive to his salon.

33   He lived in a cramped and cluttered place near the airport, tucked away in the kind of building that architectural critic Reyner Banham calls a *dingbat*. Books were all over: stacked, piled, tossed, and crated, underlined and dog eared, well worn and new. Cigarette ashes crusted with coffee in saucers or spilled over the sides of motel ashtrays. The little bedroom had, along two of its walls, bricks and boards loaded with notes, magazines, and oversized books. The kitchen joined the living room, and there was a stack of German newspapers under the sink. I had never seen anything like it: a great flophouse of language furnished by City Lights and Café le Metro. I read every title. I flipped through paperbacks and scanned jackets and memorized names: Gogol, *Finnegan's Wake*, Djuna Barnes, Jackson Pollock, *A Coney Island of the Mind*, F. O. Matthiessen's *American Renaissance*, all sorts of Freud, *Troubled Sleep*, Man Ray, *The Education of Henry Adams*, Richard Wright, *Film as Art*, William Butler Yeats, Marguerite Duras, *Redburn*, *A Season in Hell*, *Kapital*. On the cover of Alain-Fournier's *The Wanderer* was an Edward Gorey drawing of a young man on a road winding into dark trees. By the hotplate sat a strange Kafka novel called *Amerika*, in which an adolescent hero crosses the Atlantic to find the Nature Theater of Oklahoma. Art and Mark would be talking about a movie or the school newspaper, and I would be consuming my English teacher's library. It was heady stuff. I felt like a Pop Warner athlete on steroids.

34   Art, Mark, and I would buy stogies and triangulate from MacFarland's apartment to the Cinema, which now shows X-rated films but was then L.A.'s premiere art theater, and then to the musty Cherokee Bookstore in Hollywood to hobnob with beatnik homosexuals—smoking, drinking bourbon and coffee, and trying out awkward phrases we'd gleaned from our mentor's bookshelves. I was happy and precocious and a little scared as well, for Hollywood Boulevard was thick with a kind of decadence that was foreign to the South Side. After the Cherokee, we would head back to the security of MacFarland's apartment, slaphappy with hipness.

35   Let me be the first to admit that there was a good deal of adolescent passion in this embrace of the avant-garde: self-absorption, sexually charged pedantry, an elevation of the odd and abandoned. Still it was a time during which I absorbed an awful lot of information: long lists of titles, images from expressionist paintings, new wave shibboleths, snippets of philosophy, and names that read like Steve Fusco's misspellings—Goethe, Nietzsche, Kierkegaard. Now this is hardly the stuff of deep understanding. But it was an introduction, a phrase book, a Baedeker[3] to a vocabulary of ideas, and it felt good at the time to know all these words. With hindsight I realize how layered and important that knowledge was.

36   It enabled me to do things in the world. I could browse bohemian bookstores in far-off, mysterious Hollywood; I could go to the Cinema and see events through the lenses of European directors; and, most of all, I could share an evening, talk that talk, with Jack MacFarland, the man I most admired at the time. Knowledge was becoming a bonding agent. Within a year or two, the persona of the disaffected hipster would prove too cynical, too alienated to last. But for a time it was new and exciting: It provided a critical perspective on society, and it allowed me to act as though I were living beyond the limiting boundaries of South Vermont.

EXERCISES

Some of the Issues

1. Give a physical description of the neighborhood where Rose grew up.
2. How would you characterize the men who lived in the area (paragraph 7)?
3. Considering the view of life on Vermont Avenue, can you infer why Rose doesn't mention any women?
4. How do you think he felt about growing up in his neighborhood? What lines from the text support your idea?
5. The author says that his childhood days were quiet, lazy, and lonely. What kinds of neighborhood activities did attract his attention?
6. What defense mechanism did Rose develop to cope with school and the hopelessness of the neighborhood (paragraph 12)?
7. Rose spent hours with his chemistry set, yet he was disappointed that it didn't allow him "to do the things I wanted to do." Based on what you know about his life, what "things" do you suppose he had in mind?
8. According to Rose, what are the job skills that vocational education programs should teach (paragraphs 18 and 19)?
9. In paragraphs 22–24, how does Rose interpret Ken Harvey's sentence, "I just wanna be average"?

[3]Classic guidebook for travelers.

10. What kind of a person is Jack MacFarland? If you were a film director, which actor would you cast to play him?
11. What do you think was the key to MacFarland's success as a teacher?
12. The knowledge that Rose gained during his senior year enabled him "to do things in the world" and "to act as though I were living beyond the limiting boundaries of South Vermont." How does all this relate to his childhood dreams? Find lines from earlier portions of the text that support your idea.

The Way We Are Told

13. Reread Rose's description of his neighborhood (paragraphs 1–8). Which images best capture the feeling of place for you?
14. How would you characterize Rose's use of language in paragraph 18, "Students will float to the mark you set. I and the others in the vocational classes were bobbing in pretty shallow water." Can you find similar phrases in paragraphs 18–24 that continue the comparison?

Some Subjects for Writing

15. Rose describes several of his classmates in Voc. Ed. who attempted to cope with the "disorienting" atmosphere of their high school (paragraphs 20–24). Did you or any of your high school classmates develop special ways of coping with the system or with the teachers? Recount this experience.
16. In paragraphs 18–24, Rose sharply criticizes traditional vocational education programs. What kinds of programs do you think are appropriate for students who do not plan to go to college or who want to enter the job market immediately after high school?
17. Write a letter to your high school principal (you do not need to send it) explaining the ways in which the school was successful or unsuccessful in meeting your needs and those of students like you. If it seems relevant, make realistic suggestions for change.
18. Many high schools, perhaps including the one you attended, use "tracking" to place students in separate classes according to their presumed ability for academic success. Rose, as well as other educators, questions this system. Write an essay detailing the advantages or disadvantages of such a system for schools and their students. Consider the question of how and whether one can determine ahead of time if a student has the ability to succeed academically.
*19. Rose says that a mystique surrounds those who grow up in urban environments: "It's popular these days to claim you grew up on the streets" (paragraph 10). Do you agree? What cultural factors might influence this attitude? You might also want to read Nell Bernstein's "Goin' Gangsta, Choosin' Cholita."

Living in Two Worlds

Marcus Mabry

Marcus Mabry was a junior at Stanford University when he wrote this essay for the April 1988 issue of Newsweek on Campus, *a supplement to the popular newsmagazine distributed on college campuses. As he himself tells it, he comes from a poor family in New Jersey whose lives seem far removed from the life at Stanford, one of the most affluent universities in the United States. It is this wide gap between home—African-American, poor—and college—white, mainstream, and affluent—that Mabry discusses. His double identity attests to both the mobility in American society and the tensions that it may create.*

Mabry has been bureau chief for Newsweek *in Johannesburg, and before that was their Paris correspondent. He is currently a senior editor at* Newsweek International. *He is the author of* White Bucks and Black-Eyed Peas: Coming of Age Black in White America *(1995).*

1   A round, green cardboard sign hangs from a string proclaiming, "We built a proud new feeling," the slogan of a local supermarket. It is a souvenir from one of my brother's last jobs. In addition to being a bagger, he's worked at a fast-food restaurant, a gas station, a garage and a textile factory. Now, in the icy clutches of the Northeastern winter, he is unemployed. He will soon be a father. He is 19 years old.

2   In mid-December I was at Stanford, among the palm trees and weighty chores of academe. And all I wanted to do was get out. I joined the rest of the undergrads in a chorus of excitement, singing the praises of Christmas break. No classes, no midterms, no finals...and no freshmen! (I'm a resident assistant.) Awesome! I was looking forward to escaping. I never gave a thought to what I was escaping to.

3   Once I got home to New Jersey, reality returned. My dreaded freshmen had been replaced by unemployed relatives; badgering professors had been replaced by hard-working single mothers, and cold classrooms by dilapidated bedrooms and kitchens. The room in which the "proud new feeling" sign hung contained the belongings of myself, my mom and my brother. But for these two weeks it was mine. They slept downstairs on couches.

4   Most students who travel between the universes of poverty and affluence during breaks experience similar conditions, as well as the guilt, the helplessness and, sometimes, the embarrassment associated with them. Our friends are willing to listen, but most of them are unable to imagine the pain of the impoverished lives that we see every six months. Each time I return home I feel further away from the realities of poverty in America and more ashamed that they are

allowed to persist. What frightens me most is not that the American socioeconomic system permits poverty to continue, but that by participating in that system I share some of the blame.

5   Last year I lived in an on-campus apartment, with a (relatively) modern
bathroom, kitchen and two bedrooms. Using summer earnings, I added some
expensive prints, a potted palm and some other plants, making the place look
like the more-than-humble abode of a New York City Yuppie. I gave dinner
parties, even a *soirée française.*[1]

6   For my roommate, a doctor's son, this kind of life was nothing extraordinary. But my mom was struggling to provide a life for herself and my brother. In
addition to working 24-hour-a-day cases as a practical nurse, she was trying to
ensure that my brother would graduate from high school and have a decent life.
She knew that she had to compete for his attention with drugs and other potentially dangerous things that can look attractive to a young man when he sees no
better future.

7   Living in my grandmother's house this Christmas break restored all the forgotten, and the never acknowledged, guilt. I had gone to boarding school on a
full scholarship since the ninth grade, so being away from poverty was not new.
But my own growing affluence has increased my distance. My friends say that I
should not feel guilty: what could I do substantially for my family at this age,
they ask. Even though I know that education is the right thing to do, I can't help
but feel, sometimes, that I have it too good. There is no reason that I deserve security and warmth, while my brother has to cope with potential unemployment
and prejudice. I, too, encounter prejudice, but it is softened by my status as a
student in an affluent and intellectual community.

8   More than my sense of guilt, my sense of helplessness increases each time I
return home. As my success leads me further away for longer periods of time,
poverty becomes harder to conceptualize and feels that much more oppressive
when I visit with it. The first night of break, I lay in our bedroom, on a couch
that let out into a bed that took up the whole room, except for a space heater. It
was a little hard to sleep because the springs from the couch stuck through at inconvenient spots. But it would have been impossible to sleep anyway because of
the groans coming from my grandmother's room next door. Only in her early
60s, she suffers from many chronic diseases and couldn't help but moan, then
pray aloud, then moan, then pray aloud.

9   This wrenching of my heart was interrupted by the 3 A.M. entry of a relative
who had been allowed to stay at the house despite rowdy behavior and threats
toward the family in the past. As he came into the house, he slammed the door,
and his heavy steps shook the second floor as he stomped into my grandmother's
room to take his place, at the foot of her bed. There he slept, without blankets
on a bare mattress. This was the first night. Later in the vacation, a Christmas

[1]Elegant party in French style.

turkey and a Christmas ham were stolen from my aunt's refrigerator on Christmas Eve. We think the thief was a relative. My mom and I decided not to exchange gifts that year because it just didn't seem festive.

10   A few days after New Year's I returned to California. The Northeast was soon hit by a blizzard. They were there, and I was here. That was the way it had to be, for now. I haven't forgotten; the ache of knowing their suffering is always there. It has to be kept deep down, or I can't find the logic in studying and partying while people, my people, are being killed by poverty. Ironically, success drives me away from those I most want to help by getting an education.

11   Somewhere in the midst of all that misery, my family has built, within me, "a proud feeling." As I travel between the two worlds it becomes harder to remember just how proud I should be—not just because of where I have come from and where I am going, but because of where they are. The fact that they survive in the world in which they live is something to be very proud of, indeed. It inspires within me a sense of tenacity and accomplishment that I hope every college graduate will someday possess.

EXERCISES

Some of the Issues

1. Describe the two worlds Mabry lives in.
2. Mabry looks forward to "escaping" from school (paragraph 2), not an unusual sentiment at the end of a semester. What is he escaping to? Considering the rest of what he tells the reader, what is the real direction of escape?
3. "Once I got home to New Jersey, reality returned" (paragraph 3). Why does Mabry refer to life in New Jersey as "reality"? Is life at Stanford not real?
4. In paragraph 8, Mabry says "More than my sense of guilt, my sense of helplessness increases each time I return home." What events does he describe that contribute to this feeling?
5. Why does Mabry say in paragraph 11 that his family built "a proud feeling" within him?

The Way We Are Told

6. Consider the order of the first two paragraphs. Why does Mabry start with his brother rather than himself?
7. In the opening and concluding paragraphs and again in paragraph 3, Mabry refers to the supermarket sign about a "proud new feeling." How does the reference change each time he uses it? How does the repetition of the phrase help him to unify the essay? Try to define the kind of pride he is talking about.

8. Account for Mabry's use of expressions like "weighty chores of academe," "awesome!" "more-than-humble abode," and "*soirée française*." From which of Mabry's two worlds do these phrases come? What does he gain by including them?

Some Subjects for Writing

9. Many people have had the experience of living in two different worlds—perhaps not the same two as Mabry's. If you have had such an experience—in family life, as a result of a job, a vacation, or some other cause—discuss your worlds and your relation to them.

10. Most students experience some change when they go to college that distances them from their family or alters their family role. Describe a change that you have either gone through or that you see yourself going through in the future.

11. Interview three students at your college who come from different ethnic or socioeconomic backgrounds. How have their college experiences varied? Write an essay in which you draw conclusions about how students' backgrounds may affect their experiences at and their adjustments to college life and academics.

Who Burns for the Perfection of Paper

Martín Espada

Born in Brooklyn, New York to a Puerto Rican father and a Jewish-Jehovah's Witness mother, poet and essayist Martín Espada was raised in the working class housing projects of East New York. Espada's own life experiences provide the subject matter for much of his creative work, which focuses heavily on issues of class, ethnicity, and social justice. His sense of social justice is deeply rooted in his family and upbringing. In his essay Zapata's Disciple and Perfect Brie, *Espada traces the influence of his father's activism and Puerto Rican identity on the development of his own social conscience, saying "My father's social class was defined by the opportunities denied him because of racism, and the opportunities he created for himself in spite of racism."*

Espada's work history is interesting and varied. He has worked as a night desk clerk at a transient hotel, telephone solicitor, gas station attendant, bouncer, bartender, and tenants' rights attorney, among other jobs. He is currently a professor of English at the University of Massachusetts at Amherst. This poem is informed both by his experience as a factory worker at a company that made yellow legal pads and by his time as a law student. It is reprinted from his poetry collection entitled City of Coughing and Dead Radiators *(1993).*

At sixteen, I worked after high school hours
at a printing plant
that manufactured legal pads:
Yellow paper
5   stacked seven feet high
and leaning
as I slipped cardboard
between the pages,
then brushed red glue
10   up and down the stack.
No gloves: fingertips required
for the perfection of paper,
smoothing the exact rectangle.
Sluggish by 9 PM, the hands
15   would slide along suddenly sharp paper,
and gather slits thinner than the crevices

of the skin, hidden.
Then the glue would sting,
hands oozing
20   till both palms burned
at the punchclock.

Ten years later, in law school,
I knew that every legal pad
was glued with the sting of hidden cuts,
25   that every open lawbook
was a pair of hands
upturned and burning.

EXERCISES

Some of the Issues

1. Why does Espada emphasize the idea of perfection? What does he say is required in order for the paper to achieve perfection?
2. The making of legal pads may seem like an odd topic for a poem. Why does Espada think it's important?
3. Where does Espada use alliteration? How does this help the flow of the poem?
4. In the middle of the poem, Espada moves from the first person to the third person. Why do you suppose he does this? What effect does it have on the reader?
5. How do you interpret the last stanza of the poem? What images does Espada evoke? How does it follow from the rest of the poem?

Some Subjects for Writing

6. Do you think many of Espada's law school classmates shared his experience of working in a factory? Describe a situation where you had an insight into an experience that you felt others around you might not have. Describe how you gained that experience, and how it affected your feelings about or your approach to that situation.

PART III
FAMILIES

The American family once considered the norm in the postwar generation of the 1940s and 1950s is now the minority. The traditional family in which children grow up in the same household with two biological parents who are married to each other is being replaced by an array of differently formed families. The selections in Chapter 3 call into question assumptions about what makes a "normal" family, and ask whether indeed such a thing has ever existed.

Dan Savage, a gay man raising a son, confronts his own assumptions about gender and sexual orientation as he muses on what kinds of toys and clothes his son should have. In "The Mommy Wars," Susan Douglas and Meredith Michaels compare media images of celebrity moms with those of welfare mothers. Their tone is humorous (though the point is serious) as they argue that these images are an important reflection of societal attitudes about class, celebrity, and motherhood.

In "Families," Jane Howard gives ten characteristics she believes all good families must have. Her definition of family includes non-traditional families, such as families based on friendship. In "Where Are the Good Old Days," Stephanie Coontz challenges the notion that there ever was such a thing as a "traditional" family.

In "Choosing a Mate," Ruth Breen tells the story of her marriage, arranged by her parents. She compares arranged marriages to "love" marriages and concludes that they are equally likely to succeed. Alfred Kazin recounts the story of his eastern European immigrant family living in the tenements of New York City early in the twentieth century. His family is held together by the ceaseless work and worry of his mother. Finally, in a short poem by Theodore Roethke, we get a brief glimpse of a child's memory of his father, a memory filled with mixed emotions.

Role Reversal

Dan Savage

Dan Savage is best known as the author of "Savage Love," a weekly syndi-cated sex advice column that appears in alternative newspapers across the country. Savage, who is openly gay, began dispensing advice in 1991 in The Stranger, *a Seattle alternative weekly where he remains an editor. Savage's column is known for its caustic wit combined with practical common sense. Many of his columns have been collected into a book,* Savage Love: Straight Answers from America's Most Popular Sex Columnist *(1997).*

In 1998, Dan and his partner Terry adopted a son, DJ, through open adoption, a process in which an adoptive family often maintains contact with birth parents throughout the life of the child. Savage describes the experience of adopting DJ in his book The Kid: What Happened After My Boyfriend and I Decided To Go Get Pregnant: An Adoption Story *(1999). This se-lection, originally published in* The New York Times, *describes in a humor-ous way the struggles parents go through in addressing the complex issue of gender roles in a child's upbringing.*

1   She was homeless by choice and seven months pregnant by accident when she selected my boyfriend and me from our adoption agency's pool of pre-screened parent wannabes. Six weeks later, the three of us sat in a recovery room at the hospital taking turns holding our son, DJ. Some adoptive parents abuse pronouns ("*our* son," "*my* child") to establish possession; it's as if they're saying, "Our child now, not her child anymore." But doing an open adoption means embracing the "most plural" definition of every plural pronoun, at least where your child is concerned. When I say "our" son, his mother is included. We may be DJ's full-time parents, but she is his parent, too, and stealth-hostile pronouns can't change that.

2   But one parent was missing that day in the hospital.

3   When DJ's mom was a 19-year-old street kid, she had hooked up with Bac-chus, our son's biological father, for a few weeks one summer. By the time she realized she was pregnant, the god of wine was gone. When we adopted DJ, Bacchus didn't know he was a father—or that his son had been adopted by a gay couple. We were tense when Bacchus surfaced in New Orleans, appropriately enough, shortly before DJ's first birthday, but in the end Bacchus wanted only what we had agreed to give his mother: pictures a few times a year and the occa-sional visit. DJ met his biological father, whose real name is Jacob, in a hotel off Bourbon Street a few weeks later. When Jacob's own dad, a truck driver living in Texas, called to thank us for taking "good care of my grandson," we started

sending him pictures too. The gay thing didn't appear to be an issue with Jacob or his father. It never came up.

4   Since the day we brought DJ home from the hospital, people have been asking us if we're going to bring DJ up gay. The idea that two gay men, of all people, would even think it possible for a parent to select their child's sexual orientation is absurd. Didn't our own parents try that on us? Didn't it fail? Yet the question is put to us by the most unlikely people; relatives present at our long-ago coming-out dramas; friends we assumed to be more sophisticated. And as a result of hearing it so many times, my boyfriend and I have come to feel . . . scrutinized.

5   So watching my son tear into an unexpected late bonus round of Christmas gifts, I couldn't help wondering if the gay thing was coming up. Last month, Jacob's father and his father's new wife sent an enormous package filled with a toy workbench, a battery-powered toy drill, a battery-powered toy saw, a hammer and two screwdrivers. It looked to my slightly paranoid eyes like a grow-up-straight care package from some concerned grandparents. (Of course, as my boyfriend points out, there's a good chance DJ's biograndparents bought him tools because DJ's a boy.)

6   Most hip, modern, urban parents have a sense of humor about sex roles. Not us. I had given the sons of straight friends little pink dresses as baby gifts for years. "Don't assume anything," I wanted each pink dress to say. Almost all of my friends put their sons in their pink dresses once and took a picture before exchanging them. A few payback pink dresses arrived in the first weeks we had DJ, but we didn't have a single pink-dress photo-op. If we put him in a dress, my God, people might think we were trying to make him gay.

7   Walking home with DJ the day his preschool teacher painted DJ's fingernails red, I wanted to scream, "I didn't do it!" Then there was the neighbor who started calling our sons, who play together, "cute little boyfriends," much to her husband's consternation—and mine. A friend threatened to give DJ a "Future Hooters Girl" T-shirt on his birthday until I told him it would wind up at Goodwill faster than a crate of eight-track tapes.

8   So if DJ's Texan grandparents sent tools because they worry his gay dads are buying him nothing but Barbie dolls, well, their fears are misplaced. All we buy DJ are trucks and planes and cars and trains and blocks—which, as it turns out, is all DJ wants. He's a standard-issue boy, not a sissy like I was. Of course, I would love him just as much if he were into dolls, even if I have to admit it's a relief that he isn't.

9   But if he wanted dolls I would give him dolls; if he wanted to paint his nails red and wear a "Future Hooters Girl" T-shirt to school, I would let him. But I would still worry that people might think that my boyfriend and I were, as a relative put it, "pushing DJ in *that* direction." So I guess we're lucky DJ loves—adores—his new tools. He could still grow up gay; I know plenty of adult gay men who played with toolboxes when they were boys. I never did, but I'm playing with them now. Being DJ's dad has forced me to take a belated interest in all

the boy stuff I wouldn't touch when I was a kid. I spend an awful lot of time on the floor with my son these days playing with cars and trucks, blocks and Legos, hammers and saws. DJ is the kind of boy I never was, and now, thanks to my son, so am I.

EXERCISES

Some of the Issues

1. Why does Savage emphasize the pronoun "our" in paragraph 1? Why does he feel that parents often abuse the pronoun? What does he imply about the significance of language?
2. Why does Savage recount the responses of DJ's father and grandfather to their adoption?
3. What questions do people keep asking Savage and his boyfriend (paragraph 4)? Why does Savage find this question "absurd"? What does he imply when he writes: "Didn't our own parents try that on us?"
4. What kinds of conflicts does Savage feel about the kinds of gifts he and other people buy for his son? Why does he buy his friends' boys pink dresses, but then refuse to dress his son in one for a "photo-op"?
5. How does choice fit into Savage's decisions about what kinds of toys DJ plays with and the kinds of clothes he wears? Does Savage think that the toys and clothes a child is exposed to have no impact on their understanding of gender roles?
6. What does Savage's last paragraph tell us about his own interests as a child? How does this fit in with the ideas presented in the rest of the essay?
7. What does Savage appear to value in parenting? What, in the end, has the most influence on a child?

The Way We Are Told

8. Why do you think Savage tells us DJ's father's nickname is Bacchus (the Greek god of wine), before he tells us his real name, Jacob?
9. What is the tone of the essay? How does the tone affect your interpretation?
10. Savage's thesis is implied rather than stated directly. If you had to come up with a thesis for the essay, what would it be?

Some Subjects for Writing

11. Visit a local toy store or a toy section of a department store. Determine which products are marketed to girls and which ones are marketed to boys.

Write an essay in which you analyze the assumptions about gender that lie behind the marketing. You should consider not only the product itself (including what it does and what it looks like), but also the design of and the text written on the packaging of the product.

12. Interview several of your peers about the kinds of toys they played with when they were children and how they feel it affected their lives. If they have children or expect to have children, include questions about what kinds of toys they will and won't buy for them. Using specific examples from their interviews, write an essay in which you analyze their responses.

The Mommy Wars

Susan Douglas and Meredith Michaels

Susan Douglas and Meredith Michaels are both teachers; Douglas a professor of communication studies at the University of Michigan and Michaels a philosophy professor at Smith College in Massachusetts. Douglas is the author of several books, including Where the Girls Are: Growing Up Female With the Mass Media, *a look at the pop culture that fed women of the baby boom generation with images that simultaneously acknowledged a blossoming feminist awareness and reinforced sex-role stereotypes. Michaels is the co-author of three books of philosophy. Together they have collaborated on a book,* Bringing Up Baby: Motherhood and Media in Contemporary Culture, *which expands upon some of the issues raised in this essay.*

Originally published in Ms *magazine in 2000, this selection addresses how images of motherhood are constructed in the media, specifically in this case in the magazines we all see as we wait in line at the supermarket checkout. The authors set up a dramatic comparison between media portrayals (and, by extension, societal expectations) of two different "kinds" of mothers. Glamorous celebrity moms such as Kirstie Alley, Christie Brinkley, and Jodie Foster, they claim, are held to very different standards than welfare moms who are trying to do the same job (raising children) under considerably harsher circumstances.*

Welfare reform was a hotly debated topic in the 1990s, leading up to the passage by Congress in 1996 of the Personal Responsibility and Work Opportunity Reconciliation Act, which radically transformed the nation's welfare system. It limited the length of time families could stay on welfare and shifted the focus of welfare programs from entitlement to job preparation programs. There was an explosion of media coverage on the topic, including the profiles of welfare mothers that Douglas and Michaels respond to in this essay. Though experts on both sides of the debate admit that welfare reform has been of somewhat mixed success, the 1996 legislation was reauthorized by Congress in 2002.

1   It's 5:22 P.M. You're in the grocery check-out line. Your three-year-old is writhing on the floor, screaming, because you have refused to buy her a Teletubby pinwheel. Your six-year-old is whining, repeatedly, in a voice that could saw through cement, "But mommy, puleeze, puleeze," because you have not bought him the latest Lunchables, which features as the four food groups: chips, a candy bar, fake cheese, and artificial coloring.

2   To distract yourself, and to avoid the glares of other shoppers who have already deemed you the worst mother in America, you leaf through *People* magazine. Inside, Uma Thurman gushes, "Motherhood is sexy." Moving on to *Good Housekeeping*, Vanna White says of her child, "When I hear his cry at 6:30 in the

morning, I have a smile on my face, and I'm not an early riser." Brought back to reality by stereophonic wailing, you feel about as sexy and euphoric as Rush Limbaugh in a thong.

3　　Meanwhile, *Newsweek*, also at the check-out line, offers a different view of motherhood. In one of the many stories about welfare mothers that proliferated until "welfare reform" was passed in 1996, you meet Valerie, 27, and "the three children she has by different absentee fathers." She used to live with her mother, "who, at 42, has six grandchildren." But now Valerie resides with other families, all of whom "live side-by-side in open trash-filled apartments." Hey, maybe you're not such a failure after all.

4　　Motherhood has been one of the biggest media fixations of the past two decades. And this is what so many of us have been pulled between when we see accounts of motherhood in the media: celebrity moms who are perfect, most of them white, always rich, happy, and in control, the role models we should emulate, versus welfare mothers who are irresponsible, unmarried, usually black or Latina—as if there were no white single mothers on the dole—poor, miserable, and out of control, the bad examples we should scorn.

5　　Beginning in the late 1970s, with the founding of *People* and *Us*, and exploding with a vengeance in the '90s with *InStyle*, the celebrity-mom profile has spread like head lice through popular magazines, especially women's. "For me, happiness is having a baby," gushed Marie Osmond on a 1983 cover of *Good Housekeeping*, and Linda Evans added in *Ladies' Home Journal*, "All I want is a husband and baby." These celeb biographies, increasingly presented as instruction manuals for how the rest of us should live our lives, began to proliferate just as there was a dramatic rise in the number of women who worked outside the home while raising small children. Pulled between established wisdom—if you worked outside the home before your children entered kindergarten you were bound to raise an ax murderer—and the economic and psychic need to work, many of these mothers were searching for guidance. And celebrity mom magazine articles seemed to provide it.

6　　Celebrity moms were perfect for the times. They epitomized two ideals that sat in uneasy but fruitful alliance. On the one hand, they exemplified the unbridled materialism and elitism the Reagan era had spawned. On the other, they represented the feminist dream of women being able to have a family and a job outside the home without being branded traitors to true womanhood. Magazine editors apparently figured they could use stars to sell magazines and to serve as role models.

7　　But now, in the year 2000, things have gotten out of control. Celebrity moms are everywhere, beaming from the comfy serenity and perfection of their lives as they give multiple interviews about their "miracle babies," what an unadulterated joy motherhood is, and all the things they do with their kids to ensure they will be perfectly normal Nobel laureates by the age of 12.

8　　These stories are hardly reassuring. They make the rest of us feel that our own lives are, as the great seventeenth century philosopher Thomas Hobbes put it, nasty, brutish, and short. So why should we care about something so banal as the celebrity mom juggernaut? One answer is that it bulldozed through so much of American popular culture just when working mothers, single mothers, and welfare mothers were identified, especially by conservative male pundits, as the cause of everything bad, from the epidemic of drug use to the national debt to rising crime rates. Remember all the hand-wringing by George Will, William Bennett, and Allan Bloom[1] about America's "moral decay"? The biggest culprit, of course, was the single welfare mother. These guys attacked celebrity single mothers now and then, but the mud never stuck—not even, heaven help us, on that fictional celebrity single mother Murphy Brown.[2]

9   As the push "to end welfare as we know it" gained momentum and reached its climax in the welfare reform of 1996, the canonized celebrity mom and de-monized welfare mother became ever more potent symbols, working in power-ful opposition to each other. We rarely saw these very different mothers in the same publication, or even considered them in the same breath. Celebrity moms graced the covers of magazines designed for self-realization and escape; welfare mothers were the object of endless stories in newspapers and newsmagazines and on the nightly news that focused on public policy and its relation to the ten-uous state of morality in America.

10   But what if we put these portrayals side by side and compare what these differ-ent mothers were made to stand for? Could it be that the tsunami of celebrity-mom profiles helped, however inadvertently, to justify punitive policies toward welfare mothers and their children? While the "you *can* have it all" ethos of these pieces made the rest of us feel like failures as mothers, and upped the ante in the eyes of employers and coworkers about how much working mothers can handle, a little side-by-side reading also exposes some rather daunting hypocrisy. Often, one group is glamorized and the other castigated for precisely the same behavior.

11   Let's take a look at a celebrity mom first. Kirstie Alley, for example. It's 1994. The star of *Cheers* and the *Look Who's Talking* movies graces the cover of *InStyle*, a magazine that pays fawning tribute to the charming idiosyncrasies and lifestyle choices of our nation's most glamorous. Among Kirstie's recent choices is the purchase of her third house. *InStyle* advises us respectfully that "as with all of her houses, Kirstie paid cash." On a tour of her new Bangor, Maine, retreat (the renovation of which was paid for by a quick voice-over job she did for Sub-aru), we discover that both Kirstie and her house are "at once down-to-earth and whimsical."

12   Kirstie must be down-to-earth, of course, because now, at long last, she is a mother. Her "playful sense of style" is made evident by the decoupage grapes

---

[1]Conservative social critics.

[2]1990s television character who stirred up controversy when she became a single mom.

that grace her son True's high chair. "It was painted and cracked to make it look old," *InStyle* informs us. (Why not simply rely on natural toddler effluvia to give the chair that petroglyph look?) True has just turned one; his whimsical high chair faces an equally whimsical ceramic pig holding a blackboard on which a new word appears each day to encourage his reading.

13   In our tour through Kirstie's hideaway, we encounter an entourage—decorators, a nanny, a cook, and various personal assistants. Kirstie spends True's two-hour nap time working out with her personal trainer and then being served a healthful, fat-free lunch by the cook. Lounging in her living room (painted to "echo" the surrounding firs and elms), reflecting on the challenges of motherhood, Kirstie gushes, "Being a mother has given me a whole new purpose. Every day when I wake up it's like Christmas morning to me, and seeing life through True's eyes gives me a whole new way of looking at the world." Perfect house. Perfect husband. Perfect child. Perfect career. Perfect life. Kirstie is a perfect mother. *InStyle* invites you to curl up on the sofa with Kirstie, but then implies that you'd probably just spill your tea on it.

14   Forward to 1997. There's Kirstie again, now the star of the television series *Veronica's Closet*, beaming at us once more from *InStyle*. "A new man, a new show, a brand-new life," proclaims the cover. Since 1994, her island mansion has "become a place to play." Each of the 15 bedrooms is decorated with Kirstie's "eclectic and playful eye." According to *InStyle*, most people would have found decorating this 16,000-square-foot house daunting, but not Kirstie. "I'm very fast," she explains. "I don't shop. I just point: boom, boom, boom." Having outgrown his high chair, True now has his own miniature lobster boat. In addition, he and his new sister, Lillie, can frolic in their personal nursery-rhyme garden, complete with Mother Goose figures especially commissioned by "fun-loving" Kirstie because, as she puts it, "I hope to give my children a spirit of play."

15   Kirstie swears by the facial treatment she receives every morning on her terrace as the fog burns off Penobscot Bay. It involves "blasting her face with oxygen and enzymes . . . through a plastic hose hooked up to two pressurized tanks." Though her life was perfect in 1994, she has since set aside her husband, Parker Stevenson, in favor of her "soul mate," James Wilder, who "is a cross between Houdini, Errol Flynn, and Marlon Brando." Apparently Kirstie uses the same technique for choosing her lovers as she does for choosing sofa fabrics. With James, "It was like comet to comet. Boom . . ."

16   Not that we ought to single out Kirstie (although such self-serving bilge makes it irresistible). Celebrity-mom profiles are almost all alike and haven't changed much over the years, except that the houses and toys are more lavish. Celebrity moms are shown embracing motherhood after years of sweating under klieg lights, which apparently brings them in touch with their true, essential, feminine natures. Most important, motherhood is a powerfully transforming experience, akin to seeing God. It always changes these women, and always for the better. "I feel more enriched and compassionate toward others since having my son," says Elle McPherson.

17   *Ladies Home Journal* tells us that Christie Brinkley's third child, daughter Sailor (her father, Brinkley's fourth husband, is a descendant of Captain Cook), "barely tipping the scale at eight pounds . . . has become Brinkley's anchor, a midlife miracle well worth waiting for." Of her second child, Jack (from her third marriage, which lasted only a few months), Christie was equally lyrical: "It's like I went to hell and came back with this angel."

18   We assume that most (but not all) of these celebrity moms are not trying to gloat, or to rub our noses in our own poor lifestyle choices (which invariably include the failure to choose being thin, white, gorgeous, and rich). And we've all said mushy things about how much our kids mean to us, especially in the immediate aftermath of birth, before the months of sleep deprivation and projectile vomiting produce a slightly more jaundiced view of the joys of motherhood.

19   But there's little deviation in the celebrity mom profile: it is a sturdily ossified genre, and those who choose to contribute to it must embody and emphasize certain traits. She is everything that you—poor, stupid, incompetent, slob—are not: serene, resourceful, contented, transformed, perky, fun-loving, talented, nurturing, selfless, organized, spontaneous, thin, fit, pore-free, well-rested, well-manicured, on-the-go, sexy, and rich. She has absolutely no ambivalence about motherhood, would prefer to spend all her time with her kids if only she could, and finds that when she comes home from a draining day, her children recharge her as if they were Energizers. She is never furious, hysterical, or uncertain. She is never a bitch. She is June Cleaver[3] with cleavage and a successful career. In a 1997 cover story titled "The New Sexy Moms," *People* told us that "postpartum depression isn't an option for such celebrity moms as Whitney Houston, Madonna, and supermodel Niki Taylor." Being subjected to sleep deprivation and raging hormones was a choice for these women, and they just said no.

20   The celebrity-mom profile is predicated on the interview, in which we hear extensively from the mother herself. This is a media form designed to showcase the mother's subjective processes and inner life and, thus, to celebrate her distinctive individuality. We're meant to hang on her every word, no matter how banal. She hasn't fallen through the cracks, ended up part of some vast, nameless, harried horde like the rest of us. What makes her such a great mother and enviable person is her ability to take action, make smart choices, and impose discipline on herself while being loving and spontaneous with her kids. The myth of the determined individual, fully capable of vaulting over all sorts of economic, political, and social barriers, is beautifully burnished in these profiles. It's all up to you, if only you'll try, try, and try again. There are no such things in this gauzy world as economic inequalities, institutional sexism, racism, or class privilege. Nor are there tired, pissed-off partners or kids who've just yelled, "I hate you! I wish you were dead!"

---

[3]1950s TV ideal of the perfect mother.

21　　　Celebrity children don't wreak havoc with work, they enhance it and even fortify their mothers' bargaining position with the boss. Says actress Gigi Rice, "Now, if they want you to do a job, you say, 'Well, my baby comes with me.' What are they going to say—no?" In addition, *People* tells us, "Contractually mandated star perks typically include first-class airfare for the entire entourage, a separate trailer for the kiddies and a 24-hour limousine on standby to ferry them wherever they want to go, paid hotel accommodations for the nanny, even a nanny allowance." Sounds just like your workplace, *n'est-ce pas?*

22　　　Celebrity moms exemplify what motherhood has become in our intensified consumer culture: a competition. They rekindle habits of mind, pitting women against women, that the women's movement sought to end, leaving the notion of sisterhood in the dust. More perniciously, these portraits resurrect so many of the stereotypes about women we hoped to deep-six 30 years ago: that women are, by genetic composition, nurturing and maternal, that they love all children and prefer motherhood to anything, especially work—so they should be the main ones responsible for raising the kids. In the pages of the glossies, motherhood becomes a contest in which the reader is always the loser. Why do Kirstie and Cindy and Whitney love being mothers in some unequivocal way that you do not? Because they're good and you're bad.

23　Ah, but you could be worse. What about media motherhood on the other side of the tracks? Celebrity mom profiles place us on the outside looking in; stories about welfare mothers invite us to look down from on high. Welfare mothers have not been the subject of honey-hued profiles in glossy magazines. They are not the subjects of their own lives, but objects of journalistic scrutiny. We don't hear about these women's maternal practices—what do they do with their kids to nurture them, educate them, soothe them, or keep them happy. It is simply assumed that these women don't have inner lives. Emotions are not ascribed to them; we don't hear them laugh or see their eyes well up with tears. One of the most frequent verbs used to describe them is "complain," as when they complain about losing health care for their kids when they go off welfare. When they are quoted, it is not their feelings about the transformative powers of motherhood to which we are made privy. Rather, we hear their relentless complaints about "the system."

24　　　In many articles about welfare, we don't hear from the mothers at all, but instead from academic experts who study them, or from politicians whose careers are devoted to bashing them. The iconography of the welfare mother is completely different, too—she's not photographed holding her child up in the air, whizzing her about. In fact, she's rarely, if ever, shown smiling at all. It's as if the photographer yelled "scowl" just before clicking the shutter.

25　　　These mothers are shown as sphinx-like, monolithic, part of a pathetic historical pattern known, familiarly, as "the cycle of dependency." In a major article in *Newsweek* in August 1993 titled "The Endangered Family," we learn that "For many African Americans, marriage and childbearing do not go together." Not to mention the 25 percent of white women for whom they don't go together either, or the celebrity single mothers like Jodie Foster, Madonna, and Farrah Fawcett.

26   It isn't just that the conservative right has succeeded in stereotyping welfare mothers as lazy, promiscuous parasites; the media in which these mothers appear provide no point of identification with them. At best, these mothers are pitiable. At worst, they are reprehensible opposites of the other mothers we see so much of, the new standard-bearers of ideal motherhood—the doting, conscientious celebrities for whom motherhood is a gateway to heaven.

27   During the height of welfare bashing in the Reagan, Bush, and Clinton administrations, the stereotype of the "welfare queen" gained mythological status. But there were other, less obvious, journalistic devices that served equally well to dehumanize poor mothers and their children. Unsavory designations proliferated with a vengeance: "chronic dependents," "the chronically jobless," "welfare mothers in training," "hard-core welfare recipients," "never-married mothers," "welfare careerists," and "welfare recidivists" became characters in a distinctly American political melodrama. Poor women weren't individuals; instead their life stories became case-studies of moral decay, giving substance to the inevitable barrage of statistics peppering the media's presentation of "Life on the Dole." In publications everywhere, we met the poster mother for welfare reform. She only had a first name, she lived in the urban decay of New York, Chicago, or Detroit, she was not married, she had a pile of kids each with a different absent father, and she spent her day painting her nails, smoking cigarettes, and feeding Pepsi to her baby.

28   As sociologists have pointed out, even though there consistently have been more white people than black on welfare, the news media began, in the mid-1960s, to rely almost exclusively on pictures of African Americans to illustrate stories about welfare, reinforcing the stereotype that most welfare recipients are black. Occasionally readers are introduced to the runner-up in the poster competition: the white welfare mother, whose story varies only in that she lives in a trailer in some godforsaken place we have never heard of and is really, really fat.

29   For example, in a 1995 edition of CBS's *48 Hours,* titled "The Rage Over Welfare," we met two overweight white women who live on welfare in New Hampshire. The very first shots—just to let us know the kind of lazy, selfish mothers we are in for—are close-ups of hands shuffling a deck of playing cards and, next, a mom lighting a cigarette. The white male journalist badgers one of the women, who says she can't work because she has epilepsy and arthritis in both knees. "People with epilepsy work. People with bad knees work. People do," he scolds. As she answers, "I don't know what kind of a job I could find," the camera again cuts to her hands shuffling the cards, suggesting, perhaps, a bright future in the casino industry if she'd only apply herself.

30   Or there's Denise B., one of the "True Faces of Welfare," age 29, with five daughters, from ages one to 13. "All, after the first, were conceived on welfare—conceived perhaps deliberately," *Readers Digest* sniffs, conjuring up

the image of Denise doing some quick math calculations, saying to herself, Oh boy, an extra 60 bucks a month, and then running out to find someone to get her pregnant. The other thing we learn about Denise is that she's a leech. Why not get a job, even though she has toddlers? Because she's lazy. "To get a good job, she would first have to go to school, then earn her way up to a high salary," *Reader's Digest* reminds us, and then lets the ingrate, Denise, speak. "'That's going to take time,' she says, 'It's a lot of work and I ain't guaranteed to get nothing.'" What we learn of Denise's inner life is that she's a calculating cynic. Her kids don't make her feel like every day is Christmas; no, we're supposed to think she uses her kids to get something for nothing.

31   Even the New York *Times'* Jason De Parle, one of the more sympathetic white male journalists to cover welfare, gets blinded by class privilege. Roslyn Hale, he wrote in 1994, who had been trying to get off welfare, had a succession of jobs that "alternatively invite and discourage public sympathy." She had worked as a maid and as a clerk in a convenience store during the overnight shift when drunks came in and threatened her with a knife. Hale "blames economics for her problems," De Parle reports, since these were crappy jobs that paid only minimum wage. "And sometimes she blames herself. 'I have an attitude,' she admitted." Hello? What middle-class woman would not have "an attitude" after having been threatened at knife-point or being expected to be grateful for such jobs?

32   In the Boston *Globe's* "Welfare Reform Through a Child's Eyes" we see little Alicia, who now has a room of her own, Barbies, four kittens, and a ferret because her mother got a job. But although this story appears to be through the child's eyes (never the mother's), it's actually through the judgmental eyes of the press. Sure, the mom has quit drinking, quit crack, and is now working at a nursing center. But the apartment is "suffused with the aroma of animal droppings and her mother's cigarette smoke." Presumably everyone but welfare mothers and former welfare mothers know how to make their litter boxes smell like gardenias.

33   One of the sentences most commonly used to characterize the welfare mother is "Tanya, who has ___ children by ___ different men . . ." (you fill in the blanks). Their lives are reduced to the number of successful impregnations by multiple partners—like zoo animals, but unlike Christie Brinkley, although she has exactly the same reproductive M.O. And while the celebrity magazines gush that Christie, Kirstie, and Cindy are sexier than ever, a welfare mother's sexuality is depicted as her downfall.

34   In the last three years, we've seen the dismantling of the nation's welfare system. Meanwhile, the resentment over the ridiculous standards we're supposed to meet is rising. Sure, many of us ridicule these preposterous portraits of celebrity mom-dom, and we gloated when the monumentally self-righteous "I read the Bible to Cody" Kathie Lee Gifford got her various comeuppances. But the problem is bigger than that: the standards set by celebrity motherhood as touted by the media, with their powerful emphasis on individual will, choice,

and responsibility, severely undercut sympathy for poor mothers and their children. Both media characterizations have made it easier for middle-class and upper-middle-class women—especially working women facing speed-ups at work and a decline in leisure time—to resent welfare mothers instead of identifying with them and their struggles.

35   Why does the media offer us this vision? Not surprising, many reporters bought into the myths that began in the Reagan era, with its dogma of trickle-down economics, its attacks on the poor and people of color, and its antifeminist backlash, through which patriarchy got a new name—family values. Becoming rich and famous came to be the ultimate personal achievement. Reagan's message was simple—the outlandish accumulation of wealth by the few is the basis of a strong economy.

36   In that context, celebrity-mom profiles haven't been just harmless dreck that helps sell magazines. They have encouraged self-loathing, rather than reassurance, in those of us financially comfortable enough not to have to worry about where our kids' next meals are coming from. And they play a subtle but important role in encouraging so many of us to think about motherhood as an individual achievement and a test of individual will and self-discipline. That mind-set—the one that promotes individual responsibility over community and societal obligations—justifies letting poor women and their children fend for themselves until mom makes the right lifestyle choices.

37   These stories suggest that we, too, can make it to the summit if we just get up earlier, laugh more, and buy the right products. These stories are about leaving others behind, down below. Phony images of joyful, ever-nurturing celebrity moms sitting side-by-side in the newsstands next to humorless, scowling welfare mothers naturalize a pecking order in which some kids deserve to eat well, have access to a doctor, or go to Disney World, and others do not. Under the glossy veneer of maternal joy, generosity, and love lurks the worst sort of narcissism that insists it's every woman for herself. Paying lip service to a collagen-injected feminism, celebrity momism trivializes the struggles and hopes of real women, and kisses off sisterhood as hopelessly out of style.

EXERCISES

Some of the Issues

1. What scenario do the authors describe in their opening paragraphs? Why did they choose this particular setting?
2. According to the authors, what social, economic, and political factors have contributed to the rise in popularity of celebrity mom profiles? Why has motherhood "been one of the biggest media fixations of the past two decades" (paragraph 5)?

3. According to the authors, what effect do the celebrity mom profiles have on mothers who read them? What are your responses to reading profiles of celebrities?

4. The authors suggest that the media's contrasting treatment of privileged and poor women has influenced legislation. What exactly is their claim? What evidence do they provide in later parts of the essay? Do you find this evidence convincing?

✗5. What do the authors mean when they state: "Often one group is glamorized and the other castigated for precisely the same behavior" (paragraph 10)? How do they support their claim? Can you think of other situations where the media generally portray one group in a more positive light than another for a similar behavior?

6. How do the authors describe Kirstie Alley's home, as depicted in *InStyle* magazine (paragraphs 11–16)? Why do they feel these details are significant?

7. What impression do the authors want to give of Kirstie Alley? Is their critique aimed at her, at the magazine, or at both? Given what you know of these kinds of profiles, do you think the authors are justified in their views? Use specific examples to back up your point.

8. Summarize what the authors see as the difference between the celebrity mom profiles and the newspaper descriptions of welfare mothers. Why do the authors view these comparisons as significant or revealing?

9. What do the authors see as some of the myths and distortions often generated by the media in their depictions of welfare mothers? Why do they feel these distortions can be harmful?

10. According to the authors, what kind of "mind-set" do celebrity mom profiles help promote (paragraph 36)? Why are they so strongly against it?

11. Collect four or five depictions of both celebrities and people who are not celebrities from various publications. In small groups, analyze the differences between the various depictions. How are the people portrayed? What kinds of details does each one include and exclude? Also consider the publication in which it appeared. In other words, what is the audience, and how might that affect how it is written?

The Way We Are Told

12. To whom are the authors speaking in the opening paragraphs? Who is the "you"?

13. Why might the authors put the words "welfare reform" in quotation marks? What seems to be their attitude toward this "reform"?

14. How do the authors use comparison and contrast to back up their argument? Is it effective? Why or why not?

15. How would you characterize the authors' tone? Does the tone shift at all in different points in the reading? Use specific examples to back up your answers.

16. Who do you feel is the primary audience for this piece? How do you know this? To what extent does the piece speak to readers beyond its primary audience?

Some Subjects for Writing

17. Write your own satire of a celebrity profile that plays up certain aspects of his or her identity. Use both satire and hyperbole to try to demonstrate how certain kinds of media often emphasize specific characteristics of celebrities in order to create an image. You might choose to include images with your piece that also play up these characteristics. (By making a collage or using a scanner and computer photography program, you could piece together parts of different images to make your commentary more effective.)

18. Using Douglas's and Michaels's method of comparison and contrast as a model, write an essay in which you analyze portrayals of people who are similar in some way but whose depictions in the media may vary in significant ways. You may look at depictions of men and women who are in the same profession, or of a group of people who do similar things or have similar behaviors but who are from different socio-economic classes. Like Douglas and Michaels, develop your thesis by trying to get at what you think might be significant about the differences you see in these portrayals.

*19. Read Joshua Gamson's "Do Ask, Do Tell" and consider the impact the media has in formulating stereotypes based on class, race, ethnicity, gender, and sexual orientation. Using examples from both the Gamson piece and "The Mommy Wars" along with examples from other readings and your own experience, write an essay in which you examine what kind of influence the media have in formulating people's thoughts and beliefs.

Families

Jane Howard

Jane Howard, (1935–96) was a reporter, editor, writer, and college teacher. Among her books are Please Touch: A Guided Tour of the Human Potential Movement *(1970), the autobiographical* A Different Woman *(1973),* Families *(1978), and* Margaret Mead: A Life *(1984).*

Howard explains ten characteristics good families should have. Her definition of a family includes not only the one you are born into but also those you may develop through close friendships. Though this essay was written in 1978, many of the issues it raises continue to be part of popular dialogue about what makes a family.

1   Each of us is born into one family not of our choosing. If we're going to go around devising new ones, we might as well have the luxury of picking their members ourselves. Clever picking might result in new families whose benefits would surpass or at least equal those of the old. The new ones by definition cannot spawn us—as soon as they do that, they stop being new—but there is plenty they can do. I have seen them work wonders. As a member in reasonable standing of six or seven tribes in addition to the one I was born to, I have been trying to figure which earmarks are common to both kinds of families.

2   (1) Good families have a chief, or a heroine, or a founder—someone around whom others cluster, whose achievements as the Yiddish word has it, let them *kvell*,[1] and whose example spurs them on to like feats. Some blood dynasties produce such figures regularly; others languish for as many as five generations between demigods, wondering with each new pregnancy whether this, at last, might be the messianic baby who will redeem us. Look, is there not something gubernatorial about her footstep, or musical about the way he bangs with his spoon on his cup? All clans, of all kinds, need such a figure now and then. Sometimes clans based on water rather than blood harbor several such personages at one time. The Bloomsbury Group[2] in London six decades ago was not much hampered by its lack of a temporal history.

3   (2) Good families have a switchboard operator—someone like my mother who cannot help but keep track of what all the others are up to, who plays

---

[1] To boast about accomplishments.
[2] Close-knit group of prominent London intellectuals, writers, and artists of the first quarter of the twentieth century.

Houston Mission Control to everyone else's Apollo. This role, like the forego-
ing one, is assumed rather than assigned. Someone always volunteers for it.
That person often also has the instincts of an archivist, and feels driven to keep
scrapbooks and photograph albums up to date, so that the clan can see proof of
its own continuity.

4   (3) Good families are much to all their members, but everything to none.
Good families are fortresses with many windows and doors to the outer world.
The blood clans I feel most drawn to were founded by <u>parents who are nearly as
devoted to whatever it is they do outside as they are to each other and their chil-
dren</u>. Their curiosity and passion are contagious. Everybody, where they live, is
busy. Paint is spattered on eyeglasses. Mud lurks under fingernails. Person-to-
person calls come in the middle of the night from Tokyo and Brussels. Catchers'
mitts, ballet slippers, overdue library books and other signs of extrafamilial concerns are everywhere.

[margin note: INTERESTS OUTSIDE THE FAMILY]

5   (4) Good families are <u>hospitable</u>. Knowing that hosts need guests as much
as guests need hosts, they are generous with honorary memberships for friends,
whom they urge to come early and often and to stay late. Such clans exude a
vivid sense of surrounding rings of relatives, neighbors, teachers, students and
godparents, any of whom at any time might break or slide into the inner circle.
Inside that circle a wholesome, <u>tacit emotional feudalism develops: you give me
protection, I'll give you fealty</u>. Such treaties begin with, but soon go far beyond,
the jolly exchange of pie at Thanksgiving for cake on birthdays. It means you
can ask me to supervise your children for the fortnight you will be in the hospital, and that however inconvenient this might be for me, I shall manage to. It
means I can phone you on what for me is a dreary, wretched Sunday afternoon
and for you is the eve of a deadline, knowing you will tell me to come right over,
if only to watch you type. It means we need not dissemble. ("To yield to seeming," as Buber[3] wrote, "is man's essential cowardice, to resist it is his essential
courage . . . one must at times pay dearly for life lived from the being, but it is
never too dear.")

[margin note: PEOPLE ALLOWED IN]

6   (5) <u>Good families deal squarely with direness</u>. Pity the tribe that doesn't
have, and cherish, at least one flamboyant eccentric. Pity too the one that sup-
poses it can avoid for long the woes to which all flesh is heir. Lunacy, bank-
ruptcy, suicide and other unthinkable fates sooner or later afflict the noblest of
clans with an undertow of gloom. Family life is a set of givens, someone once
told me, and it takes courage to see certain givens as blessings rather than as
curses. Contradictions and inconsistencies are givens, too. So is the war against
what the Oregon patriarch Kenneth Babbs calls malarkey. "There's always
malarkey lurking, bubbles in the cesspool, fetid bubbles that pop and smell. But

[margin note: HONESTY ABOUT FAMILY DIFFICULTIES]

[3]Martin Buber (1878–1965) religious philosopher, influenced by the Hassidic Jewish tradition,
whose views proclaimed the importance of a close personal relationship between God and
man.

I don't put up with malarkey, between my stepkids and my natural ones or any-where else in the family."

7   (6) Good families prize their rituals. Nothing welds a family more than these. Rituals are vital especially for clans without histories, because they evoke a past, imply a future, and hint at continuity. No line in the Seder service at Passover[4] reassures more than the last: "Next year in Jerusalem!" A clan be-comes more of a clan each time it gathers to observe a fixed ritual (Christmas, birthdays, Thanksgiving, and so on), grieve at a funeral (anyone may come to most funerals; those who do declare their tribalness), and devises a new rite of *Rituals* its own. Equinox breakfasts and all-white dinners can be at least as welding as Memorial Day parades. Several of us in the old *Life* magazine years used to meet for lunch every Pearl Harbor Day, preferably to eat some politically neutral fare like smorgasbord, to "forgive" our only ancestrally Japanese colleague Irene Kubota Neves. For that and other reasons we became, and remain, a sort of family.

8   "Rituals," a California friend of mine said, "aren't just externals and holi-days. They are the performances of our lives. They are a kind of shorthand. They can't be decreed. My mother used to try to decree them. She'd make such a goddamn fuss over what we talked about at dinner, aiming at Topics of Com-mon Interest, topics that celebrated our cohesion as a family. These perfor-mances were always hollow, because the phenomenology of the moment got sacrificed for the *idea* of the moment. Real rituals are discovered in retrospect. They emerge around constitutive moments, moments that only happen once, around whose memory meanings cluster. You don't choose those moments. They choose themselves." A lucky clan includes a born mythologizer, like my blood sister, who has the gift of apprehending such a moment when she sees it, and who cannot help but invent new rituals everywhere she goes.

9   (7) Good families are affectionate. This is of course a matter of style. I know clans whose members greet each other with gingerly handshakes or, in what *Affectionate* pass for kisses, with hurried brushes of side jawbones, as if the object were to touch not the lips but the ears. I don't see how such people manage. "The tribe that does not hug," as someone who has been part of many *ad hoc* families re-cently wrote to me, "is no tribe at all. More and more I realize that everybody, regardless of age, needs to be hugged and comforted in a brotherly or sisterly way now and then. Preferably now."

10   (8) Good families have a sense of place, which these days is not achieved *Home-Base* easily. As Susanne Langer wrote in 1957, "Most people have no home that is a *or Family* symbol of their childhood, not even a definite memory of one place to serve that *Seat* purpose . . . all the old symbols are gone." Once I asked a roomful of supper guests who, if anyone, felt any strong pull to any certain spot on the face of the earth. Everyone was silent, except for a visitor from Bavaria. The rest of us

---

[4]Jewish festival that commemorates the Israelites' exodus from Egypt.

seemed to know all too well what Walker Percy means in *The Moviegoer* when he tells of the "genie-soul of the place which every place has or else is not a place [and which] wherever you go, you must meet and master or else be met and mastered." All that meeting and mastering saps plenty of strength. It also underscores our need for tribal bases of the sort which soaring real estate taxes and splintering families have made all but obsolete.

11   So what are we to do, those of us whose habit and pleasure and doom is our tendency, as a Georgia lady put it, to "fly off at every other whipstitch?" Think in terms of movable feasts, for a start. Live here, wherever here may be, as if we were going to belong here for the rest of our lives. Learn to hallow whatever ground we happen to stand on or land on. Like medieval knights who took their *INNA-MARIE* tapestries along on Crusades, like modern Afghanis with their yurts, we must pack such totems and icons as we can to make short-term quarters feel like home. Pillows, small rugs, watercolors can dispel much of the chilling anonymity of a sublet apartment or motel room. When we can, we should live in rooms with stoves or fireplaces or anyway candlelight. The ancient saying still is true: Extinguished hearth, extinguished family. Round tables help, too, and as a friend of mine once put it, so do "too many comfortable chairs, with surfaces to put feet on, arranged so as to encourage a maximum of eye contact." Such rooms inspire good talk, of which good clans can never have enough.

12   (9) Good families, not just the blood kind, find some way to connect with posterity. "To forge a link in the humble chain of being, encircling heirs to ancestors," as Michael Novak has written, "is to walk within a circle of magic as primitive as humans knew in caves." He is talking of course about babies, feeling them *PASSING DOWN TO A YOUNGER GENERATION* leap in wombs, giving them suck. Parenthood, however, is a state which some miss by chance and others by design, and a vocation to which not all are called. Some of us, like the novelist Richard P. Brickner, "look on as others name their children who in turn name their own lives, devising their own flags from their parents' cloth." What are we who lack children to do? Build houses? Plant trees? Write books or symphonies or laws? Perhaps, but even if we do these things, there still should be children on the sidelines, if not at the center, of our lives. It is a sadly impoverished tribe that does not allow access to, and make much of, some children. Not too much, of course: it has truly been said that never in history have so many educated people devoted so much attention to so few children. Attention, in excess, can turn to fawning, which isn't much better than neglect. Still, if we don't regularly see and talk to and laugh with people who can expect to outlive us by twenty years or so, we had better get busy and find some.

13   (10) Good families also honor their elders. The wider the age range, the *HONOR THEIR ELDERS SAME (SEE RELATION) OF CONTINUITY)* stronger the tribe. Jean-Paul Sartre[5] and Margaret Mead,[6] to name two spectacularly confident former children, have both remarked on the central importance

[5](1905–80) French existential philosopher and author.
[6](1901–78) Popular American anthropologist known for her work in comparing habits and beliefs of varied cultures.

of grandparents in their own early lives. Grandparents now are in much more abundant supply than they were a generation or two ago when old age was more rare. If actual grandparents are not at hand, no family should have too hard a time finding substitute ones to whom to give unfeigned homage. The Soviet Union's enchantment with day care centers, I have heard, stems at least in part from the state's eagerness to keep children away from their presumably subversive grandparents. Let that be a lesson to clans based on interest as well as to those based on genes.

EXERCISES

Some of the Issues

1. In paragraph 1, and elsewhere in her book *Families,* Howard suggests that people should build their own families, "devising new ones" with friends, supplementing (or replacing) natural families. What do you think of her idea?

2. In offering her 10 "earmarks . . . common to both kinds of families" does she distinguish at any time between "natural" and "new" families? If so, in what way?

3. Look at each of the 10 points, and consider if each one is convincing. If you agree with Howard, try to add evidence from your own experience. If you disagree, try to develop counterarguments. Are there any points you would add? Why?

*4. Read Alfred Kazin's "The Kitchen." Which of the 10 points fit that family and why?

5. Howard's definitions are implicitly based on mainstream American culture. On the basis of your experience or reading, would you say that her definitions hold for families in other cultures?

The Way We Are Told

6. Each of the 10 points begins in exactly the same way. What is the effect of this repetition?

7. Describe how each of the points is constructed. How is the content arranged? How consistent is the arrangement?

8. Howard frequently uses a specific example to talk about a general idea, for example the last two sentences of point 3; or, in point 4, "you can ask me to supervise your children for the fortnight you will be in the hospital." Find other examples. What is their effect?

Some Subjects for Writing

9. Select a topic similar to Howard's, for example, "The good citizen," or "An educated person," or "An effective teacher." Then treat it as Howard

might, developing the points one by one that together constitute a definition of the subject.

10. Some writers and sociologists have compared gangs to families. In your opinion, are gangs families? Argue for or against that proposition.

11. Howard's definition of families includes families of friends, as well as the family that she was born into. She also talks about the virtues of choosing "new families whose benefits would surpass or at least equal those of one's birth family." What role do close friendships play in life? Is that role similar to or different from roles played by one's blood relationships? You may want to consider whether or not friendships play the same role in the lives of men and women.

Where Are the Good Old Days?

Stephanie Coontz

Born in 1944, Stephanie Coontz is a writer and college professor whose work often addresses the myths and realities of the American family. In this essay, she investigates how families were structured at various points in history, and concludes that our nostalgia for the "good old days" of family life (as embodied in the 1950s ideal of two parents, married to each other, supporting their children comfortably on one income) is nostalgia based on an imagined reality, not an actual one. Coontz points out that the 1950s were perhaps the most atypical decade in terms of family structure, and that throughout American history, families have existed in an infinite variety of configurations. If we look at the big picture of the American family, we find an enormous variety of experiences, and to presume the prevalence of one kind of "ideal" family is to long for "good old days" that indeed never were.

Coontz is the author of several books, including The Way We Never Were: American Families and the Nostalgia Trap *(1992) and* The Way We Really Are: Coming to Terms with America's Changing Families *(1997), both of which address in greater detail some of the ideas in this essay.*

1   The American family is under siege. To listen to the rhetoric of recent months, we have all fallen down on the job. We're selfish; too preoccupied with our own gratification to raise our children properly. We are ungrateful; we want a handout, not a hand.

2   If only we'd buckle down, stay on the straight and narrow, keep our feet on the ground, our shoulder to the wheel, our eye on the ball, our nose to the grindstone. Then everything would be all right, just as it was in the family-friendly '50s, when we could settle down in front of the television after an honest day's work and see our lives reflected in shows like Ozzie and Harriet and Father Knows Best.[1]

3   But American families have been under siege more often than not during the past 300 years. Moreover, they have always been diverse, both in structure and ethnicity. No family type has been able to protect its members from the

---

[1] 1950s television shows that epitomized the ideal, middle-class American family.

roller-coaster rides of economic setbacks or social change. Changes that improved the lives and fortunes of one family type or individual often resulted in losses for another.

4   A man employed in the auto industry, for example, would have been better off financially in the 1950s than now, but his retired parents would be better off today. If he had a strong taste for power, he might prefer Colonial times, when a man was the undisputed monarch of the household and any disobedience by wife, child, or servant was punishable by whipping. But woe betide that man if he wasn't born to property. In those days, men without estates could be told what to wear, where to live, and whom to associate with.

5   His wife, on the other hand, might have been happier in the 1850s, when she might have afforded two or three servants. We can be pretty sure, though, that the black or Irish servants of that day would not have found the times so agreeable. And today's children, even those scarred by divorce, might well want to stay put rather than live in the late 19th century, when nearly half of them died before they reached their late teens.

A HISTORY OF TRADEOFFS

6   These kinds of tradeoffs have characterized American family life from the beginning. Several distinctly different types of families already coexisted in Colonial times: On the East Coast, the Iroquois lived in longhouses with large extended families. Small families were more common among the nomadic Indian groups, where marital separation, though frequent, caused no social stigma or loss of access to group resources. African-American slaves, whose nuclear families had been torn apart, built extended family networks through ritual co-parenting, the adoption of orphans, and complex naming patterns designed to preserve links among families across space and time.

7   White Colonial families were also diverse: High death rates meant that a majority spent some time in a stepfamily. Even in intact families, membership ebbed and flowed; many children left their parents' home well before puberty to work as servants or apprentices to other households. Colonial family values didn't sentimentalize childhood. Mothers were far less involved in caring for their children than modern working women, typically delegating the task to servants or older siblings. Children living away from home usually wrote to their fathers, sometimes adding a postscript asking him to "give my regards to my mother, your wife."

A REVOLUTION OF SORTS

8   Patriarchal authority started to collapse at the beginning of the Revolutionary War: The rate of premarital conception soared and children began to marry out of birth order. Small family farms and shops flourished and, as in Colonial days,

a wife's work was valued as highly as her husband's. The revolutionary ferment also produced the first stirrings of feminism and civil rights. A popular 1773 Massachusetts almanac declared: "Then equal Laws let custom find, and neither Sex oppress: More Freedom give to Womankind or to Mankind give less." New Jersey women had the right to vote after the Revolution. In several states slaves won their freedom when they sued, citing the Declaration of Independence.

9   But commercial progress undermined these movements. The spread of international trade networks and the invention of the cotton gin in 1793 increased slavery's profits. Ironically, when revolutionary commitment to basic human equality went head-to-head with economic dependence on slavery, the result was an increase in racism: Apologists now justified slavery on the grounds that blacks were less than human. This attitude spilled over to free blacks, who gradually lost both their foothold in the artisan trades and the legal rights they'd enjoyed in early Colonial times. The subsequent deterioration in their status worked to the advantage of Irish immigrants, previously considered nonwhite and an immoral underclass.

10   Feminist ideals also faded as industrialization and wage labor took work away from the small family farms and businesses, excluding middle-class wives from their former economic partnerships. For the first time, men became known as breadwinners. By the post-Civil War era of 1870 through 1890, the participation of married women in the labor force was at an all-time low; social commentators labeled those wives who took part in political or economic life sexual degenerates or "semi-hermaphrodites."

WOMEN LOSE; CHILDREN LOSE MORE

11   As women left the workforce children entered it by the thousands, often laboring in abysmal conditions up to ten hours a day. In the North, they worked in factories or tenement workshops. As late as 1900, 120,000 children worked in Pennsylvania's mines and factories. In the South, states passed "apprentice" laws binding black children out as unpaid laborers , often under the pretext that their parents neglected them. Plantation owners (whose wives and daughters encased themselves in corsets and grew their fingernails long) accused their former female slaves of "loaferism" when they resisted field labor in order to stay closer to home with their children.

12   So for every 19th-century middle-class family that was able to nurture its women and children comfortably inside the family circle, there was an Irish or German girl scrubbing floors, a Welsh boy mining coal, a black girl doing laundry, a black mother and child picking cotton, and a Jewish or Italian daughter making dresses, cigars, or artificial flowers in a sweatshop.

13   Meanwhile, self-styled "child-saver" charity workers, whose definition of an unfit parent had more to do with religion, ethnicity, or poverty than behavior, removed other children from their families. They sent these "orphans" to live with Western farmers who needed extra hands—or merely dumped them

in a farm town with a dollar and an earnest lecture about escaping the evils of city life.

THE OUTER FAMILY CIRCLE

14   Even in the comfortable middle-class households of the late 19th century, norms and values were far different from those we ascribe to "traditional" families. Many households took in boarders, lodgers, or unmarried relatives. The nuclear family wasn't the primary focus of emotional life. The Victorian insistence on separate spheres for men and women made male-female relations extremely stilted, so women commonly turned to other women for their most intimate relationships. A woman's diary would rhapsodize for pages about a female friend, explaining how they carved their initials on a tree, and then remark, "Accepted the marriage proposal of Mr. R. last night" without further comment. Romantic friendships were also common among young middle-class men, who often recorded that they missed sleeping with a college roommate and laying an arm across his bosom. No one considered such relationships a sign of homosexuality; indeed, the term wasn't even invented until the late 19th century.

15   Not that 19th-century Americans were asexual: By midcentury New York City had one prostitute for every 64 men; the mayor of Savannah estimated his city had one for every 39. Perhaps prostitution's spread was inevitable at a time when the middle class referred to the "white meat" and "dark meat" of chicken to spare ladies the embarrassment of hearing the terms "breast" or "thigh."

THE ADVENT OF THE COUPLE

16   The early 20th century brought more changes. Now the emotional focus shifted to the husband and wife. World War I combined with a resurgence of feminism to hasten the collapse of Victorian values, but we can't underestimate the role the emergence of a mass consumer market played: Advertisers quickly found that romance and sexual titillation worked wonders for the bottom line.

17   Marriage experts and the clergy, concerned that longer lifespans would put a strain on marriages, denounced same-sex friendships as competitors to love; people were expected to direct all their emotional, altruistic and sensual impulses into marriage. While this brought new intimacy and sexual satisfaction to married life, it also introduced two trends that disturbed observers. One was an increased dissatisfaction with what used to be considered adequate relationships. Great expectations, social historian Elaine Tyler May points out in her book of the same name, could generate great disappointments. It's no surprise that the U. S. has had both the highest consumption of romance novels and the highest divorce rates in the world since the early part of the 20th century.

18   The second consequence of this new cult of married bliss was the emergence of an independent and increasingly sexualized youth culture. In the late 19th century, middle-class courtship revolved around the institution of "call-

ing." A boy was invited to call by the girl or her parents. It was as inappropriate then for a boy to hint he'd like to be asked over as it was in the 1950s for a girl to hint she'd like to be asked out. By the mid-1920s, calling had been almost totally replaced by dating, which took young people away from parental control but made a girl far more dependent on the boy's initiative. Parents especially worried about the moral dangers the automobile posed—and with reason: A middle-class boy was increasingly likely to have his first sexual encounter with a girlfriend rather than a prostitute.

19   The early part of the century brought a different set of changes to America's working class. In the 1920s, for the first time, a majority of children were born to male-breadwinner, female-homemaker families. Child labor laws and the spread of mass education allowed more parents to keep their children out of the workforce. Numerous immigrant families, however, continued to pull their offspring out of school so they could help support the family, often arousing intense generational conflicts. African-American families kept their children in school longer than other families in those groups, but their wives were much more likely to work outside the home.

THERE GOES THE FAMILY

20   In all sectors of society, these changes created a sense of foreboding. Is Marriage on the Skids? asked one magazine article of the times; What Is the Family Still Good For? fretted another. Popular commentators harkened back to the "good old days," bemoaning the sexual revolution, the fragility of nuclear-family ties, the cult of youthful romance, and the threat of the "emancipated woman."

21   The stock market crash, the Great Depression, and the advent of World War II moved such fears to the back burner. During the '30s and '40s, family trends fluctuated from one extreme to another. Depression hardship—contrary to its television portrayal on The Waltons—usually failed to make family and community life stronger. Divorce rates fell, but desertion and domestic violence rose sharply; economic stress often translated into punitive parenting that left children with emotional scars still apparent to social researchers decades later. Murder rates in the '30s were as high as in the 1980s; rates of marriages and births plummeted.

22   WWII started a marriage boom, but by 1946 the number of divorces was double that in 1941. This time the social commentators blamed working women, interfering in-laws and, above all, inadequate mothers. In 1946, psychiatrist Edward Strecker published *Their Mothers' Sons: The Psychiatrist Examines an American Problem*, which argued that women who were old-fashioned "moms" instead of modern "mothers" were emasculating American boys.

23   Moms, he said disapprovingly, were immature and unstable and sought emotional recompense for the disappointments of their own lives. They took care of aging parents and tried to exert too much control over their children. Mothers, on the other hand, put their parents in nursing homes and derived all their satisfaction from the nuclear family while cheerfully urging independence

on their children. Without motherhood, said the experts, a woman's life meant nothing. Too much mothering, though, would destroy her own marriage and her son's life. These new values put women in an emotional doublebind, and it's hardly surprising that tranquilizers, which came on the scene in the '50s, were marketed and prescribed almost exclusively to housewives.

THE '50s: PARADISE LOST?

24   Such were the economic and cultural ups and downs that created the 1950s. If that single decade had actually represented the "tradition" it would be reasonable to argue that the family has indeed collapsed. By the mid 1950s, the age of marriage and parenthood had dropped dramatically, divorce rates bottomed out and the birthrate, one sociologist has recently noted, "approached that of India." The proportion of children in Ozzie-and-Harriet type families reached an all-time high of 60 percent.

25   Today, in contrast, a majority of mothers, including those with preschool children, work outside the home. Fifty percent of children live with both biological parents, almost one quarter live with single parents and more than 21 percent are in stepfamilies. Three quarters of today's 18–24-year-olds have never been married, while almost 50 percent of all first marriages—and 60 percent of remarriages—will end in divorce. Married couples wait longer to bear children and have fewer of them. For the first time there are more married couples without children than with them. Less than one quarter of contemporary marriages are supported by one wage earner.

26   Taking the 1950s as the traditional norm, however, overstates both the novelty of modern family life and the continuity of tradition. The 1950s was the most atypical decade in the entire history of American marriage and family life. In some ways, today's families are closer to older patterns than were '50s families. The median age at first marriage today is about the same as it was at the beginning of the century, while the proportion of never-married people is actually lower. The number of women who are coproviders and the proportion of children living in stepfamilies are both closer to that of Colonial days than the 1950s. Even the ethnic diversity among modern families is closer to the patterns of the early part of this century than to the demographics of the 1950s. And the time a modern working mother devotes to childcare is higher than in Colonial or Revolutionary days.

27   The 1950s family, in other words, was not at all traditional; nor was it always idyllic. Though many people found satisfactions in family life during that period, we now know the experiences of many groups and individuals were denied. Problems such as alcoholism, battering, and incest were swept under the rug. So was discrimination against ethnic groups, political dissidents, women, elders, gays, lesbians, religious minorities and the handicapped. Rates of divorce and unwed motherhood were low, but that did not prevent 30 percent of American children from living in poverty, a higher figure than at present.

IT'S ALL RELATIVE

28 Why then, do many people remember the 1950s as so much easier than today? One reason is that after the hardships of the Depression and WWII, things were improving on many fronts. Though poverty rates were higher than today, they were falling. Economic inequality was also decreasing. The teenage birthrate was almost twice as high in 1957 as today, but most young men could afford to marry. Violence against African-Americans was appallingly widespread, yet many blacks got jobs in the expanding manufacturing industries and for the first time found an alternative to Southern agriculture's peonage.

29 What we forget when politicians tell us we should revive the 1950s family is that the social stability of that period was due less to its distinctive family forms than to its unique socioeconomic and political climate. High rates of unionization, heavy corporate investment in manufacturing, and generous government assistance in the form of public-works projects, veterans' benefits, student loans and housing subsidies gave young families a tremendous jump start, created predictable paths out of poverty, and led to unprecedented increases in real wages. By the time the "traditional male breadwinner" reached age 30, in both the 1950s and '60s, he could pay the principal and interest on a median-priced home on only 15–18 percent of his income. Social Security promised a much-needed safety net for the elderly, formerly the poorest segment of the population. These economic carrots combined with the sticks of McCarthyism and segregation to keep social dissent on the back burner.

THE NEW TRENDS

30 Because the '60s were a time of social protest, many people forget that families still made economic gains throughout the decade. Older workers and home-owners continued to build security for their retirement years. The postwar boom and government subsidies cut child poverty in half from 1949 to 1959. It was halved again, to its lowest levels ever, from 1959 to 1969. The high point of health and nutrition for poor children came in 1970, a period that coincided with the peak years of the Great Society, not the high point of the '50s family.

31 Since 1973, however, a new phase has emerged. Some things have continued to improve: High school graduation rates are at an all-time high; minority test scores rose steadily from 1970 to 1990; poverty rates among the elderly have continued to fall while life expectancy has risen.

32 Other trends show mixed results: The easy availability of divorce has freed individuals from oppressive or even abusive marriages, but many divorces have caused emotional and economic suffering for both children and adults. Women have found new satisfaction at work, and there's considerable evidence that children can benefit from having a working mother, but the failure of businesses— and some husbands—to adjust to working mothers' needs has caused much family stress and discord.

33   In still other areas, the news is quite bleak. Children have now replaced seniors as the poorest segment of the population; the depth and concentration of child poverty has increased over the past 20 years so it's now at 1965 levels. Many of the gains ethnic groups made in the 1960s and '70s have been eroded.

34   History suggests that most of these setbacks originate in social and economic forces rather than in the collapse of some largely mythical traditional family. Perhaps the most powerful of these sources is the breakdown of America's implicit postwar wage bargain with the working class, where corporations ensured labor stability by increasing employment, rewarding increased productivity with higher wages, and investing in jobs and community infrastructure. At the same time, the federal government subsidized home ownership and higher education.

35   Since 1973, however, real wages have fallen for most families. It increasingly requires the work of two earners to achieve the modest upward mobility one could provide in the 1950s and '60s. Unemployment rates have risen steadily as corporations have abandoned the communities that grew up around them, seeking cheap labor overseas or in nonunionized sectors of the South. Involuntary part-time work has soared. As *Time* magazine noted in 1993, the predictable job ladders of the '50s and '60s have been sawed off: "Companies are portable, workers are throwaway." A different article in the same issue found, "Long-term commitments . . . are anathema to the modern corporation."

36   During the 1980s the gap between the rich and middle-class widened in 46 states, and each year since 1986 has set a new postwar record for the gap between rich and poor. In 1980 a CEO earned 30 to 40 times as much as the average worker, by 1994 he earned 187 times as much. Meanwhile, the real wages of a young male high school graduate are lower today than those earned by his 1963 counterpart.

37   These economic changes are not driven by the rise in divorce and unwed motherhood. Decaying wage and job structures—not changing family structures—have caused the overwhelming bulk of income redistribution. And contrary to what has been called a new bipartisan consensus, marriage is not the solution to poverty. According to sociologist Donald J. Hernandez, Ph.D., formerly with the U. S. Census Bureau, even if every child in America were reunited with both biological parents, two thirds of those who are poor today would still be poor.

OUR UNCERTAIN FUTURE

38   History's lessons are both positive and negative. We can take comfort from the fact that American families have always been in flux and that a wide variety of family forms and values have worked well for different groups at different times. There's no reason to assume that recent changes are entirely destructive. Families have always been vulnerable to rapid economic change and have always needed economic and emotional support from beyond their own small bound-

aries. Our challenge is to grapple with the sweeping transformations we're currently undergoing. History demonstrates it's not as simple as returning to one or another family form from the past. Though there are many precedents for successfully reorganizing family life, there are no clear answers to the issues facing us as we enter the 21st century.

EXERCISES

Some of the Issues

1. Does Coontz believe most of what she writes in the first two paragraphs? If not, who does she assume does believe it?
2. What does Coontz mean by the word "rhetoric" in the first paragraph? Where does the issue of rhetoric come up again in other parts of the essay?
3. According to Coontz, what decade do people think of when they think of the ideal family? Do you think this is still true for your generation?
4. What does Coontz mean by the statement, "No family type has been able to protect its members from the roller-coaster rides of economic setbacks and social change" (paragraph 3)? What does the statement indicate about what Coontz believes to be the relationship between social forces and the more intimate lives of families?
5. According to Coontz, what impact did the American Revolution have on the American family? How and why did the ideals of the revolution fade?
6. When and why did men become known as breadwinners (paragraph 10)?
7. What group replaced women in the workforce in the late 1800s? What kinds of work did they do?
8. How does Coontz characterize the Victorian family and intimate relationships during Victorian times (paragraph 14)? When did Victorian values start to change and why?
9. What effect did the consumer market have on marriage and romantic relationships in the twentieth century?
*10. How were mothers characterized in the 1940s? How does this compare to the characterizations of motherhood discussed in Susan Douglas's and Meredith Michaels's "The Mommy Wars"?
11. Why is it ironic that the family of the 1950s is considered to be the norm?
12. What does Coontz feel is our challenge today? How does this challenge relate to her thesis?
13. How would you characterize the "ideal" family if such a thing exists? Did the Coontz essay in any way change your perception of the family? If so, how?
14. What similarities do you see between today's family and Coontz's descriptions of the family in earlier periods? Give specific examples to back up your answer.

15. Find articles, photos, and advertisements that describe or show families and bring your examples to class. In groups of three or four, compare your examples and consider the messages they convey and underlying assumptions they make about the contemporary family.

16. In several parts of this essay, Coontz points to the fact that depictions of the "ideal" of the American family leave out large segments of the actual population. Who is left out at various times? Are there groups that seem to be always left out?

The Way We Are Told

17. How does Coontz set up her thesis statement? What is she arguing against?

18. Coontz deliberately employs several clichés in paragraph 2. What purpose does this device serve?

19. Coontz often uses two techniques, compare and contrast and cause and effect, to back up her thesis. Find examples of both.

20. Consider the title of the essay. Why do you think Coontz chose this as a title?

Some Subjects for Writing

21. Interview friends and relatives, including at least one person from a generation other than your own, about the specifics of family life during their childhood. Does their experience—and your own—correspond with Coontz's depiction of family life? Using specific examples, write an essay in which you present and analyze your findings.

*22. Read Susan Douglas's and Meredith Michaels's "The Mommy Wars" in which the authors analyze the differences between media images of celebrity moms and those of welfare mothers. Note how Douglas and Michaels draw their examples from different kinds of publications and consider how they compare and contrast the profiles of people from different social and economic classes. Using their methodology as a model, find three or four profiles of American families from various backgrounds in magazines and newspapers. Keeping in mind whom the profiles are about and where they appear, write a paper in which you analyze the messages that these profiles convey.

23. Coontz's analysis of the history of the American family covers a large amount of ground in a relatively short essay, providing only what she sees as the relevant facts about specific eras in order to back up her points. With the help of your instructor, write a research paper that explores the family during one era in more depth. Develop your thesis based on what you determine to be the key factors that influenced the family at that time.

Choosing a Mate

Ruth Breen

Born in Israel, Ruth Breen was a student at Brooklyn College in New York when she wrote this essay. She came to the United States with her family as a teenager and was married shortly thereafter. At the time she wrote this essay, she had five children.

Breen, a Hassidic Jew, tells the story of her marriage—arranged by her family when she was seventeen. Although, as Breen says, Americans typically think of arranged marriages as a thing of the past, they are still quite common in Orthodox Jewish communities.

Breen argues in this essay that, though the view of marriage in her community seems at odds with the "modern world's" notion of marriage founded on romantic love, in reality her marriage and the ones she knows in her community are not so different from "love" marriages.

1   *Choice* is not one of the terms I would use to describe my marriage. This is not to say that I was forced into marrying my husband. It is just that I associate the word *choice* with some sort of selection. To choose is to select from among many, or at least, between two. It is pick out one's favorite: one's favorite pickle from the pickles in the jar, one's favorite dress, one's favorite man. But my husband was not picked out. I knew no other; I experienced no one else.

2   When people discuss arranged marriages, they usually refer to them as part of history, gone with the crinolines and hand-kissing. I don't usually volunteer the fact that my marriage was officially arranged—in New York, in the eighties. I keep silent because trying to explain my community's marriage rituals to those who are accustomed to modern notions of love is useless. The cultural gap is so great that I usually find no common ground to stand on. When it comes to love and marriage, Hassidic ideologies and values seem to be the very opposite of the modern world's view.

3   I was two weeks past my seventeenth birthday when I was engaged to be married. Before I met my husband, I had never spoken to "boys." My own brother was only four years old, and my male cousins were even younger. I went to an all-girls school. We discussed boys all the time, of course, but boys were truly as abstract and alien as Martians. Most of our information came from the "Romance" section in the public library.

4   One evening, while I was doing my homework, my father came into the room. He told me that a matchmaker had called and offered a *shiduch* (an arranged date). "Do you want to get married, Ruthie?" he asked.

5   Of course I wanted to get married. I also wanted to fly to the moon and to be in a Hollywood motion picture. I was seventeen. I wanted adventure; I wanted fun. A boy would definitely be an adventure.

6   And there would be whipped cream too: presents, a white gown, I, the center of attraction, blossoming with youth, astonishing with beauty. I definitely wanted to get married. I would have no more curfew. I would buy cases and cases of orange soda. I would watch T.V. anytime, any channel that I wanted. I would eat chocolates on the living room couch. I would be independent.

7   The "boy," whose name I couldn't remember, or was yet to know, was studying in Israel. He would have to come to New York to meet me. But meeting me would be a final step. Before that, for three weeks, my parents were busy investigating his background, his grades in school, his habits, his friends, his family's history, his health—I even knew the names of his teachers in elementary school—but I still had not seen him. There was an "executive conference" between both sets of parents to discuss who would pay for what, and who would support us, and for how long. Then there was an "exam" that I had to pass—meeting his parents. Finally, the future bridegroom arrived.

8   When I saw my husband, Michael, for the first time, I thought, "So this is the face I will see for the rest of my life; this is the father of my children." But we still did not speak. Then we were left alone in the room. When we spoke, it was no different than what one would expect. I told him a few jokes, he smiled. We had some cake. I could have said that I didn't like him, but how could I know? He was a stranger. I could have said that I needed more time, but my mother was already cutting up cake for the party. I was not forced, but my grandparents were already on the plane, coming to congratulate us.

9   I met my husband, Michael, on Saturday evening. Sunday, at noon, we were engaged to be married. I received a diamond ring. We smiled a lot at each other. I was in seventh heaven, but I didn't know him at all.

10   My story is not unique. Tens of thousands of boys and girls in Hassidic communities are married that way. Did I expect love and passion? I don't remember. Did I doubt that he was the "the one"? Maybe, for an hour. Am I happy? Yes, we are both happy. We fell in love exactly five weeks after we were married. We went through the same initial euphorias, the same first fight, the same delicious reconciliation—but we were already married. We grew together. We practiced everything on each other. Eleven years have passed, and I am the only woman Michael has ever touched. I was always the only one.

11   My parents chose for me. I will probably choose for my children. Of the 32 girls in my class at school, all married by arrangement. Two are divorced. The rest, still married, would probably fit any standard statistics of happy or miserable marriages.

12   Intellectually, arranged marriages may seem a prescription for failure. Emotionally, arranged marriages may seem unfair, anti-love and anti-romance. In spite of all, our couples find enough happiness to stick together. They learn to love and desire, to bond and connect. They have candlelight dinners and secret

silly jokes. They give cards to each other and buy flowers for Sabbath. They go on romantic vacations. They love, they lust, they fight, they leave. Their marriages are as strong and as weak as "love" marriages are. Love comes in different ways, yet people love the same all over the world, and against all odds.

EXERCISES

Some of the Issues

1. How does Breen define "choice" in the introductory paragraph? Why is it important that she define this word? How does her definition differ from others we might use?
2. In paragraph 2, why does the author not usually volunteer the fact that her marriage was officially arranged?
3. Looking at paragraphs 5 and 6, what does the author imagine marriage to be? Do you think her images of married life are different from or similar to those of most seventeen-year-olds?
4. What was your reaction to the authors' description of the marriage and courting process described in paragraphs 7 through 9?
5. Were you surprised to read that the author anticipates arranging marriages for her own children? Why or why not?
6. What claims does Breen make about the success of arranged marriages? Were her claims convincing to you?

The Way We Are Told

7. The thesis of this essay is implied rather than stated directly. If you were to develop a one-sentence thesis, what might it be?
8. Why does the author put the word *boys* in quotation marks (paragraph 3)? How do the quotes indicate her feelings?
9. Looking at paragraphs 4 though 7, how does the author build up anticipation about the marriage?
10. Analyze the tone of the writing. How does the author control the tone to indicate how she felt before, during, and after the marriage?
11. Consider possible audiences for this essay. What kinds of attitudes was the author anticipating on the part of her audience?

Some Subjects for Writing

12. What was your initial reaction to the essay? Taking into consideration both the author's and your own view of marriage, analyze both the benefits and drawbacks of arranged marriages.
13. What, in your opinion, is most important in a successful marriage: love, physical attraction, commitment, communication? Is marriage something one has to "work on"?

The Kitchen

Alfred Kazin

Alfred Kazin (1915–98) was born in Brooklyn, New York to eastern European parents. He was a scholar, critic, and cultural historian who taught at several universities, last at the City University of New York. He held several distinguished fellowships and was a member of the American Academy of Arts and Sciences. His books include On Native Grounds *(1942),* The Inmost Leaf *(1955),* Starting Out in the Thirties *(1965),* New York Jew *(1978), and* An American Procession *(1984). Selections from Kazin's journals were published as* A Lifetime Burning in Every Moment: From the Journals of Alfred Kazin *(1996).*

In this selection from A Walker in the City *(1957), Kazin describes the setting in which he grew up. It was not unusual for its time and place: a tenement district in a large American city, peopled with immigrants from eastern Europe, working hard, struggling for a life for themselves and, more importantly, for their children.*

The large-scale immigration that brought as many as one million new inhabitants annually from Europe to America lasted from the 1880s to the First World War. The majority of the immigrants in those years came from eastern, southern, and central Europe. They included large numbers of Jewish families like Kazin's, escaping not only the stifling poverty of their regions but also the outright persecution to which they were subjected in Czarist Russia.

1   In Brownsville tenements the kitchen is always the largest room and the center of the household. As a child I felt we lived in a kitchen to which four other rooms were annexed. My mother, a "home" dressmaker, had her workshop in the kitchen. She told me once that she had begun dressmaking in Poland at thirteen; as far back as I can remember, she was always making dresses for the local women. She had an innate sense of design, a quick eye for all the subtleties in the latest fashions, even when she despised them, and great boldness. For three or four dollars she would study the fashion magazines with a customer, go with the customer to the remnants store on Belmont Avenue to pick out the material, argue the owner down—all remnants stores, for some reason, were supposed to be shady, as if the owners dealt in stolen goods—and then for days would patiently fit and baste and sew and fit again. Our apartment was always full of women in their housedresses sitting around the kitchen table waiting for a fitting. My little bedroom next to the kitchen was the fitting room. The sewing machine, an old nut-brown Singer with golden scrolls painted along the black arm and engraved along the two tiers of little drawers massed with needles and

thread on each side of the treadle, stood next to the window and the great coal-black stove which up to my last year in college was our main source of heat. By December the two outer bedrooms were closed off, and used to chill bottles of milk and cream, cold borscht and jellied calves' feet.

2 The kitchen held our lives together. My mother worked in it all day long, we ate in it almost all meals except the Passover *seder*,[1] I did my homework and first writing at the kitchen table, and in winter I often had a bed made up for me on three kitchen chairs near the stove. On the wall just over the table hung a long horizontal mirror that sloped to a ship's prow at each end and was lined in cherry wood. It took up the whole wall, and drew every object in the kitchen to itself. The walls were a fiercely stippled whitewash, so often rewhitened by my father in slack seasons that the paint looked as if it had been squeezed and cracked into the walls. A large electric bulb hung down the center of the kitchen at the end of a chain that had been hooked into the ceiling; the old gas ring and key still jutted out of the wall like antlers. In the corner next to the toilet was the sink at which we washed, and the square tub in which my mother did our clothes. Above it, tacked to the shelf on which were pleasantly ranged square, blue bordered white sugar and spice jars, hung calendars from the Public National Bank on Pitkin Avenue and the Minsker Progressive Branch of the Workman's Circle; receipts for the payment of insurance premiums, and household bills on a spindle; two little boxes engraved with Hebrew letters. One of these was for the poor, the other to buy back the Land of Israel. Each spring a bearded little man would suddenly appear in our kitchen, salute us with a hurried Hebrew blessing, empty the boxes (sometimes with a sidelong look of disdain if they were not full), hurriedly bless us again for remembering our less fortunate Jewish brothers and sisters, and so take his departure until the next spring, after vainly trying to persuade my mother to take still another box. We did occasionally remember to drop coins in the boxes, but this was usually only on the dreaded morning of "mid-terms" and final examinations, because my mother thought it would bring me luck. She was extremely superstitious, but embarrassed about it, and always laughed at herself whenever, on the morning of an examination, she counseled me to leave the house on my right foot. "I know it's silly," her smile seemed to say, "but what harm can it do? It may calm God down."

3 The kitchen gave a special character to our lives; my mother's character. All my memories of that kitchen are dominated by the nearness of my mother sitting all day long at her sewing machine, by the clacking of the treadle against the linoleum floor, by the patient twist of her right shoulder as she automatically pushed at the wheel with one hand or lifted the foot to free the needle where it had got stuck in a thick piece of material. The kitchen was her life. Year by year, as I began to take in her fantastic capacity for labor and her anxious zeal, I realized it was ourselves she kept stitched together. I can never remember a time

[1]Jewish festival that commemorates the Israelites' exodus from Egypt.

when she was not working. She worked because the law of her life was work, work and anxiety; she worked because she would have found life meaningless without work. She read almost no English; she could read the Yiddish paper, but never felt she had time to. We were always talking of a time when I would teach her how to read, but somehow there was never time. When I awoke in the morning she was already at her machine, or in the great morning crowd of housewives at the grocery getting fresh rolls for breakfast. When I returned from school she was at her machine, or conferring over *McCall's* with some neighborhood woman who had come in pointing hopefully to an illustration— "Mrs. Kazin! Mrs. Kazin! Make me a dress like it shows here in the picture!" When my father came home from work she had somehow mysteriously inter- rupted herself to make supper for us, and the dishes cleared and washed, was back at her machine. When I went to bed at night, often she was still there, pounding away at the treadle, hunched over the wheel, her hands steering a piece of gauze under the needle with a finesse that always contrasted sharply with her swollen hands and broken nails. Her left hand had been pierced through when as a girl she had worked in the infamous Triangle Shirtwaist Fac- tory on the East Side. A needle had gone straight through the palm, severing a large vein. They had sewn it up for her so clumsily that a tuft of flesh always lay folded over the palm.

4   The kitchen was the great machine that set our lives running; it whirred down a little only on Saturdays and holy days. From my mother's kitchen I gained my first picture of life as a white, overheated, starkly lit workshop redo- lent with Jewish cooking, crowded with women in housedresses, strewn with fashion magazines, patterns, dress material, spools of thread—and at whose cen- ter, so lashed to her machine that bolts of energy seemed to dance out of her hands and feet as she worked, my mother stamped the treadle hard against the floor, hard, hard, and silently, grimly at war, beat out the first rhythm of the world for me.

EXERCISES

Some of the Issues

1. Kazin writes about the kitchen in his childhood home. Is he writing from the point of view of a child or an adult? What indications do you have of one or the other?

2. In speaking of his mother, Kazin says, "The law of her life was work, work and anxiety." In an age in which many people's goal is self-fulfillment, this does not seem to be a happy life. Can you find any evidence as to whether Mrs. Kazin was happy or unhappy? What pleasures did she have?

3. What is the meaning of the first sentence in paragraph 4? Why does Kazin call the kitchen "the great machine"?

The Way We Are Told

4. The same two words are repeated in the first sentence of each paragraph. What purpose does that repetition serve?
5. Compare the first two paragraphs. How do they differ from each other in content and in the way they are written?
6. Kazin talks about the kitchen of his childhood home but does not describe it until the second paragraph. What would be the effect if he had started with that description?
7. Reread the second paragraph. What details does Kazin give? How are they arranged—in which kind of order? Could an artist draw a picture on the basis of Kazin's description? Could an architect draw a plan from it?
8. Kazin describes several items in detail—the sewing machine, aspects of the kitchen itself, and his mother's work. Find some adjectives that stand out because they are unusual or that add precision or feeling to his descriptions.

Some Subjects for Writing

9. Write a paragraph about a place of significance for you, using Kazin's second paragraph as your model. Try to show its significance by the way you describe it.
10. Consider the role of work in the life of Kazin's mother. If you know someone whose life seems completely tied up with some specific activity, describe that person through his or her activity.

My Papa's Waltz

Theodore Roethke

Theodore Roethke (1908–63), a widely published and much honored American poet, received a Pulitzer Prize in 1953 and a Bollingen Prize in 1958, among other awards. Two of his collections of poems, Words for the Wind *(1958) and* The Far Field *(1964), received National Book Awards. His* Collected Poems *appeared in 1966. He taught at several universities, last as Poet in Residence at the University of Washington.*

This brief poem is like a snapshot—a recollection of a moment that sums up the relationship of father and son.

The whiskey on your breath
Could make a small boy dizzy;
But I hung on like death:
Such waltzing was not easy.

5   We romped until the pans
Slid from the kitchen shelf;
My mother's countenance
Could not unfrown itself.

The hand that held my wrist
10   Was battered on one knuckle;
At every step you missed
My right ear scraped a buckle.

You beat time on my head
With a palm caked hard by dirt,
15   Then waltzed me off to bed
Still clinging to your shirt.

EXERCISES

Some of the Issues

1. Read the poem aloud several times. The poem describes a waltz—a turning dance that is usually thought of as sedate and graceful but can be dizzyingly fast. How does the rhythm of the poem suggest the dance?

2. The poem is like a snapshot—a recollection of a moment that sums up the relationship of father and son. What indications are there that the relationship was a close one, despite difficulties?

Some Subjects for Writing

3. Describe an incident from your early childhood that you remember well. In your description, try to make the reader understand how you felt about the event.

IV

DEFINING
OURSELVES

Each of us carries a number of identities. We are identified as sons or daughters, as parents, as students, as members of clubs or teams, professions or unions, religious denominations, or social classes. In some cases our particular identities will not only associate us with specific groups of people, but also type us. In American society, as multiethnic and multiracial as it is, this attribution of identity is particularly complex and often carries with it, rightly or wrongly, certain notions about the members of a group. Often, when we define ourselves, it is in reaction to these notions.

Recently, the issues of multiracial or multiethnic identity has been an important part of American conversation, though it's hardly a new phenomenon. For the first time in the 2000 census, Americans were able to identify themselves as a member of more than one racial or ethnic group. The decision to make this change in the census was a reflection of the fact that increasing numbers of Americans do not identify with only one group.

In "An Ethnic Trump," Gish Jen, a Chinese American, and her husband, of Irish descent, consider whether to send their four-year-old son to Chinese day school. The debate centers around the question of whether some identities are immutable and others are matters of choice. Robin D.G. Kelley begins his essay with the question, "So, what are you?" and concludes that this is not a simple question nor one that he feels he can answer without a more detailed history of his family background. He implies that there are many people whose answer to this question would be equally complex. Roxanne Farmanfarmaian, born of an Iranian father and a Utah Mormon mother, compares the interwoven strands of her identity with the DNA strands of the double helix, and concludes that one can't be separated from the other.

In "A Slow Walk of Trees," Toni Morrison traces her own sense of identity and her view of the world as an African American back to her grandparents, who were slaves. She reinforces the notion that identity cannot exist outside of a historical context. For Nicolette Toussaint, partially deaf since childhood, deafness is a part of her identity. She must decide whether to declare her disability to others to whom it may not be immediately apparent. If she does not, she risks being misunderstood; if she does, she risks being set aside as "other."

Sometimes, other people's perceptions of us are clouded by myths and popular images. In "The Myth of the Latin Woman: I Just Met a Girl Named María," Judith Ortiz Cofer writes about the stereotypical, often demeaning images of Latinas generated by popular culture. A writer and professor raised alternately in Puerto Rico and in the United States, she has always balanced two identities, but to the outside world she is often taken to be the "María" of *West Side Story* or the "Evita" of the musical. Malcolm X describes how as a young boy in 1914 he sought to be more like the white majority by straightening his hair. Later in life he realizes how degrading the process was and decides to take pride in his African-American identity.

If identities can be multiple and can change over time, to what extent can they be chosen? In her article "Goin' Gangsta, Choosin' Cholita," Nell Bernstein examines teenagers in Northern California. Many of them claim an identity they were not born into or emphasize only one of several identities. In much the same way one might try on clothes, these teenagers may be reacting to social change by trying to join the group that they consider to be most powerful in their own world.

In the poem that ends the chapter, Wendy Rose, of Hopi-Miwok ancestry, uses a news story of the sale of her people's bones to a museum as a symbol of the stealing of Native American lands and culture. Though the museum may tout it as a preservation of Native American identity, Rose describes it as a violation motivated by financial gain rather that cultural respect.

An Ethnic Trump

Gish Jen

Born in 1956, Gish Jen grew up Chinese-American in predominantly Jewish suburbs of New York City. She graduated from Harvard College and received her master's degree in creative writing from the University of Iowa Writer's Workshop.

Jen is the author of two novels, Typical American *(1991) and, most recently,* Mona in the Promised Land *(1996)—both of which humorously chronicle the coming of age of young Chinese Americans as they struggle with issues of family and ethnic identity. Her newest work is a collection of short stories entitled* Who's Irish? *(1999).*

In this essay, Jen raises the question of why certain ethnicities "trump" others—why her son, for example, whose heritage is both Irish and Chinese, attends a Chinese culture school and not an Irish one. Jen concludes that one of the reasons might be "the relative distance of certain cultures from mainstream America." Most Irish Americans today are descended from ancestors who came to the United States during the great wave of Irish immigration in the mid-1800s. Though Irish immigrants were seen as outsiders by mainstream American culture at the time, they have since become more accepted and assimilated. Though there have been Chinese immigrants to the United States since the Gold Rush of 1847, most Chinese Americans trace their arrival to this country to much more recent times.

1   That my son, Luke, age 4, goes to Chinese-culture school seems inevitable to most people, even though his father is of Irish descent. For certain ethnicities trump others; Chinese, for example, trumps Irish. This has something to do with the relative distance of certain cultures from mainstream American culture, but it also has to do with race. For as we all know, it is not only certain ethnicities that trump others but certain colors: black trumps white, for example, always and forever; a mulatto is not a kind of white person, but a kind of black person.

2   And so it is, too, that my son is considered a kind of Asian person whose manifest destiny is to embrace Asian things. The Chinese language. Chinese food. Chinese New Year. No one cares whether he speaks Gaelic or wears green on St. Patrick's Day. For though Luke's skin is fair, and his features mixed, people see his straight black hair and "know" who he is.

3   But is this how we should define ourselves, by other people's perceptions? My husband, Dave, and I had originally hoped for Luke to grow up embracing his whole complex ethnic heritage. We had hoped to pass on to him values and habits of mind that had actually survived in both of us.

4   Then one day, Luke combed his black hair and said he was turning it yellow. Another day, a fellow mother reported that her son had invited all blond-
haired children like himself to his birthday party. And yet another day, Luke was
happily scooting around the Cambridge Common playground when a pair of
older boys, apparently brothers, blocked his way. "You're Chinese!" they
shouted, leaning on the hood of Luke's scooter car. "You are! You're Chinese!"
So brazen were these kids, that even when I, an adult, intervened, they continued to shout. Luke answered, "No, I'm not!"—to no avail; it was not clear if the
boys even heard him. Then the boys' mother called to them from some distance
away, outside the fence, and though her voice was no louder than Luke's, they
left obediently.

5   Behind them opened a great, rippling quiet, like the wash of a battleship.

6   Luke and I immediately went over things he could say if anything like that
ever happened again. I told him that he was 100 percent American, even though
I knew from my own childhood in Yonkers that these words would be met only
with derision. It was a sorry chore. Since then I have not asked him about the incident, hoping that he has forgotten about it, and wishing that I could, too. For I
wish I could forget the sight of those kids' fingers on the hood of Luke's little car.
I wish I could forget their loud attack, but also Luke's soft defense: *No, I'm not.*

7   Chinese-culture school. After dozens of phone calls, I was elated to discover
the Greater Boston Chinese Cultural Association nearby in west Newton. The
school takes children at 3, has a wonderful sense of community and is housed in
a center paid for, in part, by great karaoke fund-raising events. (Never mind
what the Japanese meant to the Chinese in the old world. In this world, people
donate at least $200 each for a chance at the mike, and the singing goes on all
night.) There are even vendors who bring home-style Chinese food to sell after
class—stuff you can't get in a restaurant. Dave and I couldn't wait for the second
class, and a chance to buy more *bao* for our freezer.

8   But in the car on the way to the second class, Luke announced that he didn't
want to go to Chinese school anymore. He said that the teacher talked mostly
about ducks and bears and that he wasn't interested in ducks and bears. And I
knew this was true. I knew that Luke was interested only in whales and ships.
And what's more, I knew we wouldn't push him to take swimming lessons if he
didn't want to, or music. Chinese school was a wonderful thing, but there was a
way in which we were accepting it as somehow non-optional. Was that right?
Hadn't we always said that we didn't want our son to see himself as more essentially Chinese than Irish?

9   Yet we didn't want him to deny his Chinese heritage, either. And if there
were going to be incidents on the playground, we wanted him to at least know
what Chinese meant. So when Luke said again that he didn't want to go to Chinese school, I said, "Oh, really?" Later on we could try to teach him to define
himself irrespective of race. For now, though, he was going to Chinese school. I
exchanged glances with Dave. And then together, in a most carefully casual
manner, we squinted at the road and kept going.

EXERCISES

Some of the Issues

1. What does the author mean when she says that certain ethnicities trump others? Do you agree with this statement?
2. What incidents does the author describe in paragraph 4? Why are they significant and how do they relate to each other?
3. In the end, does the author come to see Chinese school as optional for her son?
4. What are both the literal and figurative meanings of the last line?
5. What are some of the issues Jen brings up concerning families with parents of different ethnic, religious, or racial groups? What are your feelings on this issue?

The Way We Are Told

6. What is the tone of the essay? Why might Jen have chosen this tone?
7. How does Jen use humor in paragraphs 7 and 8?
8. Throughout the essay, Jen uses direct quotations to emphasize certain points or ideas. Where does she use them, and are they effective?

Some Subjects for Writing

9. Jen concludes that, at least for now, Chinese school is not an option for Luke in the same way swimming and music lessons are. Were certain schools, events, or programs not optional for you as a child because they were highly significant to your family? Write a narrative in which you describe this experience. From your perspective as an adult, analyze its importance in your life.
10. Consider what it means to be multiracial or multiethnic. Is it important that people choose to identify more strongly with one aspect of their ethnic identity, or is it possible for people to see themselves as comprised of many identities, histories, and backgrounds?

The People in Me

Robin D.G. Kelley

Robin D.G. Kelley spent the earliest years of his life in New York's Harlem and later moved with his family to Seattle before settling in Pasadena, California. He attended college at California State University in Long Beach, where he chose four different majors before settling on history, and still managed to earn his degree in three years. Within four years of graduating college he had earned both a masters and a doctorate in history from UCLA.

Kelley is a social historian whose work focuses on how black people, particularly in America, have defined the notion of liberation and the strategies they've developed to achieve it. He has a keen interest in grass roots movements and on how culture, especially popular culture like hip-hop music and graffiti, expresses people's desire for liberation.

Kelley is currently Professor of History and Africana Studies at New York University, but much of his writing has been published outside of academic circles. He has written for the Nation, Monthly Review, The New York Times Magazine, *and the* Voice Literary Supplement, *among others. He is the author of several books about history and popular culture, most recently* Yo' Mama's DisFunktional! Fighting the Culture Wars in Urban America *(1997). This selection was originally published in* ColorLines, *a magazine about race and culture.*

1   "So, what are you?" I don't know how many times people have asked me that. "Are you Puerto Rican? Dominican? Indian or something? You must be mixed." My stock answer has rarely changed: "My mom is from Jamaica but grew up in New York, and my father was from North Carolina but grew up in Boston. Both black."

2   My family has lived with "the question" for as long as I can remember. We're "exotics," all cursed with "good hair" and strange accents—we don't sound like we from da Souf or the Norwth, and don't have that West Coast-by-way-of-Texas Calabama thang going on. The only one with the real West Indian singsong vibe is my grandmother, who looks even more East Indian than my sisters. Whatever Jamaican patois my mom possessed was pummeled out of her by cruel preteens who never had sensitivity seminars in diversity. The result for us was a nondescript way of talking, walking, and being that made us not black enough, not white enough—just a bunch of not-quite-nappy-headed enigmas.

3   My mother never fit the "black momma" media image. A beautiful, demure, light brown woman, she didn't drink, smoke, curse, or say things like "Lawd Jesus" or "hallelujah," nor did she cook chitlins or gumbo. A vegetarian, she played

the harmonium (a foot-pumped miniature organ), spoke softly with textbook diction, meditated, followed the teachings of Paramahansa Yogananda, and had wild hair like Chaka Khan. She burned incense in our tiny Harlem apartment, sometimes walked the streets barefoot, and, when she could afford it, cooked foods from the East.

4   To this day, my big sister gets misidentified for Pakistani or Bengali or Ethiopian. (Of course, changing her name from Sheral Anne Kelley to Makani Themba has not helped.) Not long ago, an Oakland cab driver, apparently a Sikh who had immigrated from India, treated my sister like dirt until he discovered that she was not a "scoundrel from Sri Lanka," but a common black American. Talk about ironic: How often are black women spared indignities *because* they are African American?

5   "What are you?" dogged my little brother more than any of us. He came out looking just like his father, who was white. In the black communities of Los Angeles and Pasadena, my baby bro' had to fight his way into blackness, usually winning only when he invited his friends to the house. When he got tired of this, he became what people thought he was—a cool white boy. Today he lives in Tokyo, speaks fluent Japanese, and is happily married to a Japanese woman (who is actually Korean passing as Japanese!). He stands as the perfect example of our mulattoness: a black boy trapped in a white body who speaks English with a slight Japanese accent and has a son who will spend his life confronting "the question."

6   Although folk had trouble naming us, we were never blanks or aliens in a "black world." We were and are "polycultural," and I'm talking about all peoples in the Western world. It is not skin, hair, walk, or talk that renders black people so diverse. Rather, it is the fact that most of them are products of different "cultures"—living cultures, not dead ones. These cultures live in and through us every day, with almost no self-consciousness about hierarchy or meaning. "Polycultural" works better than "multicultural," which implies that cultures are fixed, discrete entities that exist side by side—a kind of zoological approach to culture. Such a view obscures power relations, but often reifies race and gender differences.

7   Black people were polycultural from the get-go. Most of our ancestors came to these shores not as Africans, but as Ibo, Yoruba, Hausa, Kongo, Bambara, Mende, Mandingo, and so on. Some of our ancestors came as Spanish, Portuguese, French, Dutch, Irish, English, Italian. And more than a few of us, in North America as well as in the Caribbean and Latin America, have Asian and Native American roots.

8   Our lines of biological descent are about as pure as O.J.'s blood sample, and our cultural lines of descent are about as mixed up as a pot of gumbo. What we know as "black culture" has always been fluid and hybrid. In Harlem in the late 1960s and 1970s, Nehru suits were as popular—and as "black"—as dashikis, and martial arts films placed Bruce Lee among a pantheon of black heroes that included Walt Frazier of the New York Knicks and Richard Rountree, who played

John Shaft in blaxploitation cinema. How do we understand the zoot suit—or the conk—without the pachuco culture of Mexican American youth, or low riders in black communities without Chicanos? How can we discuss black visual artists in the interwar years without reference to the Mexican muralists, or the radical graphics tradition dating back to the late 19th century, or the Latin American artists influenced by surrealism?

9   Vague notions of "Eastern" religion and philosophy, as well as a variety of Orientalist assumptions, were far more important to the formation of the Lost-Found Nation of Islam than anything coming out of Africa. And Rastafarians drew many of their ideas from South Asians, from vegetarianism to marijuana, which was introduced into Jamaica by Indians. Major black movements like Garveyism and the African Blood Brotherhood are also the products of global developments. We won't understand these movements until we see them as part of a dialogue with Irish nationalists from the Easter Rebellion,[1] Russian and Jewish émigrés from the 1905 and 1917 revolutions, and Asian socialists like India's M.N. Roy and Japan's Sen Katayama.

10   Indeed, I'm not sure we can even limit ourselves to Earth. How do we make sense of musicians Sun Ra, George Clinton, and Lee "Scratch" Perry or, for that matter, the Nation of Islam, when we consider the fact that space travel and notions of intergalactic exchange constitute a key source of their ideas?

11   So-called "mixed race" children are not the only ones with a claim to multiple heritages. All of us are inheritors of European, African, Native American, and Asian pasts, even if we can't exactly trace our bloodlines to these continents.

12   To some people that's a dangerous concept. Too many Europeans don't want to acknowledge that Africans helped create so-called Western civilization, that they are both indebted to and descendants of those they enslaved. They don't want to see the world as One—a tiny little globe where people and cultures are always on the move, where nothing stays still no matter how many times we name it. To acknowledge our polycultural heritage and cultural dynamism is not to give up our black identity. It does mean expanding our definition of blackness, taking our history more seriously, and looking at the rich diversity within us with new eyes.

13   So next time you see me, don't ask where I'm from or what I am, unless you're ready to sit through a long-ass lecture. As singer/songwriter Abbey Lincoln once put it, "I've got some people in me."

[1]Irish war for independence in 1916.

EXERCISES

Some of the Issues

1. In paragraph 2, Kelley describes his family as "not-quite-nappy-headed enigmas." What does he mean by this? What details does he use to back up his claim?

2. How does Kelley describe his mother in paragraph 3? What is significant about her interests?

3. Why does Kelley see irony in the way his sister is treated by the Sikh cab driver (paragraph 4)?

4. Kelley uses the term "polycultural" (paragraph 6). What does he mean by this term? Why does he feel it works better than the work "multicultural"?

5. How does Kelley go on to complicate the issue of culture? What does he mean by the term "rich diversity" (paragraph 12)?

6. Have you ever been asked "the question"? Describe the time(s) you have been asked it, and analyze the situation. Who asked you and under what circumstances? What do you think was the person's reason for asking it?

7. Another question people often ask to type strangers is, "What do you do?" Do you see ways in which this is similar to the "What are you?" question?

The Way We Are Told

8. Kelley begins his essay with what he later refers to as "the question": "So what are you?" Why do you think he does this? To whom is he speaking?

9. Why does the author put quotation marks around the words "exotics" and "good hair" in paragraph 2, and "black momma" in paragraph 3?

10. What would you say Kelley's attitude is toward "the question"? What is it about the tone of the essay that indicates this? Use specific examples from the reading to back up your claim.

11. Kelley does not state his thesis directly. If you were to come up with a one- or two-sentence thesis for this essay, what would it be?

Some Subjects for Writing

12. Write about your response to a frequently asked question that is, at least in some ways, similar to the question, "What are you?" Some examples might be, "What do you do?" "How old are you?" "Where are you from?" Do you ever feel like people want to know more than just the factual answer when they ask it?

*13. Multiracial and multiethnic identity has become an important topic of late, particularly with the change in the 2000 census that allowed respondents to identify themselves as a member of more than one ethnic/racial group. Read Gish Jen's "An Ethnic Trump" and Roxane Farmanfarmaian's "The Double Helix." How do their perspectives on the issue differ? In what ways do the authors agree or disagree? Focus on the language and the terms they use, and cite specific examples from each reading.

The Double Helix

Roxane Farmanfarmaian

Half Iranian and half American Mormon, Roxane Farmanfarmaian was raised in Holland and went to college in the United States. Her father Manucher Farmanfarmaian, who she describes in this essay as having had a harem as a family, was born in Iran in 1917 to an aristocratic family. He eventually rose to a high position in the Iranian government and was influential in the creation of OPEC, the alliance of oil-producing nations. Like many Iranians with means, he fled the country in 1979 when the Ayatollah Khomeini came to power in a fundamentalist revolution. Together, Roxane and her father co-authored an account of his experiences in Iran entitled Blood and Oil: Inside the Shah's Iran *(1998).*

Farmanfarmaian is currently a journalist who has written for many publications, including The *New York Times,* Interview, Time *and* USA Today. *She also co-founded and wrote for* The Iranian, *an independent news magazine in Iran before the revolution. This essay is taken from* Half *and* Half *(1998), an anthology of essays by authors who grew up binational, biracial or bicultural. In it, Farmanfarmaian describes her experience growing up between her American and Iranian worlds, never quite feeling at home in either, though acknowledging that in spite of their enormous differences, they also have some unexpected similarities.*

1   Call me the foreigner. Though I was born a child of deep, strong roots, I have no sense of cultural belonging. I grew up in Europe, in a country that was not my own. In my parents' homelands, on the other hand, I felt no sense of self-recognition. Their worlds were thousands of miles apart, and both extreme. "What home is this?" I would wonder, seeing nothing of myself in them. And yet, like haunting background music that I could barely hear, the symmetries between my parents' worlds, repeated with uncanny consistency, implied a unity I could not grasp. Was there a purpose to their patterns, I wondered, seeing nothing beyond the haphazard coincidence of nature. Or was it simply that one always searches for parallels, trying to find the familiar in the unknown?

2   As a child, I was oblivious to the contradictions between my ancestral worlds. But as I grew older, I felt increasingly lost among the people who were supposed to be my countrymen, and at sea in the cities that held my heritage.

3   My mother was born a Mormon, my father a Muslim. This almost always is cause for amazement in those just brought into the know. I respond like a spitting snake, pointing out that the religions share not only their initial *M*s, but

that their women wear special garments, that they both eschew certain foods, and, of course, that they both believe in the practice of polygamy.

4   Polygamy was, in fact, one of the elements that brought my parents together when they met in New York back in the fifties. My father, an outspoken critic of Iran's regime at the time, was cooling his heels as an exile, living in a small apartment on the Upper East Side of Manhattan. My mother, fresh from Salt Lake City, was attending Columbia University's Teachers College while making ends meet as a governess. They met at a production of T.S. Eliot's *Murder in the Cathedral* being staged in the university's chapel. A few weeks later, he invited her to his apartment for tea. There, in the powder room, she saw a watercolor of Brigham Young sitting in the middle of a wide bed, a line of wives stretching out on either side of him. Stunned to see the father of the Latter-day Saints so prominently displayed in the home of a Muslim, she let out a cry.

5   "It reminds me of my father," he explained. "He had a harem—with nine wives."

6   The parallels between the worlds of my parents did not end with Brigham Young. Once, while I was still in college, I flew from Tehran directly to Salt Lake City. It was not something I'd really planned to do. I'd spent the summer in Iran, and flew into New York intending to go straight on to university. But somehow I'd miscalculated my dates and, upon arrival, realized that classes did not start for another week. I called my mother from Kennedy Airport. As mothers will, she told me to come right out. Sixteen hours after stepping onto an Iran Air flight out of Tehran—and because of the time change, only a few hours later in the afternoon—I stepped off an America West flight in Salt Lake City.

7   I could have been disembarking at the same place I had boarded from. The mountains, rising into the twilight, were twins of the ones I'd just left. The ranges were both snowcapped, with the cities' lights running down their slopes like molten lava into the dusty plain. The air was the same dry air, tinged with the taste of salt from the wind off the saline lakes that lay embedded in their deserts. Iran's brackish lake lay farther off than Salt Lake City's, and dried up and cracked in the summer. But still, it gave off the same acrid smell.

8   It always struck me as one of those ironies that I, so tenuously American, should be from Utah, such a totally American place and yet, in all the United States, there is no more foreign a place, either. My mother's family are apiarists, and it is the honeycomb that is the emblem of Utah. It is also home to the Rainbow Arch, which graces so many of the posters hanging in travel agencies around the world. Yet it is the Mormon religion that is the true hallmark of Utah. And Mormons make other Americans feel slightly uncomfortable. Maybe it's the fact that the Book of Mormon is drawn from golden tablets which were miraculously unearthed by the teenaged Joseph Smith in the forests of New York, and which then as miraculously disappeared again before anyone else could see them. Or perhaps it is because Mormons don't drink coffee because they're not supposed to consume caffeine, but have been allowed to drink Coca-Cola ever since the church bought a goodly number of the company's shares.

Or, most onerous of all, is it because, in the midst of a perfectly normal conversation, the Mormon missionary zeal will suddenly spring out like an attacking pit bull, forcing the victim to wriggle away as best he or she can?

9   To be fair, both faiths are deceptive in order to get around their rigid doctrines. Is it any more self-serving on the part of the Mormon religion to ban the consumption of alcohol and yet allow private clubs to serve liquor to anyone who joins for a day, a week, or a month, than for the Muslim religion to ban prostitution but allow the purchase of a wife for a day, a week, or a month?

10   Not surprisingly, for a person born into two of the most fanatic religions in the world, I turned out rather religiously bland. To be honest, neither of my parents is particularly devout. I am glad of it. But it did weaken my footing in trying to find my place in their cultures. In Utah, strong religious conviction is imperative: you are either of the faith or not, and if not, and you've chosen to leave the faith behind, you even have a name—you are a "Jack Mormon." Feeling freed from the manacles of religion—especially such a controlling one—I considered myself above my Salt Lake relatives. Without realizing it, I replaced my need to belong with preemptive disdain—an attitude that ensured that I could not be rejected because I'd already done the rejecting. This was dangerously self-serving, but since I lived abroad, I did not need to reckon with this false sense of superiority for many years. Instead, as an expat based in Holland, I hopped blithely from one nation to another, simultaneously from nowhere and everywhere like so many others of my ilk: the army brats, the Eurotrash, the diplomatic crowd, and all the rest who were the human equivalents of the Eurodollar. In The Hague, midway between my parent's homelands, I attended an American school and thought of myself as American. Yet, when my friends said they were from Ohio or Texas, I did not say I was from Utah. No, I was just generally American.

11   Culture shock, with a capital *C*, came when I moved to the States for college. The realization that I was not American, no matter how general, was blistering. I didn't understand the Whopper jokes; I didn't know who Topper[1] was; I'd never seen a Corvair. When Easter came around, and everyone gathered to watch *The Wizard of Oz* on TV, I retired alone to my room, unable to relate to a movie whose characters bore no resemblance to the way I'd imagined them since childhood, and alienated by a culture that had fostered a tradition around a film I'd never seen.

12   That first year of college was one of the loneliest of my life.

13   After living through it, however, I was more American than I'd ever been. At the same time, I made an important discovery: that I was rather happy I wasn't as American as I'd previously thought I wanted to be. The America that had held such an aura for me was the one defined by Tootsie Rolls, and Ked sneakers, and even *Bonanza*—none of which could easily be obtained, or viewed, abroad. Once I was in America, however, these became commonplace, along with the avalanche of other products that filled the supermarkets and the time on TV. I soon felt saturated with the consumerism and the waste, and tired of

[1]1950s television character

the constant advertisements, and the claims to be the biggest and the best in the world. Perhaps one has to be a foreigner to clearly see a culture. For me, the emphasis on "things" ran through American life like too much fat in an overrich meal. It was a constant irritant, and I recoiled, hankering for the more family-oriented, simpler life I'd grown up with. I was different from most other Americans, I realized, in some ways I did not want to change.

14   When it came to feeling Persian, on the other hand, I thought I had no illusions. I was, to my own mind, clearly an outsider. I did not speak the language; I had no Iranian friends; I did not pretend to know the culture. This was before the revolution and the hostage crisis. It was not politically incorrect yet to be from Iran. Still, there were pitfalls. Deep inside, unnamed, unrecognized, I had a sense of entitlement. Because my father's family was large and powerful, because it had been instrumental in Persia's modern history, and could track its ancestors back as far as the 800s, I felt the country was stamped upon my bones. Like brown hair or a flair for languages, I believed I had somehow genetically inherited an innate Persian sensibility. Though outwardly I was a foreigner, I subconsciously presumed that once I returned to my fatherland, I would quickly feel I belonged.

15   I was mistaken. This was made crystal clear the summer I spent in Tehran before I flew on to Salt Lake City. It was the first time I'd gone alone, the first time I'd gone without my father there. And I was lost. My savvy as a world traveler forsook me. I was more estranged in Iran than anywhere I'd ever been.

16   My roommate from college came through to visit for a couple weeks. It was an opportunity to explore Iran, and, acting the knowledgeable host, I suggested we travel to Yazd, the capital of the Zoroastrians, a midsize town located somewhere in the middle of the central plain. Upon our arrival, we drove to the one hotel I'd been told existed there, only to find it shut. Thank God I'd thought to get the name of a friend of a friend before leaving Tehran, and he kindly put us up for the night in his office. To this day, I don't know where regular tourists stay when visiting Yazd's Zoroastrian fire monuments and its houses with their unusual wind towers.

17   Our first night, we went to the local bazaar, a dark cavernous place, and bought dried figs for dinner. We slept on cots set up in the office hallway. The next night, we did the same. Two nights were enough. The following morning, we decided to decamp to Isfahan, where I knew there were sumptuous mosques, a glittering bazaar, and a four-star hotel called the Shah Abbas in an old, stately caravansary.

18   The friend of a friend said he'd drive us. In fact, it was his chauffeur at the wheel, while he sat in the front seat and talked at us for six hours as we drove across the bleached stones of the desert.

19   "I went to the University of Nebraska," he said. "I lived for four years at the Holiday Inn. I never had to make my bed. And I ate french fries and ice cream every night for dinner."

20   I looked out the window, mortified, as though he epitomized all Persians and his words reflected directly on me. My roommate, on the other hand, thought him a fool—if a kindly one—and simply ignored him.

21   Going to Isfahan was a good choice. Though neither of us could understand the words, we listened to a storyteller in the hotel courtyard that evening, his singsong voice punctuated by the hubbly-bubbly pipes being smoked by many of the other listeners. The air was languid, the stars close, and we could always tell when we'd reached a good part in the story because the smokers would suddenly start inhaling quickly and the pipes would gurgle loudly in unison.

22   The next day, however, my sense of equilibrium vanished at the airport. Expecting to get a routine confirmation of our ticket change through Isfahan, I was met with a typical Middle Eastern scene: a mobbed departure desk, no one in line, everyone shouting at the harried clerk, who paid no mind to who was first or second but only to whoever shoved their tickets most insistently into his face. Instantly, I knew I'd gone about the tickets all wrong. I should have had them confirmed earlier by someone in the hotel, paid a little bakshish,[2] and avoided this scene altogether. Instead, I now had to claw my way through this melee. I felt I had let my roommate down—acting as though I knew my way around when in fact I was just an impostor, as ill at ease as she—if not more so—among my countrymen.

23   It was not until three years later, caught amid revolution and religious revival, my Persian family fleeing and my American countrymen taken hostage, that I came to understand my roots as an Iranian. I'd moved there just in time to catch the turmoil. Thank God I did, for it was the last chance I had to get to know the country. I stayed for two years. As Iran lurched toward political Islam, I developed a circle of friends, published a liberal English-language magazine, and traveled to hot spots around the country. Despite the guns in the streets, I grew used to driving around in the back alleyways, and came to understand the women in their tentlike chadors. Once, on a visit to the holy city of Qom, I even wore one myself, which caught the wind in its folds and elicited catcalls from some youths lurking nearby.

24   The revolution caught me once again in a personal conflict of national identity: Iran rejecting America—or was it the other way around? I was as much at risk of being arrested in the streets of Tehran for being an American as for being a member of the Persian elite. I felt shame for both my countries. But at last, I felt love for one.

25   That stay in Iran was a watershed for me. Although the country was lurching in a direction I could not condone, I felt a common identity with the passions and sentiments of the people. I loved the Persian wit, the street jokes about Ayatollah Khomeini and his wife and all the other mullahs who were so

[2]Bribe.

seriously taking over the country. I loved the ancient architecture, the food, and the strange third-world contrasts that would serve up a camel train caught in a traffic jam on the Tehran beltway. As more and more of my family fled the revolution, while I stayed, I felt less and less the impostor. In the past, everyone had seemed so much more "Persian" than I was. Now, I felt I knew something about Iran that only an Iranian could know—which gave me a sense of credibility. I no longer felt embarrassed that others spoke the language better than I did, or had memories of childhood summers on the Caspian, or had gone on camel trips across the desert. They had left, while I stayed on to experience the turmoil—and the baring of the country's soul. I knew what the villagers were saying about the demonstrations, how people reacted to the postrevolution drivel on TV, and where the last place was in town to get a glass of wine with dinner. I no longer needed to pretend that I belonged.

26   And yet, in my heart of hearts, I knew that it was more than that. Such intimate details I knew about Utah, too, and still I did not feel the same sense of belonging there. One summer in particular I had tapped its inner sanctum, selling encyclopedias door to door in hundred-degree heat. I saw inside the houses of hundreds of people, spoke to them about their families and their hopes, and asked them for money. They were good people, generous people, who gave me water and cake, and lived with too many children and too little time. But I did not feel they were my people.

27   Was it the sense of history that permeated all aspects of Iran that I related to so well? Was it the excitement of revolution that gave me a sense of real involvement? Or was it the fact that I had to lose Iran, and that I would have felt the same about Utah if it instead had been the one I had had to leave? I do not know. But when the Iranian revolution ejected me, and most of my Persian family, I left with a heavy heart, knowing that I was at last leaving a homeland behind me.

28   Today, I still cannot go back to Iran. The political situation makes me at once an outcast and a wanted woman. Finally, however, I understand the symmetry that, like a double helix, seems to turn my mother's country back into my father's, and back again. I have come to grips with my need for reflected identity. Though Utah never has drawn me the way Iran did, it now offers me the legacy of both. Now every time I fly into Salt Lake City and disembark from the plane, I look up at the mountains, and at the city cascading down their slopes, and for one fleeting moment I taste the salt air and feel I'm stepping onto the dusty plain of Tehran.

EXERCISES

Some of the Issues

1. How does Farmanfarmaian define the question of home in paragraph 1?
2. What kinds of parallels does Farmanfarmaian see between her parents' worlds?

3. Why does Farmanfarmaian say that Utah is at once "such a totally American place, and yet, in all the United States there is no more foreign a place, either" (paragraph 8)?
4. In paragraph 10, Farmanfarmaian describes herself as "just generally American." How does this differ from the way other students at the American school in The Hague describe themselves? Why in paragraph 11 does she say that she changed her mind about being American?
5. For Farmanfarmaian, what role does popular culture play in the formation of people's identity (paragraphs 11–13)?
6. How does Farmanfarmaian describe her first visit alone to Iran? What does she learn from it?
7. What does Farmanfarmaian mean when she writes, "But at last I felt love for one" in paragraph 24? What makes that feeling complex? What does Farmanfarmaian say she loves about Iran and what circumstances lead her to his realization?
8. In paragraph 1, Farmanfarmaian makes a distinction between "roots" and a sense of "cultural belonging." The essay is, in many ways, an elaboration on this specific claim. Using specific examples from the reading, show how she distinguishes between the two.
9. What does the title refer to? Do you think it's an appropriate title?

The Way We Are Told

10. Farmanfarmaian's opening sentence speaks directly to the reader. What is she asking us to do? What is the effect?
11. Look carefully at the paragraphs where Farmanfarmaian's writing is particularly descriptive (for example, paragraph 7). What techniques does she use? Do the images work for you? Why or why not?
12. Farmanfarmaian often uses short sentences to punctuate her ideas. Find instances where she does this. How do they help her make her point?

Some Subjects for Writing

13. To what extent is identity tied to a specific place? Write an essay in which you explore the extent to which your own identity developed out of the place or places you grew up.
*14. In paragraph 10, Farmanfarmaian describes herself as "simultaneously from nowhere and everywhere." Read Pico Iyer's "Home is Everyplace." How are her views and experiences similar to those of Iyer? What might account for the differences? Explain your answer using specific examples from the texts.

A Slow Walk of Trees

Toni Morrison

Toni Morrison was born in 1931 in Lorrain, Ohio, a small town near Cleveland. She received a B.A. degree from Howard University and an M.A. from Cornell. Morrison is well known for her novels, including The Bluest Eye *(1969),* Sula *(1973),* Song of Solomon *(1977),* Beloved *(1987), and* Paradise *(1998). Morrison has won both the Pulitzer Prize and the Nobel Prize for Literature.*

The article included here was first published in the New York Times Magazine *on July 4, 1976, the date of the American bicentennial. Morrison describes as well as contrasts the attitudes of her grandparents and parents toward the discrimination that was a central factor in their lives. In each of the two generations, she explains, the male had an essentially pessimistic outlook that nothing could be done; the female, on the other hand, set out to cope with whatever particular adversity was likely to befall her family. At the same time, Morrison sees a generational difference between the views of her grandparents and her parents that indicates some progress: an increased belief in the possibility of assuming control of their lives.*

1 His name was John Solomon Willis, and when at age 5 he heard from the old folks that "the Emancipation Proclamation was coming," he crawled under the bed. It was his earliest recollection of what was to be his habitual response to the promise of white people: horror and an instinctive yearning for safety. He was my grandfather, a musician who managed to hold on to his violin but not his land. He lost all 88 acres of his Indian mother's inheritance to legal predators who built their fortunes on the likes of him. He was an unreconstructed black pessimist who, in spite of or because of emancipation, was convinced for 85 years that there was no hope whatever for black people in this country. His rancor was legitimate, for he, John Solomon, was not only an artist but a first-rate carpenter and farmer, reduced to sending home to his family money he had made playing the violin because he was not able to find work. And this during the years when almost half the black male population were skilled craftsmen who lost their jobs to white ex-convicts and immigrant farmers.

2 His wife, however, was of a quite different frame of mind and believed that all things could be improved by faith in Jesus and an effort of the will. So it was she, Ardelia Willis, who sneaked her seven children out of the back window into the darkness, rather than permit the patron of their sharecropper's existence to become their executioner as well, and headed north in 1912, when 99.2 percent of all black people in the U.S. were native-born and only 60 percent of white Americans were. And it was Ardelia who told her husband that they could not

stay in the Kentucky town they ended up in because the teacher didn't know long division.

3   They have been dead now for 30 years and more and I still don't know which of them came closer to the truth about the possibilities of life for black people in this country. One of their grandchildren is a tenured professor at Princeton. Another, who suffered from what the Peruvian poet called "anger that breaks a man into children," was picked up just as he entered his teens and emotionally lobotomized by the reformatories and mental institutions specifically designed to serve him. Neither John Solomon nor Ardelia lived long enough to despair over one or swell with pride over the other. But if they were alive today each would have selected and collected enough evidence to support the accuracy of the other's original point of view. And it would be difficult to convince either one that the other was right.

4   Some of the monstrous events that took place in John Solomon's America have been duplicated in alarming detail in my own America. There was the public murder of a President in a theater in 1865 and the public murder of another President on television in 1963. The Civil War of 1861 had its encore as the civil rights movement of 1960. The torture and mutilation of a black West Point Cadet (Cadet Johnson Whittaker) in 1880 had its rerun with the 1970's murders of students at Jackson State College, Texas Southern and Southern University in Baton Rouge. And in 1976 we watch for what must be the thousandth time a pitched battle between the children of slaves and the children of immigrants— only this time, it is not the New York draft riots of 1863, but the busing turmoil in Paul Revere's home town, Boston.

5   Hopeless, he'd said. Hopeless. For he was certain that white people of every political, religious, geographical and economic background would band together against black people everywhere when they felt the threat of our progress. And a hundred years after he sought safety from the white man's "promise," somebody put a bullet in Martin Luther King's brain. And not long before that some excellent samples of the master race demonstrated their courage and virility by dynamiting some little black girls to death. If he were here now, my grandfather, he would shake his head, close his eyes and pull out his violin—too polite to say, "I told you so." And his wife would pay attention to the music but not to the sadness in her husband's eyes, for she would see what she expected to see—not the occasional historical repetition, but, *like the slow walk of certain species of trees from the flatlands up into the mountains,* she would see the signs of irrevocable and permanent change. She, who pulled her girls out of an inadequate school in the Cumberland Mountains, knew all along that the gentlemen from Alabama who had killed the little girls would be rounded up. And it wouldn't surprise her in the least to know that the number of black college graduates jumped 12 percent in the last three years: 47 percent in 20 years. That there are 140 black mayors in this country; 14 black judges in the District Circuit, 4 in the Courts of Appeals and one on the Supreme Court. That there are 17 blacks in Congress, one in the Senate; 276 in state legislatures—223 in

state houses, 53 in state senates. That there are 112 elected black police chiefs and sheriffs, 1 Pulitzer Prize winner; 1 winner of the Prix de Rome; a dozen or so winners of the Guggenheim; 4 deans of predominantly white colleges. . . . Oh, her list would go on and on. But so would John Solomon's sweet sad music.

6   While my grandparents held opposite views on whether the fortunes of black people were improving, my own parents struck similarly opposed postures, but from another slant. They differed about whether the moral fiber of white people would ever improve. Quite a different argument. The old folks argued about how and if black people could improve themselves, who could be counted on to help us, who would hinder us and so on. My parents took issue over the question of whether it was possible for white people to improve. They assumed that black people were the humans of the globe, but had serious doubts about the quality and existence of white humanity. Thus my father, distrusting every word and every gesture of every white man on earth, assumed that the white man who crept up the stairs one afternoon had come to molest his daughters and threw him down the stairs and then our tricycle after him. (I think my father was wrong, but considering what I have seen since, it may have been very healthy for me to have witnessed that as my first black-white encounter.) My mother, however, *believed* in them—their possibilities. So when the meal we got on relief was bug-ridden, she wrote a long letter to Franklin Delano Roosevelt. And when white bill collectors came to our door, it was she who received them civilly and explained in a sweet voice that we were people of honor and that the debt would be taken care of. Her message to Roosevelt got through—our meal improved. Her message to the bill collectors did not always get through and there was occasional violence when my father (self-exiled to the bedroom for fear he could not hold his temper) would hear that her reasonableness had failed. My mother was always wounded by these scenes, for she thought the bill collector knew that she loved good credit more than life and that being in arrears on a payment horrified her probably more than it did him. So she thought he was rude because he was white. For years she walked to utility companies and department stores to pay bills in person and even now she does not seem convinced that checks are legal tender. My father loved excellence, worked hard (he held three jobs at once for 17 years) and was so outraged by the suggestion of personal slackness that he could explain it to himself only in terms of racism. He was a fastidious worker who was frightened of one thing: unemployment. I can remember now the doomsday-cum-graveyard sound of "laid off" and how the minute school was out he asked us, "Where you workin'?" Both my parents believed that all succor and aid came from themselves and their neighborhood, since "they"—white people in charge and those not in charge but in obstructionist positions—were in some way fundamentally, genetically corrupt.

7   So I grew up in a basically racist household with more than a child's share of contempt for white people. And for each white friend I acquired who made a small crack in that contempt, there was another who repaired it. For each one

who related to me as a person, there was one who in my presence at least, became actively "white." And like most black people of my generation, I suffer from racial vertigo that can be cured only by taking what one needs from one's ancestors. John Solomon's cynicism and his deployment of his art as both weapon and solace, Ardelia's faith in the magic that can be wrought by sheer effort of the will; my mother's open-mindedness in each new encounter and her habit of trying reasonableness first; my father's temper, his impatience and his efforts to keep "them" (throw them) out of his life. And it is out of these learned and selected attitudes that I look at the quality of life for my people in this country now. These widely disparate and sometimes conflicting views, I suspect, were held not only by me, but by most black people. Some I know are clearer in their positions, have not sullied their anger with optimism or dirtied their hope with despair. But most of us are plagued by a sense of being worn shell-thin by constant repression and hostility as well as the impression of being buoyed by visible testimony of tremendous strides. There *is* repetition of the grotesque in our history. And there *is* the miraculous walk of trees. The question is whether our walk is progress or merely movement. O.J. Simpson leaning on a Hertz car *is* better than the Gold Dust Twins on the back of a soap box. But is "Good Times" better than Stepin Fetchit? Has the first order of business been taken care of? Does the law of the land work for us?

EXERCISES

Some of the Issues

1. Toni Morrison describes her grandfather as a pessimist and says that "his rancor was legitimate." Why does she call it legitimate? Toward whom was it directed?
2. What was the difference in basic outlook between Morrison's grandfather and grandmother? What did her grandmother believe? How does the author show that she lived up to her beliefs?
3. Why does Morrison cite the lives of John Solomon and Ardelia's two grandchildren in paragraph 3? How do these lives relate to her grandparents' beliefs? In what way does Morrison think these lives would have affected her grandparents' beliefs?
4. Reread paragraph 4. What bearing does what Morrison tells here have on the grandparents' views?
5. After rereading paragraph 5, explain the title of the essay. Whose beliefs does Morrison reflect in this paragraph?
6. Explain the distinction Morrison makes between the views of her grandparents and her parents. What is the difference between the views of her father and mother?
7. Morrison says: "So I grew up in a basically racist household." How does Morrison trace her views back to the influence of her parents and grandparents?

The Way We Are Told

8. Morrison uses a mix of personal anecdotes and more general observations, including statistics, to support her thesis. How are these used to support the idea of black progress or the lack of it?
9. As Morrison tells it, one each of her parents and grandparents was an optimist, the other a pessimist. Try to determine Morrison's own stand. Whose side is she on?

Some Subjects for Writing

10. How would you characterize your own family's outlook on life? Is it more on the optimistic or pessimistic side? How have your family's attitudes influenced you?
11. Which point of view, the optimistic one of Morrison's grandmother or the pessimistic one of her grandfather, best accounts for the trend in race relations in the United States in the past ten years? Cite specific events in the news or changes in media representation, or draw from personal experience and family history.

Hearing the Sweetest Songs

Nicolette Toussaint

Nicolette Toussaint is a writer, painter, and political activist who lives in San Francisco. This essay originally appeared in a 1994 issue of Newsweek.

Toussaint, who is hearing impaired, describes her experience of having a disability that "doesn't announce itself." Toussaint examines the advantages and disadvantages of choosing whether to "pass" as a nondisabled person or to announce her disability openly. In doing so she calls into question society's reactions to and acceptance of disability. As Toussaint concludes, "We're all just temporarily abled, and every one of us, if we live long enough, will become disabled in some way."

1 Every year when I was a child, a man brought a big, black, squeaking machine to school. When he discovered I couldn't hear all his peeps and squeaks, he would get very excited. The nurse would draw a chart with a deep canyon in it. Then I would listen to the squeaks two or three times, while the adults—who were all acting very, very nice—would watch me raise my hand. Sometimes I couldn't tell whether I heard the squeaks or just imagined them, but I liked being the center of attention.

2 My parents said I lost my hearing to pneumonia as a baby; but I knew I hadn't *lost* anything. None of my parts had dropped off. Nothing had changed: if I wanted to listen to Beethoven, I could put my head between the speakers and turn the dial up to 7, I could hear jets at the airport a block away. I could hear my mom when she was in the same room—if I wanted to. I could even hear my cat purr if I put my good ear right on top of him.

3 I wasn't aware of *not* hearing until I began to wear a hearing aid at the age of 30. It shattered my peace: shoes creaking, papers crackling, pencils tapping, phones ringing, refrigerators humming, people cracking knuckles, clearing throats and blowing noses! Cars, bikes, dogs, cats, kids all seemed to appear from nowhere and fly right at me.

4 I was constantly startled, unnerved, agitated—exhausted. I felt as though inquisitorial Nazis in an old World War II film were burning the side of my head with a merciless white spotlight. Under that onslaught, I had to break down and confess: I couldn't hear. Suddenly, I began to discover many things I couldn't do.

5 I couldn't identify sounds. One afternoon, while lying on my side watching a football game on TV, I kept hearing a noise that sounded like my cat playing with a flexible-spring doorstop. I checked, but the cat was asleep. Finally, I happened

to lift my head as the noise occurred. Heard through my good ear, the metallic buzz turned out to be the referee's whistle.

6   I couldn't tell where sounds came from. I couldn't find my phone under the blizzard of papers on my desk. The more it rang, the deeper I dug, I shoveled mounds of paper onto the floor and finally had to track it down by following the cord from the wall.

7   When I lived alone, I felt helpless because I couldn't hear alarm clocks, vulnerable because I couldn't hear the front door open and frightened because I wouldn't hear a burglar until it was too late.

8   Then one day I missed a job interview because of the phone. I had gotten off the subway 20 minutes early, eager and dressed to the nines. But the address I had written down didn't exist! I must have misheard it: I searched the street, becoming overheated, late and frantic, knowing that if I confessed that I couldn't hear on the phone, I would make my odds of getting hired even worse.

9   For the first time, I felt unequal, disadvantaged and disabled. Now that I had something to compare, I knew that I *had* lost something; not just my hearing, but my independence and my sense of wholeness. I had always hated to be seen as inferior, so I never mentioned my lack of hearing. Unlike a wheelchair or a white cane, my disability doesn't announce itself. For most of my life, I chose to pass as abled, and I thought I did it quite well.

10   But after I got the hearing aid, a business friend said, "You know, Nicolette, you think you get away with not hearing, but you don't. Sometimes in meetings you answer the wrong question. People don't know you can't hear, so they think you're daydreaming, eccentric, stupid—or just plain rude. It would be better to just tell them."

11   I wondered about that then, and I still do. If I tell, I risk being seen as *un*able rather than *dis*abled. Sometimes, when I say I can't hear, the waiter will turn to my companion and say, "What does she want?" as though I have lost my power of speech.

12   If I tell, people may see *only* my disability. Once someone is labeled "deaf," "crippled," "mute" or "aged," that's too often all they are. I'm a writer, a painter, a slapdash housekeeper, a gardener who grows wondrous roses; my hearing is just part of the whole. It's a tender part, and you should handle it with care. But like most people with a disability, I don't mind if you ask about it.

13   In fact, you should ask, because it's an important part of me, something my friends see as part of my character. My friend Anne always rests a hand on my elbow in parking lots, since several times, drivers who assume that I hear them have nearly run me over. When I hold my head at a certain angle, my husband, Mason, will say, 'It's a plane" or 'It's a siren." And my mother loves to laugh about the things I *thought* I heard: last week I was told that "the Minotaurs in the garden are getting out of hand." I imagined capering bullmen and I was disappointed to learn that all we had in the garden were overgrown "baby tears."

14   Not hearing can be funny, or frustrating. And once in a while, it can be the cause of something truly transcendent. One morning at the shore I was listening

to the ocean when Mason said, "Hear the bird?" What bird? I listened hard until I heard a faint, unbirdlike, croaking sound. If he hadn't mentioned it, I would never have noticed it. As I listened, slowly I began to hear—or perhaps imagine—a distant song. Did I *really* hear it? Or just hear in my heart when he shared with me? I don't care. Songs imagined are as sweet as songs heard, and songs shared are sweeter still.

15   That sharing is what I want for all of us. We're all just temporarily abled, and everyone of us, if we live long enough, will become disabled in some way. Those of us who have gotten there first can tell you how to cope with phones and alarm clocks. About ways of holding a book, opening a door and leaning on a crutch all at the same time. And what it's like to give up in despair on Thursday, then begin all over again on Friday, because there's no other choice—and because the roses are beginning to bud in the garden.

16   These are conversations we all should have, and it's not that hard to begin. Just let me see your lips when you speak. Stay in the same room. Don't shout. And ask what you want to know.

EXERCISES

Some of the Issues

1. In paragraphs 1 and 2 Toussaint talks about her childhood attitudes toward her loss of hearing. How did her attitudes differ from those of the adults around her?
2. In paragraphs 3 through 9 Toussaint tells what happened when she began wearing a hearing aid at age thirty. How did things change? How did she feel about the changes?
3. Why does Toussaint question whether she should tell people about her disability when they may not immediately notice it (paragraphs 11 and 12)? Having read the rest of the essay, what do you think her solution was?
4. In paragraph 14, Toussaint describes an important moment in her life—a bird's song that she may or may not have actually heard—and says "Songs imagined are as sweet as songs heard, and songs shared are sweeter still." What does she mean? Do you agree?
5. What, according to Toussaint, do all of us share (paragraph 15)?
6. Throughout the essay Toussaint mentions both positive and negative aspects of her disability. What are they?
7. Did Toussaint's essay influence how you consider and talk about either your own or others' disabilities? In what way?

The Way We Are Told

8. What do you think Toussaint gains by beginning her essay with a description of her childhood?

9. Many good writers use sensual details, describing what they see, hear, smell, or touch to add vividness to their writing. More often than not, the details writers provide are mostly visual. Give several examples of the sensual details Toussaint uses.

10. Toussaint gives several examples of sounds that she interprets differently than a person with normal hearing might. What does she gain by telling you of her "mistakes"?

Some Subjects for Writing

11. Toussaint is keenly aware of the sounds around her. Many of us with normal hearing block out some of the sounds around us. Increase your own awareness of sound by finding a place where you can close your eyes and listen for several minutes at a time. Concentrate on the sounds around you. Write a description of the place focusing on details of sound.

12. Toussaint tells how her hearing loss has had both positive and negative consequences. Many of us have experienced some physical challenge, whether genetic or caused by illness or injury. Some of these challenges, like poor eyesight, can be temporarily or permanently corrected; some cannot. Also, as Toussaint reminds us, we are all "temporarily abled" since our abilities will diminish with age. Write about how you, or someone you know, has coped with a loss of ability.

13. Research what your school or community does to provide for people with serious disabilities. If possible, interview people who are disabled or get information from groups that represent the disabled. Evaluate the effectiveness of current provisions.

The Myth of the Latin Woman: I Just Met a Girl Named María

Judith Ortiz Cofer

Judith Ortiz Cofer was born in 1952 in Hormigueros, Puerto Rico, and emigrated with her family to the United States in 1956 when her father joined the U.S. Navy and was assigned to a ship in Brooklyn Yard. Cofer's family returned frequently to Puerto Rico to stay with relatives while her father was away at sea.

Cofer has published several volumes of poetry and has said of her poems, "The 'infinite variety' and power of language interest me. I never cease to experiment with it. As a native Puerto Rican, my first language was Spanish. It was a challenge, not only to learn English, but to master it enough to teach it and—the ultimate goal—to write poetry in it."

Cofer is the author of Silent Dancing: A Partial Remembrance of a Puerto Rican Childhood *(1990). This essay is taken from* The Latin Deli: Telling the Lives of Barrio Women *(1993), a collection of stories, poems, and essays that describe the cultural duality of growing up both Puerto Rican and American. Cofer is also the author of* An Island Like You: Stories of the Barrio *(1995),* The Year of Our Revolution, *a collection of short stories and poems (1998), and* Woman In Front of the Sun: On Becoming a Writer *(2000). She is currently Professor of English at the University of Georgia.*

The song referred to in the title of this essay is from West Side Story, *a popular Broadway musical and film about two teenagers who fall in love despite their different ethnic backgrounds and allegiances to rival gangs.*

1   On a bus trip to London from Oxford University where I was earning some graduate credits one summer, a young man, obviously fresh from a pub, spotted me and as if struck by inspiration went down on his knees in the aisle. With both hands over his heart he broke into an Irish tenor's rendition of "María" from *West Side Story.* My politely amused fellow passengers gave his lovely voice the round of gentle applause it deserved. Though I was not quite as amused, I managed my version of an English smile: no show of teeth, no extreme contortions of the facial muscles—I was at this time of my life practicing reserve and cool. Oh, that British control, how I coveted it. But María had followed me to

London, reminding me of a prime fact of my life: you can leave the Island, master the English language, and travel as far as you can, but if you are a Latina, especially one like me who so obviously belongs to Rita Moreno's gene pool, the Island travels with you.

2   This is sometimes a very good thing—it may win you that extra minute of someone's attention. But with some people, the same things can make *you* an island—not so much a tropical paradise as an Alcatraz, a place nobody wants to visit. As a Puerto Rican girl growing up in the United States and wanting like most children to "belong," I resented the stereotype that my Hispanic appearance called forth from many people I met.

3   Our family lived in a large urban center in New Jersey during the sixties, where life was designed as a microcosm of my parents' casas on the island. We spoke in Spanish, we ate Puerto Rican food bought at the bodega, and we practiced strict Catholicism complete with Saturday confession and Sunday mass at a church where our parents were accommodated into a one-hour Spanish mass slot, performed by a Chinese priest trained as a missionary for Latin America.

4   As a girl I was kept under strict surveillance, since virtue and modesty were, by cultural equation, the same as family honor. As a teenager I was instructed on how to behave as a proper señorita. But it was a conflicting message girls got, since the Puerto Rican mothers also encouraged their daughters to look and act like women and to dress in clothes our Anglo friends and their mothers found too "mature" for our age. It was, and is, cultural, yet I often felt humiliated when I appeared at an American friend's party wearing a dress more suitable to a semiformal than to a playroom birthday celebration. At Puerto Rican festivities, neither the music nor the colors we wore could be too loud. I still experience a vague sense of letdown when I'm invited to a "party" and it turns out to be a marathon conversation in hushed tones rather than a fiesta with salsa, laughter, and dancing—the kind of celebration I remember from my childhood.

5   I remember Career Day in our high school, when teachers told us to come dressed as if for a job interview. It quickly became obvious that to the barrio girls, "dressing up" sometimes meant wearing ornate jewelry and clothing that would be more appropriate (by mainstream standards) for the company Christmas party than as daily office attire. That morning I had agonized in front of my closet, trying to figure out what a "career girl" would wear because, essentially, except for Marlo Thomas on TV, I had no models on which to base my decision. I knew how to dress for school: at the Catholic school I attended we all wore uniforms; I knew how to dress for Sunday mass, and I knew what dresses to wear for parties at my relatives' homes. Though I do not recall the precise details of my Career Day outfit, it must have been a composite of the above choices. But I remember a comment my friend (an Italian-American) made in later years that coalesced my impressions of that day. She said that at the business school she was attending the Puerto Rican girls always stood out for wearing "everything at once." She meant, of course, too much jewelry, too many accessories. On that day at school, we were simply made the negative models by the nuns who were

themselves not credible fashion experts to any of us. But it was painfully obvious to me that to the others, in their tailored skirts and silk blouses, we must have seemed "hopeless" and "vulgar." Though I now know that most adolescents feel out of step much of the time, I also know that for the Puerto Rican girls of my generation that sense was intensified. The way our teachers and classmates looked at us that day in school was just a taste of the culture clash that awaited us in the real world, where prospective employers and men on the street would often misinterpret our tight skirts and jingling bracelets as a come-on.

6   Mixed cultural signals have perpetuated certain stereotypes—for example, that of the Hispanic woman as the "Hot Tamale" or sexual firebrand. It is a one-dimensional view that the media have found easy to promote. In their special vocabulary, advertisers have designated "sizzling" and "smoldering" as the adjectives of choice for describing not only the foods but also the women of Latin America. From conversations in my house I recall hearing about the harassment that Puerto Rican women endured in factories where the "boss men" talked to them as if sexual innuendo was all they understood and, worse, often gave them the choice of submitting to advances or being fired.

7   It is custom, however, not chromosomes, that leads us to choose scarlet over pale pink. As young girls, we were influenced in our decisions about clothes and colors by the women—older sisters and mothers who had grown up on a tropical island where the natural environment was a riot of primary colors, where showing your skin was one way to keep cool as well as to look sexy. Most important of all, on the island, women perhaps felt freer to dress and move more provocatively, since, in most cases, they were protected by the traditions, mores, and laws of a Spanish/Catholic system of morality and machismo whose main rule was: *You may look at my sister, but if you touch her I will kill you.* The extended family and church structure could provide a young woman with a circle of safety in her small pueblo on the island; if a man "wronged" a girl, everyone would close in to save her family honor.

8   This is what I have gleaned from my discussions as an adult with older Puerto Rican women. They have told me about dressing in their best party clothes on Saturday nights and going to the town's plaza to promenade with their girlfriends in front of the boys they liked. The males were thus given an opportunity to admire the women and to express their admiration in the form of *piropos:* erotically charged street poems they composed on the spot. I have been subjected to a few piropos while visiting the Island, and they can be outrageous, although custom dictates that they must never cross into obscenity. This ritual, as I understand it, also entails a show of studied indifference on the woman's part; if she is "decent," she must not acknowledge the man's impassioned words. So I do understand how things can be lost in translation. When a Puerto Rican girl dressed in her idea of what is attractive meets a man from the mainstream culture who has been trained to react to certain types of clothing as a sexual signal, a clash is likely to take place. The line I first heard based on this aspect of the myth happened when the boy who took me to my first formal dance leaned

over to plant a sloppy overeager kiss painfully on my mouth, and when I didn't respond with sufficient passion said in a resentful tone: "I thought you Latin girls were supposed to mature early"—my first instance of being thought of as a fruit or vegetable—I was supposed to *ripen*, not just grow into womanhood like other girls.

9   It is surprising to some of my professional friends that some people, including those who should know better, still put others "in their place." Though rarer, these incidents are still commonplace in my life. It happened to me most recently during a stay at a very classy metropolitan hotel favored by young professional couples for their weddings. Late one evening after the theater, as I walked toward my room with my new colleague (a woman with whom I was coordinating an arts program), a middle-aged man in a tuxedo, a young girl in satin and lace on his arm, stepped directly into our path. With his champagne glass extended toward me, he exclaimed, "Evita!"

10   Our way blocked, my companion and I listened as the man half-recited, half-bellowed "Don't Cry for Me, Argentina." When he finished, the young girl said: "How about a round of applause for my daddy?" We complied, hoping this would bring the silly spectacle to a close. I was becoming aware that our little group was attracting the attention of the other guests. "Daddy" must have perceived this too, and he once more barred the way as we tried to walk past him. He began to shout-sing a ditty to the tune of "La Bamba"—except the lyrics were about a girl named María whose exploits all rhymed with her name and gonorrhea. The girl kept saying "Oh, Daddy" and looking at me with pleading eyes. She wanted me to laugh along with the others. My companion and I stood silently waiting for the man to end his offensive song. When he finished, I looked not at him but at his daughter. I advised her calmly never to ask her father what he had done in the army. Then I walked between them and to my room. My friend complimented me on my cool handling of the situation. I confessed to her that I really had wanted to push the jerk into the swimming pool. I knew that this same man—probably a corporate executive, well educated, even worldly by most standards—would not have been likely to regale a white woman with a dirty song in public. He would perhaps have checked his impulse by assuming that she could be somebody's wife or mother, or at least *somebody* who might take offense. But to him, I was just an Evita or a María: merely a character in his cartoon-populated universe.

11   Because of my education and my proficiency with the English language, I have acquired many mechanisms for dealing with the anger I experience. This was not true for my parents, nor is it true for the many Latin women working at menial jobs who must put up with stereotypes about our ethnic group such as: "They make good domestics." This is another facet of the myth of the Latin woman in the United States. Its origin is simple to deduce. Work as domestics, waitressing, and factory jobs are all that's available to women with little English and few skills. The myth of the Hispanic menial has been sustained by the same media phenomenon that made "Mammy" from *Gone with the Wind* America's

idea of the black woman for generations; María, the housemaid or counter girl, is now indelibly etched into the national psyche. The big and the little screens have presented us with the picture of the funny Hispanic maid, mispronouncing words and cooking up a spicy storm in a shiny California kitchen.

12   This media-engendered image of the Latina in the United States has been documented by feminist Hispanic scholars, who claim that such portrayals are partially responsible for the denial of opportunities for upward mobility among Latinas in the professions. I have a Chicana friend working on a Ph.D. in philosophy at a major university. She says her doctor still shakes his head in puzzled amazement at all the "big words" she uses. Since I do not wear my diplomas around my neck for all to see, I too have on occasion been sent to that "kitchen," where some think I obviously belong.

13   One such incident that has stayed with me, though I recognize it as a minor offense, happened on the day of my first public poetry reading. It took place in Miami in a boat-restaurant where we were having lunch before the event. I was nervous and excited as I walked in with my notebook in my hand. An older woman motioned me to her table. Thinking (foolish me) that she wanted me to autograph a copy of my brand new slender volume of verse, I went over. She ordered a cup of coffee from me, assuming that I was the waitress. Easy enough to mistake my poems for menus, I suppose. I know that it wasn't an intentional act of cruelty, yet of all the good things that happened that day, I remember that scene most clearly, because it reminded me of what I had to overcome before anyone would take me seriously. In retrospect I understand that my anger gave my reading fire, that I have almost always taken doubts in my abilities as a challenge—and that the result is, most times, a feeling of satisfaction at having won a convert when I see the cold, appraising eyes warm to my words, the body language change, the smile that indicates that I have opened some avenue for communication. That day I read to that woman and her lowered eyes told me that she was embarrassed at her little faux pas, and when I willed her to look up at me, it was my victory, and she graciously allowed me to punish her with my full attention. We shook hands at the end of the reading, and I never saw her again. She has probably forgotten the whole thing but maybe not.

14   Yet I am one of the lucky ones. My parents made it possible for me to acquire a stronger footing in the mainstream culture by giving me the chance at an education. And, books and art have saved me from the harsher forms of ethnic and racial prejudice that many of my Hispanic *compañeras* have had to endure. I travel a lot around the United States, reading from my books of poetry and my novel, and the reception I most often receive is one of positive interest by people who want to know more about my culture. There are, however, thousands of Latinas without the privilege of an education or the entrée into society that I have. For them life is a struggle against the misconceptions perpetuated by the myth of the Latina as whore, domestic or criminal. We cannot change this by legislating the way people look at us. The transformation, as I see it, has to occur at a much more individual level. My personal goal in my public life is to

try to replace the old pervasive stereotypes and myths about Latinas with a much more interesting set of realities. Every time I give a reading, I hope the stories I tell, the dreams and fears I examine in my work, can achieve some universal truth which will get my audience past the particulars of my skin color, my accent, or my clothes.

15   I once wrote a poem in which I called us Latinas "God's brown daughters." This poem is really a prayer of sorts, offered upward, but also, through the human-to-human channel of art, outward. It is a prayer for communication, and for respect. In it, Latin women pray "in Spanish to an Anglo God / with a Jewish heritage," and they are "fervently hoping / that if not omnipotent, / at least He be bilingual."

EXERCISES

Some of the Issues

1. How does Cofer react to the young man's serenade in paragraph 1?
2. In paragraphs 2 through 5, Cofer talks about her childhood in New Jersey where she received different cultural signals from her Puerto Rican family than from the Anglo world outside. What were these signals? How were they confusing to her?
3. What are the stereotypes of Latin women that the American media perpetuate (paragraph 6)? Can you think of others besides the ones Cofer mentions?
4. According to Cofer, what behaviors or customs are interpreted differently in Puerto Rico than in the United States? Why? Can you give other examples of behaviors that have different meanings in different cultures?
5. What role do stereotypes play in explaining the behavior of the man in the tuxedo (paragraphs 9–10) and the woman at the poetry reading (paragraph 13)? What is your own opinion of how stereotypes are formed in our culture?
*6. Cofer says that she is "one of the lucky ones" (paragraph 14). What does she believe her privileges allow her to do? You may want to compare her viewpoint with that expressed in Aurora Levins Morales's "Class Poem."
7. To what extent is the stereotyping Cofer experiences based on her being a woman? How are stereotypes about Latin men different? How are stereotypes about women in other cultures the same or different?

The Way We Are Told

8. Like many writers, Cofer begins with a story. How does this narrative help illustrate her point?
9. Cofer uses references to Latina and black women in popular culture (María, Evita, and Mammy in *Gone with the Wind*) to indicate stereotypical roles that mainstream culture assigns to minority women. Were you familiar with the references? If not, was it easy for you to associate Cofer's ideas with other stereotypical images in the media?

Some Subjects for Writing

10. In "The Myth of the Latin Woman" Cofer explores how that myth prevents people from seeing her as who she is. Analyze common stereotypes that are applied to people belonging to a particular group. These stereotypes can be based on race, ethnicity, gender, or sexual preference, but you can also use, for example, stereotypes about athletes, intellectuals, or lawyers.

11. What role do the media play in stereotyping? Find one or more examples of newspaper or magazine articles, television shows, or movies that you believe reinforce misconceptions about a particular group in American society. Explain in detail the nature of the misrepresentations.

*12. Gloria Naylor, in "The Meaning of a Word," writes about how the same word can be affectionate in the context of family but deeply hurtful when said by someone else. Cofer also talks about actions that can have different meanings in different contexts. Describe a situation in which your own behavior, or the behavior of someone toward you, was affected by context.

Hair

Malcolm X

Malcolm X, born in Omaha, Nebraska, in 1925, changed his name from Malcolm Little when he joined Elijah Muhammad's Black Muslims, in which he eventually moved up to become second in command. He broke with the Muslims because of major differences in policy and established an organization of his own. Soon after that he was assassinated at a public meeting, on February 21, 1965. The Autobiography of Malcolm X, written with Alex Haley (later more widely known as the author of Roots *), was published in 1964. The selection reprinted here is from one of the early parts of the book and records an experience during Malcolm X's junior high school years in Michigan, in 1941. He gives the reader what amounts to a recipe, but a recipe on two levels: he describes in detail the painful process of "conking," straightening hair, that he as a boy subjected himself to. On a more fundamental level it was, as he says, a "big step toward self-degradation."*

1   Shorty soon decided that my hair was finally long enough to be conked. He had promised to school me in how to beat the barbershop's three- and four-dollar price by making up congolene, and then conking ourselves.

2   I took the little list of ingredients he had printed out for me, and went to a grocery store, where I got a can of Red Devil lye, two eggs, and two medium-sized white potatoes. Then at a drugstore near the poolroom, I asked for a large jar of vaseline, a large bar of soap, a large-toothed comb and a fine-toothed comb, one of those rubber hoses with a metal spray-head, a rubber apron and a pair of gloves.

3   "Going to lay on that first conk?" the drugstore man asked me. I proudly told him, grinning, "Right!"

4   Shorty paid six dollars a week for a room in his cousin's shabby apartment. His cousin wasn't at home. "It's like the pad's mine, he spends so much time with his woman," Shorty said. "Now, you watch me—"

5   He peeled the potatoes and thin-sliced them into a quart-sized Mason fruit jar, then started stirring them with a wooden spoon as he gradually poured in a little over half the can of lye. "Never use a metal spoon; the lye will turn it black," he told me.

6   A jelly-like, starchy-looking glop resulted from the lye and potatoes, and Shorty broke in the two eggs, stirring real fast—his own conk and dark face bent down close. The congolene turned pale-yellowish. "Feel the jar," Shorty said. I cupped my hand against the outside, and snatched it away. "Damn right, it's hot, that's the lye," he said. "So you know it's going to burn when I comb it in—it burns *bad*. But the longer you can stand it, the straighter the hair."

7   He made me sit down, and he tied the string of the new rubber apron tightly around my neck, and combed up my bush of hair. Then, from the big vaseline jar, he took a handful and massaged it hard all through my hair and into the scalp. He also thickly vaselined my neck, ears and forehead. "When I get to washing out your head, be sure to tell me anywhere you feel any little stinging," Shorty warned me, washing his hands, then pulling on the rubber gloves, and tying on his own rubber apron. "You always got to remember that any congolene left in burns a sore into your head."

8   The congolene just felt warm when Shorty started combing it in. But then my head caught fire.

9   I gritted my teeth and tried to pull the sides of the kitchen table together. The comb felt as if it was raking my skin off.

10   My eyes watered, my nose was running. I couldn't stand it any longer; I bolted to the washbasin. I was cursing Shorty with every name I could think of when he got the spray going and started soap-lathering my head.

11   He lathered and spray-rinsed, lathered and spray-rinsed, maybe ten or twelve times, each time gradually closing the hot-water faucet, until the rinse was cold, and that helped some.

12   "You feel any stinging spots?"

13   "No," I managed to say. My knees were trembling.

14   "Sit back down, then. I think we got it all out okay."

15   The flame came back as Shorty, with a thick towel, started drying my head, rubbing hard. "*Easy, man, easy*" I kept shouting.

16   "The first time's always worst. You get used to it better before long. You took it real good, homeboy. You got a good conk."

17   When Shorty let me stand up and see in the mirror, my hair hung down in limp, damp strings. My scalp still flamed, but not as badly; I could bear it. He draped the towel around my shoulders, over my rubber apron, and began again vaselining my hair.

18   I could feel him combing, straight back, first the big comb, then the fine-tooth one.

19   Then, he was using a razor, very delicately, on the back of my neck. Then, finally, shaping the sideburns.

20   My first view in the mirror blotted out the hurting. I'd seen some pretty conks, but when it's the first time, on your *own* head, the transformation, after the lifetime of kinks, is staggering.

21   The mirror reflected Shorty behind me. We both were grinning and sweating. And on top of my head was this thick, smooth sheen of shining red hair— real red—as straight as any white man's.

22   How ridiculous I was! Stupid enough to stand there simply lost in admiration of my hair now looking "white," reflected in the mirror in Shorty's room. I vowed that I'd never again be without a conk, and I never was for many years.

23   This was my first really big step toward self-degradation: when I endured all of that pain, literally burning my flesh to have it look like a white man's hair.

I had joined that multitude of Negro men and women in America who are brainwashed into believing that the black people are "inferior"—and white people "superior"—that they will even violate and mutilate their God-created bodies to try to look "pretty" by white standards.

cosmetic surgery?

EXERCISES

Some of the Issues

1. What is a conk and why did Malcolm X want it?
2. Why does Malcolm X describe the process of buying the ingredients and of applying them in such detail?
3. What is the thesis of this short selection? With what arguments, information, or assertions does Malcolm X support his thesis?

The Way We Are Told

4. The selection divides into two very different parts. What are they? How do they differ?
5. The main part of the selection is a description of a process. How is it arranged? What qualities of instruction, even of a recipe, does it have? How and where does it differ from a recipe?

Some Subjects for Writing

6. Malcolm X describes a process that shows, among other things, that people will go to great lengths to conform. Develop a short essay describing, in a straightforward, neutral manner, some example of how people will subject themselves to pain, inconvenience, and embarrassment to conform to some fashion or idea.
7. Rewrite your previous essay, but take a strong stand indicating approval or disapproval of the process.
8. Write an essay examining the rewards American society offers for conforming, or the penalties for not conforming.

Goin' Gangsta, Choosin' Cholita: Teens Today "Claim" a Racial Identity

Nell Bernstein

Nell Bernstein, a San Francisco journalist, is an editor at Pacific News Service, and was formerly editor of Youth Outlook!, *a San Francisco journal of teen life. She has written for* Mother Jones, The San Fransisco Bay Guardian, *and the online magazine* Salon. *She has studied and written extensively on children in foster care, and has written a book,* A Rage to Do Better: Listening to Young People from the Foster Care System *(2000). This essay originally appeared in a 1994 issue of* West *magazine, the Sunday supplement to the* San Jose Mercury News.*

In "Goin' Gangsta, Choosin' Cholita," Bernstein describes what she calls the "hybridization" of American teenagers, and explores the idea that among today's teenagers, identity is seen as a choice, not determined by what community, race, or heritage you were born into. For many of the Northern California teens interviewed in this essay, identity is seen as something as changeable as clothing, musical taste, or vocabulary; a lifestyle rather than a birthright.

1   Her lipstick is dark, the lip liner even darker, nearly black. In baggy pants, a blue plaid Pendleton, her bangs pulled back tight off her forehead, 15-year-old April is a perfect cholita, a Mexican gangsta girl.

2   But April Miller is Anglo. "And I don't like it!" she complains. "I'd rather be Mexican."

3   April's father wanders into the family room of their home in San Leandro, California, a suburb near Oakland. "Hey, cholita," he teases. "Go get a suntan. We'll put you in a barrio and see how much you like it."

4   A large, sandy-haired man with "April" tattooed on one arm and "Kelly"—the name of his older daughter—on the other, Miller spent 21 years working in a San Leandro glass factory that shut down and moved to Mexico a couple of years ago. He recently got a job in another factory, but he expects NAFTA to swallow that one, too.

5   "Sooner or later we'll all get nailed," he says. "Just another stab in the back of the American middle class."

6   Later, April gets her revenge: "Hey, Mr. White Man's Last Stand," she teases. "Wait till you see how well I manage my welfare check. You'll be asking me for money."

7   A once almost exclusively white, now increasingly Latin and black working-class suburb, San Leandro borders on predominantly black East Oakland. For decades, the boundary was strictly policed and practically impermeable. In 1970 April Miller's hometown was 97 percent white. By 1990 San Leandro was 65 percent white, 6 percent black, 15 percent Hispanic, and 13 percent Asian or Pacific Islander. With minorities moving into suburbs in growing numbers and cities becoming ever more diverse, the boundary between city and suburb is dissolving, and suburban teenagers are changing with the times.

8   In April's bedroom, her past and present selves lie in layers, the pink walls of girlhood almost obscured, Guns N' Roses and Pearl Jam posters overlaid by rappers Paris and Ice Cube. "I don't have a big enough attitude to be a black girl," says April, explaining her current choice of ethnic identification. What matters is that she thinks the choice is hers. For April and her friends, identity is not a matter of where you come from, what you were born into, what color your skin is. It's what you wear, the music you listen to, the words you use—everything to which you pledge allegiance, no matter how fleetingly.

10   The hybridization of American teens has become talk show fodder, with "wiggers"—white kids who dress and talk "black"—appearing on TV in full gangsta regalia. In Indiana a group of white high school girls raised a national stir when they triggered an imitation race war at their virtually all white high school last fall simply by dressing "black."

11   In many parts of the country, it's television and radio, not neighbors, that introduce teens to the allure of ethnic difference. But in California, which demographers predict will be the first state with no racial majority by the year 2000, the influences are more immediate. The California public schools are the most diverse in the country: 42 percent white, 36 percent Hispanic, 9 percent black, 8 percent Asian.

12   Sometimes young people fight over their differences. Students at virtually any school in the Bay Area can recount the details of at least one "race riot" in which a conflict between individuals escalated into a battle between their clans. More often, though, teens would rather join than fight. Adolescence, after all, is the period when you're most inclined to mimic the power closest at hand, from stealing your older sister's clothes to copying the ruling clique at school.

13   White skaters and Mexican would-be gangbangers listen to gangsta rap and call each other "nigga" as term of endearment; white girls sometimes affect Spanish accents; blond cheerleaders claim Cherokee ancestors.

14   "Claiming" is the central concept here. A Vietnamese teen in Hayward, another Oakland suburb, "claims" Oakland—and by implication blackness—because he lived there as a child. A law-abiding white kid "claims" a Mexican gang he says he hangs with. A brown-skinned girl with a Mexican father and a

white mother "claims" her Mexican side, while her fair-skinned sister "claims" white. The word comes up over and over, as if identity were territory, the self a kind of turf.

15   At a restaurant in a minimall in Hayward, Nicole Huffstutler, 13, sits with her friends and describes herself as "Indian, German, French, Welsh, and, um . . . American": "If somebody says anything like 'Yeah, you're just a peckerwood,' I'll walk up and I'll say 'white pride!' 'Cause I'm proud of my race, and I wouldn't wanna be any other race."

16   "Claiming" white has become a matter of principle for Heather, too, who says she's "sick of the majority looking at us like we're less than them." (Hayward schools were 51 percent white in 1990, down from 77 percent in 1980, and whites are now the minority in many schools.)

17   Asked if she knows that nonwhites have not traditionally been referred to as "the majority" in America, Heather gets exasperated: "I hear that all the time, every day. They say, 'Well, you guys controlled us for many years, and it's time for us to control you.' Every day."

18   When Jennifer Vargas—a small, brown-skinned girl in purple jeans who quietly eats her salad while Heather talks—softly announces that she's "mostly Mexican," she gets in trouble with her friends.

19   "No, you're not!" scolds Heather.

20   "I'm mostly Indian and Mexican," Jennifer continues, flatly. "I'm very little . . . I'm mostly . . ."

21   "Your mom's white!" Nicole reminds her sharply. "She has blond hair."

22   "That's what I mean," Nicole adds. "People think that white is a bad thing. They think that white is a bad race. So she's trying to claim more Mexican than white."

23   "I have very little white in me," Jennifer repeats. "I have mostly my dad's side, 'cause I look like him and stuff. And most of my friends think that me and my brother and sister aren't related, 'cause they look more like my mom."

24   "But you guys are all the same race, you just look different," Nicole insists. She stops eating and frowns. "OK, you're half and half each what your parents have. So you're equal as your brother and sister, you just look different. And you should be proud of what you are—every little piece and bit of what you are. Even if you were Afghan or whatever, you should be proud of it."

25   Will Mosley, Heather's 17-year-old brother, says he and his friends listen to rap groups like Compton's Most Wanted, NWA, and Above the Law because they "sing about life"—that is, what happens in Oakland, Los Angeles, anyplace but where Will is sitting today, an empty Round Table Pizza in a minimall.

26   "No matter what race you are," Will says, "if you live like we do, then that's the kind of music you like."

27   And how do they live?

28   "We don't live bad or anything," Will admits. "We live in a pretty good neighborhood, there's no violence or crime. I was just . . . we're just city people, I guess."

29   Will and his friend Adolfo Garcia, 16, say they've outgrown trying to be something they're not. "When I was 11 or 12," Will says, "I thought I was becoming a big gangsta and stuff. Because I liked that music, and thought it was the coolest, I wanted to become that. I wore big clothes, like you wear in jail. But then I kind of woke up. I looked at myself and thought, 'Who am I trying to be?'"

30   They may have outgrown blatant mimicry, but Will and his friends remain convinced that they can live in a suburban tract house with a well-kept lawn on a tree-lined street in "not a bad neighborhood" and still call themselves "city" people on the basis of musical tastes. "City" for these young people means crime, graffiti, drugs. The kids are law-abiding, but these activities connote what Will admiringly calls "action." With pride in his voice, Will predicts that "in a couple of years, Hayward will be like Oakland. It's starting to get more known, because of crime and things. I think it'll be bigger, more things happening, more crime, more graffiti, stealing cars."

31   "That's good," chimes in 15-year-old Matt Jenkins whose new beeper—an item that once connoted gangsta chic but now means little more than an active social life—goes off periodically. "More fun."

32   The three young men imagine with disdain life in a gangsta-free zone. "Too bland, too boring," Adolfo says. "You have to have something going on. You can't just have everyday life."

33   "Mowing your lawn," Matt sneers.

34   "Like Beaver Cleaver's house," Adolfo adds. "It's too clean out here."

35   Not only white kids believe that identity is a matter of choice or taste, or that the power of "claiming" can transcend ethnicity. The Manor Park Locos—a group of mostly Mexican-Americans who hang out in San Leandro's Manor Park—say they descend from the Manor Lords, tough white guys who ruled the neighborhood a generation ago.

36   They "are like our . . . uncles and dads, the older generation," says Jesse Martinez, 14. "We're what they were when they were around, except we're Mexican."

37   "There's three generations," says Oso, Jesse's younger brother. "There's Manor Lords, Manor Park Locos, and Manor Park Pee Wees." The Pee Wees consist mainly of the Locos' younger brothers, eager kids who circle the older boys on bikes and brag about "punking people."

38   Unlike Will Mosley, the Locos find little glamour in city life. They survey the changing suburban landscape and see not "action" or "more fun" but frightening decline. Though most of them are not yet 18, the Locos are already nostalgic, longing for a Beaver Cleaver past that white kids who mimic them would scoff at.

39   Walking through nearly empty Manor Park, with its eucalyptus stands, its softball diamond and tennis courts, Jesse's friend Alex, the only Asian in the group, waves his arms in a gesture of futility. "A few years ago, every bench was filled," he says. "Now no one comes here. I guess it's because of everything that's going on. My parents paid a lot for this house, and I want it to be nice for them. I just hope this doesn't turn into Oakland."

40   Glancing across the park at April Miller's street, Jesse says he knows what the white cholitas are about. "It's not a racial thing," he explains. "It's just all the most popular people out here are Mexican. We're just the gangstas that everyone knows. I guess those girls wanna be known."

41   Not every young Californian embraces the new racial hybridism. Andrea Jones, 20, an African-American who grew up in the Bay Area suburbs of Union City and Hayward, is unimpressed by what she sees mainly as shallow mimicry. "It's full of posers out here," she says. "When *Boyz N the Hood* came out on video, it was sold out for weeks. The boys all wanna be black, the girls all wanna be Mexican. It's the glamour."

42   Driving down the quiet, shaded streets of her old neighborhood in Union City, Andrea spots two white preteen boys in Raiders jackets and hugely baggy pants strutting erratically down the empty sidewalk. "Look at them," she says. "Dislocated."

43   She knows why. "In a lot of these schools out here, it's hard being white," she says. "I don't think these kids were prepared for the backlash that is going on, all the pride now in people of color's ethnicity, and our boldness with it. They have nothing like that, no identity, nothing they can say they're proud of.

44   "So they latch onto their great-grandmother who's a Cherokee, or they take on the most stereotypical aspects of being black or Mexican. It's beautiful to appreciate different aspects of other people's culture—that's like the dream of what the 21st century should be. But to garnish yourself with pop culture stereotypes just to blend—that's really sad."

45   Roland Krevocheza, 18, graduated last year from Arroyo High School in San Leandro. He is Mexican on his mother's side, Eastern European on his father's. In the new hierarchies, it may be mixed kids like Roland who have the hardest time finding their place, even as their numbers grow. (One in five marriages in California is between people of different races.) They can always be called "wannabes," no matter what they claim.

46   "I'll state all my nationalities," Roland says. But he takes a greater interest in his father's side, his Ukrainian, Romanian, and Czech ancestors. "It's more unique," he explains. "Mexican culture is all around me. We eat Mexican food all the time, I hear stories from my grandmother. I see the low-riders and stuff. I'm already part of it. I'm not trying to be; I am."

47   His darker-skinned brother "says he's not proud to be white," Roland adds. "He calls me 'Mr. Nazi.'" In the room the two share, the American flags and the reproduction of the Bill of Rights are Roland's; the Public Enemy poster belongs to his brother.

48   Roland has good reason to mistrust gangsta attitudes. In his junior year in high school, he was one of several Arroyo students who were beaten up outside the school at lunchtime by a group of Samoans who came in cars from Oakland. Roland wound up with a split lip, a concussion, and a broken tailbone. Later he was told that the assault was "gang-related"—that the Samoans were beating up anyone wearing red.

49   "Rappers, I don't like them," Roland says. "I think they're a bad influence on kids. It makes kids think they're all tough and bad."

50   Those who, like Roland, dismiss the gangsta and cholo styles as affectations can point to the fact that several companies market overpriced knockoffs of "ghetto wear" targeted at teens.

51   But there's also something going on out here that transcends adolescent faddishness and pop culture exoticism. When white kids call their parents "racist" for nagging them about their baggy pants; when they learn Spanish to talk to their boyfriends; when Mexican-American boys feel themselves descended in spirit from white "uncles"; when children of mixed marriages insist that they are whatever race they say they are, all of them are more than just confused.

52   They're inching toward what Andrea Jones calls "the dream of what the 21st century should be." In the ever more diverse communities of Northern California, they're also facing the complicated reality of what their 21st century will be.

53   Meanwhile, in the living room of the Miller family's San Leandro home, the argument continues unabated. "You don't know what you are," April's father has told her more than once. But she just keeps on telling him he doesn't know what time it is.

EXERCISES

Some of the Issues

1. Paragraphs 1 through 9 describe April Miller's choice of identity. Given what you know about April's life, why do you think she makes the choice she does? Do you think her reasons are valid?
2. What is April's father's reaction to her choice? What might account for the differences in their feelings?
3. What are the demographic changes the author describes in paragraphs 7, 11, and 16? How might these changes affect people's attitudes toward race and identity?
4. What does the author say about power in paragraph 12? How does her analysis relate to other ideas presented in the article?
5. Paragraphs 10 through 14 give other examples of teenagers "claiming" new racial or ethnic identities. Who claims what and why? How can "claiming" cause conflict?
6. Examine the discussion between Nicole, Heather, and Jennifer about claiming (paragraphs 15 through 24). On what basis does each young woman make her claim?
7. Paragraphs 25 through 34 recount the discussion between Heather's older brother and his friends about identity. How might you account for their attitudes? What is your reaction to them?

8. Paragraphs 35 through 40 look at "claiming" through the eyes of a group of young Mexican-Americans, Jesse and the others in "The Manor Park Locos." Compare and contrast their attitudes with those of the other teenagers in the essay. What is Jesse's explanation for white cholitas like April Miller?

9. Why is Andrea Jones critical (paragraphs 41 through 44)? Do you agree with her analysis?

10. Paragraphs 45 through 50 examine the views of Roland Krevocheza and his brother. How do they define themselves and why?

11. After examining the varying views of the Californians in Bernstein's article, do you agree with her that "there's something also going on here that transcends adolescent faddishness and pop culture exoticism"?

12. Do you see the changes Bernstein describes in your own part of the country? If so, describe what you think is happening.

13. Do you think April and her friends are inching toward "the dream of what the 21st century should be" (paragraphs 44 and 52)? Why or why not?

The Way We Are Told

14. Why do you think the author chose to begin and end with the story of April Miller and her father?

15. How does Bernstein use the various quotes and dialog to present different but often related perspectives?

16. What do you feel is the author's opinion of the teenagers she describes? How do you draw your conclusions?

Some Subjects for Writing

17. Choose one of the persons quoted in this article. Write a letter to that person either agreeing or disagreeing with the views he or she expresses and explaining why.

18. Each one of us chooses some aspects of our personalities to emphasize and present to the world as more "real" than others. Discuss your choice of clothes, music, and behavior. What do you want these choices to say about you and your character? If your ideas about your identity have changed over time, explain how and why.

19. Taking into consideration some of the issues brought up in the article, interview a group of teenagers about their views on identity. Develop a series of question beforehand and ask follow-up questions during the interview. You will probably want to use a tape recorder. Then, write an essay in which you analyze the opinions of the teenagers you interviewed.

Three Thousand Dollar Death Song

Wendy Rose

Wendy Rose, of Hopi and Miwok ancestry, was born in Oakland, California, in 1948. She received B.A. and M.A. degrees from the University of California at Berkeley. A visual artist, poet, and anthropologist, she is a frequent contributor of articles to anthologies and journals. She has published several volumes of poetry, including Going to War with All My Relations *(1993),* Bone Dance *(1994), and* Now Poof She Is Gone *(1994). Rose writes of herself, "I have often been identified as a 'protest poet' and although something in me frowns a little at being so neatly categorized, that is largely the truth."*

In the following poem, taken from Lost Copper *(1980), Rose examines the cost incurred, both material and spiritual, when museums collect and display Native American mummies, skeletons, artifacts, and sacred objects. For many of Native American ancestry, the exhibiting of these remains is a continued source of pain and disrespect. In recent years, Native activists and other groups have demanded that museums return bones for reburial; in 1990 a federal law took effect requiring the return of these items to the tribe or association.*

> *"Nineteen American Indian Skeletons from Nevada . . . valued at $3,000 . . ."*
> —Museum invoice, 1975

Is it in cold hard cash? the kind
that dusts the insides of mens' pockets
lying silver-polished surface along the cloth.
Or in bills? papering the wallets of they
5   who thread the night with dark words. Or
checks? paper promises weighing the same
as words spoken once on the other side
of the grown grass and dammed rivers
of history. However it goes, it goes.
10   Through my body it goes
assessing each nerve, running its edges
along my arteries, planning ahead
for whose hands will rip me

15   into pieces of dusty red paper,
      whose hands will smooth or smatter me
      into traces of rubble. Invoiced now,
      it's official how our bones are valued
      that stretch out pointing to sunrise
      or are flexed into one last foetal bend,
20   that are removed and tossed about,
      catalogued, numbered with black ink
      on newly-white foreheads.
      As we were formed to the white soldier's voice,
      so we explode under white students' hands.
25   Death is a long trail of days
      in our fleshless prison.

      From this distant point we watch our bones
      auctioned with our careful beadwork,
      our quilled medicine bundles, even the bridles
30   of our shot-down horses. You: who have
      priced us, you who have removed us: at what cost?
      What price the pits where our bones share
      a single bit of memory, how one century
      turns our dead into specimens, our history
35   into dust, our survivors into clowns.
      Our memory might be catching, you know;
      picture the mortars, the arrowheads, the labrets[1]
      shaking off their labels like bears
      suddenly awake to find the seasons have ended
40   while they slept. Watch them touch each other,
      measure reality, march out the museum door!
      Watch as they lift their faces
      and smell about for us; watch our bones rise
      to meet them and mount the horses once again!
45   The cost, then, will be paid
      for our sweetgrass-smelling having-been
      in clam shell beads and steatite,
      dentalia[2] and woodpecker scalp, turquoise
      and copper, blood and oil, coal
50   and uranium, children, a universe
      of stolen things.

[1]*Labrets* are ornaments of wood or bone worn in a hole pierced through the lip.
[2]*Dentalia* refers to any marine mollusk resembling a tooth.

EXERCISES

Some of the Issues

1. How does Rose contrast the value of the skeletons to Native Americans with their value to others?
2. How does Rose describe the museum's physical treatment of Native American skeletons and cultural artifacts? How is that treatment symbolic of the treatment of Native American people?
3. Beginning in line 36, Rose describes a fantasy in which the bones will rise. What does she imagine them doing?
4. The word "cost" occurs several times in the poem. How does its meaning change throughout the poem?
5. Look at the list of "stolen things" at the end of the poem. In what order are items placed? Why?
6. How might museum officials justify a display of Native American skeletons and traditional art on the basis of its educational value?

Some Subjects for Writing

7. Write about an object that has meaning to you aside from its monetary value. What is its history and what makes it valuable to you?
*8. In "On Seeing England for the First Time," Jamaica Kincaid writes of being immersed in the culture of a colonial power while her own culture was ignored. Consider the case of a Native American child growing up in America. Would that child's experience be similar or dissimilar to Kincaid's? In what ways?

PART V

AMERICAN ENCOUNTERS

O ur lives and identities are shaped by encounters with people, places and cultures. For better or worse, our most formative experiences can come from the challenges posed by our interactions with and reactions to that which is unfamiliar to us. In this chapter, writers explore how specific encounters have shaped their lives and ideas. Their encounters force them to question their assumptions and to confront other people's assumptions about them.

For immigrants to America, their move to the United States can be one of their most transformative encounters. In "Walking in Lucky Shoes" Bette Bao Lord reflects on her positive (or lucky) feelings about her own encounters in the United States, while lamenting the fact that racism and bigotry are still the source of negative encounters for many here in America. Ultimately, she poses the question that Michel Guillaume St. Jean de Crèvecoeur asked two hundred years earlier: "What is an American?" but comes up with a more conflicted and complicated answer. Crèvecoeur had come as a young man to the "New World" and settled in the French colony of Louisiana. In his *Letters from an American Farmer* (1782), he defines the new creature, the American, as different in any number of ways from his classbound, traditional European ancestors. In defining "What is an American?" Crèvecoeur celebrates the creation of what he views as an almost classless society, in which persons can reach whatever position in life their abilities allow. A modern, and much lighter, view of what America "means" is found in the selection called "Recapture the Flag: 34 Reasons to Love America," a series of statements that demonstrate the variety of ways people define what is American.

We all know by the time we reach our teens, and sometimes much sooner, that difference is often viewed as threatening. Through ignorance and fear of the unknown, our worst selves can emerge. Brent Staples, a tall African-American man, becomes a fearsome entity with whom pedestrians avoid making eye contact. Piri Thomas recalls being on "Alien Turf"—the new kid, a Puerto Rican—in an Italian neighborhood. Walter White describes how his family's house became a target of a mob during a race riot in Atlanta early in this century.

In "Black Like Them" Malcolm Gladwell compares the lives of African-Americans and West Indian black immigrants to the United States. How does each group define itself? How are their encounters with the white majority different? In a complex essay, Galdwell uses his own family history and the work of scholars to reflect on the kinds of racism experienced by both groups. Jeanne Wakatsuki Houston, with her husband, records her own experience in a historical event: the internment of Japanese-Americans on the West Coast at the beginning of World War II. Likewise, in the poem at the end of the unit, Dwight Okita recalls the irrational fears foisted on other Americans to justify the Japanese-American relocation policy.

Walking in Lucky Shoes

Bette Bao Lord

Bette Bao Lord was born on November 3, 1938, in Shanghai, China, where her father worked as an official of the Nationalist Chinese government. She immigrated to the United States in 1946, attended Tufts University, and completed a law degree at Fletcher School of Law and Diplomacy in 1960.

Lord was awarded the American Book Award for her first novel, Spring Moon *(1982). She originally planned the book as a nonfiction account of her 1973 journey to China. However, fearing that her family in China might suffer reprisals from leaders of the Cultural Revolution, she decided to write a historical novel instead. The novel chronicles five generations of the Chang family, whose lives witness the eradication of the traditional Chinese family structure and the disappearance of the upper-middle class. Lord is also the author of a memoir,* Legacies: A Chinese Mosaic *(1990) and another novel,* The Middle Heart *(1996).*

In the following Newsweek *guest editorial "My Turn," Lord emphasizes that multiculturalism is a national strength that has the potential both to make us proud of our diverse ancestries and to bind us together. She believes Americans can be different as individuals, but all members of the same family.*

1   I confess, novelists have a fetish. We can't resist shoes. Indeed, we spend our lives recalling the pairs we have shed and snatching others off unsuspecting souls. We're not proud. We're not particular. Whether it's Air Jordans or the clodhoppers of Frankenstein, Imelda's[1] gross collection or one glass slipper, we covet them all. There's no cure for this affliction. To create characters, we must traipse around and around in our heads sporting lost or stolen shoes.

2   At 8, I sailed for America from Shanghai without a passing acquaintance of A, B or C, wearing scruffy brown oxfords. Little did I know then that they were as magical as those glittering red pumps that propelled Dorothy down the yellow brick road.

3   Only yesterday, it seems, resting my chin on the rails of the SS Marylinx, I peered into the mist for *Mei Guo*, Beautiful Country. It refused to appear. Then, in a blink, there was the Golden Gate,[2] more like the portals to Heaven than the arches of a man-made bridge.

---

[1]Imelda Marcos, wife of former president/dictator of the Philippines, famous for her enormous shoe collection.

[2]Long bridge at the entrance to San Francisco Bay.

4   Only yesterday, standing at PS 8[3] in Brooklyn, I was bewitched—others, alas, were bothered and bewildered—when I proclaimed:

> I pledge a lesson to the frog of
>   the United States of America.
> And to the wee puppet for witch's hands.
>   One Asian, in the vestibule,
> with little tea and just rice for all.

5   Although I mangled the language, the message was not lost. Not on someone wearing immigrant shoes.

6   Only yesterday, rounding third base in galoshes, I swallowed a barrelful of tears wondering what wrong I had committed to anger my teammates so. Why were they all madly screaming at me to go home, go home?

7   Only yesterday, listening in pink cotton mules to Red Barber broadcasting from Ebbetts Field, I vaulted over the Milky Way as my hero, Jackie Robinson, stole home.

8   Only yesterday, enduring the pinch of new Mary Janes at my grammar-school graduation, I felt as tall as the Statue of Liberty, reciting Walt Whitman:[4] "I hear America singing, the varied carols I hear . . . Each singing what belongs to him or her and to none else. . . ."

9   Today I cherish every unstylish pair of shoes that took me up a road cleared by the footfalls of millions of immigrants before me—to a room of my own. For America has granted me many a dream, even one that I never dared to dream—returning to the land of my birth in 1989 as the wife of the American ambassador. Citizens of Beijing were astounded to see that I was not a *yang guei ze*, foreign devil, with a tall nose and ghostly skin and bumpy hair colored in outlandish hues. I looked Chinese, I spoke Chinese, and after being in my company they accused me of being a fake, of being just another member of the clan.

10   I do not believe that the loss of one's native culture is the price one must pay for becoming an American. On the contrary, I feel doubly blessed. I can choose from two rich cultures those parts that suit my mood or the occasion best. And unbelievable as it may seem, shoes tinted red, white and blue go dandy with them all.

11   Recently I spoke at my alma mater. There were many more Asian faces in that one audience than there were enrolled at Tufts University when I cavorted in white suede shoes to cheer the Jumbos to victory. One asked, "Will you tell us about your encounters with racial prejudice?" I had no ready answers. I thought hard. Sure, I had been roughed up at school. Sure, I had failed at work. Sure, I had at times felt powerless. But had prejudice against the shade of my skin and the shape of my eyes caused these woes? Unable to show off the wounds I had

---

[3]Public schools in New York City are designated by number.
[4](1819–92) American poet whose work celebrated both individual worth and human diversity.

endured at the hands of racists, I could only cite a scene from my husband's 25th reunion at Yale eight years ago. Throughout that weekend, I sensed I was being watched. But even after the tall, burly man finally introduced himself, I did not recognize his face or name. He hemmed and hawed, then announced that he had flown from Colorado to apologize to me. I could not imagine why. Apparently at a party in the early '60s, he had hectored me to cease dating his WASP[5] classmate.

12   Someone else at Tufts asked, "How do you think of yourself? As a Chinese or as an American?" Without thinking, I blurted out the truth: "Bette Bao Lord." Did I imagine the collective sigh of relief that swept through the auditorium? I think not. Perhaps I am the exception that proves the rule. Perhaps I am blind to insult and injury. Perhaps I am not alone. No doubt I have been lucky. Others have not been as fortunate. They had little choice but to wear ill-fitting shoes warped by prejudice, to start down a less traveled road strewn with broken promises and littered with regrets, haunted by racism and awash with tears. Where could that road possibly lead? Nowhere but to a nation, divided, without liberty and no justice at all.

13   The Berlin wall[6] is down, but between East Harlem and West Hempstead, between the huddled masses of yesterday and today, the walls go up and up. Has the cold war ended abroad only to usher in heated racial and tribal conflicts at home? No, I believe we shall overcome. But only when:

14   We engage our diversity to yield a nation greater than the sum of its parts.

15   We can be different as sisters and brothers are, and belong to the same family.

16   We bless, not shame, America, our home.

17   A home, no doubt, where skeletons nest in closets and the roof leaks, where foundations must be shored and rooms added. But a home where legacies conceived by the forefathers are tendered from generation to generation to have and to hold. Legacies not of gold but as intangible and inalienable and invaluable as laughter and hope.

18   We the people can do just that—if we clear the smoke of ethnic chauvinism and fears by braving our journey to that "City Upon a Hill" in each other's shoes.

EXERCISES

Some of the Issues

1. How do you characterize Lord's attitude and emotions toward America?
2. In paragraph 9, why did the Chinese accuse her of being a "a fake"? What point does she make by mentioning this experience?

---

[5]White Anglo-Saxon Protestant.
[6]Built in 1961, it separated East and West Berlin until it was torn down in 1989.

3. In paragraph 11, what is significant about the man from Colorado's apology to her at her husband's 25th Yale reunion?
4. After she blurts out her name in the auditorium at Tufts University (paragraph 12) she perceives a "collective sigh of relief" from the audience. Why?

The Way We Are Told

5. The essay is structured chronologically. What stylistic device does Lord use to mark time transitions?
6. In paragraph 1, Lord introduces the shoe metaphor and then intersperses literal and figurative examples of shoes throughout the essay. Select instances of each use and show how they contribute to the thesis.
7. Give examples of Lord's uses of humor in paragraphs 4 through 6. Do you find them funny? Believable?

Some Subjects for Writing

8. In your opinion, is Lord simply "walking in lucky shoes"? What role does luck play in her life? What other factors may have contributed to her success?
9. In the final paragraph, Lord is optimistic that Americans will overcome racial conflicts. Are you hopeful that this will be accomplished in the near future? Why or why not?

What Is an American?

Michel Guillaume St. Jean de Crèvecoeur

Michel Guillaume St. Jean de Crèvecoeur (1735–1813) came as a young man to the New World, settling at first in the French colony of Louisiane, which at that time stretched in a huge arc from the mouth of the St. Lawrence River in the north to the mouth of the Mississippi in the south. In the Seven Years War (1756–63), called the French and Indian Wars in America, he fought under Montcalm against the British. When the colonies passed into British hands, he remained and settled as a farmer in Vermont. The Revolutionary War found him on the side of the loyalists. Crèvecoeur returned to France permanently in 1790. His Letters from an American Farmer, *written in French, was published in 1782 and is among the earliest descriptions of life in America.*

Crèvecoeur defines and describes what he sees as the virtues and advantages America possesses as compared to the Europe of his day. He sees a prosperous agricultural society, virtually classless, in which persons can reach whatever position in life their abilities allow. He contrasts this to the Old World with its ingrained class structure, where a man (or woman) is born to wealth and high status or to poverty and lifelong drudgery, with no way to escape. He sees America as a young, mobile society in contrast to the static world from which the new man, the American, has made his escape.

1   I wish I could be acquainted with the feelings and thoughts which must agitate the heart and present themselves to the mind of an enlightened Englishman, when he first lands on this continent. He must greatly rejoice, that he lived at a time to see this fair country discovered and settled; he must necessarily feel a share of national pride, when he views the chain of settlements which embellishes these extended shores. When he says to himself, this is the work of my countrymen, who, when convulsed by factions, afflicted by a variety of miseries and wants, restless and impatient, took refuge here. They brought along with them their national genius, to which they principally owe what liberty they enjoy, and what substance they possess. Here he sees the industry of his native country, displayed in a new manner, and traces in their works the embryos of all the arts, sciences, and ingenuity which flourish in Europe. Here he beholds fair cities, substantial villages, extensive fields, an immense country filled with decent houses, good roads, orchards, meadows, and bridges, where an hundred years ago all was wild, woody, and uncultivated!

2   What a train of pleasing ideas this fair spectacle must suggest! It is a prospect which must inspire a good citizen with the most heartfelt pleasure.

The difficulty consists in the manner of viewing so extensive a scene. He is arrived on a new continent; a modern society offers itself to his contemplation, different from what he had hitherto seen. It is not composed, as in Europe, of great lords who possess every thing, and of a herd of people who have nothing. Here are no aristocratical families, no courts, no kings, no bishops, no ecclesiastical dominion, no invisible power giving to a few a very visible one; no great manufacturers employing thousands, no great refinements of luxury. The rich and the poor are not so far removed from each other as they are in Europe.

3   Some few towns excepted, we are all tillers of the earth, from Nova Scotia to West Florida. We are a people of cultivators, scattered over an immense territory, communicating with each other by means of good roads and navigable rivers, united by the silken bands of mild government, all respecting the laws without dreading their power, because they are equitable. We are all animated with the spirit of industry, which is unfettered, and unrestrained, because each person works for himself. If he travels through our rural districts, he views not the hostile castle, and the haughty mansion, contrasted with the clay-built hut and miserable cabin, where cattle and men help to keep each other warm, and dwell in meanness, smoke, and indigence. A pleasing uniformity of decent competence appears throughout our habitations. The meanest of our log-houses is a dry and comfortable habitation. Lawyer or merchant are the fairest titles our towns afford; that of a farmer is the only appellation of the rural inhabitants of our country. It must take some time ere he can reconcile himself to our dictionary, which is but short in words of dignity, and names of honour. There, on a Sunday, he sees a congregation of respectable farmers and their wives, all clad in neat homespun, well mounted, or riding in their own humble waggons. There is not among them an esquire, saving the unlettered magistrate. There he sees a parson as simple as his flock, a farmer who does not riot on the labour of others. We have no princes, for whom we toil, starve, and bleed: we are the most perfect society now existing in the world. Here man is free as he ought to be; nor is this pleasing equality so transitory as many others are. Many ages will not see the shores of our great lakes replenished with inland nations, nor the unknown bounds of North America entirely peopled. Who can tell how far it extends? Who can tell the millions of men whom it will feed and contain? for no European foot has as yet travelled half the extent of this mighty continent?

4   The next wish of this traveller will be to know whence came all these people? They are a mixture of English, Scotch, Irish, Dutch, Germans, and Swedes. From this promiscuous breed, the race now called Americans have arisen. The eastern provinces must indeed be excepted, as being the unmixed descendants of Englishmen. I have heard many wish they had been more intermixed also: for my part, I am no wisher; and think it much better as it has happened. They exhibit a most conspicuous figure in this great and variegated picture; they too enter for a great share in the pleasing perspective displayed in these thirteen provinces. I know it is fashionable to reflect on them; but I respect them for

what they have done; for the accuracy and wisdom with which they have settled their territory; for the decency of their manners; for their early love of letters; their ancient college, the first in this hemisphere; for their industry, which to me, who am but a farmer, is the criterion of every thing. There never was a people, situated as they are, who, with so ungrateful a soil, have done more in so short a time. Do you think that the monarchical ingredients which are more prevalent in other governments, have purged them from all foul stains? Their histories assert the contrary.

5   In this great American asylum, the poor of Europe have by some means met together, and in consequence of various causes; to what purpose should they ask one another, what countrymen they are? Alas, two thirds of them had no country. Can a wretch who wanders about, who works and starves, whose life is a continual scene of sore affliction of pinching penury; can that man call England or any other kingdom his country? A country that had no bread for him, whose fields procured him no harvest, who met with nothing but the frowns of the rich, the severity of the laws, with jails and punishments; who owned not a single foot of the extensive surface of this planet? No! Urged by a variety of motives, here they came. Everything has tended to regenerate them; new laws, a new mode of living, a new social system; here they are become men: in Europe they were as so many useless plants, wanting vegetative mould, and refreshing showers; they withered, and were mowed down by want, hunger, and war: but now, by the power of transplantation, like all other plants, they have taken root and flourished! Formerly they were not numbered in any civil list of their country, except in those of the poor; here they rank as citizens. By what invisible power has this surprizing metamorphosis been performed? By that of the laws and that of their industry. The laws, the indulgent laws, protect them as they arrive, stamping on them the symbol of adoption; they receive ample rewards for their labours; these accumulated rewards procure them lands; those lands confer on them the title of freemen; and to that title every benefit is affixed which men can possibly require. This is the great operation daily performed by our laws. From whence proceed these laws? From our government. Whence that government? It is derived from the original genius and strong desire of the people, ratified and confirmed by government. This is the great chain which links us all, this is the picture which every province exhibits.

6   What attachment can a poor European emigrant have for a country where he had nothing? The knowledge of the language, the love of a few kindred as poor as himself, were the only cords that tied him: his country is now that which gives him land, bread, protection, and consequence: *Ubi panis ibi patria*,[1] is the motto of all emigrants. What then is the American, this new man? He is either an European, or the descendant of an European; hence that strange mixture of

---

[1] Where bread is, there is my country.

blood, which you will find in no other country. I could point out to you a man, whose grandfather was an Englishman, whose wife was Dutch, whose son married a French woman, and whose present four sons have now four wives of different nations. *He* is an American, who, leaving behind him all his ancient prejudices and manners, receives new ones from the new mode of life he has embraced, the new government he obeys, and the new rank he holds. He becomes an American by being received in the broad lap of our great *Alma Mater.*

7   Here individuals of all nations are melted into a new race of men, whose labours and posterity will one day cause great change in the world. Americans are the western pilgrims, who are carrying along with them that great mass of arts, sciences, vigour, and industry, which began long since in the east; they will finish the great circle. The Americans were once scattered all over Europe; here they are incorporated into one of the finest systems of population which has ever appeared, and which will hereafter become distinct by the power of the different climates they inhabit. The American ought, therefore, to love this country much better than that wherein either he or his forefathers were born. Here the rewards of his industry follow with equal steps the progress of his labour; his labour is founded on the basis of nature, *self-interest*; can it want a stronger allurement? Wives and children, who before in vain demanded of him a morsel of bread, now, fat and frolicsome, gladly help their father to clear those fields whence exuberant crops are to arise to feed and to clothe them all; without any part being claimed, either by a despotic prince, a rich abbot, or a mighty lord. Here religion demands but little of him; a small voluntary salary to the minister, and gratitude to God; can he refuse these? The American is a new man, who acts upon new principles; he must therefore entertain new ideas, and form new opinions. From involuntary idleness, servile dependence, penury, and useless labour, he has passed to toils of a very different nature, rewarded by ample subsistence.—This is an American.

EXERCISES

Some of the Issues

1. Why should the "enlightened Englishman" rejoice at landing in America?
2. What is the central idea of the second paragraph? How does it relate to the first? How does it carry Crèvecoeur's ideas beyond the first paragraph?
3. Consider the last sentence in paragraph 2 and explain how it is expanded on in paragraph 3.
4. Paragraph 3 makes its point by means of contrasts. What are they?
5. Paragraphs 4 and 5 classify the people who came to America, but in two different ways. Paragraph 4 discusses national origins. How are Americans described in paragraph 5?

6. In paragraphs 6 and 7 Crèvecoeur asserts that these diverse Europeans are "melted into a new race of men"—Americans. How does that process take place? (Note the word "melted.")
7. Make a list of the contrasts Crèvecoeur makes or clearly implies between Europe and America. Then attempt to organize and classify them into major groupings.

The Way We Are Told

8. Why does Crèvecoeur create the character of the "enlightened Englishman" to report on America in paragraph 1, instead of continuing to use the first person singular, as he does in the opening sentence?
9. Crèvecoeur tries to convince the reader of the superiority of Americans and their institutions. Who, would you say, are his readers? What are their likely beliefs? How does Crèvecoeur respond to these beliefs?
10. Crèvecoeur uses rhetorical questions, exclamations, and repetition of words and phrases to strengthen his case. Find examples of each.

Some Subjects for Writing

11. Write an essay in praise of some institution that you admire. Select those aspects that seem important to you, organize them in some logical order, and write your description, stressing the favorable facts rather than giving your opinions.
12. Crèvecoeur presents the American as an ideal "new man," free of the shackles of history imposed on him in Europe. In an essay examine the extent to which the American can still be described in Crèvecoeur's terms today.
13. Crèvecoeur may have been the first to use the word *melt* to describe the fusion of people of different nationalities into a new "race of men"—Americans. The term *melting pot* has become a cliché representing that process. More recently some observers have cast doubts on the extent of that process and preferred the analogy of the salad bowl or mosaic to the melting pot. What are the implications of each of these terms? Write an essay discussing what term you might use to describe America and why.

Recapture the Flag: 34 Reasons to Love America

This list was selected from a longer one that appeared in the Minneapolis/ St. Paul alternative weekly newspaper City Pages *on the day before Independence Day, July 3, 1991. Some of the items on the list might be considered traditional, whereas others are quite unconventional; together they attempt to capture the American mosaic.*

1. The hometown team on a winning streak
2. Pancakes (not crepes)
3. *Roe v. Wade*
4. Thurgood Marshall
5. American cranks—quirky thinkers with transformative visions: Gertrude Stein, William Burroughs, Howlin' Wolf, Henry Thoreau, R. Crumb, Charlie Parker, Abbie Hoffman, Charlotte Perkins Gilman, Lester Bangs, Jill Johnston, Dorothy Parker, Emma Goldman, Hunter S. Thompson, Josephine Baker, Walt Whitman, Lenny Bruce
6. Corn on the cob
7. The idea of the road as a place to reinvent yourself, a train of thought running from Robert Johnson through Kerouac to *Thelma & Louise*
8. Cool, dark bars where the bartender knows your name
9. Computer hackers
10. Dairy Queen
11. Soul food, po' boy sandwiches: Cuisine made from the cheap and unwanted
12. Elvis Presley. He had to invent himself first, because what he chased after—an amped-up fusion of black and white musics with deep, surreptitious roots—wasn't supposed to exist at all. When Elvis happened, the pitched reaction didn't portend only rock & roll; it foreshadowed a chain of events from the Selma marches to the Reagan backlash
13. Pioneers of social frontiers: Jackie Robinson, Queer Nation, AIM, Malcolm X, Angela Davis, Harriet Tubman, the Radical Faeries, Betty Friedan, Sojourner Truth, C.O.Y.O.T.E., Elizabeth Cady Stanton, Martin Luther King Jr.
14. The front porch or stoop: Gossip, swings, neighbor-spying, gin & tonics

15. The way immigration transforms the nation's eating habits: Wieners, potatoes, pizza, chow mein, spaghetti, tacos, egg rolls, curry, mock duck, pad thai

16. The phenomenal growth of popular literature written by women over the last 30 years: Adrienne Rich, Anne Tyler, Marge Piercy, Toni Morrison, Ursula LeGuin, Alice Hoffman, Maxine Hong Kingston, Audre Lorde, Gloria Naylor, Amy Tan, Kaye Gibbons, Louise Erdrich, Terry McMillan, Alice Walker, etc., etc., etc.

17. People who don't force you to love America

18. Blues, gospel, country & western, jazz, rock, bluegrass, soul, disco, rap, zydeco . . . strains from different cultures tossed together on the long, long road from Memphis to Chicago, Abilene to Hoboken, Detroit to L.A.

19. The land

20. Roadside diners with biscuits and gravy and bottomless glasses of iced tea

21. The richness of speech as you cross from state to state, region to region, sometimes city block to city block

22. All the highways in the Great Plains that curve into extravagant, sprawling space

23. The desperate courage of AIDS activists in the 1980s

24. Louis Armstrong, William Faulkner, Duke Ellington, Billie Holiday, Raymond Chandler, Ray Charles, John Ford and John Wayne, Alfred Stieglitz, Georgia O'Keeffe, Flannery O'Connor, Jimmie Rodgers, Aretha Franklin, Babe Ruth, Hank Williams, Muddy Waters, Robert Frank, Allen Ginsberg, Ishmael Reed, James Brown, Orson Welles, Jackson Pollock: While too much of white America still looked nervously to Europe, they helped shape a culture of breathtaking scope, vibrancy, and vulgar energy

25. Michael Jordan

26. The Vietnam War Memorial, for the lesson it takes to heart: Its egalitarianism, the air of loss, the way it ennobles war deaths without glorifying them

27. The verse of Woody Guthrie's "This Land Is Your Land" that most people never heard, which captured the spirit of the whole song: "Was a big high wall there that tried to stop me/A sign was painted said: Private Property/But on the back side it didn't say nothing/This land was made for you and me"

28. James Baldwin, the best thinker on race in the second half of this century, maybe the best essayist of his age, period: the writer most committed to working out his horrific ambivalence toward his motherland: America, not Africa

29. Earth First!

30. The Ramones: At a time when American rock & roll was becoming unbearably ponderous (Eagles, America, Jackson Browne), they melded '60s girl-group singing with Bay City Rollers pop chants, surf licks, and MC5 buzzsaw guitars, to create a whole new genre—cartoon rock. Gabba gabba hey

31. All-night grocery stores

32. Roadside monuments: Driving down the highway you spot something unusual on the horizon. It doesn't look like a tree exactly; it's definitely not a billboard. As you get closer, you figure it out—a 30-foot-high talking cow

33. Backyard barbecues: Swat the flies. Drop a burger in the dirt. Serve it anyway

34. Avon ladies, door-to-door encyclopedia salesmen, and Mary Kay pink Cadillacs

EXERCISES

Some of the Issues

1. Say which reasons are your favorites and why.
2. The title states that these are reasons to "love" America. Not everyone would agree that all 34 are positive qualities. What do you think?
3. Many of the people, places and things listed in this essay may be unfamiliar to you. Gather in groups of four or five and share your knowledge of who and what they are. Divide up those that are still unknown and use the Internet to look them up. Share your findings in the next class.

The Way We Are Told

4. What can you infer about the composers of this list? What values and beliefs are inherent in their choices?
5. Do you think this list was generated by people your age? Justify your answer.

Some Subjects for Writing

6. In a small group, brainstorm your own list of reasons to love (or not love) America. Discuss which categories you might add or expand on.
7. Use your own list or the one provided here to write about one representative trait that you think Americans can be proud of.

Night Walker

Brent Staples

Brent Staples was born in 1951 in Chester, Pennsylvania. He holds a Ph.D. degree in psychology from the University of Chicago and is a member of the editorial board of the New York Times *and the author of* Parallel Time: A Memoir *(1991). The selection reprinted here appeared originally in* Ms. *magazine in September 1986. In it Staples describes repeated experiences he had taking walks at night. A tall African-American man, he aroused the fear of other pedestrians as well as drivers who saw him as the stereotypical mugger.*

1   My first victim was a woman—white, well dressed, probably in her early twenties. I came upon her late one evening on a deserted street in Hyde Park, a relatively affluent neighborhood in an otherwise mean, impoverished section of Chicago. As I swung onto the avenue behind her, there seemed to be a discreet, uninflammatory distance between us. Not so. She cast back a worried glance. To her, the youngish black man—a broad six feet two inches with a beard and billowing hair, both hands shoved into the pockets of a bulky military jacket—seemed menacingly close. After a few more quick glimpses, she picked up her pace and was soon running in earnest. Within seconds she disappeared into a cross street.

2   That was more than a decade ago. I was 22 years old, a graduate student newly arrived at the University of Chicago. It was in the echo of that terrified woman's footfalls that I first began to know the unwieldy inheritance I'd come into—the ability to alter public space in ugly ways. It was clear that she thought herself the quarry of a mugger, a rapist, or worse. Suffering a bout of insomnia, however, I was stalking sleep, not defenseless wayfarers. As a softy who is scarcely able to take a knife to a raw chicken—let alone hold it to a person's throat—I was surprised, embarrassed, and dismayed all at once. Her flight made me feel like an accomplice in tyranny. It also made it clear that I was indistinguishable from the muggers who occasionally seeped into the area from the surrounding ghetto. That first encounter, and those that followed, signified that a vast, unnerving gulf lay between nighttime pedestrians—particularly women—and me. And I soon gathered that being perceived as dangerous is a hazard in itself. I only needed to turn a corner into a dicey situation, or crowd some frightened, armed person in a foyer somewhere, or make an errant move after being pulled over by a policeman. Where fear and weapons meet—and they often do in urban America—there is always the possibility of death.

3   In that first year, my first away from my hometown, I was to become thoroughly familiar with the language of fear. At dark, shadowy intersections in Chicago, I could cross in front of a car stopped at a traffic light and elicit the *thunk, thunk, thunk, thunk* of the driver—black, white, male, or female—hammering down the door locks. On less traveled streets after dark, I grew accustomed to but never comfortable with people who crossed to the other side of the street rather than pass me. Then there were the standard unpleasantries with police, doormen, bouncers, cab drivers, and others whose business it is to screen out troublesome individuals *before* there is any nastiness.

4   I moved to New York nearly two years ago and I have remained an avid night walker. In central Manhattan, the near-constant crowd cover minimizes tense one-on-one street encounters. Elsewhere—visiting friends in SoHo, where sidewalks are narrow and tightly spaced buildings shut out the sky—things can get very taut indeed.

5   After dark on the warrenlike streets of Brooklyn where I live, women seem to set their faces on neutral and, with their purse straps strung across their chests bandolier style, they forge ahead as though bracing themselves against being tackled. I understand, of course, that the danger they perceive is not a hallucination. Women are particularly vulnerable to street violence, and young black males are drastically overrepresented among the perpetrators of that violence. Yet these truths are no solace against the kind of alienation that comes of being ever the suspect, against being set apart, a fearsome entity with whom pedestrians avoid making eye contact.

6   It is not altogether clear to me how I reached the ripe old age of 22 without being conscious of the lethality nighttime pedestrians attributed to me. Perhaps it was because in Chester, Pennsylvania, the small, angry industrial town where I came of age in the 1960s, I was scarcely noticeable against a backdrop of gang warfare, street knifings, and murders. I grew up one of the good boys, had perhaps a half-dozen fist fights. In retrospect, my shyness of combat has clear sources.

7   Many things go into the making of a young thug. One of those things is the consummation of the male romance with the power to intimidate. An infant discovers that random flailings send the baby bottle flying out of the crib and crashing to the floor. Delighted, the joyful babe repeats those motions again and again, seeking to duplicate the feat. Just so, I recall the points at which some of my boyhood friends were finally seduced by the perception of themselves as tough guys. When a mark cowered and surrendered his money without resistance, myth and reality merged—and paid off. It is, after all, only manly to embrace the power to frighten and intimidate. We, as men, are not supposed to give an inch of our lane on the highway; we are to seize the fighter's edge in work and in play and even in love; we are to be valiant in the face of hostile forces.

8   Unfortunately, poor and powerless young men seem to take all this nonsense literally. As a boy, I saw countless tough guys locked away; I have since

buried several, too. They were babies, really—a teenage cousin, a brother of 22, a childhood friend in his mid-twenties—all gone down in episodes of bravado played out in the streets. I came to doubt the virtues of intimidation early on. I chose, perhaps even unconsciously, to remain a shadow—timid, but a survivor.

9   The fearsomeness mistakenly attributed to me in public places often has a perilous flavor. The most frightening of these confusions occurred in the late 1970s and early 1980s when I worked as a journalist in Chicago. One day, rushing into the office of a magazine I was writing for with a deadline story in hand, I was mistaken for a burglar. The office manager called security and, with an ad hoc posse, pursued me through the labyrinthine halls, nearly to my editor's door. I had no way of proving who I was. I could only move briskly toward the company of someone who knew me.

10   Another time I was on assignment for a local paper and killing time before an interview. I entered a jewelry store on the city's affluent Near North Side. The proprietor excused herself and returned with an enormous red Doberman pinscher straining at the end of a leash. She stood, the dog extended toward me, silent to my questions, her eyes bulging nearly out of her head. I took a cursory look around, nodded, and bade her good night. Relatively speaking, however, I never fared as badly as another black male journalist. He went to nearby Waukegan, Illinois, a couple of summers ago to work on a story about a murderer who was born there. Mistaking the reporter for the killer, police hauled him from his car at gunpoint and but for his press credentials would probably have tried to book him. Such episodes are not uncommon. Black men trade tales like this all the time.

11   In "My Negro Problem—And Ours" Podhoretz[1] writes that the hatred he feels for blacks makes itself known to him through a variety of avenues—one being his discomfort with that "special brand of paranoid touchiness" to which he says blacks are prone. No doubt he is speaking here of black men. In time, I learned to smother the rage I felt at so often being taken for a criminal. Not to do so would surely have led to madness—via that special "paranoid touchiness" that so annoyed Podhoretz at the time he wrote the essay.

12   I began to take precautions to make myself less threatening. I move about with care, particularly late in the evening. I give a wide berth to nervous people on subway platforms during the wee hours, particularly when I have exchanged business clothes for jeans. If I happen to be entering a building behind some people who appear skittish, I may walk by, letting them clear the lobby before I return, so as not to seem to be following them. I have been calm and extremely congenial on those rare occasions when I've been pulled over by the police.

---

[1]This well-known essay by Norman Podhoretz was published in 1963 in *Commentary* magazine. The article recounts Podhoretz's experience growing up as a poor Jew in New York City and describes both his fear and envy of African-American youth, whom he felt held the power in his neighborhood.

13   And on late-evening constitutionals along streets less traveled by, I employ what has proved to be an excellent tension-reducing measure: I whistle melodies from Beethoven and Vivaldi and the more popular classical composers. Even steely New Yorkers hunching toward nighttime destinations seem to relax, and occasionally they even join in the tune. Virtually everybody seems to sense that a mugger wouldn't be warbling bright, sunny selections from Vivaldi's *Four Seasons*. It is my equivalent of the cowbell that hikers wear when they know they are in bear country.

EXERCISES

Some of the Issues

1. How does Staples first discover his "ability to alter public space" (paragraph 2)?
2. What is Staples's reaction to the way he is perceived by strangers on his nightly walks? Does he show that he understands the feelings of some of those who fear him? Does he also show anger? Where?
3. What does Staples tell us about himself? About his childhood? How does this knowledge emphasize the contrast between his real self and the way he is often perceived by strangers?
4. How does Staples respond to Norman Podhoretz's contention that black men have a "special brand of paranoid touchiness" (paragraph 11)?
5. What has Staples learned to do to reduce the tension of passersby? Why does he choose the music he does? Does it solve his problem?

The Way We Are Told

6. Staples starts with an anecdote. Why does he use the word "victim" in the first sentence? Is there really a "victim"?
7. Identify examples drawn from Staples's own experience. How are they used to support the generalizations he makes?

Some Subjects for Writing

8. Write about a time when someone misjudged you or something you did. What were the circumstances? How did you feel? What was the resolution? What did you learn from the experience?
9. Observe and reflect on your own neighborhood. Write an essay in which you examine to what extent "outsiders" are welcome in your community. You may want to focus on one incident or examine a particular public place in your area.
10. In 1903 W.E.B. DuBois, one of the most prominent African-American intellectuals, predicted that the "problem of the Twentieth Century is the problem of the color line." To what extent do you believe he was right?

Alien Turf

Piri Thomas

Piri Thomas was born in Spanish Harlem in 1928 and grew up in its world of gangs, drugs, and petty crime. In his teens he became an addict, was convicted of attempted armed robbery, and served six years of a fifteen-year sentence. After his release, he began to work for drug rehabilitation programs in New York and Puerto Rico and developed a career as a writer. The autobiographical Down These Mean Streets *(1967), from which the following selection is taken, was his first book. A sequel,* Savior, Savior, Hold My Hand, *was published in 1972.*

Thomas tells the reader about an event in his childhood, one that many young people will have experienced: being the new kid on the block. But when the block is in a poor neighborhood and when, moreover, the new kid is from a background different from the prevailing culture, then the mix can turn explosive.

1 Sometimes you don't fit in. Like if you're a Puerto Rican on an Italian block. After my new baby brother, Ricardo, died of some kind of germs, Poppa moved us from 111th Street to Italian turf on 114th Street between Second and Third Avenue. I guess Poppa wanted to get Momma away from the hard memories of the old pad.

2 I sure missed 111th Street, where everybody acted, walked, and talked like me. But on 114th Street everything went all right for a while. There were a few dirty looks from the spaghetti-an'-sauce cats, but no big sweat. Till that one day I was on my way home from school and almost had reached my stoop when someone called: "Hey, you dirty fuckin' spic."

3 The words hit my ears and almost made me curse Poppa at the same time. I turned around real slow and found my face pushing in the finger of an Italian kid about my age. He had five or six of his friends with him.

4 "Hey, you," he said, "What nationality are ya?"

5 I looked at him and wondered which nationality to pick. And one of his friends said, "Ah, Rocky, he's black enuff to be a nigger. Ain't that what you is, kid?"

6 My voice was almost shy in its anger. "I'm Puerto Rican," I said. "I was born here." I wanted to shout it, but it came out like a whisper.

7 "Right here inna street?" Rocky sneered. "Ya mean right here inna middle of da street?"

8 They all laughed. I hated them. I shook my head slowly from side to side.

9 "Uh-uh," I said softly. "I was born inna hospital—inna bed."

10   "Umm, *paisan*[1]—born inna bed," Rocky said.

11   I didn't like Rocky Italiano's voice. "Inna hospital," I whispered, and all the time my eyes were trying to cut down the long distance from this trouble to my stoop. But it was no good; I was hemmed in by Rocky's friends. I couldn't help thinking about kids getting wasted for moving into a block belonging to other people.

12   "What hospital, *paisan?*" Bad Rocky pushed.

13   "Harlem Hospital," I answered, wishing like all hell that it was 5 o'clock instead of just 3 o'clock, 'cause Poppa came home at 5. I looked around for some friendly faces belonging to grown-up people, but the elders were all busy yakking away in Italian. I couldn't help thinking how much like Spanish it sounded. Shit, that should make us something like relatives.

14   "Harlem Hospital?" said a voice. "I knew he was a nigger."

15   "Yeah," said another voice from an expert on color. "That's the hospital where all them black bastards get born at."

16   I dug three Italian elders looking at us from across the street and I felt saved. But that went out the window when they just smiled and went on talking. I couldn't decide whether they had smiled because this new whatever-he-was was gonna get his ass kicked or because they were pleased that their kids were welcoming a new kid to their country. An older man nodded his head at Rocky, who smiled back. I wondered if that was a signal for my funeral to begin.

17   "Ain't that right, kid?" Rocky pressed. "Ain't that where all black people get born?"

18   I dug some of Rocky's boys grinding and pushing and punching closed fists against open hands. I figured they were looking to shake me up, so I straightened up my humble voice and made like proud. "There's all kinds of people born there. Colored people, Puerto Ricans like me, an'—even spaghetti-benders like you."

19   "That's a dirty fuckin' lie"—*bash*, I felt Rocky's fist smack into my mouth— "You dirty fuckin' spic."

20   I got dizzy and then more dizzy when fists started to fly from everywhere and only toward me. I swung back, *splat, bish*—my fist hit some face and I wished I hadn't, 'cause then I started getting kicked.

21   I heard people yelling in Italian and English and I wondered if maybe it was 'cause I hadn't fought fair in having hit that one guy. But it wasn't. The voices were trying to help me.

22   "Whas'sa matta, you no-good kids, leeva da kid alone," a man said. I looked through a swelling eye and dug some Italians pushing their kids off me with slaps. One even kicked a kid in the ass. I could have loved them if I didn't hate them so fuckin' much.

23   "You all right, kiddo?" asked the man.

[1]Buddy.

24   "Where you live, boy?" said another one.

25   "Is the *bambino*[2] hurt?" asked a woman.

26   I didn't look at any of them. I felt dizzy. I didn't want to open my mouth to talk, 'cause I was fighting to keep from puking up. I just hoped my face was cool-looking. I walked away from the group of strangers. I reached my stoop and started to climb the steps.

27   "Hey, spic," came a shout from across the street. I started to turn to the voice and changed my mind. "Spic" wasn't my name. I knew that voice, though. It was Rocky's. "We'll see ya again, spic," he said.

28   I wanted to do something tough, like spitting in their direction. But you gotta have spit in your mouth in order to spit, and my mouth was hurt dry. I just stood there with my back to them.

29   "Hey, your old man just better be the janitor in that fuckin' building."

30   Another voice added, "Hey, you got any pretty sisters? We might let ya stay onna block."

31   Another voice mocked, "Aw, fer Chrissake, where ya ever hear of one of them black broads being pretty?"

32   I heard the laughter. I turned around and looked at them. Rocky made some kind of dirty sign by putting his left hand in the crook of his right arm while twisting his closed fist in the air.

33   Another voice said, "Fuck it, we'll just cover the bitch's face with the flag an' fuck'er for old glory."

34   All I could think of was how I'd like to kill each of them two or three times. I found some spit in my mouth and splattered it in their direction and went inside.

35   Momma was cooking, and the smell of rice and beans was beating the smell of Parmesan cheese from the other apartments. I let myself into our new pad. I tried to walk fast past Momma so I could wash up, but she saw me.

36   "My God, Piri, what happened?" she cried.

37   "Just a little fight in school, Momma. You know how it is, Momma, I'm new in school an' . . ." I made myself laugh. Then I made myself say, "But Moms, I whipped the living _____ outta two guys, an' one was bigger'n me."

38   "*Bendito*,[3] Piri, I raise my family in Christian way. Not to fight. Christ says to turn the other cheek."

39   "Sure, Momma." I smiled and went and showered, feeling sore at Poppa for bringing us into spaghetti country. I felt my face with easy fingers and thought about all the running back and forth from school that was in store for me.

40   I sat down to dinner and listened to Momma talk about Christian living without really hearing her. All I could think of was that I hadda go out in that street again. I made up my mind to go out right after I finished eating. I had to, shook up or not; cats like me had to show heart.

[2]Child.
[3]Blessed.

41   "Be back, Moms," I said after dinner. "I'm going out on the stoop." I got halfway to the stoop and turned and went back to our apartment. I knocked.

42   "Who is it?" Momma asked.

43   "Me, Momma."

44   She opened the door. "*¿Qué pasa?*"[4] she asked.

45   "Nothing, Momma, I just forgot something," I said. I went into the bedroom and fiddled around and finally copped a funny book and walked out the door again. But this time I made sure the switch on the lock was open, just in case I had to get back real quick. I walked out on that stoop as cool as could be, feeling braver with the lock open.

46   There was no sign of Rocky and his killers. After awhile I saw Poppa coming down the street. He walked like beat tired. Poppa hated his pick-and-shovel job with the WPA. He couldn't even hear the name WPA without getting a fever. *Funny,* I thought, *Poppa's the same like me, a stone Puerto Rican, and nobody in this block even pays him a mind. Maybe older people get along better'n us kids.*

47   Poppa was climbing the stoop. "Hi, Poppa," I said.

48   "How's it going, son? Hey, you sure look a little lumped up. What happened?"

49   I looked at Poppa and started to talk it outta me all at once and stopped, 'cause I heard my voice start to sound scared, and that was no good.

50   "Slow down, son," Poppa said. "Take it easy." He sat down on the stoop and made a motion for me to do the same. He listened and I talked. I gained confidence. I went from a tone of being shook up by the Italians to a tone of being a better fighter than Joe Louis and Pedro Montanez lumped together, with Kid Chocolate thrown in for extra.

51   "So that's what happened," I concluded. "And it looks like only the beginning. Man, I ain't scared, Poppa, but like there's nothin' but Italianos on this block and there's no me's like me except for me an' our family."

52   Poppa looked tight. He shook his head from side to side and mumbled something about another Puerto Rican family that lived a coupla doors down from us.

53   I thought, *What good would that do me, unless they prayed over my dead body in Spanish?* But I said, "Man! That's great. Before ya know it, there'll be a whole bunch of us moving in, huh?"

54   Poppa grunted something and got up. "Staying out here, son?"

55   "Yeah, Poppa, for a little while longer."

56   From that day on I grew eyes all over my head. Anytime I hit that street for anything, I looked straight ahead, behind me and from side to side all at the same time. Sometimes I ran into Rocky and his boys—the cat was never without his boys—but they never made a move to snag me. They just grinned at me like a bunch of hungry alley cats that could get to their mouse anytime they wanted.

---

[4]What's happening?

That's what they made me feel like—a mouse. Not like a smart house mouse but like a white house pet that ain't got no business in the middle of cat country but don't know better 'cause he grew thinking he was a cat—which wasn't far from wrong 'cause he'd end up as part of the inside of some cat.

57   Rocky and his fellas got to playing a way-out game with me called "One-finger-across-the-neck-inna-slicing-motion," followed by such gentle words as "It won't be long, spico." I just looked at them blank and made it to wherever I was going.

58   I kept wishing those cats went to the same school I went to, a school that was on the border between their country and mine, and I had *amigos* there—and there I could count on them. But I couldn't ask two or three *amigos* to break into Rocky's block and help me mess up his boys. I knew 'cause I had asked them already. They had turned me down fast, and I couldn't blame them. It would have been murder, and I guess they figured one murder would be better than four.

59   I got through the days trying to play it cool and walk on by Rocky and his boys like they weren't there. One day I passed them and nothing was said. I started to let out my breath. I felt great; I hadn't been seen. Then someone yelled in a high, girlish voice, "Yoo-hoo . . . Hey, *paisan* . . . we see yoo . . ." And right behind that voice came a can of evaporated milk—whoosh, clatter. I walked cool for ten steps then started running like mad.

60   This crap kept up for a month. They tried to shake me up. Every time they threw something at me, it was just to see me jump. I decided that the next fucking time they threw something at me I was gonna play bad-o and not run. That next time came about a week later. Momma sent me off the stoop to the Italian market on 115th Street and First Avenue, deep in Italian country. Man, that was stompin' territory. But I went, walking in the style which I had copped from the colored cats I had seen, a swinging and stepping down hard at every step. Those cats were so down and cool that just walking made a way-out sound.

61   Ten minutes later I was on my way back with Momma's stuff. I got to the corner of First Avenue and 114th Street and crushed myself right into Rocky and his fellas.

62   "Well-l, fellas," Rocky said, "Lookee who's here."

63   I didn't like the sounds coming out of Rocky's fat mouth. And I didn't like the sameness of the shitty grins spreading all over the boys' faces. But I thought, *No more! No more! I ain't gonna run no more.* Even so, I looked around, like for some kind of Jesus miracle to happen. I was always looking for miracles to happen.

64   "Say, *paisan*," one guy said, "you even buying from us *paisans*, eh? Man, you must wantta be Italian."

65   Before I could bite that dopey tongue of mine, I said, "I wouldn't be a guinea on a motherfucking bet."

66   "Wha-at?" said Rocky, really surprised. I didn't blame him; I was surprised myself. His finger began digging a hole in his ear, like he hadn't heard me right. "Wha-at? Say that again?"

67   I could feel a thin hot wetness cutting itself down my leg. I had been so ashamed of being so damned scared that I had peed on myself. And then I wasn't scared any more; I felt a fuck-it-all attitude. I looked real bad at Rocky and said, "Ya heard me. I wouldn't be a guinea on a bet."

68   "Ya little sonavabitch, we'll kick the shit outta ya," said one guy, Tony, who had made a habit of asking me if I had any sen-your-ritas for sisters.

69   "Kick the shit outta me yourself if you got any heart, you mother fuckin' fucker," I screamed at him. I felt kind of happy, the kind of feeling that you get only when you got heart.

70   Big-mouth Tony just swung out, and I swung back and heard all of Momma's stuff plopping all over the street. My fist hit Tony smack dead in the mouth. He was so mad he threw a fist at me from about three feet away. I faked and jabbed and did fancy dance steps. Big-mouth put a stop to all that with a punch in my mouth. I heard the home cheers of "Yea, yea, bust that spic wide open!" Then I bloodied Tony's nose. He blinked and sniffed without putting his hands to his nose, and I remembered Poppa telling me, "Son, if you're ever fighting somebody an' you punch him in the nose, and he just blinks an' sniffs without holding his nose, you can do one of two things: fight like hell or run like hell—'cause that cat's a fighter."

71   Big-mouth came at me and we grabbed each other and pushed and pulled and shoved. *Poppa,* I thought, *I ain't gonna cop out. I'm a fighter, too.* I pulled away from Tony and blew my fist into his belly. He puffed and butted my nose with his head. I sniffed back. *Poppa, I didn't put my hands to my nose.* I hit Tony again in that same weak spot. He bent over in the middle and went down to his knees.

72   Big-mouth got up as fast as he could, and I was thinking how much heart he had. But I ran toward him like my life depended on it; I wanted to cool him. Too late. I saw his hand grab a fistful of ground asphalt which had been piled nearby to fix a pothole in the street. I tried to duck; I should have closed my eyes instead. The shitty-gritty stuff hit my face, and I felt the scrappy pain make itself a part of my eyes. I screamed and grabbed for two eyes with one hand, while the other I beat some kind of helpless tune on air that just couldn't be hurt. I heard Rocky's voice shouting, "Ya scum bag, ya didn't have to fight the spic dirty; you could've fucked him up fair and square!" I couldn't see. I heard a fist hit a face, then Big-mouth's voice: "Whatta ya hittin' me for?" and then Rocky's voice: "*Putana!*[5] I ought ta knock all your fuckin' teeth out."

73   I felt hands grabbing at me between my screams. I punched out. *I'm gonna get killed,* I thought. Then I heard many voices: "Hold it, kid." "We ain't gonna hurt ya." "Je-*sus,* don't rub your eyes." "Ooooohhhh, shit, his eyes is fulla that shit."

74   *You're fuckin' right,* I thought, *and it hurts like* coño.

---

[5]Whore.

75 I heard a woman's voice now: "Take him to a hospital." And an old man asked: "How did it happen?"

76 "Momma, Momma," I cried.

77 "Comon, kid," Rocky said, taking my hand. "Lemme take ya home." I fought for the right to rub my eyes. "Grab his other hand, Vincent," Rocky said. I tried to rub my eyes with my eyelids. I could feel hurt tears cutting down my cheeks. "Come on, kid, we ain't gonna hurt ya," Rocky tried to assure me. "Swear to our mudders. We just wanna take ya home."

78 I made myself believe him, and trying not to make pain noises, I let myself be led home. I wondered if I was gonna be blind like Mr. Silva, who went around from door to door selling dish towels and brooms, his son leading him around.

79 "You okay, kid?" Rocky asked.

80 "Yeah," what was left of me said.

81 "A-huh," mumbled Big-mouth.

82 "He got much heart for a nigger," somebody else said.

83 A *spic*, I thought.

84 "For anybody," Rocky said. "Here we are kid," he added. "Watch your step."

85 I was like carried up the steps. "What's your apartment number?" Rocky asked.

86 "One-B—inna back—ground floor," I said, and I was led there. Somebody knocked on Momma's door. Then I heard running feet and Rocky's voice yelling back, "Don't rat, huh, kid?" And I was alone.

87 I heard the door open and Momma say, "*Bueno*, Piri, come in." I didn't move. I couldn't. There was a long pause; I could hear Momma's fright. "My God," she said finally "What's happened?" Then she took a closer look. "Aieeee," she screamed. "*¡Dios mío!*"[6]

88 "I was playing with some kids, Momma," I said, "an' I got some dirt in my eyes." I tried to make my voice come out without the pain, like a man.

89 "*Dios eterno*[7]—your eyes!"

90 "What's the matter? What's the matter?" Poppa called from the bedroom.

91 "*¡Está ciego!*[8]" Momma screamed. "He is blind!"

92 I heard Poppa knocking things over as he came running. Sis began to cry. Blind, hurting tears were jumping out of my eyes. "Whattya mean, he's blind?" Poppa said as he stormed into the kitchen. "What happened?" Poppa's voice was both scared and mad.

93 "Playing, Poppa."

[6]My God.
[7]Eternal God.
[8]He's blind!

94   "Whatta ya mean, 'playing'?" Poppa's English sounded different when he got warm.

95   "Just playing, Poppa."

96   "Playing? Playing got all that dirt in your eyes? I bet my ass. Them damn Ee-ta-liano kids ganged up on you again." Poppa squeezed my head between the fingers of one hand. "That settles it—we're moving outta this damn section, outta this damn block, outta this damn shit."

97   *Shit*, I thought, *Poppa's sure cursin' up a storm.* I could hear him slapping the side of his leg, like he always did when he got real mad.

98   "Son," he said, "you're gonna point them out to me."

99   "Point who out, Poppa? I was playin' an'—"

100   "Stop talkin' to him and take him to the hospital!" Momma screamed.

101   "*Pobrecito,*[9] poor Piri," cooed my little sister.

102   "You sure, son?" Poppa asked. "You was only playing?"

103   "Shit, Poppa, I said I was."

104   *Smack*—Poppa was so scared and mad, he let it out in the slap to the side of my face.

105   "*¡Bestia!* ani-*mul!*" Momma cried. "He's blind, and you hit him!"

106   "I'm sorry, son, I'm sorry," Poppa said in a voice like almost crying. I heard him running back into the bedroom yelling, "Where's my pants?"

107   Momma grabbed away fingers that were trying to wipe away the hurt in my eyes. "*Caramba*, no rub, no rub," she said, kissing me. She told Sis to get a rag and wet it with cold water.

108   Poppa came running back into the kitchen. "Let's go, son, let's go. Jesus! I didn't mean to smack ya, I really didn't," he said, his big hand rubbing and grabbing my hair gently.

109   "Here's the rag, Momma," said Sis.

110   "What's that for?" asked Poppa.

111   "To put on his eyes," Momma said.

112   I heard the smack of a wet rag, *blapt*, against the kitchen wall. "We can't put nothing on his eyes. It might make them worse. Come on, son," Poppa said nervously, lifting me up in his big arms. I felt like a little baby, like I didn't hurt so bad. I wanted to stay there, but I said, "Let me down, Poppa, I ain't no kid."

113   "Shut up," Poppa said softly. "I know you ain't but it's faster this way."

114   "Which hospeetal are you taking him to?" Momma asked.

115   "Nearest one," Poppa answered as we went out the door. He carried me through the hall and out into the street, where the bright sunlight made a red hurting color through the crap in my eyes. I heard voices on the stoop and on the sidewalk: "Is that the boy?"

116   "A-huh. He's probably blinded."

---

[9] You poor boy.

117   "We'll get a cab, son," Poppa said. His voice loved me. I heard Rocky yelling from across the street, "We're pulling for ya, kid. Remember what we . . ." The rest was lost to Poppa's long legs running down to the corner of Third Avenue. He hailed a taxi and we zoomed off toward Harlem Hospital. I felt the cab make all kinds of sudden stops and turns.

118   "How do you feel, *hijo?*"[10] Poppa asked.

119   "It burns like hell."

120   "You'll be okay," he said, and as an afterthought added, "Don't curse, son."

121   I heard cars honking and the Third Avenue el roaring above us. I knew we were in Puerto Rican turf, 'cause I could hear our language.

122   "Son."

123   "Yeah, Poppa."

124   "Don't rub your eyes, fer Christ sake." He held my skinny wrists in his one hand, and everything got quiet between us.

125   The cab got to Harlem Hospital. I heard change being handled and the door opening and Poppa thanking the cabbie for getting here fast. "Hope the kid'll be okay," the driver said.

126   *I will be*, I thought, *I ain't gonna be like Mr. Silva.*

127   Poppa took me in his arms again and started running. "Where's emergency mister?" he asked someone.

128   "To your left and straight away," said a voice.

129   "Thanks a lot," Poppa said, and we were running again.

130   "Emergency?" Poppa said when we stopped.

131   "Yes, sir," said a girl's voice. "What's the matter?"

132   "My boy's got his eyes full of ground-up tar an'—"

133   "What's the matter?" said a man's voice.

134   "Youngster with ground tar in his eyes, doctor."

135   "We'll take him, mister. You just put him down here and go with the nurse. She'll take down the information. Uh, you the father?"

136   "That's right, doctor."

137   "Okay, just put him down here."

138   "Poppa, don't leave me," I cried.

139   "Sh, son, I ain't leaving you. I'm just going to fill out some papers, an' I'll be right back."

140   I nodded my head up and down and was wheeled away. When the rolling stretcher stopped, somebody stuck a needle in me and I got sleepy and started thinking about Rocky and his boys, and Poppa's slap, and how great Poppa was, and how my eyes didn't hurt no more . . .

141   I woke up in a room blind with darkness. The only lights were the ones inside my head. I put my fingers to my eyes and felt bandages. "Let them be, sonny," said a woman's voice.

---

[10]Son.

142   I wanted to ask the voice if they had taken my eyes out, but I didn't. I was afraid the voice would say yes.

143   "Let them be, sonny," the nurse said, pulling my hand away from the bandages. "You're all right. The doctor put the bandages on to keep the light out. They'll be off real soon. Don't you worry none, sonny."

144   I wished she would stop calling me sonny. "Where's Poppa?" I asked cool like.

145   "He's outside, sonny. Would you like me to send him in?"

146   I nodded. "Yeah." I heard walking-away shoes, a door opening, a whisper, and shoes walking back toward me. "How do you feel, *hijo?*" Poppa asked.

147   "It hurts like shit, Poppa."

148   "It's just for awhile, son, and then off come the bandages. Everything's gonna be all right."

149   I thought, *Poppa didn't tell me to stop cursing.*

150   "And son, I thought I told you to stop cursing," he added.

151   I smiled. Poppa hadn't forgotten. Suddenly I realized that all I had on was a hospital gown. "Poppa, where's my clothes?" I asked.

152   I got them. I'm taking them home an'—"

153   "Whatta ya mean, Poppa?" I said, like scared. "You ain't leavin' me here? I'll be damned if I stay." I was already sitting up and feeling my way outta bed. Poppa grabbed me and pushed me back. His voice wasn't mad or scared any more. It was happy and soft, like Momma's.

154   "Hey," he said, "get your ass back in bed or they'll have to put a bandage there too."

155   "Poppa," I pleaded. "I don't care, wallop me as much as you want, just take me home."

156   "Hey, I thought you said you wasn't no kid. Hell, you ain't scared of being alone?"

157   Inside my head there was a running of *Yeah, yeah, yeah*, but I answered, "Naw, Poppa, it's just that Momma's gonna worry and she'll get sick an' everything, and—"

158   "Won't work, son," Poppa broke in with a laugh.

159   I kept quiet.

160   "It's only for a couple days. We'll come and see you an' everybody'll bring you things."

161   I got interested but played it smooth. "What kinda things, Poppa?"

162   Poppa shrugged his shoulders and spread his big arms apart and answered me like he was surprised that I should ask. "Uh . . . fruits and . . . candy and ice cream. And Momma will probably bring you chicken soup."

163   I shook my head sadly, "Poppa, you know I don't like chicken soup."

164   "So we won't bring chicken soup. We'll bring what you like. Goddammit, whatta ya like?"

165   "I'd like the first things you talked about, Poppa," I said softly. "But instead of soup I'd like"—I held my breath back, then shot it out—"some roller skates!"

166   Poppa let out a whistle. Roller skates were about $1.50, and that was rice and beans for more than a few days. Then he said, "All right, son, soon as you get home, you got 'em."

167   But he had agreed too quickly. I shook my head from side to side. Shit, I was gonna push all the way for the roller skates. It wasn't every day you'd get hurt bad enough to ask for something so little like a pair of roller skates. I wanted them right away.

168   "Fer Christ sakes," Poppa protested, "you can't use 'em in here. Why, some kid will probably steal 'em on you." But Poppa's voice died out slowly in a "you win" tone as I just kept shaking my head from side to side. "Bring 'em tomorrow," he finally mumbled, "but that's it."

169   "Thanks, Poppa."

170   "Don't ask for no more."

171   My eyes were starting to hurt like mad again. The fun was starting to go outta the game between Poppa and me. I made a face.

172   "Does it hurt, son?"

173   "Naw, Poppa. I can take it." I thought how I was like a cat in a movie about Indians, taking it like a champ, tied to a stake and getting like burned toast.

174   Poppa sounded relieved. "Yeah, it's only at first it hurts." His hand touched my foot. "Well, I'll be going now . . ." Poppa rubbed my foot gently and then slapped me the same gentle way on the side of my leg. "Be good, son," he said and walked away. I heard the door open and the nurse telling him about how they were gonna move me to the ward 'cause I was out of danger. "Son," Poppa called back, "you're *un hombre*."[11]

175   I felt proud as hell.

176   "Poppa."

177   "Yeah, son?"

178   "You won't forget to bring the roller skates, huh?"

179   Poppa laughed, "Yeah, son."

180   I heard the door close.

EXERCISES

Some of the Issues

1. How do the first two sentences set the scene?
2. Piri wants to project a certain self-image in front of the gang. Characterize it.
3. Until the climactic fight, the cat-and-mouse game that Rocky's gang plays goes through several stages. Determine what these stages are and how Piri reacts to them.

[11]A man.

4. How do the adults (those in the street as well as Piri's parents) react to the situation at the various stages? How does Piri deal with his parents' reactions in particular?
5. How does Rocky's attitude toward Piri change after one of the gang members throws the asphalt? What causes the change?
6. What is the significance of Thomas calling himself a "spic" in paragraph 83?
7. Explain Piri's reaction to "spic" and "nigger." Is Piri's desire to be identified as a Puerto Rican a matter of pride or practicality?
8. What is the importance of being "*un hombre,*" of having "heart"? How does Piri prove himself a man? By whose standards?

The Way We Are Told

9. There is almost no description in this selection; it is all action and dialog. Thomas nevertheless manages to convey some strong impressions of individuals and their attitudes. How does he do it? Cite some examples.
*10. Both Maya Angelou ("Graduation") and Thomas tell their stories from an adolescent's point of view. Apart from the content, how do the two stories differ? Use specific examples.

Some Subjects for Writing

11. Write about a conflict that you have had. Set the scene and then use mostly dialog to tell your story. See if you can make the voices authentic.
*12. The term "rite of passage" is usually used to indicate the ceremony marking the formal change of a young person from childhood to adulthood, such as a confirmation or *bar mitzvah,* though it is not always a religious ceremony. Write an essay arguing that Angelou's graduation and Thomas's big fight (or one or the other) were such rites of passage.

I Learn What I Am

Walter White

*Walter White was born in Atlanta, Georgia, in 1893. He joined the NAACP
early in its development and served as its head from 1931 until his death in
1955. The following excerpt is taken from his autobiography,* A Man Called
White *(1948).*

*The events White describes took place in his childhood, at the beginning
of the twentieth century. The year was 1906 and he was living in Atlanta
with his large family, near the line that separated the white community from
his own. His father, an employee of the U.S. Postal Service, kept the house in
immaculate repair, its white picket fence symbolizing the American Dream.
When a race riot erupted in Atlanta, their house became a target of the mob.
White tells the dramatic story of those two days.*

1   There were nine light-skinned Negroes in my family: mother, father, five
sisters, an older brother, George, and myself. The house in which I discovered what it meant to be a Negro was located on Houston Street, three blocks
from the Candler Building, Atlanta's first skyscraper, which bore the name of
the ex-drug clerk who had become a millionaire from the sale of Coca-Cola. Below us lived none but Negroes; toward town all but a very few were white. Ours
was an eight room, two-story frame house which stood out in its surroundings
not because of its opulence but by contrast with the drabness and unpaintedness
of the other dwellings in a deteriorating neighborhood.

2   Only Father kept his house painted, the picket fence repaired, the board
fence separating our place from those on either side whitewashed, the grass
neatly trimmed, and flower beds abloom. Mother's passion for neatness was
even more pronounced and it seemed to me that I was always the victim of her
determination to see no single blade of grass longer than the others or any one
of the pickets in the front fence less shiny with paint than its mates. This spic-
and-spanness became increasingly apparent as the rest of the neighborhood became more down-at-heel, and resulted, as we were to learn, in sullen envy
among some of our white neighbors. It was the violent expression of that resentment against a Negro family neater than themselves which set the pattern of our
lives.

3   On a day in September 1906, when I was thirteen, we were taught that
there is no isolation from life. The unseasonably oppressive heat of an Indian
summer day hung like a steaming blanket over Atlanta. My sisters and I had
casually commented upon the unusual quietness. It seemed to stay Mother's
volubility and reduced Father, who was more taciturn, to monosyllables. But,

as I remember it, no other sense of impending trouble impinged upon our consciousness.

4   I had read the inflammatory headlines in the *Atlanta News* and the more restrained ones in the *Atlanta Constitution* which reported alleged rapes and other crimes committed by Negroes. But these were so standard and familiar that they made—as I look back on it now—little impression. The stories were more frequent, however, and consisted of eight-column streamers instead of the usual two- or four-column ones.

5   Father was a mail collector. His tour of duty was from three to eleven P.M. He made his rounds in a little cart into which one climbed from a step in the rear. I used to drive the cart for him from two until seven, leaving him at the point nearest our home on Houston Street, to return home either for study or sleep. That day Father decided that I should not go with him. I appealed to Mother, who thought it might be all right, provided Father sent me home before dark because, she said, "I don't think they would dare start anything before nightfall." Father told me as we made the rounds that ominous rumors of a race riot that night were sweeping the town. But I was too young that morning to understand the background of the riot. I became much older during the next thirty-six hours, under circumstances which I now recognize as the inevitable outcome of what had preceded. . . .

6   During the afternoon preceding the riot little bands of sullen, evil-looking men talked excitedly on street corners all over downtown Atlanta. Around seven o'clock my father and I were driving toward a mail box at the corner of Peachtree and Houston Streets when there came from near-by Pryor Street a roar the like of which I had never heard before, but which sent a sensation of mingled fear and excitement coursing through my body. I asked permission of Father to go and see what the trouble was. He bluntly ordered me to stay in the cart. A little later we drove down Atlanta's main business thoroughfare, Peachtree Street. Again we heard the terrifying cries, this time near at hand and coming toward us. We saw a lame Negro bootblack from Herndon's barber shop pathetically trying to outrun a mob of whites. Less than a hundred yards from us the chase ended. We saw clubs and fists descending to the accompaniment of savage shouting and cursing. Suddenly a voice cried, "There goes another nigger!" Its work done, the mob went after the new prey. The body with the withered foot lay dead in a pool of blood on the street.

7   Father's apprehension and mine steadily increased during the evening, although the fact that our skins were white kept us from attack. Another circumstance favored us—the mob had not yet grown violent enough to attack United States government property. But I could see Father's relief when he punched the time clock at eleven P.M. and got into the cart to go home. He wanted to go the back way down Forsyth Street, but I begged him, in my childish excitement and ignorance, to drive down Marietta to Five Points, the heart of Atlanta's business district, where the crowds were densest and the yells loudest. No sooner had we turned into Marietta Street, however, than we saw careening toward us an un-

dertaker's barouche. Crouched in the rear of the vehicle were three Negroes clinging to the sides of the carriage as it lunged and swerved. On the driver's seat crouched a white man, the reins held taut in his left hand. A huge whip was gripped in his right. Alternately he lashed the horses and, without looking backward, swung the whip in savage swoops in the faces of members of the mob as they lunged at the carriage determined to seize the three Negroes.

8 There was no time for us to get out of its path, so sudden and swift was the appearance of the vehicle. The hub cap of the right rear wheel of the barouche hit the right side of our much lighter wagon. Father and I instinctively threw our weight and kept the cart from turning completely over. Our mare was a Texas mustang which, frightened by the sudden blow, lunged in the air as Father clung to the reins. Good fortune was with us. The cart settled back on its four wheels as Father said in a voice which brooked no dissent, "We are going home the back way and not down Marietta."

9 But again on Pryor Street we heard the cry of the mob. Close to us and in our direction ran a stout and elderly woman who cooked at a downtown white hotel. Fifty yards behind, a mob which filled the street from curb to curb was closing in. Father handed the reins to me and, though he was of slight stature, reached down and lifted the woman into the cart. I did not need to be told to lash the mare to the fastest speed she could muster.

10 The church bells tolled the next morning for Sunday service. But no one in Atlanta believed for a moment that the hatred and lust for blood had been appeased. Like skulls on a cannibal's hut the hats and caps of victims of the mob of the night before had been hung on the iron hooks of telegraph poles. None could tell whether each hat represented a dead Negro. But we knew that some of those who had worn the hats would never again wear any.

11 Late in the afternoon friends of my father's came to warn of more trouble that night. They told us that plans had been perfected for a mob to form on Peachtree Street just after nightfall to march down Houston Street to what the white people called "Darktown," three blocks or so below our house, "to clean out the niggers." There had never been a firearm in our house before that day. Father was reluctant even in those circumstances to violate the law, but he at last gave in at Mother's insistence.

12 We turned out the lights early, as did all our neighbors. No one removed his clothes or thought of sleep. Apprehension was tangible. We could almost touch its cold and clammy surface. Toward midnight the unnatural quiet was broken by a roar that grew steadily in volume. Even today I grow tense in remembering it.

13 Father told mother to take my sisters, the youngest of them only six, to the rear of the house, which offered more protection from stones and bullets. My brother George was away, so Father and I, the only males in the house, took our places at the front windows of the parlor. The windows opened on a porch along the front side of the house, which in turn gave onto a narrow lawn that sloped down to the street and a picket fence. There was a crash as Negroes

smashed the street lamp at the corner of Houston and Piedmont Avenue down the street. In a very few minutes the vanguard of the mob, some of them bearing torches, appeared. A voice which we recognized as that of the son of the grocer with whom we had traded for many years yelled, "That's where that nigger mail carrier lives! Let's burn it down! It's too nice for a nigger to live in!" In the eerie light Father turned his drawn face toward me. In a voice as quiet as though he were asking me to pass him the sugar at the breakfast table, he said, "Son, don't shoot until the first man puts his foot on the lawn and then—don't you miss!"

14   In the flickering light the mob swayed, paused, and began to flow toward us. In that instant there opened up within me a great awareness; I knew then who I was. I was a Negro, a human being with an invisible pigmentation which marked me a person to be hunted, hanged, abused, discriminated against, kept in poverty and ignorance, in order that those whose skin was white would have readily at hand a proof of their superiority, a proof patent and inclusive, accessible to the moron and the idiot as well as to the wise man and the genius. No matter how low a white man fell, he could always hold fast to the smug conviction that he was superior to two-thirds of the world's population, for those two-thirds were not white.

15   It made no difference how intelligent or talented my millions of brothers and I were, or how virtuously we lived. A curse like that of Judas was upon us, a mark of degradation fashioned with heavenly authority. There were white men who said Negroes had no souls, and who proved it by the Bible. Some of these now were approaching us, intent upon burning our house.

16   Theirs was a world of contrasts in values: superior and inferior, profit and loss, cooperative and noncooperative, civilized and aboriginal, white and black. If you were on the wrong end of the comparison, if you were inferior, if you were noncooperative, if you were aboriginal, if you were black, then you were marked for excision, expulsion, or extinction. I was a Negro; I was therefore that part of history which opposed the good, the just, and the enlightened. I was a Persian, falling before the hordes of Alexander. I was a Carthaginian, extinguished by the Legions of Rome. I was a Frenchman at Waterloo, an Anglo-Saxon at Hastings, a Confederate at Vicksburg. I was the defeated, wherever and whenever there was a defeat.

17   Yet as a boy there in the darkness amid the tightening fright, I knew the inexplicable thing—that my skin was as white as the skin of those who were coming at me.

18   The mob moved toward the lawn. I tried to aim my gun, wondering what it would feel like to kill a man. Suddenly there was a volley of shots. The mob hesitated, stopped. Some friends of my father's had barricaded themselves in a two-story brick building just below our house. It was they who had fired. Some of the mobsmen, still blood-thirsty, shouted, "Let's go get the nigger." Others, afraid now for their safety, held back. Our friends, noting the hesitation, fired another volley. The mob broke and retreated up Houston Street.

19   In the quiet that followed I put my gun aside and tried to relax. But a tension different from anything I had ever known possessed me. I was gripped by the knowledge of my identity, and in the depths of my soul I was vaguely aware that I was glad of it. I was sick with loathing for the hatred which had flared before me that night and come so close to making me a killer; but I was glad I was not one of those who hated; I was glad I was not one of those made sick and murderous by pride. I was glad I was not one of those whose story is in the history of the world, a record of bloodshed, rapine, and pillage. I was glad my mind and spirit were part of the races that had not fully awakened, and who therefore had still before them the opportunity to write a record of virtue as a memorandum to Armageddon.[1]

20   It was all just a feeling then, inarticulate and melancholy, yet reassuring in the way that death and sleep are reassuring, and I have clung to it now for nearly half a century.

EXERCISES

Some of the Issues

1. In paragraph 1 White explains the location of his house in Atlanta. What is most important about the location?
2. In paragraph 2 White describes the appearance of the house and yard. Why is it important for him to stress the difference between it and its surroundings?
3. What does White mean when he says in paragraph 3, "we were taught that there is no isolation from life"?
4. In paragraph 4 White describes the headlines in the newspapers. How do they change in the days before the riot? Does he imply that his family believed what the papers said or not?
5. In paragraphs 5 through 13 there are indications that the riots are neither new nor isolated, unique occasions. Find these indicators.
6. In what ways do the actions of the mob differ between the first and second day of the rioting?
7. Where are the police?
8. In paragraphs 14 through 17 White interrupts his account of the mob's actions to describe his thoughts and feelings of bitterness. Contrast them to his thoughts in paragraphs 19 and 20, after the mob had fled and the danger was—temporarily—past.

[1]Biblical reference to the final battle between good and evil; total defeat. Generally refers to a massive conflict of slaughter.

The Way We Are Told

9. White gives his description of home and neighborhood in two separate paragraphs (1 and 2). How do the paragraphs differ?
10. How does White begin to build suspense in paragraph 3? How do paragraphs 4 and 5 also prepare the reader for what is to come?
11. Paragraph 6 gives the first description of a specific event, using several words and phrases that have emotional impact. Cite four or five of these.
12. In paragraph 9 White describes another episode of rescue. See if there are any words here, like those in paragraph 6, that have emotional connotations.
13. How does White heighten the suspense in the final paragraphs of the essay?

Some Subjects for Writing

14. Have you ever felt yourself in real danger? If so, try to describe the circumstances in two ways: give an objective description of the events and then rewrite your essay, trying to heighten the effect by the careful use of emotionally effective words and phrases. (You will find that the overuse of emotional words diminishes rather than enhances the effect.)
15. White describes his experience in the Atlanta riots as a turning point in his life. Describe an experience in your own life that profoundly changed your values.
*16. Read Maya Angelou's "Graduation." Both she and White record bad experiences that turned into a kind of victory in the end; both indicate that the victory is not final but needs to be fought for again and again. Write an essay in which you compare these experiences and their meaning to White and Angelou.

Black Like Them

Malcolm Gladwell

Malcolm Gladwell was born in 1963 in England, grew up in Canada, and graduated from the University of Toronto in 1984. "Black Like Them" originally appeared in the New Yorker in 1996, where Gladwell is a staff writer. He is also the author of a book, The Tipping Point: How Little Things Can Make A Big Difference (2000).

Gladwell begins his essay by telling the story of his cousins Rosie and Noel, immigrants from Jamaica who have settled in New York City. Gladwell explores the question of why West Indians and American blacks are treated differently in the United States, and why they perceive themselves as fitting into American society in a different way. Drawing from family experience, historical information, and sociological studies, Gladwell uses the experience of West Indian blacks to investigate both the roots and the pervasiveness of racism in the U.S.

1   My cousin Rosie and her husband, Noel, live in a two-bedroom bungalow on Argyle Avenue, in Uniondale, on the west end of Long Island. When they came to America, twelve years ago, they lived in a basement apartment a dozen or so blocks away, next to their church. At the time, they were both taking classes at the New York Institute of Technology, which was right nearby. But after they graduated, and Rosie got a job managing a fast-food place and Noel got a job in asbestos removal, they managed to save a little money and bought the house on Argyle Avenue.

2   From the outside, their home looks fairly plain. It's in a part of Uniondale that has a lot of tract housing from just after the war, and most of the houses are alike—squat and square, with aluminum siding, maybe a dormer window in the attic, and a small patch of lawn out front. But there is a beautiful park down the street, the public schools are supposed to be good, and Rosie and Noel have built a new garage and renovated the basement. Now that Noel has started his own business, as an environmental engineer, he has his office down there—Suite 2B, it says on his stationery—and every morning he puts on his tie and goes down the stairs to make calls and work on the computer. If Noel's business takes off, Rosie says, she would like to move to a bigger house, in Garden City, which is one town over. She says this even though Garden City is mostly white. In fact, when she told one of her girlfriends, a black American, about this idea, her friend said that she was crazy—that Garden City was no place for a black person. But that is just the point. Rosie and Noel are from Jamaica. They don't consider themselves black at all.

3   This doesn't mean that my cousins haven't sometimes been lumped together with American blacks. Noel had a job once removing asbestos at Kennedy Airport, and his boss there called him "nigger" and cut his hours. But Noel didn't take it personally. That boss, he says, didn't like women or Jews, either, or people with college degrees—or even himself, for that matter. Another time, Noel found out that a white guy working next to him in the same job and with the same qualifications was making ten thousand dollars a year more than he was. He quit the next day. Noel knows that racism is out there. It's just that he doesn't quite understand—or accept—the categories on which it depends.

4   To a West Indian, black is a literal description: you are black if your skin is black. Noel's father, for example, is black. But his mother had a white father, and she herself was fair-skinned and could pass. As for Rosie, her mother and my mother, who are twins, thought of themselves while they were growing up as "middle-class brown," which is to say that they are about the same shade as Colin Powell. That's because our maternal grandfather was part Jewish, in addition to all kinds of other things, and Grandma, though she was a good deal darker than he was, had enough Scottish blood in her to have been born with straight hair. Rosie's mother married another brown Jamaican, and that makes Rosie a light chocolate. As for my mother, she married an Englishman, making everything that much more complicated, since by the racial categories of my own heritage I am one thing and by the racial categories of America I am another. Once, when Rosie and Noel came to visit me while I was living in Washington, D.C., Noel asked me to show him "where the black people lived," and I was confused for a moment until I realized that he was using "black" in the American sense, and so was asking in the same way that someone visiting Manhattan might ask where Chinatown was. That the people he wanted to see were in many cases racially indistinguishable from him didn't matter. The facts of his genealogy, of his nationality, of his status as an immigrant made him, in his own eyes, different.

5   This question of who West Indians are and how they define themselves may seem trivial, like racial hairsplitting. But it is not trivial. In the past twenty years, the number of West Indians in America has exploded. There are now half a million in the New York area alone and, despite their recent arrival, they make substantially more money than American blacks. They live in better neighborhoods. Their families are stronger. In the New York area, in fact, West Indians fare about as well as Chinese and Korean immigrants. That is why the Caribbean invasion and the issue of West Indian identity have become such controversial issues. What does it say about the nature of racism that another group of blacks, who have the same legacy of slavery as their American counterparts and are physically indistinguishable from them, can come here and succeed as well as the Chinese and the Koreans do? Is overcoming racism as simple as doing what Noel does, which is to dismiss it, to hold himself above it, to brave it and move on?

6   These are difficult questions, not merely for what they imply about American blacks but for the ways in which they appear to contradict conventional

views of what prejudice is. Racism, after all, is supposed to be indiscriminate. For example, sociologists have observed that the more blacks there are in a community the more negative the whites' attitudes will be. Blacks in Denver have a far easier time than blacks in, say, Cleveland. Lynchings in the South at the turn of this century, to give another example, were far more common in counties where there was a large black population than in areas where whites were in the majority. Prejudice is the crudest of weapons, a reaction against blacks in the aggregate that grows as the perception of black threat grows. If that is the case, however, the addition of hundreds of thousands of new black immigrants to the New York area should have made things worse for people like Rosie and Noel, not better. And, if racism is so indiscriminate in its application, why is one group of blacks flourishing and the other not?

7   The implication of West Indian success is that racism does not really exist at all—at least, not in the form that we have assumed it does. The implication is that the key factor in understanding racial prejudice is not the behavior and attitudes of whites but the behavior and attitudes of blacks—not white discrimination but black culture. It implies that when the conservatives in Congress say the responsibility for ending urban poverty lies not with collective action but with the poor themselves they are right.

8   I think of this sometimes when I go with Rosie and Noel to their church, which is in Hempstead, just a mile away. It was once a white church, but in the past decade or so it has been taken over by immigrants from the Caribbean. They have so swelled its membership that the church has bought much of the surrounding property and is about to add a hundred seats to its sanctuary. The pastor, though, is white, and when the band up front is playing and the congregation is in full West Indian form the pastor sometimes seems out of place, as if he cannot move in time with the music. I always wonder how long the white minister at Rosie and Noel's church will last—whether there won't be some kind of groundswell among the congregation to replace him with one of their own. But Noel tells me the issue has never really come up. Noel says, in fact, that he's happier with a white minister, for the same reasons that he's happy with his neighborhood, where the people across the way are Polish and another neighbor is Hispanic and still another is a black American. He doesn't want to be shut off from everyone else, isolated within the narrow confines of his race. He wants to be part of the world, and when he says these things it is awfully tempting to credit that attitude with what he and Rosie have accomplished.

9   Is this confidence, this optimism, this equanimity all that separates the poorest of American blacks from a house on Argyle Avenue?

* * * * *

10   In 1994, Philip Kasinitz, a sociologist at Manhattan's Hunter College, and Jan Rosenberg, who teaches at Long Island University, conducted a study of the Red Hook area of Brooklyn, a neighborhood of around thirteen or fourteen

thousand which lies between the waterfront and the Gowanus Expressway. Red Hook has a large public-housing project at its center, and around the project, in the streets that line the waterfront, are several hundred thriving blue-collar businesses—warehouses, shipping companies, small manufacturers, and contractors. The object of the study was to resolve what Kasinitz and Rosenberg saw as the paradox of Red Hook: despite Red Hooks seemingly fortuitous conjunction of unskilled labor and blue-collar jobs, very few of the Puerto Ricans and African-Americans from the neighborhood ever found work in the bustling economy of their own back yard.

11   After dozens of interviews with local employers, the two researchers uncovered a persistent pattern of what they call positive discrimination. It was not that the employers did not like blacks and Hispanics. It was that they had developed an elaborate mechanism for distinguishing between those they felt were "good" blacks and those they felt were "bad" blacks, between those they judged to be "good" Hispanics and those they considered "bad" Hispanics. "Good" meant that you came from outside the neighborhood, because employers identified locals with the crime and dissipation they saw on the streets around them. "Good" also meant that you were an immigrant, because employers felt that being an immigrant implied a loyalty and a willingness to work and learn not found among the native-born. In Red Hook, the good Hispanics are Mexican and South American, not Puerto Rican. And the good blacks are West Indian.

12   The Harvard sociologist Mary C. Waters conducted a similar study, in 1993, which looked at a food-service company in Manhattan where West Indian workers have steadily displaced African-Americans in the past few years. The transcripts of her interviews with the company managers make fascinating reading, providing an intimate view of the perceptions that govern the urban workplace. Listen to one forty-year-old white male manager on the subject of West Indians:

> They tend more to shy away from doing all of the illegal things because they have such strict rules down in their countries and jails. And they're nothing like here. So like, they're like really paranoid to do something wrong. They seem to be very, very self-conscious of it. No matter what they have to do, if they have to try and work three jobs, they do. They won't go into drugs or anything like that.

13   Or listen to this, from a fifty-three-year-old white female manager:

> I work closely with this one girl who's from Trinidad. And she told me when she first came here to live with her sister and cousin, she had two children. And she said I'm here four years and we've reached our goals. And what was your goal? For her two children to each have their own bedroom. Now she has a three bedroom apartment and she said that's one of the goals she was shooting for. . . . If that was an American, they would say, I reached my goal. I bought a Cadillac.

14   This idea of the West Indian as a kind of superior black is not a new one. When the first wave of Caribbean immigrants came to New York and Boston, in the early nineteen-hundreds, other blacks dubbed them Jewmaicans, in derisive reference to the emphasis they placed on hard work and education. In the nineteen-eighties, the economist Thomas Sowell gave the idea a serious intellectual imprimatur by arguing that the West Indian advantage was a historical legacy of Caribbean slave culture. According to Sowell, in the American South slaveowners tended to hire managers who were married, in order to limit the problems created by sexual relations between overseers and slave women. But the West Indies were a hardship post, without a large and settled white population. There the overseers tended to be bachelors, and, with white women scarce, there was far more commingling of the races. The resulting large group of coloreds soon formed a kind of proto-middle class, performing various kinds of skilled and sophisticated tasks that there were not enough whites around to do, as there were in the American South. They were carpenters, masons, plumbers, and small businessmen, many years in advance of their American counterparts, developing skills that required education and initiative.

15   My mother and Rosie's mother came from this colored class. Their parents were schoolteachers in a tiny village buried in the hills of central Jamaica. My grandmother's and grandfather's salaries combined put them, at best, on the lower rungs of the middle class. But their expectations went well beyond that. In my grandfather's library were Dickens and Maupassant. My mother and her sister were pushed to win scholarships to a proper English-style boarding school at the other end of the island; and later, when my mother graduated, it was taken for granted that she would attend university in England, even though the cost of tuition and passage meant that my grandmother had to borrow a small fortune from the Chinese grocer down the road.

16   My grandparents had ambitions for their children, but it was a special kind of ambition, born of a certainty that American blacks did not have—that their values were the same as those of society as a whole, and that hard work and talent could actually be rewarded. In my mother's first year at boarding school, she looked up "Negro" in the eleventh edition of the Encyclopedia Britannica. "In certain . . . characteristics . . . the negro would appear to stand on a lower evolutionary plane than the white man," she read. And the entry continued:

> The mental constitution of the negro is very similar to that of a child, normally good-natured and cheerful, but subject to sudden fits of emotion and passion during which he is capable of performing acts of singular atrocity, impressionable, vain, but often exhibiting in the capacity of servant a dog-like fidelity which has stood the supreme test.

17   All black people of my mother's generation—and of generations before and since—have necessarily faced a moment like this, when they are confronted for the first time with the allegation of their inferiority. But, at least in my mother's

case, her school was integrated, and that meant she knew black girls who were more intelligent than white girls, and she knew how she measured against the world around her. At least she lived in a country that had blacks and browns in every position of authority, so her personal experience gave the lie to what she read in the encyclopedia. This, I think, is what Noel means when he says that he cannot quite appreciate what it is that weighs black Americans down, because he encountered the debilitating effects of racism late, when he was much stronger. He came of age in a country where he belonged to the majority.

18   When I was growing up, my mother sometimes read to my brothers and me from the work of Louise Bennett, the great Jamaican poet of my mother's generation. The poem I remember best is about two women—one black and one white—in a hair salon, the black woman getting her hair straightened and, next to her, the white woman getting her hair curled:

> same time me mind start 'tink
> 'bout me and de white woman
> how me tek out me natural perm
> and she put in false one

19   There is no anger or resentment here, only irony and playfulness—the two races captured in a shared moment of absurdity. Then comes the twist. The black woman is paying less to look white than the white woman is to look black:

> de two a we da tek a risk
> what rain or shine will bring
> but fe har risk is t're poun'
> fi me onle five shillin'

20   In the nineteen-twenties, the garment trade in New York was first integrated by West Indian women, because, the legend goes, they would see the sign on the door saying "No blacks need apply" and simply walk on in. When I look back on Bennett's poem, I think I understand how they found the courage to do that.

21   It is tempting to use the West Indian story as evidence that discrimination doesn't really exist—as proof that the only thing inner-city African-Americans have to do to be welcomed as warmly as West Indians in places like Red Hook is to make the necessary cultural adjustments. If West Indians are different, as they clearly are, then it is easy to imagine that those differences are the reason for their success—that their refusal to be bowed is what lets them walk on by the signs that prohibit them or move to neighborhoods that black Americans would shy away from. It also seems hard to see how the West Indian story is in any way consistent with the idea of racism as an indiscriminate, pernicious threat aimed at all black people.

22   But here is where things become more difficult, and where what seems obvious about West Indian achievement turns out not to be obvious at all. One of the striking things in the Red Hook study, for example, is the emphasis that the employers appeared to place on hiring outsiders—Irish or Russian or Mexican or West Indian immigrants from places far from Red Hook. The reason for this was not, the researchers argue, that the employers had any great familiarity with the cultures of those immigrants. They had none, and that was the point. They were drawn to the unfamiliar because what was familiar to them—the projects of Red Hook—was anathema. The Columbia University anthropologist Katherine Newman makes the same observation in a recent study of two fast-food restaurants in Harlem. She compared the hundreds of people who applied for jobs at those restaurants with the few people who were actually hired, and found, among other things, that how far an applicant lived from the job site made a huge difference. Of those applicants who lived less than two miles from the restaurant, ten per cent were hired. Of those who lived more than two miles from the restaurant, nearly forty per cent were hired. As Newman puts it, employers preferred the ghetto they didn't know to the ghetto they did.

23   Neither study describes a workplace where individual attitudes make a big difference, or where the clunky and impersonal prejudices that characterize traditional racism have been discarded. They sound like places where old-style racism and appreciation of immigrant values are somehow bound up together. Listen to another white manager who was interviewed by Mary Waters:

> Island blacks who come over, they're immigrant. They may not have such a good life where they are so they gonna try to strive to better themselves and I think there's a lot of American blacks out there who feel we owe them. And enough is enough already. You know, this is something that happened to their ancestors, not now. I mean, we've done so much for the black people in America now that it's time that they got off their butts.

24   Here, then, are the two competing ideas about racism side by side: the manager issues a blanket condemnation of American blacks even as he holds West Indians up as a cultural ideal. The example of West Indians as "good" blacks makes the old blanket prejudice against American blacks all the easier to express. The manager can tell black Americans to get off their butts without fear of sounding, in his own ears, like a racist, because he has simultaneously celebrated island blacks for their work ethic. The success of West Indians is not proof that discrimination against American blacks does not exist. Rather, it is the means by which discrimination against American blacks is given one last, vicious twist: I am not so shallow as to despise you for the color of your skin, because I have found people your color that I like. Now I can despise you for who you are.

25   This is racism's newest mutation—multicultural racism, where one ethnic group can be played off against another. But it is wrong to call West Indians the victors in this competition, in anything but the narrowest sense. In American

history, immigrants have always profited from assimilation: as they have adopted the language and customs of this country, they have sped their passage into the mainstream. The new racism means that West Indians are the first group of people for whom that has not been true. Their advantage depends on their remaining outsiders, on remaining unfamiliar, on being distinct by custom, culture, and language from the American blacks they would otherwise resemble. There is already some evidence that the considerable economic and social advantages that West Indians hold over American blacks begin to dissipate by the second generation, when the island accent has faded, and those in positions of power who draw distinctions between good blacks and bad blacks begin to lump West Indians with everyone else. For West Indians, assimilation is tantamount to suicide. This is a cruel fate for any immigrant group, but it is especially so for West Indians, whose history and literature are already redolent with the themes of dispossession and loss, with the long search for identity and belonging. In the nineteen-twenties, Marcus Garvey[1] sought community in the idea of Africa. Bob Marley, the Jamaican reggae singer, yearned for Zion. In "Rites of Passage" the Barbadian poet Edward Kamau Brathwaite writes:

> Where, then, is the nigger's
> home?
>
> In Paris Brixton Kingston
> Rome?
>
> Here?
> Or in Heaven?

26   America might have been home. But it is not: not Red Hook, anyway; not Harlem; not even Argyle Avenue.

27   There is also no small measure of guilt here, for West Indians cannot escape the fact that their success has come, to some extent, at the expense of American blacks, and that as they have noisily differentiated themselves from African-Americans—promoting the stereotype of themselves as the good blacks—they have made it easier for whites to join in. It does not help matters that the same kinds of distinctions between good and bad blacks which govern the immigrant experience here have always lurked just below the surface of life in the West Indies as well. It was the infusion of white blood that gave the colored class its status in the Caribbean, and the members of this class have never forgotten that, nor have they failed, in a thousand subtle ways, to distance themselves from those around them who experienced a darker and less privileged past.

28   In my mother's house, in Harewood, the family often passed around a pencilled drawing of two of my great-grandparents; she was part Jewish, and he was

---

[1](1887–1940) Black nationalist who was born in Jamaica and lived in the United States after 1916.

part Scottish. The other side—the African side—was never mentioned. My grandmother was the ringleader in this. She prized my grandfather's light skin, but she also suffered as a result of this standard. "She's nice, you know, but she's too dark," her mother-in-law would say of her. The most telling story of all, though, is the story of one of my mother's relatives, whom I'll call Aunt Joan, who was as fair as my great-grandmother was. Aunt Joan married what in Jamaica is called an Injun—a man with a dark complexion that is redeemed from pure Africanness by straight, fine black hair. She had two daughters by him— handsome girls with dark complexions. But he died young, and one day, while she was travelling on a train to visit her daughter, she met and took an interest in a light-skinned man in the same railway car. What happened next is something that Aunt Joan told only my mother, years later, with the greatest of shame. When she got off the train, she walked right by her daughter, disowning her own flesh and blood, because she did not want a man so light-skinned and desirable to know that she had borne a daughter so dark.

29   My mother, in the nineteen-sixties, wrote a book about her experiences. It was entitled *Brown Face, Big Master*, the brown face referring to her and the big master, in the Jamaican dialect, referring to God. Sons, of course, are hardly objective on the achievements of their mothers, but there is one passage in the book that I find unforgettable, because it is such an eloquent testimony to the moral precariousness of the Jamaican colored class—to the mixture of confusion and guilt that attends its position as beneficiary of racism's distinctions. The passage describes a time just after my mother and father were married, when they were living in London and my eldest brother was still a baby. They were looking for an apartment, and after a long search my father found one in a London suburb. On the day after they moved in, however, the landlady ordered them out. "You didn't tell me your wife was colored," she told my father, in a rage.

30   In her book my mother describes her long struggle to make sense of this humiliation, to reconcile her experience with her faith. In the end, she was forced to acknowledge that anger was not an option—that as a Jamaican "middle-class brown," and a descendant of Aunt Joan, she could hardly reproach another for the impulse to divide good black from bad black:

> I complained to God in so many words: "Here I was, the wounded representa-
> tive of the negro race in our struggle to be accounted free and equal with the
> dominating whites!" And God was amused; my prayer did not ring true with
> Him. I would try again. And then God said, "Have you not done the same
> thing? Remember this one and that one, people whom you have slighted or
> avoided or treated less considerately than others because they were different
> superficially, and you were ashamed to be identified with them. Have you not
> been glad that you are not more colored than you are? Grateful that you are
> not black?" My anger and hate against the landlady melted. I was no better
> than she was, nor worse for that matter. . . . We were both guilty of the sin of
> self-regard, the pride and the exclusiveness by which we cut some people off
> from ourselves.

31   I grew up in Canada, in a little farming town an hour and a half outside of Toronto. My father teaches mathematics at a nearby university, and my mother is a therapist. For many years, she was the only black person in town, but I cannot remember wondering or worrying, or even thinking, about this fact. Back then, color meant only good things. It meant my cousins in Jamaica. It meant the graduate students from Africa and India my father would bring home from the university. My own color was not something I ever thought much about, either, because it seemed such a stray fact. Blacks knew what I was. They could discern the hint of Africa beneath my fair skin. But it was a kind of secret—something that they would ask me about quietly when no one else was around. ("Where you from?" an older black man once asked me. "Ontario," I said, not thinking. "No," he replied. "Where you *from?*" And then I understood and told him, and he nodded as if he had already known. "We was speculatin' about your heritage," he said.) But whites never guessed, and even after I informed them it never seemed to make a difference. Why would it? In a town that is ninety-nine per cent white, one modest alleged splash of color hardly amounts to a threat.

32   But things changed when I left for Toronto to attend college. This was during the early nineteen-eighties, when West Indians were immigrating to Canada in droves, and Toronto had become second only to New York as the Jamaican expatriates' capital in North America. At school, in the dining hall, I was served by Jamaicans. The infamous Jane-Finch projects, in northern Toronto, were considered the Jamaican projects. The drug trade then taking off was said to be the Jamaican drug trade. In the popular imagination, Jamaicans were—and are—welfare queens and gun-toting gangsters and dissolute youths. In Ontario, blacks accused of crimes are released by the police eighteen per cent of the time; whites are released twenty-nine per cent of the time. In drug-trafficking and importing cases, blacks are twenty-seven times as likely as whites to be jailed before their trial takes place, and twenty times as likely to be imprisoned on drug-possession charges.

33   After I had moved to the United States, I puzzled over this seeming contradiction—how West Indians celebrated in New York for their industry and drive could represent, just five hundred miles northwest, crime and dissipation. Didn't Torontonians see what was special and different in West Indian culture? But that was a naïve question. The West Indians were the first significant brush with blackness that white, smug, comfortable Torontonians had ever had. They had no bad blacks to contrast with the newcomers, no African-Americans to serve as a safety valve for their prejudices, no way to perform America's crude racial triage.

34   Not long ago, I sat in a coffee shop with someone I knew vaguely from college, who, like me, had moved to New York from Toronto. He began to speak of the threat that he felt Toronto now faced. It was the Jamaicans, he said. They were a bad seed. He was, of course, oblivious of my background. I said nothing, though, and he launched into a long explanation of how, in slave times, Jamaica was the island where all the most troublesome and obstreperous slaves were sent, and how that accounted for their particularly nasty disposition today.

35   I have told that story many times since, usually as a joke, because it was funny in an appalling way—particularly when I informed him much, much later that my mother was Jamaican. I tell the story that way because otherwise it is too painful. There must be people in Toronto just like Rosie and Noel, with the same attitudes and aspirations, who want to live in a neighborhood as nice as Argyle Avenue, who want to build a new garage and renovate their basement and set up their own business downstairs. But it is not completely up to them, is it? What has happened to Jamaicans in Toronto is proof that what has happened to Jamaicans here is not the end of racism, or even the beginning of the end of racism, but an accident of history and geography. In America, there is someone else to despise. In Canada, there is not. In the new racism, as in the old, somebody always has to be the nigger.

EXERCISES

Some of the Issues

1. Examine the description of Rosie and Noel's house and office in paragraph 2. What is your image of Rosie and Noel? How do the beginning paragraphs serve as an introduction to the ideas presented in the article?

2. According to the author, what are some of the reasons behind Noel's response to racism (paragraph 3)?

3. Summarize the differences the author describes between the West Indian definition of black and the American definition (paragraph 4).

4. Reread paragraphs 5 through 7. What are some of the other immigrant groups to which the author compares West Indians? Why are some of the questions raised by Gladwell "difficult"?

5. What are the conclusions of each of the studies Gladwell discusses in paragraphs 10 through 13 and 22 through 24? How does he use these conclusions to support his ideas?

6. What are the differences between the history and culture of American blacks and those of West Indians, particularly Gladwell's family (paragraphs 14 and 15)?

7. What happened when Gladwell's mother looked up the word "Negro" in the encyclopedia? How did her personal experience give "the lie to what she read" (paragraph 17)?

8. In paragraph 21, the author writes, "It is tempting to use the West Indian story as evidence that discrimination doesn't really exist." How does the author go on to question this "evidence"?

9. How does the author define "multicultural racism" in paragraph 25? Why are West Indians not "the victims in this competition, in anything but the narrowest sense"?

10. In paragraphs 31 through 35, Gladwell compares the history and treatment of Canadian West Indians to that of American West Indians. What is Gladwell trying to point out through these comparisons?

The Way We Are Told

11. The author waits until the end of paragraph 2 to tell us that Rosie and Noel are from Jamaica. What is the effect of doing so?
12. How does Gladwell combine the use of personal and family history with more objective sources? Do you find the mixture effective?
13. Gladwell concludes his essay with a strong statement. How does he build his evidence for this statement throughout the essay? Why might he have chosen not to make this statement toward the beginning?
14. We are not absolutely sure of Gladwell's point until the middle or even the end of his essay. In fact, we might initially suspect that Gladwell is making an opposite point to the one he finally makes. What might he gain from structuring the essay this way?

Some Subjects for Writing

15. Interview two or more relatives or friends who either immigrated to the United States or identify with a specific ethnic or racial group. Keeping in mind some of the issues Gladwell raises, focus on both their self-image and identity as well as how they perceive themselves to be treated by others. Make sure you develop a series of questions beforehand and, as you are interviewing, ask follow-up questions that might help your subjects elaborate on, explain, or analyze their experience. Write an essay in which you recount their stories and compare their experiences.

Arrival at Manzanar

Jeanne Wakatsuki Houston
and James D. Houston

Like Walter White in an earlier selection, Jeanne Wakatsuki was caught up in a historical event. The year was 1942, the place California. A few months before, the Japanese had attacked the United States, bombing Pearl Harbor and overrunning U.S. possessions in the Pacific. The war was going badly; the U.S. forces and those of its allies were in retreat all over the area. Popular anger and fear turned against the Japanese-Americans living on the West Coast. President Franklin D. Roosevelt signed an executive order to intern those thousands of U.S. citizens—men, women, and children. They were rounded up at short notice, had to leave their homes and businesses, either selling them or abandoning them outright. They were shipped off to internment camps; Manzanar was one of them. They had to spend the war years there, all except those men who volunteered for the army. The battalion formed by these Japanese-Americans, fighting in Italy, became the most decorated U.S. Army unit in the war.

The internment of Americans of Japanese descent increasingly became a subject of controversy and criticism in the decades following the war. In 1987 the U.S. Congress finally passed an act that made some restitution to the former internees; it acknowledged that what was done to them had been wrong and included a payment of $20,000 to each of the survivors of the camps, that is, to those who were still alive after more than 40 years.

Jean Wakatsuki, born in California in 1935, was seven years old when she, together with her family, was sent to the internment camp at Manzanar. She remained there until age eleven. After high school she studied sociology and journalism at San Jose State College, where she met her husband, James D. Houston, a novelist. Together they wrote Farewell to Manzanar, *published in 1973, as a record of life in the camp and of its impact on her and her family. The following is a selection from it.*

1   In December of 1941 Papa's disappearance didn't bother me nearly so much as the world I soon found myself in.

2   He had been a jack-of-all-trades. When I was born he was farming near Inglewood. Later, when he started fishing, we moved to Ocean Park, near Santa Monica, and until they picked him up, that's where we lived, in a big frame house with a brick fireplace, a block back from the beach. We were the only Japanese family in the neighborhood. Papa liked it that way. He didn't want to be labeled or grouped by anyone. But with him gone and no way of knowing

what to expect, my mother moved all of us down to Terminal Island. Woody already lived there, and one of my older sisters had married a Terminal Island boy. Mama's first concern now was to keep the family together; and once the war began, she felt safer there than isolated racially in Ocean Park. But for me, at age seven, the island was a country as foreign as India or Arabia would have been. It was the first time I had lived among other Japanese, or gone to school with them, and I was terrified all the time.

3   This was partly Papa's fault. One of his threats to keep us younger kids in line was "I'm going to sell you to the Chinaman." When I had entered kindergarten two years earlier, I was the only Oriental in the class. They sat me next to a Caucasian girl who happened to have very slanted eyes. I looked at her and began to scream, certain Papa had sold me out at last. My fear of her ran so deep I could not speak of it, even to Mama, couldn't explain why I was screaming. For two weeks I had nightmares about this girl, until the teachers finally moved me to the other side of the room. And it was still with me, this fear of Oriental faces, when we moved to Terminal Island.

4   In those days it was a company town, a ghetto owned and controlled by the canneries. The men went after fish, and whenever the boats came back—day or night—the women would be called to process the catch while it was fresh. One in the afternoon or four in the morning, it made no difference. My mother had to go to work right after we moved there. I can still hear the whistle—two toots for French's, three for Van Camp's—and she and Chizu[1] would be out of bed in the middle of the night, heading for the cannery.

5   The house we lived in was nothing more than a shack, a barracks with single plank walls and rough wooden floors, like the cheapest kind of migrant workers' housing. The people around us were hard-working, boisterous, a little proud of their nickname, *yo-go-re*, which meant literally *uncouth one*, or roughneck, or dead-end kid. They not only spoke Japanese exclusively, they spoke a dialect peculiar to Kyushu, where their families had come from in Japan, a rough, fisherman's language, full of oaths and insults. Instead of saying *ba-ka-ta-re*, a common insult meaning *stupid*, Terminal Islanders would say *ba-ka-ya-ro*, a coarser and exclusively masculine use of the word, which implies gross stupidity. They would swagger and pick on outsiders and persecute anyone who didn't speak as they did. That was what made my own time there so hateful. I had never spoken anything but English, and the other kids in the second grade despised me for it. They were tough and mean, like ghetto kids anywhere. Each day after school I dreaded their ambush. My brother Kiyo, three years older, would wait for me at the door, where we would decide whether to run straight home together, or split up, or try a new and unexpected route.

[1] Woody's wife, the author's sister-in-law.

6   None of these kids ever actually attacked. It was the threat that frightened us, their fearful looks, and the noises they would make, like miniature Samurai,[2] in a language we couldn't understand.

7   At the time it seemed we had been living under this reign of fear for years. In fact, we lived there about two months. Late in February the navy decided to clear Terminal Island completely. Even though most of us were American-born, it was dangerous having that many Orientals so close to the Long Beach Naval Station, on the opposite end of the island. We had known something like this was coming. But, like Papa's arrest, not much could be done ahead of time. There were four of us kids still young enough to be living with Mama, plus Granny, her mother, sixty-five then, speaking no English, and nearly blind. Mama didn't know where else she could get work, and we had nowhere else to move *to*. On February 25 the choice was made for us. We were given forty-eight hours to clear out.

8   The secondhand dealers had been prowling around for weeks, like wolves, offering humiliating prices for goods and furniture they knew many of us would have to sell sooner or later. Mama had left all but her most valuable possessions in Ocean Park, simply because she had nowhere to put them. She had brought along her pottery, her silver, heirlooms like the kimonos Granny had brought from Japan, tea sets, lacquered tables, and one fine old set of china, blue and white porcelain, almost translucent. On the day we were leaving, Woody's car was so crammed with boxes and luggage and kids we had just run out of room. Mama had to sell this china.

9   One of the dealers offered her fifteen dollars for it. She said it was a full setting for twelve and worth at least two hundred. He said fifteen was his top price. Mama started to quiver. Her eyes blazed up at him. She had been packing all night and trying to calm down Granny, who didn't understand why we were moving again and what all the rush was about. Mama's nerves were shot, and now navy jeeps were patrolling the streets. She didn't say another word. She just glared at this man, all the rage and frustration channeled at him through her eyes.

10   He watched her for a moment and said he was sure he couldn't pay more than seventeen fifty for that china. She reached into the red velvet case, took out a dinner plate and hurled it at the floor right in front of his feet.

11   The man leaped back shouting, "Hey! Hey, don't do that! Those are valuable dishes!"

12   Mama took out another dinner plate and hurled it at the floor, then another and another, never moving, never opening her mouth, just quivering and glaring at the retreating dealer, with tears streaming down her cheeks. He finally turned and scuttled out the door, heading for the next house. When he was

[2]Japanese warrior class from the twelfth to the end of the nineteenth century.

gone she stood there smashing cups and bowls and platters until the whole set lay in scattered blue and white fragments across the wooden floor.

13   The name Manzanar meant nothing to us when we left Boyle Heights. We didn't know where it was or what it was. We went because the government ordered us to. And, in the case of my older brothers and sisters, we went with a certain amount of relief. They had all heard stories of Japanese homes being attacked, of beatings in the streets of California towns. They were as frightened of the Caucasians as Caucasians were of us. Moving, under what appeared to be government protection, to an area less directly threatened by the war seemed not such a bad idea at all. For some it actually sounded like a fine adventure.

14   Our pickup point was a Buddhist church in Los Angeles. It was very early, and misty, when we got there with our luggage. Mama had bought heavy coats for all of us. She grew up in eastern Washington and knew that anywhere inland in early April would be cold. I was proud of my new coat, and I remember sitting on a duffel bag trying to be friendly with the Greyhound driver. I smiled at him. He didn't smile back. He was befriending no one. Someone tied a numbered tag to my collar and to the duffel bag (each family was given a number, and that became our official designation until the camps were closed), someone else passed out box lunches for the trip, and we climbed aboard.

15   I had never been outside Los Angeles County, never traveled more than ten miles from the coast, had never even ridden on a bus. I was full of excitement, the way any kid would be, and wanted to look out the window. But for the first few hours the shades were drawn. Around me other people played cards, read magazines, dozed, waiting. I settled back, waiting too, and finally fell asleep. The bus felt very secure to me. Almost half its passengers were immediate relatives. Mama and my older brothers had succeeded in keeping most of us together, on the same bus, headed for the same camp. I didn't realize until much later what a job that was. The strategy had been, first, to have everyone living in the same district when the evacuation began, and then to get all of us included under the same family number, even though names had been changed by marriage. Many families weren't as lucky as ours and suffered months of anguish while trying to arrange transfers from one camp to another.

16   We rode all day. By the time we reached our destination, the shades were up. It was late afternoon. The first thing I saw was a yellow swirl across a blurred, reddish setting sun. The bus was being pelted by what sounded like splattering rain. It wasn't rain. This was my first look at something I would soon know very well, a billowing flurry of dust and sand churned up by the wind through Owens Valley.

17   We drove past a barbed-wire fence, through a gate, and into an open space where trunks and sacks and packages had been dumped from the baggage trucks that drove out ahead of us. I could see a few tents set up, the first rows of black barracks, and beyond them, blurred by sand, rows of barracks that seemed to spread for miles across this plain. People were sitting on cartons or milling around, with their backs to the wind, waiting to see which friends or relatives

might be on this bus. As we approached, they turned or stood up, and some moved toward us expectantly. But inside the bus no one stirred. No one waved or spoke. They just stared out the windows, ominously silent. I didn't understand this. Hadn't we finally arrived, our whole family intact? I opened a window, leaned out, and yelled happily "Hey! This whole bus is full of Wakatsukis!"

18   Outside, the greeters smiled. Inside there was an explosion of laughter, hysterical, tension-breaking laughter that left my brothers choking and whacking each other across the shoulders.

19   We had pulled up just in time for dinner. The mess halls weren't completed yet. An outdoor chow line snaked around a half-finished building that broke a good part of the wind. They issued us army mess kits, the round metal kind that fold over, and plopped in scoops of canned Vienna sausage, canned string beans, steamed rice that had been cooked too long, and on top of the rice a serving of canned apricots. The Caucasian servers were thinking the fruit poured over rice would make a good dessert. Among the Japanese, of course, rice is never eaten with sweet foods, only with salty or savory foods. Few of us could eat such a mixture. But at this point no one dared protest. It would have been impolite. I was horrified when I saw the apricot syrup seeping through my little mound of rice. I opened my mouth to complain. My mother jabbed me in the back to keep quiet. We moved on through the line and joined the others squatting in the lee of half-raised walls, dabbing courteously at what was, for almost everyone there, an inedible concoction.

20   After dinner we were taken to Block 16, a cluster of fifteen barracks that had just been finished a day or so earlier—although finished was hardly the word for it. The shacks were built of one thickness of pine planking covered with tarpaper. They sat on concrete footings, with about two feet of open space between the floorboards and the ground. Gaps showed between the planks, and as the weeks passed and the green wood dried out, the gaps widened. Knotholes gaped in the uncovered floor.

21   Each barracks was divided into six units, sixteen by twenty feet, about the size of a living room, with one bare bulb hanging from the ceiling and an oil stove for heat. We were assigned two of these for the twelve people in our family group; and our official family "number" was enlarged by three digits—16 plus the number of this barracks. We were issued steel army cots, two brown army blankets each, and some mattress covers, which my brothers stuffed with straw.

22   The first task was to divide up what space we had for sleeping. Bill and Woody contributed a blanket each and partitioned off the first room: one side for Bill and Tomi, one side for Woody and Chizu and their baby girl. Woody also got the stove, for heating formulas.

23   The people who had it hardest during the first few months were young couples like these, many of whom had married just before the evacuation began, in order not to be separated and sent to different camps. Our two rooms were crowded, but at least it was all in the family. My oldest sister and her husband

were shoved into one of those sixteen-by-twenty-foot compartments with six people they had never seen before—two other couples, one recently married like themselves, the other with two teenage boys. Partitioning off a room like that wasn't easy. It was bitter cold when we arrived, and the wind did not abate. All they had to use for room dividers were those army blankets, two of which were barely enough to keep one person warm. They argued over whose blanket should be sacrificed and later argued about noise at night—the parents wanted their boys asleep by 9:00 P.M.—and they continued arguing over matters like that for six months, until my sister and her husband left to harvest sugar beets in Idaho. It was grueling work up there, and wages were pitiful, but when the call came through camp for workers to alleviate the wartime labor shortage, it sounded better than their life at Manzanar. They knew they'd have, if nothing else, a room, perhaps a cabin of their own.

24   That first night in Block 16, the rest of us squeezed into the second room—Granny, Lillian, age fourteen, Ray, thirteen, May, eleven, Kiyo, ten, Mama, and me. I didn't mind this at all at the time. Being youngest meant I got to sleep with Mama. And before we went to bed I had a great time jumping up and down on the mattress. The boys had stuffed so much straw into hers, we had to flatten it some so we wouldn't slide off. I slept with her every night after that until Papa came back.

EXERCISES

Some of the Issues

1. What do the first three paragraphs tell us about Houston's family?
2. Paragraphs 3 through 7 explain her fears. What are they? What would you imagine would be the mother's fears in this period?
3. What does the story about the secondhand dealer (paragraphs 8 through 12) tell us about the situation of Japanese-Americans at that time? What does it tell us about Houston's mother?
4. Examine the actions of the camp officials. To what extent can the authorities be said to be deliberately cruel? Unthoughtful? Uninformed about cultural differences? Cite specific details to support your view.
*5. Read Maxine Hong Kingston's "Girlhood among Ghosts." Both Kingston and Houston grew up in California at about the same time. In what way are their two experiences similar? How do they differ?

The Way We Are Told

6. In paragraphs 20 through 24 Houston gives a detailed description of the barracks. Does her description contain any words or phrases that express emotions? Justify their presence or absence.

Some Subjects for Writing

7. Jeanne Wakatsuki Houston describes the bus ride to Manzanar from a child's point of view, as an adventure, almost fun, and not as a tragedy. Recall an incident of your childhood that would look different to you now (a fire, getting lost in a strange neighborhood). Describe it from a child's point of view and end with a paragraph explaining how you view the same incident as an adult.

8. Write about a time you, or your family, experienced a challenge or unexpected change. How did you or others react to change at that time? Looking back on the experience, did it produce changes in individuals in your family or in the family structure as a whole?

9. At one point, all the members of Jeanne Wakatsuki's family had to live in one room along with five strangers. In an essay consider how important having your own space and privacy is to you. Describe your present arrangements and the extent to which you might like to change them.

*10. Jeanne Wakatsuki Houston (with James D. Houston) and Dwight Okita recount two experiences of Japanese-American children who were interned during World War II. With the help of your instructor, research and write a paper on the experience of Japanese-Americans during the war.

In Response to Executive Order 9066: All Americans of Japanese Descent Must Report to Relocation Centers

Dwight Okita

*Dwight Okita was born in Chicago in 1958. A poet and playwright, he has had three plays—*The Salad Bowl Dance, The Rainy Season, *and* Richard Speck—*produced. In 1992, he published a collection of poetry,* Crossing with the Light.

Okita's mother was among the thousands of Japanese-Americans who were interned shortly after the United States entered World War II. This poem is written in his mother's voice.

Dear Sirs:
Of course I'll come. I've packed my galoshes
and three packets of tomato seeds. Janet calls them
"love apples." My father says where we're going
5   they won't grow.

I am a fourteen-year-old girl with bad spelling
and a messy room. If it helps any, I will tell you
I have always felt funny using chopsticks
and my favorite food is hot dogs.
10   My best friend is a white girl named Denise—
we look at boys together. She sat in front of me
all through grade school because of our names:
O'Connor, Ozawa. I know the back of Denise's head very well.

I tell her she's going bald. She tells me I copy on tests.
We are best friends.
I saw Denise today in Geography class.
She was sitting on the other side of the room.
"You're trying to start a war," she said, "giving secrets away
to the Enemy, Why can't you keep your big mouth shut?"
I didn't know what to say.
I gave her a packet of tomato seeds
and asked her to plant them for me, told her
when the first tomato ripened
she'd miss me.

EXERCISES

Some of the Issues

1. How do the tone and contents of the letter contrast with the title?
2. Okita's poem is written in the voice of a fourteen-year-old girl. What indications do we have that she sees the world as a "typical" American teenager? Why is this important to the ideas presented in the poem?
3. What does Denise say in lines 18 through 19? Does she make any sense? How do her comments reflect the government's policy toward Japanese-Americans?
4. What is the tone set by the opening lines of the letter? Does that tone change by the end of the poem?
5. What is the significance of the tomato seeds?
*6. Read Jeanne Wakatsuki Houston's account of her family's internment at Manzanar. What additional evidence does it give of how the government at that time misunderstood the "threat" posed by Japanese-Americans?

Some Subjects for Writing

*7. Read Jeanne Wakatsuki Houston and James D. Houston's "Arrival at Manzanar." Imagine yourself as a child or adolescent who is suddenly placed into a new and unfriendly environment. Write an imaginary journal entry for either the day before, or the day of, your arrival. Make sure your entry includes some direct or indirect indication of your age and your life before internment.

PART VI

CHANGING PLACES

Changing places, transplanting ourselves into another context, can sharpen our awareness and appreciation of cultural differences and give us insight into our own culture. It's rare, however, that we can step easily into someone else's shoes. Usually, we carry with us a sense of our history even if that history fades or evolves over time. All of the pieces in this chapter are written by people whose change of place has significantly altered their lives and thinking. Some of them changed places temporarily, whereas others took up permanent residence in their new setting, even if they hadn't originally intended it that way. Some were transplanted by their own choice. Others were forced by circumstances to leave one place and find a new one. In some cases it was a combination of both.

The first two pieces are about people who have changed places by immigrating to the United States. Bharati Mukherjee shows us "Two Ways to Belong in America" by comparing and contrasting the different choices she and her sister made after moving to the United States from India as young adults. The author decides to put down roots by becoming a U.S. citizen. Her sister, who has lived in the U.S. for just as long, decides to remain an expatriate and maintain stronger ties to her native country. In "Amérka, Amérka," Anton Shammas illustrates how immigrants can live in this country and keep their native traditions if they so chose. "This country is big," he says, "it has room not only for the newcomers, but for their portable homelands."

Other selections illustrate the knowledge that can be gained by encountering a culture whose values are very different from those of one's own. Mark Salzman, a young American teaching English in China, discovers that his students have a different view of the "truth" about the role of their country and his in world affairs. Although the differences in worldview keep communication with the students on a friendly but superficial level, Salzman gains a deeper understanding of life in China through his meeting with a young woman doctor.

Their immediate sympathy for one another bridges the cultural gap between them. John David Morley's story about an Englishman living in Japan builds on the two cultures' different uses of space to present two different views of privacy, and concept of self. Laura Bohannan, an anthropologist, addresses the question of differences in cultural interpretation and proves that no story is universal. The western values enshrined in Shakespeare's *Hamlet* are apparently obvious, but only to westerners. The prince of Denmark's behavior is seen in a completely different way by the tribe she observes in Africa. George Orwell, a British colonial officer sent to Burma, discovers, as he says, "the real motives for which despotic governments act."

Jamaica Kincaid, in "On Seeing England for the First Time," writes about her childhood in Antigua, then a British colony. For Kincaid, colonial rule meant that her own culture was forcibly replaced by an alien and "colder" culture. In school she was so immersed in study of English geography, English history, and the lives and customs of the people of England that she could not "see" her own island. When she actually travels to England as an adult, her resentment at the culture foisted upon her and other colonials bursts out. Jonathan Swift also reflects on the colonial experience. In an essay written 250 years ago, Jonathan Swift makes a proposal that is more outrageous than "modest" to convince the English to rethink the way they treat the Irish.

In the poem that ends the section, Gloria Anzaldúa explores living with several different and perhaps warring identities, crossing categories of race, ethnicity, and gender roles that others consider fixed. To live in the borderlands between cultures is to live in a dangerous place, but it is the only place that Anzaldúa feels she can be free. We cross many borders when we change places, both physical and metaphorical.

Two Ways to Belong in America

Bharati Mukherjee

Born in 1940 in Calcutta, India, Bharati Mukherjee came to the United States in 1961 to study writing at the University of Iowa after attending college at the University of Calcutta. She has lived in many places across the United States and Canada and has taught at several universities, including Columbia University and the University of California at Berkeley. She is the author of many books of fiction and nonfiction, including most recently the novels The Holder of the World *(1993) and* Leave It To Me *(1997). Much of her work portrays the experiences of Indian and other immigrants in North American Culture. Mukherjee became a Canadian citizen in 1972 and a United States citizen in 1988.*

This essay, Mukherjee's "tale of two sisters," originally appeared in the New York Times *in 1996. The "current debate over the status of immigrants" she mentions in the first paragraph of her essay refers to legislation being debated at the time which called for new restrictions on immigration. The Illegal Immigration Reform and Immigrant Responsibility Act, which became law in 1996, toughened border enforcement and made it more difficult for refugees to gain asylum. It also greatly expanded the grounds for deporting even long-resident immigrants and created harsh penalties for resident aliens who return to their country without U.S. permission, even in circumstances such as serious illness or death of a family member. In the years since, Congress has passed legislation that mitigates some of the harsher parts of the original law, although many of them still remain in force.*

1   This is a tale of two sisters from Calcutta, Mira and Bharati, who have lived in the United States for some 35 years, but who find themselves on different sides in the current debate over the status of immigrants. I am an American citizen and she is not. I am moved that thousands of long-term residents are finally taking the oath of citizenship. She is not.

2   Mira arrived in Detroit in 1960 to study child psychology and pre-school education. I followed her a year later to study creative writing at the University of Iowa. When we left India, we were almost identical in appearance and attitude. We dressed alike, in saris; we expressed identical views on politics, social issues, love, and marriage in the same Calcutta convent-school accent. We would endure our two years in America, secure our degrees, then return to India to marry the grooms of our father's choosing.

3   Instead, Mira married an Indian student in 1962 who was getting his business administration degree at Wayne State University. They soon acquired the labor certifications necessary for the green card[1] of hassle-free residence and employment.

4   Mira still lives in Detroit, works in the Southfield, Mich., school system, and has become nationally recognized for her contributions in the fields of pre-school education and parent-teacher relationships. After 36 years as a legal immigrant in this country, she clings passionately to her Indian citizenship and hopes to go home to India when she retires.

5   In Iowa City in 1963, I married a fellow student, an American of Canadian parentage. Because of the accident of his North Dakota birth, I bypassed labor-certification requirements and the race-related "quota" system that favored the applicant's country of origin over his or her merit. I was prepared for (and even welcomed) the emotional strain that came with marrying outside my ethnic community. In 33 years of marriage, we have lived in every part of North America. By choosing a husband who was not my father's selection, I was opting for fluidity, self-invention, blue jeans and T-shirts, and renouncing 3,000 years (at least) of caste-observant, "pure culture" marriage in the Mukherjee family. My books have often been read as unapologetic (and in some quarters overenthusiastic) texts for cultural and psychological "mongrelization." It's a word I celebrate.

6   Mira and I have stayed sisterly close by phone. In our regular Sunday morning conversations, we are unguardedly affectionate. I am her only blood relative on this continent. We expect to see each other through the looming crises of aging and ill health without being asked. Long before Vice President Gore's "Citizenship U.S.A." drive, we'd had our polite arguments over the ethics of retaining an overseas citizenship while expecting the permanent protection and economic benefits that come with living and working in America.

7   Like well-raised sisters, we never said what was really on our minds, but we probably pitied one another. She, for the lack of structure in my life, the erasure of Indianness, the absence of an unvarying daily core. I, for the narrowness of her perspective, her uninvolvement with the mythic depths or the superficial pop culture of this society. But, now, with the scapegoatings of "aliens" (documented or illegal) on the increase, and the targeting of long-term legal immigrants like Mira for new scrutiny and new self-consciousness, she and I find ourselves unable to maintain the same polite discretion. We were always unacknowledged adversaries, and we are now, more than ever, sisters.

8   "I feel used," Mira raged on the phone the other night. "I feel manipulated and discarded. This is such an unfair way to treat a person who was invited to stay and work here because of her talent. My employer went to the I.N.S. and

[1]Official card, originally green, issued by the United States government to foreign nationals permitting them to work legally.

petitioned for the labor certification. For over 30 years, I've invested my creativity and professional skills into the improvement of *this* country's pre-school system. I've obeyed all the rules, I've paid my taxes, I love my work, I love my students, I love the friends I've made. How dare America now change its rules in midstream? If America wants to make new rules curtailing benefits of legal immigrants, they should apply only to immigrants who arrive after those rules are already in place."

9   To my ears, it sounded like the description of a long-enduring, comfortable yet loveless marriage, without risk or recklessness. Have we the right to demand, and to expect, that we be loved? (That, to me, is the subtext of the arguments by immigration advocates.) My sister is an expatriate, professionally generous and creative, socially courteous and gracious, and that's as far as her Americanization can go. She is here to maintain an identity, not to transform it.

10   I asked her if she would follow the example of others who have decided to become citizens because of the anti-immigration bills in Congress. And here, she surprised me. "If America wants to play the manipulative game, I'll play it, too," she snapped. "I'll become a U.S. citizen for now, then change back to India when I'm ready to go home. I feel some kind of irrational attachment to India that I don't to America. Until all this hysteria against legal immigrants, I was totally happy. Having my green card meant I could visit any place in the world I wanted to and then come back to a job that's satisfying and that I do very well."

11   In one family, from two sisters alike as peas in a pod, there could not be a wider divergence of immigrant experience. America spoke to me—I married it—I embraced the demotion from expatriate aristocrat to immigrant nobody, surrendering those thousands of years of "pure culture," the saris, the delightfully accented English. She retained them all. Which of us is the freak?

12   Mira's voice, I realized, is the voice not just of the immigrant South Asian community but of an immigrant community of the millions who have stayed rooted in one job, one city, one house, one ancestral culture, one cuisine, for the entirety of their productive years. She speaks for greater numbers than I possibly can. Only the fluency of her English and the anger, rather than fear, born of confidence from her education, differentiate her from the seamstresses, the domestics, the technicians, the shop owners, the millions of hard-working but effectively silenced documented immigrants as well as their less fortunate "illegal" bothers and sisters.

13   Nearly 20 years ago, when I was living in my husband's ancestral homeland of Canada, I was always well-employed but never allowed to feel part of the local Quebec or larger Canadian society. Then, through a Green Paper that invited a national referendum on the unwanted side effects of "nontraditional" immigration, the Government officially turned against its immigrant communities, particularly those from South Asia.

14   I felt then the same sense of betrayal that Mira feels now. I will never forget the pain of that sudden turning, and the casual racist outbursts the Green Paper

elicited. That sense of betrayal had its desired effect and drove me, and thousands like me, from the country.

15   Mira and I differ, however, in the ways in which we hope to interact with the country that we have chosen to live in. She is happier to live in America as expatriate Indian than as an immigrant American. I need to feel like a part of the community I have adopted (as I tried to feel in Canada as well). I need to put roots down, to vote and make the difference that I can. The price that the immigrant willingly pays, and that the exile avoids, is the trauma of self-transformation.

EXERCISES

Some of the Issues

1. In what ways were Mukherjee and her sister the same when they left India? How did their choices and perspectives eventually differ? In what ways did they remain similar?
2. How does Mukherjee feel about having married someone who is not from her own ethnic community? How does she describe her life in paragraph 5?
3. For what does Mukherjee feel she and her sister probably pity each other (paragraph 7)? Why does she admit this now?
4. What argument does Mira make in paragraph 8? How does Mukherjee respond to it?
5. Who does Mukherjee feel Mira's voice represents (paragraph 12)?
6. To what extent does Mukherjee sympathize with Mira? Why?

The Way We Are Told

7. Mukherjee begins her piece in the third person then reveals that she is actually referring to herself and her sister. Why do you think she does this?
8. Why does Mukherjee put the words "pure culture" in quotation marks (paragraph 11)?
9. Consider the title. Why does Mukherjee use the word "belong" as opposed to "live" or "reside"? What does the word "belong" imply?
10. Mukherjee uses a personal story to make a more general point. What is she arguing for?

Some Subjects for Writing

11. Mukherjee tells the story of two sisters who were "alike as peas in a pod" but ended up taking different paths when they came to the United States. Write a narrative about two people you know (this could include yourself) who were close but who had very different experiences when they entered a new context or setting. Your narrative should not only recount what happened; it should also analyze what might account for those differences in

experiences. Like Mukherjee, you might write about moving to a different country, city, or state, or you might talk about another move such as the transition from grammar school to high school or from high school to college.

12. "Two Ways to Belong in America" was written in response to a congressional proposal to deny government benefits to resident aliens. Consider a piece of legislation that you feel has had or might have a personal impact on your life or the life of someone close to you. Write an essay in which, like Mukherjee, you explore the complicated ways in which changes in laws and regulations can impact people's everyday lives.

Amérka, Amérka:
A Palestinian Abroad
in the Land of the Free

Anton Shammas

Anton Shammas is a Palestinian born in Israel in 1950. He attended Hebrew University and came to the United States in 1987 as a Rockefeller Fellow at the University of Michigan. He is the author of the novel Arabesques *(1989) and has published numerous essays. Shammas teaches in the Department of Near Eastern Studies at the University of Michigan.*

Historic Palestine, on the eastern coast of the Mediterranean, is sacred land to three major religions—Judaism, Christianity, and Islam—and, throughout history, ownership of this land has been often and bitterly contested. After the Second World War, the part of Palestine known as the West Bank was administered by Jordan and known as West Jordan. Since the Israeli victory in the war of 1967, it has been occupied by Israel. The majority of inhabitants of the West Bank are Palestinian Arabs, though there are Israeli settlements in several communities.

In 1988, Jordan, under King Hussein, relinquished all of its claims to the Palestine Liberation Organization (now called the Palestinian Authority), which proclaimed a Palestinian state. In 1993, Israel and the PLO signed a peace agreement calling for the withdrawal of Israeli troops from areas of the West Bank, though when this book was published, the tensions and conflict had again reached a critical point.

In this essay published in Harper's *magazine in 1991, Shammas speaks of Arab immigrants who, although physically separated from their home in the Middle East, carry with them the spiritual and cultural heritage of their "lost Palestine."*

1   Some years ago, in San Francisco, I heard the following tale from a young, American-educated Palestinian engineer. We had found a rustic, trendy place and managed to find a quiet table. Over lukewarm beers, rather than small cups of lukewarm cardamomed coffee, we talked about his family, which had wandered adrift in the Arab world for some time before finding its moorings on the West Coast, and in particular of a relative of his living to the south of San Francisco whom we were planning to visit the following day. We never did make that visit—that is a story, too—but the story about this man has fluttered inside my head ever since.

2   We will call him Abu-Khalil. Imagine him as a fortysomething Palestinian (he is now past sixty) whose West Bank homeland was, once again in his lifetime, caving in on him in June 1967 after what the Arabs call the Defeat of Hazieran 5 and the Israelis and Americans call the Six-Day War.[1] Where was he to spend the occupation years of his life? Where could he get as far away from the Israeli "benign" presence as his captive mind could go? The choices were essentially two: He could cross the Allenby Bridge to His Majesty's Jordan,[2] or he could take an unhijackable flight west, from Ben-Gurion Airport. He chose the latter, a plane that would carry him to the faraway U.S.A.— to those members of his large family (Arabs always seem to have *large* families) who had discovered the New World centuries after Columbus. (They had discovered the New World, as they would tell him later, in a sort of belated westbound revenge for the eastbound expulsion of their great ancestors from Andalusia/Spain the same year that Columbus's Spanish ships arrived on the shores of his imaginary India.)

3   To continue our tale: Abu-Khalil lands in San Francisco one warm September afternoon, clad in a heavy black coat that does not astonish his waiting relatives a bit, since they are familiar with the man's eccentricities. But what about the security guys at Ben-Gurion Airport? Didn't the out-of-season coat merit suspicion and a frisking? Apparently not. Abu-Khalil is, as far as I can tell, the only Palestinian to have seeped out through the thick security screenings at Ben-Gurion Airport—née Lydda—unsearched. How else to account for the fact that he had managed to carry on board with him a veritable Little Palestine— flora, fauna, and all?

4   His bags were heavy with small plants and seeds that went undetected by Israeli security. (It should be said, of course, that flora poised to explode is not what they look for in a Palestinian's luggage at Ben-Gurion Airport.) As for U.S. Customs Form 6059B, which inbound foreigners are graciously asked to fill out before they land—it prohibits passengers from importing "fruits, vegetables, plants, plant products, soil, meats, meat products, birds, snails, and other live animals and animal products"—our passenger, to the best of the storyteller's authorial knowledge (and mine), could not read English, and no American officer, lawful or otherwise, bothered to verify his declarations—albeit not made— through questioning, much less through physical search, these being two procedures that Palestinians are much accustomed to in their comings and goings in the Middle East.

5   So that's how Abu-Khalil managed to bring to California some representative plants of Palestine, many still rooted in their original, fecund soil. It seems,

[1]Two names (Arab and Israeli, respectively) for the armed conflict between Israel, Jordan, Syria, and Egypt in June of 1967.

[2]The West Bank had been administered by the neighboring country of Jordan under its king, Hussein, from 1949 until Israeli victory in 1967.

however, that he took pride mainly—think of it as a feather in his kaffiyeh[3]—in his having managed to smuggle out of the West Bank, through Israel, and into the United States seven representative birds of his homeland. The duri, the hassoun, the sununu, the shahrur, the bulbul, the summan, and the hudhud, small-talk companion to King Solomon himself—they all surrounded him now in California, re-chirping Palestine away in his ears from inside their unlocked American cages. "They will not leave their open cages," Abu-Khalil would say, or so the story went, "till I leave mine."

6   Abu-Khalil's was a cage of his own making; he has not left it to this very day. But I was mainly interested in the birds, in their mute, wondrous migration. In the years that followed, I asked the storyteller, did they forget their mother chirp? Did they eventually adopt the mellow sounds of California? And how, I asked, did he manage to smuggle in these birds in the first place? "Well," said my friend, "he had a coat of many pockets, you see."

7   I found the story hard to believe at the time; but one has to trust the story-teller, even a Palestinian. After all, where else could the birds of Palestine go "after the last sky," in the words of the poet Mahmoud Darwish, but to the Land of the Free.

8   My storyteller and I belong to a different generation from Abu-Khalil's. We, and others like us, are too young to think of smuggling roots and soil, though not young enough to forget all about the birds we left behind. We travel light, empty-pocketed, with the vanity of those who think home is a portable idea, something that dwells mainly in the mind or within a text. Celebrating the modern powers of imagination and of fiction, we have lost faith in our old idols—memory, storytelling. We are not even sure anymore whether there ever was a home out there, a territory, a homeland. We owe allegiance to no memory; and we have adopted as our anthem Derek Walcott's perhaps-too-often-quoted line: "I had no nation now but the imagination." Our language, Arabic, was de-territorialized by another, and only later did we realize that Arabic does not even have a word for "territory." The act of de-territorialization, then, took place outside our language, so we could not talk, much less write, about our plight in our mother tongue. Now we need the language of the Other for that, the language that can categorize the new reality and sort it out for us in upper and lower cases; the language that can re-territorialize us, as imaginary as that might be, giving us some allegedly solid ground. It is English for my San Francisco storyteller-friend, French for others, Hebrew for me: the unlocked cages of our own choices. In short, we are Palestine's post-Abu-Khalilians, if you like.

9   Many Middle Eastern Abu-Khalils have immigrated to the U.S.A. over the years, driven out of their respective homelands by wars, greedy foreigners, and pangs of poverty. At the turn of the century, when the Ottomans—who had been ruling the Middle East since 1517—were practicing some refined forms of

[3]Arab headdress.

their famine policy, Arabs left their homes and families and sailed to the Americas. Brazil and Argentina had their charm; Michigan, too. Today, Michigan is home to the largest Arab-American community in North America. If you were to take a stroll through the streets of Dearborn, a south-by-southwest suburb of Detroit, the signs and names might remind you of some ancient legend.

10   Bereft of names and deeds, these Arabs came to Michigan to make names for themselves as a twentieth-century self-mocking variation on the old Mesopotamian tradition of the *shuma shakanu,* the preservation of one's name and deeds. That also was the original aim of those who followed Nimrod the Hunter in his biblical endeavor to reach heaven and said, "Let us make us a name for ourselves" (Gen. 11:4). An American heaven of sorts and, in this case, an American name; no concealed Nimrods.

11   Hoping for a happier ending than the biblical one, they have come from places whose names Mark Twain, the great American nomenclator, traveling with "the innocents abroad" some 123 years ago, found impossible to pronounce. "One of the great drawbacks to this country," he wrote in September 1867, from Palestine, "is its distressing names that nobody can get the hang of . . . . You may make a stagger of pronouncing these names, but they will bring any Christian to grief that tries to spell them. I have an idea that if I can only simplify the nomenclature of this country, it will be of the greatest service to Americans who may travel here in the future."

12   This may account for the notorious Hollywood tradition, many years after tongue-in-cheek Twain, of assuming that all men Middle Eastern—if fortunate enough to actually have names of their own in the films—should be called Abdul. (In fact, Abdul is but the first half of a common Middle Eastern compound.) So all these anonymous Abduls are here now, trying, so far away from home, to complete their names, in a new world that has been practicing the renaming of things now for five centuries and counting.

* * * * *

13   From Fassuta, my small village in the Galilee,[4] émigrés went mainly to Brazil and Argentina. My grandfather and his brothers and brother-in-law left for Argentina in 1896, only to return home, empty-handed, a year later. Then, on the eve of the First World War, my grandfather tried his luck again, this time on his own, heading once more to Argentina (at least that's what he told my grandmother the night before he took off), where he vanished for about ten years, leaving behind three daughters and three sons, all of them hungry. His youngest son, my uncle Jiryes, followed in his footsteps in 1928, leaving his wife and child behind, never to come back.

14   One of my childhood heroes, an old villager whom we, the children of Fassuta, always blamed for having invented school, had actually been to Salt Lake City. I don't have the foggiest idea what he did there for three years before the

[4]Region in what is now Northern Israel, on the border of Syria.

Depression; his deeds remain a sealed and, I suspect, quite salty book, but he certainly did not betray the Catholic faith, no sir. I still remember him in the late 1950s, breathing down my neck during Mass at the village's church. He used to wear impeccable white American shirts under his Arab *abaya*,[5] even some thirty years after he had returned to the village. But that was the only American fingerprint on him; the rest was Middle Eastern.

15   The most famous American immigrant from my village, though, was M., my aunt Najeebeh's brother-in-law, Najeebeh being my father's sister. I hate to be finicky about the exact relationship, but that is simply the way it is in Arabic: There are different words to refer to the father's and the mother's side of the family. At any rate, M. left the village in the early 1920s and came back to visit his brothers some forty years later, with his non-Arabic-speaking sons. As a matter of fact, he was the only one of a long, winding line of immigrants who had really made it, or "had it fixed," as the Galileans would say. He came to own a chain of fast-food restaurants, quite famous in the Midwest. Before I myself left the Mideast for these parts, I went to see his nephews—my cousins—in the village and promised them, under oath, that I would certainly look M. up one day and introduce myself, or at least pop into one of his restaurants and, naturally, ask for a free meal. I have not yet done the former and am still keeping the latter for a rainy Michigan day. However, whenever I come across his chain's emblem, a plump plastic boy holding a plate high above his plumply combed head, I remember my late aunt Najeebeh and think how disconcerted she would be had she known what kind of a mnemonic-device-in-the-form-of-a-cultural-shock she had become for her nephew, in faraway Amérka, as it is called in my part of the world.

16   Upon first arriving in Amérka, one of my first cultural shocks was the otherwise trivial American fact that shirts had not only a neck size but also a sleeve size. Fassuta's Salt Lake City visitor and I, we both come from a culture where, insofar as shirts are concerned, one's arm length doesn't matter much. People in the Middle East are still immersed in figuring out the length of their postcolonial borders, personal and otherwise, and all indications show that a long time will elapse before they start paying attention to the lonely business of their sleeve size.

17   Which may or may not have something to do with the fact that in a culture with an oral background of storytelling, where choices continue, even in postcolonial times, to be made for you (be they by God, fate, nature, or the ruler), you don't enjoy the luxuries of the novel's world, where characters make their own choices and have to live, subsequently, with the consequences, sleeve size and all. The storyteller's world revolves around memory; the novelist's, around imagination. And what people in places like the Middle East are struggling to do, I think, is to shrug off the bondage of their memory and decolonize their

---

[5]A cloak.

imagination. So, in this regard, for a Middle Easterner to have a sleeve size would be a sign of such a decolonization.

18   My first stroll ever on American soil took place in a park along the Iowa River, in Iowa City. I was thirty years old, and there were so many things I had not seen before. On that day I saw my first squirrel. There are many jittery, frail creatures in the Middle East, but, to the best of my zoological knowledge, there are no squirrels. However, people do talk of the *sinjabi*, the squirrelish color. I remember thinking, during my walk, that if there were no squirrels in the Middle East, how come the Arabs use the word *sinjabi?*

19   Not long after the day I took my walk, I found out, as I had expected, that there were *sinjabs* in Iran and that the word *sinjabi* was derived from the Persian, a language that had given Arabic, long before the Koran, so many beautiful words. Some 1,300 years later, at the very time of my stay in Iowa, the Ayatollah Khomeini[6] was busy squirreling away some ideas about a new order, about the Mesopotamian tradition of the *shuma shakanu*. A half-world away, Salman Rushdie[7] was, apparently, squirreling away some counter-ideas of his own. It was not hard to imagine, later, who would play the Crackers, and who—or on whose—Nuts.

20   My Galilean friend J., not to be confused with the biblical author, came to America some sixteen years ago. We'd met at the Hebrew University in Jerusalem, in the early Seventies. He was my instructor in the Introduction to Arabic literature course, and I'm still indebted to him for teaching me the first steps of academic research and, most importantly, for being so decent a friend as to have unabashedly explained to me how I would never have the proper discipline.

21   At that time he was mulling over the idea that he should perhaps come to this country to work on a Ph.D. in modern Arabic literature. Once he had made up his mind, he started frantically looking for a wife with whom to share the burden of American self-exile. I asked him once whether it wouldn't be wiser to find himself an already naturalized American lady, to which he replied: "I'm looking for a woman that when I put my weary head against her arm, I want to hear her blood murmuring in Arabic." He did eventually find one, and they both immigrated to Amérka and have been happily listening to each other's blood ever since.

22   J. was looking for the blood tongue, for the primordial language, wherein the names of things, long before the confusion of tongues, were so deeply lodged in the things they designated that no human eye could decipher the sign. Had he been a Cabalist, he would have believed that what God introduced into the world was written words, not murmurings of blood. But J. came from the

[6](1900–89) Shiite Muslim religious leader who had a powerful influence in Iran, especially after it became an Islamic republic in 1979.
[7](1947–) Indian-born British novelist whose book *The Satanic Verses* (1988) enraged many Muslims, including the Ayatollah Khomeini, who called for his death.

oral Middle East to the literate West, and he knew upon arriving in Amérka that he would be expected to trade in his mother tongue and keep the secret language circulating only in his veins.

23   I saw the already "naturalized" J. again, in Jerusalem, some ten years after he'd left. At the end of a very long night of catching up, he picked up a Hebrew literary magazine from my desk and browsed through it. Something caught his eye; he paused for a moment. "What is *this* doing here?" "This" turned out to be an ad for a famous Israeli brand of women's underwear. I wasn't sure what he meant. It was a full-page ad, an exact replica of the famous photograph of Marilyn Monroe standing on a grate in the street, her dress blowing above her waist. "You know what the reference is to, right?" I asked. No, he did not. And I thought, How could a bright guy like J. live for so long in the U.S.A., be an *American citizen*, and not be familiar with what I thought were the basics of American iconography?

24   I had been settled for a year in Ann Arbor when I went to visit J. and his wife in Ohio. Having just returned from a short visit to our Galilee home, I brought J., who has a green thumb, what he had asked me to: some local lubia peas for his thriving backyard garden. We were reminiscing late at night, with Fayruz, the famous Lebanese singer, on the stereo in the background and some Middle Eastern munchies on the coffee table, when I suddenly remembered that night in Jerusalem years before and the ad with the Marilyn knockoff. It would be nice if you did recognize the American icon, I thought to myself, but it is nice too that you can live in this country for decades without being forced to go native. You can always pick up your own fold of the huge map and chart yourself into it.

25   Now it is my fourth year in Ann Arbor. I moved in early in September of 1987, and for three months my relationship with the squirrels outside my window was quite good. "Quite good," as my English professor at the Hebrew University in Jerusalem used to say, means "yes, good, but there's no need to be so excited about it." So I was developing an unexciting relationship with these creatures, especially with one of them, whom I told myself I was able to tell from the others, although they all did look alike, if I may say so without prejudice. Anyway, I would open the door early in the morning to pick up the *New York Times* from the doorstep, and he would be goofing around its blue, transparent wrap (that's how the paper is home-delivered in Michigan), unalarmed by my invasion of *his* kingdom.

26   But one morning, as I reached down for the paper, he froze, all of a sudden, in the middle of one of his silly gesticulations, gaping at me in utter terror, and then fled away as if I were about to—well, throw a stone at him. Maybe it was a morning in December 1987, and he had peeked at the *Times*. Maybe I will never cease to look east for my images and metaphors.

27   For J., for my friend in San Francisco, for me, the Old World will never cease to hold us hostage in this way. Sometimes I think that no matter how deep

I have traveled *into* the American life, I still carry my own miniature Abu-Khalils in my pockets and a miniature Middle East in my mind. There is little space for Amérka in the most private of my maps.

28   And speaking of maps, how many adult Americans know where the "heartbroken piece of territory" Mark Twain was talking about actually is?

29   Still, would it matter if they did?

30   I don't think it would. After all, modern colonialism (sometimes euphemistically referred to as "our American interests"), unlike its old-fashioned, European counterpart, is not geographically oriented. Geographical literacy is defunct; its demise was caused by the invention of the remote control. And if you happen to live in this vast country, your sense of geography is necessarily numbed by what Aldous Huxley would have called one's "local validity." Paradoxically, the vastness of the land provides Americans with a continental alibi. A look at the map of the U.S.A. from, say, a Palestinian point of view would psychologically suffice to make a clear-cut distinction between the American people and their government's policy. Unlike England, for instance, where every Brit seems to be living in London and has something or another to do with the business of running the rather rusty machinery of a worn-out colonialism, there is an utter distinction when it comes to the United States between the Americans on Capitol Hill and the *real* Americans who, on a good day, want absolutely nothing to do with Washington's follies.

31   Maybe that's why Abu-Khalil can feel at home in California, surrounded by the artifacts of his lost Palestine. This country is *big*; it has enough room not only for the newcomers but also for their portable homelands. Among other achievements, Amérka has made homesickness obsolete.

EXERCISES

Some of the Issues

1. What is the significance of Abu-Khalil's smuggling seven birds out of Palestine to the United States? What do these birds represent?
2. How is Shammas's concept of home different from Abu-Khalil's? What historical events have shaped younger Arabs' views?
3. Explain what Shammas means by "unlocked cages of our own choices" in paragraph 8.
4. How does Shammas distinguish the storyteller from the novelist in paragraphs 8 and 17?
5. In paragraph 17, Shammas asserts that many Middle Easterners are struggling to cast off "the bondage of their memory and decolonize their imagination." What are the political implications of this statement?
6. Shammas's friend J. married an Arab woman before coming to America. Why is it important for him to keep "the secret language circulating only in his veins" (paragraph 22)?

7. In paragraph 23, what is the source of his friend J.'s confusion over the underwear ad in the Hebrew literary magazine? How does his friend's ignorance strike Shammas?
8. How do you understand the last line, "Amérka has made homesickness obsolete?"

The Way We Are Told

9. How does the squirrel metaphor in paragraphs 18 and 19 and 25–27 relate to the Middle Eastern experience?
10. Shammas uses part of Mark Twain's description of Palestine as that "most hopeless, dreary, heartbroken piece of territory out of Arizona" to underscore the fact that many Americans are geographically illiterate. He cites this American characteristic as a possible advantage. Why?
11. Find several examples of the author's humorous or sarcastic tone.
12. In paragraph 23, why is the word *naturalized* in quotation marks?

Some Subjects for Writing

13. If you were forced to leave home, what objects would you take with you? Write an essay in which you describe the objects and explain your choices.
14. "... Home is a portable idea, something that dwells mainly in the mind or within a text" (paragraph 8). In an essay, consider what home means to you and develop a personal definition of "home." Illustrate your idea with your experience and, if appropriate, the experiences of Shammas and other authors in *Crossing Cultures*.

Teacher Mark

Mark Salzman

Mark Salzman, scholar of Chinese language and literature, screenwriter, actor, and martial arts expert, was born in Greenwich, Connecticut, in 1959. Not long after his graduation from Yale University in 1982, he took a job teaching English in Changsha, the capital of Hunan province in China. The following selection is taken from his memoir of that experience, Iron and Silk: A Young American Encounters Swordsmen, Bureaucrats, and Other Citizens of Contemporary China *(1987). He is also the author of three novels,* The Laughing Sutra *(1991),* The Soloist, *(1994) and* Lying Awake *(2000), and a memoir,* Lost in Place: Growing Up Absurd in Suburbia *(1995).*

The early and mid-1980s were marked by rapid changes in the People's Republic of China. The country, with more than one billion people—by far the most populous on earth—was rapidly opening up to the outside world, particularly the industrialized West. Tens of thousands of Chinese university students were coming to study in Western countries, including the United States. Western corporations were encouraged to develop commerce and industry with, and in, China. The communist government that had ruled the country since the revolution in 1949 was experimenting with capitalist incentives for economic development. The country seemed to be moving from a rigidly socialist system under a dictatorial regime to an intellectual opening up that promised changes in a democratic direction. In 1989 the impatience with the slow pace of that opening-up process, as well as anger about corruption and favoritism in the government, led to huge protest demonstrations led by hundreds of thousands of students. In the late spring of 1989 these movements were harshly suppressed.

Salzman describes a time when the opening up seemed in full flower and likely to continue. The Cultural Revolution referred to in paragraph 41 was a time of great upheaval and destruction in the 1960s. Bands of young women and men, called the Red Guards, roamed the country out of control, dispensing what they considered justice. Education came to a standstill as millions of teachers, students, and professionals were sent to work as peasants in the countryside under the harshest conditions.

The Gulag Archipelago *(paragraph 50) by the Russian novelist Aleksandr Solzhenitsyn is a description—and severe indictment—of the concentration camps in the Soviet Union under Josef Stalin, in which millions of people lived and died.*

1   In 1982, I graduated from Yale University as a Chinese literature major. I was fluent in Mandarin and nearly so in Cantonese, had struggled through a fair

amount of classical Chinese and had translated the works of Huang Po-Fei, a modern poet. Oddly, though, I had no real desire to go to China; it sounded like a giant penal colony to me, and besides, I have never liked traveling much. I applied to the Yale-China Association because I needed a job, and was assigned to teach English at Hunan Medical College in Changsha, a sooty, industrial city of more than a million people and the capital of the southern province of Hunan.

2   When I arrived in Changsha, the temperature was above 100 degrees. I was 22 years old and homesick. The college assigned three classes to me: 26 doctors and teachers of medicine; four men and one woman identified as "the Middle-Aged English Teachers," and 25 medical students, ages 22 to 28. I was entirely unsure what to expect from them; the reverse, I would learn, was also true.

3   Their English ability ranged from nearly fluent to practically hopeless. At the end of the first week the Class Monitor for the class of doctors read aloud the results of their "Suggestions for Better Study" meeting: "Dear Teacher Mark. You are an active boy! Your lessons are very humorous and very wonderful. To improve our class, may we suggest that in the future, we (1) spend more time reading (2) spend more time listening (3) spend more time writing, and (4) spend more time speaking. Also, some students feel you are moving too quickly through the book. However, some students request that you speed up a little, because the material is too elementary. We hope we can struggle together to overcome these contradictions! Thank you, our dear teacher."

4   On the first day of class, when I asked the Middle-Aged English Teachers to introduce themselves to me, each chose instead to introduce the person sitting next to him. Teacher Xu began: "Teacher Cai was a wonderful dancer when he was a young man. He is famous in our college because he has a beautiful wife." Teacher Cai hit Teacher Xu and said, "Teacher Xu is always late to class, and he is afraid of his wife!"

5   "I am not!"

6   "Oh, but you are!"

7   Teacher Zhang pointed to Teacher Zhu. "Teacher Zhu was a navy man," he said. "But he can't swim! And Teacher Du is very fat. So we call her Fatty Du—she has the most powerful voice in our college!" Fatty Du beamed with pride and said, "And Teacher Zhang's special characteristic is that he is afraid of me!"

8   "I am not!"

9   "Oh, but you are!"

10   On an afternoon some weeks later, I asked them to open their textbooks to a chapter entitled "War," which contained photographs of World War II, including one of the atomic bomb explosion over Hiroshima.

11   "Teacher Zhu," I said, "Can you tell us something about your experiences during the war?"

12   Teacher Zhu, an aspiring Communist Party member, stood up and smiled.

13   "Yes," he said. Then he hesitated. "This is a picture of the atom bomb, isn't it?"

14   "Yes."

15   He smiled stiffly. "Teacher Mark—how do you feel, knowing your country dropped an atom bomb on innocent people?"

16   My face turned red with embarrassment at having the question put so personally, but I tried to remain detached.

17   "This is a good question, Teacher Zhu. I can tell you that in America, many people disagree about this. Not everyone thinks it was the right thing to do, although most people think that it saved lives."

18   "How did it save lives?"

19   "Well, by ending the war quickly."

20   Here, Teacher Zhu looked around the room at his classmates.

21   "But Teacher Mark. It is a fact that the Japanese had already surrendered to the Communist Eighth Route Army of China. America put the bomb on Japan to make the world think America was the . . ."

22   "The victor!" shouted Fatty Du.

23   "Yes, the victor," said Teacher Zhu.

24   I must have stood gaping for a long time, for the other students began to laugh.

25   "Teacher Zhu," I asked, "how do you know this is a fact?"

26   "Because that is what our newspapers say!"

27   "I see. But our newspapers tell a different story. How can we know which newspaper has told the truth?"

28   Here he seemed relieved.

29   "That is easy! Our newspapers are controlled by the people, but your newspapers are owned by capitalist organizations, so of course they make things up to support themselves."

30   My mouth opened and closed a few times. Fatty Du, apparently believing that the truth had been too much for me, came to my aid.

31   "It doesn't matter! Any capitalist country would do that. It is not just your country!"

32   My head swimming, I asked her if she thought only capitalist countries lied in the papers.

33   "Oh, of course not! The Russians do it, too. But here in China, we have no reason to lie in the papers. When we make a mistake, we admit it! As for war, there is nothing to lie about. China has never attacked a nation. It has only defended its borders. We love peace. If we were the most powerful country in the world, think how peaceful the world would be!"

34   I agreed that war was a terrible thing and said I was glad that China and the United States had become friendly. The class applauded my speech.

35   "Teacher Mark—can I trouble you? I have a relative. She is my wife's cousin. She is a doctor visiting from Harbin. She speaks very good English and is very interested in learning more. Could I take her here to practice with you? It would only be once or twice."

36   Because of the overwhelming number of relatives and friends of students, not to mention perfect strangers, who wanted to learn English, I had to be protective of my time. I explained this to my student and apologized for not being able to help him.

37   "This is terrible," he said, smiling sheepishly.

38   "Why?" I asked.

39   "Because . . . I already told her you would."

40   I tried to let my annoyance show, but the harder I frowned, the more broadly he smiled, so at last I agreed to meet with her once.

41   "Her name is Little Mi," he said, much relieved. "She is very smart and strong-willed. She was always the leader of her class and was even the head of the Communist Youth League in her school. During the Cultural Revolution, she volunteered to go to the countryside. There she almost starved to death. At last she had a chance to go to medical school. She was the smartest in her class."

42   Little Mi sounded like a terrific bore; I cleared my throat, hoping that my student would simply arrange a time and let me be, but he continued. "Her specialty was pediatrics. She wanted to work with children. When the time came for job assignments after graduation, though, some people started a rumor that she and some of the other English students read Western literature in their spare time instead of studying medicine. They were accused of *fang yang pi!*"—imitating Westerners.

43   "So instead of being sent to a good hospital, she was sent to a small family planning clinic outside of the city. There she mostly assists doctors with abortions. That is how she works with children. But saddest of all, she has leukemia. Truly, she has eaten bitter all her life. When can I bring her?"

44   I told him they could come to my office in the Foreign Languages Building that evening. He thanked me extravagantly and withdrew.

45   At the appointed time someone knocked. I braced myself for an hour of grammar questions and opened the door. There stood Little Mi, who could not have been much older than I, with a purple scarf wrapped around her head like a Russian peasant woman. She was petite, unsmiling and beautiful. She looked at me without blinking.

46   "Are you Teacher Mark?" she asked in an even, low voice.

47   "Yes—please come in." She walked in, sat down and said in fluent English, "My cousin's husband apologizes for not being able to come. His adviser called him in for a meeting. Do you mind that I came alone?"

48   "Not at all. What can I do for you?"

49   "Well," she said, looking at the bookshelf next to her, "I love to read, but it is difficult to find good books in English. I wonder if you would be so kind as to lend me a book or two, which I can send back to you from Harbin as soon as I finish them." I told her to pick whatever she liked from my shelf. As she went through the books she talked about the foreign novels she had enjoyed; "Of Mice and Men," "From Here To Eternity" and "The Gulag Archipelago."

50   "How did you get 'The Gulag Archipelago'?" I asked her.

51   "It wasn't easy," she answered. "I hear that Americans are shocked by what they read in it. Is that true?"

52   "Yes, weren't you?"

53   "Not really," she answered quietly.

54   I remembered the story of her life my student had told. "You are a pretty tough girl, aren't you?" I said.

55   She looked up from the magazine she had been leafing through with a surprised expression, then covered her mouth with her hand and giggled nervously. "How terrible! I'm not like that at all!"

56   We talked for over an hour, and she picked a few books to take with her. When she got up to leave, I asked her when she would return to Harbin.

57   "The day after tomorrow."

58   Against all better judgment I asked her to come visit me again the next evening. She eyed me closely, said "Thank you—I will," then disappeared into the unlit hallway. I listened to her footsteps as she made her way down the stairs and out of the deserted building. Then from the window I watched her shadowy figure cross the athletic field.

59   She came the next night at exactly the same time. I had brought for her a few books of photographs of the United States, and she marveled at the color pictures taken in New England during the fall: "How beautiful," she said. "Just like a dream."

60   I could not openly stare at her, so I gazed at her hand as she turned the pages of the book, listened to her voice, and occasionally glanced at her face when she asked me something.

61   We talked and talked, then she seemed to remember something and looked at her watch. It was after 10 o'clock—nearly two hours had passed. She gasped, suddenly worried. "I've missed the last bus!"

62   She was staying in a hospital on the other side of the river, at least a two-hour walk. It was a bitter cold night. On foot, she would get back after midnight and arouse considerable suspicion. The only thing to do was put her on the back of a bicycle and ride her. That in itself would not attract attention, since that is how most Chinese families travel around town. I had seen families of five on one bicycle many times, and young couples ride this way for want of anything else to do at night. The woman usually rides sidesaddle on the rack over the rear wheel with her arms around the man's waist, leaning her shoulder and face against his back.

63   A Chinese woman riding that way on a bicycle powered by a Caucasian male would attract attention, however. I put on my thick padded Red Army coat, tucked my hair under a Mao hat, wore a surgical mask (as many Chinese do, to keep dust out of their lungs), and put on a pair of Chinese sunglasses, the kind that *liumang*—young punks—wear. Little Mi wrapped her scarf around her head and left the building first.

64   Five minutes later, I went out, rode fast through the gate of our college, and saw her down the street, shrouded in the haze of dust kicked up by a coal truck. I pulled alongside her and she jumped on before I stopped.

65   The street was crowded. Neither of us said a word. Trucks, buses and jeeps flung themselves madly through the streets, bicycles wove around us, and pedestrians darted in front of us, cursing the *liumang*. Finally I turned onto the road that ran along the river, and the crowd thinned out. It was a horrible road, with potholes everywhere that I could not see in time to avoid. She, too shy to put her arms around my waist, had been balancing herself across the rack, but when we hit an especially deep rut I heard her yelp and felt her grab on to me. Regaining her balance, she began to loosen her grip, but I quickly steered into another pothole and told her to hold on. Very slowly, I felt her leaning her shoulder against my back. When at last her face touched my coat, I could feel her cheek through it.

66   We reached the steep bridge and I started the climb. About halfway up she told me to stop riding, that we could walk up the bridge to give me a rest. At the top, we stopped to lean against the rail and look at the lights of the city. Trucks and jeeps were our only company.

67   "Does this remind you of America?" she asked, gesturing toward the city lights with her chin.

68   "Yes, a little."

69   "Do you miss home?"

70   "Very much. But I'll be home very soon. And when I get home, I will miss Changsha."

71   "Really? But China is so . . . no you tell me—what is China like?"

72   "The lights are dimmer here."

73   "Yes," she said quietly, "and we are boring people, aren't we?" Only her eyes showed above the scarf wrapped around her face. I asked her if she thought she was boring, and her eyes wrinkled with laughter.

74   "I am not boring. I believe I am a very interesting girl. Do you think so?"

75   "Yes, I think so." She had pale skin, and I could see her eyelids blush.

76   "When you go back to America, will you live with your parents?"

77   "No."

78   "Why not?"

79   "I'm too old! They would think it was strange if I didn't live on my own."

80   "How wonderful! I wish my parents felt that way. I will have to live with them forever."

81   "Forever?"

82   "Of course! Chinese parents love their children, but they also think that children are like furniture. They own you, and you must make them comfortable until they decide to let you go. I cannot marry, so I will have to take care of them forever. I am almost 30 years old, and I must do whatever they say. So I sit in my room and dream. In my imagination I am free, and I can do wonder things!"

83   "Like what?"

84   She cocked her head to one side and raised one eyebrow.

85   "Do you tell people your dreams?"

86   "Yes, sometimes."

87   She laughed and said, "I'm not going to tell you my dreams."

88   We were silent awhile, then she suddenly asked me if I was a sad man or a happy man.

89   "That's hard to say—sometimes I'm happy, sometimes I'm sad. Mostly, I just worry."

90   "Worry? What do you worry about?"

91   "I don't know—everything, I guess. Mostly about wasting time."

92   "How strange! My cousin's husband says that you work very hard."

93   "I like to keep busy. That way I don't have time to worry."

94   "I can't understand that. You are such a free man—you can travel all over the world as you like, make friends everywhere. You are a fool not to be happy, especially when so many people depend on it."

95   "What do you mean?"

96   "My relative says that your nickname in the college is *huoshenxian*—an immortal in human form—because you are so . . . different. Your lectures make everyone laugh, and you make people feel happy all the time. This is very unusual."

97   I asked her if she was happy or sad. She raised one eyebrow again, looking not quite at me.

98   "I don't have as many reasons to be happy as you." She looked at her watch and shook her head. "I must get back—we have to hurry." As I turned toward the bicycle she leaned very close to me, almost touching her face against mine, looking straight into my eyes, and said, "I have an idea."

99   I could feel her breath against my throat.

100   "Let's coast down the bridge," she said. "Fast! No brakes!"

101   I got on the bicycle.

102   "Are you getting on?" I asked her.

103   "Just a minute. At the bottom I'll get off, so I'll say goodbye now."

104   "I should at least take you to the gate of the hospital."

105   "No, that wouldn't be a good idea. Someone might see me and ask who you were. At the bottom of the bridge I'll hop off, and you turn around. I won't see you again, so thank you. It was fun meeting you. You should stop worrying." She jumped on, pressed her face against my back, held me like a vice, and said, "Now—go! As fast as you can!"

EXERCISES

Some of the Issues

1. How did Salzman feel about going to China before traveling there? What was his preparation for the job of teaching English?

2. Describe Salzman's English classes. How appropriate are the doctors' suggestions? How did the middle-aged English teachers introduce one another?
3. What differing views of history are revealed in paragraphs 13–34?
4. What impression did Salzman have of Little Mi before meeting her? What do you learn about her past? About the effects of the Cultural Revolution?
5. What is Salzman's reaction when he finds out that Little Mi has read *The Gulag Archipelago?*
6. How is Little Mi's personality revealed to us? What indications are there of a change in Salzman's feelings?
7. The final conversation between Salzman and Little Mi reveals many differences in their lives and attitudes toward living. What are they? Do you think Salzman and Little Mi understand each other in spite of their differences?

The Way We Are Told

8. At first sight Salzman seems simply to be recording his conversations and impressions. Yet, in doing so, he lets the reader know quite clearly what he feels. How does Salzman express his point of view? Try to find some examples.
9. In paragraph 15 Teacher Zhu confronts Salzman with a question about dropping the atom bomb on Hiroshima. Examine the rest of the discussion between Salzman and the teachers. How does Salzman show that they, far from wanting a confrontation on that topic, go out of their way to "help" him understand?

Some Subjects for Writing

10. Salzman and Little Mi lead lives that are very far apart. Before their meeting Salzman expects her to be a bore. Yet, in the few hours they spend together, they bridge the wide gap between them. Describe a situation in which your own anticipation or first impression of someone turned out to be wrong.
11. Write about a meeting with someone that led to a turning point in your life. Try to convey the importance of the meeting mostly through the use of dialogue. Since you will probably not remember the exact words that were said, you may, like all writers, invent words as long as they are true to the experience.

Living in a Japanese Home

John David Morley

John David Morley was born in Singapore in 1948, of British parents, and educated at Oxford University. His earliest job was as tutor to the children of Elizabeth Taylor and Richard Burton when they were filming in Mexico. His interest in theater led him to Japanese theater and eventually to Japanese culture in general. He taught himself Japanese, studied at the Language Research Institute at Waseda University in Tokyo, and then went to work for Japanese Television as liaison officer, interpreter, and researcher, stationed in Munich, Germany. In 1985 he published a novel, Pictures from the Water Trade: Adventures of a Westerner in Japan, *from which this selection is taken. The novel is based on some of his own experiences.*

The Japanese island empire successfully managed to isolate itself from foreign influences until the middle of the nineteenth century. Once that isolation had been breached, however, Japan moved rapidly to catch up with the Western world, not only by industrializing but also by following the major powers' expansionist policies. Japan fought a successful war with Russia (1905), occupied and eventually annexed Korea (1910), and, in the 1930s, occupied Manchuria and large parts of China. After its surprise attack on Pearl Harbor (December 7, 1941), Japan had spectacular initial successes in World War II, occupying the Philippines, Indochina, Indonesia, Burma, and Singapore. Defeated and virtually destroyed in the later phases of the war, Japan was occupied by the U.S. Army under General Douglas MacArthur, whose administration of the islands is primarily responsible for converting Japan into a constitutional monarchy with a parliamentary government. Japan's economic recovery was spectacular—today, despite an economic downturn beginning in the 1990s, Japan is still the second largest world economic power. Japan's success is all the more remarkable when one considers that the country has almost no natural resources of its own on its crowded islands. With its size smaller than California, it has 125 million inhabitants, about half as many as the United States. Japanese society is highly homogeneous, has a very low crime rate, a very high level of literacy, and is considered very hard-working.

1   The introduction was arranged through a mutual acquaintance, Yoshida, at the private university where Boon was taking language courses and where

Sugama was employed on the administrative staff. They met one afternoon in the office of their acquaintance and inspected each other warily for ten minutes.

2   "Nice weather," said Boon facetiously as he shook hands with Sugama. Outside it was pouring with rain.

3   "Nice weather?" repeated Sugama doubtfully, glancing out of the window. "But it's raining."

4   It was not a good start.

5   Sugama had just moved into a new apartment. It was large enough for two, he said, but he was looking for someone to share the expenses. This straightforward information arrived laboriously, in bits and pieces, sandwiched between snippets of Sugama's personal history and vague professions of friendship, irritating to Boon, because at the time he felt they sounded merely sententious. All this passed back and forth between Sugama and Boon through the mouth of their mutual friend, as Boon understood almost no Japanese and Sugama's English, though well-intentioned, was for the most part impenetrable.

6   It made no odds to Boon where he lived or with whom. All he wanted was a Japanese-speaking environment in order to absorb the language as quickly as possible. He had asked for a family, but none was available.

7   One windy afternoon in mid-October the three of them met outside the gates of the university and set off to have a look at Sugama's new apartment. It was explained to Boon that cheap apartments in Tokyo were very hard to come by, the only reasonable accommodation available being confined to housing estates subsidized by the government. Boon wondered how a relatively prosperous bachelor like Sugama managed to qualify for government-subsidized housing. Sugama admitted that this was in fact only possible because his grandfather would also be living there. It was the first Boon had heard of the matter and he was rather taken aback.

8   It turned out, however, that the grandfather would "very seldom" be there—in fact, that he wouldn't live there at all. He would only be there on paper, he and his grandson constituting a "family." That was the point. "You must *say* he is there," said Sugama emphatically.

9   The grandfather lived a couple of hundred miles away, and although he never once during the next two years set foot in the apartment he still managed to be the bane of Boon's life. A constant stream of representatives from charities, government agencies and old people's clubs, on average one or two a month, came knocking on the door, asking to speak to grandfather. At first grandfather was simply "not in" or had "gone for a walk," but as time passed and the flow of visitors never faltered, Boon found himself having to resort to more drastic measures. Grandfather began to make long visits to his home in the country; he had not yet returned because he didn't feel up to making the journey; his health gradually deteriorated. Finally Boon decided to have him invalided, and for a long time his condition remained "grave." On grandfather's behalf Boon received the condolences of all these visitors, and occasionally even presents.

10   Two years later grandfather did in fact die. Boon was thus exonerated, but in the meantime he had got to know grandfather well and had become rather fond of him. He attended his funeral with mixed feelings.

11   Sugama had acquired tenure of his government-subsidized apartment by a stroke of luck. He had won a ticket in a lottery. These apartments were much sought after, and in true Japanese style their distribution among hundreds of thousands of applicants was discreetly left to fate. The typical tenant was a young couple with one or two children, who would occupy the apartment for ten or fifteen years, often under conditions of bleak frugality, in order to save money to buy a house. Although the rent was not immoderate, prices generally in Tokyo were high, and it was a mystery to Boon how such people managed to live at all. Among the lottery winners there were inevitably also those people for whom the acquisition of an apartment was just a prize, an unexpected bonus, to be exploited as a financial investment. It was no problem for these nominal tenants to sub-let their apartments at prices well above the going rate.

12   Boon had never lived on a housing estate and his first view of the tall concrete compound where over fifty thousand people lived did little to reassure him. Thousands of winner families were accommodated in about a dozen rectangular blocks, each between ten and fifteen stories high, apparently in no way different (which disappointed Boon most of all) from similar housing compounds in Birmingham or Berlin. He had naively expected Japanese concrete to be different, to have a different colour, perhaps, or a more exotic shape.

13   But when Sugama let them into the apartment and Boon saw the interior he immediately took heart: this was unmistakably Japanese. Taking off their shoes in the tiny box-like hall, the three of them padded reverently through the kitchen into the *tatami*[1] rooms.

14   "Smell of fresh *tatami*," pronounced Sugama, wrinkling his nose.

15   Boon was ecstatic. Over the close-woven pale gold straw matting lay a very faint greenish shimmer, sometimes perceptible and sometimes not, apparently in response to infinitesimal shifts in the texture of the falling light. The *tatami* was quite unlike a carpet or any other form of floor-covering he had ever seen. It seemed to be alive, humming with colours he could sense rather than see, like a greening tree in the brief interval between winter and spring. He stepped on to it and felt the fibres recoil, sinking under the weight of his feet, slowly and softly.

16   "You can see green?" asked Sugama, squatting down.

17   "Yes indeed."

18   "Fresh *tatami*. Smell of grass, green colour. But not for long, few weeks only."

19   "What exactly is it?"

20   "Yes."

[1]Woven straw matting used as a floor covering in Japanese homes.

21   Boon turned to Yoshida and repeated the question, who in turn asked Sugama and conferred with him at length.

22   "*Tatami* comes from *oritatamu*, which means to fold up. So it's a kind of matting you can fold up."

23   "Made of straw."

24   "Yes."

25   "How long does it last?"

26   Long consultation.

27   "He says this is not so good quality. Last maybe four, five years."

28   "And then what?"

29   "New *tatami*. Quite expensive, you see. But very practical."

30   The three *tatami* rooms were divided by a series of *fusuma*, sliding screens made of paper and light wood. These screens were decorated at the base with simple grass and flower motifs; a natural extension, it occurred to Boon, of the grass-like *tatami* laid out in-between. Sugama explained that the *fusuma* were usually kept closed in winter, and in summer, in order to have "nice breeze," they could be removed altogether. He also showed Boon the *shoji*, a type of sliding screen similar to the *fusuma* but more simple: an open wooden grid covered on one side with semi-transparent paper, primitive but rather beautiful. There was only one small section of *shoji* in the whole apartment; almost as a token, thought Boon, and he wondered why.

31   With the exception of a few one- and two-room apartments every house that Boon ever visited in Japan was designed to incorporate these three common elements: *tatami*, *fusuma* and *shoji*. In the houses of rich people the *tatami* might last longer, the *fusuma* decorations might be more costly, but the basic concept was the same. The interior design of all houses being much the same, it was not surprising to find certain similarities in the behavior and attitudes of the people who lived in them.

32   The most striking feature of the Japanese house was lack of privacy: the lack of individual, inviolable space. In winter, when the *fusuma* were kept closed, any sound above a whisper was clearly audible on the other side, and of course in summer they were usually removed altogether. It is impossible to live under such conditions for very long without a common household identity emerging which naturally takes precedence over individual wishes. This enforced family unity was still held up to Boon as an ideal, but in practice it was ambivalent, as much a yoke as a bond.

33   There was no such thing as the individual's private room, no bedroom, dining- or sitting-room as such, since in the traditional Japanese house there was no furniture determining that a room should be reserved for any particular function. A person slept in a room, for example, without thinking of it as a bedroom or as his room. In the morning his bedding would be rolled up and stored away in a cupboard; a small table known as the *kotatsu*, which could also be plugged into the mains to provide heating, was moved back into the centre of the room and here the family ate, drank, worked and relaxed for the rest of the

day. Although it was becoming standard practice in modern Japan for children to have their own rooms, many middle-aged and nearly all older Japanese still lived this way. They regarded themselves as "one flesh," their property as common to all; the *uchi* (household, home) was constituted according to a principle of indivisibility. The system of moveable screens meant that the rooms could be used by all the family and for all purposes: walls were built round the *uchi*, not inside it.

34   Boon later discovered analogies between this concept of house and the Japanese concept of self. The Japanese carried his house around in his mouth and produced it in everyday conversation, using the word *uchi* to mean "I," the representative of my house in the world outside. His self-awareness was naturally expressed as corporate individuality, hazy about quite what that included, very clear about what it did not.

35   *Ittaikan*, the traditional view of the corporate *uchi* as one flesh, had unmistakably passed into decline in modern Japan. A watery sentiment remained, lacking the conviction that had once made the communal *uchi* as self-evident in practice as it was in principle. This was probably why people had become acutely aware of the problem of space, although they did not necessarily have less space now than they had had before. A tendency to restrict the spatial requirements of daily life quite voluntarily had been evident in Japan long before land became scarce. When the tea-room was first introduced during the Muromachi period (early fourteenth to late sixteenth century) the specification of its size was four and a half mats, but in the course of time this was reduced to one mat (two square metres). The reasons for this kind of scaling down were purely aesthetic. It was believed that only within a space as modest as this could the spirit of *wabi*, a taste for the simple and quiet, be truly cultivated.

36   The almost wearying sameness about all the homes which Boon visited, despite differences in the wealth and status of their owners, prompted a rather unexpected conclusion: the classlessness of the Japanese house. The widespread use of traditional materials, the preservation of traditional structures, even if in such contracted forms as to have become merely symbolic, suggested a consensus about the basic requirements of daily life which was very remarkable, and which presumably held implications for Japanese society as a whole. Boon's insight into that society was acquired very slowly, after he had spent a great deal of time sitting on the *tatami* mats and looking through the sliding *fusuma* doors which had struck him as no more than pleasing curiosities on his first visit to a Japanese-style home.

EXERCISES

Some of the Issues

1. Describe the first meeting of Boon and Sugama. Why did Boon consider it "not a good start"?

2. Describe the selection process for government-subsidized housing in Japan—very different from Western practices. Can you find a rationale for the Japanese system?
3. On entering the new apartment Sugama wrinkles his nose while Boon is ecstatic. What accounts for their difference in attitude?
4. What are the key elements of the Japanese home? What are the advantages of this mode of living? What disadvantages does it have?
5. How does the arrangement condition the lives of the people who live in it? How does it reflect Japanese values?
6. Morley says that the most striking feature of the Japanese house is lack of privacy. Later he speaks of the classlessness of the Japanese home. How does he illustrate his two points?

The Way We Are Told

7. The author does not at any time refer to Western conditions and attitudes; yet they are constantly implied in his discussion of events, contacts with people, and descriptions of living conditions. Give some examples.
8. What does the author achieve by his gradual revelation of the truth about Sugama's grandfather?
9. The story is told by Boon, a fictional British visitor, but the experiences presumably reflect Morley's own. What does the author gain by creating Boon to tell his story?

Some Subjects for Writing

10. How important is privacy to you? How did the physical environment in which you grew up shape your attitudes?
11. Compare and contrast the Western or American concept of privacy to the Japanese view as described by Morley. How does the physical environment of the Japanese home support Japanese notions of privacy? In describing the American living space, you might think of the "ideal" American family home, a bedroom for each child, preferably with a private bath, and a kitchen and family room as places for the family to gather.

Shakespeare in the Bush

Laura Bohannan

*Laura Bohannan, born in New York City in 1922, was a professor of anthro-
pology at the University of Illinois in Chicago. She received her doctorate
from Oxford University and later did field work with various peoples in
Africa, including the Tiv, a tribe in central Nigeria, with whom this story is
concerned. Under the pseudonym Elenore Smith Bowen, she has published a
novel about anthropological field work,* Return to Laughter.

*The Tiv, who have a tradition of storytelling (accompanied by beer
drinking) during the rainy season, asked their visitor to tell a story. She
chose Shakespeare's* Hamlet, *believing that its universality would make it
comprehensible, even in a culture very different from the one in which it was
originally conceived. This assumption turned out to be quite wrong.*

1   Just before I left Oxford for the Tiv in West Africa, conversation turned to the
season at Stratford. "You Americans," said a friend, "often have difficulty
with Shakespeare. He was, after all, a very English poet, and one can easily misinterpret the universal by misunderstanding the particular."

2   I protested that human nature is pretty much the same the whole world
over; at least the general plot and motivation of the greater tragedies would always be clear—everywhere—although some details of custom might have to be
explained and difficulties of translation might produce other slight changes. To
end an argument we could not conclude, my friend gave me a copy of *Hamlet* to
study in the African bush: it would, he hoped, lift my mind above its primitive
surroundings, and possibly I might, by prolonged meditation, achieve the grace
of correct interpretation.

3   It was my second field trip to that African tribe, and I thought myself ready
to live in one of its remote sections—an area difficult to cross even on foot. I
eventually settled on the hillock of a very knowledgeable old man, the head of a
homestead of some hundred and forty people, all of whom were either his close
relatives or their wives and children. Like the other elders of the vicinity, the old
man spent most of his time performing ceremonies seldom seen these days in
the more accessible parts of the tribe. I was delighted. Soon there would be
three months of enforced isolation and leisure, between the harvest that takes
place just before the rising of the swamps and the clearing of new farms when
the water goes down. Then, I thought, they would have even more time to perform ceremonies and explain them to me.

4   I was quite mistaken. Most of the ceremonies demanded the presence of elders from several homesteads. As the swamps rose, the old men found it too difficult to walk from one homestead to the next, and the ceremonies gradually

ceased. As the swamps rose even higher, all activities but one came to an end. The women brewed beer from maize and millet. Men, women, and children sat on their hillocks and drank it.

5   People began to drink at dawn. By midmorning the whole homestead was singing, dancing, and drumming. When it rained, people had to sit inside their huts: there they drank and sang or they drank and told stories. In any case, by noon or before, I either had to join the party or retire to my own hut and my books. "One does not discuss serious matters when there is beer. Come, drink with us." Since I lacked their capacity for the thick native beer, I spent more and more time with *Hamlet*. Before the end of the second month, grace descended on me. I was quite sure that *Hamlet* had only one possible interpretation, and that one universally obvious.

6   Early every morning, in the hope of having some serious talk before the beer party, I used to call on the old man at his reception hut—a circle of posts supporting a thatched roof above a low mud wall to keep out wind and rain. One day I crawled through the low doorway and found most of the men of the homestead sitting huddled in their ragged cloths on stools, low plank beds, and reclining chairs, warming themselves against the chill of the rain around a smoky fire. In the center were three pots of beer. The party, had started.

7   The old man greeted me cordially, "Sit down and drink." I accepted a large calabash full of beer, poured some into a small drinking gourd, and tossed it down. Then I poured some more into the same gourd for the man second in seniority to my host before I handed my calabash over to a young man for further distribution. Important people shouldn't ladle beer themselves.

8   "It is better like this," the old man said, looking at me approvingly, and plucking at the thatch that had caught in my hair. "You should sit and drink with us more often. Your servants tell me that when you are not with us, you sit inside your hut looking at a paper."

9   The old man was acquainted with four kinds of "papers": tax receipts, bride price receipts, court fee receipts, and letters. The messenger who brought him letters from the chief used them mainly as a badge of office, for he always knew what was in them and told the old man. Personal letters for the few who had relatives in the government or mission stations were kept until someone went to a large market where there was a letter writer and reader. Since my arrival, letters were brought to me to be read. A few men also brought me bride price receipts, privately, with requests to change the figures to a higher sum. I found moral arguments were of no avail, since in-laws are fair game, and the technical hazards of forgery difficult to explain to an illiterate people. I did not wish them to think me silly enough to look at any such paper for days on end, and I hastily explained that my "paper" was one of the "things of long ago" of my country.

10   "Ah," said the old man. "Tell us."

11   I protested that I was not a storyteller. Storytelling is a skilled art among them; their standards are high, and the audiences critical—and vocal in their criticism. I protested in vain. This morning they wanted to hear a story while

they drank. They threatened to tell me no more stories until I told them one of mine. Finally, the old man promised that no one would criticize my style "for we know you are struggling with our language." "But," put in one of the elders, "you must explain what we do not understand, as we do when we tell you our stories." Realizing that here was my chance to prove *Hamlet* universally intelligible, I agreed.

12   The old man handed me some more beer to help me on with my storytelling. Men filled their long wooden pipes and knocked coals from the fire to place in the pipe bowls; then, puffing contentedly, they sat back to listen. I began in the proper style.

13   "Not yesterday, not yesterday, but long ago, a thing occurred. One night three men were keeping watch outside the homestead of the great chief, when suddenly they saw the former chief approach them."

14   "Why was he no longer the chief?"

15   "He was dead," I explained. "That is why they were troubled and afraid when they saw him."

16   "Impossible," began one of the elders, handing his pipe on to his neighbor, who interrupted, "Of course it wasn't the dead chief. It was an omen sent by a witch. Go on."

17   Slightly shaken, I continued. "One of these three was a man who knew things"—the closest translation for scholar, but unfortunately it also meant witch. The second elder looked triumphantly at the first. "So he spoke to the dead chief saying, 'Tell us what we must do so you may rest in your grave,' but the dead chief did not answer. He vanished, and they could see him no more. Then the man who knew things—his name was Horatio—said this event was the affair of the dead chief's son, Hamlet."

18   There was a general shaking of heads round the circle. "Had the dead chief no living brothers? Or was this son the chief?"

19   "No," I replied. "That is, he had one living brother who became the chief when the elder brother died."

20   The old men muttered: such omens were matters for chiefs and elders, not for youngsters; no good could come of going behind a chief's back; clearly Horatio was not a man who knew things.

21   "Yes, he was," I insisted, shooing a chicken away from my beer. "In our country the son is next to the father. The dead chief's younger brother had become the great chief. He had also married his elder brother's widow only about a month after the funeral."

22   "He did well," the old man beamed and announced to the others, "I told you that if we knew more about Europeans, we would find they really were very like us. In our country also," he added to me, "the younger brother marries the elder brother's widow and becomes the father of his children. Now, if your uncle, who married your widowed mother, is your father's full brother, then he will be a real father to you. Did Hamlet's father and uncle have one mother?"

23   His question barely penetrated my mind; I was too upset and thrown too far off balance by having one of the most important elements of *Hamlet* knocked straight out of the picture. Rather uncertainly I said that I thought they had the same mother, but I wasn't sure—the story didn't say. The old man told me severely that these genealogical details made all the difference and that when I got home I must ask the elders about it. He shouted out the door to one of his younger wives to bring his goatskin bag.

24   Determined to save what I could of the mother motif, I took a deep breath and began again. "The son Hamlet was very sad because his mother had married again so quickly. There was no need for her to do so, and it is our custom for a widow not to go to her next husband until she has mourned for two years."

25   "Two years is too long," objected the wife, who had appeared with the old man's battered goatskin bag. "Who will hoe your farms for you while you have no husband?"

26   "Hamlet," I retorted without thinking, "was old enough to hoe his mother's farms himself. There was no need for her to remarry." No one looked convinced. I gave up. "His mother and the great chief told Hamlet not to be sad, for the great chief himself would be a father to Hamlet. Furthermore, Hamlet would be the next chief: therefore he must stay to learn the things of a chief. Hamlet agreed to remain, and all the rest went off to drink beer."

27   While I paused, perplexed at how to render Hamlet's disgusted soliloquy to an audience convinced that Claudius and Gertrude had behaved in the best possible manner, one of the younger men asked me who had married the other wives of the dead chief.

28   "He had no other wives," I told him.

29   "But a chief must have many wives! How else can he brew beer and prepare food for all his guests?"

30   I said firmly that in our country even chiefs had only one wife, that they had servants to do their work, and that they paid them from tax money.

31   It was better, they returned, for a chief to have many wives and sons who would help him hoe his farms and feed his people; then everyone loved the chief who gave much and took nothing—taxes were a bad thing.

32   I agreed with the last comment, but for the rest fell back on their favorite way of fobbing off my questions: "That is the way it is done, so that is how we do it."

33   I decided to skip the soliloquy. Even if Claudius was here thought quite right to marry his brother's widow, there remained the poison motif, and I knew they would disapprove of fratricide. More hopefully I resumed, "That night Hamlet kept watch with the three who had seen his dead father. The dead chief again appeared, and although the others were afraid, Hamlet followed his dead father off to one side. When they were alone, Hamlet's dead father spoke."

34   "Omens can't talk!" The old man was emphatic.

35   "Hamlet's dead father wasn't an omen. Seeing him might have been an omen, but he was not." My audience looked as confused as I sounded. "It *was* Hamlet's dead father. It was a thing we call a 'ghost.'" I had to use the English

word, for unlike many of the neighboring tribes, these people didn't believe in the survival after death of any individuating part of the personality.

36   "What is a 'ghost'? An omen?"

37   "No, a 'ghost' is someone who is dead but who walks around and can talk, and people can hear him and see him but not touch him."

38   They objected. "One can touch zombis."

39   "No, no! It was not a dead body the witches had animated to sacrifice and eat. No one else made Hamlet's dead father walk. He did it himself."

40   "Dead men can't walk," protested my audience as one man.

41   I was quite willing to compromise. "A 'ghost' is the dead man's shadow."

42   But again they objected. "Dead men cast no shadows."

43   "They do in my country," I snapped.

44   The old man quelled the babble of disbelief that arose immediately and told me with that insincere, but courteous, agreement one extends to the fancies of the young, ignorant, and superstitious, "No doubt in your country the dead can also walk without being zombis." From the depths of his bag he produced a withered fragment of kola nut, bit off one end to show it wasn't poisoned, and handed me the rest as a peace offering.

45   "Anyhow," I resumed, "Hamlet's dead father said that his own brother, the one who became chief, had poisoned him. He wanted Hamlet to avenge him. Hamlet believed this in his heart, for he did not like his father's brother." I took another swallow of beer. "In the country of the great chief, living in the same homestead, for it was a very large one, was an important elder who was often with the chief to advise and help him. His name was Polonius. Hamlet was courting his daughter, but her father and her brother . . . [I cast hastily about for some tribal analogy] warned her not to let Hamlet visit her when she was alone on her farm, for he would be a great chief and so could not marry her."

46   "Why not?" asked the wife, who had settled down on the edge of the old man's chair. He frowned at her for asking stupid questions and growled, "They live in the same homestead."

47   "That was not the reason," I informed them. "Polonius was a stranger who lived in the homestead because he helped the chief, not because he was a relative."

48   "Then why couldn't Hamlet marry her?"

49   "He could have," I explained, "But Polonius didn't think he would. After all, Hamlet was a man of great importance who ought to marry a chief's daughter, for in his country a man could have only one wife. Polonius was afraid that if Hamlet made love to his daughter, then no one else would give a high price for her."

50   "That might be true," remarked one of the shrewder elders, "but a chief's son would give his mistress's father enough presents and patronage to more than make up the difference. Polonius sounds like a fool to me."

51   "Many people think he was," I agreed. "Meanwhile Polonius sent his son Laertes off to Paris to learn the things of that country, for it was the homestead of a very great chief indeed. Because he was afraid that Laertes might waste a lot

of money on beer and women and gambling, or get into trouble by fighting, he sent one of his servants to Paris secretly, to spy out what Laertes was doing. One day Hamlet came upon Polonius's daughter Ophelia. He behaved so oddly he frightened her. Indeed"—I was fumbling for words to express the dubious quality of Hamlet's madness—"the chief and many others had also noticed that when Hamlet talked one could understand the words but not what they meant. Many people thought that he had become mad." My audience suddenly became much more attentive. "The great chief wanted to know what was wrong with Hamlet, so he sent for two of Hamlet's age mates [school friends would have taken long explanation] to talk to Hamlet and find out what troubled his heart. Hamlet, seeing that they had been bribed by the chief to betray him, told them nothing. Polonius, however, insisted that Hamlet was mad because he had been forbidden to see Ophelia, whom he loved."

52   "Why," inquired a bewildered voice, "should anyone bewitch Hamlet on that account?"

53   "Bewitch him?"

54   "Yes, only witchcraft can make anyone mad, unless, of course, one sees the beings that lurk in the forest."

55   I stopped being a storyteller, took out my notebook and demanded to be told more about these two causes of madness. Even while they spoke and I jotted notes, I tried to calculate the effect of this new factor on the plot. Hamlet had not been exposed to the beings that lurk in the forests. Only his relatives in the male line could bewitch him. Barring relatives not mentioned by Shakespeare, it had to be Claudius who was attempting to harm him. And, of course, it was.

56   For the moment I staved off questions by saying that the great chief also refused to believe that Hamlet was mad for the love of Ophelia and nothing else. "He was sure that something much more important was troubling Hamlet's heart."

57   "Now Hamlet's age mates," I continued, "had brought with them a famous storyteller. Hamlet decided to have this man tell the chief and all his homestead a story about a man who had poisoned his brother because he desired his brother's wife and wished to be chief himself. Hamlet was sure the great chief could not hear the story without making a sign if he was indeed guilty, and then he would discover whether his dead father had told him the truth."

58   The old man interrupted, with deep cunning, "Why should a father lie to his son?" he asked.

59   I hedged: "Hamlet wasn't sure that it really was his dead father." It was impossible to say anything, in that language, about devil-inspired visions.

60   "You mean," he said, "it actually was an omen, and he knew witches sometimes send false ones. Hamlet was a fool not to go to one skilled in reading omens and divining the truth in the first place. A man-who-sees-the-truth could have told him how his father died, if he really had been poisoned, and if there was witchcraft in it; then Hamlet could have called the elders to settle the matter."

61   The shrewd elder ventured to disagree. "Because his father's brother was a great chief, one-who-sees-the-truth might therefore have been afraid to tell it. I think it was for that reason that a friend of Hamlet's father—a witch and an elder—sent an omen so his friend's son would know. Was the omen true?"

62   "Yes," I said, abandoning ghosts and the devil; a witch-sent omen it would have to be. "It was true, for when the storyteller was telling his tale before all the homestead, the great chief rose in fear. Afraid that Hamlet knew his secret he planned to have him killed."

63   The stage set of the next bit presented some difficulties of translation. I began cautiously. "The great chief told Hamlet's mother to find out from her son what he knew. But because a woman's children are always first in her heart, he had the important elder Polonius hide behind a cloth that hung against the wall of Hamlet's mother's sleeping hut. Hamlet started to scold his mother for what she had done."

64   There was a shocked murmur from everyone. A man should never scold his mother.

65   "She called out in fear, and Polonius moved behind the cloth. Shouting, 'A rat!' Hamlet took his machete and slashed through the cloth." I paused for dramatic effect. "He had killed Polonius!"

66   The old men looked at each other in supreme disgust. "That Polonius truly was a fool and a man who knew nothing! What child would not know enough to shout, 'It's me!'" With a pang, I remembered that these people are ardent hunters, always armed with bow, arrow, and machete; at the first rustle in the grass an arrow is aimed and ready, and the hunter shouts "Game!" If no human voice answers immediately, the arrow speeds on its way. Like a good hunter Hamlet had shouted, "A rat!"

67   I rushed in to save Polonius's reputation. "Polonius did speak. Hamlet heard him. But he thought it was the chief and wished to kill him to avenge his father. He had meant to kill him earlier that evening . . ." I broke down, unable to describe to these pagans, who had no belief in individual afterlife, the difference between dying at one's prayers and dying "unhousell'd, disappointed, unaneled."

68   This time I had shocked my audience seriously. "For a man to raise his hand against his father's brother and the one who had become his father—that is a terrible thing. The elders ought to let such a man be bewitched."

69   I nibbled at my kola nut in some perplexity, then pointed out that after all the man had killed Hamlet's father.

70   "No," pronounced the old man, speaking less to me than to the young men sitting behind the elders. "If your father's brother has killed your father, you must appeal to your father's age mates; *they* may avenge him. No man may use violence against his senior relatives." Another thought struck him. "But if his father's brother had indeed been wicked enough to bewitch Hamlet and make him mad that would be a good story indeed, for it would be his fault that Hamlet, being mad, no longer had any sense and thus was ready to kill his father's brother."

71   There was a murmur of applause. *Hamlet* was again a good story to them, but it no longer seemed quite the same story to me. As I thought over the coming complications of plot and motive, I lost courage and decided to skim over dangerous ground quickly.

72   "The great chief," I went on, "was not sorry that Hamlet had killed Polonius. It gave him a reason to send Hamlet away, with his two treacherous age mates, with letters to a chief of a far country, saying that Hamlet should be killed. But Hamlet changed the writing on their papers, so that the chief killed his age mates instead." I encountered a reproachful glare from one of the men whom I had told undetectable forgery was not merely immoral but beyond human skill. I looked the other way.

73   "Before Hamlet could return, Laertes came back for his father's funeral. The great chief told him Hamlet had killed Polonius. Laertes swore to kill Hamlet because of this, and because his sister Ophelia, hearing her father had been killed by the man she loved, went mad and drowned in the river."

74   "Have you already forgotten what we told you?" The old man was reproachful. "One cannot take vengeance on a madman; Hamlet killed Polonius in his madness. As for the girl, she not only went mad, she was drowned. Only witches can make people drown. Water itself can't hurt anything. It is merely something one drinks and bathes in."

75   I began to get cross. "If you don't like the story, I'll stop."

76   The old man made soothing noises and himself poured me some more beer. "You tell the story well, and we are listening. But it is clear that the elders of your country have never told you what the story really means. No, don't interrupt! We believe you when you say your marriage customs are different, or your clothes and weapons. But people are the same everywhere; therefore, there are always witches and it is we, the elders, who know how witches work. We told you it was the great chief who wished to kill Hamlet, and now your own words have proved us right. Who were Ophelia's male relatives?"

77   "There were only her father and her brother." Hamlet was clearly out of my hands.

78   "There must have been many more; this also you must ask of your elders when you get back to your country. From what you tell us, since Polonius was dead, it must have been Laertes who killed Ophelia, although I do not see the reason for it."

79   We had emptied one pot of beer, and the old men argued the point with slightly tipsy interest. Finally one of them demanded of me, "What did the servant of Polonius say on his return?"

80   With difficulty I recollected Reynaldo and his mission. "I don't think he did return before Polonius was killed."

81   "Listen," said the elder, "and I will tell you how it was and how your story will go, then you may tell me if I am right. Polonius knew his son would get into trouble, and so he did. He had many fines to pay for fighting, and debts from gambling. But he had only two ways of getting money quickly. One was to marry off his sister at once, but it is difficult to find a man who will marry a

woman desired by the son of a chief. For if the chief's heir commits adultery with your wife, what can you do? Only a fool calls a case against a man who will someday be his judge. Therefore Laertes had to take the second way: he killed his sister by witchcraft, drowning her so he could secretly sell her body to the witches."

82   I raised an objection. "They found her body and buried it. Indeed Laertes jumped into the grave to see his sister once more—so, you see, the body was truly there. Hamlet, who had just come back, jumped in after him."

83   "What did I tell you?" The elder appealed to the others. "Laertes was up to no good with his sister's body. Hamlet prevented him, because the chief's heir, like a chief, does not wish any other man to grow rich and powerful. Laertes would be angry, because he would have killed his sister without benefit to himself. In our country he would try to kill Hamlet for that reason. Is this not what happened?"

84   "More or less," I admitted. "When the great chief found Hamlet was still alive, he encouraged Laertes to try to kill Hamlet and arranged a fight with machetes between them. In the fight both the young men were wounded to death. Hamlet's mother drank the poisoned beer that the chief meant for Hamlet in case he won the fight. When he saw his mother die of poison, Hamlet, dying, managed to kill his father's brother with his machete."

85   "You see, I was right!" exclaimed the elder.

86   "That was a very good story," added the old man, "and you told it with very few mistakes. There was just one more error, at the very end. The poison Hamlet's mother drank was obviously meant for the survivor of the fight, whichever it was. If Laertes had won, the great chief would have poisoned him, for no one would know that he arranged Hamlet's death. Then, too, he need not fear Laertes' witchcraft; it takes a strong heart to kill one's only sister by witchcraft.

87   "Sometime," concluded the old man, gathering his ragged toga about him, "you must tell us some more stories of your country. We, who are elders, will instruct you in their true meaning, so that when you return to your own land your elders will see that you have not been sitting in the bush, but among those who know things and who have taught you wisdom."

EXERCISES

Some of the Issues

1. In paragraphs 1 and 2 Bohannan and a friend discuss human nature in relation to Shakespeare's *Hamlet.* What are their opinions?
2. Read paragraphs 3 through 6. What were Bohannan's expectations for her second field trip to the Tiv, and why were they mistaken? How do her plans change?
3. What is the significance of the discussion about "papers" in paragraphs 8 and 9? How does it foretell that the Tiv's interpretation of *Hamlet* may differ from Bohannan's (and ours)?

4. In a number of instances, Bohannan shows that she is knowledgeable about the social customs of the Tiv and is trying to conform to them. Give some specific instances.

5. In paragraphs 24–32 two differences between the Tiv and Western cultural presumptions are made clear: they relate to the period of mourning for the dead and to the number of wives a chief may have. In what way does the Tiv's view on these matters differ from Western views? Does their view have any advantages for their culture?

6. The Tiv elders are shocked at several parts of the story of *Hamlet*. What specific instances can you cite? Do their moral perceptions differ from ours in those instances?

7. Bohannan makes several efforts to make *Hamlet* more intelligible or acceptable to the Tiv. What are some of these? Does she succeed?

8. Both Bohannan (paragraph 2) and the chief (paragraph 76) say that human nature is much the same everywhere. What evidence do you find in the essay to support or contradict these assertions?

The Way We Are Told

9. Bohannan begins her essay with a conversation with a friend at Oxford. Do you feel this is an effective way to begin?

10. Several times in her essay Bohannan expresses surprise at the Tiv's reaction to her story. Is it possible that she was in reality not as surprised as she indicates?

Some Subjects for Writing

11. Bohannan does her best to adapt the story of Hamlet to the experiences, customs, and feelings of the Tiv. Have you ever had the experience of having to adapt yourself in some way to a situation in which the rules and assumptions differed greatly from your own? Tell the story.

12. Describe a particular American event or activity to someone who has never experienced it. Topics might be Thanksgiving, a rock concert, a barbecue, a commencement exercise.

*13. Read "A Modest Proposal" by Jonathan Swift. In an essay demonstrate that both Bohannan and Swift adopt poses in order to make their arguments effectively.

Shooting an Elephant

George Orwell

George Orwell (the pseudonym of Eric Arthur Blair) was an English journalist, critic, and novelist. Born in 1903 in India, he was educated in England at Eton College. He served with the Indian Imperial Police in Burma from 1922 to 1927. This essay is based on his experience there.

Orwell returned to England in 1927 and turned to writing but with little success. He lived in great poverty for some time, as described in his first published book, Down and Out in Paris and London *(1933). In the mid-1930s he fought on the side of the Republic in the Spanish Civil War, was wounded and wrote of his experience in* Homage to Catalonia *(1938). Success finally came late in his life with* Animal Farm *(1945) and* 1984, *both of which expressed his concerns about totalitarian governments.* 1984 *was published in 1949, the year before his death from tuberculosis.*

In Orwell's time, Burma was a part of the Indian Empire under British rule. When India gained independence in 1947, Burma became a separate, sovereign state. About the size of Texas with a population of forty million, this country, now called Myanmar, is ruled by a heavy-handed military dictatorship, and is largely closed off from the rest of the world.

1   In Moulmein, in lower Burma, I was hated by large numbers of people—the only time in my life that I have been important enough for this to happen to me. I was sub-divisional police officer of the town, and in an aimless, petty kind of way anti-European feeling was very bitter. No one had the guts to raise a riot, but if a European woman went through the bazaars alone somebody would probably spit betel juice over her dress. As a police officer I was an obvious target and was baited whenever it seemed safe to do so. When a nimble Burman tripped me up on the football field and the referee (another Burman) looked the other way, the crowd yelled with hideous laughter. This happened more than once. In the end the sneering yellow faces of young men that met me everywhere, the insults hooted after me when I was at a safe distance, got badly on my nerves. The young Buddhist priests were the worst of all. There were several thousands of them in the town and none of them seemed to have anything to do except stand on street corners and jeer at Europeans.

2   All this was perplexing and upsetting. For at that time I had already made up my mind that imperialism was an evil thing and the sooner I chucked up my job and got out of it the better. Theoretically—and secretly, of course—I was all for the Burmese and all against their oppressors, the British. As for the job I was doing, I hated it more bitterly than I can perhaps make clear. In a job like that

you see the dirty work of Empire at close quarters. The wretched prisoners huddling in the stinking cages of the lockups, the gray, cowed faces of the long-term convicts, the scarred buttocks of the men who had been flogged with bamboos—all these oppressed me with an intolerable sense of guilt. But I could get nothing into perspective. I was young and ill-educated and I had had to think out my problems in the utter silence that is imposed on every Englishman in the East. I did not even know that the British Empire is dying, still less did I know that it is a great deal better than the younger empires that are going to supplant it. All I knew was that I was stuck between my hatred of the empire I served and my rage against the evil-spirited little beasts who tried to make my job impossible. With one part of my mind I thought of the British Raj[1] as an un-breakable tyranny, as something clamped down, in *saecula saeculorum,*[2] upon the will of prostrate peoples; with another part I thought that the greatest joy in the world would be to drive a bayonet into a Buddhist priest's guts. Feelings like these are the normal by-products of imperialism; ask any Anglo-Indian official, if you can catch him off duty.

3   One day something happened which in a roundabout way was enlightening. It was a tiny incident in itself, but it gave me a better glimpse than I had had be-fore of the real nature of imperialism—the real motives for which despotic governments act. Early one morning the sub-inspector at a police station the other end of the town rang me up on the 'phone and said that an elephant was rav-aging the bazaar. Would I please come and do something about it? I did not know what I could do, but I wanted to see what was happening and I got on to a pony and started out. I took my rifle, an old .44 Winchester and much too small to kill an elephant, but I thought the noise might be useful *in terrorem.*[3] Various Burmans stopped me on the way and told me about the elephant's doings. It was not, of course, a wild elephant, but a tame one which had gone "must." It had been chained up, as tame elephants always are when their attack of "must" is due, but on the previous night it had broken its chain and escaped. Its mahout,[4] the only person who could manage it when it was in that state, had set out in pursuit, but had taken the wrong direction and was now twelve hours' journey away, and in the morning the elephant had suddenly reappeared in the town. The Burmese population had no weapons and were quite helpless against it. It had already destroyed somebody's bamboo hut, killed a cow and raided some fruit-stalls and devoured the stock; also it had met the municipal rubbish van and, when the driver jumped out and took to his heels, had turned the van over and inflicted violences upon it.

4   The Burmese sub-inspector and some Indian constables were waiting for me in the quarter where the elephant had been seen. It was a very poor quarter,

---

[1]British rule over India, Pakistan, and Burma until 1947. (Raj is the Hindi word for reign.)
[2]For all time.
[3]To spread terror.
[4]Elephant keeper and driver.

a labyrinth of squalid bamboo huts, thatched with palm-leaf, winding all over a steep hillside. I remember that it was a cloudy, stuffy morning at the beginning of the rains. We began questioning the people as to where the elephant had gone and, as usual, failed to get any definite information. That is invariably the case in the East; a story always sounds clear enough at a distance, but the nearer you get to the scene of events the vaguer it becomes. Some of the people said that the elephant had gone in one direction, some said that he had gone in another, some professed not even to have heard of any elephant. I had almost made up my mind that the whole story was a pack of lies, when we heard yells a little distance away. There was a loud, scandalized cry of "Go away, child! Go away this instant!" and an old woman with a switch in her hand came round the corner of a hut, violently shooing away a crowd of naked children. Some more women followed, clicking their tongues and exclaiming; evidently there was something that the children ought not to have seen. I rounded the hut and saw a man's dead body sprawling in the mud. He was an Indian, a black Dravidian coolie,[5] almost naked, and he could not have been dead many minutes. The people said that the elephant had come suddenly upon him round the corner of the hut, caught him with its trunk, put its foot on his back and ground him into the earth. This was the rainy season and the ground was soft; and his face had scored a trench a foot deep and a couple yards long. He was lying on his belly with arms crucified and head sharply twisted to one side. His face was coated with mud, the eyes wide open, the teeth bared and grinning with an expression of unendurable agony. (Never tell me, by the way, that the dead look peaceful. Most of the corpses I have seen looked devilish.) The friction of the great beast's foot had stripped the skin from his back as neatly as one skins a rabbit. As soon as I saw the dead man I sent an orderly to a friend's house nearby to borrow an elephant rifle. I had already sent back the pony, not wanting it to go mad with fright and throw me if it smelt the elephant.

5   The orderly came back in a few minutes with a rifle and five cartridges, and meanwhile some Burmans had arrived and told us that the elephant was in the paddy fields below, only a few hundred yards away. As I started forward practically the whole population of the quarter flocked out of the houses and followed me. They had seen the rifle and were all shouting excitedly that I was going to shoot the elephant. They had not shown much interest in the elephant when he was merely ravaging their homes, but it was different now that he was going to be shot. It was a bit of fun to them, as it would be to an English crowd; besides they wanted the meat. It made me vaguely uneasy. I had no intention of shooting the elephant—I had merely sent for the rifle to defend myself if necessary—and it is always unnerving to have a crowd following you. I marched down the hill, looking and feeling a fool, with the rifle over my shoulder and an ever-growing army of people jostling at my heels. At the bottom, when you got away from the huts, there was a metalled road and beyond that a miry waste of paddy

[5]Native laborer of south India.

fields a thousand yards across, not yet ploughed but soggy from the first rains and dotted with coarse grass. The elephant was standing eight yards from the road, his left side towards us. He took not the slightest notice of the crowd's approach. He was tearing up bunches of grass, beating them against his knees to clean them and stuffing them into his mouth.

6   I had halted on the road. As soon as I saw the elephant I knew with perfect certainty that I ought not to shoot him. It is a serious matter to shoot a working elephant—it is comparable to destroying a huge and costly piece of machinery—and obviously one ought not to do it if it can possibly be avoided. And at that distance, peacefully eating, the elephant looked no more dangerous than a cow. I thought then and I think now that his attack of "must" was already passing off; in which case he would merely wander harmlessly about until the mahout came back and caught him. Moreover, I did not in the least want to shoot him. I decided that I would watch him for a little while to make sure that he did not turn savage again, and then go home.

7   But at that moment I glanced round at the crowd that had followed me. It was an immense crowd, two thousand at the least and growing every minute. It blocked the road for a long distance on either side. I looked at the sea of yellow faces above the garish clothes—faces all happy and excited over this bit of fun, all certain that the elephant was going to be shot. They were watching me as they would watch a conjurer about to perform a trick. They did not like me, but with the magical rifle in my hands I was momentarily worth watching. And suddenly I realized that I should have to shoot the elephant after all. The people expected it of me and I had got to do it; I could feel their two thousand wills pressing me forward, irresistibly. And it was at this moment, as I stood there with the rifle in my hands, that I first grasped the hollowness, the futility of the white man's dominion in the East. Here was I, the white man with his gun, standing in front of the unarmed native crowd—seemingly the leading actor of the piece; but in reality I was only an absurd puppet pushed to and fro by the will of those yellow faces behind. I perceived in this moment that when the white man turns tyrant it is his own freedom that he destroys. He becomes a sort of hollow, posing dummy, the conventionalized figure of a sahib.[6] For it is the condition of his rule that he shall spend his life in trying to impress the "natives," and so in every crisis he has got to do what the "natives" expect of him. He wears a mask, and his face grows to fit it. I had got to shoot the elephant. I had committed myself to doing it when I sent for the rifle. A sahib has got to act like a sahib; he has got to appear resolute, to know his own mind and do definite things. To come all that way, rifle in hand, with two thousand people marching at my heels, and then to trail feebly away, having done nothing—no, that was impossible. The crowd would laugh at me. And my whole life, every white man's life in the East, was one long struggle not to be laughed at.

[6]Term formerly used by inhabitants of colonial India to address Europeans.

8   But I did not want to shoot the elephant. I watched him beating his bunch of grass against his knees, with that preoccupied grandmotherly air that elephants have. It seemed to me that it would be murder to shoot him. At that age I was not squeamish about killing animals, but I had never shot an elephant and never wanted to. (Somehow it always seems worse to kill a *large* animal.) Besides, there was the beast's owner to be considered. Alive, the elephant was worth at least a hundred pounds; dead, he would only be worth the value of his tusks, five pounds, possibly. But I had got to act quickly. I turned to some experienced-looking Burmans who had been there when we arrived, and asked them how the elephant had been behaving. They all said the same thing: he took no notice of you if you left him alone, but he might charge if you went too close to him.

9   It was perfectly clear to me what I ought to do. I ought to walk up to within, say, twenty-five yards of the elephant and test his behavior. If he charged, I could shoot; if he took no notice of me, it would be safe to leave him until the mahout came back. But also I knew that I was going to do no such thing. I was a poor shot with a rifle and the ground was soft mud into which one would sink at every step. If the elephant charged and I missed him, I should have about as much chance as a toad under a steam-roller. But even then I was not thinking particularly of my own skin, only of the watchful yellow faces behind. For at that moment, with the crowd watching me, I was not afraid in the ordinary sense, as I would have been if I had been alone. A white man mustn't be frightened in front of "natives"; and so, in general, he isn't frightened. The sole thought in my mind was that if anything went wrong those two thousand Burmans would see me pursued, caught, trampled on and reduced to a grinning corpse like that Indian up the hill. And if that happened it was quite probable that some of them would laugh. That would never do. There was only one alternative. I shoved the cartridges into the magazine and lay down on the road to get a better aim.

10   The crowd grew very still, and a deep, low, happy sigh, as of people who see the theatre curtain go up at last, breathed from innumerable throats. They were going to have their bit of fun after all. The rifle was a beautiful German thing with cross-hair sights. I did not then know that in shooting an elephant one would shoot to cut an imaginary bar running from ear-hole to ear-hole. I ought, therefore, as the elephant was sideways on, to have aimed straight at his ear-hole; actually I aimed several inches in front of this, thinking the brain would be further forward.

11   When I pulled the trigger I did not hear the bang or feel the kick—one never does when a shot goes home—but I heard the devilish roar of glee that went up from the crowd. In that instant, in too short a time, one would have thought, even for the bullet to get there, a mysterious, terrible change had come over the elephant. He neither stirred nor fell, but every line of his body had altered. He looked suddenly stricken, shrunken, immensely old, as though the frightful impact of the bullet had paralyzed him without knocking him down. At

last, after what seemed a long time—it might have been five seconds, I dare say—he sagged flabbily to his knees. His mouth slobbered. An enormous senility seemed to have settled upon him. One could have imagined him thousands of years old. I fired again into the same spot. At the second shot he did not collapse but climbed with desperate slowness to his feet and stood weakly upright, with legs sagging and head drooping. I fired a third time. That was the shot that did for him. You could see the agony of it jolt his whole body and knock the last remnant of strength from his legs. But in falling he seemed for a moment to rise, for as his hind legs collapsed beneath him he seemed to tower upward like a huge rock toppling, his trunk reaching skywards like a tree. He trumpeted, for the first and only time. And then down he came, his belly towards me, with a crash that seemed to shake the ground even where I lay.

12   I got up. The Burmans were already racing past me across the mud. It was obvious that the elephant would never rise again, but he was not dead. He was breathing very rhythmically with long rattling gasps, his great mound of a side painfully rising and falling. His mouth was wide open—I could see far down into caverns of pale pink throat. I waited a long time for him to die, but his breathing did not weaken. Finally I fired my two remaining shots into the spot where I thought his heart must be. The thick blood welled out of him like red velvet, but still he did not die. His body did not even jerk when the shots hit him, the tortured breathing continued without a pause. He was dying, very slowly and in great agony, but in some world remote from me where not even a bullet could damage him further. I felt that I had got to put an end to that dreadful noise. It seemed dreadful to see the great beast lying there, powerless to move and yet powerless to die, and not even to be able to finish him. I send back for my small rifle and poured shot after shot into his heart and down his throat. They seemed to make no impression. The tortured gasps continued as steadily as the ticking of a clock.

13   In the end I could not stand it any longer and went away. I heard later that it took him half an hour to die. Burmans were bringing dahs[7] and baskets even before I left, and I was told they had stripped his body almost to the bones by the afternoon.

14   Afterwards, of course, there were endless discussions about the shooting of the elephant. The owner was furious, but he was only an Indian and could do nothing. Besides, legally I had done the right thing, for a mad elephant has to be killed, like a mad dog, if its owner fails to control it. Among the Europeans opinion was divided. The older men said I was right, the younger men said it was a damn shame to shoot an elephant for killing a coolie, because an elephant was worth more than any damn Coringhee coolie. And afterwards I was very glad that the coolie had been killed; it put me legally in the right and it gave me a sufficient pretext for shooting the elephant. I often wondered whether any of the others grasped that I had done it solely to avoid looking a fool.

---

[7]Large heavy knives used in Burma.

EXERCISES

Some of the Issues

1. Before Orwell begins to tell the story of the shooting of the elephant, he uses two paragraphs to talk about feelings: the feelings of the Burmese toward him as a colonial officer, and his own "perplexing and upsetting" feelings toward the Burmese. Why are Orwell's feelings complex and contradictory? How does this discussion of attitudes set the scene for the narrative that follows?

2. The main topic or theme of the essay is stated in the first few sentences of paragraph 3. After reading the whole essay, explain why the incident Orwell describes gave him "a better glimpse . . . of the real nature of imperialism." What, according to Orwell, are "the real motives for which despotic governments act"?

3. In paragraph 7 Orwell says, "I perceived in this moment that when the white man turns tyrant it is his own freedom that he destroys." Explain the meaning of this sentence; how does it apply to the story Orwell tells?

The Way We Are Told

4. When Orwell begins to tell the story of the elephant, in paragraph 3, he continues to reveal his attitude toward the Burmese in various indirect ways. Try to show how he does this.

5. In paragraph 4 Orwell describes the dead coolie in considerable detail. Later, in paragraphs 11 and 12, he goes on to describe the elephant's death in even greater detail. Compare the two descriptions.

6. In paragraphs 5 through 9 Orwell discusses his plans and options regarding the elephant. Paragraphs 5 and 6, however, differ greatly from 7, 8, and 9, in both content and treatment. Characterize the difference.

7. The largest section of Orwell's essay describes an event that takes place within a short period of time. Estimate the time lapse from the moment Orwell sent for the rifle (end of paragraph 4) to the moment he turns away (paragraph 13).

8. Consider Orwell's tone in the last paragraph. What evidence is there that he is being ironic?

Some Subjects for Writing

9. In paragraphs 11 and 12 Orwell describes in detail an event that took only a few minutes. The abundance of sensory detail about the incident brings us closer to seeing it as Orwell did. Recall a dramatic moment in your life, a time when you needed to act quickly. Recreate that moment in writing by giving details about what you saw, heard, felt, and smelled. Try to bring the reader there.

10. Have you ever been placed in a situation in which you were forced to do something that you did not entirely agree with? For example, an employee must often carry out the policies of his or her employer even while disagreeing with them. Write an essay describing such an incident and detail your feelings before, during, and after.

11. Orwell is placed in a position of authority but finds that it restricts his scope of action rather than expands it. Write an essay that asserts the truth of this apparent contradiction. Try to find examples of other situations in which the possession of power limits the possessor.

On Seeing England for the First Time

Jamaica Kincaid

Jamaica Kincaid was born Elaine Potter Richardson in St. Johns, Antigua, in 1949; she left that country at seventeen to become an au pair (a live-in babysitter) in New York City. She did not return to Antigua to visit until almost twenty years later.

Kincaid is the author of three novels: Annie John *(1985),* Lucy *(1990), and* Autobiography of My Mother *(1996), and a book of short stories,* At the Bottom of the River *(1983). She is also the author of a memoir,* My Brother *(1997), and* A Small Place *(1988), a long essay about Antigua in which she explores the effects of colonialism and how the rule of the British Empire has shaped the identity of her native country and its people.*

Antigua is an independent island state in the eastern Caribbean. The country was colonized in 1632, when the British established a settlement there. It remained a British colony until it became an internally self-governing state in association with Great Britain in 1967, and declared its independence in 1981.

Like A Small Place, *"On Seeing England for the First Time" explores the moral, psychological, cultural, and economic devastation brought on by the rule of a colonial power. The essay describes Kincaid's experience of first visiting England as an adult, comparing her experience of that country to the familiarity she had consciously or unconsciously absorbed by growing up under British rule.*

1   When I saw England for the first time, I was a child in school sitting at a desk. The England I was looking at was laid out on a map gently, beautifully, delicately, a very special jewel; it lay on a bed of sky blue—the background of the map—its yellow form mysterious, because though it looked like a leg of mutton, it could not really look like anything so familiar as a leg of mutton because it was England—with shadings of pink and green, unlike any shadings of pink and green I had seen before, squiggly veins of red running in every direction. England was a special jewel all right, and only special people got to wear it. The people who got to wear England were English people. They wore it well and they wore it everywhere: in jungles, in deserts, on plains, on top of the highest mountains, on all the oceans, on all the seas, in places where they were not welcome, in places they should not have been. When my teacher had pinned

this map up on the blackboard, she said, "This is England"—and she said it with authority, seriousness, and adoration, and we all sat up. It was as if she had said, "This is Jerusalem, the place you will go to when you die but only if you have been good." We understood then—we were meant to understand then—that England was to be our source of myth and the source from which we got our sense of reality, our sense of what was meaningful, our sense of what was meaningless—and much about our own lives and much about the very idea of us headed that last list.

2   At the time I was a child sitting at my desk seeing England for the first time, I was already very familiar with the greatness of it. Each morning before I left for school, I ate a breakfast of half a grapefruit, an egg, bread and butter and a slice of cheese, and a cup of cocoa; or half a grapefruit, a bowl of oat porridge, bread and butter and a slice of cheese, and a cup of cocoa. The can of cocoa was often left on the table in front of me. It had written on it the name of the company, the year the company was established, and the words "Made in England." Those words, "Made in England," were written on the box the oats came in too. They would also have been written on the box the shoes I was wearing came in; a bolt of gray linen cloth lying on the shelf of a store from which my mother had bought three yards to make the uniform that I was wearing had written along its edge those three words. The shoes I wore were made in England; so were my socks and cotton undergarments and the satin ribbons I wore tied at the end of two plaits of my hair. My father, who might have sat next to me at breakfast, was a carpenter and cabinet maker. The shoes he wore to work would have been made in England, as were his khaki shirt and trousers, his underpants and undershirt, his socks and brown felt hat. Felt was not the proper material from which a hat that was expected to provide shade from the hot sun should be made, but my father must have seen and admired a picture of an Englishman wearing such a hat in England, and this picture that he saw must have been so compelling that it caused him to wear the wrong hat for a hot climate most of his long life. And this hat—a brown felt hat—became so central to his character that it was the first thing he put on in the morning as he stepped out of bed and the last thing he took off before he stepped back into bed at night. As we sat at breakfast a car might go by. The car, a Hillman or a Zephyr, was made in England. The very idea of the meal itself, breakfast, and its substantial quality and quantity was an idea from England; we somehow knew that in England they began the day with this meal called breakfast and a proper breakfast was a big breakfast. No one I knew liked eating so much food so early in the day; it made us feel sleepy, tired. But this breakfast business was Made in England like almost everything else that surrounded us, the exceptions being the sea, the sky, and the air we breathed.

3   At the time I saw this map—seeing England for the first time—I did not say to myself, "Ah, so that's what it looks like," because there was no longing in me to put a shape to those three words that ran through every part of my life, no matter how small; for me to have had such a longing would have meant that I

lived in a certain atmosphere, an atmosphere in which those three words were felt as a burden. But I did not live in such an atmosphere. My father's brown felt hat would develop a hole in its crown, the lining would separate from the hat itself, and six weeks before he thought that he could not be seen wearing it—he was a very vain man—he would order another hat from England. And my mother taught me to eat my food in the English way: the knife in the right hand, the fork in the left, my elbows held still close to my side, the food carefully balanced on my fork and then brought up to my mouth. When I had finally mastered it, I overheard her saying to a friend, "Did you see how nicely she can eat?" But I knew then that I enjoyed my food more when I ate it with my bare hands, and I continued to do so when she wasn't looking. And when my teacher showed us the map, she asked us to study it carefully, because no test we would ever take would be complete without this statement: "Draw a map of England."

4   I did not know then that the statement "Draw a map of England" was something far worse than a declaration of war, for in fact a flat-out declaration of war would have put me on alert, and again in fact, there was no need for war—I had long ago been conquered. I did not know then that this statement was part of a process that would result in my erasure, not my physical erasure, but my erasure all the same. I did not know then that this statement was meant to make me feel in awe and small whenever I heard the word "England": awe at its existence, small because I was not from it. I did not know very much of anything then—certainly not what a blessing it was that I was unable to draw a map of England correctly.

5   After that there were many times of seeing England for the first time. I saw England in history. I knew the names of all the kings of England. I knew the names of their children, their wives, their disappointments, their triumphs, the names of people who betrayed them, I knew the dates on which they were born and the dates they died. I knew their conquests and was made to feel glad if I figured in them; I knew their defeats. I knew the details of the year 1066 (the Battle of Hastings, the end of the reign of the Anglo-Saxon kings) before I knew the details of the year 1832 (the year slavery was abolished). It wasn't as bad as I make it sound now; it was worse. I did like so much hearing again and again how Alfred the Great, traveling in disguise, had been left to watch cakes, and because he wasn't used to this the cakes got burned, and Alfred burned his hands pulling them out of the fire, and the woman who had left him to watch the cakes screamed at him. I loved King Alfred. My grandfather was named after him; his son, my uncle, was named after King Alfred; my brother is named after King Alfred. And so there are three people in my family named after a man they have never met, a man who died over ten centuries ago. The first view I got of England then was not unlike the first view received by the person who named my grandfather.

6   This view, though—the naming of the kings, their deeds, their disappointments—was the vivid view, the forceful view. There were other views, subtler

ones, softer, almost not there—but these were the ones that made the most last-ing impression on me, these were the ones that made me really feel like nothing. "When morning touched the sky" was one phrase, for no morning touched the sky where I lived. The mornings where I lived came on abruptly, with a shock of heat and loud noises. "Evening approaches" was another, but the evenings where I lived did not approach; in fact, I had no evening—I had night and I had day and they came and went in a mechanical way: on, off; on, off. And then there were gentle mountains and low blue skies and moors over which people took walks for nothing but pleasure, when where I lived a walk was an act of la-bor, a burden, something only death or the automobile could relieve. And there were things that a small turn of a head could convey—entire worlds, whole lives would depend on this thing, a certain turn of a head. Everyday life could be quite tiring, more tiring than anything I was told not to do. I was told not to gossip, but they did that all the time. And they ate so much food, violating an-other of those rules they taught me: do not indulge in gluttony. And the foods they ate actually: if only sometime I could eat cold cuts after theater, cold cuts of lamb and mint sauce, and Yorkshire pudding and scones, and clotted cream, and sausages that came from up-country (imagine, "up-country"). And having trou-bling thoughts at twilight, a good time to have troubling thoughts, apparently; and servants who stole and left in the middle of a crisis, who were born with a limp or some other kind of deformity, not nourished properly in their mother's womb (that last part I figured out for myself; the point was, oh to have an un-trustworthy servant); and wonderful cobbled streets onto which solid front doors opened; and people whose eyes were blue and who had fair skins and who smelled only of lavender, or sometimes sweet pea or primrose. And those flow-ers with those names: delphiniums, foxgloves, tulips, daffodils, floribunda, pe-onies; in bloom, a striking display, being cut and placed in large glass bowls, crystal, decorating rooms so large twenty families the size of mine could fit in comfortably but used only for passing through. And the weather was so remark-able because the rain fell gently always, only occasionally in deep gusts, and it colored the air various shades of gray, each an appealing shade for a dress to be worn when a portrait was being painted; and when it rained at twilight, wonder-ful things happened: people bumped into each other unexpectedly and that would lead to all sorts of turns of events—a plot, the mere weather caused plots. I saw that people rushed: they rushed to catch trains, they rushed toward each other and away from each other; they rushed and rushed and rushed. That word: rushed! I did not know what it was to do that. It was too hot to do that, and so I came to envy people who would rush, even though it had no meaning to me to do such a thing. But there they are again. They loved their children; their children were sent to their own rooms as a punishment, rooms larger than my entire house. They were special, everything about them said so, even their clothes; their clothes rustled, swished, soothed. The world was theirs, not mine; everything told me so.

7   If now as I speak of all this I give the impression of someone on the outside looking in, nose pressed up against a glass window, that is wrong. My nose was pressed up against a glass window all right, but there was an iron vise at the back of my neck forcing my head to stay in place. To avert my gaze was to fall back into something from which I had been rescued, a hole filled with nothing, and that was the word for everything about me, nothing. The reality of my life was conquests, subjugation, humiliation, enforced amnesia. I was forced to forget. Just for instance, this: I lived in a part of St. John's, Antigua, called Ovals. Ovals was made up of five streets, each of them named after a famous English seaman—to be quite frank, an officially sanctioned criminal: Rodney Street (after George Rodney), Nelson Street (after Horatio Nelson), Drake Street (after Francis Drake), Hood Street, and Hawkins Street (after John Hawkins). But John Hawkins was knighted after a trip he made to Africa, opening up a new trade, the slave trade. He was then entitled to wear as his crest a Negro bound with a cord. Every single person living on Hawkins Street was descended from a slave. John Hawkins's ship, the one in which he transported the people he had bought and kidnapped, was called *The Jesus*. He later became the treasurer of the Royal Navy and rear admiral.

8   Again, the reality of my life, the life I led at the time I was being shown these views of England for the first time, for the second time, for the one-hundred-millionth time, was this: the sun shone with what sometimes seemed to be a deliberate cruelty; we must have done something to deserve that. My dresses did not rustle in the evening air as I strolled to the theater (I had no evening, I had no theater; my dresses were made of a cheap cotton, the weave of which would give way after not too many washings). I got up in the morning, I did my chores (fetched water from the public pipe for my mother, swept the yard), I washed myself, I went to a woman to have my hair combed freshly every day (because before we were allowed into our classroom our teachers would inspect us, and children who had not bathed that day, or had dirt under their fingernails, or whose hair had not been combed anew that day, might not be allowed to attend class). I ate that breakfast. I walked to school. At school we gathered in an auditorium and sang a hymn, "All Things Bright and Beautiful," and looking down on us as we sang were portraits of the Queen of England and her husband; they wore jewels and medals and they smiled. I was a Brownie. At each meeting we would form a little group around a flagpole, and after raising the Union Jack, we would say, "I promise to do my best, to do my duty to God and the Queen, to help other people every day and obey the scouts' law."

9   Who were these people and why had I never seen them, I mean really seen them, in the place where they lived? I had never been to England. No one I knew had ever been to England, or I should say, no one I knew had ever been and returned to tell me about it. All the people I knew who had gone to England had stayed there. Sometimes they left behind them their small children, never to see them again. England! I had seen England's representatives. I had

seen the governor general at the public grounds at a ceremony celebrating the Queen's birthday. I had seen an old princess and I had seen a young princess. They had both been extremely not beautiful, but who of us would have told them that? I had never seen England, really seen it, I had only met a representative, seen a picture, read books, memorized its history. I had never set foot, my own foot, in it.

10   The space between the idea of something and its reality is always wide and deep and dark. The longer they are kept apart—idea of thing, reality of thing—the wider the width, the deeper the depth, the thicker and darker the darkness. This space starts out empty, there is nothing in it, but it rapidly becomes filled up with obsession or desire or hatred or love—sometimes all of these things, sometimes some of these things, sometimes only one of these things. The existence of the world as I came to know it was a result of this: idea of thing over here, reality of thing way, way over there. There was Christopher Columbus, an unlikable man, an unpleasant man, a liar (and so, of course, a thief) surrounded by maps and schemes and plans, and there was the reality on the other side of that width, that depth, that darkness. He became obsessed, he became filled with desire, the hatred came later, love was never a part of it. Eventually, his idea met the longed for reality. That the idea of something and its reality are often two completely different things is something no one ever remembers; and so when they meet and find that they are not compatible, the weaker of the two, idea or reality, dies. That idea Christopher Columbus had was more powerful than the reality he met, and so the reality he met died.

11   And so finally, when I was a grown-up woman, the mother of two children, the wife of someone, a person who resides in a powerful country that takes up more than its fair share of a continent, the owner of a house with many rooms in it and of two automobiles, with the desire and will (which I very much act upon) to take from the world more than I give back to it, more than I deserve, more than I need, finally then, I saw England, the real England, not a picture, not a painting, not through a story in a book, but England, for the first time. In me, the space between the idea of it and its reality had become filled with hatred, and so when at last I saw it I wanted to take it into my hands and tear it into little pieces and then crumble it up as if it were clay, child's clay. That was impossible, and so I could only indulge in not-favorable opinions.

12   There were monuments everywhere; they commemorated victories, battles fought between them and the people who lived across the sea from them, all vile people, fought over which of them would have dominion over the people who looked like me. The monuments were useless to them now, people sat on them and ate their lunch. They were like markers on an old useless trail, like a piece of old string tied to a finger to jog the memory, like old decoration in an old house, dirty, useless, in the way. Their skins were so pale, it made them look so fragile, so weak, so ugly. What if I had the power to simply banish them from their land, send boat after boatload of them on a voyage that in fact had no des-

tination, force them to live in a place where the sun's presence was a constant? This would rid them of their pale complexion and make them look more like me, make them look more like the people I love and treasure and hold dear, and more like the people who occupy the near and far reaches of my imagination, my history, my geography, and reduce them and everything they have ever known to figurines as evidence that I was in divine favor, what if all this was in my power? Could I resist it? No one ever has.

13   And they were rude, they were rude to each other. They didn't like each other very much. They didn't like each other in the way they didn't like me, and it occurred to me that their dislike for me was one of the few things they agreed on.

14   I was on a train in England with a friend, an English woman. Before we were in England she liked me very much. In England she didn't like me at all. She didn't like the claim I said I had on England, she didn't like the views I had of England. I didn't like England, she didn't like England, but she didn't like me not liking it too. She said, "I want to show you my England, I want to show you the England that I know and love." I had told her many times before that I knew England and I didn't want to love it anyway. She no longer lived in England; it was her own country, but it had not been kind to her, so she left. On the train, the conductor was rude to her; she asked something, and he responded in a rude way. She became ashamed. She was ashamed at the way he treated her; she was ashamed at the way he behaved. "This is the new England," she said. But I liked the conductor being rude; his behavior seemed quite appropriate. Earlier this had happened: we had gone to a store to buy a shirt for my husband; it was meant to be a special present, a special shirt to wear on special occasions. This was a store where the Prince of Wales has his shirts made, but the shirts sold in this store are beautiful all the same. I found a shirt I thought my husband would like and I wanted to buy him a tie to go with it. When I couldn't decide which one to choose, the salesman showed me a new set. He was very pleased with these, he said, because they bore the crest of the Prince of Wales, and the Prince of Wales had never allowed his crest to decorate an article of clothing before. There was something in the way he said it; his tone was slavish, reverential, awed. It made me feel angry; I wanted to hit him. I didn't do that. I said, my husband and I hate princes, my husband would never wear anything that had a prince's anything on it. My friend stiffened. The salesman stiffened. They both drew themselves in, away from me. My friend told me that the prince was a symbol of her Englishness, and I could see that I had caused offense. I looked at her. She was an English person, the sort of English person I used to know at home, the sort who was nobody in England but somebody when they came to live among the people like me. There were many people I could have seen England with; that I was seeing it with this particular person, a person who reminded me of the people who showed me England long ago as I sat in church or at my desk, made me feel silent and afraid, for I wondered if, all these years of our friendship, I had had a friend or had been in the thrall of a racial memory.

15   I went to Bath—we, my friend and I, did this, but though we were together, I was no longer with her. The landscape was almost as familiar as my own hand, but I had never been in this place before, so how could that be again? And the streets of Bath were familiar, too, but I had never walked on them before. It was all those years of reading, starting with Roman Britain. Why did I have to know about Roman Britain? It was of no real use to me, a person living on a hot, drought-ridden island, and it is of no use to me now, and yet my head is filled with this nonsense, Roman Britain. In Bath, I drank tea in a room I had read about in a novel written in the eighteenth century. In this very same room, young women wearing those dresses that rustled and so on danced and flirted and sometimes disgraced themselves with young men, soldiers, sailors, who were on their way to Bristol or someplace like that, so many places like that where so many adventures, the outcome of which was not good for me, began. Bristol, England. A sentence that began "That night the ship sailed from Bristol, England" would end not so good for me. And then I was driving through the countryside in an English motorcar, on narrow winding roads, and they were so familiar, though I had never been on them before; and through little villages the names of which I somehow knew so well though I had never been there before. And the countryside did have all those hedges and hedges, fields hedged in. I was marveling at all the toil of it, the planting of the hedges to begin with and then the care of it, all that clipping, year after year of clipping, and I wondered at the lives of the people who would have to do this, because wherever I see and feel the hands that hold up the world, I see and feel myself and all the people who look like me. And I said, "Those hedges" and my friend said that someone, a woman named Mrs. Rothchild, worried that the hedges weren't being taken care of properly; the farmers couldn't afford or find the help to keep up the hedges, and often they replaced them with wire fencing. I might have said to that, well if Mrs. Rothchild doesn't like the wire fencing, why doesn't she take care of the hedges herself, but I didn't. And then in those fields that were now hemmed in by wire fencing that a privileged woman didn't like was planted a vile yellow flowering bush that produced an oil, and my friend said that Mrs. Rothchild didn't like this either; it ruined the English countryside, it ruined the traditional look of the English countryside.

16   It was not at that moment that I wished every sentence, everything I knew, that began with England would end with "and then it all died; we don't know how, it just all died." At that moment, I was thinking, who are these people who forced me to think of them all the time, who forced me to think that the world I knew was incomplete, or without substance, or did not measure up because it was not England; that I was incomplete, or without substance, and did not measure up because I was not English. Who were these people? The person sitting next to me couldn't give me a clue; no one person could. In any case, if I had said to her, I find England ugly, I hate England; the weather is like a jail sentence, the English are a very ugly people, the food in England is like a jail sentence, the hair of English people is so straight, so dead looking, the English

have an unbearable smell so different from the smell of people I know, real people of course, she would have said that I was a person full of prejudice. Apart from the fact that it is I—that is, the people who look like me—who made her aware of the unpleasantness of such a thing, the idea of such a thing, prejudice, she would have been only partly right, sort of right: I may be capable of prejudice, but my prejudices have no weight to them, my prejudices have no force behind them, my prejudices remain opinions, my prejudices remain my personal opinion. And a great feeling of rage and disappointment came over me as I looked at England, my head full of personal opinions that could not have public, my public, approval. The people I come from are powerless to do evil on grand scale.

17   The moment I wished every sentence, everything I knew, that began with England would end with "and then it all died, we don't know how, it just all died" was when I saw the white cliffs of Dover. I had sung hymns and recited poems that were about a longing to see the white cliffs of Dover again. At the time I sang the hymns and recited the poems, I could really long to see them again because I had never seen them at all, nor had anyone around me at the time. But there we were, groups of people longing for something we had never seen. And so there they were, the white cliffs, but they were not that pearly majestic thing I used to sing about, that thing that created such a feeling in these people that when they died in the place where I lived they had themselves buried facing a direction that would allow them to see the white cliffs of Dover when they were resurrected, as surely they would be. The white cliffs of Dover, when finally I saw them, were cliffs, but they were not white; you would only call them that if the word "white" meant something special to you; they were dirty and they were steep; they were so steep, the correct height from which all my views of England, starting with the map before me in my classroom and ending with the trip I had just taken, should jump and die and disappear forever.

EXERCISES

Some of the Issues

1. The first paragraph describes the way Kincaid, as a child, first "saw" England. What was she supposed to feel? What indications are there of what she actually did feel?
2. Cite several examples of how Antiguans adopted English dress, food, and customs even when clearly inappropriate for their own needs. What would account for these practices?
3. Why is the teacher's command to draw a map of England "far worse than a declaration of war" (paragraph 4)?
4. In paragraphs 5 and 6, Kincaid tells of all the facts she learned in school about England. Why doesn't she mention learning anything about Antigua in school?

5. In paragraph 7, why does Kincaid think that she would fall into a "hole filled with nothing" if she were to avert her gaze from the glass window?
6. How can a "famous" English seaman and the officially sanctioned criminal (paragraph 7) be the same person?
7. In paragraph 10 Kincaid talks about the idea versus the reality of Columbus. How, according to Kincaid, did ideas overpower reality?
8. When Kincaid finally travels to England, how has she changed from her childhood self? How has she remained the same?
9. How do Kincaid's feelings differ from those of her English friend (paragraphs 14-16)? Why do those feelings become literally "unspeakable"?
10. In the final two paragraphs, Kincaid expresses anger so strong that she wishes England and the English were dead. Trace the development of that anger and its sources. Do you think her anger is justified? Why or why not?

The Way We Are Told

11. How does Kincaid make use of the multiple meanings of "see" in the title and throughout the essay?
12. Kincaid's essay uses multiple contrasts: between imported customs and everyday life; between history written by the conquerors and by the conquered; between what she feels about England and what she is expected to feel. How does the structure of the essay help to underline those contrasts?
13. Why is it important that the white cliffs of Dover are not really white?
14. Kincaid's last sentence refers back to the map described in her beginning paragraph. Is this an effective conclusion?

Some Subjects for Writing

15. Write about an experience in your own life that was radically different from what you had been led to expect. Compare your expectations with the reality you found.
16. Describe a current or historical event from two radically different points of view: that of those who have benefited from it and that of those who have not.
17. In the library, gather basic information about Antigua or a country that is now or has recently been a colony. Then with your instructor plan a research project that explores some aspect of the history of colonialism in that country.

A Modest Proposal

Jonathan Swift

Jonathan Swift (1667–1745) is the author of Gulliver's Travels *(1726). Born in Dublin of a Protestant family in a Catholic country, he was educated at Trinity College, Dublin, and Oxford University. He was ordained in the Anglican Church and eventually became Dean of St. Patrick's Cathedral in Dublin. One of the great satirists of English literature, he attacked religious as well as social and educational corruption in his books* A Tale of a Tub *and* Gulliver's Travels. *In his "A Modest Proposal" Swift addresses himself to the English absentee rulers of Ireland.*

"This great town" in the first paragraph refers to Dublin. The last sentence of paragraph 1 refers to the practice of poor people committing themselves, usually for a fixed number of years, to service in a military enterprise or in a colony (including the American colonies).

A MODEST PROPOSAL

For Preventing the Children of Poor People in Ireland from Being a Burden to Their Parents or Country, and for Making Them Beneficial to the Public

1   It is a melancholy object to those who walk through this great town or travel in the country, when they see the streets, the roads, and cabin doors, crowded with beggars of the female sex, followed by three, four, or six children, all in rags and importuning every passenger for an alms. These mothers, instead of being able to work for their honest livelihood, are forced to employ all their time in strolling to beg sustenance for their helpless infants, who, as they grow up, either turn thieves for want of work, or leave their dear native country to fight for the Pretender[1] in Spain, or sell themselves to the Barbadoes.[2]

2   I think it is agreed by all parties that this prodigious number of children in the arms, or on the backs, or at the heels of their mothers, and frequently of their fathers, is in the present deplorable state of the kingdom a very great additional grievance; and therefore whoever could find out a fair, cheap, and easy method of making these children sound, useful members of the commonwealth would deserve so well of the public as to have his statue set up for a preserver of the nation.

[1]Reference to James Edward Stuart (1688–1766)—known as "the Old Pretender"—a Catholic who laid claim to the British throne though he was exiled in France.
[2]Irish often sailed to Barbados and exchanged labor for their passage.

3   But my intention is very far from being confined to provide only for the children of professed beggars; it is of a much greater extent, and shall take in the whole number of infants at a certain age who are born of parents in effect as little able to support them as those who demand our charity in the streets.

4   As to my own part, having turned my thoughts for many years upon this important subject, and maturely weighed the several schemes of other projectors, I have always found them grossly mistaken in their computation. It is true, a child just dropped from its dam may be supported by her milk for a solar year, with little other nourishment; at most not above the value of two shillings, which the mother may certainly get, or the value in scraps, by her lawful occupation of begging; and it is exactly at one year old that I propose to provide for them in such a manner as instead of being a charge upon their parents or the parish, or wanting food and raiment for the rest of their lives, they shall on the contrary contribute to the feeding, and partly to the clothing, of many thousands.

5   There is likewise another great advantage in my scheme, that it will prevent those voluntary abortions, and that horrid practice of women murdering their bastard children, alas, too frequent among us, sacrificing the poor innocent babes, I doubt, more to avoid the expense than the shame, which would move tears and pity in the most savage and inhuman breast.

6   The number of souls in this kingdom being usually reckoned one million and a half, of these I calculate there may be about two hundred thousand couples whose wives are breeders; from which number I subtract thirty thousand couples who are able to maintain their own children, although I apprehend there cannot be so many under the present distress of the kingdom; but this being granted, there will remain an hundred and seventy thousand breeders. I again subtract fifty thousand for those women who miscarry, or whose children die by accident or disease within the year. There only remain an hundred and twenty thousand children of poor parents annually born. The question therefore is, how this number shall be reared and provided for, which, as I have already said, under the present situation of affairs, is utterly impossible by all the methods hitherto proposed. For we can neither employ them in handicraft nor agriculture; we neither build houses (I mean in the country) nor cultivate land. They can very seldom pick up a livelihood by stealing till they arrive at six years old, except where they are of towardly parts; although I confess they learn the rudiments much earlier, during which time they can however be looked upon only as probationers, as I have been informed by a principal gentleman in the country of Cavan, who protested to me that he never knew above one or two instances under the age of six, even in a part of the kingdom so renowned for the quickest proficiency in that art.

7   I am assured by our merchants that a boy or a girl before twelve years old is no salable commodity; and even when they come to this age, they will not yield above three pounds, or three pounds and half a crown at most on the Exchange;

which cannot turn to account either to the parents or the kingdom, the charge of nutriment and rags having been at least four times that value.

8   I shall now therefore humbly propose my own thoughts, which I hope will not be liable to the least objection.

9   I have been assured by a very knowing American of my acquaintance in London, that a young healthy child well nursed is at a year old a most delicious, nourishing, and wholesome food, whether stewed, roasted, baked, or boiled; and I make not doubt that it will equally serve in a fricassee or a ragout.

10   I do therefore humbly offer it to public consideration that of the hundred and twenty thousand children, already computed, twenty thousand may be reserved for breed, whereof only one fourth part to be males, which is more than we allow to sheep, black cattle, or swine; and my reason is that these children are seldom the fruits of marriage, a circumstance not much regarded by our savages, therefore one male will be sufficient to serve four females. That the remaining hundred thousand may at a year old be offered in sale to the persons of quality and fortune through the kingdom, always advising the mother to let them suck plentifully in the last month, so as to render them plump and fat for a good table. A child will make two dishes at an entertainment for friends; and when the family dines alone, the fore or hind quarter will make a reasonable dish, and seasoned with a little pepper or salt will be very good boiled on the fourth day, especially in winter.

11   I have reckoned upon a medium that a child just born will weigh twelve pounds, and in a solar year if tolerably nursed increaseth to twenty-eight pounds.

12   I grant this food will be somewhat dear, and therefore very proper for landlords, who, as they have already devoured most of the parents, seem to have the best title to the children.

13   Infant's flesh will be in season throughout the year, but more plentiful in March, and a little before and after. For we are told by a grave author, an eminent French physician, that fish being a prolific diet, there are more children born in Roman Catholic countries about nine months after Lent, than at any other season; therefore, reckoning a year after Lent, the markets will be more glutted than usual, because the number of popish infants is at least three to one in this kingdom; and therefore it will have one other collateral advantage, by lessening the number of Papists among us.

14   I have already computed the charge of nursing a beggar's child (in which list I reckon all cottagers, laborers, and four fifths of the farmers) to be about two shillings per annum, rags included; and I believe no gentleman would repine to give ten shillings for the carcass of a good fat child, which, as I have said, will make four dishes of excellent nutritive meat, when he hath only some particular friend or his own family to dine with him. Thus the squire will learn to be a good landlord, and grow popular among the tenants; the mother will have eight shillings net profit, and be fit for work till she produces another child.

15   Those who are more thrifty (as I must confess the times require) may flay the carcass; the skin of which artificially dressed will make admirable gloves for ladies, and summer boots for fine gentlemen.

16   As to our city of Dublin, shambles[3] may be appointed for this purpose in the most convenient parts of it, and butchers we may be assured will not be wanting; although I rather recommend buying the children alive, and dressing them hot from the knife as we do roasting pigs.

17   A very worthy person, a true lover of this country, and whose virtues I highly esteem, was lately pleased in discoursing on this matter to offer a refinement upon my scheme. He said that many gentlemen of his kingdom, having of late destroyed their deer, he conceived that the want of venison might be well supplied by the bodies of young lads and maidens, not exceeding fourteen years of age nor under twelve, so great a number of both sexes in every county being now ready to starve for want of work and service; and these to be disposed of by their parents, if alive, or otherwise by their nearest relations. But with due deference to so excellent a friend and so deserving a patriot, I cannot be altogether in his sentiments; for as to the males, my American acquaintance assured me from frequent experience that their flesh was generally tough and lean, like that of our schoolboys, by continual exercise, and their taste disagreeable; and to fatten them would not answer the charge. Then as to the females, it would, I think with humble submission, be a loss to the public, because they soon would become breeders themselves; and besides, it is not improbable that some scrupulous people might be apt to censure such a practice (although indeed very unjustly) as a little bordering upon cruelty; which, I confess, hath always been with me the strongest objection against any project, how well soever intended.

18   But in order to justify my friend, he confessed that this expedient was put into his head by the famous Psalmanazar, a native of the island Formosa, who came from thence to London above twenty years ago, and in conversation told my friend that in his country when any young person happened to be put to death, the executioner sold the carcass to the persons of quality as a prime dainty; and that in his time the body of a plump girl of fifteen, who was crucified for an attempt to poison the emperor, was sold to his Imperial Majesty's prime minister of state, and other great mandarins of the court, in joints from the gibbet, at four hundred crowns. Neither indeed can I deny that if the same use were made of several plump young girls in this town, who without one single groat to their fortunes cannot stir abroad without a chair,[4] and appear at the playhouse and assemblies in foreign fineries which they never will pay for, the kingdom would not be the worse.

19   Some persons of a desponding spirit are in great concern about that vast number of poor people who are aged, diseased, or maimed, and I have been de-

---

[3]Slaughterhouses.
[4]A portable chair carried by two people on foot.

sired to employ my thoughts what course may be taken to ease the nation of so grievous an encumbrance. But I am not in the least pain upon that matter, because it is very well known that they are every day dying and rotting by cold and famine, and filth and vermin, as fast as can be reasonably expected. And as to the younger laborers, they are now in almost as hopeful a condition. They cannot get work, and consequently pine away for want of nourishment to a degree that if any time they are accidentally hired to common labor, they have not strength to perform it; and thus the country and themselves are happily delivered from the evils to come.

20   I have too long digressed, and therefore shall return to my subject. I think the advantages by the proposal which I have made are obvious and many, as well as of the highest importance.

21   For first, as I have already observed, it would greatly lessen the number of Papists, with whom we are yearly overrun, being the principal breeders of the nation as well as our most dangerous enemies; and who stay at home on purpose to deliver the kingdom to the Pretender, hoping to take their advantage by the absence of so many good Protestants, who have chosen rather to leave their country than to stay at home and pay tithes against their conscience to an Episcopal curate.

22   Secondly, the poorer tenants will have something valuable of their own, which by law may be made liable to distress, and help to pay their landlord's rent, their corn and cattle being already seized and money a thing unknown.

23   Thirdly, whereas the maintenance of an hundred thousand children, from two years old and upwards, cannot be computed at less than ten shillings a piece per annum, the nation's stock will be thereby increased fifty thousand pounds per annum, besides the profit of a new dish introduced to the tables of all gentlemen of fortune in the kingdom who have any refinement in taste. And the money will circulate among ourselves, the goods being entirely of our own growth and manufacture.

24   Fourthly, the constant breeders, besides the gain of eight shillings sterling per annum by the sale of their children, will be rid of the charge for maintaining them after the first year.

25   Fifthly, this food would likewise bring great custom to taverns, where the vintners will certainly be so prudent as to procure the best receipts for dressing it to perfection, and consequently have their houses frequented by all the fine gentlemen, who justly value themselves upon their knowledge in good eating; and a skillful cook, who understands how to oblige his guests, will contrive to make it as expensive as they please.

26   Sixthly, this would be a great inducement to marriage, which all wise nations have either encouraged by rewards or enforced by laws and penalties. It would increase the care and tenderness of mothers toward their children, when they were sure of a settlement for life to the poor babes, provided in some sort by the public, to their annual profit instead of expense. We should see an honest emulation among the married women, which of them could bring the fattest

child to the market. Men would become as fond of their wives during the time of their pregnancy as they are now of their mares in foal, their cows in calf, or sows when they are ready to farrow; nor offer to beat or kick them (as is too frequent a practice) for fear of a miscarriage.

27   Many other advantages might be enumerated. For instance, the addition of some thousand carcasses in our exportation of barreled beef, the propagation of swine's flesh, and improvements in the art of making good bacon, so much wanted among us by the great destruction of pigs, too frequent at our tables, which are no way comparable in taste or magnificence to a well-grown, fat, yearling child, which roasted whole will make a considerable figure at a lord mayor's feast or any other public entertainment. But this and many others I omit, being studious of brevity.

28   Supposing that one thousand families in this city would be constant customers for infants' flesh, besides others who might have it at merry meetings, particularly weddings and christenings, I compute that Dublin would take off annually about twenty thousand carcasses, and the rest of the kingdom (where probably they will be sold somewhat cheaper) the remaining eighty thousand.

29   I can think of no one objection that will possibly be raised against this proposal, unless it should be urged that the number of people will be thereby much lessened in the kingdom. This I freely own, and it was indeed one principal design in offering it to the world. I desire the reader will observe, and I calculate my remedy for this one individual kingdom of Ireland and for no other that ever was, is, or I think ever can be upon earth. Therefore, let no man talk to me of other expedients: of taxing our absentees at five shillings a pound: of using neither clothes nor household furniture except what is of our own growth and manufacture: of utterly rejecting the materials and instruments that promote foreign luxury: of curing the expensiveness of pride, vanity, idleness, and gaming in our women: of introducing a vein of parsimony, prudence, and temperance: of learning to love our country, in the want of which we differ even from Laplanders and the inhabitants of Topinamboo: of quitting our animosities and factions, nor acting any longer like the Jews, who were murdering one another at the very moment their city was taken: of being a little cautious not to sell our country and conscience for nothing: of teaching landlords to have at least one degree of mercy toward their tenants: lastly, of putting a spirit of honesty, industry, and skill into our shopkeepers; who, if a resolution could not be taken to buy only our native goods, would immediately unite to cheat and exact upon us in the price, the measure, and the goodness, nor could ever yet be brought to make one fair proposal of just dealing, though often and earnestly invited to it.

30   Therefore, I repeat, let no man talk to me of these and the like expedients, til he hath at least some glimpse of hope that there will ever be some hearty and sincere attempt to put them in practice.

31   But as to myself, having been wearied out for many years with offering vain, idle, visionary thoughts, and at length utterly despairing of success, I fortunately

32   fell upon this proposal, which, as it is wholly new, so it hath something solid and real, of no expense and little trouble, full in our own power, and whereby we can incur no danger in disobliging England. For this kind of commodity will not bear exportation, the flesh being of too tender a consistence to admit a long continuance in salt, although perhaps I could name a country which would be glad to eat up our whole nation without it.

32   After all, I am not so violently bent upon my own opinion as to reject any offer proposed by wise men, which shall be found equally innocent, cheap, easy, and effectual. But before something of that kind shall be advanced in contradiction to my scheme, and offering a better, I desire the author or authors will be pleased maturely to consider two points. First, as things now stand, how they will be able to find food and raiment for an hundred thousand useless mouths and backs. And secondly, there being a round million of creatures in human figure throughout this kingdom, whose sole subsistence put into a common stock would leave them in debt two millions of pounds sterling, adding those who are beggars by profession to the bulk of farmers, cottagers, and laborers, with their wives and children who are beggars in effect; I desire those politicians who dislike my overture, and may perhaps be so bold to attempt an answer, that they will first ask the parents of these mortals whether they would not at this day think it a great happiness to have been sold for food at a year old in this manner I prescribe, and thereby have avoided such a perpetual scene of misfortunes as they have since gone through by the oppression of landlords, the impossibility of paying rent without money or trade, the want of common sustenance, with neither house nor clothes to cover them from the inclemencies of the weather, and the most inevitable prospect of entailing the like or greater miseries upon their breed forever.

33   I profess, in the sincerity of my heart, that I have not the least personal interest in endeavoring to promote this necessary work, having no other motive than the public good of my country, by advancing our trade, providing for infants, relieving the poor, and giving some pleasure to the rich. I have no children by which I can propose to get a single penny; the youngest being nine years old, and my wife past childbearing.

EXERCISES

Some of the Issues

1. Paragraphs 1 through 6 are an introduction. What is the main point the author wants to make?
2. Paragraph 7 is a transition. Before you have read the rest, what might it foretell?
3. The short paragraph 8 is the beginning of the real proposal; and paragraph 9, its central idea. Explain that idea.

4. Paragraph 10 expands the proposal in 9. It relates in particular to paragraph 6. Why are all these statistical calculations important? What do they contribute to the impact of the essay?
5. Look back to paragraph 5. What hints of the idea to come do you now find in it?
6. Paragraphs 15 through 17 offer refinements on the main theme. What are they?
7. Examine the logic of each of the advantages of the proposal, as listed in paragraphs 21 through 26. Why is the lessening of the number of Papists a particular advantage?
8. In paragraph 29, when the essay turns to possible objections, which are the ones that are omitted completely? Why? Why does the narrator so vehemently concentrate on Ireland in this paragraph?
9. In paragraph 29 other remedies are also proposed for solving the plight of Ireland. What distinguishes them from the one the narrator is advocating?

The Way We Are Told

10. Readers of this essay will for a time take Swift's observations at face value. At what point in the essay are they likely to change their minds?
11. Swift creates a narrator whose modest proposal this is. Try to imagine him: What kind of person might he be? What might be his profession? Consider some of the phrases he uses, his obsession with statistics and the financial aspects of the problem, and his attention to detail.
12. In paragraph 4, in the narrator's choice of words, you find the first hint of what is to come. Locate it. Do you find an echo in paragraph 6?
13. Having made his proposal boldly in paragraph 9, the narrator develops it in paragraphs 10 through 14. Paragraphs 15 through 17 heighten the effect. Consider the choice of images in these paragraphs.

Some Subjects for Writing

14. Do you have any modest proposals as to what to do with teachers, younger brothers or sisters, former boyfriends or girlfriends, or anyone else?
15. Write an essay in which you attempt to change somebody's mind. You may use irony, as Swift does, exaggerating the consequences of the other side's position. Or you may write more objectively, proposing a real solution to the problem. Your challenge, a difficult one, is to get a person who disagrees with you to take your argument seriously.

To live in
the Borderlands
means you . . .

Gloria Anzaldúa

Gloria Anzaldúa describes herself as a "Chicana tejana lesbian-feminist poet and fiction writer." She has taught Chicana studies, feminist studies, and creative writing at various universities, and has conducted writing workshops around the country.

> *She is editor of* Making Face Making Soul/Haciendo Caras: Creative and Critical Perspectives by Women of Color *(1990) and coeditor of* This Bridge Called My Back: Writings by Radical Women of Color *(1981). She is also the author of a novel,* La Prieta *(the dark one) published in 1997. This poem is taken from* Borderlands/La Frontera: The New Mestiza *(1987), a collection of prose and poetry that describes the author's childhood along the Texas-Mexico border, growing up between two cultures, Anglo and Mexican, equally at home and alien in both. Anzaldúa speaks of an actual physical border, but expands her metaphor to include the psychological "borderlands" that occur whenever two or more cultures coexist together.*

To live in the Borderlands means you . . .

are neither *hispana india negra española*
ni gabacha, eres mestiza, mulata,[1] half-breed
caught in the crossfire between camps
while carrying all five races on your back
not knowing which side to turn to, run from;

To live in the Borderlands means knowing
that the *india* in you, betrayed for 500 years,
is no longer speaking to you,
that *mexicanas* call you *rajetas,*[2]

---

[1]Hispanic, Indian (Native American), black, Spanish nor white (*gabacha* is the Hispanic term for a white woman), you are of mixed blood, mulatto.
[2]Split.

that denying the Anglo inside you
is as bad as having denied the Indian or Black;

Cuando vives en la frontera[3]
people walk through you, the wind steals your voice,
15   you're a *burra, buey,*[4] scapegoat,
forerunner of a new race,
half and half—both woman and man, neither—
a new gender;

To live in the Borderlands means to
20   put *chile* in the borscht,
eat whole wheat *tortillas,*
speak Tex-Mex with a Brooklyn accent;
be stopped by *la migra*[5] at the border checkpoints;

Living in the Borderlands means you fight hard to
25   resist the gold elixir beckoning from the bottle,
the pull of the gun barrel,
the rope crushing the hollow of your throat;

In the Borderlands
you are the battleground
30   where enemies are kin to each other;
you are at home, a stranger,
the border disputes have been settled
the volley of shots have shattered the truce
you are wounded, lost in action
35   dead, fighting back;

To live in the Borderlands means
the mill with the razor white teeth wants to shred off
your olive-red skin, crush out the kernel, your heart
pound you pinch you roll you out
40   smelling like white bread but dead;

To survive the Borderlands
you must live *sin fronteras*[6]
be a crossroads.

[3]When you live in the borderlands.
[4]Donkey, ox.
[5]Immigration officials—specifically U.S. immigration officials.
[6]Without borders.

EXERCISES

Some of the Issues

1. The title of Anzaldúa's poem is also its beginning line and is repeated, with some variation, again and again. What is the effect of the near repetition and of the changes?
2. What might Anzaldúa gain by her use of Spanish words?
3. Throughout the poem, Anzaldúa speaks of borders within herself, and borders imposed by the outside world. What are these? Why is it sometimes difficult to tell the difference?
4. Anzaldúa often uses contradictory images in her poem. For example, in the third stanza she is both "a scapegoat" and the "forerunner of a new race." Find other pairs of opposing images. What is their effect?
5. What is "the mill with the razor white teeth" (line 37) and what is its danger?
6. What is Anzaldúa's suggestion for survival? What does she mean by it?
7. Although the author speaks of the difficulty of living in the borderlands, there are also indications of optimism. Which do you see as the principal message of the poem?
*8. Read Aurora Levins Morales's "Class Poem." Like Anzaldúa, she writes about her various heritages and their relationship to her current identity. What similarities and differences do you see between the two authors' points of view?
*9. Read Pico Iyer's "Home Is Every Place." Both authors talk about borders and use geography as a symbol of their own identity. Compare and contrast their views.

Some Subjects for Writing

10. Although not all of us are of mixed or battling heritages, most of us have felt split—"rajetas"—at some point in our lives. For example, we may feel both allegiance to and conflict with the identities prescribed by our family's traditions, our religion, our social class, or our society's ideas about appropriate gender roles. In an essay, describe a way in which you see yourself on the border of any of these identities or others important to you.
11. Do you think society is becoming more or less accepting of people who cross conventional roles of race, ethnicity, or gender? Why or why not? Write an essay giving evidence to support your views.

PART **VII**

HOW WE LIVE

We are, in many ways, defined by the world around us. Changes in technology, law, economics, and social custom alter the way we live our everyday lives. At the same time, our daily lives and decisions help shape and define social and political changes. Though the essays in this section deal with a variety of issues—from work to cable television—each addresses the relationship between our personal lives and our social and political environments. Taken together, these essays demonstrate that how we live is both a reflection of the world and a catalyst for changing it.

Two of the authors in this section address the issue of how changes in technology impact our lives, identities, and our sense of home. Geraldine Brooks focuses on her town of Waterford, Virginia, and, using both irony and humor, recounts the story of how the townspeople fought back against the local cable company. In "Unplugged," she demonstrates that we, as individuals and communities, can make decisions that allow us to shape our environments regardless of larger changes in technology and communication. In "Home Is Every Place," Pico Iyer describes his life as a member of a new breed of "transcontinental warriors," people for whom every place is equally familiar and strange. For Iyer, who sees himself living in an increasingly small and interconnected world, home can no longer be defined through our connection to place and nationality.

Brooks and Iyer also reflect on time, and how technology has affected the speed of life. In "Tempo: The Speed of Life," Robert Levine describes different cultures' perceptions of time and the differing pace at which people live their lives in various places around the world. He concludes with thought-provoking questions that allow us to question the tempo at which we live our own lives.

The next two essays look at two specific aspects of how we live, one from a personal perspective and the other from a more general viewpoint. Lars Eighner's description of "scavenging" in "On Dumpster Diving" becomes a commentary on both homelessness and on wastefulness in American society. Through his vivid and meticulous description of his daily dives into the dumpster, Eighner delivers a poignant commentary on consumer society and the irony of homelessness in a country of abundance. Barbara Brandt, in "Less is More: A Call for Shorter Work Hours," analyzes the American impulse toward overwork and advocates a change to a thirty-hour work week. According to Brandt, "Americans often assume that overwork is an inevitable fact of life," and we too easily accept this assumption without considering the sacrifices we make in terms of our families, communities, and personal leisure.

In "Town-Building Is No Mickey Mouse Operation," Michael Pollan takes us to the Disney-created town of Celebration, Florida, and asks whether an ideal community can be successfully engineered, or whether a community is constantly evolving and, as he puts it, "messy." For Pollan, Celebration gets at the heart of what democracy means in a consumer-oriented society.

This section ends with a poem that celebrates both everyday experience and personal identity. Through describing moments in lives of friends and family that have touched upon her own life, Aurora Levins Morales, in "Class Poem," credits others for helping her define herself and allowing her to be proud of both her privilege and her heritage.

Unplugged

Geraldine Brooks

*Geraldine Brooks is a native of Australia and a graduate of Sydney Univer-
sity and the Columbia University School of Journalism. She has spent extensive time in the Middle East, is a former foreign correspondent for the* Wall
Street Journal, *and is the author of* Nine Parts of Desire *(1995), a book
about Arab women, a memoir,* Foreign Correspondence: A Pen Pal's Journey From Down Under to All Over *(1998) and a novel,* Year of Wonders: A Novel of the Plague *(2001).*

*In "Unplugged," Brooks reflects on the question of whether to bring ca-
ble television to Waterford, the small town in Virginia where she lives. The
residents of Waterford are seen as eccentric because they choose to reject
"more than seventy channels of the finest programming available" and question whether the information and entertainment brought to us by mass media
expands our horizons or compromises our individuality.*

1   Jake came to dinner a few weeks ago. We talked about the nine muses, and
why tragedy is important in human storytelling. Jake has been reading a lot
of Greek mythology lately. He's eight. A few nights later, Jake's dad, Mike, and I
walked up the hill to the old schoolhouse for a Citizens' Association meeting
about bringing cable TV to Waterford, a town of 250 people in the foothills of
Virginia's Blue Ridge Mountains. The hills do terrible things to TV reception.

2   The president of the cable company had come to tell us that it probably
wasn't a moneymaker for him to string the cable all the way out to our eighty-
some houses, but he felt it was only right to give us the chance to partake of
the rich offerings of his service. He passed around the latest full-color guide
describing what we were missing that month. The cover featured Melanie Griffith.
If we had cable, we would have been able to watch her in the movie *Milk
Money.*

3   Mike's house on Main Street doesn't have a TV. But like most houses here,
it has broad views of farmland rolling away to the wooded hillside, and big, old
maples in the garden. From the high meadow behind town you can look at the
Catoctin Creek as it wends through the valley, and see why the young Pennsylvania Quaker, Amos Janney, figured back in 1733 that this would be a fine place
to build a mill.

4   The mill is still there, and like most buildings in town, it has American history written into the horsehair mortar holding up its walls. Just opposite, there's
a stone house whose Quaker inhabitant found slaves a worse evil than war, even
though fighting for the Union caused him to be read out of Meeting for violating pacifist principles. The Baptist church on the High Street still has bullet

holes in the bricks from the skirmish that took place there between the Confederates and Waterford's Loudoun Rangers, the only regiment raised in Virginia that fought on the Union side.

5   There aren't many Quakers here now, but they left behind a tradition of stubborn singularity. The townspeople—farmers and carpenters who've always lived here, artists and software designers who've arrived more recently—like the fact that this place is different: always has been, always will.

6   At the Citizens' Association meeting, the cable guy brags about how his service offers "more than seventy channels of the finest programming available." Mike, beside me, fidgets on his chair. Suddenly, he's speaking, softly and diffidently, as he always does.

7   "People here have time to talk to each other. I'm proud of our bad TV reception because it gets us out of our houses, and I'd kind of hate that to change because there's nine different football games to watch. Personally, I'd rather go fishing than watch the fishing channel."

8   The cable man doesn't realize that this is one of those Martin Luther moments, and that Mike has just nailed the theses to the door. His tone, when he replies, is unctuously patronizing.

9   "Well, that's your opinion and you're certainly entitled to it. But do you have a child?" Mike nods. "Then you should think about his future. He's going to be at a disadvantage when he gets to college and has to compete with young people who've been exposed to all the marvelous information that cable can bring them."

10   People who know Mike's boy Jake burst into loud guffaws. "That's bullshit!" shouts our neighbor Phil, sitting in back. And suddenly the tone of the meeting has changed, changed utterly. If Waterford could stand up to the Confederate States of America, it certainly can stand up to Cablevision of Loudoun County.

11   Someone who has just moved out here from a suburb that has Cablevision is on her feet, saying what a bunch of crap the programs are, and how she had canceled her subscription after a couple of months.

12   "Haven't you ever heard of books?" someone else shouts. "There's more 'marvelous information' in the local library than's on seven hundred cable channels!" Last year, the county decided that Waterford was too small to warrant visits from the Bookmobile. We had a meeting about that, too. Our neighbors Casey and Jeff donated the front room of their house—a bay-windowed storefront that used to be the village milliner—so we'd have a place to put a cooperative library.

13   That meeting wasn't nearly as loud as this one. The decibels don't come down until someone gets us off on a discussion of the life of Thomas Jefferson, and whether one could say it was impoverished for lack of television.

14   People barely notice when the cable man melts away. The next speaker is our neighbor Mary, who wants to tell us about laying rumble strips to slow the traffic through town. "Well," she says, raising an eyebrow, "I'm not sure I want to get up in front of *this* crowd!"

15   The next morning, when we meet up at the post office to pick up our mail, a few of us allow that we feel a bit sheepish about more or less running the cable man out of town. But then we look up at the ugly tangle of power lines—one of the few twentieth-century intrusions in town—and consider how one more big thick cable running along up there would make it even more unsightly, and less likely that we'll ever realize the village's long-standing dream of getting the things buried.

16   Marie, who lives right across from the post office, grows a morning glory vine every spring. She trains it up the power pole in front of her balcony, and lets the wires become a trellis for a cascade of royal blue blooms. In summer, a team from the power company came out intending to chop the vine down. Marie gave them each a cup of tea and a fresh-baked scone, then put them on the phone with the local agricultural extension agent, who explained that morning glory is a tender annual that will be gone with the first frost. The team finished their tea, and decided they'd leave the flowers be.

17   In less than a week, word of the Waterford Cable Rebellion filtered to the outside world. It seems we're the first town in the United States to resist it. Reporters from the *Washington Post*, CBS news, Fox network, and even South Korean TV showed up and filed bemused, "can-you-believe-it" features about the bunch of oddball hayseeds who don't want cable.

18   It's become eccentric not to want every place to be just like every other place. It isn't just the cable. Waterford is battling a new law that says the eighty buildings here, which have done just fine for 250 years without addresses, must now post three-inch-high, light-reflecting, five-digit street numbers to fit in with a county-wide grid system. One tiny lane has all of three cottages. But the first house will have to post a number that makes it 15545 Butchers Row.

19   Perhaps we'd have a better chance of holding on to what's here if the history it represented was linked with the museum-like grand estate of some long-ago rich man. But what's here isn't grand. These cottages and ice houses and root cellars are the templates of ordinary lives.

20   The old rooms have a way of slowly shaping you to fit them. You arrive here thinking you simply must have more built-in closets, but instead find yourself shedding your excess wardrobe. You open up the old stone-lined, hand-dug well so your arms can feel the effort of hauling a full water-bucket up thirty feet. I suppose, if we had cable, I could be watching *Body by Jake* on the Family Channel instead.

21   Down on Main Street, my neighbor Jake is toning his biceps by helping his dad stack the woodpile. I think I'll amble down there and have a word with him about a Corinthian king named Sisyphus.

EXERCISES

Some of the Issues

1. Brooks briefly describes two scenarios in her opening paragraph. How do they serve as introduction to the essay?

2. What historical events or moments does Brooks recount? How does she use this history to help her make her point?
3. Why is it ironic that the cable representative refers specifically to Mike's child in paragraph 9?
*4. Consider Brooks's statement: "It's become eccentric not to want every place to be just like every other place" (paragraph 18). For a different point of view, read Pico Iyer's "Home Is Every Place." What are the perspectives presented by each author? What are your own views on the subject?
5. Brooks presents a very positive view of Waterford. Some might see her as romantic or overly resistant to change. What do you think?

The Way We Are Told

6. Why do you suppose Brooks chose this title for the essay?
7. What tone does Brooks use to portray the cable representative in paragraph 2? Where else in the essay do you notice a similar tone?
8. Brooks's thesis is implied rather than directly stated. If you were to develop a thesis statement for her essay, what might it be?

Some Subjects for Writing

9. Brooks presents two different views of cable television: those of the cable representative and those of the townspeople and herself. Whose views come closest to your own? Write an essay in which you defend or criticize the role television plays in our society. Although you should present a strong defense of your opinion, make sure to consider other viewpoints.
*10. In Pico Iyer's "Home Is Every Place," the author's sense of attachment to place clearly differs from Brooks's. Consider your own attachment to a place, or various places. How has it helped to shape your identity?

Home Is Every Place

Pico Iyer

Pico Iyer was born in Oxford, England, in 1957 to Indian parents. The son of two college professors, he was educated in the elite British public school system and at Oxford and Harvard Universities. He later became an American citizen.

Iyer has written a novel, Cuba and the Night *(1995), and several volumes of travel literature. These chronicle his journeys through various parts of Asia, and include* Video Night in Kathmandu: And Other Reports from the Not-So-Far East *(1988) and* The Lady and the Monk: Four Seasons in Kyoto *(1991). Much of his writing focuses on the ways in which Western culture has infiltrated the Asian world.*

Iyer has said of his work, "Writing should be an act of communication more than of mere self-expression—a telling of a story rather than a flourishing of skills. The less conscious one is of being 'a writer,' the better the writing. . . . Writing, in fact, should ideally be as spontaneous and urgent as a letter to a lover, or a message to a friend who has just lost a parent. And because of the ways a writer is obliged to tap the private selves that even those closest to him never see, writing is, in the end, the oddest of anomalies; an intimate letter to a stranger."

This essay originally appeared in Homeground *(1996), an anthology of writings about the concept of "home." Iyer uses terms such as "transit loungers" and "privileged homeless" to describe a group of people, himself included, for whom the idea of home is not tied to a particular place, and who feel equally at home (or not at home) in many places. Iyer asserts that the modern world, with its blending of cultures and its distances shortened by fax, phone, and airplane, is increasingly made for people like him: "resident aliens of the world, impermanent residents of nowhere." By describing himself as a member of this tribe of nomads who supposedly lack a specific national or cultural identity, Iyer, in a sense, claims a home for himself.*

1   By the time I was nine, I was already used to going to school by trans-Atlantic plane, to sleeping in airports, to shuttling back and forth, three times a year, between my parents' (Indian) home in California and my boarding school in England. Throughout the time I was growing up, I was never within 6,000 miles of the nearest relative—and came, therefore, to learn how to define relations in non-familial ways. From the time I was a teenager, I took it for granted that I could take my budget vacations (as I did) in Bolivia and Tibet, China and Morocco. It never seemed strange to me that a girlfriend might be on the other side of a continent or sea.

2   It was only recently that I realized that all these habits of mind and life would scarcely have been imaginable in my parents' youth; the very facts and facilities that shape my world are all distinctly new developments, and mark me as a modern type.

3   It was only recently, in fact, that I realized that I am an example, perhaps, of an entirely new breed of people, a transcontinental tribe of wanderers that is multiplying as fast as international phone lines and Frequent Flyer programs. We are the Transit Loungers, forever heading to the Departure Gate, forever orbiting the world. We buy our interests duty-free, we eat our food on plastic plates, we watch the world through borrowed headphones. We pass through countries as through revolving doors, resident aliens of the world, impermanent residents of nowhere. Nothing is strange to us, and nowhere is foreign. We are visitors even in our own homes.

4   This is not, I think, a function of affluence so much as of simple circumstance. I am not, that is, a jet-setter pursuing vacations from Marbella[1] to Phuket;[2] I am simply a fairly typical product of a movable sensibility, living and working in a world that is itself increasingly small and increasingly mongrel. I am a multinational soul on a multicultural globe where more and more countries are as polyglot and restless as airports. Taking planes seems as natural to me as picking up the phone, or going to school; I fold up my self and carry it around with me as if it were an overnight case.

5   The modern world seems increasingly made for people like me. I can plop myself down anywhere and find myself in the same relation of familiarity and strangeness: Lusaka,[3] after all, is scarcely more strange to me than the foreigners' England in which I was born; the America where I am registered as an "alien"; and the almost unvisited India that people tell me is my home. I can fly from London to San Francisco to Osaka and feel myself no more a foreigner in one place than another; all of them are just locations—pavilions in some intercontinental Expo—and I can work or live or love in any one of them. All have Holiday Inns, direct-dial phones, CNN, and DHL. All have sushi and Thai restaurants, Kentucky Fried Chicken and Coke. My office is as close as the nearest fax machine or modem. Roppongi is West Hollywood is Leblon.[4]

6   This kind of life offers an unprecedented sense of freedom and mobility: tied down to nowhere, we can pick and choose among locations. Ours is the first generation that can go off to visit Tibet for a week, or meet Tibetans down the street; ours is the first generation to be able to go to Nigeria for a holiday to find our roots or to find they are not there. At the lowest level, this new internationalism also means that I can get on a plane in Los Angeles, get off a few hours later in Jakarta, check into a Hilton, order a cheeseburger in English, and pay

---

[1]Coastal town in southern Spain.
[2]Island off southern Thailand.
[3]Capital of Zambia.
[4]Entertainment districts in Tokyo, Los Angeles, and Rio de Janeiro, respectively.

for it all with an American Express card. At the next level, it means that I can meet, in the Hilton coffee shop, an Indonesian businessman who is as conversant as I am with Michael Kinsley and Magic Johnson and Madonna. At a deeper level, it means that I need never feel estranged. If all the world is alien to us, all the world is home.

7   I have learned, in fact, to love foreignness. In any place I visit, I have the privileges of an outsider: I am an object of interest, and even fascination; I am a person set apart, able to enjoy the benefits of the place without paying the taxes. And the places themselves seem glamorous to me, romantic, as seen through foreign eyes: distance on both sides lends enchantment. Policemen let me off speeding tickets, girls want to hear the stories of my life, pedestrians will gladly point me to the nearest Golden Arches. Perpetual foreigners in the transit lounge, we enjoy a kind of diplomatic immunity; and, living off room service in our hotel rooms, we are never obliged to grow up, or even, really, to be ourselves.

8   Thus, many of us learn to exult in the blessings of belonging to what feels like a whole new race. It is a race, as Salman Rushdie[5] says, of "people who root themselves in ideas rather than places, in memories as much as in material things; people who have been obliged to define themselves—because they are so defined by others—by their otherness; people in whose deepest selves strange fusions occur, unprecedented unions between what they were and where they find themselves." And when people argue that our very notion of wonder is eroded, that alienness itself is as seriously endangered as the wilderness, that more and more of the world is turning into a single synthetic monoculture, I am not worried: a Japanese version of a French fashion is something new, I say, not quite Japanese and not truly French. Comme des Garcons hybrids are the art form of the time.

9   And yet, sometimes, I stop myself and think. What kind of heart is being produced by these new changes? And must I always be a None of the Above? When the stewardess comes down the aisle with disembarkation forms, what do I fill in? My passport says one thing, my face another; my accent contradicts my eyes. Place of Residence, Final Destination, even Marital Status are not much easier to fill in; usually I just tick "Other."

10   And beneath all the boxes, where do we place ourselves? How does one fix a moving object on a map? I am not an exile, really, nor an immigrant; not deracinated, I think, any more than I am rooted. I have not fled the oppression of war, nor found ostracism in the places where I do alight; I can scarcely feel severed from a home I have barely known. Yet is "citizen of the world" enough to comfort me? And does taking my home as every place make it easier to sleep at night?

11   Alienation, we are taught from kindergarten, is the condition of the time. This is the century of exiles and refugees, of boat people and statelessness; the time

[5](1947–) Indian-born British novelist whose book *The Satanic Verses* (1988) enraged many Muslims. He was forced into hiding by death threats.

when traditions have been abolished, and men become closer to machines. This is the century of estrangement: more than a third of all Afghans live outside Afghanistan; the second city of the Khmers is a refugee camp; the second tongue of Beverly Hills is Farsi. The very notion of nation-states is outdated; many of us are as crosshatched within as Beirut.

12   We airport-hoppers can, in fact, go through the world as through a house of wonders, picking up something at every stop, and taking the whole globe as our playpen, or our supermarket (and even if we don't go to the world, the world will increasingly come to us: just down the street, almost wherever we are, are nori[6] and salsa, tiramisu and *naan*[7]). We don't have a home, we have a hundred homes. And we can mix and match as the situation demands. "Nobody's history is my history," Kazuo Ishiguro, a great spokesman for the privileged homeless, once said to me, and then went on, "Whenever it was convenient for me to become very Japanese, I could become very Japanese, and then, when I wanted to drop it, I would just become this ordinary Englishman." Instantly, I felt a shock of recognition: I have a wardrobe of selves from which to choose. And I savor the luxury of being able to be an Indian in Cuba (where people are starving for yoga and Tagore[8]), or an American in Thailand, to be an Englishman in New York.

13   And so we go on circling the world, six miles above the ground, displaced from time, above the clouds, with all our needs attended to. We listen to announcements given in three languages. We confirm our reservations at every stop. We disembark at airports that are self-sufficient communities, with hotels, gymnasia, and places of worship. At customs we have nothing to declare but ourselves.

14   But what is the price we pay for all of this? I sometimes think that this mobile way of life is as novel as high-rises, or the video monitors that are rewiring our consciousness. And even as we fret about the changes our progress wreaks in the air and on the airwaves, in forests and on streets, we hardly worry about the changes it is working in ourselves, the new kind of soul that is being born out of a new kind of life. Yet this could be the most dangerous development of all, and not only because it is the least examined.

15   For us in the Transit Lounge, disorientation is as alien as affiliation. We become professional observers, able to see the merits and deficiencies of anywhere, to balance our parents' viewpoints with their enemies' position. Yes, we say, of course it's terrible, but look at the situation from Saddam's point of view. I understand how you feel, but the Chinese had their own cultural reasons for Tiananmen Square.[9] Fervor comes to seem to us the most foreign place of all.

16   Seasoned experts at dispassion, we are less good at involvement, or suspensions of disbelief; at, in fact, the abolition of distance. We are masters of the aer-

[6]Japanese seaweed.
[7]Indian bread.
[8]Rabindranath Tagore (1861–1941), Indian poet who won the Nobel prize for literature in 1913.
[9]Student demonstrations in 1989 that were suppressed by the Chinese government.

ial perspective, but touching down becomes more difficult. Unable to get stirred by the raising of a flag, we are sometimes unable to see how anyone could be stirred. I sometimes think that this is how Rushdie, the great analyst of this condition, somehow became its victim. He had juggled homes for so long, so adroitly, that he forgot how the world looks to someone who is rooted, in country or belief. He had chosen to live so far from affiliation that he could no longer see why people choose affiliation in the first place. Besides, being part of no society means one is accountable to no one, and need respect no laws outside one's own. If single-nation people can be fanatical as terrorists, we can end up ineffectual as peacekeepers.

17   We become, in fact, strangers to belief itself, unable to comprehend many of the rages and dogmas that animate (and unite) people. Conflict itself seems inexplicable to us sometimes, simply because partisanship is; we have the agnostic's inability to retrace the steps of faith. I could not begin to fathom why some Moslems would think of murder after hearing about *The Satanic Verses;* yet sometimes I force myself to recall that it is we, in our floating skepticism, who are the exceptions, that in China or Iran, in Korea or Peru, it is not so strange to give up one's life for a cause.

18   We end up, then, a little like nonaligned nations, confirming our reservations at every step. We tell ourselves, self-servingly, that nationalism breeds monsters, and choose to ignore the fact that internationalism breeds them too. Ours is the culpability not of the assassin, but of the bystander who takes a snapshot of the murder. Or, when the revolution catches fire, hops on the next plane out.

19   In any case, the issues in the Transit Lounge are passing; a few hours from now, they'll be a thousand miles away. Besides, this is a foreign country, we have no interests here. The only thing we have to fear are hijackers—passionate people with beliefs.

20   Sometimes, though, just sometimes, I am brought up short by symptoms of my condition. They are not major things, but they are peculiar ones, and ones that would not have been so common 50 years ago. I have never bought a house of any kind, and my ideal domestic environment, I sometimes tell my friends, is a hotel-room. I have never voted, or ever wanted to vote, and I eat in restaurants three times a day. I have never supported a nation (in the Olympic Games, say), or represented "my country" in anything. Even my name is weirdly international, because my "real name' is one that makes sense only in the home where I have never lived.

21   I choose to live in America in part, I think, because it feels more alien the longer I stay there. I love being in Japan because it reminds me, at every turn, of my foreignness. When I want to see if any place is home, I must subject the candidates to a battery of tests. Home is the place of which one has memories but no expectations.

22   If I have any deeper home, it is, I suppose, in English. My language is the house I carry round with me as a snail his shell; and in my lesser moments I try to forget that mine is not the language spoken in America, or even, really, by any member of my family.

23   Yet even here, I find, I cannot place my accent, or reproduce it as I can the tones of others. And I am so used to modifying my English inflections according to whom I am talking to—an American, an Englishman, a villager in Nepal, a receptionist in Paris—that I scarcely know what kind of voice I have.

24   I wonder, sometimes, if this new kind of non-affiliation may not be alien to something fundamental in the human state. The refugee at least harbors passionate feelings about the world he has left—and generally seeks to return there; the exile at least is propelled by some kind of strong emotion away from the old country and towards the new—indifference is not an exile emotion. But what does the Transit Lounger feel? What are the issues that we would die for? What are the passions that we would live for?

25   Airports are among the only sites in public life where emotions are hugely sanctioned, in block capitals. We see people weep, shout, kiss in airports; we see them at the furthest edges of excitement and exhaustion. Airports are privileged spaces where we can see the primal states writ large—fear, recognition, hope. But there are some of us, perhaps, sitting at the Departure Gate, boarding passes in hand, watching the destinations ticking over, who feel neither the pain of separation nor the exultation of wonder; who alight with the same emotions with which we embarked; who go down to the baggage carousel and watch our lives circling, circling, circling, waiting to be claimed.

EXERCISES

Some of the Issues

1. How does Iyer describe his life in paragraph 1?
2. In paragraph 3, Iyer defines himself as part of a new "breed" of people that he calls a "transcontinental tribe of wanderers"? Why does he use these terms? What other terms does he use to describe himself and others like him?
3. Iyer speculates that his situation is not "a function of affluence" (paragraph 4). To what extent do you agree with him?
4. Looking at paragraph 5, consider the extent to which chains, franchises, and modern technology affect the "smallness" of the world.
5. How does the perspective of the essay change in paragraph 9?
6. Viewing the essay as a whole, what does Iyer mean when he describes himself and those like him as "seasoned experts at dispassion" (paragraph 16)?
7. Looking at the whole essay, summarize what Iyer describes as both the benefits and drawbacks of being a "Transit Lounger."
8. How does Iyer define home throughout the essay? What role does language play in Iyer's conception of home?
*9. Read Anton Shammas's "Amérka, Amérka." What is the difference between Shammas's idea of a "portable" home (Shammas, paragraph 8) and Iyer's?

10. Working in small groups, use an atlas to find all the places Iyer mentions in his essay. On a blank map of the world, mark all of the places you find. Discuss what you know about these places or the images you have of them.

The Way We Are Told

11. Consider the title. How well does it describe the ideas discussed in the essay? What are some other titles Iyer might have used?
12. Paragraphs 9 and 10 offer a series of questions. What purpose do they serve? How do they help guide the reader?
13. The author uses descriptive language, but never describes one place in detail. Why is this appropriate to the essay?
14. What metaphor does Iyer use in his concluding paragraph? How does this metaphor help summarize his ideas?

Some Subjects for Writing

15. In paragraph 12, Iyer writes, "Even if we don't go to the world, the world will increasingly come to us." How true is this of the place you live now? Describe your city or town by painting a vivid picture of the various cultures and nationalities represented.
16. Reflecting on your relationship to your family, culture, nationality, and the place you were born, write an essay in which you provide your own definition of home.
*17. In Geraldine Brooks's "Unplugged," the argument of the cablevision man is that the media can broaden the town's perspective on the world. The townspeople reject his argument. Looking at both Iyer and Brooks, and thinking about your own perspective, write an essay in which you analyze how the media can influence our perceptions of community and identity.

Tempo:
The Speed of Life

Robert Levine

Does everyone in the world share the same perception of time? In this essay, Robert Levine, a social psychologist who has devoted his career to studying the psychology of time and the pace of life, asks us to explore a dimension of our experience we normally take for granted: our perception of time.

Levine first became intrigued by the idea of studying time as a visiting professor at a Brazilian university in the 1970s. There he found the pace of life so slow as to be maddening, even compared to the laid-back northern California town where he made his home. In Brazil, Levine's students often wandered into class long after the scheduled hour, and it was perfectly acceptable to arrive several hours late for an appointment.

Levine's current studies focus on how places differ in their pace and conception of time. In this essay, he describes his methods for measuring the pace of life, timing, for instance, how long it takes to buy a stamp at the post office or measuring how accurate bank clocks are in the downtown area of a city. His experiments, ingenious yet simple, lead him to draw conclusions about what social, economic, and cultural factors determine the tempo of a particular place.

This selection is the first chapter of Levine's book The Geography of Time: The Temporal Misadventures of a Social Psychologist or, How Every Culture Views Time Just a Little Bit Differently. *Levine is a professor of psychology at California State University in Fresno and has published articles in* Psychology Today, Discover, *and* American Scientist.

The question of tempo . . . depends not only on the factors of personal taste and skill but to some extent upon the individual instrument and the room or hall involved in the performance.

Willard Palmer,
Chopin: An Introduction to His Piano Works

1   The pace of life is the flow or movement of time that people experience. It is characterized by rhythms (what is the pattern of work time to down time? is there a regularity to social activities?), by sequences (is it work before play or the other way around?), and by synchronies (to what extent are people and their activities attuned to one another?). But first and foremost, the pace of life is a matter of tempo.

2   The term "tempo" is borrowed from music theory, where it refers to the rate or speed at which a piece is performed. Musical tempo, like the time of personal experience, is extremely subjective. At the top of virtually every classical score, the composer inserts a nonquantitative tempo mark—*largo* or *adagio* to suggest a slow tempo, *allegro* or *presto* for fast tempos, *accelerando* or *ritardando* for changing tempos. There is even a directive called *tempo rubato*—literally translated as "stolen time"—which calls for a give-and-take in tempo between two hands. But unless the composer specifies a metronome setting (which most classical composers did not or could not do, as the metronome was not marketed until 1816), the precise metric translation of notation is open to widely varying interpretation. Depending on the speed at which the performer sets the metronome, Chopin's *Minute Waltz* may take up to two minutes to play.

3   The same is true for human time. We may play the same notes in the same sequence, but there is always that question of tempo. It depends upon the person, the task and the setting. One student may stay up all night to learn the same material that a gifted friend absorbs in a evening. The novelist might wait patiently for his next image, while his fellow writer at the newspaper races from deadline to deadline. Given an hour to spare with their child, one parent uses it to read aloud; another teams up in a demanding video game. My college student cousin travels to Europe for two months while his businessman father hurries across the same route in two weeks.

4   The speed may be measured over brief and immediate periods of time, as when one experiences rapidly oncoming traffic or an upcoming deadline, or over longer, more sustained intervals, such as when we speak of the accelerating tempo of twentieth-century living. Alvin Toffler, for example, in his popular book *Future Shock*, addresses the subject of tempo when he speaks of the psychic disruption that is caused by too much change in too short a time. The trauma is not caused by the shock of change per se, but by the rate of change. Whether considered over the short or the long term, and no matter how it is measured, there are vast cultural, historical, and individual differences in the tempo of life.

TIME SIGNATURES AROUND THE WORLD

> The further East I travel the sloppier the perception of time becomes. It irritates me in Poland and drives me gibbering in the USSR.
>
> Anonymous British Traveler

5   Adjusting to an alien tempo can pose as many difficulties as learning a foreign language. In one particularly telling study of the roots of culture shock, sociologists James Spradley and Mark Phillips asked a group of returning Peace Corps volunteers to rank 33 items as to the amount of cultural adjustment each had required of them. The list included a wide range of items familiar to travel paranoids, such as the "type of food eaten," "personal cleanliness of most people," "the number of people of your own race" and "the general standard of living."

But aside from mastering the foreign language, the two greatest difficulties for volunteers concerned social time: "the general pace of life," followed by one of it most significant components, "how punctual most people are."[1]

6   Neil Altman was one of these temporally disoriented Peace Corps volunteers. Altman, who is now a clinical psychologist in New York City, served a term as an agricultural consultant in a village in the South of India. "When we first got to India," he recalls, "I used to go to the local horticulture office to get seeds and the like. I'd go into the office of the head guy to request what I wanted, but would find six or eight people sitting around his desk, each person with some business to transact, presumably. I would impatiently state my purpose: 'Good morning, Mr. Kahn, could I get some tomato seeds, please?' 'Good morning, Volunteer *sahib*, won't you join us for some tea?' So I would have no choice but to sit down and wait while some servant ran out to get me tea. Then Mr. Kahn would inquire about my wife, etc., and then all the assembled people would have a million questions about my life, about America, etc., etc., etc. It would be hard to know how to ask for my tomato seeds again without being rude. Eventually, after an hour or two I would decide to risk being rude anyway. I would get my seeds and be on my way, noting that none of the people sitting around the desk had gotten any of their business taken care of."[2]

7   My own travels to the third world have led to the same confrontations with tempo. Sometimes it seems life in these countries is one long wait: for buses and trains, for entry and exit visas, for dinner, for toilets. Once, when trying to get to the train station in New Delhi, I waited 45 minutes for a bus so crowded that I had to hang on an extra two stops until I could force my way off. From there, I walked back to the station, where I waited nearly another hour to buy my train ticket. When I finally got to the window, the cashier greeted me with the traditional *"Namaste"* and immediately flipped up a sign that read "Closed for Lunch" (in English, I might add). With my blood pressure headed for Kashmir, I turned around to gather support for my case. But all of my compatriots were already sitting on the floor, with their blankets spread out, eating picnic lunches. "What can I do?' I asked a couple next to me. "You can join us for lunch," they answered. After several false starts to nowhere, I finally did.

8   When the ticket window reopened, I found my position in line had been taken by a family of six. They offered me peanuts and blessed me in Hindi. When I asked them to give me my place back, the eldest male smiled politely and mumbled something that I swear sounded like "When Shiva flies to Miami Beach." When I finally got to the ticket window, I was told that my train was sold out. And all this work for a train that was not going to leave for three more days. I eventually did get a ticket (oh, the miracles that a little *baksheesh* [bribery] can accomplish). But even with a ticket, I was told to come to the station an hour early, only to find I had to push through several waves of crowds to ask someone to get out of my reserved seat. Needless to say, the train left late and arrived even later, none of which mattered, because the gentleman I was scheduled to meet at the station was even later than me.

9   There is an inscription on the narrow-gauge Darjeeling Himalayan Express that reads: "'slow' is spelled with four letters; So is 'life.' 'Speed' is spelled with five letters; So is 'death.'" Really.

10   Intercultural struggles over tempo are found all over the world. My colleague Alan Button, for example, tells how he was once late for an appointment while traveling in Russia. His guide began shouting to the cab driver a Russia phrase (*Pay yeh kaly*) meaning "Get there yesterday" or literally, "Let's went." His guide advised him that the literal translations of words like "hurry" and "rush" simply do not carry the urgency in Russian that they do in English. If he had merely ordered the driver to "Get there as soon as you can," Button was told, he would arrive even later then he did. As it turns out, he arrived very late, but still found that he was some twenty minutes earlier than the fellow he was scheduled to meet.

11   The literature is filled with accounts of rushing, time-is-money travelers whose racing leaves the baffled residents of slower worlds running for cover. During my year in Brazil, it seemed as if I heard no more frequent words from my laid-back hosts than their pleading advice: *"Calma, Bobby, calma."* No matter how hard I tried to slow down, there almost always seemed to come the breathless *"Calma, por favor"*—sometimes as an appeal, other times offered with head-shaking pity. And I was simply moving at the tempo of a college professor from Fresno—hardly America's prototype of hurriedness.

12   James Jones, a fellow social psychologist from the University of Rhode Island, had a similar experience when he was living in the West Indian nation of Trinidad several years ago. He had traveled to Trinidad on a Guggenheim Fellowship to study its people's humor. But what he learned more than anything was that he was always seriously out of step. Latecomers to appointments, he reports, would greet his impatience with comments like: "Eh mon, what's your hurry, nuh? De sea ain goin' no place. Relax mon, a'm comin' to yuh just now." "So," as Jones put it, "I wait." Perhaps the most remarkable similarity in Jones's and my experiences was the profound results they had for our careers. Although we both had limited success in achieving the original goals of our projects—his to study humor in Trinidad and mine to study social perception in Brazil—these interests soon receded into the background. The more compelling puzzle, to both the traveler and the social psychologist in each of us, was the richness of the social time we encountered and our confusion with it. As a result, the study of time has become the focus of each of our research programs. Jones has gone on to become an international authority on the psychology of time perspective, and I have remained obsessed with studying the pace of life.

ELEMENTS OF TEMPO

13   What characteristics of places and cultures makes them faster or slower? To answer this question, my own research group has recently completed a series of studies comparing the pace of life in 31 different countries from throughout the

world. The results of these experiments, coupled with research findings from other social scientists, establish several factors that are critical in the establishment of tempo norms.

14   Let me briefly describe how my studies were conducted. In each country, we went into one or more of the major cities in order to measure three indicators of the tempo of life.[3] (For simplicity, Hong Kong is referred to here as a country despite its colonial status.)[4] First, we measured the average walking speed of randomly selected pedestrians over a distance of 60 feet. The measurements were made on clear summer days during main business hours, usually during the morning rush, in at least two locations on main downtown streets. Locations were chosen that were flat, unobstructed, had broad sidewalks, and were sufficiently uncrowded that pedestrians could potentially walk at their own preferred maximum speed. In order to control for the effects of socializing, only pedestrians walking alone were used. Neither subjects with clear physical handicaps nor those who appeared to be window shopping were timed. A minimum of 35 walkers of each sex were clocked in each city.

15   The second experiment focused on an example of speed in the workplace: the time it took postal clerks to fulfill a standard request for stamps. In each city, we presented clerks with a note in the local language requesting a common stamp—the now standard 32-center in the United States, for example. They were also handed paper money—the equivalent of a $5 bill. We measured the elapsed time between the passing of the note and the completion of the request.

16   Third, as an estimate of a city's interest in clock time, we observed the accuracy of 15 randomly selected bank clocks in main downtown areas in each city. Times on the 15 clocks were compared to those reported by the phone company.

17   The three scores for each country were then statistically combined into an overall pace-of-life score.

18   From these experiments and the research of others, one can determine five principal factors that determine the tempo of cultures around the world. People are prone to move faster in places with vital economies, a high degree of industrialization, larger populations, cooler climates, and a cultural orientation toward individualism.

Economic Well-Being
The healthier a place's economy, the faster its tempo.

As a city grows larger, the value of its inhabitants' time increases with the city's increasing wage rate and cost of living, so that economizing on time becomes more urgent, and life becomes more hurried and harried.

Irving Hoch[5]

19   The number one determinant of a place's tempo is economics. Without question, the strongest and most consistent finding in our experiments is that places with vital economies tend to have faster tempos. The fastest people we found

were in the wealthier North American, Northern European, and Asian nations. The slowest were in third-world countries, particularly those in South and Central America and the Middle East.

20   Faster overall tempos are highly related to a country's economic well-being on every level: to the economic health of the country as a whole (as measured by gross domestic product per capita); to the economic well-being actually experienced by the average citizen (as measured by purchasing power parity, which is an estimate of how much the average income earned in a country is capable of purchasing); and to how well people are able to fulfill their minimum needs (measured by average caloric intake).[6] People from richer and poorer nations do, in fact, march to different drummers.

21   We can speculate about the direction of causality between the tempo of life and economic conditions. Most likely, the arrow points both ways. Places with active economies put greater value on time, and places that value time will be more likely to have active economies. Economic variables and the tempo tend to be mutual reinforcing; they come in a package.

22   We don't need to travel to other countries to see the connection between economics and tempo. Some of the most telling evidence for the economic explanation appears in subcultures within countries. In the United States, for example, many economically impoverished minority groups make a point of distinguishing their own shared temporal norms from those of the prevailing Anglo-American majority. American Indians like to speak of "living on Indian time." Mexican-Americans differentiate between *hora inglesa*—which refers to the actual time on the clock—and *hora mexicana*—which treats the time on the clock considerably more casually.

23   African-Americans often distinguish their own culture's sense of time—what they sometimes refer to by the no longer fashionable term "colored people's time" (CPT)—from the majority standard of "white people's time." Jules Henry, an anthropologist, spent more than a year during the 1960's conducting interviews with mostly poor African-American families living in a St. Louis housing development. One of the strongest distinctions his interviewees made between their own lives and those of the surrounding Anglo community concerned their self-described CPT. "According to C.P. time," Henry explains, "a scheduled event may occur at any moment over a wide spread of hours—or perhaps not at all." Henry's interviewees were quick to point out how sharply this contrasted with the highly organized, precisely scheduled world of white people.[7]

24   The sociologist John Horton applies a more contemporary slant to CPT, using it to refer to "cool people's time." The term "cool people" refers to the "sporadically unemployed young Black street corner population." Horton spent two years interviewing many of these street people. "Characteristically," he reports,

> the street person gets up late, hits the street in the late morning or early afternoon, and works his way to the set. This is a place for relaxed social activity. Hanging on the set with the boys is the major way of passing time and waiting

until some necessary or desirable action occurs. . . . On the set yesterday merges into today, and tomorrow is an emptiness to be filled in through the pursuit of bread and excitement.[8]

25   The prevailing tempo, in other words, is very slow. As Horton makes clear, however, the street people are adept at speeding up their tempos when the situation calls for it. The street dude, according to Horton, is on time by the standard clock whenever he cares to be and is not on time when he doesn't want to be. Most often, the latter is the case. Time for the cool person is "dead" when resources are low—such as when money is tight, or when he's in jail. But time is "alive" whenever and wherever there is "action." The tempo is slow early in the week, when money is tight, but accelerates exponentially on Friday and Saturday nights.[9]

The Degree of Industrialization
The more developed the country, the less free time per day.

What kind of rule is this? The more timesaving machinery there is, the more pressed a person is for time.

Sebastian De Grazia
Of Time, Work, and Leisure

26   We should not be surprised that the wealthier places in our experiments have faster norms. Economic vitality is closely tied to industrialization. Historically, in fact, the single most crucial watershed event in the acceleration of the tempo of the Western world was the Industrial Revolution.

27   It is one of the great ironies of modern times that, with all of our timesaving creations, people have less time to themselves than ever before. Life in the Middle Ages is usually portrayed as bleak and dreary, but one commodity people had more of than their successors was leisure time. Until the Industrial Revolution, in fact, most evidence suggests that people showed little inclination to work. In Europe through the Middle Ages, the average number of holidays per year was around 115 days. It is interesting to note that still today, poorer countries take more holidays, on the average, than richer ones.

28   It has often been the very creations intended to save time that have been most responsible for increasing the workload. Recent research indicates that farm wives in the 1920's, who were without electricity, spent significantly less time at housework than did suburban women, with all their modern machinery, in the latter half of the century. One reason for this is that almost every technical advance seems to be accompanied by a rise in expectations. For example, when cheap window glass was introduced in Holland at the end of the seventeenth century it became impossible to ignore the dirt that accumulated indoors. Today's vacuum cleaners and other products have raised peoples' cleanliness standards even higher; in so doing; they demand that people invest the time needed to propel these products against the suddenly defeatable household grit and bacteria.[10] So much for better living through Westinghouse.

29   It is telling to observe how modern conveniences have affected the way people use their time. A study by anthropologist Allen Johnson, for example, compared the use of time among the Machiguenga Indians to that of workers living in France. The French workers, he found, spend more time at work and consuming things (eating, reading, watching television), but have considerably less free time than the Machiguenga workers. These differences are true for both men and women. French men spend four times as many hours consuming the fruits of their labors, but pay a stiff price for these goodies: They have four hours less free time per day than their Machiguenga counterparts. Perhaps most tellingly, Johnson found that the conveniences of modern living extract an extremely high toll in the time required for their maintenance. The Machiguenga give three to four times more of their production time at home to manufacturing (for example, baskets and cloth) than they do to maintenance work (doing the laundry, cleaning, making repairs). The French pattern is almost exactly the reverse. In the end, as the anthropologist Marvin Harris observed, modern appliances are "labor-saving devices that don't save work."

30   Johnson, borrowing from recent economic theory, argues that industrialization produces an evolutionary progression from a "time surplus" to a "time affluence" to a "time famine" society, which is how he characterizes most developed countries. The ultimate effect, Johnson argues, is on the tempo of people's lives:

> As a result of producing and consuming more, we are experiencing an increasing scarcity of time. This works in the following way. Increasing efficiency in production means that each individual must produce more goods per hour; increased productivity means . . . that to keep the system going we must consume more goods. Free time gets converted into consumption time because time spent neither producing nor consuming comes increasingly to be viewed as wasted . . . The increase in the value of time (its increasing scarcity) is felt subjectively as an increase in tempo or pace. We are always in danger of being slow on the production line or late to work; and in our leisure we are always in danger of wasting time.[11]

31   At the slow extreme of the tempo continuum are the Stone Age economics of the so-called primitive agricultural and hunting-gathering societies. The Kapauku of Papua, for example, don't believe in working two consecutive days. The !Kung Bushmen work two-and-a-half days per week, typically six hours a day. In the Sandwich Islands, men work only four hours per day.[12]

32   On average, studies show, women in less advanced economies work an average of 15 to 20 hours per week, and men put in about 15 hours. The shift to plow cultivation, which requires feeding and caring for draft animals, pushes the work week of men to 25 to 30 hours. It requires one day for a Dobe woman in Australia to gather enough food to feed her family for three days. The rest of the time is her own—to visit, entertain, work on her embroidery, or, as is often the case, to do nothing at all.

33   There are some underdeveloped cultures where the clock seems to stand still, if it exists at all. Edward Hall, an anthropologist, relates the story of a Afghani man in Kabul who could not locate a brother with whom he had an appointment. An investigation by a member of the American embassy eventually revealed the root of the problem: The two brothers had agreed to meet in Kabul, but had neglected to specify what year.[13] What often surprises clock-watching Anglo-Europeans most about this story is to learn just how many people in the world fail to see the humor in Hall's story; most are quite understanding and sympathetic toward the miscommunication.

34   But it would be a gross generalization to conclude that industrialization and tempo are one and the same. Sometimes the tempos of third-world cultures can be strikingly different, even between seemingly similar neighbors. The anthropologist Paul Bohannan, for example, has researched tribal greeting styles.[14] In one study, he compared the Tiv of Nigeria to their neighbors, the Hausa. The Tiv, he found, are fast people. They waste little time with perfunctory rituals such as greetings. They like to get their hellos out of the way quickly and get right down to business. Living right next to these third-world Type A's are their neighbors, the Hausas, who would not think of depriving a greeting of its rightful duration. Bohannan tells of having once observed an English anthropologist and a Hausa string out their hellos for 20 minutes. They both seemed to enjoy the ritual, the intricacies of which they had been practicing and perfecting for many years.

35   Rules governing how soon a greeting should begin may also vary. Sushila Niles, currently a psychology instructor at Northern Territory University in Darwin, Australia, tells about an unpleasant encounter with a government official during her stay as a teacher in an African country. After being sent in by the man's secretary, Niles found him in conversation with someone else. "I stood aside politely," she recalls. "Suddenly he turned to me and said 'What, madam, no greeting?' I had breached all conventions of social interaction by not greeting him the moment I stepped into his office. I said that I had been brought up to believe that interrupting was rude. But he was not mollified."[15]

36   Stephen Buggie, a professor of psychology at Presbyterian College in South Carolina, spent three years teaching in Zambia and nine years in Malawi. "In Zambia," he recalls, "the tempo of life is generally slow, with casual regard towards punctuality and time. But walking speed in downtown Lusaka (the capital and largest city) is fast, as an individual deterrent against rampant pickpocketing. Neighboring Malawi is very different. Meetings there start more promptly than in Zambia. Malawi's Life President, Kamuzu Banda, practiced medicine in Scotland for 30 years before entering politics back home. He rules the country absolutely and is a stickler for punctuality. Back in the 1970's he made it illegal for public clocks to display inaccurate time. Broken clocks were supposed to be removed or covered with a shroud."[16]

Population Size
Bigger cities have faster tempos.

37   After economic well-being, the single strongest predictor of differences in the tempo of places is population size. Studies have shown over and over again that, on the whole, people in bigger cities move faster than their counterparts from smaller places.[17]

38   In one of the earliest studies of this type, Herbert Wright, as part of his "City-Town" project, observed the behavior of children in typical city supermarkets and in small-town grocery stores. One of the strongest differences between the two environments turned out to be walking speed. The average city child walked nearly twice as fast through the supermarket as the town child did through the smaller grocery. The town children spent three times as much time interacting with clerks and other shoppers. They also spent significantly more time physically touching objects in the market.[18]

39   Australian psychologist Paul Amato found comparable differences on the other side of the world, in New Guinea. In an interesting series of experiments, Amato observed pedestrian walking speed, the speed with which change was given in European shops, and the elapsed time of betel-nut transactions in open market places in a large city (Port Moresby) and two rural towns (Wewak and Mount Hagen). The urban locale clocked in with faster speeds on the walking measure and betel-nut transactions. There were no urban-rural differences on the change measure—tellingly, no one in any of the locales in New Guinea seemed at all interested in this sort of activity.[19]

40   The definitive treatise on the association between walking speed and population size comes from a series of international studies by psychologist Marc Bornstein and his colleagues. In their first group of experiments, Bornstein's team observed walking speeds in main downtown locations in a total of 25 cities spread across Czechoslovakia, France, Germany, Greece, Israel, and the United States. They found an astonishingly high relationship between population size and walking speed across this heterogeneous collection of cities. (In statistical terms, they found a correlation of $r = .91$ between population size and the walking speed, with 1.00 being the highest correlation possible; in other words, an almost perfect relationship.)[20]

41   When strong mathematical relationships occur in cross-cultural studies of this type, they beg for replication. Answering this challenge, Bornstein conducted a second series of studies. He applied the conditions of his earlier investigation to a new sample of cities and towns in Ireland, Scotland, and the United States. Once again, he found that there was an extremely strong correlation between population size and walking speed ($r = .88$). Bornstein argues that "a highly predictable relationship seems to exist between the pace of life that characterizes a locale and the size of its population."[21] Given Bornstein's results— one does not often discover correlations of this magnitude in the inherently noisy science of social psychology—it is difficult to argue with his conclusion.

Climate
Hotter places are slower.

42   There is also considerable validity to the old stereotype about life being slower in warmer places.[22] All of the slowest nations in our 31-country study—Mexico, Brazil, and Indonesia were the slowest of all—have tropical climates. These are the sort of places that people from the fastest countries—Switzerland, Ireland, Germany—look toward for their winter vacations. Looking at the 31 countries as a whole, we found a strong relationship between the climate (as measured by average maximum temperatures)[23] of cities and how slow they were on our measures.

43   Some people believe that the slow tempo of warm places has an ergonomic explanation—that it results from a general lack of energy. Certainly, anyone who has been through a heat wave knows that high temperatures can wear one down. Others hypothesize that the slowness has an evolutionary/economic sensibility. They argue that people in warmer places don't need to work as hard. They require fewer and less costly belongings—fewer clothes, simpler homes, so why bother to rush? Then there are people who believe that warmer climates simply encourage taking time to enjoy life. Whatever the explanation, it is clear that hotter places are much more likely to have slower tempos.

Cultural Values
Individualistic cultures move faster than those that emphasize collectivism.

44   A culture's basic value system is also reflected in its norms about tempo. Probably the strongest cultural differences concern what is known as individualism versus collectivism: whether the basic cultural orientation is toward the individual and the nuclear family or to a larger collective. The United States is a classic individualistic culture. Traditional Asia, on the other hand, tends to focus on the collective. In Pakistan and India, for example, many people share large homes with extended families—something on the order of individual apartments with shared kitchen facilities. In Tibet and Nepal, families live together, and it is common for brothers to share the same wife—an economically convenient arrangement for Sherpas (porters) who spend most of their lives away from home. In some collectivistic cultures, the sense of family extends toward the entire village, or even the national "tribe." Many cross-cultural psychologists believe that the individualism-collectivism continuum is, in fact, the single most significant characteristic of the social patterns of a culture.

45   Harry Triandis, a social psychologist at the University of Illinois who is considered the foremost expert on the topic of individualism-collectivism, has found that individualistic cultures, compared to collectivist ones, put more emphasis on achievement than on affiliation.[24] The focus on achievement usually leads to a time-is-money mindset, which in turn results in an urgency to make every moment count. In cultures where social relationships take precedence, however, there is a more relaxed attitude toward time. Collectivist cultures, then, should be characterized by slower tempos. We test this prediction in our

31-country study by comparing each country's individualism-collectivism scores[25] to their times on our three experiments. Our results confirmed the hypothesis: greater individualism was highly related to faster tempos.

46   A focus on people, as we shall see in subsequent chapters, is often at odds with a tempo dictated by schedules and the time on the clock. In some collectivist cultures, in fact, time urgency is not only deemphasized but treated with downright hostility. The anthropologist Pierre Bourdieu, for example, has studied the Kabyle people, a collectivist society in Algeria. The Kabyle, he found, want nothing to do with speed. They despise any semblance of haste in their social affairs, regarding it as a "lack of decorum combined with diabolical ambition." The clock is referred to as "the devil's mill."[26]

THE BEAT OF YOUR OWN DRUM

Time travels in divers paces with divers persons

William Shakespeare,
As You Like It

47   My focus is on the pace of life as it differs between cultures and places. Obviously, however, there are also vast differences in tempo between individuals within the same culture, as well as between those living in the same town or city. Neighbors may vary in both their personal preferences and in the tempo of life they actually experience.

48   Most of the attention to individual differences has centered on the concept of time urgency—the struggle to achieve as much as possible in the shortest period of time. Time urgency is one of the defining components of a Type A behavior pattern. Meyer Friedman and Ray Rosenman described the coronary-prone personality as being impatient, having a tendency to walk quickly, eat quickly, do two things at once, and to take pride in always being punctual.[27] The most widely used test of Type A behavior, the Jenkins Activity Survey, measures these characteristics with a "Speed and Impatience" scale.[28] Several more recent Type A scales have been developed, with labels such as "Time Urgency," "Perpetual Activation,"[29] and "Timelock."[30] All of these tests find extensive individual differences in the degree to which people are concerned with making every moment count.

49   But we need to be careful not to overgeneralize about "fast" and "slow" people. As is the case for cultures, each individual's pace may vary sharply according to the time, the place, and what they are doing. If you would like an accurate gauge of your own tendency towards time urgency, it is important to look into a wide range of behaviors. You might began by thinking about yourself in these ten areas:

50   • Concern with clock time: Compared to most people, are you particularly aware of the time on the clock? Do you, for example, frequently glance at

your watch? Or, on the other hand, are you the sort of person who some-times forgets the time or even what day of the week it is?

51 • Speech patterns: How rushed is your speech? Do you tend to speak faster than other people? When someone takes too long to get to the point while speaking, do you often feel like hurrying them along? Are you a person who accepts interruptions?

52 • Eating habits: How rushed is your eating behavior? Are you often the first person finished eating at the table? Do you take time to eat three meals a day in a slow and relaxed manner?

53 • Walking speed: Do you walk faster than most people? Do fellow walkers sometimes ask you to slow down?

54 • Driving: Do you get excessively annoyed in slow traffic? When you are caught behind slow driver, do you sometimes honk or make rude ges-tures to try to speed them up?

55 • Schedules: Are you addicted to setting and /or maintaining schedules? Do you allot a specific amount of time for each activity? Do you have a fetish about punctuality?

56 • Listmaking: Are you a compulsive listmaker? When preparing for a trip, for example, do you make a list of things to do or things to bring?

57 • Nervous energy: Do you have excessive nervous energy? Are you a person who becomes irritable when you sit for an hour without doing something?

58 • Waiting: Do you get more annoyed than most people if you have to wait in line for than a couple of minutes at the bank, a store, or to be seated in a restaurant? Do you sometimes walk out of these places if you en-counter even a short wait?

59 • Alerts: Do others warn you to slow down? How often have you heard your friends or spouse tell you to take it easier, or to become less tense?

60 Nearly everyone exhibits time urgency on at least some of these questions. But if your answers indicate an overconcern with time and speed in most or all of the categories, or if you are particularly extreme in even a few areas, then you would probably be classified as a time-urgent personality.[31]

61 When the sense of time urgency becomes extreme and habitual—when peo-ple feel compelled to rush even in the absence of real external pressures—it may lead to what cardiac psychologists Diane Ulmer and Leonard Schwartzburd call

"hurry sickness."[32] If you are curious whether your case has progressed to this advanced stage, look for these three symptoms:

62   Do you notice . . .

63   • . . . deterioration of personality, marked primarily by loss of interest in aspects of life except for those connected with achievement of goals and by a preoccupation with numbers, with a growing tendency to evaluate life in terms of quantity rather than quality?

64   • . . . racing-mind syndrome, characterized by rapid, shifting thoughts that gradually erode the ability to focus and concentrate and create disruption of sleep?

65   • . . . loss of ability to accumulate pleasant memories, mainly due to either a preoccupation with future events or rumination about past events, with little attention to the present? Focusing on the present is often limited to crises or problems; therefore memories accumulated tend be of unpleasant situations.

66   Ulmer and Schwartzburd have found that "yes" answers to these questions warrant a diagnosis of hurry sickness. People with this "disease" suffer a wide range of difficulties, ranging from health problems, particularly those related to cardiovascular system, to the fragmentation of social relationships and to a low sense of self-worth.

67   But the concept of hurry sickness vastly overgeneralizes the consequences of living life at a fast tempo. There is a saying that to a hammer, everything looks like a nail. And if you are a cardiac psychologist, you see behavior through the template of disease. A rapid tempo in itself, however, does not necessarily spell disease. The relationship between time pressure, time urgency, and hurry sickness is no more single-arrowed for individuals than it is for cultures: external time pressure does not always lead to a sense of time urgency, nor do either of the two invariably produce the symptoms of hurry sickness.

68   Tempo cannot be reduced to simply the presence or absence of a problem. My students and I have developed a test that measures individual differences in tempo in a broader sense.[33] We have found that the tempo of personal experience separates into five different categories, only one of which is time urgency. When asked about the tempo of their lives, people consider questions about time urgency but they also focus on the speed they perceive in their workplace, the speed they perceive outside their workplace, the level of activity they prefer in their lives, and the tempo they prefer in their surrounding environment.

69   It is telling that people's responses on any of these temporal matters are not very predictive of their responses on the others. This suggests that each of the five categories are distinct facets of the general tempo of life people experience. Most important, we have found that fast or slow tempos per se may have less to

do with developing hurry sickness than the fit between the personal temperament categories and those concerning physical realities. For example, people with high activity level preferences tend to actually be better off with speedy lifestyles and environments. Also, the balance between the tempo people experience inside the workplace compared to that in their personal lives may be more important for their psychological and physical health than whether they work in a highly time-pressured job or a more relaxed one.

70   To assess the tempo of your life within this larger picture, you might ask yourself these additional questions:

71   Do you feel that the tempo of life is too fast, too slow, or just right when it comes to . . .

72   • . . . your school or work life?

73   • . . . the city or town where you live?

74   • . . . your home life?

75   • . . . your social life?

76   • . . . your life as a whole?

77   You don't need a psychologist to interpret your answers to these questions. The fact is that what is too fast for one person spells boredom for another. And the pressure of one moment can be a stimulant at the next. For every Charles Darwin ("A man who wastes one hour of time has not discovered the meaning of life") we hear from Oscar Levant ("So little time, so little to do"). If left alone, would you take your life at a leisurely tempo? Do you find today's rapid tempo stimulating? Do you feel like people are always rushing you along and making you do things faster than you would like to? Does your work or school often demand that you put in more time than you prefer? Do you like the energy and excitement of big cities, or if you had your way, would you prefer to live in a slow-paced environment?

78   There is no inherent good or bad to an individual tempo. What we make of time is a very personal matter.

BEYOND TEMPO

> What then, is time? If no one asks me, I know. If I wish to explain it to someone who asks, I know it not.
>
> St. Augustine
> *Confessions, Book II Sec. 14.*

79   The terms "tempo" and "pace of life" are sometimes used interchangeably. In fact, the speed of our lives does often color the entirety of our temporal expe-

rience. A study by the psychologist Marilyn Dapkus underscores the salience of one's tempo.[34] Dapkus, who was interested in learning what type of concepts people use to describe their experience of time, interviewed a group of adults about the full range of their temporal awareness. She found that people tended to frame their responses in terms of tempo, no matter what area of temporal experience they were addressing. When asked about "change and continuity" in life, for example, a typical response was:

> As you get older, people say time appears to go faster. When my boy lives one extra year, that's 10 percent of his life, but when I live one extra year that's only 2 percent of my life.

80   When addressing the temporal concept that time is limited, a subject responded:

> My husband doesn't feel as rushed as I do; he's more relaxed, he takes it in stride if time runs out. He can say, "That's that," but I'd be trying to cram in one more thing.

81   In music, attributes like tempo and rhythm are distinct entities. They can be analyzed independently. In the world of social time, however, the lines are less clear cut.

82   But the pace of life people experience goes beyond tempo. The pace of life is a tangled arrangement of cadences, of perpetually changing rhythms and sequences, stresses and calms, cycles and spikes. It may be regular or irregular, and in or out of synch with its surroundings. The pace of life transcends simple measures of fast or slow. It is this overlaying and interconnectedness of tempo with the many dimensions of social time, I believe, that constitutes the pace of life that people experience.

Notes

[1]Spradley, J. P., and Phillips, M. (1972). Culture and stress: A quantitative analysis. *American Anthropologist* 74, 518–29.

[2]Personal communication, January 16, 1996.

[3]In most countries, data were collected in either the largest city or a rival major city: Amsterdam (The Netherlands), Athens (Greece), Budapest (Hungary), Dublin (Ireland), Frankfurt (Germany), Guanzhou (China), Hong Kong (Hong Kong).

[4]Jakarta (Indonesia), London (England), Mexico City (Mexico), Nairobi (Kenya), New York City (U.S.A.), Paris (France), Rio de Janeiro (Brazil), Rome (Italy), San Jose (Costa Rica), San Salvador (El Salvador), Seoul (South Korea), Singapore (Singapore), Stockholm (Sweden), Taipei (Taiwan), Tokyo (Japan), Toronto (Canada), and Vienna (Austria). In four other countries for various reasons, the observations were made in more than one city. In Poland, data were collected in Wroclaw, Lodz, Poznan, Lublin, and Warsaw. In Switzerland, measures

were taken in both Bern and Zurich. In Syria and Jordan, most observations were made in the capital cities of Damascus and Amman, but some were done in secondary population centers. In each of these cases, data from the different cities were combined for that country. Data for all countries were collected during the summer or other warm-weather months of the year, over the period 1992–95.

[5]Hoch, I. (1976). City size effects, trends and policies. *Science* 193, 856–63, 857. For further discussion of the economic hypothesis, see: Bornstein, M. H. (1979). The pace of life: Revisited. *International Journal of Psychology* 14, 83–90.

[6]Statistics were based on the most recent available data from the World Band. World Bank (1994). *The World Bank Atlas: 1995.* Washington, D.C.: World Bank.

[7]Henry, J. (1965, March/April). White people's time—colored people's time. *Trans-Action* 2, 31–34.

[8]Ibid., p. 24.

[9]Horton, J. (1972). Time and cool people. In Kochman, T. (ed.), *Rappin and Stylin' Out,* 19–31. Urbana, Ill.: University of Illinois Press.

[10]Hunt, S. (1984, May 25). Why tribal peoples and peasants of the Middle Ages had more free time than we do. *Maine Times,* p. 40.

[11]Johnson, A. (1978, September). In search of the affluent society. *Human Nature,* 50–59.

[12]Schor, J. B. (1991). *The Overworked American.* New York: Basic Books, 10.

[13]Hall, E. T. (1959). *The Silent Language.* New York: Doubleday.

[14]Bohannan, P. (1980). Time, rhythm, and pace. *Science* 80, 1, 18–20.

[15]Niles, S. E-mail posting on *Intercultural Network,* May 19, 1995.

[16]Personal communication, November 21, 1993.

[17]Since our 31 countries study was based chiefly on the largest city in each country, it did not provide a particularly strong retest of the population size hypothesis.

[18]Wright, H. F. (1961). The city-town project: A study of children in communities differing in size. Unpublished grant report.

[19]Amato, P. R. (1983). The effects of urbanization on interpersonal behavior. *Journal of Cross-Cultural Psychology* 14, 353–67.

[20]Bornstein, M. H. (1979). The pace of life: Revisited. *International Journal of Psychology* 14, 83–90.

[21]Bornstein, M., and Bornstein, H. (1976). The pace of life. *Nature* 259, pp. 557–59.

[22]Some evidence for this hypothesis may also be found in a study by: Hoel, L. A. (1968). Pedestrian travel rates in central business districts. *Traffic Engineer* 38, 10–13.

[23]More sophisticated temperature-humidity indices are not readily available for many international cities.

[24]Triandis, H. (1994). *Culture and Social Behavior.* New York: McGraw-Hill.

[25]Individualism-collectivism scores were provided by Harry Triandis.

[26]Bourdieu, Pierre (1963). The attitude of the Algerian peasant toward time. In: Pitt-Rivers, J. (ed.) *Mediterranean Countrymen,* 55–72. Paris: Mouton.

[27]Friedman, M., and Rosenman, R. H. (1959). Association of specific overt behavior patterns with blood and cardiovascular findings. *Journal of the American Medical Association* 240, 761–63.

[28]Jenkins, C. D., Zyzanski, S. J., and Rosenman, R. H. (1979). *Jenkins Activity Survey: Form C.* New York: Psychological Corporation.

[29]Wright, L., McCurdy, S., and Rogoll, G. (1992). The TUPA Scale: A self-report measure for the Type A subcomponent of time urgency and perpetual activation. *Psychological Assessment* 4, 352–56.

[30]Keyes, R. (1991). *Timelock.* New York: HarperCollins.

[31]For more detailed self-evaluation measures of time urgency, two good sources are: Landy, F. J., Restegary, H., Thayer, J., and Colvin, C. (1991). Time urgency: The construct and its meaning. *Journal of Applied Psychology* 76, 644–57; or: Friedman, M., Fleischmann, N., and Price, V. (1996). Diagnosis of Type A behavior pattern. In Robert Allan and Stephen Scheidt (eds.), *Heart and Mind: The Practice of Cardiac Psychology*, 179–96. Washington, D.C.: American Psychological Association.

[32]Ulmer, D. K., and Schwartzburd, L. (1996). Treatment of time pathologies. In Robert Allan and Stephen Scheidt (eds.), *Heart and Mind: The Practice of Cardiac Psychology*, 329–62. Washington, D.C.: American Psychological Association.

[33]For further information about the scale, see: Levine, R., and Conover, L. (1992, July). The pace of life scale: Development of a measure of individual differences in the pace of life. Paper presented to the International Society for the Study of Time, Normandy, France; and: Soles, J. R., Eyssell, K., Norenzayan, A., and Levine, R. (1994, April). Personality correlates of the pace of life. Paper presented at the meetings of the Western Psychological Association, Kona, Hawaii.

[34]Dapkus, M. (1985). A thematic analysis of the experience of time. *Journal of Personality and Social Psychology* 49, 408–19.

EXERCISES

Some of the Issues

1. How does Levine define the term "tempo"? Why is it essential to our understanding of "the pace of life"? How is the music analogy an apt one?
2. What were the two most difficult adjustments for Peace Corps volunteers besides mastering the language of a foreign country (paragraph 5)? Were you surprised to find this out?
3. What methodologies did Levine use to determine the tempo of a place (paragraphs 13–18)? What do you think of these methodologies?
4. In paragraph 18, Levine writes: "People are prone to move faster in places with vital economies, a high degree of industrialization, larger populations, cooler climates, and a cultural orientation toward individualism." Is there anything in your own experience that would cause to you to agree or disagree with this conclusion?
5. To what does Levine attribute the disappearance of leisure time? Why does time saving-machinery lead to less leisure time?
6. What do the terms "time surplus," "time affluence," and "time famine" mean (paragraph 30)?
7. Summarize the factors that affect the tempo of life. Which seem most valid to you? Why?

8. Write down your responses to Levine's questions in paragraphs 50–59 in the five different contexts listed in paragraph 72 through 76. In groups of three or four, compare your answers.

9. From your own perspective, what are the advantages and disadvantages of having a faster tempo of life? Use specific examples to back up your point.

10. Do you see the tempo of life in the United States as having changed at all in your lifetime? If you do see change, to what do you attribute these changes? Interview a relative or friend from an earlier generation and ask them the same questions.

The Way We Are Told

11. How does Levine combine research and narrative?

12. Can you find instances where Levine uses humor? How do these moments help set the tone of the chapter?

13. Levine uses bullet points at times in the text. Why does he use them? In what contexts are they appropriate or useful in writing?

14. Look back at Levine's use of epigraphs (opening quotations for each section). What purpose do these opening quotations serve?

15. Find at least three specific claims the author makes. What evidence does he use to support those claims?

16. Look carefully at Levine's end notes. What additional information do they provide?

Some Subjects for Writing

17. Conduct an experiment where you apply the measures Levine describes in paragraphs 13 through 18 to two different areas within traveling distance of where you live (perhaps a neighborhood and a downtown area or a suburban area and an urban one). Write an essay in which you compare your findings. You might also come up with other measures appropriate to the specific sites you're looking at or adjust Levine's measures.

18. Write an essay in which you examine the impact of technology on our perceptions and use of time. You should consider not only whether or not technology affects the tempo of our lives, but also how newer innovations may increase or decrease our leisure time. Some examples of increasingly popular technologies whose impacts you might consider are cell phones, laptop computers, and other more portable means of communication.

*19. Drawing examples from Levine's chapter, your own experience, and other readings such as Barbara Brandt's "The Call for Shorter Work Hours" and Pico Iyer's "Home Is Every Place," write an essay in which you develop your own claims about the tempo of contemporary life and how it affects the quality of life.

On Dumpster Diving

Lars Eighner

Lars Eighner was born in 1948 in Corpus Christi, Texas. "On Dumpster Diving" is excerpted from Travels with Lizbeth, *a chronicle of Eighner's three years as a homeless person. Lizbeth is the author's dog and traveling companion. Typed on equipment found in the garbage,* Travels with Lizbeth *began as a series of letters to friends describing the events that took Eighner from a job in a mental institution to life as a homeless person. The book is written as a series of vignettes because, as the author says, "A homeless life has no story line."*

In a sober tone punctuated with sharp detail, Eighner describes, analyzes, and philosophizes about the things we as a society discard. Often these are things Eighner finds perfectly usable. Although the author doesn't directly draw conclusions for the reader, his careful descriptions of what we consider "garbage" make a statement about our "disposable" society and about what we value, whether we are homeless or not.

Eighner received much acclaim for Travels with Lizbeth *and its unique point of view. He is no longer homeless and lives in Austin, Texas. He has written several books of gay erotic fiction, and his most recent book is a novel,* Pawn to Queen Four *(1994).*

1   Long before I began Dumpster diving I was impressed with Dumpsters, enough so that I wrote the Merriam-Webster research service to discover what I could about the word *Dumpster*. I learned from them that it is a proprietary word belonging to the Dempster Dumpster company. Since then I have dutifully capitalized the word, although it was lowercased in almost all the citations Merriam-Webster photocopied for me. Dempster's word is too apt. I have never heard these things called anything but Dumpsters. I do not know anyone who knows the generic name for these objects. From time to time I have heard a wino or hobo give some corrupted credit to the original and call them Dipsy Dumpsters.

2   I began Dumpster diving about a year before I became homeless.

3   I prefer the word *scavenging* and use the word *scrounging* when I mean to be obscure. I have heard people, evidently meaning to be polite, use the word *foraging*, but I prefer to reserve that word for gathering nuts and berries and such, which I do also according to the season and the opportunity. *Dumpster diving* seems to me to be a little too cute and, in my case, inaccurate because I lack the athletic ability to lower myself into the Dumpsters as the true divers do, much to their increased profit.

4   I like the frankness of the word *scavenging*, which I can hardly think of without picturing a big black snail on an aquarium wall. I live from the refuse of others. I am a scavenger. I think it a sound and honorable niche, although if I could I would naturally prefer to live the comfortable consumer life, perhaps—and only perhaps—as a slightly less wasteful consumer, owing to what I have learned as a scavenger.

5   While Lizbeth and I were still living in the shack on Avenue B as my savings ran out, I put almost all my sporadic income into rent. The necessities of daily life I began to extract from Dumpsters. Yes, we ate from them. Except for jeans, all my clothes came from Dumpsters. Boom boxes, candles, bedding, toilet paper, a virgin male love doll, medicine, books, a typewriter, dishes, furnishings, and change, sometimes amounting to many dollars—I acquired many things from the Dumpsters.

6   I have learned much as a scavenger. I mean to put some of what I have learned down here, beginning with the practical art of Dumpster diving and proceeding to the abstract.

7   What is safe to eat?

8   After all, the finding of objects is becoming something of an urban art. Even respectable employed people will sometimes find something tempting sticking out of a Dumpster or standing beside one. Quite a number of people, not all of them of the bohemian type, are willing to brag that they found this or that piece in the trash. But eating from Dumpsters is what separates the dilettanti from the professionals. Eating safely from the Dumpsters involves three principles: using the senses and common sense to evaluate the condition of the found materials, knowing the Dumpsters of a given area and checking them regularly, and seeking always to answer the question "Why was this discarded?"

9   Perhaps everyone who has a kitchen and a regular supply of groceries has, at one time or another, made a sandwich and eaten half of it before discovering mold on the bread or got a mouthful of milk before realizing the milk had turned. Nothing of the sort is likely to happen to a Dumpster diver because he is constantly reminded that most food is discarded for a reason. Yet a lot of perfectly good food can be found in Dumpsters.

10   Canned goods, for example, turn up fairly often in the Dumpsters I frequent. All except the most phobic people would be willing to eat from a can, even if it came from a Dumpster. Canned goods are among the safest of foods to be found in Dumpsters but are not utterly foolproof.

11   Although very rare with modern canning methods, botulism is a possibility. Most other forms of food poisoning seldom do lasting harm to a healthy person, but botulism is almost certainly fatal and often the first symptom is death. Except for carbonated beverages, all canned goods should contain a slight vacuum and suck air when first punctured. Bulging, rusty, and dented cans and cans that spew when punctured should be avoided, especially when the contents are not very acidic or syrupy.

12　　Heat can break down the botulin, but this requires much more cooking than most people do to canned goods. To the extent that botulism occurs at all, of course, it can occur in cans on pantry shelves as well as in cans from Dumpsters. Need I say that home-canned goods are simply too risky to be recommended.

13　　From time to time one of my companions, aware of the source of my provisions, will ask, "Do you think these crackers are really safe to eat?" For some reason it is most often the crackers they ask about.

14　　This question has always made me angry. Of course I would not offer my companion anything I had doubts about. But more than that, I wonder why he cannot evaluate the condition of the crackers for himself. I have no special knowledge and I have been wrong before. Since he knows where the food comes from, it seems to me he ought to assume some of the responsibility for deciding what he will put in his mouth. For myself I have few qualms about dry foods such as crackers, cookies, cereal, chips, and pasta if they are free of visible contaminates and still dry and crisp. Most often such things are found in the original packaging, which is not so much a positive sign as it is the absence of a negative one.

15　　Raw fruits and vegetables with intact skins seem perfectly safe to me, excluding of course the obviously rotten. Many are discarded for minor imperfections that can be pared away. Leafy vegetables, grapes, cauliflower, broccoli, and similar things may be contaminated by liquids and may be impractical to wash.

16　　Candy, especially hard candy, is usually safe if it has not drawn ants. Chocolate is often discarded only because it has become discolored as the cocoa butter de-emulsified. Candying, after all, is one method of food preservation because pathogens do not like very sugary substances.

17　　All of these foods might be found in any Dumpster and can be evaluated with some confidence largely on the basis of appearance. Beyond these are foods that cannot be correctly evaluated without additional information.

18　　I began scavenging by pulling pizzas out of the Dumpster behind a pizza delivery shop. In general, prepared food requires caution, but in this case I knew when the shop closed and went to the Dumpster as soon as the last of the help left.

19　　Such shops often get prank orders; both the orders and the products made to fill them are called *bogus*. Because help seldom stays long at these places, pizzas are often made with the wrong topping, refused on delivery for being cold, or baked incorrectly. The products to be discarded are boxed up because inventory is kept by counting boxes: A boxed pizza can be written off; an unboxed pizza does not exist.

20　　I never placed a bogus order to increase the supply of pizzas and I believe no one else was scavenging in this Dumpster. But the people in the shop became suspicious and began to retain their garbage in the shop overnight. While it lasted I had a steady supply of fresh, sometimes warm pizza. Because I knew the Dumpster I knew the source of the pizza, and because I visited the Dumpster regularly I knew what was fresh and what was yesterday's.

21　　The area I frequent is inhabited by many affluent college students. I am not here by chance; the Dumpsters in this area are very rich. Students throw out many good things, including food. In particular they tend to throw everything out when they move at the end of a semester, before and after breaks, and around midterm, when many of them despair of college. So I find it advantageous to keep an eye on the academic calendar.

22   Students throw food away around breaks because they do not know whether it has spoiled or will spoil before they return. A typical discard is a half jar of peanut butter. In fact, nonorganic peanut butter does not require refrigeration and is unlikely to spoil in any reasonable time. The student does not know that, and since it is Daddy's money, the student decides not to take a chance. Opened containers require caution and some attention to the question, "Why was this discarded?" But in the case of discards from student apartments, the answer may be that the item was thrown out through carelessness, ignorance, or wastefulness. This can sometimes be deduced when the item is found with many others, including some that are obviously perfectly good.

23   Some students, and others, approach defrosting a freezer by chucking out the whole lot. Not only do the circumstances of such a find tell the story, but also the mass of frozen goods stays cold for a long time and items may be found still frozen or freshly thawed.

24   Yogurt, cheese, and sour cream are items that are often thrown out while they are still good. Occasionally I find a cheese with a spot of mold, which of course I just pare off, and because it is obvious why such a cheese was discarded, I treat it with less suspicion than an apparently perfect cheese found in similar circumstances. Yogurt is often discarded, still sealed, only because the expiration date on the carton had passed. This is one of my favorite finds because yogurt will keep for several days, even in warm weather.

25   Students throw out canned goods and staples at the end of semesters and when they give up college at midterm. Drugs, pornography, spirits, and the like are often discarded when parents are expected—Dad's Day, for example. And spirits also turn up after big party weekends, presumably discarded by the newly reformed. Wine and spirits, of course, keep perfectly well even once opened, but the same cannot be said of beer.

26   My test for carbonated soft drinks is whether they still fizz vigorously. Many juices or other beverages are too acidic or too syrupy to cause much concern, provided they are not visibly contaminated. I have discovered nasty molds in vegetable juices, even when the product was found under its original seal; I recommend that such products be decanted slowly into a clear glass. Liquids always require some care. One hot day I found a large jug of Pat O'Brien's Hurricane mix. The jug had been opened but was still ice cold. I drank three large glasses before it became apparent to me that someone had added the rum to the mix, and not a little rum. I never tasted the rum, and by the time I began to feel the effects I had already ingested a very large quantity of the beverage. Some divers would have considered this a boon, but being suddenly intoxicated in a public place in the early afternoon is not my idea of a good time.

27   I have heard of people maliciously contaminating discarded food and even handouts, but mostly I have heard of this from people with vivid imaginations who have had no experience with the Dumpsters themselves. Just before the pizza shop stopped discarding its garbage at night, jalapeños began showing up on most of the thrown-out pizzas. If indeed this was meant to discourage me, it was a wasted effort because I am a native Texan.

28   For myself, I avoid game, poultry, pork, and egg-based foods, whether I find them raw or cooked. I seldom have the means to cook what I find, but when I do I avail myself of plentiful supplies of beef, which is often in very good condition. I suppose fish becomes disagreeable before it becomes dangerous. Lizbeth is happy to have any such thing that is past its prime and, in fact, does not recognize fish as food until it is quite strong.

29   Home leftovers, as opposed to surpluses from restaurants, are very often bad. Evidently, especially among students, there is a common type of personality that carefully wraps up even the smallest leftover and shoves it into the back of the refrigerator for six months or so before discarding it. Characteristic of this type are the reused jars and margarine tubs to which the remains are committed. I avoid ethnic foods I am unfamiliar with. If I do not know what it is supposed to look like when it is good, I cannot be certain I will be able to tell if it is bad.

30   No matter how careful I am I still get dysentery at least once a month, oftener in warm weather. I do not want to paint too romantic a picture. Dumpster diving has serious drawbacks as a way of life.

31   I learned to scavenge gradually, on my own. Since then I have initiated several companions into the trade. I have learned that there is a predictable series of stages a person goes through in learning to scavenge.

32   At first the new scavenger is filled with disgust and self-loathing. He is ashamed of being seen and may lurk around, trying to duck behind things, or he may try to dive at night. (In fact, most people instinctively look away from a scavenger. By skulking around, the novice calls attention to himself and arouses suspicion. Diving at night is ineffective and needlessly messy.)

33   Every grain of rice seems to be a maggot. Everything seems to stink. He can wipe the egg yolk off the found can, but he cannot erase from his mind the stigma of eating garbage.

34   That stage passes with experience. The scavenger finds a pair of running shoes that fit and look and smell brand-new. He finds a pocket calculator in perfect working order. He finds pristine ice cream, still frozen, more than he can eat or keep. He begins to understand: People throw away perfectly good stuff, a lot of perfectly good stuff.

35   At this stage, Dumpster shyness begins to dissipate. The diver, after all, has the last laugh. He is finding all manner of good things that are his for the taking. Those who disparage his profession are the fools, not he.

36   He may begin to hang on to some perfectly good things for which he has neither a use nor a market. Then he begins to take note of the things that are not

perfectly good but are nearly so. He mates a Walkman with broken earphones and one that is missing a battery cover. He picks up things that he can repair.

37   At this stage he may become lost and never recover. Dumpsters are full of things of some potential value to someone and also of things that never have much intrinsic value but are interesting. All the Dumpster divers I have known come to the point of trying to acquire everything they touch. Why not take it, they reason, since it is all free? This is, of course, hopeless. Most divers come to realize that they must restrict themselves to items of relatively immediate utility. But in some cases the diver simply cannot control himself. I have met several of these pack-rat types. Their ideas of the values of various pieces of junk verge on the psychotic. Every bit of glass may be a diamond, they think, and all that glisters, gold.

38   I tend to gain weight when I am scavenging. Partly this is because I always find far more pizza and doughnuts than water-packed tuna, nonfat yogurt, and fresh vegetables. Also I have not developed much faith in the reliability of Dumpsters as a food source, although it has been proven to me many times. I tend to eat as if I have no idea where my next meal is coming from. But mostly I just hate to see food go to waste and so I eat much more than I should. Something like this drives the obsession to collect junk.

39   As for collecting objects, I usually restrict myself to collecting one kind of small object at a time, such as pocket calculators, sunglasses, or campaign buttons. To live on the street I must anticipate my needs to a certain extent: I must pick up and save warm bedding I find in August because it will not be found in Dumpsters in November. As I have no access to health care, I often hoard essential drugs, such as antibiotics and antihistamines. (This course can be recommended only to those with some grounding in pharmacology. Antibiotics, for example, even when indicated are worse than useless if taken in insufficient amounts.) But even if I had a home with extensive storage space, I could not save everything that might be valuable in some contingency.

40   I have proprietary feelings about my Dumpsters. As I have mentioned, it is no accident that I scavenge from ones where good finds are common. But my limited experience with Dumpsters in other areas suggests to me that even in poorer areas, Dumpsters, if attended with sufficient diligence, can be made to yield a livelihood. The rich students discard perfectly good kiwifruit; poorer people discard perfectly good apples. Slacks and Polo shirts are found in the one place; jeans and T-shirts in the other. The population of competitors rather than the affluence of the dumpers most affects the feasibility of survival by scavenging. The large number of competitors is what puts me off the idea of trying to scavenge in places like Los Angeles.

41   Curiously, I do not mind my direct competition, other scavengers, so much as I hate the can scroungers.

42   People scrounge cans because they have to have a little cash. I have tried scrounging cans with an able-bodied companion. Afoot a can scrounger simply cannot make more than a few dollars a day. One can extract the necessities of

life from the Dumpsters directly with far less effort than would be required to accumulate the equivalent value in cans. (These observations may not hold in places with container redemption laws.)

43   Can scroungers, then, are people who must have small amounts of cash. These are drug addicts and winos, mostly the latter because the amounts of cash are so small. Spirits and drugs do, like all other commodities, turn up in Dumpsters and the scavenger will from time to time have a half bottle of a rather good wine with his dinner. But the wino cannot survive on these occasional finds; he must have his daily dose to stave off the DTs. All the cans he can carry will buy about three bottles of Wild Irish Rose.

44   I do not begrudge them the cans, but can scroungers tend to tear up the Dumpsters, mixing the contents and littering the area. They become so specialized that they can see only cans. They earn my contempt by passing up change, canned goods, and readily hockable items.

45   There are precious few courtesies among scavengers. But it is common practice to set aside surplus items: pairs of shoes, clothing, canned goods, and such. A true scavenger hates to see good stuff go to waste, and what he cannot use he leaves in good condition in plain sight.

46   Can scroungers lay waste to everything in their path and will stir one of a pair of good shoes to the bottom of a Dumpster, to be lost or ruined in the muck. Can scroungers will even go through individual garbage cans, something I have never seen a scavenger do.

47   Individual garbage cans are set out on the public easement only on garbage days. On other days going through them requires trespassing close to a dwelling. Going through individual garbage cans without scattering litter is almost impossible. Litter is likely to reduce the public's tolerance of scavenging. Individual cans are simply not as productive as Dumpsters; people in houses and duplexes do not move so often and for some reason do not tend to discard as much useful material. Moreover, the time required to go through one garbage can that serves one household is not much less than the time required to go through a Dumpster that contains the refuse of twenty apartments.

48   But my strongest reservation about going through individual garbage cans is that this seems to me a very personal kind of invasion to which I would object if I were a householder. Although many things in Dumpsters are obviously meant never to come to light, a Dumpster is somehow less personal.

49   I avoid trying to draw conclusions about the people who dump in the Dumpsters I frequent. I think it would be unethical to do so, although I know many people will find the idea of scavenger ethics too funny for words.

50   Dumpsters contain bank statements, correspondence, and other documents, just as anyone might expect. But there are also less obvious sources of information. Pill bottles, for example. The labels bear the name of the patient, the name of the doctor, and the name of the drug. AIDS drugs and antipsychotic medicines, to name but two groups, are specific and are seldom prescribed for

any other disorders. The plastic compacts for birth-control pills usually have complete label information.

51   Despite all of this sensitive information, I have had only one apartment resident object to my going through the Dumpster. In that case it turned out the resident was a university athlete who was taking bets and who was afraid I would turn up his wager slips.

52   Occasionally a find tells a story. I once found a small paper bag containing some unused condoms, several partial tubes of flavored sexual lubricants, a partially used compact of birth-control pills, and the torn pieces of a picture of a young man. Clearly she was through with him and planning to give up sex altogether.

53   Dumpster things are often sad—abandoned teddy bears, shredded wedding books, despaired-of sales kits. I find many pets lying in state in Dumpsters. Although I hope to get off the streets so that Lizbeth can have a long and comfortable old age, I know this hope is not very realistic. So I suppose when her time comes she too will go into a Dumpster. I will have no better place for her. And after all, it is fitting, since for most of her life her livelihood has come from the Dumpster. When she finds something I think is safe that has been spilled from a Dumpster, I let her have it. She already knows the route around the best ones. I like to think that if she survives me she will have a chance of evading the dog catcher and of finding her sustenance on the route.

54   Silly vanities also come to rest in the Dumpsters. I am a rather accomplished needleworker. I get a lot of material from the Dumpsters. Evidently sorority girls, hoping to impress someone, perhaps themselves, with their mastery of a womanly art, buy a lot of embroider-by-number kits, work a few stitches horribly, and eventually discard the whole mess. I pull out their stitches, turn the canvas over, and work an original design. Do not think I refrain from chuckling as I make gifts from these kits.

55   I find diaries and journals. I have often thought of compiling a book of literary found objects. And perhaps I will one day. But what I find is hopelessly commonplace and bad without being, even unconsciously, camp. College students also discard their papers. I am horrified to discover the kind of paper that now merits an A in an undergraduate course. I am grateful, however, for the number of good books and magazines the students throw out.

56   In the area I know best I have never discovered vermin in the Dumpsters, but there are two kinds of kitty surprise. One is alley cats whom I meet as they leap, claws first, out of Dumpsters. This is especially thrilling when I have Lizbeth in tow. The other kind of kitty surprise is a plastic garbage bag filled with some ponderous, amorphous mass. This always proves to be used cat litter.

57   City bees harvest doughnut glaze and this makes the Dumpster at the doughnut shop more interesting. My faith in the instinctive wisdom of animals is always shaken when ever I see Lizbeth attempt to catch a bee in her mouth, which she does whenever bees are present. Evidently some birds find Dumpsters profitable, for birdie surprise is almost as common as kitty surprise of the first kind. In hunting season all kinds of small game turn up in Dumpsters, some

of it, sadly, not entirely dead. Curiously, summer and winter, maggots are uncommon.

58   The worse of the living and near-living hazards of the Dumpsters are the fire ants. The food they claim is not much of a loss, but they are vicious and aggressive. It is very easy to brush against some surface of the Dumpster and pick up half a dozen or more fire ants, usually in some sensitive area such as the underarm. One advantage of bringing Lizbeth along as I make Dumpster rounds is that, for obvious reasons, she is very alert to ground-based fire ants. When Lizbeth recognizes a fire-ant infestation around our feet, she does the Dance of the Zillion Fire Ants. I have learned not to ignore this warning from Lizbeth, whether I perceive the tiny ants or not, but to remove ourselves at Lizbeth's first pas de bourée. All the more so because the ants are the worst in the summer months when I wear flip-flops if I have them. (Perhaps someone will misunderstand this. Lizbeth does the Dance of the Zillion Fire Ants when she recognizes more fire ants than she cares to eat, not when she is being bitten. Since I have learned to react promptly, she does not get bitten at all. It is the isolated patrol of fire ants that falls in Lizbeth's range that deserves pity. She finds them quite tasty.)

59   By far the best way to go through a Dumpster is to lower yourself into it. Most of the good stuff tends to settle at the bottom because it is usually weightier than the rubbish. My more athletic companions have often demonstrated to me that they can extract much good material from a Dumpster I have already been over.

60   To those psychologically or physically unprepared to enter a Dumpster, I recommend a stout stick, preferably with some barb or hook at one end. The hook can be used to grab plastic garbage bags. When I find canned goods or other objects loose at the bottom of a Dumpster, I lower a bag into it, roll the desired object into the bag, and then hoist the bag out—a procedure more easily described than executed. Much Dumpster diving is a matter of experience for which nothing will do except practice.

61   Dumpster diving is outdoor work, often surprisingly pleasant. It is not entirely predictable; things of interest turn up every day and some days there are finds of great value. I am always very pleased when I can turn up exactly the thing I most wanted to find. Yet in spite of the element of chance, scavenging more than most other pursuits tends to yield returns in some proportion to the effort and intelligence brought to bear. It is very sweet to turn up a few dollars in change from a Dumpster that has just been gone over by a wino.

62   The land is now covered with cities. The cities are full of Dumpsters. If a member of the canine race is ever able to know what it is doing, then Lizbeth knows that when we go around to the Dumpsters, we are hunting. I think of scavenging as a modern form of self-reliance. In any event, after having survived nearly ten years of government service, where everything is geared to the lowest common denominator, I find it refreshing to have work that rewards initiative and effort. Certainly I would be happy to have a sinecure again, but I am no longer heartbroken that I left one.

63   I find from the experience of scavenging two rather deep lessons. The first
is to take what you can use and let the rest go by. I have come to think that there
is no value in the abstract. A thing I cannot use or make useful, perhaps by trad-
ing, has no value however rare or fine it may be. I mean useful in a broad
sense—some art I would find useful and some otherwise.

64   I was shocked to realize that some things are not worth acquiring, but now I
think it is so. Some material things are white elephants that eat up the possessor's substance. The second lesson is the transience of material being. This has
not quite converted me to a dualist, but it has made some headway in that direction. I do not suppose that ideas are immortal, but certainly mental things are
longer lived than other material things.

65   Once I was the sort of person who invests objects with sentimental value.
Now I no longer have those objects, but I have the sentiments yet.

66   Many times in our travels I have lost everything but the clothes I was wearing and Lizbeth. The things I find in Dumpsters, the love letters and rag dolls
of so many lives, remind me of this lesson. Now I hardly pick up a thing without
envisioning the time I will cast it aside. This I think is a healthy state of mind.
Almost everything I have now has already been cast out at least once, proving
that what I own is valueless to someone.

67   Anyway, I find my desire to grab for the gaudy bauble has been largely
sated. I think this is an attitude I share with the very wealthy—we both know
there is plenty more where what we have came from. Between us are the rat-
race millions who nightly scavenge the cable channels looking for they know
not what.

68   I am sorry for them.

EXERCISES

Some of the Issues

1. Why might Eighner begin his essay by defining words and terms?
2. In paragraphs 7 through 30, Eighner describes how to select safe food
    from Dumpsters. What information do you recall from his descriptions?
    How does Eighner establish his authority on the issue of Dumpster div-
    ing? What indications does he give that his judgment is not infallible?
3. What is Eighner's attitude toward the students in the neighborhood where
    he scavenges (paragraphs 21 through 25)? How did you, as a student, react
    to his comments?
4. What does Eighner say are the stages people go through as scavengers
    (paragraphs 31 through 37)?
5. Who are the scavengers Eighner disapproves of and why? Do you feel he is
    too judgmental?

6. What reasons does Eighner give for not scavenging in individual garbage cans? Can you think of a similar way in which you set boundaries for respecting the privacy of others?
7. What does Eighner feel he shares with the wealthy (paragraph 67)? How does he describe the "rat-race millions" and why does he feel sorry for them?
8. Eighner tells us in paragraph 4 that, as a scavenger, he has learned how wasteful consumers can be. Having finished his essay, summarize what he has learned about wastefulness, citing examples from throughout the text.
9. What are some of the ethical issues Eighner raises in this essay? What do you think of Eighner's sense of ethics?
10. What were your responses to this essay? Did it change your perceptions of the homeless in any way?

The Way We Are Told

11. "On Dumpster Diving" could be classified as a "process" essay, a type of writing that describes how to do something. How does Eighner use this form to tell us more than simply "how to" scavenge?
12. What is the tone of the essay? Does it vary?
13. Eighner gives detailed descriptions throughout the essay. What is their effect?

Some Subjects for Writing

14. Describe how to do something that you do well. Begin in a way that establishes your authority on the issue. If possible, choose something that is important to you, but whose value to others may not be obvious.
15. What provisions should be made for the homeless? Should they be allowed to share public buildings such as libraries, or sleep in sheltered areas of buildings, train, subway, or bus stations? Should churches open space for them? Write an essay explaining your views.
16. Do you feel there is too much wastefulness in American society? Give evidence based on personal experience and observations. For example, you may want to observe the habits of students in your school cafeteria, patrons in a local restaurant, or employees in your workplace.

Less Is More: A Call for Shorter Work Hours

Barbara Brandt

Barbara Brandt is a community organizer and social change activist who lives in the Boston area and focuses her work on issues of gender, community, economics, and environment. She is the author of Whole Life Economics: Revaluing Daily Life *(1995). This essay was written in conjunction with a collective called the "Shorter Work Time Group," of which Brandt was a member, and appeared in the* Utne Reader *as part of a section on work.*

Brandt argues that increases in technology such as computers and fax machines, while they initially seem to offer us more convenience, save us time, and decrease our workload, have actually increased the pace of our lives and raised our standards of productivity. Brandt makes the case that, while the typical American work week—eight hours a day, forty hours a week—seems to most Americans like "the natural rhythm of the universe," we could all benefit from a conception of work that included more free time to care for families, explore hobbies and interests, and develop community.

1   America is suffering from overwork. Too many of us are too busy, trying to squeeze more into each day while having less to show for it. Although our growing time crunch is often portrayed as a personal dilemma, it is in fact a major social problem that has reached crisis proportions over the past 20 years.

2   The simple fact is that Americans today—both women and men—are spending too much time at work, to the detriment of their homes, their families, their personal lives, and their communities. The American Dream promised that our individual hard work paired with the advances of modern technology would bring about the good life for all. Glorious visions of the leisure society were touted throughout the '50s and '60s. But now most people are working more than ever before, while still struggling to meet their economic commitments. Ironically, the many advances in technology, such as computers and fax machines, rather than reducing our workload, seem to have speeded up our lives at work. At the same time, technology has equipped us with "conveniences" like microwave ovens and frozen dinners that merely enable us to adopt a similar frantic pace in our home lives so we can cope with more hours at paid work.

3   A recent spate of articles in the mainstream media has focused on the new problems of overwork and lack of time. Unfortunately, overwork is often portrayed as a special problem of yuppies and professionals on the fast track. In re-

ality, the unequal distribution of work and time in America today reflects the decline in both standard of living and quality of life for most Americans. Families whose members never see each other, women who work a double shift (first on the job, then at home), workers who need more flexible work schedules, and unemployed and underemployed people who need more work are all casualties of the crisis of overwork.

4   Americans often assume that overwork is an inevitable fact of life—like death and taxes. Yet a closer look at other times and other nations offers some startling surprises.

5   Anthropologists have observed that in pre-industrial (particularly hunting and gathering) societies, people generally spend 3 to 4 hours a day, 15 to 20 hours a week, doing the work necessary to maintain life. The rest of the time is spent in socializing, partying, playing, storytelling, and artistic or religious activities. The ancient Romans celebrated 175 public festivals a year in which everyone participated, and people in the Middle Ages had at least 115.

6   In our era, almost every other industrialized nation (except Japan) has fewer annual working hours and longer vacations than the United States. This includes all of Western Europe, where many nations enjoy thriving economies and standards of living equal to or higher than ours. Jeremy Brecher and Tim Costello, writing in *Z Magazine* (Oct. 1990), note that "European unions during the 1980s made a powerful and largely successful push to cut working hours. In 1987 German metalworkers struck and won a 37.5-hour week; many are now winning a 35-hour week. In 1990, hundreds of thousands of British workers have won a 37-hour week."

7   In an article about work-time in the *Boston Globe*, Suzanne Gordon notes that workers in other industrialized countries "enjoy—as a statutory right— longer vacations [than in the U.S.] from the moment they enter the work force. In Canada, workers are legally entitled to two weeks off their first year on the job. . . . After two or three years of employment, most get three weeks of vacation. After 10 years, it's up to four, and by 20 years, Canadian workers are off for five weeks. In Germany, statutes guarantee 18 days minimum for everyone, but most workers get five or six weeks. The same is true in Scandinavian countries, and in France."

8   In contrast to the extreme American emphasis on productivity and commitment, which results in many workers, especially in professional-level jobs, not taking the vacations coming to them, Gordon notes that "In countries that are America's most successful competitors in the global marketplace, all working people, whether lawyers or teachers, CEOs or janitors, take the vacations to which they are entitled by law. 'No one in West Germany,' a West German embassy's officer explains, 'no matter how high up they are, would ever say they couldn't afford to take a vacation. Everyone takes their vacation.'"

9   And in Japan, where dedication to the job is legendary, Gordon notes that the Japanese themselves are beginning to consider their national workaholism a

serious social problem leading to stress-related illnesses and even death. As a result, the Japanese government recently established a commission whose goal is to promote shorter working hours and more leisure time.

10   Most other industrialized nations also have better family-leave policies than the United States, and in a number of other countries workers benefit from innovative time-scheduling opportunities such as sabbaticals.

11   While the idea of a shorter workweek and longer vacations sounds appealing to most people, any movement to enact shorter work-time as a public policy will encounter surprising pockets of resistance, not just from business leaders but even from some workers. Perhaps the most formidable barrier to more free time for Americans is the widespread mind-set that the 40-hour workweek, 8 hours a day, 5 days a week, 50 weeks a year, is a natural rhythm of the universe. This view is reinforced by the media's complete silence regarding the shorter work-time and more favorable vacation and family-leave policies of other countries. This lack of information, and our leaders' reluctance to suggest that the United States can learn from any other nation (except workaholic Japan) is one reason why more Americans don't identify overwork as a major problem or clamor for fewer hours and more vacation. Monika Bauerlein, a journalist originally from Germany now living in Minneapolis, exclaims, "I can't believe that people here aren't rioting in the streets over having only two weeks of vacation a year."

12   A second obstacle to launching a powerful shorter work-time movement is America's deeply ingrained work ethic, or its modern incarnation, the workaholic syndrome. The work ethic fosters the widely held belief that people's work is their most important activity and that people who do not work long and hard are lazy, unproductive, and worthless.

13   For many Americans today, paid work is not just a way to make money but is a crucial source of their self-worth. Many of us identify ourselves almost entirely by the kind of work we do. Work still has a powerful psychological and spiritual hold over our lives—and talk of shorter work-time may seem somehow morally suspicious.

14   Because we are so deeply a work-oriented society, leisure-time activities—such as play, relaxation, engaging in cultural and artistic pursuits, or just quiet contemplation and "doing nothing"—are not looked on as essential and worthwhile components of life. Of course, for the majority of working women who must work a second shift at home, much of the time spent outside of paid work is not leisure anyway. Also much of our non-work time is spent not just in personal renewal, but in building and maintaining essential social ties—with family, friends, and the larger community.

15   Today, as mothers and fathers spend more and more time on the job, we are beginning to recognize the deleterious effects—especially on our young people—of the breakdown of social ties and community in American life. But unfortunately, our nation reacts to these problems by calling for more paid professionals—more police, more psychiatrists, more experts—without recognizing the possi-

bility that shorter work hours and more free time could enable us to do much of the necessary rebuilding and healing, with much more gratifying and longer-lasting results.

16   Of course, the stiffest opposition to cutting work hours comes not from citizens but from business. Employers are reluctant to alter the 8-hour day, 40-hour workweek, 50 weeks a year because it seems easier and more profitable for employers to hire fewer employees for longer hours rather than more employees—each of whom would also require health insurance and other benefits—with flexible schedules and work arrangements.

17   Harvard University economist Juliet B. Schor, who has been studying issues of work and leisure in America, reminds us that we cannot ignore the larger relationship between unemployment and overwork: While many of us work too much, others are unable to find paid work at all. Schor points out that "workers who work longer hours lose more income when they lose their jobs. The threat of job loss is an important determinant of management's power on the shop floor." A system that offers only two options—long work hours or unemployment—serves as both a carrot and a stick. Those lucky enough to get full-time jobs are bribed into docile compliance with the boss, while the spectre of unemployment always looms as the ultimate punishment for the unruly.

18   Some observers suggest that keeping people divided into "the employed" and "the unemployed" creates feelings of resentment and inferiority/superiority between the two groups, thus focusing their discontent and blame on each other rather than on the corporations and political figures who actually dictate our nation's economic policies.

19   Our role as consumers contributes to keeping the average work week from falling. In an economic system in which addictive buying is the basis of corporate profits, working a full 40 hours or more each week for 50 weeks a year gives us just enough time to stumble home and dazedly—almost automatically—shop; but not enough time to think about deeper issues or to work effectively for social change. From the point of view of corporations and policymakers, shorter work time may be bad for the economy, because people with enhanced free time may begin to find other things to do with it besides mindlessly buying products. It takes more free time to grow vegetables, cook meals from scratch, sew clothes, or repair broken items than it does to just buy these things at the mall.

20   Any serious proposal to give employed Americans a break by cutting into the eight-hour work day is certain to be met with anguished cries about international competitiveness. The United States seems gripped by the fear that our nation has lost its economic dominance, and pundits, policymakers, and business leaders tell us that no sacrifice is too great if it puts America on top again.

21   As arguments like this are put forward (and we can expect them to increase in the years to come), we need to remember two things. First, even if America maintained its dominance (whatever that means) and the economy were booming again, this would be no guarantee that the gains—be they in

wages, in employment opportunities, or in leisure—would be distributed equitably between upper management and everyone else. Second, the entire issue of competitiveness is suspect when it pits poorly treated workers in one country against poorly treated workers in another; and when the vast majority of economic power, anyway, is in the control of enormous multinational corporations that have no loyalty to the people of any land.

EXERCISES

Some of the Issues

1. What was your immediate reaction to Brandt's first paragraph? Do you agree or disagree? Why or why not?
2. What does Brandt see as the irony of modern technology (paragraph 2)? How, in your opinion, has technology changed our commitments to work, family, and community?
3. According to Brandt, who in America suffers from overwork (paragraph 3)?
4. In paragraphs 4 through 10 Brandt contrasts the work habits or preindustrial and other industrialized nations with those of the United States. Why does she make these comparisons?
5. In paragraphs 11 through 15, Brandt discusses two reasons why individuals resist a shorter workweek. What are they? Do you agree with her comments on the "work ethic"?
6. Why are employers reluctant to alter the eight-hour day (paragraph 16)?
7. According to Brandt and Juliet B. Schor, how does overwork divide us (paragraphs 16 through 19) and which groups are pitted against each other (paragraph 21)? What are the consequences of this division?
8. According to Brandt, what role do corporations play in encouraging consumption and keeping the workweek long (paragraph 19)? Do you agree with her analysis?

The Way We Are Told

9. Brandt makes certain points in her argument by first stating a common assumption and then presenting evidence against that assumption. Find places in the essay where she does this. Does it make her argument more effective?
10. How does Brandt use comparison and contrast to provide evidence for her argument?

Some Subjects for Writing

11. In a journal, document your own work habits for three or four days. Take note of how much time you devote to your work, school, leisure, family,

and community. Using examples and descriptions from your journal, write an essay in which you define and examine your own work habits.

12. Interview three or four people from different social or cultural backgrounds about their work habits. Make sure to prepare a list of questions beforehand and ask follow-up questions during the interview. Write an essay in which you compare and contrast their attitudes toward both work and leisure.

13. Do you agree with Brandt that Americans overvalue the "work ethic" and undervalue leisure-time activities? Write an essay explaining your views.

14. In a section of the article not reprinted here, Brandt makes specific proposals for shortening the workweek to thirty hours. Write a persuasive essay in which you argue for or against a shorter workweek. Make sure to back up your claims with specific evidence, and to qualify your argument by showing that you understand the other side.

Town-Building Is No Mickey Mouse Operation

Michael Pollan

Michael Pollan grew up on Long Island and graduated from Bennington College in Vermont. He studied at Oxford University in England before receiving a master's degree in English at Columbia University in New York. He is an editor-at-large at Harper's *magazine and a contributing writer at* The New York Times, *where this essay was first published. He writes often on gardening, environmentalism, and nature. His most recent book is* The Botany of Desire: A Plant's Eye View of the World *(2001).*

In this essay, Pollan visits the town of Celebration, a planned community built by the Walt Disney Company on former swampland in southern Florida. Celebration is an example of a recent movement in city planning called "New Urbanism." A response to the prevalence of alienating and isolating suburban sprawl and the perceived lack of community in American life, this philosophy of architecture and planning seeks to create community by designing street life, schools, stores and governing structures as well as buildings. Perhaps the most famous example of this type of town planning is the community of Seaside, Florida, whose idyllic streets served as the set for the movie "The Truman Show."

Pollan investigates whether it is indeed possible to manufacture a community through detailed planning and control of social and physical structures. What happens, Pollan asks, when the inevitable unpredictability of life starts to take over and a manufactured community starts acting like a real one? Real community, Pollan posits, cannot be controlled. It is, as he says, "messy, ever-changing, and invariably political."

1 The sun was barely up over the brand-new town of Celebration, Fla. and the Rotarians[1] had gathered in the clubhouse at the golf course for their weekly breakfast meeting. I'd come fully expecting to meet a bunch of white guys in polo shirts who'd remind me of my father, and there were quite enough of them. And

---

[1]Worldwide organization of business people and professionals dedicated to community service.

yet right there across the table sat several other Celebration Rotarians who, in age and outlook and appearance, reminded me a whole lot more of, well, me.

2   Only two years ago, the spot on which we were getting acquainted, these implausible Rotarians and I, was an impenetrable cypress swamp on the farthest edge of Walt Disney World. Now there is a handsome and lively town (population 1,500, eventually to reach 20,000) built by Disney, which has deployed its considerable capital and place-making skills to create, in the choral refrain of just about every company executive I met, "not just a housing development but a community." Viewed from that perspective, Celebration is nothing more than an elaborate contraption for the production of *Rotarians*—for transforming isolated and disaffected American suburbanites (not unlike myself) into civic-minded members of a community. By one measure the contraption seemed to be working: scarcely 18 months after the first family moved in, Celebration has become ground for a luxuriant growth of scout troops, religious groups and hobbyist clubs of every conceivable stripe. No doubt any housing development that markets itself as an old-fashioned town would tend to attract more than its share of joiners. There is, too, the fact that Disney has been quietly working behind the scenes (for there is always a "backstage" at Disney) to seed and nourish all these groups. But none of this explained the presence, across from me at breakfast, of someone like Todd Hill—an urbane landscape architect from Atlanta who doesn't fit anyone's stereotype of a Rotary member. Hill is, by his own lights, living proof that the "neotraditional" design of a subdivision can transform a young urban professional into what can best be described as a neo-Rotarian.

3   "Before I moved here I was not a big volunteer type," he told me over microbrewed beers on his porch one evening. "I worked all the time." Hill, who is 37, and his wife, Lisa, live on Mulberry Street in a Charleston side row, one of the six historical-house styles permitted in Celebration. They moved here from a condo in Atlanta, and their home has a two-career, no-kids sparseness about it—lightly inhabited, with somewhat less in the way of furniture than high-end home audio and video equipment.

4   As a design professional, Hill had long been familiar with the ideas of neotraditionalism, the planning movement, also known as the New Urbanism, whose principles Disney has drawn upon in building Celebration; his experience living here has already convinced him that "it works"—that walkable streets, attractive public spaces and close-by downtown can profoundly affect people's daily lives.

5   "It's a physical thing that becomes a spiritual thing," Hill said, by way of explaining his belated discovery of his Rotarian self. "About two months after we moved to Celebration, I was back in Atlanta on a job, and it hit me: for the first time in my life, I felt as though I was part of a community. That's when I decided I should join something. Me! When I first went to Rotary, I thought it was going to be, you know, Fred Flintstone in the bullhorn hat. I mean, what was all this 'fellowship' stuff? It's kind of hokey, and I'm not ordinarily that kind of person, but I see it as a community thing."

6   "Community" is a word we hear a lot these days, not only in the speeches of the President and in books by self-described "communitarian" thinkers in several different fields, but also in the focus groups and brochures of real-estate developers. (Community has emerged as one of the "features" most prized by new home buyers, according to the trade journal *Builder.*) Americans seem to sense, and regret, the fraying of our "civil society"—the informal network of clubs, volunteer groups and civic and religious organizations that traditionally knit a community together.

7   The town of Celebration represents the Disney Company's ambitious answer to the perceived lack of community in American life, but it is an answer that raises a couple of difficult questions. To what extent can redesigning the physical world we inhabit—the streets, public spaces and buildings—foster a greater sense of community? And what exactly does "a sense of" mean here?—for the word community hardly ever goes abroad in Celebration without that dubious prefix.

8   Disney occupies a special place in the American landscape and culture. Few companies are as skillful at making places, at shaping the physical environment to affect our behavior. Disney's theme parks deserve credit for helping to keep alive not only a large part of America's vernacular architecture but, on Main Street, the very experience of walkable streets and pleasing public places—this at precisely the time when Americans were abandoning real Main Streets for their cars and suburban cul-de-sacs. But Disney's expertise is in building theme parks for paying guests, not towns for citizens. A real community is messy, ever changing and inevitably political—three adjectives that pretty much sum up everything the culture of Disney cannot abide. Very soon after the first homeowners moved into Celebration, Disney got its first taste of the unpredictability of community life, and of the difference between consumers and citizens. A bruising controversy erupted over the curriculum at the Celebration public school, and Disney suddenly found itself in a most unfamiliar environment, one that has tested the company's vaunted skills at managing reality.

9   Disney's expertise at making places and synthesizing urban experience cannot be separated from its legendary obsession with control; it is, even more than most, a corporation that lives by scripts of its own scrupulous devising. At Celebration, however, Disney has set in motion a story whose script it can only partly control. It is this experiment that I recently traveled to Celebration to observe: just how does a corporation go about manufacturing a community? And what happens when it actually succeeds, and that community starts to act like one?

THE STREET

10   One Sunday afternoon, I took a long walk through the streets of Celebration, hoping to understand just what Robert A.M. Stern meant when he told me that "the street is the key to everything else we're trying to accomplish here." Stern is, along with Jaquelin Robertson, a fellow New York architect, Celebration's

master planner; the two laid out the town's network of streets, its downtown commercial district, its parks and school and "wellness center." If a neotraditional town like Celebration represents a technology for the creation of community, the street, Stern was suggesting, is its most crucial component—its flywheel or microprocessor.

11   The streets of Celebration are loosely gridded, which means lots of stop signs, and narrow enough to force cars to crawl, so a pedestrian senses at once that he belongs here. The first thing I noticed as I headed up Longmeadow toward Hippodrome Park was just how much there is to look at. The houses are close enough to one another, and sufficiently varied in style, to unfold before the pedestrian in a pleasing rhythm. Even the grandest houses—and Longmeadow is a street of "Estate Homes"—are on tiny lots pulled up to the curb, and their faces engage the passerby with ceremonial front doors, nicely detailed windows and columns and sociable front porches.

12   Though I spotted no porch sitters on my walk, I spoke to several residents who swear by their porches, especially in the winter, when Orlando's temperatures and mosquitoes let up. Lise Juneman, a young mother of two, said her family "spends every Saturday morning out on the porch, having coffee, playing Barbies with the girls, catching up with neighbors strolling by." A cliche, perhaps, but not an unappealing one.

13   Stern had spoken of the importance of making the street into an outdoor room—a public space in its own right, not just a connector—and the best of Celebration's streets have already achieved this quality. The orderly ranks of trees (Disney has planted thousands of handsome, mature specimens) present a unifying street wall, the dead faces of garages have been banished to backyards (where they are accessible by service alleys) and the house fronts have been carefully scaled so as not to overwhelm the space. I found it easy to strike up conversations on the street, and my notebook quickly filled with slightly astonished testimonials to the forgotten pleasures of small-town life: "I used to just wave at my neighbors from the car. Now we stop and gossip on the corner." "Everyone's so friendly here, it's like the first week of college."

14   If the typical suburb represents a king of monoculture, street after street of architecturally and socioeconomically identical houses, Celebration has already achieved a striking degree of diversity. During my walk, I strolled down a street of million-dollar homes facing the golf course, and then turned to find a lane of modest cottages that sell for a fifth as much; walking another block or two, I came to a broad crescent of town-house apartments that rent for as little as $600 a month. This sort of diversity, while limited—there are no poor in Celebration, and the town is extremely white—is nevertheless rare today in the suburbs, where it is an article of the real-estate faith that people will live next door only to neighbors of the same class. In Celebration, houses of roughly the same price do face each other across a street, but the service alleys behind those houses deliberately mix high and low, forcing the surgeon and the firefighter to mingle while taking out the trash or getting into their cars. Stern spoke of deliberately

setting up such encounters as one of the many ways that "design can help to orchestrate community."

15   This is, of course, a very old utopian idea, with deep roots in the American landscape: that the proper arrangement of streets and houses can help usher in a specific sort of community. When, in the 1630s, the Puritans established a town on Massachusetts Bay, they specified exactly how far from the meeting house anyone could build—no more than a mile and a half—and laid out their village in concentric circles to enforce the social compact. In our own century, a long succession of middle-class utopias—Radburn, N.J.; Reston, Va.; Columbia, Md.; Levittown, N.Y., and countless unheralded others—have been staked out, plotted and built on blank stretches of land in the conviction that a considered arrangement of streets, houses, public spaces and, increasingly these days, walls and gates will help to realize a specific vision of the good society. In the mid-60's, Walt Disney decided he had something to add to this tradition. He originally conceived Epcot (an acronym for Experimental Protoype Community of Tomorrow) not as a theme park but as a high-tech model city of 20,000 residents. But it was not to be: shortly after his death in 1966, company executives, no doubt worried about profit margins and the likelihood that a city populated by real people might prove more difficult to manage than a theme park, decided to shelve Walt's utopia.

16   Today, Disney executives from Michael Eisner, the company's chairman, on down speak of Celebration as the fulfillment of Walt Disney's old dream to build a City on a Hill—a model held up to the world.

17   "Eisner was very clear from the beginning that he didn't want to do just another residential community," Bob Shinn said over dinner downtown at Max's Cafe. Shinn is senior vice president of Walt Disney Imagineering, giving him responsibility for the company's operations in Florida. "With Celebration, we're giving something back, trying to blaze a trail to improve American family life, education and health. This project allows us to fulfill Walt's idea for a town of tomorrow."

18   Of course, fulfilling the founder's vision was not the only motivation for building Celebration: if it is a City on a Hill, it is at the same time an element in a larger corporate strategy and, very simply, a $2.5 billion real-estate deal, a creative way of packaging and selling Florida swampland. (Disney paid approximately $200 an acre for this land in the 60s, it is selling quarter-acre lots at Celebration for upward of $80,000.)

19   According to Tom Lewis, perhaps the Disney executive most closely involved with Celebration's early planning, the town had its more earthly origins on Wall Street, in the bloody battle for control of Disney in the early 80s. Part of what made the corporation such an attractive takeover target was the vast acreage of undeveloped real estate it owned in Orlando—the theme parks and hotels occupied only a small fraction of the company's 27,000-acre holdings. After Michael Eisner took over the company in 1984, he ordered a study of the

real estate that determined that some 10,000 acres of it, lying on the south side of Route 192, would never be needed by Walt Disney World. Developing that land in some way would render Disney that much less attractive to a raider.

20　　Another consideration was the fact that Disney's relations with local governments in central Florida had grown somewhat strained. Walt Disney World occupies a state-chartered and virtually sovereign municipality called Reedy Creek Improvement District, which contributes relatively little in the way of taxes to Osceola County, one of the two counties it straddles. By "de-annexing" the 10,000 acres and populating them with taxpayers, Disney could please local governments and smooth the approval process for future theme-park projects, like its new Animal Kingdom. (Had Celebration remained within Reedy Creek, it would also have given Disney's private municipality something it can't afford to have: independent voters.)

21　　Of course, Disney could have accomplished these goals far more cheaply and easily by building a conventional housing development or resort community—and this is where the company's old utopian streak probably came into play. In a bit of local lore cherished by Celebration residents and executives alike, Eisner is said to have instructed his real-estate-development team that Celebration—the town's name was chosen from a focus-grouped list by Eisner and his wife—needs to make money for stockholders, but if it's not going to be state of the art, Disney shouldn't bother.

22　　The state of the art has changed considerably since Walt Disney's time. Disney's corporate vision of the future has undergone a revolution since 1966, from Epcot's sleek technological sublime (the city of tomorrow was to have people movers and a vast dome overhead) to neotraditionalism. Perhaps most closely identified with Seaside, the Florida resort community designed in the 80s by Andres Duany and Elizabeth Plater-Zybek, neotraditional town planning has until now enjoyed rather more success nationally with the media than the marketplace. Many New Urbanists are counting on Disney's success at Celebration to sell developers and home buyers on the idea that the next American utopia should look like a neotraditional town.

23　　They could be right. Some 5,000 home buyers entered a lottery for the privilege of purchasing the first 350 homes at Celebration, and sales since then have been brisk enough (Celebration is currently the fastest-selling development in its price range in the Orlando area) to catch the attention of developers and planning officials from across the nation. Indeed, walking the streets of Celebration, bumping into visitors from all over the world doing much the same thing I was, I realized that Disney's town has already become what Disney's founder intended—a stop on the architectural tour of the American future.

24　　It was hard not to come away from that tour impressed by the extraordinary care Disney has taken in every aspect of the town's physical design. And yet by the end of my walk the very designed-ness of Celebration had started to weigh on me. Eventually the streetscape began to feel a little *too* perfect, a little too considered. After a while my eye longed for something not quite so orchestrated.

25   From my research I knew that every last visual detail my eyes had taken in during my two-hour walk, from the precise ratio of lawn to perennials in the front yards to the scrollwork on the Victorian porches to the exact relationship of column, capital and entablature on the facades of every Colonial Revival, had been stipulated—had in fact been spelled out in the gorgeous and obsessively detailed "Pattern Book" that governs every facet of architectural and even horti-cultural life at Celebration. I knew all that, yet now I felt it, too, and how it felt was packaged, less than real, somewhat more like a theme park than a town.

26   When I offered these impressions to Robert Stern, he said, wait for "the buildings to take on the patina of age, the landscaping to get luxurious" and for time to put its mark on a place that is still very, very new. I noticed that he spoke of time leaving its mark, not people. In fact, no one can make the slightest change to his house's exterior without first obtaining written permission from the company; even the choice of trees and shrubs is subject to approval, and will remain so indefinitely. That doesn't leave much room for history.

27   "Will Celebration always look so newly minted? That's a real question," Stern acknowledged. "They do have people power-washing the streets at night"—which is exactly what they do in the theme parks. But then the archi-tect, who also happens to sit on Disney's board, remembered himself. "Your know it's a really sad commentary," he said, "that for something to look 'real,' it has to be run-down." That is one sort of history, certainly, though not the one I had in mind.

DOWNTOWN

28   From the air, Celebration vaguely resembles a river delta, with the residential lanes flowing south and collecting at the head of Market Street, a commercial thoroughfare lined with stately palms that carry down to a pretty man-made lake. The whole neotraditional town idea is predicated on providing residents with a vibrant downtown area, a center of social gravity. Downtown Celebration is a sleepy little grid of streets lined with upscale shops and restaurants, a two-screen movie theater (designed by Cesar Pelli), a bank (by Robert Venturi), a neat toy of a post office (Michael Graves) and a visitors' center (really a sales of-fice, designed by the late Charles Moore). Leaving aside these generally whimsi-cal "signature" buildings, downtown resembles a miniature Santa Barbara—vaguely historical, lots of pastel stucco (actually a synthetic material call Dryvit), with most of the parking deftly hidden behind Main Street.

29   It is tempting to dismiss Celebration's downtown as a shopping mall with-out a roof, but that wouldn't be quite accurate: for one thing, there are no big national chains (most of the shops are appealing mom and pop operations); for another, there are rental apartments and a handful of offices above the shops. Andres Duany judges it "a spectacular achievement."

30   Many residents regard living within a five-minute walk of downtown as one of the best things about life at Celebration. "I am much less dependent on my

car," Lise Juneman said; some, like Ramond Chiaramonte, have actually scaled back their fleets. Kids in particular enjoy a freedom in Celebration that is almost inconceivable today anywhere else. By the time children have reached the age of 10 or so, most parents are willing to let them wander freely, and after-school hours once filled with television are now taken up with Rollerblading to the parks and pool or expeditions downtown, where preteens go to check out the clothes at Village Mercantile or cadge samples of the coffee coolers at Barnie's.

31   For grown-ups, downtown offers a quasi-urban experience that can't be had elsewhere in the suburbs. Brian Haas and his wife, Dianne, are doctors who met while in medical school in Manhattan in the 80s. Career took the Haases to the Orlando area, but both miss the experience of walking to bars and jazz clubs in New York. They can get some of that here, Brian said.

32   "We're a high-powered New York-Washington couple," he explained, as I joined him early one morning for breakfast before he walked his children Julian and Zachary, to school. "Morning Edition" was on the radio, that week's New Yorker on the kitchen counter. Except for the cavernous space, the Haas home could easily pass for the apartment of an overscheduled two-income Manhattan family.

33   "I'm an inveterate New Yorker," Brian said. "I could not at first imagine ever living in a Disney town—too Mickey Mouse, to use a cynical New Yorker's expression. But cynicism is often a mask for frustrated idealism. After visiting Celebration, I realized there were virtues to Disney's involvement. With all the publicity"—and here he gestured in my direction—"they can't afford to let Celebration fail."

34   After a while I began to see how someone as "high powered" as Brian Haas, a busy surgeon who probably devotes very little time in a day to doubt, might learn to suspend disbelief about something like the urbanity of his adopted hometown. "It's the best of New York," Brian declared. And then, a moment later, "I love it because of the kids." Which is, of course, the classic pre-neotraditional rationale for moving to the suburbs.

35   So what is Celebration? A town or a suburb? A subdivision with a few streets of restaurants and shops, or a plausible alternative to the general sprawl of suburban cul-de-sacs spilling their cars onto commercial strips? From one perspective, Celebration allows people like Brian Haas, Todd Hill, Lise Juneman and their children to have a different life style than they would in a subdivision without a town center. Yet one has only to climb the tower at the visitors' center to see that the new town is really just one more in a series of residential pods hanging off the classic suburban strip—in this case, Route 192—by a single asphalt thread. Like all but a very few New Urbanist projects, Disney's town offers few real places to shop—there's no hardware store or pharmacy—and few serious employment opportunities; it also leaves the larger patterns of transportation undisturbed. Celebration might look like a railroad suburb, and its residents may walk downtown on the weekends, but on Monday morning most of them will have no choice but to climb back into their cars for the half-hour commute to Orlando.

36   Rosemary Cordingley laughed when I asked her whether she felt as though she lived in a town: "Oh, yes, a new town! We're pioneers! Please. I can't even get my hair cut downtown. Oh, it's very nice, you can walk to the movies with your friends—that part is great. But a town? It's not even close."

THE SCHOOL

37   Celebration School, a dignified campus of classrooms linked by covered walk-ways, is right in the middle of town. In brochures for Celebration, Disney resur-rects Walt Disney's dream of "a school of tomorrow" and depicts its K–12 public school "as a model for education into the next century." Florida schools are notoriously poor, and the promise of a "state-of-the-art school" in central Florida has proven to be the town's strongest selling point—the main reason home buyers are prepared to pay a 25 percent to 40 percent premium over com-parable real estate to live in Celebration.

38   Given the expectations, it isn't surprising that the school should have emerged as the first real test of Disney's management and Celebration's com-munity. Very soon after school opened in fall '96, a couple dozen parents began expressing dissatisfaction about the quality of the education their children were receiving. Many objected to the school's notably progressive curriculum: there are multi-age classrooms; reading is taught using the "whole language" method; tests are few, and there are "narrative assessments" instead of grades. ("This is a place," the principal said, "where nobody fails.")

39   Some of these approaches are quite controversial—the state of California, for example, is currently abandoning whole language in the face of plummeting reading scores, and while multi-age classrooms are catching on in places, com-bining six grades in one space is virtually unheard of. So why would Disney have opted for such a radical school, particularly in a neotraditional town? Possibly because a more conventional school would have been hard to distinguish from any other Osceloa County public school.

40   At any rate, problems—or, as the company prefers to call them, "growing pains"—emerged right away. A group of some 30 parents began meeting to dis-cuss their concerns and push for changes—hardly an unusual occurrence, but Celebration is an unusual place, and it all but suffered a nervous breakdown. Here was a faction of its young community flexing its muscles for the first time, and it gave everyone a chance to see how Disney would react. As parents trooped in to complain, executives listened patiently, even sympathetically, but finally disclaimed responsibility—this was, after all, public school, and the com-pany had its hands tied. All of which was true, but did little to assuage the anger of parents who had put so much faith in Disney.

41   For Roger Burton, a successful small-business owner who had moved his family to Celebration from Chicago largely because of the school, the episode was disillusioning. "Sure it was a public school, but we figured if Disney was be-

hind it, it would be as fabulous as everything else they do," he said. "I knew Celebration was going to be a very controlled situation, but controlled in a good way. But as soon as you run into a problem, you find there is no mechanism to change things. The only person you can call is a corporate vice president, but he's not interested in the school, not really. He's interested in selling real estate."

42   Frustrated at the lack of response, Burton and a group of his neighbors began speaking out in the press. Celebration residents have discovered that they possess a powerful political tool few of the rest of us can lay claim to: merely by picking up the phone, they can put a local school squabble on the front page and the evening news. The press descended on the Celebration School story, and Disney realized it had a problem.

43   Soon after the first negative articles appeared, the great majority of Celebration residents suddenly rose up in full-throated support of the school, though just how spontaneously is open to question. One Disney executive told me that "the negative publicity galvanized the whole community in support of the school," but several residents see Disney's hand behind a lot of the galvanizing. Jackson Mumey, one of the parents most articulate in support of the school, was put on the Disney payroll as an "educational consultant"; he gave interviews to the press, educated benighted parents about the curriculum and helped organize something called the Dream Team—a parents organization that lent moral support to the teachers, who were thought to be demoralized by the controversy. A plane was hired to fly a "Great Job Bobbi" banner above downtown Celebration on Teacher Appreciation Day. (Bobbi Vogel, the principal, quit not long after, as did 6 of the 19 teachers.)

44   Brent Herrington, Celebration's "community services manager," emerged as one of the school's biggest cheerleaders. Herrington is paid by Disney to manage town affairs, but professes to represent "all the stakeholders." From his office in town hall, Herrington helped to organize a series of "pep rallies" and picnics for the teachers and helped raise funds to buy them small gifts—things like Celebration School jerseys.

45   All of this might seem harmless enough, yet there was a dark side to the frenzied show of support. At one point early in the controversy, Herrington used his monthly newsletter to solicit contributions for a "positive parents" fund, and school boosters soon took to calling themselves "the positive parents." Surely this was an insidious choice of words, for it immediately cast critics of the school as "negative parents." Dissent had been framed as destructive. The critics took to calling themselves "refuseniks."

46   Tensions quickly mounted, to the point where "the Hatfields and McCoys"—as Brian Haas described the warring factions—virtually stopped speaking to one another. "As soon as you say anything," Burton told me, "you become an outcast. If you don't like Celebration, you should leave, people would say. Keep quiet or get out." Rosemary Cordingley, another school critic, told of being harangued on the street by Margo Schwartz, a single mother in her 40s who emerged as one of the most vociferous "positives." I can imagine it, for when

Schwartz spotted me on Water Street interviewing a refusenik, she strode up to us and, jabbing her index finger at my notebook, informed me that "Beulah here was one of the negative ones who only wants to bash this place." (Schwartz and I had never met before.)

47   Cordingley refers to the positive parents as the "pixie-dust" brigade.

48   "Those of us who weren't quite so sprinkled with pixie dust were ostracized," Cordingley said. "And it was orchestrated by Disney. We were treated in a very ugly manner. There was a lot of talk about property values. Instead of facing up to the problems—and believe me, the majority agrees there are problems—they hold pep rallies! Disneymania is fine at the park, but not in a school." Cordingley pulled her children out of school, and now drives them 25 miles to a parochial school. All told, some 30 children—16 percent of the total—withdrew from Celebration School last year, and the defections have continued.

49   Joseph Palacios, who has been active in efforts to reform the school, lays much of the blame for the polarization of the community at the steps of town hall: "A real town manager isn't going to try to create division in his community, but Brent Herrington did exactly that. Brent treated everyone as either positive or negative, and if you were negative, he would literally turn his back on you on the street. Your phone calls to town hall wouldn't get returned." Palacios, the father of a second grader, was one of the few residents willing to criticize Herrington on the record, but three others reported similar treatment.

50   "Brent is supposed to represent all of us," Palacios said, "but it became clear during the school fight that he's representing Disney." Asked about this, Herrington told me, "This perception is mistaken." It would appear, however, that "community building" has been less of a priority than damage control. Large unscripted public meetings where residents might speak freely have been scrupulously avoided; in their place Disney has held "focus groups" about the school.

51   Perhaps the most telling episode in the whole school drama came a year ago when a handful of families—including Roger Burton's—decided to pack up and leave Celebration. According to the contract that buyers sign, a homeowner may not profit from the sale of a house held less than one year unless he can prove hardship. Disney offered to exempt the disgruntled families from the rule but only on condition of signing an agreement promising never to reveal their reasons for leaving Celebration. "They were treating me like a Russian dissident," Rich Adams said. "You know, 'Sign here and you can go.'" Adams, who was one of the first to move to Celebration, became the first to move out. In the end, he signed nothing and Disney did nothing to stop him or the others. Herrington said that in retrospect the confidentiality agreement "probably wasn't the best choice."

TOWN HALL

52   Celebration's town hall is prominently situated at the head of Market Street, and to see it for the first time is to wonder if its architecture doesn't represent

one of wily old Philip Johnson's more clever inside jokes. Johnson's design begins with the obligatory white columns, the same ones that have symbolized democratic values in American civic architecture since the time of Thomas Jefferson. Yet Johnson has taken this venerable convention and multiplied it ad absurdum, until the entrance to Celebration's town hall is all but lost in the shadowy forest of columns—52 of them in all. A straightforward symbol of republican self-government is thus transformed into a disconcerting image of obscurity. It couldn't be more fitting, for Celebration's town hall is privately owned—by Disney.

53   "Town hall offers residents one-stop shopping for services" is how Tom Lewis, the Disney executive, characterizes what happens in the building; "shopping" is not a bad metaphor either, because the whole panoply of municipal services—everything from garbage pickup to street lighting, from the provision of recreational facilities and (a portion of) public safety to the enforcement of town rules—has been privatized at Celebration, as indeed they have been at hundreds of thousands of other master-planned communities across America.

54   The responsibility for managing these private governments—for that is what they are—generally falls to a homeowners' association whose board is elected by the residents. Homeowners' associations are now the fastest-growing form of political organization in the country, forming a kind of alternative political universe in which one of every eight Americans now resides.

55   The Celebration homeowners' association has its offices in the town hall, and that is where I met the town manager, Brent Herrington, the man Tom Lewis called "sort of the Mayor of Celebration." Herrington is a big, bluff 37-year-old Texan whose friendly demeanor was hard to reconcile with the image of Disney enforcer that several residents had painted. He is a product of the master-planned world: he grew up in Kingwood, a "highly amenitized" community of Houston, and has spent most of his working life as a professional manager of various master-planned developments.

56   When I mentioned to Herrington that I'd heard him described as Celebration's Mayor, he smiled and demurred. "I'm more like a small-town-manager— I'm the go-to guy, but I don't see myself as a politician." Indeed, Herrington sees running a town like Celebration not as a matter of politics at all, but of "good communication and consensus building."

57   In Herrington's view, his actions during the school crisis fall squarely under that heading. When I suggested that some residents felt he had taken sides, and that the rhetoric of "positive parents" is perhaps not as post-political as it sounds, Herrington said, "There was no perception on my part or the developer's part that we were pursuing a controversial path or taking sides."

58   Surely the most ticklish part of Herrington's job is enforcing the myriad rules that typically govern life in a master-planned community. To anyone living outside the walls of such a community, these rules can sound outrageous, but inside residents generally view them favorably, as a way to keep property values

high at a time when many suburbs have entered a period of decline. As one Celebration resident explained it, "The rules are there to make sure your neighbor's front yard doesn't turn into 'Sanford and Son.'" It should be said that this was the only racist remark I heard at Celebration.

59 All the rules governing life at Celebration would (in fact do) fill a book, but here are some of the more striking: All visible window coverings must be either white or off-white. A resident may hold only one garage sale in any 12-month period. A single political sign (measuring 18 by 24 inches) may be posted for 45 days prior to an election. Any activity that "detracts from the overall appearance of the properties" is prohibited—including the parking of residents' pickup trucks on the street.

60 "A violation is usually just an oversight" Herrington explained. "We try to solve problems as neighbors."

61 While I was walking around Celebration, I noticed some bright red curtains in the windows of a new Victorian on Longmeadow. Only then did I fully grasp the import of a cryptic little item I'd spotted in Herrington's monthly newsletter: "Please refrain from using colored or patterned material in the windows. This can look pretty 'icky' from the street!"

62 Icky?! So this is the voice of private government in the 90s? It all struck me as fairly creepy, Big Brother with a smiley face, but then I am probably not temperamentally suited to life in Celebration. As Kenneth Wong, president of Walt Disney Imagineering, pointedly reminded me, "Everyone is here on a voluntary basis."

63 Master Planner Stern is vigorous in his defense of Celebration's rules: "In a freewheeling capitalist society, you need controls—you can't have community without them. It's right there in Tocqueville: in the absence of an aristocratic hierarchy, you need firm rules to maintain decorum. I'm convinced these controls are actually liberating to people. It makes them feel their investment is safe. Regimentation can release you."

64 The best defense of the regulatory regime at Celebration is that the people here have chosen to live under it and, if not now then eventually, those people can vote to change it. At least that's what I kept hearing from both the past and current "mayors" of Celebration. "In 8 or 10 years," Herrington assured me, "all the power will revert to the homeowners." Lewis said the same thing.

65 But it turns out that matters are not quite that simple. Buried in the legal thickets of Celebration's "Covenants, Codes and Restrictions," the quasi-constitution that all home buyers are required to sign, can be found the underlying political script Disney wrote for the future of its town, and it reads very differently from the public script about community building and participation that company executives lay out for residents and reporters.

66 For while it is true that Celebration residents will eventually elect the directors of the homeowners' association, the covenants guarantee that that body will remain a creature of Disney's for as long as the company wishes—specifically, for as long as it owns a single acre of land within, or adjacent to, Celebration.

The homeowners' association cannot change any rule or restriction in Celebration "without prior notice to and the written approval of the Celebration Company," according to the covenants. Disney further retains the right to control every aspect of the physical character of Celebration for as long as it wishes to. Thus, however vital the community that evolves in Celebration turns out to be, ultimate power over its affairs will remain backstage, with Disney.

67   "It is absolute top-down control," said Evan McKenzie, a lawyer and expert on homeowners' associations, when I showed him the copy of the covenants I had obtained from a sales agent. "The homeowners are powerless against the association and the association is powerless against Disney. I can't imagine anything more undemocratic."

68   When I went back to Tom Lewis for clarification, he said that, as far as he understood, Celebration's covenants were "standard master-planned community boilerplate" and referred me to Wayne S. Hyatt, the Atlanta lawyer who was the principal author of them. Hyatt specializes in master-planned governments; he is, in effect, the "framer" of Celebration's constitution, which he has described in speeches to professional groups as "progressive," part of a "shift from people and property management to building community."

69   Only after I cited specific articles of the covenants did Hyatt acknowledge that Disney would indeed retain a veto over the homeowners' association indefinitely and that this was unusual. "The residents can still make decisions, but the veto stays with the developer," he said. I asked him if he saw any contradiction between the goal of building community and the fact that Disney planned to keep that community's representative body on a short and permanent leash.

70   "Not at all," he replied. "This will result in more progressive governance: you can't change things arbitrarily to my detriment, and I can't change things arbitrarily to your detriment. It's a system of checks and balances. This is not a dictatorial Disney. This is a participatory Disney."

71   For many residents, it is precisely Disney's participation that attracted them to Celebration in the first place. Most people I met expressed complete confidence in Disney's ability to run the town just as well as it runs its other enterprises. "Who's going to do a better job of it?" a prospective homeowner I met at the visitors' center asked me. "The *homeowners?* Come on!" Lise Juneman said: "Disney gives me a sense of security. They will insure a quality product, and keep property values up."

72   Somewhat sheepishly, I started asking everybody I met if they felt they were living in a democracy. To a great extent, the answers I got depended on where a resident stood on the school issue. Predictably, school critics did not feel they were living in a democracy; the far more numerous "positive parents" did. But what was striking was that the two groups held entirely different conceptions of what a democracy is. Critics like Rosemary Cordingley and Joseph Palacios described democracy in terms of power and voting, rights and self-rule, the traditional copybook maxims learned in elementary school.

73   The "positives" spoke with equal fervor of something more . . . well, neo. "It is definitely a democracy," Margo Schwartz said, "because we can go to town hall and express our feelings. It's a very responsive government."

74   Tom Lewis said, "Democracy is being listened to, so I'd say it's clearly a democracy." Charlie Rogers, a Rotarian who heads up the Sun Trust Bank branch in town, told me: "Everyone's input is welcome. Disney's doing an excellent job of staying in the background. Behind the scenes they're doing a lot, and while they have to control things, I think they really want to step back."

75   It may be Disney's boldest innovation at Celebration to have established a rather novel form of democracy, one that is based on consumerist, rather than republican, principles. For many of the people I met at Celebration, the measure of democracy is not self-rule but responsiveness—they're prepared to surrender power over their lives to a corporation as long as that corporation remains sensitive to their needs. This is the streamlined, focus-grouped responsiveness of elected government—which for many Americans was discredited a long time ago. Of course, the consumerist democracy holds only as long as the interests of the corporation and the consumer are one. So far, this has largely been the case, if only because all the community's "stakeholders" have dedicated themselves to the proposition of maintaining high property values—which is one way, I suppose, to define the public interest.

76   Todd Hill's answer to my question about democracy was slightly different than his neighbors' and, befitting his general post-modern slant on life, completely without illusion and undefensive. "This is no democracy, I know that. But, hey," he shrugged, "it's the 90s." Hill sees no necessary connection between community, which he cherishes, and self-rule, which is . . . old.

77   Maybe Hill is right. Maybe Disney has developed a new kind of community for the 90s, one that has been shorn of politics and transformed into a commodity—something people buy and consume rather than produce, an amenity rather than an achievement. Certainly Celebration is, as many residents noted, an "apolitical" place. Mention the word "politics" to people here, and they will talk about "divisiveness"; for in this view, politics is the enemy of community, rather than its natural expression.

78   I put this idea to Daniel Kemmis, who served until recently as the Mayor of Missoula, Mont. (population 88,520), and is the author of two books about community and place. "I don't believe you can create genuine community in the absence of self-government," he said. "Community finally depends on people taking responsibility for their own lives and the place where they live. That's a messy, troublesome—and also deeply satisfying—process."

79   "The interesting question here is, What will people do with the civic skills they're apt to acquire in this community? My guess is they will put them to political use—that there will be building pressure for the people to have more of a say."

80   Kemmis hasn't been to Celebration, but he may be onto something. For Disney seems to have set in motion two powerful forces that are bound sooner

or later to collide. They have built a most impressive landscape of community—a place expressly designed to encourage neighbors to engage one another, to form associations and acquire the "civic virtues"—yet they have built it atop a subsoil of authoritarianism, which limits participation to only the most trivial matters of that community's business.

81   Why would Disney do two such contradictory things—undercut the very community it has worked so hard to create? Tocqueville suggested an answer 150 years ago when he pointed out that "civil associations . . . facilitate political association" by teaching people the "strength that they may acquire by uniting together."

82   It may be that the very same contraption that produces neo-Rotarians like Todd Hill will eventually produce political activists, too.

83   If Disney truly believed in its benign, post-political vision of community—as an end in itself, as something that confines its energies to block parties and rotary meetings—it would never have bothered to make everyone in it sign such an onerous constitution. But Disney, who is nothing if not an astute observer of the American character, understands that sooner or later the people of Celebration will find their political voice, and when they do they're likely to make a mess of the company's carefully crafted script.

84   In a future history of the town of Celebration, the skirmish over the schools may well mark the beginning of that process. Certainly the episode has been a political education. "A real town has a voting process," Rosemary Cordingley said, "but this place is run by Disney. Could it ever change? There might have to be an uprising first." For now, people like Cordingley are keeping their heads down. "Last year was traumatic," she explained. There's talk among residents of an informal "moratorium on bad press." But politics could rear its head again at any time.

85   No doubt the school crisis has been an education for Disney, too. Brian Haas, who is generally supportive of the company, believes that "Disney has learned a lesson—that this isn't just selling someone on a theme park. You're playing with people's lives." That's one lesson. Another is that a community of citizens is a lot more difficult to control than a community of employees or tourists, especially when those citizens have access to the microphones of national publicity. Robert Stern mentioned that the company has been "amazed" by the amount of attention, good and bad, its City on a Hill has received, and is now "mindful of the fact its name will forever be linked with Celebration." To a degree Disney couldn't have foreseen, it has tied its good corporate name to the destiny of this town—and therefore to the deeds and words of people like Roger Burton, Rosemary Cordingley and Joseph Palacios. For a company like Disney to suddenly find itself in such an environment—volatile and, despite heroic efforts, ultimately unscriptable—must be disconcerting, to say the very least.

86   When I first visited Celebration early in 1996, before any people had moved in, there was enthusiastic off-the-record talk among executives of rolling

Disney towns out nationally. Not anymore: Celebration is an experiment the company has decided it won't repeat.

87   Indeed, there are signs, subtle but unmistakable, that the company would like nothing better than to put a little distance between itself and its unruly new community. Early in the fall, a crew of workers climbed the fake water tower at the entrance to Celebration and took down a banner proclaiming "Disney's Town of Celebration." Now there are just the words "Town of Celebration." It got people talking, so in last month's newsletter, Brent Herrington wrote an item aimed at dispelling the rumor "that Disney may be 'pulling out of Celebration.'" There's nothing to it, Disney's sort-of Mayor wrote; the company has merely been "eager for the public to begin recognizing Celebration as a real, thriving community with its own unique identity."

EXERCISES

Some of the Issues

1. What do the Rotarians signify for Pollan? Why is he surprised to find that some of them look like him?
2. What existed on the land before Celebration was built (paragraph 2)? According to Pollan, why did Disney build Celebration?
3. Why is the refrain "not just a housing development but a community" so important? What is Pollan's reaction to this idea? What is your response to it?
4. To what planning movement is Celebration connected (paragraph 4)? Based on your understanding of Celebration, what do you understand to be the principles behind this movement?
5. In paragraph 7, Pollan raises two key questions. Reflecting on both Pollan's article and your experiences, what is your response to these questions?
6. Why does the architect Robert A.M. Stern say, "The street is the key to everything else we're trying to accomplish here"(paragraph 10)? What is the significance of the street in Celebration?
7. What does Pollan have to say about the level of diversity in Celebration?
8. Pollan describes Celebration as connected to "a very old utopian idea" (paragraph 15)? How does he relate this idea to the history of planned communities?
9. What makes Celebration look less than real for Pollan? What would it take for a place to look or seem "real" to you?
10. Why does Pollan point out that residents of Celebration need to drive to Orlando for work (paragraph 35)? Does this in some ways contradict the goals of the town? Why or why not?
11. Summarize the controversy over the school in Celebration. Why does Pollan use the school as an example?
12. Why does Pollan say that "shopping" is not a bad metaphor for what residents can do at the town hall? How does shopping become a theme in other parts of the article?

13. What does Pollan predict will happen in Celebration? Do you agree or disagree? Why or why not?
14. What is Pollan's view of Celebration as a place to live? Find specific examples where he indicates his view, either directly or indirectly.

The Way We Are Told

15. What research methods did Pollan use in order to gain information about Celebration? Does the information and background he provides seem sufficient?
16. Make a list of the people Pollan interviewed for the article. Why do you suppose he chose these subjects? In your opinion, do these subjects help provide a well-rounded view of what's happening in the town?
17. What words or terms does Pollan repeat throughout the essay? Why does he repeat them?

Some Subjects for Writing

18. How are communities formed? To what extent can a community be constructed through city ordinances, marketing, and design? Using your own current community or the community in which you grew up as an example (this could include your current university community), write an essay examining the ways in which the physical space works to help or hinder the sense of community there. Are there other factors that might account for the way the area functions as a community?
19. One of the planners of Celebration, Robert A.M. Stern, makes the claim that towns or cities require a degree of regimentation and order to function properly (paragraph 63). Some view the degree of order at Celebration as overbearing and perhaps anti-democratic. Think of your college or university as a kind of town and analyze how it functions in terms of the degree of order or regulation. What kinds of rules and regulations exist? In your mind, are these rules necessary to create order, or do they impinge on people's freedom? You might choose to focus on a specific place, such as the dorms, or a specific issue, such as the amount of required courses.
*20. Compare the town Geraldine Brooks describes in "Unplugged" with the town of Celebration. How do these two places differ as communities? To what factors do you attribute the difference? Use specific examples from both texts to back up your answer.

Class Poem

Aurora Levins Morales

Aurora Levins Morales was born in 1954 in Indiera Baja, Puerto Rico, the daughter of an American Jewish father and a Puerto Rican mother, both Communists. She came to the United States at the age of thirteen. Much of her work focuses on the many strands that, woven together, make up her identity. This poem originally appeared in Getting Home Alive *(1986), a book of poetry she coauthored with her mother, Rosario Morales. Her latest book is* Remedies: Stories of Earth and Iron from the History of Puertoriqueñas *(1998).*

The author currently lives in the San Francisco Bay Area where she works as a teacher, writer, and performer.

This is my poem in celebration of my middle class privilege
This is my poem to say out loud
I'm glad I had food, and shelter, and shoes,
glad I had books and travel, glad there was air and light
5   and room for poetry.

This poem is for Tita, my best friend
who played in the dirt with me
and married at eighteen (which was late) and who was a scientist
but instead she bore six children   and four of them died
10   Who wanted to know the exact location of color
in the hibiscus petal, and patiently peeled away the thinnest,
most translucent layers to find it
and who works in a douche bag factory in Maricao.

This poem is for the hunger of my mother
15   discovering books at thirteen in the New York Public Library
who taught me to read when I was five
and when we lived on a coffee farm
subscribed to a mail-order library,
who read the Blackwell's catalogue
20   like a menu of delights
and when we moved from Puerto Rico to the States
we packed 100 boxes of books and 40 of everything else.

This poem is for my father's immigrant Jewish family.
For my great-grandfather Abe Sackman

25   who worked in Bridgeport making nurse's uniforms
and came home only on weekends, for years, and who painted
on bits of old wooden crates, with housepaint,
birds and flowers for his great-grandchildren
and scenes of his old-country childhood.

30   This poem celebrates my father the scientist
who left the microscope within reach,
with whom I discovered the pomegranate eye of the fruitfly,
and yes, the exact location of color in a leaf.

This poem celebrates my brother the artist
35   who began to draw when he was two,
and so my parents bought him reams of paper
and when he used them up, bought him more,
and today it's a silkscreen workshop
and posters that travel around the world,
40   and I'm glad for him   and for Pop with his housepaints
and Tita staining the cement with crushed flowers
searching for color
and my mother shutting out the cries of her first-born
ten minutes at a time
45   to sketch the roofs and elevated tracks
in red-brown pastels.

This is for Norma
who died of parasites in her stomach when she was four
I remember because her mother wailed her name
50   screaming and sobbing
one whole afternoon in the road in front of our school
and for Angélica
who caught on fire while stealing kerosene for her family
and died in pain
55   because the hospital she was finally taken to
knew she was poor
and would not give her the oxygen she needed to live
but wrapped her in greased sheets
so that she suffocated.

60   This is a poem against the wrapped sheets,
against guilt.

This is a poem to say:
my choosing to suffer gives nothing

to Tita and Norma and Angélica
65   and that not to use the tongue, the self-confidence, the training
my privilege bought me
is to die again for people who are already dead
and who wanted to live.

And in case anyone here confuses the paraphernalia
70   with the thing itself
let me add that I lived with rats and termites
no carpet   no stereo   no TV
that the bath came in buckets and was heated on the stove
that I read by kerosene lamp and had Sears mail-order clothes
75   and that that has nothing to do
with the fact of my privilege.

Understand, I know exactly what I got: protection and choice
and I am through apologizing.
I am going to strip apology from my voice
80   my posture
my apartment
my clothing
my dreams
because the voice that says the only true puertorican
85   is a dead or dying puertorican
is the enemy's voice—
the voice that says
"How can you let yourself shine when Tita, when millions
are daily suffocating in those greased sheets . . ."
90   I refuse to join them there.
I will not suffocate.
I will not hold back.
Yes, I had books and food and shelter and medicine
and I intend to survive.

EXERCISES

Some of the Issues

1. Morales begins her poem by saying that she will be grateful "out loud" for her middle-class privilege. Why do you think it may have been difficult in the past for her to say some of the things she now says publicly?
2. In her poem, Morales celebrates several persons who have contributed to her life by deed or by example. How and why are they important to her?

3. In line 61 Morales mentions guilt. Why would anyone expect her to feel guilty? In Morales's view, or in your own, is there anything to be gained from feeling guilt?
4. What does Morales mean when she writes "in case anyone here confuses the paraphernalia with the thing itself" (lines 69–70)?
5. What is the "enemy's" voice in the last stanza of the poem? Why does she refuse to listen to it?
6. What are the possible meanings of the title?

Some Subjects for Writing

7. Write an essay (or a poem) in which you celebrate some aspect of your identity. You can even begin with the line "This essay is in celebration of . . ."
8. Who has influenced you in determining the values you now hold? Write about one or more persons whose ideas and/or actions have played an important role in your life. Be sure to cite specific actions or to quote things people have said.
9. Morales talks about a turning point in the way she views her experience—she is through apologizing. Was there a moment in your life when you changed the way you viewed things? What was the change? How did it change you?

PART VIII

COMMUNICATING

How do we communicate? The first answer that is likely to come to most people's minds is through language: we speak, we listen, we read, we write. When we think further, we become increasingly aware that we also communicate in nonverbal ways, through gestures and other visual images. Increasingly, advances in technology—videos, faxes, E-mail, cell phones, voice mail, etc.— have in some ways decreased the necessity of personal, physical contact and have changed the ways in which our messages are relayed. On the other hand, the internet and E-mail can allow us to share intimate details of our lives almost instantaneously with people we would otherwise never interact with in real life. These changes in communication also raise questions about the influence of technology on culture itself. Do changes in communication bring us closer to understanding each other or do they threaten to erode our cultural differences? Or both?

In general, communication is rarely a simple or straightforward endeavor. An obvious example might be if you speak only English and the person you wish to talk to speaks only Japanese. Communication will be limited—although you might be able to understand to some extent by means of gestures. But often the complexities are more subtle. With speakers of the same language, problems may be the result of dialectal or intracultural differences, that is, language distinctions between subgroups. Gloria Naylor, in the first selection, alerts the reader to one such example concerning the use of an incendiary word that takes on different meanings within the African-American community.

Amy Tan, in "Mother Tongue," talks about the effect of growing up in a world of mixed languages, including her mother's ungrammatical but richly expressive Chinese-influenced English. Tan's first attempts as a fiction writer used a stiff and formal style completely unlike the speech she had heard around her. Her real career as a novelist begins when she takes advantage of all the Englishes she grew up with and writes with her mother as the imagined audience.

In "Lost in Translation," Eva Hoffman feels the pain of nostalgia as she remembers the friends she left in Poland and the sense of strangeness and discomfort with her dual identity. She struggles with what language to write in, the Polish of her past, which for her is becoming a "dead" language, or the English of her present. In the end she chooses English. Ian Buruma takes on the issue of languages that are literally dying out or disappearing from the world, and challenges some of the ideas of the "ecolinguists," linguists who equate the preservation of languages with the preservation of the environment and living species. Buruma concludes that language evolves and that we limit ourselves by taking an overly-preservationist view of languages.

The next three essays turn our eyes toward the media. Jack G. Shaheen analyzes the media's one-sided view of Arabs, who he claims are usually viewed stereotypically as oil sheiks or terrorists and seldom as real people. Alexis Bloom explores what happens when foreign television comes to Bhutan, a country that has prided itself on its isolation from the rest of the world. She looks not only at the television's impact on people's interests and attitudes in Bhutan, but also proposes that it might influence how the Bhutanese communicate with one another through stories. She points out that as "sitcoms and action films become more popular, this transmission becomes more fragile." In "Do Ask, Do Tell," Joshua Gamson describes daytime television talk shows, one of the few platforms for the discussion of the lives of gay and lesbians by gays and lesbians themselves. He concludes that, despite the exploitative nature of some of these shows, they do more good than harm in shaping public attitudes toward sexual orientation.

In the poem that ends the book, Lisel Mueller shows us how the words we use and the stories we tell shape our lives.

The Meaning of a Word

Gloria Naylor

Gloria Naylor, a native of New York City, was born in 1950 and educated at Brooklyn College and Yale. She has taught at George Washington, New York, and Boston universities. Her first novel, The Women of Brewster Place *(1982), won an American Book Award. Since then she has written* Linden Hills *(1985),* Mama Day *(1988),* Bailey's Cafe *(1992), and* The Men of Brewster Place *(1998). She is also the editor of* Children of the Night: The Best Short Stories by Black Writers 1967 to the Present *(1996). The essay included here appeared in* The New York Times *on February 20, 1986.*

The word whose meaning Naylor learned was nigger. *She explains that she had heard it used quite comfortably by friends and relatives, but the way it was uttered to her by a white child in school was so different that she at first did not realize that it was the same word.*

1   Language is the subject. It is the written form with which I've managed to keep the wolf away from the door and, in diaries, to keep my sanity. In spite of this, I consider the written word inferior to the spoken, and much of the frustration experienced by novelists is the awareness that whatever we manage to capture in even the most transcendent passages falls far short of the richness of life. Dialogue achieves its power in the dynamics of a fleeting moment of sight, sound, smell and touch.

2   I'm not going to enter the debate here about whether it is language that shapes reality or vice versa. That battle is doomed to be waged whenever we seek intermittent reprieve from the chicken and egg dispute. I will simply take the position that the spoken word, like the written word, amounts to a nonsensical arrangement of sounds or letters without a consensus that assigns "meaning." And building from the meanings of what we hear, we order reality. Words themselves are innocuous; it is the consensus that gives them true power.

3   I remember the first time I heard the word nigger. In my third-grade class, our math tests were being passed down the rows, and as I handed the papers to a little boy in back of me, I remarked that once again he had received a much lower mark than I did. He snatched his test from me and spit out that word. Had he called me a nymphomaniac or a necrophiliac, I couldn't have been more puzzled. I didn't know what a nigger was, but I knew that whatever it meant, it was something he shouldn't have called me. This was verified when I raised my hand, and in a loud voice repeated what he had said and watched the teacher

scold him for using a "bad" word. I was later to go home and ask the inevitable question that every black parent must face—"Mommy, what does 'nigger' mean?"

4   And what exactly did it mean? Thinking back, I realize that this could not have been the first time the word was used in my presence. I was part of a large extended family that had migrated from the rural South after World War II and formed a close-knit network that gravitated around my maternal grandparents. Their ground-floor apartment in one of the buildings they owned in Harlem was a weekend mecca for my immediate family, along with countless aunts, uncles and cousins who brought along assorted friends. It was a bustling and open house with assorted neighbors and tenants popping in and out to exchange bits of gossip, pick up an old quarrel or referee the ongoing checkers game in which my grandmother cheated shamelessly. They were all there to let down their hair and put up their feet after a week of labor in the factories, laundries and shipyards of New York.

5   Amid the clamor, which could reach deafening proportions—two or three conversations going on simultaneously, punctuated by the sound of a baby's crying somewhere in the back rooms or out on the street—there was still a rigid set of rules about what was said and how. Older children were sent out of the living room when it was time to get into the juicy details about "you-know-who" up on the third floor who had gone and gotten herself "p-r-e-g-n-a-n-t!" But my parents, knowing that I could spell well beyond my years, always demanded that I follow the others out to play. Beyond sexual misconduct and death, everything else was considered harmless for our young ears. And so among the anecdotes of the triumphs and disappointments in the various workings of their lives, the word nigger was used in my presence, but it was set within contexts and inflections that caused it to register in my mind as something else.

6   In the singular, the word was always applied to a man who had distinguished himself in some situation that brought their approval for his strength, intelligence or drive:

7   "Did Johnny *really* do that?"

8   "I'm telling you, that nigger pulled in $6,000 of overtime last year. Said he got enough for a down payment on a house."

9   When used with a possessive adjective by a woman—"my nigger"—it became a term of endearment for husband or boyfriend. But it could be more than just a term applied to a man. In their mouths it became the pure essence of manhood—a disembodied force that channeled their past history of struggle and present survival against the odds into a victorious statement of being: "Yeah, that old foreman found out quick enough—you don't mess with a nigger."

10   In the plural, it became a description of some group within the community that have overstepped the bounds of decency as my family defined it: Parents who neglected their children, a drunken couple who fought in public, people who simply refused to look for work, those with excessively dirty mouths or unkempt households were all "trifling niggers." This particular circle could

forgive hard times, unemployment, the occasional bout of depression—they had gone through all of that themselves—but the unforgivable sin was a lack of self-respect.

11   A woman could never be a "nigger" in the singular, with its connotation of confirming worth. The noun girl was its closest equivalent in that sense, but only when used in direct address and regardless of the gender doing the addressing. "Girl" was a token of respect for a woman. The one-syllable word was drawn out to sound like three in recognition of the extra ounce of wit, nerve or daring that the woman had shown in the situation under discussion.

12   "G-i-r-l, stop. You mean you said that to his face?"

13   But if the word was used in a third-person reference or shortened so that it almost snapped out of my mouth, it always involved some element of communal disapproval. And age became an important factor in these exchanges. It was only between individuals of the same generation, or from an older person to a younger (but never the other way around), that "girl" would be considered a compliment.

14   I don't agree with the argument that use of the word nigger at this social stratum of the black community was an internalization of racism. The dynamics were the exact opposite: the people in my grandmother's living room took a word that whites used to signify worthlessness or degradation and rendered it impotent. Gathering there together, they transformed "nigger" to signify the varied and complex human beings they knew themselves to be. If the word was to disappear totally from the mouths of even the most liberal of white society, no one in that room was naïve enough to believe it would disappear from white minds. Meeting the word head-on, they proved it had absolutely nothing to do with the way they were determined to live their lives.

15   So there must have been dozens of times that the word "nigger" was spoken in front of me before I reached the third grade. But I didn't "hear" it until it was said by a small pair of lips that had already learned it could be a way to humiliate me. That was the word I went home and asked my mother about. And since she knew that I had to grow up in America, she took me in her lap and explained.

EXERCISES

Some of the Issues

1. What reasons does Naylor give for considering the spoken word superior to the written? Do you agree or disagree?
2. Reread paragraph 2. What, according to Naylor, gives meaning to words? Do you agree or disagree?
3. In paragraph 3 the author tells a story from her experience as a child. How does it relate to the general statement on language that she made in the first two paragraphs? What is it that made Naylor think that she had been called a "bad" word?

4. At the end of paragraph 5 and in the examples that follow Naylor demonstrates that she had heard the word "nigger" before the boy in her class used it. Why did the previous uses register with her as something different?

The Way We Are Told

5. Naylor starts with a general statement—"Language is the subject"—which she then expands on in paragraphs 1 and 2. What focus does this beginning give her essay? How would the focus differ if she started with the anecdote in paragraph 3?
6. Naylor asserts that "the written word is inferior to the spoken." What devices does she use to help the reader *hear* the dialogue?
7. The essay consists of three parts: paragraphs 1 and 2, 3–13, and 14 and 15. The first is a general statement and the second an anecdote followed by records of conversations. How does the third part relate to the preceding two?

Some Subjects for Writing

8. Many words differ in their meaning depending on the circumstances in which they are used. Write a brief essay on the different words applied to a particular nationality or ethnic group and explain their impact.
*9. "Sticks and stones may break my bones but words can never hurt me." Do you have any experiences that would either confirm or deny the truth of that saying? You may also want to read Countee Cullen's poem "Incident."
10. Do you think teachers should set limits on language permitted in the classroom? Why or why not?

Mother Tongue

Amy Tan

Amy Tan was born in Oakland, California, in 1952, two years after her parents came to the United States from China.

Amy Tan's literary career was not planned—she first began writing fiction as a form of self-therapy. Considered a workaholic by her friends, Tan had been working 90 hours a week as a freelance technical writer; she hoped to eradicate her tendency to overwork by instead immersing herself in fiction writing. Her first efforts were stories, one of which secured her a place in a fiction writers' workshop. Tan's first novel, the semi-autobiographical The Joy Luck Club, *was published in 1989 and made into a very successful film. It tells the story of the lives of four Chinese women and their American daughters in California.*

Amy Tan's writing focuses on the lives of Chinese-American women; her novels introduce characters who are ambivalent, as she once was, about their Chinese background. Tan remarked in an interview that though she once tried to distance herself from her ethnicity, writing The Joy Luck Club *helped her discover "how very Chinese I was. And how much had stayed with me that I had tried to deny."*

Tan has since written three other novels, The Kitchen God's Wife *(1991),* The Hundred Secret Senses *(1996), and* The Bone Setter's Daughter *(2001).*

1 I am not a scholar of English or literature. I cannot give you much more than personal opinions on the English language and its variations in this country or others.

2 I am a writer. And by that definition, I am someone who has always loved language. I am fascinated by language in daily life. I spend a great deal of my time thinking about the power of language—the way it can evoke an emotion, a visual image, a complex idea, or a simple truth. Language is the tool of my trade. And I use them all—all the Englishes I grew up with.

Recently, I was made keenly aware of the different Englishes I do use. I was giving a talk to a large group of people, the same talk I had already given to half a dozen other groups. The nature of the talk was about my writing, my life, and my book, *The Joy Luck Club.* The talk was going along well enough, until I remembered one major difference that made the whole talk sound wrong. My mother was in the room. And it was perhaps the first time she had heard me give a lengthy speech, using the kind of English I have never used with her. I was saying things like, "The intersection of memory upon imagination" and "There is an aspect of my fiction that relates to thus-and-thus"—a speech filled with carefully wrought grammatical phrases, burdened, it suddenly seemed to me, with nominalized forms, past perfect tenses, conditional phrases, all the forms of standard English that I had learned in school and through books, the forms of English I did not use at home with my mother.

4   Just last week, I was walking down the street with my mother, and I again found myself conscious of the English I was using, the English I do use with her. We were talking about the price of new and used furniture and I heard myself saying this: "Not waste money that way." My husband was with us as well, and he didn't notice any switch in my English. And then I realized why. It's because over the twenty years we've been together I've often used that same kind of English with him, and sometimes he even uses it with me. It has become our language of intimacy, a different sort of English that relates to family talk, the language I grew up with.

5   So you'll have some idea of what this family talk I heard sounds like, I'll quote what my mother said during a recent conversation which I videotaped and then transcribed. During this conversation, my mother was talking about a political gangster in Shanghai who had the same last name as her family's, Du, and how the gangster in his early years wanted to be adopted by her family, which was rich by comparison. Later, the gangster became more powerful, far richer than my mother's family, and one day showed up at my mother's wedding to pay his respects. Here's what she said in part:

6   "Du Yusong having business like fruit stand. Like off the street kind. He is Du like Du Zong—but not Tsung-ming Island people. The local people call putong, the river east side, he belong to that side local people. That man want to ask Du Zong father take him in like become own family. Du Zong father wasn't look down on him, but didn't take seriously, until that man big like become a mafia. Now important person, very hard to inviting him. Chinese way, came only to show respect, don't stay for dinner. Respect for making big celebration, he shows up. Mean gives lots of respect. Chinese custom. Chinese social life that way. If too important won't have to stay too long. He come to my wedding. I didn't see, I heard it. I gone to boy's side, they have YMCA dinner. Chinese age I was nineteen."

7   You should know that my mother's expressive command of English belies how much she actually understands. She reads the *Forbes* report, listens to *Wall Street Week*, converses daily with her stockbroker, reads all of Shirley MacLaine's books with ease—all kinds of things I can't begin to understand. Yet some of my friends tell me they understand 50 percent of what my mother says. Some say they understand 80 to 90 percent. Some say they understand none of it, as if she were speaking pure Chinese. But to me, my mother's English is perfectly clear, perfectly natural. It's my mother tongue. Her language, as I hear it, is vivid, direct, full of observation and imagery. That was the language that helped shape the way I saw things, expressed things, made sense of the world.

8   Lately, I've been giving more thought to the kind of English my mother speaks. Like others, I have described it to people as "broken" or "fractured" English. But I wince when I say that. It has always bothered me that I can think of no way to describe it other than "broken," as if it were damaged and needed to be fixed, as if it lacked a certain wholeness and soundness. I've heard other terms used, "limited English," for example. But they seem just as bad, as if everything is limited, including people's perceptions of the limited English speaker.

9   I know this for a fact, because when I was growing up, my mother's "limited" English limited my perception of her. I was ashamed of her English. I believed that her English reflected the quality of what she had to say. That is, because she expressed them imperfectly her thoughts were imperfect. And I had plenty of empirical evidence to support me: the fact that people in department stores, at banks, and at restaurants did not take her seriously, did not give her good service, pretended not to understand her, or even acted as if they did not hear her.

10   My mother has long realized the limitations of her English as well. When I was fifteen, she used to have me call people on the phone to pretend I was she. In this guise, I was forced to ask for information or even to complain and yell at people who had been rude to her. One time it was a call to her stockbroker in New York. She had cashed out her small portfolio and it just so happened we were going to go to New York the next week, our very first trip outside California. I had to get on the phone and say in an adolescent voice that was not very convincing, "This is Mrs. Tan."

11   And my mother was standing in the back whispering loudly, "Why he don't send me check, already two weeks late. So mad he lie to me, losing me money."

12   And then I said in perfect English, "Yes, I'm getting rather concerned. You had agreed to send the check two weeks ago, but it hasn't arrived."

13   Then she began to talk more loudly. "What he want, I come to New York tell him front of his boss, you cheating me?" And I was trying to calm her down, make her be quiet, while telling the stockbroker, "I can't tolerate any more excuses. If I don't receive the check immediately, I am going to have to speak to your manager when I'm in New York next week." And sure enough, the following week there we were in front of this astonished stockbroker, and I was sitting there red-faced and quiet, and my mother, the real Mrs. Tan, was shouting at his boss in her impeccable broken English.

14   We used a similar routine just five days ago, for a situation that was far less humorous. My mother had gone to the hospital for an appointment, to find out about a benign brain tumor a CAT scan had revealed a month ago. She said she had spoken very good English, her best English, no mistakes. Still, she said, the hospital did not apologize when they said they had lost the CAT scan and she had come for nothing. She said they did not seem to have any sympathy when she told them she was anxious to know the exact diagnosis, since her husband and son had both died of brain tumors. She said they would not give

her any more information until the next time and she would have to make another appointment for that. So she said she would not leave until the doctor called her daughter. She wouldn't budge. And when the doctor finally called her daughter, me, who spoke in perfect English—lo and behold—we had assurances the CAT scan would be found, promises that a conference call on Monday would be held, and apologies for any suffering my mother had gone through for a most regrettable mistake.

15   I think my mother's English almost had an effect on limiting my possibilities in life as well. Sociologists and linguists probably will tell you that a person's developing language skills are more influenced by peers. But I do think that the language spoken in the family, especially in immigrant families which are more insular, plays a large role in shaping the language of the child. And I believe that it affected my results on achievement tests, IQ tests, and the SAT. While my English skills were never judged as poor, compared to math, English could not be considered my strong suit. In grade school I did moderately well, getting perhaps B's, sometimes B-pluses, in English and scoring perhaps in the sixtieth or seventieth percentile on achievement tests. But those scores were not good enough to override the opinion that my true abilities lay in math and science, because in those areas I achieved A's and scored in the ninetieth percentile or higher.

16   This was understandable. Math is precise; there is only one correct answer. Whereas, for me at least, the answers on English tests were always a judgment call, a matter of opinion and personal experience. Those tests were constructed around items like fill-in-the-blank sentence completion, such as, "Even though Tom was _____, Mary thought he was _____." And the correct answer always seemed to be the most bland combinations of thoughts, for example, "Even though Tom was shy, Mary thought he was charming," with the grammatical structure "even though" limiting the correct answer to some sort of semantic opposites, so you wouldn't get answers like, "Even though Tom was foolish, Mary thought he was ridiculous." Well, according to my mother, there were very few limitations as to what Tom could have been and what Mary might have thought of him. So I never did well on tests like that.

17   The same was true with word analogies, pairs of words in which you were supposed to find some sort of logical, semantic relationship—for example, "*Sunset* is to *nightfall* as _____ is to _____." And here you would be presented with a list of four possible pairs, one of which showed the same kind of relationship: *red* is to *stoplight, bus* is to *arrival, chills* is to *fever, yawn* is to *boring.* Well, I could never think that way. I knew what the tests were asking, but I could not block out of my mind the images already created by the first pair, "*sunset* is to *nightfall*"—and I would see a burst of colors against a darkening sky, the moon rising, the lowering of a curtain of stars. And all the other pairs of words—red, bus, stoplight, boring—just threw up a mass of confusing images, making it impossible for me to sort out something as logical as saying: "A sunset precedes nightfall" is the same as "a chill precedes a fever." The only way I would have

gotten that answer right would have been to imagine an associative situation, for example, my being disobedient and staying out past sunset, catching a chill at night, which turns into feverish pneumonia as punishment, which indeed did happen to me.

18   I have been thinking about all this lately, about my mother's English, about achievement tests. Because lately I've been asked, as a writer, why there are not more Asian Americans represented in American literature. Why are there few Asian Americans enrolled in creative writing programs? Why do so many Chinese students go into engineering? Well, these are broad sociological questions I can't begin to answer. But I have noticed in surveys—in fact, just last week— that Asian students, as a whole, always do significantly better on math achievement tests than in English. And this makes me think that there are other Asian-American students whose English spoken in the home might also be described as "broken" or "limited." And perhaps they also have teachers who are steering them away from writing and into math and science, which is what happened to me.

19   Fortunately, I happen to be rebellious in nature and enjoy the challenge of disproving assumptions made about me. I became an English major my first year in college, after being enrolled as pre-med. I started writing nonfiction as a freelancer the week after I was told by my former boss that writing was my worst skill and I should hone my talents toward account management.

20   But it wasn't until 1985 that I finally began to write fiction. And at first I wrote using what I thought to be wittily crafted sentences, sentences that would finally prove I had mastery over the English language. Here's an example from the first draft of a story that later made its way into *The Joy Luck Club*, but without this line: "That was my mental quandary in its nascent state." A terrible line, which I can barely pronounce.

21   Fortunately, for reasons I won't get into today, I later decided I should envision a reader for the stories I would write. And the reader I decided upon was my mother, because these were stories about mothers. So with this reader in mind—and in fact she did read my early drafts—I began to write stories using all the Englishes I grew up with: the English I spoke to my mother, which for lack of a better term might be described as "simple"; the English she used with me, which for lack of a better term might be described as "broken"; my translation of her Chinese, which could certainly be described as "watered down"; and what I imagined to be her translation of her Chinese if she could speak in perfect English, her internal language, and for that I sought to preserve the essence, but neither an English nor a Chinese structure. I wanted to capture what language ability tests can never reveal: her intent, her passion, her imagery, the rhythms of her speech and the nature of her thoughts.

22   Apart from what any critic had to say about my writing, I knew I had succeeded where it counted when my mother finished reading my book and gave me her verdict: "So easy to read."

EXERCISES

Some of the Issues

1. What are some possible meanings of the title of Tan's essay?
2. In paragraph 3, how does Tan describe the language used in the speech she made?
3. In paragraph 6, Tan gives us a sample of her mother's speech transcribed from a videotape. Rewrite the paragraph in a more standard from of English. What changes did you need to make? Did you have any difficulty understanding what her mother meant?
4. Why, in paragraphs 8 and 9, does Tan object to the terms "broken" or "fractured" or "limited" English?
5. As a child, how did Tan view her mother's "limited" English (paragraph 9)? What evidence does Tan present that her childhood perception was false?
6. On two occasions, Tan's mother asks her daughter to speak on her behalf— the incident with the stockbroker (paragraphs 10–13) and the more recent incident at the hospital (paragraph 14). Describe each incident. Why are they significant?
7. In paragraphs 15 through 17 Tan talks about how growing up in a family that did not have complete control of English may have affected her ability to do well on standardized English tests. What are the examples she cites of typical questions on those tests? Do you think other imaginative people, even if they did not grow up in an immigrant family, might have trouble with such questions?
8. In paragraph 18, Tan states that she and many other Asian-Americans select, or are guided toward, careers in which mastery of language is less important than skills in math or science. What, according to Tan, are the consequences of this?
9. What were the steps in Tan's own development as a writer (paragraphs 19–22).

The Way We Are Told

10. Tan begins her essay by telling you about herself—her limitations and her interests. What does she gain by doing this?
11. Tan uses quotations at several points in the essay to illustrate both her mother's language and her own. Find several of these quotations and indicate how they help support Tan's ideas about the different Englishes she understands and uses.
12. Why does Amy Tan's mother have the last word in the essay?
13. Writing teachers have probably talked to you about the importance of imagining a reader or an audience when you write. Who does Tan say was the imagined audience for her novel? Who is the audience for this essay?

Some Subjects for Writing

14. Describe an experience in which you felt either very limited or particularly effective when speaking or writing. For example, you could describe a time you took a test and forgot everything you studied because of nervousness or a time in which you managed to explain your ideas or feelings particularly well to a friend.

15. Tan talks about the challenge of disproving early negative assumptions about her abilities as a writer. Write an essay explaining a time in which you, or someone you know, managed to succeed despite others' predictions of failure.

16. Tan tells in paragraphs 2 and 21 of her attempts to use "all the Englishes [she] grew up with." Even if we do not grow up in a bilingual family, as Tan did, we all use several versions of English, depending on audience and situations. For example, we probably use a more relaxed vocabulary and more incomplete sentences when talking with friends about a subject we know well than when we are giving a presentation in class.

    Spend some time listening to your own speech and that of others in various settings. Keep a small notebook with you to jot down what you hear as accurately as possible, or use a tape recorder. Then write up your observations in a short paper.

17. Tan cites evidence that Asian-American students often major in math, science, or engineering, even when they have talents in other areas. Find out if this is the case at your university and, if possible, interview several students about their choices of majors. You could also study sources in the library that would give you information about choice of professions by different ethnic groups. Write the results of what you have found out in a short paper, citing the sources of your information.

Lost in Translation

Eva Hoffman

Eva (Ewa) Hoffman was born in Cracow, Poland, in 1945. In 1959 her family emigrated from postwar Poland to Canada. As an adult she has taught literature and written on a variety of cultural subjects. She is the author of a memoir, Lost in Translation, A Life in a New Language *(1989), a book about eastern Europe,* Exit into History *(1994), and most recently,* Shtetl: The Life and Death of a Small Town *and* The World of Polish Jews *(1997). In this excerpt from* Lost in Translation, *she describes the anguish of an adolescent with a bicultural identity growing up in the suburbs of Vancouver.*

1 The car is full of my new friends, or at least the crowd that has more or less accepted me as one of their own, the odd "greener" tag-along. They're as lively as a group of puppies, jostling each other with sharp elbows, crawling over each other to change seats, and expressing their well-being and amiability by trying to outshout each other. It's Saturday night, or rather Saturday Night, and party spirits are obligatory. We're on our way to the local White Spot, an early Canadian version of McDonald's, where we'll engage in the barbarous—as far as I'm concerned—rite of the "drive-in." This activity of sitting in your car in a large parking lot, and having sloppy, big hamburgers brought to you on a tray, accompanied by greasy french fries bounding out of their cardboard containers, mustard, spilly catsup, and sickly smelling relish, seems to fill these peers of mine with warm, monkeyish, groupy comfort. It fills me with a finicky distaste. I feel my lips tighten into an unaccustomed thinness—which, in turn, fills me with a small dislike for myself.

2 "Come on, foreign student, cheer up," one of the boys sporting a flowery Hawaiian shirt and a crew cut tells me, poking me in the ribs good-naturedly. "What's the matter, don't you like it here?" So as the car caroms off, I try to get in the mood. I try to giggle coyly as the girls exchange insinuating glances—though usually my titter comes a telling second too late. I try to join in the general hilarity, as somebody tells the latest elephant joke. Then—it's always a mistake to try too hard—I decide to show my goodwill by telling a joke myself. Finding some interruption in which to insert my uncertain voice, I launch into a translation of some slightly off-color anecdote I'd heard my father tell in Polish, no doubt hoping to get points for being risqué as well as a good sport. But as I hear my choked-up voice straining to assert itself, as I hear myself missing every beat and rhythm that would say "funny" and "punch line," I feel a hot flush of embarrassment. I come to a lame ending. There's a silence. "I suppose that's supposed to be funny," somebody says. I recede into the car seat.

3   Ah, the humiliation, the misery of failing to amuse! The incident is as rankling to my amour propre[1] as being told I'm graceless or ugly. Telling a joke is like doing a linguistic pirouette. If you fall flat, it means not only that you don't have the wherewithal to do it well but also that you have misjudged your own skill, that you are fool enough to undertake something you can't finish—and that lack of self-control or self-knowledge is a lack of grace.

4   But these days, it takes all my will to impose any control on the words that emerge from me. I have to form entire sentences before uttering them; otherwise, I too easily get lost in the middle. My speech, I sense, sounds monotonous, deliberate, heavy—an aural mask that doesn't become me or express me at all. This willed self-control is the opposite of real mastery, which comes from a trust in your own verbal powers and allows for a free streaming of speech, for those bursts of spontaneity, the quickness of response that can rise into pleasure and overflow in humor. Laughter is the lightning rod of play, the eroticism of conversation; for now, I've lost the ability to make the sparks fly.

5   I've never been prim before, but that's how I am seen by my new peers. I don't try to tell jokes too often, I don't know the slang, I have no cool repartee. I love language too much to maul its beats, and my pride is too quick to risk the incomprehension that greets such forays. I become a very serious young person, missing the registers of wit and irony in my speech, though my mind sees ironies everywhere.

6   If primness is a small recoil of distaste at things that give others simple and hearty pleasure, then prim is what I'm really becoming. Although I'm not brave enough or hermit enough to stay home by myself every night, I'm a pretend teenager among the real stuff. There's too much in this car I don't like; I don't like the blue eye shadow on Cindy's eyelids, or the grease on Chuck's hair, or the way the car zooms off with a screech and then slows down as everyone plays we're-afraid-of-the-policeman. I don't like the way they laugh. I don't care for their "ugly" jokes, or their five-hundred-pound canary jokes, or their pickle jokes, or their elephant jokes either. And most of all, I hate having to pretend.

7   Perhaps the extra knot that strangles my voice is rage. I am enraged at the false persona I'm being stuffed into, as into some clumsy and overblown astronaut suit. I'm enraged at my adolescent friends because they can't see through the guise, can't recognize the light-footed dancer I really am. They only see this elephantine creature who too often sounds as if she's making pronouncements.

8   It will take years before I pick and choose, from the Babel[2] of American language, the style of wit that fits. It will take years of practice before its nuances and patterns snap smartly into the synapses of my brain so they can generate

[1]Self-respect.
[2]Unintelligible language. In the Biblical story, the inhabitants of Babel attempt to build a tower to reach heaven. God frustrates their attempt by confusing the languages of the builders.

verbal electricity. It will take years of observing the discreet sufferings of the corporate classes before I understand the equally discreet charm of *New Yorker* cartoons.

9   For now, when I come across a *New Yorker* issue, I stare at the drawings of well-heeled people expressing some dissatisfaction with their condition as yet another demonstration of the weirdness all around me. "What's funny about that?" my mother asks in puzzlement. "I don't know," I answer, and we both shrug and shake our heads. And, as the car veers through Vancouver's neatly shrubberied and sparsely populated streets, I know that, among my other faculties, I've lost my sense of humor. I am not about to convert my adolescent friends to anti-Russian jokes. I swallow my injury, and giggle falsely at the five-hundred-pound canary.

10   Happy as larks, we lurch toward the White Spot.

11   If you had stayed there, your hair would have been straight, and you would have worn a barrette on one side.

12   But maybe by now you would have grown it into a ponytail? Like the ones you saw on those sexy faces in the magazine you used to read?

13   I don't know. You would have been fifteen by now. Different from thirteen.

14   You would be going to the movies with Zbyszek, and maybe to a café after, where you would meet a group of friends and talk late into the night.

15   But maybe you would be having problems with Mother and Father. They wouldn't like your staying out late.

16   That would have been fun. Normal. Oh God, to be a young person trying to get away from her parents.

17   But you can't do that. You have to take care of them. Besides, with whom would you go out here? One of these churlish boys who play spin the bottle? You've become more serious than you used to be.

18   What jokes are your friends in Cracow exchanging? I can't imagine. What's Basia doing? Maybe she's beginning to act. Doing exactly what she wanted. She must be having fun.

19   But you might have become more serious even there.

20   Possible.

21   But you would have been different, very different.

22   No question.

23   And you prefer her, the Cracow Ewa.

24   Yes, I prefer her. But I can't be her. I'm losing track of her. In a few years, I'll have no idea what her hairdo would have been like.

25   But she's more real, anyway.

26   Yes, she's the real one.

27   For my birthday, Penny gives me a diary, complete with a little lock and key to keep what I write from the eyes of all intruders. It is that little lock—the visible symbol of the privacy in which the diary is meant to exist—that creates my

dilemma. If I am indeed to write something entirely for myself, in what language do I write? Several times, I open the diary and close it again. I can't decide. Writing in Polish at this point would be a little like resorting to Latin or ancient Greek—an eccentric thing to do in a diary, in which you're supposed to set down your most immediate experiences and unpremeditated thoughts in the most unmediated language. Polish is becoming a dead language, the language of the untranslatable past. But writing for nobody's eyes in English? That's like doing a school exercise, or performing in front of yourself, a slightly perverse act of self-voyeurism.

28   Because I have to choose something, I finally choose English. If I'm to write about the present, I have to write in the language of the present, even if it's not the language of the self. As a result, the diary becomes surely one of the more impersonal exercises of that sort produced by an adolescent girl. These are no sentimental effusions of rejected love, eruptions of familial anger, or consoling broodings about death. English is not the language of such emotions. Instead, I set down my reflections on the ugliness of wrestling; on the elegance of Mozart, and on how Dostoyevsky puts me in mind of El Greco. I write down Thoughts. I Write.

29   There is a certain pathos to this naïve snobbery, for the diary is an earnest attempt to create a part of my persona that I imagine I would have grown into in Polish. In the solitude of this most private act, I write, in my public language, in order to update what might have been my other self. The diary is about me and not about me at all. But on one level, it allows me to make the first jump. I learn English through writing, and, in turn, writing gives me a written self. Refracted through the double distance of English and writing, this self—my English self—becomes oddly objective; more than anything, it perceives. It exists more easily in the abstract sphere of thoughts and observations than in the world. For a while, this impersonal self, this cultural negative capability, becomes the truest thing about me. When I write, I have a real existence that is proper to the activity of writing—an existence that takes place midway between me and the sphere of artifice, art, pure language. This language is beginning to invent another me. However, I discover something odd. It seems that when I write (or, for that matter, think) in English, I am unable to use the word "I." I do not go as far as the schizophrenic "she"—but I am driven, as by a compulsion, to the double, the Siamese-twin "you."

EXERCISES

Some of the Issues

1. With what details does the author describe the "barbarous" Saturday Night at the White Spot? (paragraphs 1 and 2)?

*2. Compare Hoffman's voice in the joke-telling (paragraph 2) with Maxine Hong Kingston's voice in the school recitation in "Girlhood among

Ghosts" (paragraph 27). What stands out in each author's memory of voice?

3. What is Hoffman's definition of *prim* in paragraph 6? What do you think is the underlying reason for her primness?
4. In paragraph 8, what does Hoffman say is the key to understanding the humor in *New Yorker* cartoons? What can you infer about the author's appreciation of the cartoons today?
5. In what way does the little lock on her diary create a dilemma (paragraph 27)?
6. Describe Hoffman's "English self" (paragraph 29). How does that persona contrast with her "real self" (paragraphs 25 and 26)?
*7. What does Hoffman mean when she says she created herself through writing? You may want to read Lisel Mueller's poem "Why We Tell Stories" for another view of creating one's life through words.

The Way We Are Told

8. What analogy does the author use in paragraph 3 to describe telling a joke? Explain the comparison.
9. In paragraphs 11 through 26, there is a sudden shift in diction and in audience. What effect does this shift achieve?

Some Subjects for Writing

10. In this excerpt, Hoffman is nostalgic for her teenage friends in Cracow. Have you ever experienced a longing to go back to an earlier time or place? Describe a sound, a place, a smell, or a memory of a person that evokes nostalgic feelings for you.
11. Recount an experience from your adolescence and show what it revealed about your developing sense of self.

The Road to Babel

Ian Buruma

Ian Buruma begins this complex essay by describing an incident in his native Dutch province of Friesland, where a controversy erupts over language: Should Frisian, the old (and perhaps dying) language of Friesland be used as an official language for government business? Or, is it an outdated relic that will eventually be replaced by a more widely spoken language like Dutch or English?

Many linguists have turned their attention to languages that are in danger of dying out. In this essay, Buruma challenges what he sees as the overly narrow view of those "ecolinguists," who equate the extinction of a language with the extinction of a species or ecosystem. Buruma acknowledges the importance of language in preserving cultural heritage, and strongly asserts that a culture in which local languages are wiped out in favor of one homogenized "metropolitan" language would be, to him, "a fearful thing." But, he argues, attempting to preserve languages that people no longer speak, or attempting to guard a language from changes brought by outside influence, is an exercise in fruitless nostalgia. He ultimately argues for a pluralist view of language, where people use different languages for different purposes.

Buruma was born in Holland, a country where people commonly speak more than one language. In keeping with some of the examples he cites in this essay, he writes in English, which is not his native tongue. Buruma is best known for his writings on Asia and has authored several books on various aspects of Asian culture. He is also a prolific contributor to a variety of magazines and newspapers, including the London Times, The New York Times, *and* The New York Review of Books, *where this essay originally appeared.*

1.

1   In 1951 there was a riot in the northern Dutch province of Friesland. It was not much of a riot, really, but the reasons for it, and the consequences, were interesting. The trouble started when a judge refused to hear the testimony of a local veterinarian in Frisian. The judge couldn't understand Frisian, an old Germanic language related to Dutch, German, and English, and in any case Dutch was the official language of public affairs in Friesland. So the judge, though perhaps a little tactless, was within his rights.

2   Things were stirred up, however, by the editor of a local newspaper named Fedde Schurer, who wrote a scorching attack against the judge, comparing him to the "Saxon gang" which invaded Friesland from Germany at the end of the

fifteenth century. Schurer was prosecuted for contempt of court. A mob gathered in protest in the central square of Leeuwarden, the provincial capital. Schurer was carried around on the shoulders of his supporters. The police charged with truncheons; the fire brigade pulled out the water hoses. Schurer, the people's hero, fell through a glass window and scratched his arm. The national press began to pay attention. Metropolitan arrogance was condemned. And as a result, Frisian was recognized in 1956 as a language that could be used in the courts for the first time since the sixteenth century, when Friesland became a province of the Dutch Republic.

3   The idea for Frisian as a kind of national language was, like so much else, a product of nineteenth-century Romanticism. It had not been used in government, schools, or churches for hundreds of years. But in the late 1800s, folk poets emerged to promote the native tongue. The first Bible translation was only completed in the 1940s. Teaching the language in primary schools has been permitted since 1937 and in higher education since 1980. About 400,000 people now know Frisian—that is to say, about half the people in Friesland have at least a passive knowledge of it. You can hear it spoken on radio stations. This revival has come as a reaction against uniformity of standard Dutch, an assertion of local identity, rather like Welsh, Irish, or Catalan.

4   There is a price to pay for too much regional chauvinism. At least all Frisians are educated in Dutch. But the Catalans[1] are so keen to defend their language that Castillian Spanish[2] is often neglected; some even prefer to learn English. As a result, Barcelona is in danger of becoming a more provincial city than it should be, isolated in a linguistic fog.

5   My paternal grandfather spoke Frisian at home. Be he moved to Amsterdam to study theology, a common intellectual pursuit among gifted provincials. My father does not speak a word of Frisian. All that is left of our Frisian heritage is our name; a perverse pride in the fact that twelve hundred years ago Frisians murdered an eighty-year-old English priest named Boniface who had no business converting natives to the Roman faith; and the imperfect mastery of one sentence in Frisian, used during the old struggles against the Saxon gang, when a legendary hero named Big Pier swung his club with devastating effect. It was a password meant to weed out alien infiltrators. It goes, in English translation: "Butter, bread, and green cheese, if you can't say that, you're not a real Fries" (*Bûter, brea en griene tsiis, wa't dat net sizze kin is gjin oprjochte Fries*).

6   One of the main attractions of the native tongue, or dialect, or slang, indeed the main reason for reviving or inventing one, is the fact that outsiders don't get it. In a sense the entire language is a kind of password. If you understand, you pass.

[1]People who live in the northeast of Spain and speak their own regional language.
[2]The official language of Spain.

From a strictly regional point of view, my father and I have lost an "identity." We don't get it anymore either, we don't pass, in Friesland. That is the way of the world. Once you head for the metropole, mud of the old soil does not stick to your boots for long. I can still speak and write in Dutch, but make a living by writing in English, my mother's language. For me the metropole has shifted even farther afield than Amsterdam. This is hardly unusual either. I am just one in a crowd of Bengalis, Chinese, Germans, Cubans, Russians, Belgians, Poles, and whatnot who have gone the same route.

7   Whether we like it or not, North America has become, in a linguistic sense, the metropole of the world; the rest is periphery, even though almost a billion people—15 percent of the world's population—speak Mandarin Chinese, and 266 million speak Spanish. English is the lingua franca[3] of international business, pop music, computer technology, airline travel, and much else besides. The French don't like it, but English is now the main language spoken in meetings of the European Commission in Brussels. English is the language of Hollywood movies, the common currency of world-wide entertainment. And in more and more countries, English is becoming the language of science and higher education too, replacing Latin as the lingua franca of learning.

8   A Dutch minister of education seriously suggested some years ago that English should be the language of instruction at all Dutch universities. The idea is not new. An education minister of the Meiji government in nineteenth-century Japan had a similar, though more radical suggestion: only after English had replaced Japanese as the national language would Japan become a modern and civilized nation. His idea did not bear fruit. But as for Holland, another former Dutch minister of education recently told me he was convinced that English would be the nation's primary language in two or three generations. If he is right, Dutch will go the way of Frisian, a badge of nostalgic identity, but nothing more than that. And the danger, in that event, would be that the Dutch would become like Singaporeans, proficient in several languages, masters of none. And where the Dutch go, others might follow.

9   The domination of a metropolitan language, whether Dutch, English, Castilian, or Chinese, can indeed be a fearful thing. Identities are threatened. But in fact mastery of the native language is often a password even in the metropole itself. I am convinced that my maternal grandfather, the son of an immigrant, and thus more British than the British, deliberately mispronounced his French, lest he be mistaken for a foreigner. So language is clearly a sensitive issue; and yet I believe the fears are often misplaced, and, when they are manipulated for political ends, sinister.

10   Some are so worried about the domination of English that they use such phrases as "killer language," as though English were a kind of epidemic disease

---

[3]A common language.

striking all people dumb in their own languages. The pathological terminology is no coincidence. Those who speak of killer languages, and deplore the extinction of Mbabaran in Australia or Wappo in the American West, also use terms such as "biolinguistic diversity" and link the survival of languages to larger ecological concerns: the disappearance of the rain forests, animal life, and rare flora. Native habitats, ecolinguistics claim, sometimes with good reason, are ruined by "biological waves" of Europeans and Americans crashing through the dense but fragile world of tribes and small peoples. Experts say there are still about six thousand languages spoken of which only about six hundred are expected to survive very long.

11   Guardians of more robust languages, such as the members of the French Academy,[4] worry less about extinction than pollution. Words such as *le weekend* or *le fax* make them ill. And if you think Franglais[5] is bad, take note of Japanese, which absorbs a huge mangled vocabulary from English, as it did before from Chinese, and even Portuguese and Dutch. A strike is a *suto*, from *sutoraiki*; to quit a health-threatening habit is to make a *dokuta sutoppu* (doctor's stop); to sexually harass is to commit *seku-hara*. A personal computer is a *paso-kon*, a golfing handicap a *hande*, and so on. Creative linguistic pilfering is easy to do in Japanese, for a new verb can be created by simply sticking the verb ending *ru* at the end of any borrowed phrase, as in, say, *makuru*, to eat a McDonald's hamburger—*maku*, short for *Makudonarudo*, and *ru*. (The equivalent in French, by the way, is *bouffer un macdo*.) The interesting thing is that the Japanese, like my British grandfather, are notoriously bad at learning foreign languages, partly, I believe, for xenophobic reasons, as though paralyzed by the thought that speaking a foreign language too well would sully the purity of one's Japaneseness.

12   Keeping a language pure of outside influences is always a losing battle, for no language was ever pure in the first place. Old English was changed enormously by Norman French, but Old English was itself a mixture of Frisian, Anglian, and various Saxon dialects. The Japanese writer Tanizaki Junichiro once promoted the idea that only pure Japanese, stripped clean of Chinese loanwords, would be fine enough to convey the deepest literary expressions. Since almost 60 percent of the Japanese language consists of Chinese loanwords, this was an impractical suggestion. But he made it in the 1930s, a time of overheated nationalism, and such drives toward purification are invariably inspired more by political than literary concerns.

13   The French have been worried about Anglo-Saxon pollution for a long time. Charles Maurras, a gifted prose stylist and a poisonous philosopher who founded the ultra-right Action Française, was a grumpy spectator at the first modern Olympic Games in Athens in 1896. He was particularly incensed by the

---

[4]A society of French intellectuals who want to preserve the French language.
[5]A combination of French and English.

sound of English spoken around him, especially American English, that "disgusting patois." Indeed, he thought international sports were a bad thing, for they infected the world with noxious Anglo-Saxon expressions. Maurras, a great defender of French classical purity, took a biological view of things, just like the ecolinguists. English was rootless, cosmopolitan, and infectious, like a disease. Naturally, he was a raving anti-Semite too.

14   Flemish Belgians have waged a long battle against foreign pollution, except that in their case the linguistic enemy is French, the language of the Walloons,[6] who used to be richer and more powerful than the Flemish speakers. Flemish, a dialect of Dutch, was full of French words, just as English is, but for political reasons official Flemish pedagogues did their best to find Dutch equivalents for every French loanword. The results are rich in comic absurdity, at least to the Dutch ear. Helicopter thus becomes *wentelwiek*, literally "wheeling wing." The other result is that more and more Flemings refuse to learn French. And since few Walloons know Dutch, two Belgians meeting in Antwerp or Liège will often find themselves speaking in English.

15 The main danger, however, of linguistic purism is not absurdity so much as stagnation and lifelessness. The example of Singapore is a warning less against using English as the main language of instruction in a country where most people speak something else as well than against too much engineering. The former prime minister Lee Kaun Yew has been a ferocious watchdog in this regard, trying to ban Chinese dialects in public life, or issuing public warnings against using Sino-Malay slang while speaking English. One reason so many Singaporeans cannot speak any language really well is their self-consciousness. Forced to speak an affected 1950s BBC English in public, they lapse into a looser, slangier hybrid tongue called Singlish in private, almost as though to spite the stern headmaster. Too stiff or too slangy—neither is likely to produce great literature.

16   Singaporean BBC English is not the only example of a model frozen in time. Filipino newspapers still use American journalese of the 1930s—"Prexie nixes solons"[7] and the Indian English-language press can still read like the prewar *Manchester Guardian*. In fact, of course, BBC English as a model of how the Queen's language should be spoken no longer exists. British radio and television announcers speak in a variety of regional accents, encouraged since the 1960s, when dialect became cool. And standard English has become something known as Thames Estuary, after the eastern suburbs of London and beyond. It is a nasal, almost whining, southern middle-class English with shades of cockney. Tony Blair tends to lapse into it. Mick Jagger has spoken a *faux*-cockney version for years. Even the Queen's speech last Christmas bore traces of it.

---

[6]French-speaking people of central and southern Belgium.
[7]Slang for "President vetoes legislation."

17   In any case English, as a lingua franca of business, information technology, and entertainment, will continue to creep into other languages, just as French used to do, or German, Chinese, Sanskrit, Arabic, and Persian. English is also mutating into professional dialects that consist of nothing but jargon. Inside the institutions of the European Union, something one might call Brussels English is taking shape with its own peculiar jargon and even spelling. Airline pilots across the globe converse in an English that is comprehensible only to themselves. In some cases, it is the only English they know. This has been known to cause problems in emergencies. It is one of the reasons Japan Airlines started hiring foreign pilots.

2.

18   Jargon English is ugly, but hardly a mortal threat to the continued existence of other major languages. And even where English, mostly by reason of imperial conquest, has become a main language, the effect on native identities is by no means as clear-cut as some people suppose, or fear. India is one obvious example. English is the common language of Indian elites and the government. It is in fact the only truly national language of all India, even though it is spoken only by about 5 percent of the population. Indeed, the modern sense of Indian nationhood found one of its first and most eloquent expressions in English, in the writings of Nehru.[8] English was the language of the colonial masters, but also of many nationalists who fought for independence. And English is the language of some of the finest Indian writers today, not just those who write nostalgically from London or New York, but Indians living in Delhi, Calcutta, and Bombay.

19   To be sure, Nehru and others wanted to make Hindi into the national language. But they chose a rather artificial form of Hindi, heavily encrusted with archaic terms borrowed from Sanskrit. Some of the main proponents of this national language were not native Hindi speakers but Hindu intellectuals from Gujarat and Bengal. And in the south Hindi was not spoken at all. So it never really took hold. And few people wish to revive it, even though there are proponents of a more popular Hindi, as an official alternative to English. They have not gotten very far either.

20   The problem was put well by a south Indian, whose article, in English, was plucked by a friend of mine from the Internet. The author, named Rajeev Srinivasan, is a native speaker of Malayalam, the language of Kerala, about which he has all the Romantic sentiments of a nineteenth-century idealist. He writes: "As someone who is completely bilingual in English and Malayalam, I can say with certainty that for me, Malayalam is the language of the heart, and English of the head." Neither Hindi, nor English, he continues, could possibly express the

[8]First prime minister of independent India.

"distinct Malayali ethos, with its melancholy, brooding ways that contrast so markedly with the exuberant, tropical landscape."

21   Then, to clinch his argument about languages of the heart and the head, he quotes a poem by Sir Walter Scott:

> Breathes there the man, with soul so dead,
> Who never to himself hath said,
>   This is my own, my native land!

But even if Sir Walter Scott's words can only appeal to his head, Rajeev Srinivasan still prefers English to Hindi, for at least English connects you to the wider world, not to mention the World Wide Web, whereas Hindi would make Malayalam speakers feel like second-class citizens. Hindi, he says, is "a conquering language." The language of one old empire, then, can be useful in staving off the advances of another.

22   There are examples elsewhere of the same phenomenon. The people of East Timor,[9] whose common language now is Indonesian, or Bahassa Indonesian, wish to have another national language. The only one they can think of is Portuguese. Meanwhile, people in Irian Jaya[10] have a difficult time rising against their Indonesian masters because their many tribal languages are mutually incomprehensible. They, too, could do with a national language in their struggle for autonomy. Dutch, perhaps?

23   The Philippines is an interesting case, for it went from being a European colony to an American one. The first great Filipino novel, *Noli me tangere* by José Rizal—the bible, as it were, of Filipino identity and independence, a book drenched in modern national sentiment—was written in Spanish. More than one twentieth-century Filipino writer, expressing himself in English, has deplored the loss of Spanish as the national tongue. Some writers would like to use Tagalog. But most readers of Tagalog, mainly on the island of Luzon, prefer comic books to literary novels, however expressive of deep national sentiments. So English remains the language of the elite, and thus of most Filipino literature—though not of the movies, a more popular art.

24   Tagalog will survive for a long time, just as I expect Malayalam will. But many smaller languages continue to disappear, not all because of English. A gentleman named Tefvik Esenc, the last speaker of a Caucasian language called Ubykh, died on his farm in Turkey in 1992. Red Thundercloud, from South Carolina, ran out of people to converse with in Catawba Sioux, and died in 1996. Australia used to have 250 aboriginal languages. Soon there may be none.

---

[9]Southeast Asian territory that gained independence from Indonesia in 1999. East Timor was under Portuguese rule until 1974.

[10]Indonesian province, which was under Dutch rule for some 350 years before it gained independence in 1949.

Yiddish[11] is dying, certainly as a literary language, and Ladino[12] is almost dead. Deaths are always sad events. But I am not sure the ecolinguists always deplore these losses for the right reasons.

25   When languages die because the speakers are massacred or forced to change, this is indeed deplorable, but the ecolinguists think diversity is a good thing per se, and the loss of any language, no matter how small, and whatever the circumstances of its demise, a loss to humanity. For as Daniel Nettle and Suzanne Romaine, the authors of *Vanishing Voices* (Oxford University Press, 2000) argue: "Each language is a living museum, a monument to every culture it has been vehicle to." This is no doubt true. And living museums are fascinating for linguists and other enthusiasts. But should every living museum be preserved for its own sake? Literature may have an intrinsic value, but do spoken languages? The ecolinguists argue that they do, partly for environmental reasons. Languages, claim Nettle and Romaine, "are like the miner's canary: where languages are in danger, it is a sign of environmental distress."

26   Is this always true? The Inuit of Nunavut, formerly known as Eskimos, are indeed a threatened community, not by the Canadian government but because they are a dwindling group on the edge of the world. Their suicide rate is horrendous. But they do still speak their native language. Another expression of their identity is shooting rare Bowhead whales with .50 caliber hunting rifles. The point here is not to be facetious. The hunts are not just for the meat. They are defended on cultural grounds: shooting whales is deemed essential for the preservation of identity. This, surely, is not what the ecolinguists have in mind.

27   One reason minority languages have been threatened during the last two centuries is the rise of nationalism. France used to be a country of many languages. But the republican idea of liberty, equality, and fraternity has meant that all French citizens—and preferably the rest of the world as well—should speak French. This has been both a good and a bad thing. A common language strengthened a common sense of citizenship, which, in principle, if not always in practice, transcended race or religion. It was bad in the sense that a common language was forced on Bretons and other minorities to the detriment of their own. This was based on the fallacy that people should speak only one language, as though multilingualism should necessarily tear up the nation.

28   Nettle and Romaine say we "need to divest ourselves of the traditional equation between language, nation, and state." In fact, the word "traditional" here makes little sense. Most nation-states are not very old, and certainly not eternal. But they are right in that many languages are older than the states which adopted them. The ecolinguists prefer to think of most languages as expressions of culture, local, even tribal culture, languages of the heart, so to

---

[11]A language once spoken chiefly by Jews in Eastern Europe, which has decreased dramatically in usage since the Holocaust.

[12]Judeo-Spanish, originally spoken by Jews living in Spain. Efforts have been made to preserve both Yiddish and Ladino because of their ties to Jewish literature, poetry and music.

speak, rooted in a particular soil. The metropolitan or "global languages" on the other hand are for "communicating beyond local levels and expressing ourselves as citizens of the world"—that is, they are languages of the head.

29   This, too, is a questionable claim. German was the main language of the Austro-Hungarian Empire. More citizens of Budapest in the early twentieth century read German-language newspapers than Hungarian ones. German was presumably the language of the head. And yet some of the greatest literature and poetry to emerge from the empire was written in German by people who had not "local" Germanic roots at all. Many of them were Jews, the so-called rootless cosmopolitans, and thus perhaps the most loyal citizens of Franz Joseph's[13] realm: Kafka, Joseph Roth, Musil.

30   To equate language with the state may be wrong, but to equate it entirely with a specific local culture or common ancestry is equally wrong. Another ecolinguist, David Crystal, has a balanced view of culture and language. Language, he says, is a preeminent but not exclusive badge of identity; cultures can continue even after shifting to another language. But then, by way of assessing the catastrophic consequences of losing a language, he asks us to imagine what would have happened if Norman French had displaced Old English after 1066: no Chaucer, Shakespeare, Wordsworth, Dickens. True enough. But that is to assume that Shakespeare could only have expressed himself in English. One might as well turn this imaginary example the other way around. What if English had not displaced Irish as the main language of Ireland? No Joyce, Yeats, Wilde, Shaw. And what are we to make of Beckett, who wrote in French and English, and who, when asked whether he was British, answered *"Au contraire"*?

31   Literary genius remains a mystery. The emergence of a Nabokov or Beckett[14] cannot be rationally explained, but ancestry or nationhood surely has very little to do with it. It is generally true, of course, that you gain a feeling for the rhythm and expressiveness of a language by growing up with it, by learning nursery rhymes as a child and talking with other children at school. Literate native speakers can spot a cliché when they hear one. But none of this is essential. A Joseph Conrad can switch languages and still be great, and not because he was expressing "Polishness," let alone "Englishness."

32   When Conrad began to write his famous novels, English was the lingua franca of a great empire, but not yet of the world. Will the dominance of English produce more Conrads? One of the more interesting literary events of the last few years has been the success of Ha Jin, a Chinese writer in English. Ha was in his twenties when he came to the United States. He is perhaps no Conrad, but his prose is arresting. One of its characteristics is a kind of cultural minimalism, entirely lacking literary or cultural allusions. His novel *Waiting* was set

---

[13]Last ruler of Austro-Hungarian Empire.
[14]Nabokov, whose native language was Russian, wrote in English. Beckett, who was born in Ireland and lived in France, wrote mainly in French.

in China, so allusions connected to the English-speaking world would have looked out of place anyway. And yet one wonders whether Ha Jin's work is a harbinger of a new international English style, in which culture and language are entirely disconnected. Kazuo Ishiguro, born in Japan but raised in Britain, did not consciously switch languages (he does not speak Japanese), but he tries to avoid any allusions which can be understood only by native English speakers. He claims to write for the world. The password quality of language, in other words, is deliberately discarded.

33   The current generation of writers in English with a non-English background is living in a different world from the one inhabited by Conrad, Nabokov, or Arthur Koestler. Before World War II, writers and their readers, whether they came from London, St. Petersburg, or Budapest, still shared cultural references. Literate people had a working knowledge of the Old and New Testaments and classical mythology. There was still such a thing as European, or even Western, civilization. There is much less of that now. The common references today are both global and parochial, that is to say, they are by and large American: Hollywood, pop music, airline and computer jargon. And the consequences of this may be worse, in some respects, for Americans than for speakers of more minor languages.

34   The one big advantage of speaking Dutch or Danish, or even German or Bengali, is that one is forced to be proficient in at least one other language if one is going to function in the modern world. Even the most ardent ecolinguists do not argue for monolingualism. David Crystal speaks of "healthy bilingualism," a somewhat dubious term perhaps (the word "healthy" should be used with care), but his meaning is clear: the native tongue is about history, culture, identity, and literature, while the metropolitan language is for communicating with the wider world. The distinction can be overstated, as I said, but the ability to speak and read more than one language is surely a good thing. Reading another language allows you to understand not only what people from a different place think, but how they think. Not that thoughts or feelings are determined by language. Indeed, the more one learns to understand other languages, the more a common humanity comes into view. This does not resolve human conflict. Wars would still occur even if the whole world spoke English or Esperanto.[15] But you can only understand your own cultural, political, and social place in the world if you understand the world of others, and for that it helps to comprehend what they say.

35   In some respects, then, the metropole can be a more provincial place than the periphery. With only one language at one's disposal, even if it is the lan-

---

[15]An artificial language created in the late nineteenth century, meant to become a unifying international language.

guage of the world, others will look either very strange or deceptively similar. They speak English, eat McDonald's hamburgers, and watch Hollywood films, so they must be just like Americans. This can be as misleading as the assumption that because we cannot understand what people say, their thoughts must be foreign to us too.

36   English is the password language of an international elite, far larger in scale than French or Latin ever was. This is the result of history, of empire-building, and the power of the United States. There is nothing about the English language itself that predestined it to dominate. In some distant future, the lingua franca of business and culture could be Chinese—difficult to imagine, perhaps, but theoretically possible.

37   Millions and millions aspire to join the Anglophone elite. Perhaps one day there will be almost universal comprehension of English. But the ambition to be understood by everyone will surely be matched by an equally tenacious desire to guard one's own passwords, which cannot be so readily understood. Unlike the retired Dutch education minister, I do not expect Dutch to disappear soon as a primary language. On the contrary, I believe that the superficial uniformity of globalization will provoke the Frisian effect in many places. The Internet, which links the whole world, is seen as an imperialist bastion of English, but in fact is slowly turning into an electronic free-for-all, where people can use any language they like. Indeed the Internet is becoming a repository not just of existing languages, but of virtually extinct languages too. For it is only there, on audio links to cyberspace, that you can still hear such rare Australian Aboriginal languages as Jiwarli, whose last native speaker died in 1986. And that is why I believe that just as we cannot stop ourselves from rebuilding the Tower of Babel, it will be knocked down again and again.

EXERCISES

Some of the Issues

1. Why does Buruma begin by recounting the riot in Friesland? What caused the riot and what were its results?
2. What is the history of the Frisian language and how many people speak it now? Why, according to Buruma, has it not completely disappeared?
3. According to Buruma, what are the dangers of promoting a language spoken by only a few people in a small region (paragraph 4)?
4. How does language become a kind of "password"? Can you think of times in your experience where either you didn't know the "password" or where you did know it and other people around you didn't?
5. What does Buruma mean when he states, "Whether we like it or not, North America has become, in a linguistic sense, the metropole of the world" (paragraph 7)?

6. Who are the ecolinguists and what are their claims? What is Buruma's response to them? Use specific examples to back up your point.

7. What is "linguistic purism"? Why is it unrealistic and what does Buruma see as its main danger (paragraphs 11 through 16)?

8. How does Buruma challenge the idea that the spread of English is a threat to native identities? What examples does he use?

9. Why does Buruma find the example of the Inuit of Nunavut particularly telling (paragraph 26)?

10. What effect does Buruma feel the "superficial uniformity of globalization" (paragraph 37) will have on our attitudes toward language and identity? How does he back up his conclusion throughout the essay?

11. Give examples from the essay of ways that language can both unify and divide groups of people. In groups of three or four, compare your examples and discuss what conclusions you might draw from these examples.

*12. Both Buruma and Eva Hoffman (in "Lost in Translation") make the choice to write in English instead of their native language. What are their reasons for making that choice and how are their choices both similar and different?

The Way We Are Told

13. What kinds of evidence does Buruma use to back up his claims? How does his own experience inform his perspective?

14. What is Buruma's tone in paragraph 5 when he lists what remains of his Frisian heritage? How does the tone reflect his attitude?

15. Consider the title of the piece. How is a "road" different than a tower?

Some Subjects for Writing

16. Most of you have had the experience of learning, or trying to learn, another language. Write a narrative where you recount that experience. Was it frustrating? Satisfying? Useful? Did it offer you a "password" that you didn't have before?

17. Buruma argues that it is an advantage to be "forced" to learn another language (paragraph 34). To what extent do you agree or disagree? Write an essay in which you summarize his reasoning and give your own response to it using specific examples from both the text and your experience.

18. Write an essay in which you respond to Buruma's attitude toward language and his critique of the ecolinguists. To what extent do you agree or disagree with his perspectives? Use specific examples to back up your points.

*19. Read Eva Hoffman's "Lost in Translation." Using examples from Hoffman and other material you have read (and, if relevant, your own experience), write an essay in which you consider what might be lost and what might be gained when people stop speaking a language.

The Media's Image of Arabs

Jack G. Shaheen

Jack G. Shaheen, born in 1935, taught mass communications for many years at Southern Illinois University in Edwardsville. He has also taught at the American University in Beirut and the University of Jordan in Amman. He is the author of The TV Arab *(1984), and* Reel Bad Arabs: How Hollywood Villifies a People *(2001). This essay was written in 1992.*

Lebanon, where Shaheen's family came from, is a small country at the eastern end of the Mediterranean, bordering on Israel to the south and Syria to the east and north. Its capital, Beirut, was once known as the Paris of the Middle East, a lively, sophisticated city that was also the financial center of the region. Since that time Lebanon has been ravaged by civil war and occupation by its two neighbors.

The media's image of Arabs, Shaheen asserts, is almost invariably hostile and one-sided. It contributes to, perhaps is even responsible for, the negative stereotype Americans have of Arabs. Although this essay is several years old and was written following the events of the Gulf War, Shaheen's message has perhaps grown in importance since the attacks on the World Trade Center and the Pentagon on September 11, 2001. In a recent interview about his latest book, Shaheen asserts that the negative portrayal of Arabs "is one of the reasons why we have such a hard time separating today this lunatic fringe from the vast majority of people from that region who are pretty much like us, who want the same things we do—peace, a good education for their kids, a good time on Saturday night. As we've learned from the past with African-Americans and American Indians, when you show people as barbarians, when an act like [September 11] happens, we think all the people of the region are this way."

1   America's bogeyman is the Arab. Until the nightly news brought us TV pictures of Palestinian youth being punched and beaten, almost all portraits of Arabs seen in America were dangerously threatening. Arabs were either billionaires, bombers, bedouin bandits, belly dancers or bundles in black—rarely victims. They were hardly ever seen as ordinary people practicing law, driving taxis, singing lullabies or healing the sick. Though some TV newscasts may portray them more sympathetically now, the absence of positive media images nurtures suspicion and stereotype.

2   Historically, the Arab lacks a human face. Media images are almost invariably hostile and one-sided. They articulate to, perhaps are even responsible for, the negative stereotype Americans have of Arabs. As an Arab-American, I have found that ugly caricatures have had an enduring impact on Americans of Arab heritage. For the prejudiced, during the Gulf War, all Arabs, including some of the three million Americans with Arab roots, became to many, "camel jockeys," "ragheads" and "sandsuckers." Whenever there is a crisis in the Middle East Arab-Americans are subjected to vicious stereotyping and incidents of violence and discrimination.

3   I was sheltered from prejudicial portraits at first. My parents came from Lebanon in the 1920s; they met and married in America. Our home in the steel city of Clairton, Pennsylvania was a center for ethnic sharing—black, white, Jew and gentile. There was only one major source of screen images then, at the State movie theater where I was lucky enough to get a part-time job as an usher. But in the late 1940s, Westerns and war movies were popular, not Middle Eastern dramas. Memories of World War II were fresh, and the screen heavies were the Japanese and the Germans. True to the cliché of the times, the only good Indian was a dead Indian. But when I mimicked or mocked the bad guys, my mother cautioned me. She explained that stereotypes hurt; that they blur our vision and corrupt the imagination. "Have compassion for all people, Jackie," she said. Experience the joy of accepting people as they are, and not as they appear in films, she advised.

4   Mother was right. I can remember the Saturday afternoon when my son, Michael, who was seven, and my daughter, Michele, six, suddenly called out: "Daddy, Daddy, they've got some bad Arabs on TV." They were watching that great American morality play, TV wrestling. Akbar the Great, who liked to hear the cracking of bones, and Abdullah the Butcher, a dirty fighter who liked to inflict pain, were pinning their foes with "camel clutches." From that day on, I knew I had to try to neutralize the media caricatures.

5   I believe most researchers begin their investigations because they have strong feelings in their gut about the topic. To me, the stereotyping issue was so important I had to study it. For years I watched hordes of Arabs prowl across TV and movie screens. Yet, a vacuum existed in the literature: research on TV and movie Arabs did not exist. My research began with television because visual impressions from the tube indoctrinate the young. Once a stereotypical image becomes ingrained in a child's mind, it may never wither away.

6   Investigating television's Arabs began as a solo effort. But members of my family, friends, and colleagues assisted by calling attention to dramas I might otherwise have missed. For several years, I examined *TV Guide* and cable and satellite magazines. Daily, I searched for Arab plots and characters, then taped, studied, and categorized them. To go beyond personal observations, I interviewed more than thirty industry leaders, writers, and producers in New York and Los Angeles. In the spirit of fair-mindedness, I invited image makers, those

influential purveyors of thought and imagination, to offer sparks of decency that illuminate, rather than distort, our perception of others.

7   It hasn't been easy. Images teach youngsters whom to love, whom to hate. With my children, I have watched animated heroes Heckle and Jeckle pull the rug from under "Ali Boo-Boo, the Desert Rat," and Laverne and Shirley stop "Sheik Ha-Mean-ie" from conquering "the U.S. and the world." I have read more than 250 comic books like the "Fantastic Four" and "G.I. Combat" whose characters have sketched Arabs as "lowlifes" and "human hyenas." Negative stereotypes were everywhere. A dictionary informed my youngsters that an Arab is a "vagabond, drifter, hobo and vagrant." Whatever happened, my wife wondered, to Aladdin's[1] good genie?

8   To a child, the world is simple: good versus evil. But my children and others with Arab roots grew up without ever having seen a humane Arab on the silver screen, someone to pattern their lives after. To them, it seems easier for a camel to go through the eye of a needle than for a screen Arab to appear as a genuine human being.

9   Hollywood producers employ an instant Ali Baba[2] kit that contains scimitars, veils, sunglasses and such Arab clothing as chadors[3] and kufiyahs.[4] In the mythical "Ay-rab-land," oil wells, tents, mosques, goats and shepherds prevail. Between the sand dunes, the camera focuses on a mock-up of a palace from "Arabian Nights"—or a military air base. Recent movies suggest that Americans are at war with Arabs, forgetting the fact that out of 21 Arab nations, America is friendly with 19 of them.

10   Audiences are bombarded with rigid, repetitive and repulsive depictions that demonize and delegitimize the Arab. One reason is because since the early 1900s more than 500 feature films and scores of television programs have shaped Arab portraits.

11   I recently asked 293 secondary school teachers from five states— Massachusetts, North Carolina, Arkansas, West Virginia, and Wisconsin—to write down the names of any humane or heroic screen Arab they had seen. Five cited past portraits of Ali Baba and Sinbad; one mentioned Omar Sharif and "those Arabs" in *Lion of the Desert* and *The Wind and the Lion*. The remaining 287 teachers wrote "none."

12   Nicholas Kadi, an actor with Iraqi roots, makes his living playing terrorists in such films as the 1990 release "Navy Seals." Kadi laments that he does "little talking and a lot of threatening—threatening looks, threatening

[1]Young boy in *The Arabian Nights* who is given a magic lamp and magic ring to summon genies to fulfill all his wishes.
[2]The poor woodcutter in *The Arabian Nights* who gains entrance into the treasure cave of the forty thieves by saying the words "Open Sesame."
[3]Long black veil worn by Moslem women.
[4]Arab headdress.

gestures." On screen, he and others who play Arab villains say "America," then spit. "There are other kinds of Arabs in the world," says Kadi. "I'd like to think that some day there will be an Arab role out there for me that would be an honest portrayal."

13   The Arab remains American culture's favorite whipping boy. In his memoirs, Terrel Bell, Ronald Reagan's first secretary of education, writes about an "apparent bias among mid-level, right-wing staffers at the White House" who dismissed Arabs as "sand niggers."

14   Sadly, the racial slurs continue. Posters and bumper stickers display an Arab's skull and an atomic explosion. The tag: "Nuke their ass and take their gas."

15   At a recent teacher's conference, I met a woman from Sioux Falls, South Dakota, who told me about the persistence of discrimination. She was in the process of adopting a baby when an agency staffer warned her that the infant had a problem. When she asked whether the child was mentally ill, or physically handicapped, there was silence. Finally, the worker said: "The baby is Jordanian."

16   To me, the Arab demon of today is much like the Jewish demon of yesterday. We deplore the false portrait of Jews as a swarthy menace. Yet a similar portrait has been accepted and transferred to another group of Semites—the Arabs. Print and broadcast journalists have started to challenge this stereotype. They are now revealing more humane images of Arabs, a people who traditionally suffered from ugly myths. Others could follow that lead and retire the stereotypical Arab to a media Valhalla.[5]

17   The civil rights movement of the 1960s not only helped bring about more realistic depictions of various groups; it curbed negative images of the lazy black, the wealthy Jew, the greasy Hispanic and the corrupt Italian. These images are mercifully rare on today's screens. Conscientious imagemakers and citizens worked together to eliminate the racial mockery that had been a shameful part of the American cultural scene.

18   It would be a step in the right direction if movie and TV producers developed characters modeled after real-life Arab-Americans. We could then see a White House correspondent like Helen Thomas, whose father came from Lebanon, in "The Golden Girls," a lawyer patterned after Ralph Nader on "L.A. Law," or a Syrian-American playing tournament chess like Yasser Seirawan, the Seattle grandmaster.

19   Politicians, too, should speak out against the cardboard caricatures. They should refer to Arabs as friends, not just as moderates. And religious leaders could state that Islam, like Christianity and Judaism, maintains that all mankind is one family in the care of God. When all imagemakers rightfully begin to treat

---

[5]According to Norse mythology, the hall in which the souls of warriors who had died heroically were ensured immortality.

Arabs and all other minorities with respect and dignity, we may begin to unlearn our prejudices. The ultimate result would be an image of the Arab as neither saint nor devil, but as a fellow human being, with all the potentials and frailties that condition implies.

EXERCISES

Some of the Issues

1. What, according to the author, is the standard image of the Arab in the American media? Why is he concerned that Arabs are hardly ever portrayed as ordinary people?
2. When did Shaheen first become aware of stereotypes? Why was he not conscious of them earlier?
3. Shaheen is especially concerned about the influence of the media on his children. Why does he believe that children are particularly vulnerable to stereotypes?
4. Shaheen makes specific suggestions for changing the media image of Arabs. What are they? Do you think they would be effective?
5. In April 1995, when the federal building in Oklahoma City was bombed, killing over one hundred people, the first newspapers claimed that the suspected bombers looked "Middle Eastern." In fact, all the suspects were white Americans. What negative stereotypes would account for the false reports? What damage do such reports do?
6. Following the terrorist attacks of September 2001, there were reports of many incidents where Arab Americans, or people who were perceived to be Arab, were threatened or attacked. How might a general ignorance about Arab culture have contributed to these incidents?

The Way We Are Told

7. Cite several instances in which Shaheen supports a general assertion with specific examples drawn from his own experience.
8. Shaheen's essay concentrates on the media's treatment of Arabs, yet he mentions unfair treatment of other groups as well. What does his argument gain from this expansion?

Some Subjects for Writing

9. In an essay, describe a character in a film or TV program who belongs to a minority or disadvantaged group. In your opinion is that character presented as a stereotype, either negatively or positively? If so, what changes could be made? One way of testing your opinion is to see if the character

appears the same way to a member of the depicted group as it does to someone outside the group.

10. In another article, published in the *Los Angeles Times* in August of 1996, Shaheen criticizes depictions of Middle Easterners in several movies made for children, including Disney's *Aladdin* (1992), *The Return of Jafar* (1994), and *Kazaam* (1996). If you have seen any of these films, or can rent them, analyze the depictions of Arab characters.

*11. Fights between "good guys" and "bad guys" have always been a part of drama, fiction, movies, and television. Often the "bad guys" have been members of a group that has been historically discriminated against. Consider the depictions of Native Americans in the classic Western and what influence that might have had on attitudes toward Indian people. Furthermore, could the World War II movies in which Japanese were depicted as subhuman have had any influence on American willingness to drop two atomic bombs on Japan or to intern 100,000 Japanese-Americans (as described in selections by Jeanne Wakatsuki Houston and James D. Houston, and Dwight Okita)? Look back at Shaheen's quote in the introduction to this essay, where he refers to the events of September 11, 2001. If the media are powerful in shaping opinion, what obligation do they have to present images that will not increase prejudice? Is it enough to present minorities in a realistic way, or is it important to not present them as villains?

Switch on Bhutan

Alexis Bloom

Born in Johannesburg, South Africa in 1975, Alexis Bloom is a journalist who received her B.A. and M.A. from Cambridge University in England and a master's degree in journalism from the University of California at Berkeley. She has written for the British publications the Observer, *and the* Sunday Independent *as well as* The New York Times, *where this essay originally appeared.*

Bloom is also a documentary filmmaker and has traveled in Asia since her teens. She was intrigued when she heard in 1999 that television was coming to Bhutan, a small landlocked South Asian country that prided itself on its isolation from the cultures of most of the rest of the world, and went there to film a documentary on the phenomenon. She wrote this article based on her impressions after a four-week shoot that resulted in a short film called Switch on Bhutan.

Bhutan is a monarchy of about two million people roughly half the size of Indiana. It is bordered on the north and northwest by Tibet and India on the remainder. Bhutan is overwhelmingly rural and virtually the entire country is mountainous and about three-quarters of it is forested land.

Buddhism is Bhutan's official religion, and most aspects of life there are guided by Buddhist ethics and principles. For centuries, Bhutan followed a policy of self-imposed isolation and controlled development, with a particular focus on the preservation of its unique ancient culture, and paid little attention to the world around it. Bhutan's king, Jigme Singye Wangchuck, holds among his ideals what he has nicknamed "gross national happiness," the idea that the peaceful well being of the people is as important to a country as any economic development would be. In a speech quoted in the article, he warns the citizens of Bhutan that television can be both beneficial and harmful and cautions them to "use your good sense and judgment."

1   The impish conspirators huddle in a side street of Bhutan's capital, tearing cardboard boxes into strips. Once the strips are trimmed to size, the boys proudly hold them against their waists, like little grooms adjusting cummerbunds. With varying degrees of accuracy, they scrawl "W.W.F. Championship" across the makeshift belts.

2   "I am the Rock!" screams a child in a yellow T-shirt, grasping a pint-size opponent by the neck. "I am the champion!"

3   "I am Triple H!" his opponent squawks in reply before he's knocked to the ground.

4   Less than a mile away, boys the same age chant prayers inside a Buddhist temple. Drawing their wine-colored robes close, the monks, some as young as 5, nod and bow as the wind rattles the prayer wheels outside

5   This is still a country where rural areas look as they did in ancient times, and where, for every television antenna, a thousand prayer flags flutter. But in the villages children peer through doorways, craning to catch sight of flickering televisions. And when the young monks walk past a set, they, too, stop and stare.

6   In June 1999, from a golden podium in Bhutan's only stadium, King Jigme Singye Wangchuck welcomed the arrival of modern communications technology to his remote Buddhist kingdom, the last country in the world to legalize television. But he cautioned his citizens: "Use your good sense and judgment. Television and the Internet can be both beneficial and harmful to the individual and to society." Two years later, young Bhutanese girls learn dance steps from MTV, and the extravagant, theatrical violence of the World Wrestling Federation has unexpectedly gained a devoted audience of Buddhists.

7   "We've always been this exotic, hidden, mystical land," said Kinley Dorji, editor of the weekly Kuensel, Bhutan's only newspaper. "We've been the last Shangri-La. And suddenly you have an electronic invasion. Suddenly you have TV. And not just TV, you have 25, 30 channels. We've been pried open quite dramatically."

8   Unlike most Bhutanese, Mr. Dorji, a graduate of the Columbia School of Journalism, has ventured beyond the Himalayas. He's deeply concerned about the impact of television on what he calls "a pristine society." "We've been getting letters to the newspaper," he said. "These were letters from children who were brought up in very benign, Buddhist families. They specifically asked us about this World Wrestling Federation program. 'Why are these big men standing there hitting each other? What is the purpose of it?' The children don't understand."

9   Television is a service that just about everyone here can afford. Rinzy Dorji, Bhutan's most successful cable operator, provides 45 channels for just $5 a month—the price of a bag of dried red chilies. "We have sweepers, plumbers and people at the lowest rung of society connected to our cable line," said Rinzy Dorji (who is not related to Kinley), sitting at his desk in the office of Sigma Cable. "Even if they live in a hut or a temporary shed, they can all watch the same programs for an affordable price."

10   Customers call Mr. Dorji at home night and day; Sherub, his 15-year-old daughter, unplugs the telephones when they ring cacophonously. Demand always outstrips supply, but because of the initial cost of laying cable, Sigma Cable still runs at a loss. Mr. Dorji is one of about a half-dozen surviving cable operators; many companies, unable to make a profit, have already gone out of business.

11   Sigma's 45 channels, mostly Indian and American, include three or four Hindi movie channels, CNN, the Indian and American versions of MTV, sports

channels, Discovery, the BBC and a Chinese channel. Also included is Bhutan's only home-grown broadcast station: The Bhutan Broadcasting Society (BBS). Television was launched on the condition that the BBS provide the country with content of its own, but limited technical experience means that the BBS produces just one hour of programming a day, mostly news.

12 Surveys in Bhutan are a haphazard affair, and nobody knows exactly how many people are hooked up to cable or have satellite dishes. But owning a television set is certainly a social priority, and Rinzy Dorji estimates that within a year or so, everyone in Thimphu with a telephone connection—about 6,000 people—will also have cable television.

13 "I'm making a social contribution," Mr. Dorji said. "Children who used to do undesirable things now stay at home. Vandalism, fighting, drinking; we curb such social nuisance because most children are now glued to the TV. They don't go out as they used to."

14 Bhutan, with its policy of placing "Gross National Happiness" ahead of gross national product, is also a country where the police detain or fine adults for not wearing traditional Bhutanese dress—the knee-length gho for men, the apronlike kira for women—in public.

15 "But we'd like to wear the clothes they wear on MTV," Sherub Dorji said. "At parties we used to wear the kira, but now everybody is wearing pants. Pants and miniskirts."

16 Fortunately for Sherub's generation, the fashion police don't frequent Club X, the more long-standing of Bhutan's two discos. Young people hunch over the bar, order up Red Panda beers and potent Bhutanese gin. The sale of tobacco is prohibited in most Bhutanese provinces, but you'd never guess it from the locomotive puffing of boys with seal-slick hair. Not one person in this basement hideaway is wearing traditional clothing: leather jackets shine, halter tops are clean and pressed. And they're dancing to rock 'n' roll.

17 This is a change that Kinley Dorji laments.

18 "We have always dressed like this," he said, rubbing the heavy cloth of his robe. "But now the young people want to dress like their new heroes on television, like their favorite movie stars. A generation gap is emerging with great contrast."

19 Across the Wong Chu river, at the Center for Bhutan Studies, the only sounds are the calling of crows and the occasional rattling of a passing car. Karma Ura, the center's Oxford-educated director, studies contemporary Bhutanese culture in a traditional wooden building with a view of the Thimphu valley; it's more Swiss chalet than research center. Mr. Ura is impeccably dressed in a white-cuffed, charcoal-grey gho. Visitors to this self-styled home of Bhutanese sociology are invited to take off their shoes and don slippers sewn of local fabric.

20 "Some of us thought it was too early to introduce television into Bhutan," he said, "but we were a small minority. People argued that TV could be used to

positive effect, but I don't see much evidence of that. There is a case to be made for widening people's environment, but I see commercial television as a tool for marketing."

21   Television has undoubtedly given Bhutanese a greater understanding of the outside world: before cable, international media was limited to two-day-old newspapers from India. But with news of earthquakes and elections comes advertising. International access has a cost, Mr. Ura said, and young girls now want cosmetics. Not just any cosmetics, but the brand names they have seen on television.

22   Kinley Dorji has interviewed children about their changing habits. "They said that before they didn't know that Signal was better than Colgate," he said. "But now they do, because the television said so."

23   Mr. Ura points to the arrival of a Hallmark shop on Thimphu's main street as evidence of dramatic social change. With indignation, he says that birthdays—and the associated cards, cakes and presents—were, until now, unheard of in Bhutan. This celebration of individualism, he said, has taken root as a result of Westernization.

24   "They must reflect people's changing patterns of marking social relationships," he said. "The advent of modernization is now reinforced quite powerfully by television. And very soon you will have Christmas celebrations."

25   Bhutan strictly controls tourism: fewer than 8,000 people were granted visas to enter the country last year (still an all-time high), and each paid a fee of at least $200 a day. Officials, who use the phrase "Quality Not Quantity," fear the intrusion of foreigners. But the on-screen invaders are more ill-mannered than the trekkers. "Slowly the language of violence that's heard on TV has been introduced into everyday language," Mr. Ura said. "Language here has changed. In traditional Bhutanese society, we don't use language of violence too often— our language is highly moderated. But, that's in sharp contrast to what's available on television."

26   The Bhutanese rely heavily on spoken stories; in the style of Aesop's fables, family tales serve as vehicles for instruction in cultural values. And though they include intrigue, romance and tragedy, Mr. Ura said, very few are told for sheer entertainment. "Stories are our way of transmitting social values," he said. "Our way of showing the idealized way of living." As sitcoms and action films become more popular, this transmission becomes more fragile. "This is a society where the family depended on the grandfather's stories," Kinley Dorji said. "Suddenly this family has multiple channels to watch. I think the implication of what could happen to such a society is quite clear."

27   It's not only young people who are entranced by "Baywatch" and Hollywood films: through her pebble-thick spectacles, the wizened mother-in-law of Rinzy Dorji watches hours of television each day. Danchoe Dema says she likes the Cartoon Network, which she watches with her grandchildren. And though she doesn't understand the rules of the games shown on Rupert Murdoch's Star Sports, she says, "I see them playing, running, wrestling, having fun, and this is

entertaining." Ms. Dema confesses that amid all the excitement, she sometimes forgets to say her prayers.

EXERCISES

Some of the Issues

1. What do you think accounts for the popularity of wrestling shows in Bhutan? Does this surprise you? Why or why not?
2. Why was television illegal until 1999? Do you think there was a good reason for it? Why or why not?
3. How much programming is the local television network able to produce and why? Why is this significant?
4. Why does Rinzy Dorji see himself as making a "social contribution" (paragraph 13)? Given the current critique of television in the United States, does his statement seem strange or ironic to you?
5. How does Bloom describe the youth who frequent Club X? What do their dress and social habits indicate about changes in Bhutanese culture?
6. What do Karma Ura and Kinley Dorji see as the primary role of television? What evidence do they point to?
7. Summarize the debate between those for and against television in Bhutan.
*8. How has television influenced the language of the people of Bhutan, according to Karma Ura? Read Ian Buruma's "The Road to Babel." How might Buruma interpret this change?

The Way We Are Told

9. In paragraphs 1 through 4 Bloom contrasts two images. What implications do these contrasting images have? How do they relate to the rest of the article?
10. Bloom relies on fairly detailed descriptions. How might these descriptions help support her claims?
11. Does Bloom make a specific argument for or against having television in Bhutan? What technique does she use to present different perspectives?
12. Look at Bloom's last paragraph. Do you find it to be an effective conclusion? Why or why not?

Some Subjects for Writing

13. As an experiment, avoid watching television for five to seven days. Write a paper in which you document your experiences over these days, paying particular attention to both your changes in habits and your changes in attitude or perspectives on the world. Do you feel more or less in touch with what is going on around you?

*14. In "Unplugged," Geraldine Brooks defends her town's decision to ban the cable company. Bhutan went from having no TV to having up to 45 channels. Using these two readings along with other sources (including your experience), write an essay in which you make a claim about one possible impact of television, particularly cable television. How might television enhance or detract from people's local culture and their everyday interactions in their communities?

15. How do you interpret the policy of "placing 'Gross National Happiness' ahead of gross national product" (paragraph 14)? What implications does this policy have for Bhutan? What might it mean for such a policy to be carried out in your country? Write an essay in which you explore that possibility.

Do Ask, Do Tell

Joshua Gamson

In 1995, when this essay was written, the number and popularity of daytime "tell-all" talk shows had recently increased dramatically, with new additions to the field appearing regularly. In response to keen competition for ratings, talk shows seemed to be stretching in search of ever more provocative and controversial topics. Since this article was written, some of the shows mentioned (including the venerable Phil Donahue show, which is considered to have pioneered the format) have gone off the air. Since Gamson's article was written, there has also been an increase in portrayals of gay characters in TV series such as Will and Grace, Queer as Folk *and others, though some would argue that it is debatable whether these portrayals provide a more accurate description of gay and lesbian lives.*

The title "Do Ask, Do Tell" is a play on the Clinton Administration's policy on gays and lesbians in the military, instituted shortly after Bill Clinton's election in 1992. The "don't ask, don't tell" policy allowed gays to serve in the military as long as they stayed silent about their sexual orientation, and prohibited officers from inquiring about the sexual orientation of other service members. This policy, adopted as a compromise between gay rights advocates and those opposed to gays serving openly in the military, was a change from the former policy, which had made homosexuality grounds for immediate discharge.

Several service members have since legally challenged the policy as unconstitutional, arguing that it violates their rights to free speech and equal protection, and that there exists no evidence that shows that being gay is any impediment to serving one's country.

Joshua Gamson teaches sociology at Yale University. He is the author of Claims to Fame: Celebrity in Contemporary America *(1994) and* Freaks Talk Back: Tabloid Talk Shows and Sexual Nonconformity *(1998). This essay was first published in* The American Prospect.

1   At the end of his 22 years, when Pedro Zamora lost his capacity to speak, all sorts of people stepped into the silence created by the AIDS-related brain disease that shut him up. MTV began running a marathon of *The Real World*, its seven-kids-in-an-apartment-with-the-cameras-running show on which <u>Pedro Zamora starred as Pedro Zamora, a version of himself: openly gay, Miami Cuban, HIV-positive, youth activist.</u> MTV offered the marathon as a tribute to Zamora, which it was, and as a way to raise funds, especially crucial since Zamora, like so many people with HIV, did not have private insurance. Yet, of course, MTV was

also paying tribute to itself, capitalizing on Pedro's death without quite seeming as monstrous as all that.

2   President Clinton and Florida governor Lawton Chiles made public statements and publicized phone calls to the hospital room, praising Zamora as a heroic point of light rather than as a routinely outspoken critic of their own HIV and AIDS policies. The Clinton administration, in the midst of its clampdown on Cuban immigration, even granted visas to Zamora's three brothers and a sister in Cuba—a kindly if cynical act, given the realities of people with AIDS awaiting visas and health care in Guantánamo Bay.

3   Thus, according to *People* magazine, did Zamora reach a bittersweet ending. He was unable to see, hear, or speak, yet with his family reunited, "his dream had come true." Behind the scenes, one who was there for Zamora's last weeks told me, the family actually separated Zamora from his boyfriend—quite out of keeping with the "dreams" of Pedro's life. When Pedro had his own voice, he had spoken powerfully of how anti-gay ideology and policy, typically framed as "pro-family," contributed to teen suicides and the spread of HIV; when he died, those who spoke for him emphasized individual heroism and the triumph of the heterosexual family.

4   That others appropriated Zamora on his deathbed hardly tarnishes his accomplishment. As an MTV star, he had probably reduced suffering among lesbian and gay teenagers more, and affected their thinking more deeply, than a zillion social service programs. He spoke publicly to millions in his own words and with the backing of a reputable media institution, and he did not just tell them to wear condoms, or that AIDS is an equal-opportunity destroyer. Nor did he simply fill in the sexual blanks left by prudish government prevention campaigns. He also told them and showed them: Here is me loving my boyfriend; here is what a self-possessed gay man looks like hanging out with his roommates; here is what my Cuban family might have to say about my bringing home a black man; here is me at an AIDS demonstration, getting medical news, exchanging love vows.

5   To speak for and about yourself as a gay man or a lesbian on television, to break silences that are systematically and ubiquitously enforced in public life, is profoundly political. "Don't tell" is more than a U.S. military policy; it remains U.S. public policy, formally and informally, on sex and gender nonconformity. Sex and gender outsiders—gay men, transsexuals, lesbians, bisexuals—are constantly invited to lose their voices, or suffer the consequences (job loss, baseball bats) of using them. Outside of the occasional opening on MTV or sporadic coverage of a demonstration or a parade, if one is not Melissa Etheridge or David Geffen, opportunities to speak as a nonheterosexual, or to listen to one, are few and far between. Even if the cameras soon turn elsewhere, these moments are big breakthroughs, and they are irresistible, giddy moments for the shut up.

6   Yet, in a media culture, holding the microphone and the spotlight is a complicated sort of power, not just because people grab them back from you but be-

cause they are never really yours. If you speak, you must be prepared to be used. The voice that comes out is not quite yours: It is like listening to yourself on tape (a bit deeper, or more clipped) or to a version dubbed by your twin. It is you and it is not you. Zamora's trick, until his voice was taken, was to walk the line between talking and being dubbed. The troubling question, for the silenced and the heard alike, is whether the line is indeed walkable. Perhaps the best place to turn for answers is the main public space in which the edict to shut up is reversed: daytime television talk shows.

7   For lesbians, gay men, bisexuals, drag queens, transsexuals—and combinations thereof—watching daytime television has got to be spooky. Suddenly, there are renditions of you, chattering away in a system that otherwise ignores or steals your voice at every turn. Sally Jessy Raphael wants to know what it's like to pass as a different sex, Phil Donahue wants to support you in your battle against gay bashing, Ricki Lake wants to get you a date, Oprah Winfrey wants you to love without lying. Most of all, they all want you to talk about it publicly, just at a time when everyone else wants you not to. They are interested, if not precisely in "reality," at least not in fictional accounts. For people whose desires and identities go against the norm, this is the only spot in mainstream media culture to speak on their own terms or to hear others speaking for themselves. The fact that talk shows are so much maligned, and for so many good reasons, does not close the case.

8   The other day, I happened to tune into the *Ricki Lake Show*, the fastest-rising talk show ever. The topic: "I don't want gays around my kids." I caught the last 20 minutes of what amounted to a pro-gay screamfest. Ricki and her audience explicitly attacked a large woman who was denying visitation rights to her gay ex-husband ("I had to explain to a 9-year-old what 'gay' means"; "My child started having nightmares after he visited his father"). And they went at a young couple who believed in keeping children away from gay people on the grounds that the Bible says "homosexuals should die." The gay guests and their supporters had the last word, brought on to argue, to much audience whooping, that loving gays are a positive influence and hateful heterosexuals should stay away from children. The anti-gay guests were denounced on any number of grounds, by host, other guests, and numerous audience members: They are denying children loving influences, they are bigots, they are misinformed, they read the Bible incorrectly, they sound like Mormons, they are resentful that they have put on more weight than their exes. One suburban-looking audience member angrily addressed each "child protector" in turn, along the way coming up with a possible new pageant theme: "And as for you, Miss Homophobia . . ."

9   The show was a typical mess, with guests yelling and audiences hooting at the best one-liners about bigotry or body weight, but the virulence with which homophobia was attacked is both typical of these shows and stunning. When Lake cut off a long-sideburned man's argument that "it's a fact that the easiest way to get AIDS is by homosexual sex" ("That is not a fact, sir, that is not

correct"), I found myself ready to start the chant of "Go, Ricki! Go, Ricki!" that apparently wraps each taping. Even such elementary corrections, and even such a weird form of visibility and support, stands out sharply. Here, the homophobe is the deviant, the freak.

10   Lake's show is among the new breed of rowdy youth-oriented programs, celebrated as "rock and roll television" by veteran Geraldo Rivera and denigrated as "exploitalk" by cultural critic Neal Gabler. Their sibling shows, the older, tamer "service" programs such as *Oprah* and *Donahue*, support "alternative" sexualities and genders in quieter, but not weaker, ways. Peruse last year's *Donahue:* two teenage lesbian lovers ("Young, courageous people like yourself are blazing the way for other people," says Donahue), a gay construction worker suing his gay boss for harassment ("There's only eight states that protect sexual persuasion," his attorney reports), a bisexual minister, a black lesbian activist, and two members of the African-American theater group Pomo Afro Homos ("We're about trying to build a black gay community," says one), the stars of the gender-crossing *Priscilla, Queen of the Desert* ("I have a lot of friends that are transsexuals," declares an audience member, "and they're the neatest people"), heterosexuals whose best friends are gay, lesbians starting families, gay teens, gay cops, gay men reuniting with their high school sweethearts, a gay talk show. This is a more diverse, self-possessed, and politically outspoken group of non-heterosexuals than I might find, say, at the gay bar around the corner. I can only imagine what this means for people experiencing sexual difference where none is locally visible.

11   Certainly *Donahue* makes moves to counter its "liberal" reputation, inviting right-wing black preachers and the widely discredited "psychologist" Paul Cameron, who argues that cross-dressing preceded the fall of Rome, that people with AIDS should be quarantined, and that sexuality "is going to get us." But more often than not, Donahue himself is making statements about how "homophobia is global" and "respects no nation," how "we're beating up homosexual people, calling them names, throwing them out of apartments, jobs." The "we" being asserted is an "intolerant" population that needs to get over itself. We are, he says at times, "medieval." In fact, Donahue regularly asserts that "for an advanced, so-called industrialized nation, I think we're the worst."

12   Oprah Winfrey, the industry leader, is less concerned with the political treatment of difference; she is overwhelmingly oriented toward "honesty" and "openness," especially in interpersonal relationships. As on Lake's show, lesbians and gays are routinely included without incident in more general themes (meeting people through personal ads, fools for love, sons and daughters you never knew), and bigotry is routinely attacked. But Winfrey's distinctive mark is an attack on lies, and thus the closet comes under attack—especially the gay male closet—not just for the damage it does to those in it, but for the betrayals of women it engenders.

13   On a recent program in which a man revealed his "orientation" after 19 years of marriage, for example, both Winfrey and her audience were concerned not that Steve is gay, but that he was not honest with his wife. As Winfrey put it,

[handwritten margin notes: "Yet Don. uses the 'inclusive' which 'we,' posits still lesbians, gays, etc as outsiders"]

"For me, always the issue is how you can be more truthful in your life." One of Steve's two supportive sons echoes Winfrey ("I want people to be able to be who they are"), as does his ex-wife, whose anger is widely supported by the audience ("It makes me feel like my life has been a sham"), and the requisite psychologist ("The main thing underneath all of this is the importance of loving ourselves and being honest and authentic and real in our lives"). Being truthful, revealing secrets, learning to love oneself: These are the staples of Winfrey-style talk shows. Gay and bisexual guests find a place to speak as gays and bisexuals, and the pathology becomes not sexual "deviance" but the socially imposed closet.

14 All of this, however, should not be mistaken for dedicated friendship. Even when ideological commitments to truth and freedom are at work, the primary commitment of talk shows is, of course, to money. What makes these such inviting spots for nonconforming sex and gender identities has mostly to do with the niche talk shows have carved out for ratings. The shows are about talk; the more silence there has been on a subject, the more not-telling, the better a talk topic it is. On talk shows, as media scholar Wayne Munson points out in his book *All Talk* (Temple University Press, 1993), "differences are no longer repressed" but "become the talk show's emphasis," as the shows confront "boredom and channel clutter with constant, intensified novelty and 'reality.'" Indeed, according to Munson, Richard Mincer, *Donahue's* executive producer, encourages prospective guests "to be especially unique or different, to take advantage of rather than repress difference."

15 While they highlight different sex and gender identities, expressions, and practices, the talk shows can be a dangerous place to speak and a difficult place to get heard. With around 20 syndicated talk shows competing for audiences, shows that trade in confrontation and surprise (*Ricki Lake, Jenny Jones, Jerry Springer*) are edging out the milder, topical programs (*Oprah, Donahue*).

16 As a former *Jane Whitney Show* producer told *TV Guide*, "When you're booking guests, you're thinking, 'How much confrontation can this person provide me?' The more confrontation, the better. You want people just this side of a fistfight."

17 For members of groups already subject to violence, the visibility of television can prompt more than just a fistfight, as last year's *Jenny Jones* murder underlined. In March, when Scott Amedure appeared on a "secret admirer" episode of the *Jenny Jones Show*, the admired Jon Schmitz was apparently expecting a female admirer. Schmitz, not warming to Amedure's fantasy of tying him up in a hammock and spraying cream and champagne on his body, declared himself "100 percent heterosexual." Later, back in Michigan, he punctuated this claim by shooting Amedure with a 12-gauge shotgun, telling police that the embarrassment from the program had "eaten away" at him. Or, as he reportedly put it in his 911 call, Amedure "fucked me on national TV."

18 Critics were quick to point out that programming that creates conflict tends to exacerbate it. "The producers made professions of regret," Neal Gabler wrote in the *Los Angeles Times* after the Amedure murder, "but one suspects

what they really regretted was the killer's indecency of not having pulled out his rifle and committed the crime before their cameras." In the wake of the murder, talk show producers were likened over and over to drug dealers: Publicist Ken Maley told the *San Francisco Chronicle* that "they've got people strung out on an adrenaline rush," and "they keep raising the dosage"; sociologist Vicki Abt told *People* that "TV allows us to mainline deviance"; Michelangelo Signorile argued in *Out* that some talk show producers "are like crack dealers scouring trailer park America." True enough. Entering the unruly talk show world, one is apt to become, at best, a source of adrenaline rush, and at worst a target of violence.

19   What most reporting tended to ignore, however, was that most anti-gay violence does not require a talk show "ambush" to trigger it. Like the Oakland County, Michigan, prosecutor who argued that "*Jenny Jones*'s producers' cynical pursuit of ratings and total insensitivity to what could occur here left one person dead and Mr. Schmitz now facing life in prison," many critics focused on the "humiliating" surprise attack on Schmitz with the news that he was desired by another man. As in the image of the "straight" soldier being ogled in the shower, in this logic the revelation of same-sex desire is treated as the danger, and the desired as a victim. The talk show critics thus played to the same "don't tell" logic that makes talk shows such a necessary, if uncomfortable, refuge for some of us.

20   Although producers' pursuit of ratings is indeed, unsurprisingly, cynical and insensitive, the talk show environment is one of the very few in which the declaration of same-sex desire (and, to a lesser degree, atypical gender identity) is common, heartily defended, and often even incidental. Although they overlook this in their haste to hate trash, the critics of exploitative talk shows help illuminate the odd sort of opportunity these cacophonous settings provide. Same-sex desires become "normal" on these programs not so much because different sorts of lives become clearly visible, but because they get sucked into the spectacular whirlpool of relationship conflicts. They offer a particular kind of visibility and voice. On a recent *Ricki Lake*, it was the voice of an aggressive, screechy gay man who continually reminded viewers, between laughs at his own nasty comments, that he was a regular guy. On other days, it's the take-your-hands-off-my-woman lesbian, or the I'm-more-of-a-woman-than-you'll-ever-be transsexual. The vicious voice—shouting that we gay people can be as mean, or petty, or just plain loud, as anybody else—is the first voice talk shows promote. It's one price of entry into mainstream public visibility.

21   The guests on the talk shows seem to march in what psychologist Jeanne Heaton, co-author of *Tuning in Trouble* (Jossey-Bass, 1995), calls a "parade of pathology." Many talk shows have more than a passing resemblance to freak shows. Neal Gabler, for example, argues that guests are invited to exhibit "their deformities for attention" in a "ritual of debasement" aimed primarily at reassuring the audience of its superiority. Indeed, the evidence of dehumanization is all over the place, especially when it comes to gender crossing, as in the titles of various recent *Geraldo* programs; the calls of sideshow barkers echo in "Star-Crossed Cross-Dressers: Bizarre Stories of Transvestites and Their Lovers" and

"Outrageous Impersonators and Flamboyant Drag Queens" and "When Your Husband Wears the Dress in the Family." As long as talk shows make their bids by being, in Gabler's words, "a psychological freak show," sex and gender outsiders arguably reinforce perceptions of themselves as freaks by entering a discourse in which they may be portrayed as bizarre, outrageous, flamboyant curiosities. (Often, for example, they must relinquish their right to defend themselves to the ubiquitous talk show "experts.")

22   Talk shows do indeed trade on voyeurism, and it is no secret that those who break with sex and gender norms and fight with each other on camera help the shows win higher ratings. But there is more to the picture: the place where "freaks" talk back. It is a place where Conrad, born and living in a female body, can assert against Sally Jessy Raphael's claim that he "used and betrayed" women in order to have sex with them that women fall in love with him as a man because he considers himself a man; where months later, in a program on "our most outrageous former guests" (all gender crossers), Conrad can reappear, declare himself to have started hormone treatment, and report that the woman he allegedly "used and betrayed" has stood by him. This is a narrow opening, but an opening nonetheless, for the second voice promoted by the talk show: the proud voice of the "freak," even if the freak refuses that term. The fact that talk shows are exploitative spectacles does not negate the fact that they are also opportunities; as Munson points out, they are both spectacle and conversation. They give voice to the systematically silenced, albeit under conditions out of the speaker's control, and in tones that come out tinny, scratched, distant.

23   These voices, even when they are discounted, sometimes do more than just assert themselves. Whatever their motivations, people sometimes wind up doing more than just pulling up a chair at a noisy, crowded table. Every so often they wind up messing with sexual categories in a way that goes beyond a simple expansion of them. In addition to affirming both homosexuality and heterosexuality as normal and natural, talk show producers often make entertainment by mining the in-between: finding guests who are interesting exactly because they don't fit existing notions of "gay" and "straight" and "man" and "woman," raising the provocative suggestion that the categories are not quite working.

24   The last time I visited the *Maury Povich Show*, for instance, I found myself distracted by Jason and Tiffanie. Jason, a large 18-year-old from a small town in Ohio, was in love with Calvin. Calvin was having an affair with Jamie (Jason's twin sister, also the mother of a three-month-old), who was interested in Scott, who had sex with, as I recall, both Calvin and Tiffanie. Tiffanie, who walked on stage holding Jamie's hand, had pretty much had sex with everyone except Jamie. During group sex, Tiffanie explained, she and Jamie did not touch each other. "We're not lesbians," she loudly asserted, against the noisy protestations of some audience members.

25   The studio audience, in fact, was quick to condemn the kids, who were living together in a one-bedroom apartment with Jamie's baby. Their response was predictably accusatory: You are freaks, some people said; immoral, said others; pathetically bored and in need of a hobby, others asserted. Still other aspects of

the "discussion" assumed the validity and normality of homosexuality. Jason, who had recently attempted suicide, was told he needed therapy to help him come to terms with his sexuality, and the other boys were told they too needed to "figure themselves out." Yet much talk also struggled to attach sexual labels to an array of partnerships anarchic enough to throw all labels into disarray. "If you are not lesbians, why were you holding hands?" one woman asked Tiffanie. "If you are not gay," another audience member asked Calvin, "how is it you came to have oral sex with two young men?"

26   This mix was typically contradictory: condemnation of "immoral sex" but not so much of homosexuality per se, openly gay and bisexual teenagers speaking for themselves while their partners in homosexual activities declare heterosexual identities, a situation in which sexual categories are both assumed and up for grabs. I expect the young guests were mainly in it for the free trip to New York, and the studio audience was mainly in it for the brush with television. Yet the discussion they created, the unsettling of categorical assumptions about genders and desires, if only for a few moments in the midst of judgment and laughter, is found almost nowhere else this side of fiction.

27   The importance of these conversations, both for those who for safety must shut up about their sexual and gender identities and for those who never think about them, is certainly underestimated. The level of exploitation is certainly not. Like Pedro Zamora, one can keep one's voice for a little while, one finger on the commercial megaphone, until others inevitably step in to claim it for their own purposes. Or one can talk for show, as freak, or expert, or rowdy—limits set by the production strategies within the talk show genre.

28   Those limits, not the talk shows themselves, are really the point. The story here is not about commercial exploitation, but about just how effective the prohibition on asking and telling is in the United States, how stiff the penalties are, how unsafe this place is for people of atypical sexual and gender identities. You know you're in trouble when Sally Jessy Raphael (strained smile and forced tear behind red glasses) seems like your best bet for being heard, understood, respected, and protected. That for some of us the loopy, hollow light of talk shows seems a safe haven should give us all pause.

EXERCISES

Some of the Issues

1. What is the significance of the title of the essay?
2. What, in Gamson's view, were the benefits and drawbacks of Pedro Zamora's popularity (paragraphs 1 through 3)? How does Gamson point out the irony of Zamora's fame?
3. What does Gamson feel Zamora was able to accomplish as an MTV star (paragraph 4)?
4. What does Gamson mean when he says that the microphone and spotlight are "never really yours" (paragraph 6)?

5. For whom might watching daytime television be "spooky" (paragraph 7) and why?

6. According to Gamson, how do talk shows give more voice to gays and lesbians than other forms of media? Based on your own experience, do you agree?

7. Taking into consideration both Gamson's and your own analysis, why might talk shows be a "safe haven" for gays and lesbians?

8. What is the "primary commitment" of talk shows? What "niche" have they carved out (paragraph 14)?

9. Gamson recounts the murder of Scott Amedure in paragraphs 17–19. How does Gamson analyze the media's response to the murder? Based on Gamson's account and other knowledge you might have about the case, what are your feelings about both the incident and the media's response?

10. How do same-sex desires become "normal" on talk shows (paragraph 20), and what are the consequences of this?

11. Looking at the final paragraph, what, according to Gamson, should "give us pause"?

12. Gamson develops a complicated argument, often presenting two or more sides of the issues and examples he discusses. Working in small groups, pick a short passage that you find particularly difficult and paraphrase Gamson's words.

The Way We Are Told

13. Gamson begins by recounting and analyzing Pedro Zamora's media popularity. How do the events in Zamora's life serve as a good introduction to Gamson's article?

14. Although "Do Ask, Do Tell" is not a personal narrative, Gamson often uses the first person. Why is the author's voice or presence important to the article?

15. Gamson combines both formal and informal language. Find examples of words or passages that you would define as either formal or informal.

16. Who is the audience for this essay? On what basis do you make your conclusion?

17. Conclusions can serve different or multiple purposes: Often, they simply summarize the author's main points, highlighting important ideas. At other times, a conclusion can broaden the issue or even call into question the author's own opinions or ideas. Reread Gamson's conclusion and analyze his strategy. Why might he have chosen to end the article the way he did?

Some Subjects for Writing

18. Pick a television show you watch regularly and analyze it in terms of its treatment of gays and lesbians. To what extent does the show give voice to

diverse characters and how are the characters represented or portrayed? You may choose to compare and contrast two different shows.

19. Consider how you feel about the value and purpose of talk shows. Are they, as Neal Gabler calls them, "exploitalk," or do they serve a more important purpose? In a focused essay, present your views on the subject. Try to create, as Gamson does, an argument that takes into consideration the complexity of the issue.

20. Create a script for a talk show in which you deal with a gay or lesbian theme. Provide a description of each character, and, as you write and revise, give careful consideration to how your characters would act and respond to others on the show. In other words, try to get inside the head of each character and develop each individual voice.

Why We Tell Stories

Lisel Mueller

Lisel Mueller, who came to the United States from Germany at the age of fif-teen, is the author of several collections of poetry, as well as a volume of es-says. Her poetry collection, Alive Together: New and Selected Poems *(1996), won the Pulitzer Prize.* The Need to Hold Still *(1980), from which this poem is taken, received the National Book Award.*

For Linda Nemec Foster

1
Because we used to have leaves
and on damp days
our muscles feel a tug,
painful now, from when roots
5 pulled us into the ground

and because our children believe
they can fly, an instinct retained
from when the bones in our arms
were shaped like zithers and broke
10 neatly under their feathers

and because before we had lungs
we know how far it was to the bottom
as we floated open-eyed
like painted scarves through the scenery
15 of dreams, and because we awakened

and learned to speak

2
We sat by the fire in our caves,
and because we were poor, we made up a tale
about a treasure mountain
20 that would open only for us

and because we were always defeated,
we invented impossible riddles
only we could solve,

monsters only we could kill,
25   women who could love no one else

and because we had survived
sisters and brothers, daughters and sons,
we discovered bones that rose
from the dark earth and sang
30   as white birds in the trees

3
Because the story of our life
becomes our life

Because each of us tells
the same story
35   but tells it differently

and none of us tells it
the same way twice

Because grandmothers looking like spiders
want to enchant the children
40   and grandfathers need to convince us
what happened happened because of them

and though we listen only
haphazardly, with one ear,
we will begin our story
with the word *and*

EXERCISES

Some of the Issues

1. Part 1 of Mueller's poem tells us how we are, at least in our imaginations, connected to earlier forms of life before "we awakened /and learned to speak." Imagine that you were without language. How would that fact shape your ability to think, feel, and communicate with others?
2. Part 2 of the poem deals with the time when humans first began to talk and tell stories. Why, according to Mueller, did we invent stories? What function did they serve then? What function do they serve now?
3. Why will we "begin our story with the word *and*"?
4. What is your own answer to the question, "Why do we tell stories?" Do you agree with Mueller that the way we talk about our lives shapes the way we lead our lives? Why or why not?

*5. Read Maxine Hong Kingston's "Girlhood among Ghosts." In that selection, the author remembers a story her mother told her in which the mother cuts a section from under Kingston's tongue. The incident may never have happened, yet it appears to have deep significance in Kingston's life. How does Mueller's idea "that the story of our life becomes our life" apply to Kingston?

Some Subjects for Writing

6. Most of us remember stories our families have told again and again about our childhood. Sometimes these stories are about a funny incident, sometimes they carry a moral. Often, the repetition of the story helps to establish the family's view of that child and may shape the child's own self image. Recount a story told about you and explain its influence then and now.

Credits

Alexie, Sherman. "Indian Education," from *The Lone Ranger and Tonto Fistfight in Heaven* by Sherman Alexie, copyright © 1993 by Sherman Alexie. Used by permission of Grove /Atlantic, Inc.

Angelou, Maya. "Graduation," from *I Know Why the Caged Bird Sings* by Maya Angelou. Copyright © 1969 and renewed 1997 by Maya Angelou. Used by permission of Random House, Inc.

Anonymous, "Recapture the Flag: 34 Reasons to Love America." *City Pages* (Minneapolis, MN), July 3, 1991. Reprinted by permission of the publisher.

Anzaldúa, Gloria. "To live in the Borderlands means you . . ." from *Borderlands/La Frontera: The New Mestiza.* © 1987 by Gloria Anzaldúa. Reprinted by permission of Aunt Lute Books.

Bernstein, Nell. "Goin' Gangsta, Choosin' Cholita," by Nell Bernstein from *The San Jose Mercury News*, Nov. 13, 1994. Reprinted by permission of Pacific News Service.

Bloom, Alexis. "Switch on Bhutan," from *The New York Times*, May 13, 2001. Copyright © 2001 by the New York Times Co. Reprinted by permission.

Bohannon, Laura. "Shakespeare in the Bush," from *Natural History*, August/September, 1966, Vol. 75, No. 7, by Dr. Laura Bohannon. Reprinted by permission of the author.

Brandt, Barbara. "Less is More: A Call for a Shorter Work Week," by Barbara Brandt, from *Utne Reader;* July/Aug. 1991. Reprinted with permission of the author.

Breen, Ruth. "Choosing a Mate." Used by permission of the author.

Brooks, Geraldine. "Unplugged," by Geraldine Brooks, former foreign correspondent for *The Wall Street Journal* and author of *Nine Parts of Desire: The Hidden World of Islamic Women.* Used with permission of the author.

Buruma, Ian. "The Road to Babel." Reprinted with permission from *The New York Review of Books.* Copyright © 2001 NYREV, Inc.

Cofer, Judith Ortiz. "The Myth of the Latin Woman: I Just Met a Girl Named María," from *The Latin Deli: Prose and Poetry* by Judith Ortiz Cofer, the University of Georgia Press. Reprinted by permission.

Coontz, Stephanie. "Where Are the Good Old Days?" Reprinted by permission of the author.

Cullen, Countee. "Incident," from the book *Color* by Countee Cullen. Reprinted by permission of GRM Associates, Inc., agents for the Estate of Ida M. Cullen. Copyright 1925 by Harper & Brothers; copyright renewed 1953 by Ida M. Cullen.

Douglas, Susan and Meredith Michaels. "The Mommy Wars." Reprinted by permission of *Ms.* Magazine, © 2000.

Eighner, Lars. "On Dumpster Diving," by Lars Eighner, from *Travels With Lizbeth: Three Years On The Road and On The Streets* by Lars Eighner. Copyright © 1993 by Lars Eighner. Reprinted by permission of St. Martin's Press, L.L.C.

Espada, Martín. "Who Burns for the Perfection of Paper," from *City of Coughing and Dead Radiators* by Martín Espada. Copyright © 1993 by Martín Espada. Used by permission of W.W. Norton & Company, Inc.

Farmanfarmaian, Roxane. "Double Helix," copyright © 1998 by Roxane Farmanfarmaian from *Half and Half* by Claudine Chiawei O'Hearn. Used by permission of Pantheon Books, a division of Random House, Inc.

Gamson, Joshua. "Do Ask, Do Tell," by Joshua Gamson. Reprinted with permission from *The American Prospect*, Fall 1995. Copyright New Prospect, Inc.

Gladwell, Malcolm. "Black Like Them," by Malcolm Gladwell in *The New Yorker;* April 29–May 6, 1996. Used with permission of the publisher.

Hoffman, Eva. "Lost in Translation," by Eva Hoffman. From *Lost in Translation.* Copyright © 1989 by Eva Hoffman. Used by permission of the publisher, Dutton, an imprint of New American Library, a division of Penguin Putnam, Inc.

Houston, James D. and Jeanne Wakatsuki Houston. "Shikata Ga Nai," from *Farewell to Manzanar* by James D. Houston and Jeanne Wakatsuki Houston. Copyright © 1973 by James D. Houston. Reprinted by permission of Houghton Mifflin Company. All rights reserved.

Howard, Jane. "Families," from *Family: A Celebration* by Jane Howard. Reprinted with the permission of Simon & Schuster, Inc. Copyright © 1978 by Jane Howard.

Iyer, Pico. "Home is Every Place," by Pico Iyer, from *Homeground* (Blue Heron Publishing, Hillsboro, OR), 1996. Used with permission.

Author/Title Index